THE AGE OF FOOTBALL

Also by David Goldblatt

THE BALL IS ROUND

THE FOOTBALL BOOK

THE GAME OF OUR LIVES

FUTEBOL NATION

THE GAMES

DAVID GOLDBLATT

THE AGE OF
FOOTBALL

THE GLOBAL GAME IN
THE TWENTY-FIRST CENTURY

MACMILLAN

First published 2019 by Macmillan
an imprint of Pan Macmillan
20 New Wharf Road, London N1 9RR
Associated companies throughout the world
www.panmacmillan.com

ISBN 978-1-5098-5424-0

1 3 5 7 9 8 6 4 2

A CIP catalogue record for this book is available from the British Library.

Typeset by Jouve (UK), Milton Keynes
Printed and bound by CPI Group (UK) Ltd, Croydon, CR0 4YY

Visit **www.panmacmillan.com** to read more about all our books
and to buy them. You will also find features, author interviews and
news of any author events, and you can sign up for e-newsletters
so that you're always first to hear about our new releases.

Contents

INTRODUCTION: FOOTBALL IS FIRST

Football is first.
The craziness around football is second.
Then there is the rest of the world.

Carlos Monsiváis

The spectacle is not a collection of images, but a social relationship amongst people, mediated by images.

Guy Debord

I

Carlos Monsiváis, the late essayist and critic, was referring to the mental and emotional priorities of the Mexican press and public during the World Cup, the tournament invariably coinciding with elections to either the Senate or the Presidency itself. Extraordinary as this is, that the fate of the national football team should, for even just a month, eclipse such important political moments, and true as this is for many polities and publics, Monsiváis' epigram speaks to a more general and even stranger truth.

Football is first.

First amongst sports themselves, first amongst the world's popular cultural forms. The game is able to command the allegiance, interest and engagement of more people in more places than any other sport. The World Cup has superseded the Olympics as the spectacle of all spectacles. The NFL might just remain the biggest single-sport league financially, but European football alone has entirely outstripped its revenues and global reach, and the gap is only going to get bigger. In the three most populous nations of the earth – China, India and the United States, where just twenty years ago football held a very peripheral place in the sporting and popular cultural landscape – it has now arrived for good. In China the party has made the game the measure of the nation's development. In the United States it gathers a coalition who see a version of the nation that is normal, not exceptional; playing others rather than dominating them. In India it is emerging from beneath the blanket obsession with cricket of the last few decades as a new marker of cosmopolitanism and class distinctions.

If football's place in global sporting culture has become almost unassailable, its weight, relative to other cultural forms and industries, has also sharply risen. It bears comparison with the world's religions, not as a system of belief or alternative metaphysics, but in the scale, regularity and profundity of its cycles and rituals. Its economic footprint is hardly titanic, but European football now turns over more revenue than the European publishing or cinema industries. The game's attraction to global corporations as a vector for their brands seems unquenchable, ensuring its presence and imagery is multiplied many times over. It is an object of desire for television networks across the world. Indeed, even Amazon and Facebook, recent purchasers of football media rights, have decided that they need football more than football needs them. The level of mainstream and social media coverage accorded the game is simply vast and unending. The game attracts, at its peak, audiences that dwarf other sports, shows and genres; and when it does so, it gathers eyes and minds in acts of collective imagining like no other spectacle on offer. Everywhere, as it has for over a century, football creates and dramatizes our social identities, our amities and our antipathies. No other sport, no popular cultural form, has been subject to this degree of adulation. Football is first: the most global and most popular of popular cultural phenomenon in the twenty-first century.

In Monsiváis' reading of the game, football serves primarily as a distraction from the 'real world' of Mexican politics and the country's economic and social problems. Worse, it evokes hysteria rather than the clear-eyed reasoned thinking the latter demand. This is not an unreasonable interpretation of Mexico's relationship to football, or the rest of the world's. Football is often a distraction; in some ways that is the point: the game's locus as a place of emotional refuge, escape and otherworldliness has long been part of its purpose and pleasures. Certainly, there is no shortage of irrational, myopic, deluded and obsessive behaviour in the football world. Interpreted in this light football is rendered as a twenty-first-century version of the Roman Circus, a crude but effective instrument of rule that distracts and disables popular consciousness.

True, but the idea that the real world is actually sealed off or absent from the worlds of football and the craziness around it cannot stand. In fact, the real world of economic and political power is more present in football than ever before and, though it hides itself in a thousand ways, there is actually no greater or more transparent public theatre for exposing these forces at work. At the same time the craziness around the game should not be understood as just self-consciously ignorant hedonism and reverie. One can also read the game's irrationality not as a form of madness, but as a deeply felt refusal to accept the presence of the real world in the game as legitimate, or to allot it the seriousness it commands. Football fever can serve as a collective insistence that there are other moral logics and priorities in this world, different from and more human than the ones we so blithely award the soubriquet of the real.

Guy Debord, the melancholy kingpin of the Situationist International, recognized that presence of social relationships inside the modern media spectacle. Indeed, in his brilliant, aphoristic *Society of the Spectacle*, he came to define the phenomenon in precisely that way. The media spectacle, whatever its content, would, he predicted, bind great networks of people and institutions together by the mere consumption of imagery, and in so doing establish new relationships of domination and control. The spectacle would not just distract but commodify, blind and stupefy too. Moreover, whatever spontaneous authenticity and lived reality the subject of the spectacle might possess to begin with – be it a musical performance, religious ceremony or game of football – it would inevitably be reshaped by the forces of commerce and power to create a simulacrum, an ever more perfect and ever more fabricated, deracinated version of the real.

Written in the mid-1960s, an era of deep somnolence in French football, Debord's work gives no indication that football would furnish the pinnacle of the modern spectacle. Had he done so, he might not have drawn such bleak conclusions, for Debord and the Situationists were alert to the subversive potential of play and games. His Danish colleague, the artist Asger Jorn, invented the notion of three-sided football as a challenge to ludic orthodoxy, and as an experiment in non-binary models of social interaction, while Debord's own Game of War was an avant-garde satire on the table-top board game. Football can and does nurture monomania, ignorance, atavistic loathing and mindless stupefaction, but that does not exhaust its repertoire.

First, it remains the case that a crowd cannot, as yet, be simulated and then banished. The spectacle that we have chosen to prioritize, above all, still needs a real crowd in a real stadium, where the social relationships, networks and identities established amongst those present offer an indissoluble humanity in the face of the game's commercial transformation and control. Thus, a place remains, right at the heart of the football spectacle, where resistance to the intrusion and overweening importance of economic and political power can survive, joined by a public beyond the stadium for whom the game is more than mere consumption.

Second, football, in the end, is just a game. Games, and the logic of play that animates them, are premised on the notion that the point of play is just that: play. It is a realm, amongst many things, of experimentation, pleasure, curiosity, and one in which neither money nor power should determine who can play or how to play. If they do, we are no longer merely playing, but in some way fighting or buying or bullying. Thus, almost universally in football cultures, there is a sense that games should not be fixed; that victory should follow virtue, not wealth or power; that glory bought is glory turned to ashes; that the game is not about me or you, but about us; that success and failure are collectively made and shared; that we are only as good as our weakest link, our must vulnerable team mates and citizens. Despite its commercialization, despite its capture by the global culture industries, despite every move to make over and manicure its staging, despite every effort to make the game pay homage to power on this earth, it remains a place in which, albeit dimly, a different world can still be imagined.

It would be recondite but illuminating to take the ghosts of these two gentlemen, Monsiváis and Debord, to a game of our era; to chew the fat, to watch the match; to show Monsiváis the ineradicable and instructive presence of the real world at the heart of the game; to suggest to Debord that the digital, global might of the spectacle has yet to entirely close down the space for real human relationships and critical thought. We would be a motley crew: Monsiváis, incapacitated in later life by respiratory illness and killed by it in 2010, might well have to come in a wheelchair; Debord himself, consumed by alcohol and despair, shot himself in 1994. I imagine he will have a hole through his heart, draining away whatever wine he can find in the afterlife. Debord and I could take turns, assisting Monsiváis when needed, but perhaps you could help too? Reliability was never Debord's strong suit.

And if we were to go to just one game, we should go large: Sunday, 13 July 2014. Estadio Maracanã: Rio de Janeiro, the 2014 World Cup final. Yes, accreditation might be difficult, but the world of football is not entirely unfamiliar with the undead – some might even suggest that the game has been run by them. Either way, I'm sure our Brazilian hosts would make an accommodation for two such venerable visitors. No, I don't think they've had a connection to the internet in the afterlife. So, while we are waiting for the game to start, plenty of time to bring them up to date.

For sure, Carlos. Football is first . . .

At 7.30 p.m. GMT, Germany will play Argentina in the final of the World Cup. We've come early to avoid the crush, to take in the moment, to find our tiny place in the spectacle's spider's web. One billion people will watch this game; 3.2 billion, more than half the adults in the world, have watched some of this tournament.[1] Sure, it's not a precise cross-section – more male than female, more urban than rural – but no shared moment will come closer to who we are demographically. For a month, humanity has gathered in front of screens, crowds have taken over public and private spaces, factories have rescheduled shifts and states have changed school hours, all to accommodate the football.

In rural southern China, a forklift truck driver goes to bed straight after work, so he can rise at midnight in his shack and watch the games on his laptop. In Northern Chile, the copper mines' schedule has been changed to accommodate *La Roja*'s games, the miners gathering to watch in the works canteen. In South Korea, even at five in the morning, hundreds of thousands of Red Devils have been eating breakfast in front of the national team's matches. In Beirut, where the Lebanese have no team of their own to back, whole neighbourhoods are strung with foreign flags, rooting for Argentina or Germany. World cities, home to communities from almost every participant nation at the tournament, have been buzzing with diasporic gatherings and parties: Italians in Toronto, Nigerians in London, Mexicans in Los Angeles, Ivorians in Paris. In Berlin, hundreds of thousands are gathering and dancing along the Love Mile. In the eastern half of the city where they prefer things a little more sedate, 4,000 have brought their own sofas to Union Berlin's stadium, now decorated as a living room, with a vast TV screen at one end. In Yemen's capital Sana'a, a hiatus in the Saudi bombing campaign has allowed crowds to gather to watch the games, but tonight they still cluster under a huge concrete bridge for protection. People go where they can and do what they can to watch the game. An ancient battery-powered set serves the rubbish pickers of Cairo; a precariously rigged satellite dish catches the signal in a Syrian refugee camp. In Antarctica, British scientists gather round a short-wave radio. In Earth's orbit, 200 miles above the surface of the planet, astronauts in the International Space Station watch NASA's HD-quality feed.

Everyone has been watching, and everyone wants their say. For the first time, *Il Papa* – in this incarnation Jorge Mario Bergoglio, AKA Pope Francis, a known and serious Argentinean football fan – has sent a video of greetings and blessings to the tournament. Fidel Castro, hitherto only on public record talking about baseball, made his correspondence with Maradona public, telling *El Pibe de Oro* that 'Every day I have the pleasure of following your program, on Telesur, about the World Cup of soccer; thanks to that, I can observe the extraordinary level of that universal sport.'[2] America's President Barack Obama and Iran's President Hassan Rouhani may have been preoccupied by the terrible events unfolding in Iraq that month – amongst other things, the declaration of a new caliphate by the leader of ISIS, Abu Bakr al-Baghdadi – but both men found time to use social media platforms to signal their support for their respective national teams. Obama went with Facebook and Vine; Rouhani tweeted his support along with a picture of himself dressed, most uncharacteristically, in a football tracksuit rather than his customary clerical robes. Iran's delegation at the Vienna nuclear talks took time out from diplomacy to watch the TV broadcast of their national team playing Nigeria.[3]

In a fragmented media world, national teams' games have been attracting truly exceptional mass audiences everywhere, breaking the TV record for a football match in the USA, and topping the ratings league in Brazil, Germany, Japan and Britain. Today, the game will be live on 430 channels, in dozens of languages; another 300 audio feeds will serve thousands and thousands of radio stations. Only North Korea's screens will not be showing the game, but then state television there has released a musical montage of old football artworks in a programme that suggests the country has already won the tournament. That said, you can bet your life that the elites of Pyongyang will be watching today's game on their own private streams.

Simultaneously, the global digital chorus has been immense.[4] The semi-final between Brazil and Germany generated 35 million tweets, peaking at more than half a million a minute when Germany's fifth goal went in. Today's game will make this Twitter's busiest day ever. Facebook announced more than a billion World Cup-related inter-actions during the first half of the month-long tournament. In the first week alone, the 459 million World Cup exchanges exceeded those reported for the Sochi 2014 Winter Olympics, the Super Bowl and the Oscars combined. Over the whole tournament, 350 million people have made 3 billion posts. Even FIFA's own website, perhaps the least informative of all available outlets, has received a billion visits. No event – not a man on the moon, not the opening ceremony of any Olympic games, nor any coronation, inauguration or funeral – has held humanity's attention like this.

The craziness around football is second . . .

On the pitch below us, the players stretch, warm up and juggle the ball. Smartphones and the innumerable big screens and advertising boards demand our attention. The stands are finally filling, but it still doesn't quite feel like a crowd. Then you notice how the white shirts and the striped shirts cluster, how the gruff chants and snatches of old songs in Spanish and German rise above the mundane music from the PA; how people are finding each other by ear and eye; and you, like everyone, float in the exquisite, lightheaded zone of the unknown. It's a football game: anything can happen, and who knows how we will react when it does.

   In Bogotá, Colombia, the national team's opening victory against the Greeks initiated a city-wide bacchanalian spasm of dancing, drinking and flour-throwing that descended into multiple incidents of violence. Mayor Gustavo Petro imposed a total alcohol ban for subsequent games. At the end of the group stages, the final whistle blew in Porto Alegre and an ocean away, amongst the ancient Roman ruins of Algiers, a delirious crowd celebrated Algeria's victory over South Korea, engulfed in smoke, fireworks and magnesium flares. In Lyon and Lille, the kids from the *banlieues* torched cars and buses. In Grenoble, they were scattered by riot police with tear-gas gren-ades. The following day Mexico beat Croatia in Recife and the Chicano boulevards of downtown Los Angeles and Huntington Park filled with a sea of Mexican tricolours and a party so large that the panicky LAPD called out the riot squad. In Santiago, the partying that accompanied Chile's run to the quarter-finals reached such

heights that the government asked its citizens to refrain from barbe-
cuing to protect the city's already fragile air quality.[5]

For a month, football has functioned as a vast, polymorphous set
of rituals and a global public theatre, connecting those inside the
stadiums, the crowds occupying public space in the cities of the
world and the billions more watching on screens in their homes, all
telling and retelling, inventing and interpreting the stories it has
been generating. At times, the multi-character, multi-layer narratives
that the tournament produces, and the mad chatter of the public
running commentary on the players' characters and private lives,
have made the World Cup feel like a great global soap opera. Cameroon and Ghana were consumed by fights over money between the
players and their notoriously rapacious football officials. When the
Uruguayan Luis Suárez lost control and bit the Italian defender Giorgio Chiellini, he was globally lampooned and lauded in his home
country.

On the other hand, more complex narratives, rooted in the tex-
ture of economic and social life, have given the World Cup the range
of a multi-authored international collection of short stories and
essays. England's dismal ejection from the tournament seemed a
textbook exposition of the private opulence of the Premier League
and the public squalor of the national team. In Iran, it was the
women who came through strongest. Officially banned from viewing
football with men, they followed the national team surreptitiously in
mixed cafes and then paraded through central Tehran in defiance of
the theocracy. On the other side of the world, hundreds of thousands
of ecstatic Colombians welcomed home their team as if they were
champions rather than defeated quarter-finalists. The team's best
ever World Cup performance served as a suitable marker for a nation
finally moving beyond the protracted drug wars of the previous three
decades. Argentina's and Germany's stories are not yet concluded.

Germany, still described in the hapless clichés of efficient
machines and ruthless, clinical finishing, have been dazzling: precisely the word that the French press used to laud the Brazilians at
the 1938 World Cup when they surprised the world and showed us
what the new football looked like. Now the continental positions are
reversed. Germany, finally emerging as what it has been for decades –
the pre-eminent European power – has a football team to match its
ambitions and its character: brilliantly organized but highly flexible;

individually accomplished but telepathically networked; technically superior to the Brazilians in touch, positioning and anticipation. Their 7–1 demolition of the hosts in São Paulo in the semi-final earlier in the week is unlikely to be bettered. The backdrop to the Argentinians' almost impregnable nerve and defensive concentration on the field is President Kirchner's bitter fight with US-based vulture funds over its rescheduled debt obligations. Under immense economic pressure and looking a major debt default in the eye, the country still aims to cock a snook at the international order. Meanwhile it waits for its football messiah, Lionel Messi, finally to come alive at the World Cup, to replicate Maradona's brilliance in 1986 when they last won the title, then he too can ascend to divinity.

Then there is the rest of the world . . .

Other people's World Cup stories have been more abruptly terminated. On Sunday 15 June, the Somalian jihadi group Al-Shabaab sent two minibuses of gunmen to Mpeketoni, a small Kenyan town on the Indian Ocean. There, they machine-gunned a crowd watching France versus Honduras in a television hall, as well as attacking a hotel, bank and the police station, leaving fifty people dead.[6] In Adamawa state, in the troubled central belt of Nigeria, they had been expecting the same from Boko Haram, and big screens and public gatherings had been banned. Nonetheless, two days later, as Brazil played Mexico, a bomb went off in a motorized rickshaw parked next to a viewing party in the capital city Damaturu; the local hospital received twenty-one corpses and dealt with twenty-seven serious injuries.[7] All through the tournament, the forever war between Israel and Gaza's Palestinians has raged. On 9 July, a group gathered at the Full-Time beach cafe in Gaza to watch the semi-final between Argentina and the Netherlands, and was struck by an air-to-ground missile, leaving eight dead. Just one of 750 locations hit by the Israelis in a forty-eight-hour aerial assault, just eight lives from a death toll of at least seventy-eight. As one survivor recalled, 'We were watching news on the television, waiting for the match to begin. I heard a terrible boom and felt myself suffocating. I woke up to find myself here in hospital.'[8]

The warm-ups are ending. Time to wake up. Time to look around.

II

The sorcerers of the spectacle try to fill every last unforgiving minute with sensory stimulation, lest our thoughts should wander from illusion to reality. However, even the tightest show has its gaps and lapses, and in the hiatus between the players disappearing into the tunnel and the arrival of the flags and photographers for the anthems, there are a few seconds when the pitch is empty. Take a moment to look up and behold the tragedy of the Maracanã, for an act of architectural vandalism and cultural desecration has been performed here. Once the largest and most beautiful stadium on the planet, it has been reduced to a parody of its former self.[9] Its sinuous, two-tier elliptical structure has been gutted and replaced with an off-the-shelf single-tier stand rammed into the space. The once fabulous views of Rio's skyline, previously visible between the top of the stands and the roof, have been obliterated. The original roof, formerly the crowning glory of the building, was illegally demolished and has been replaced by a pathetic concoction of scaffolding, canopies and big screens that obscures what is left of the stadium's shape. Had you had a chance to walk around the stadium beforehand, it would have been clear that these changes were just part of a huge programme of urban rebuilding characteristic of global sporting mega-events. In the case of the Maracanã, the publicly owned stadium and its surrounding public sports facilities were refurbished with public money, only to be passed to the private sector to profit from them. Two years from now, after the Rio Olympic Games, the owners will effectively abandon the stadium, allowing it to be gutted by thieves and the pitch to turn to dust.

Lost in thought, we are all brought back to the present by the incongruous sounds of FIFA's anthem. Composed by Franz Lambert, Hesse's king of the Hammond organ, and played at every World Cup since 1994, it combines teeth-clenching Europop jauntiness with the kitschiest of ceremonial flourishes.[10] At least we are on safer musical territory with the nineteenth-century national anthems that follow, with their familiar overwrought orchestration and martial rhythms.

Quite who or what those nations are today is another matter. The camera moves along the faces of the German squad, and we see, of course, the Schweinsteigers, the Grosskreutzes and the Weiden-fellers, but this is twenty-first-century Germany. The encrusted sediments of past and present global migrations run through the team as clear as a geological section: the Polish-born Lukas Podolski and Miroslav Klose; third-generation Turkish-German Mesut Özil; Sami Khedira and Jerome Boateng, born in Stuttgart and Berlin, to German mothers and Tunisian and Ghanaian fathers, respectively; and Shkodran Mustafi, a German Muslim of Albanian descent. The wave of global migrations that accompanied decolonization and Western Europe's long post-war boom is present in many squads: England's Afro-Caribbeans, France's francophone Africans and Algerians, Belgium's Congolese and the Netherlands' Surinamese.

In the last two decades, new flows of refugees and economic migrants into Europe have made their footballing mark.[11] Brazil 2014 has seen an Italy side with their first black international and undisputed star, Mario Balotelli, and a Swiss team that is almost two-thirds of migrant descent. In geological terms, these are very recent rock formations. The ancient strata of the world's global migrations, like the European colonial destruction of indigenous Americans, are present as the almost wholly European squads of Chile and Mexico; Australia can be considered an Oceanic variant of this near-genocidal encounter. In much of the Western Hemisphere, conquest was followed by the massive importation of African slave labour, which accounts for the African-European mix of the players from Brazil, Ecuador, Honduras, Costa Rica, Colombia, Uruguay and the United States. Everywhere, the changing make-up of the national team has served as both an optimistic emblem of successful integration and a lightning rod for accusations of inauthenticity.

The Argentinians are altogether less diverse, their surnames – Demichelis and Fernandez, Di Maria and Perez – suggesting only the Italian and Spanish roots of most of the country's working classes. But unlike the Germans, who overwhelmingly play at home, these are the global helots. Just three of the squad play in Argentina. Indeed, two-thirds of the 736 players at the World Cup are economic migrants. Only the Russians and the English, neither the world's best travellers, have squads based entirely at home. At the other end of the scale, not one single Uruguayan plays in their domestic league, and just one Ghanaian and one Ivorian have stayed put. All five

African qualifiers, between them, would fail to put out a full side of home-based players.

Diverse as the origins of these players are, their destinations are highly concentrated. Europe, which furnishes less than half the teams in the competition, is home to nearly three-quarters of the players here. Forty per cent of them play in just the top five European leagues, 105 in the English Premier League alone. 130 of the players, over 15 per cent of the total, play at just ten of Europe's leading clubs. They are, of course, just the tip of a much larger global pyramid of professional footballers, the 1 per cent who earn more than $700,000 a year, and the 0.1 per cent who are bringing in the tens of millions.[12] Beneath them lies a larger second tier of players in the poorer but sustainable leagues of Mexico, the USA, mid-range European countries and East Asia. At the bottom are the vast majority of the world's professional footballers. Needless to say, the top tiers are exclusively male. Even the very best paid women professionals, few as they are, remain in the bottom strata. Here, it transpires, 45 per cent of all players are on 1,000 dollars a month or less, are often paid late, and many are playing without contracts, health care or insurance, inside institutions that are regularly cruel and abusive. And FIFA wonders why there are epidemics of match-fixing, sexual abuse and mental ill health raging in professional football?

Now is a good moment to look to the north side of the Maracanã, where, in the best seats in the house, FIFA and their special guests are standing up for the anthems. The VVIP guest list, leaked this morning on social media, makes for interesting reading.[13] Of course, there is a large phalanx of FIFA officials and members of its executive committee, all in their corporate blazers – though in retrospect the main interest here is to count how many of them have departed the scene in disgrace, and how many of them are now in jail. President Blatter, General Secretary Valcke and Vice-President Platini have all been banned from football by FIFA itself. The Spaniard Angel Villar is in prison at home, charged with the corrupt use of government funds. Jeffrey Webb, the former President of CONCACAF, and Guatemalan Rafael Salguero, previously a member of the FIFA executive, are in prison awaiting their sentences, having been convicted of money-laundering and racketeering in a New York court in 2017. The man in overall charge today, the head of the organizing committee and the

Brazilian football federation, José Maria Marin, was found very guilty of the same crimes at the same trial.

Then there is the scattering of stardust, starting with half a dozen former World Cup winners, including Italy's Fabio Cannavaro, Spain's Carles Puyol, Germany's Lothar Matthäus and, in an unusual choice, the man Zidane head-butted at the 2006 final, Marco Materazzi. Three of the musicians who had bravely put their careers and reputations on the line by performing at the dismal closing ceremony – Wyclef Jean, Shakira and Carlinhos Brown – have been let in, though one wonders why Carlos Santana, who played with them, didn't get this kind of upgrade. Maybe Sepp Blatter has something against Latino rock with a jazz vibe. He certainly has the musical tastes to explain the presence of two of Southern Europe's most achingly mainstream singing voices, Placido Domingo, the Spanish tenor, and Eros Ramazzotti, the Italian MOR singer-songwriter. Blatter's leery interest in supermodels and beauty queens, regularly appended to FIFA events, also accounts for the presence of Gisele and Adriana Lima. Likewise, the seats allocated to actors Daniel Craig and Ashton Kutcher, though here the source of their attraction is Blatter's love of handsome screen heroes. Having, in his youth, modelled himself on the louche, dinner-suited lady's man Eddie Constantine, a 1950s American B-movie actor turned cult star in francophone Europe, they must have seemed suitable contemporaries. And then there is LeBron James, because, well, he is LeBron.

Heads of state and prime ministers get their own sub-section in the VVIP list and, despite a few no-shows, it's quite a gathering. Host President Dilma Rousseff is joined by her predecessor and successor, South Africa's Jacob Zuma and Russia's Vladimir Putin. Invitations had been extended to both India's Prime Minister Narendra Modi and China's President Xi Jinping, and though both declined they assured the world that they would be watching. Germany has sent both President Gauck and Chancellor Merkel. Gauck's Argentinian counterpart, Cristina Kirchner, is a no-show, claiming to be a little under the weather. Given how bitter she has proved in political defeat at home, this may be a blessing for all. However, President Ali Bongo of Gabon and the Hungarian Prime Minister Viktor Orbán have found time in their busy schedules to drop in. President Bongo has, in fact, been here since the opening ceremony and has made a real holiday of it. Orbán is more of a connoisseur, having attended every World Cup final since 1998.

They were not alone in deeming an appearance, albeit not at the final, essential. Best represented were the Latin Americans. The leftist presidents of Ecuador, Bolivia, Chile and Uruguay – Rafael Correa, Evo Morales, Michelle Bachelet and José Mujica respectively – all dropped in. The political right was represented, too, in the shape of Paraguay's president and richest man, Horacio Cartes, Suriname's Desiré Delano Bouterse and Honduras's Juan Orlando Hernández. US Vice-President Joe Biden rolled into town to watch his team beat Ghana in Natal, before seeing President Rousseff in the capital, Brasília, where he hoped to thaw the relationship between the two states, temporarily frozen by revelations of the scale of US spying on Brazil.

African delegations were also numerous, literally in the case of the entourage that accompanied Nigerian President Goodluck Jonathan. Although not quite on the scale of the 600 that travelled with him to the United Nations in New York before the tournament, it still included a cavalcade of ministers, senators and governors. As the sharp-eyed Nigerian press noted, no provision had been made for this in the budget plans of the Nigerian football federation. Ghana, the other African qualifier to send a senior national leader, opted for Vice-President Kwesi Amissah-Arthur, although with sufficient funds assembled to send 500 selected official fans and a cook.[14] Croatia's Prime Minister, Zoran Milanović, watched his team lose the opening game to the hosts. The King and Queen of Belgium showed up for their country's game with Russia; the Dutch royal couple saw Holland play Australia; and, for good measure, the secretary-general of the United Nations, Ban Ki-moon, and the Emir of Qatar have shown their faces.

To the left and the right of the VVIP zone is a long run of corporate boxes. With twenty-two official corporate sponsors, who have paid a billion dollars between them for the privilege, that is just as well. The presence of these brands and corporations, in the boxes and on the constantly moving electronic pitch boards, is obvious, anodyne and eventually, if your brain can edit them out, invisible. What cannot be ignored, what has filled the electronic and mental circuitry of the world in the months leading up to this, is their vast spend on advertising and PR of every kind. Alongside the official sponsors and their clients, there is no shortage of rich people in this world who want a comfortable piece of the action: a good seat, an identikit five-star hotel and business-class flights. FIFA, having received about a quarter of a billion dollars from the hospitality firm MATCH, allow these parasitic rentiers to sell around 10 per cent of the tournament's tickets, bundled into gilt-edged packages for the unimaginative and well-heeled. One person who will not be there, however, is MATCH's Irish chief executive Ray Whelan. He is sitting in a police cell in Rio, arrested after he tried to escape from his Copacabana hotel via the service exit at the back. He and another twelve people have been charged with the widespread, illegal and very profitable resale of World Cup tickets, though he will be subsequently cleared of the charges.[15]

Good as the global corporates are at the game of advertising, they have nothing on the DIY efforts of global celebs. That tiresome old warhorse of self-promotion, Mick Jagger, has become an ever-present on these occasions, and young pretenders like David Beckham are equally available for the paparazzi. But both will be eclipsed today by Rihanna, who will be live-tweeting the whole match from the stands. In fact, she will be so blown away by the German's victory that she will be sharing a photo of her black-and-white Teutonic leather bra. Afterwards, she will pull celebrity privilege and meet the winners backstage, her tweet confirming that, amongst the self-regarding and self-advertising, there is no more potent elixir than football. 'I touched the cup, held the cup, kissed the cup, took a selfie wit the cup!!! I meeaan . . . what is YO bucket list looking like bruh?'[16]

Lesser narcissists have also been at work: a German neo-Nazi painted with Aryan symbols, a supporter of indigenous land rights in Brazil and an opponent of the Venezuelan government have all tried pitch invasions during the Cup. During the second half of today's final, a Russian YouTube prankster, painted with the name of his show, will storm the pitch and try to kiss German defender Benedikt Höwedes. The cameras, as always, will consign him to oblivion; a move that explains the broadcaster's occasional mid-game cut to a view of Christ the Redeemer.[17]

After the suits and the celebs and the freebies are accounted for, there is the crowd, who, if the colours of the replica shirts are anything to go by, are a three-way split between the Brazilians in yellow, the Germans in white and the Argentinians in their blue-and-white stripes. The Brazilians probably have the edge, as they have had at almost every game in the competition, wearing the national team shirt, or even club shirts, with characteristic solipsism.

Ticket prices for today, at face value, range from $440 to nearly $1,000. The ticket touts in the high-end hotel lobbies are asking for at least $5,000. So, as usual, the Brazilian contingent, from a country in which around 60 per cent of the population can claim African descent, is overwhelmingly, spellbindingly white, and for the most part wealthy. Earlier in the tournament, one correspondent at Germany–Portugal in Fortaleza thought it looked more like Kansas. Local newspapers have actually been counting, and have announced that Brazil's crowds were at least 65 per cent white. Today, it is much more. There are probably a good few Americans in the crowd, who amongst the visitors have bought more tickets than anyone else. The Germans and Argentinians come next, their presence today bolstered by innumerable last-minute purchases and scams. Whatever their methods, there would be no atmosphere without them. The black Brazilians who are here are concentrated amongst the small army of stewarding and security personnel; indeed, the ethnic make-up of the security detail that will protect the players as they climb a staircase to collect their medals at the end of the game will be 100 per cent Afro-Brazilian. In any case, the 1,500 to 2,000 on duty inside the stadium are just a small ceremonial detachment from a vast army of surveillance and repression. Over the whole month, 85,000 security personnel from the Brazilian secret services, armed forces, police and private sector have been mobilized. Today, in Rio alone, 26,000 are on duty. They are not really here to counter an external terrorist threat, but to scare their own citizens.

Like an experimental novel that features two parallel universes, the spectacle of Brazil 2014 has been running alongside the counter-spectacle of the country's small social movements sparring with the Kevlar-plated leviathan of the nation's security forces. For those with both a taste for the esoteric and access to live ninja media feeds of the protests, the few brave forays by dissidents during the tournament have served as a critical grit beneath the spectacle's glitter. Protests at the 2014 World Cup took many forms. Paul Ito's mural of a starving child served a football on a golden platter was just one of hundreds of disruptive, angry, sceptical images that showed up on Brazil's walls in the run-up to the Cup. The country's anarcho-hacktivists were busy too, bringing down the websites of the Ministries of Sport and Foreign Affairs, sponsors Hyundai Brazil, the Brazilian football federation and the Bank of Brazil, but actual demonstrations dwindled to almost nothing, a pale reflection of the much larger protests that had engulfed the 2013 Confederations Cup. On the opening day of the tournament, tiny demonstrations occurred in dozens of cities, but the only ones of any size, in São Paulo and Rio, were met by overwhelming force. In São Paulo, although miles from the opening game, they were greeted by stun grenades and riot shields. Six hundred demonstrators in Rio were pepper-sprayed and teargassed. A single stone that pockmarked the glass window of ITV's Copacabana World Cup studio that evening was as close as they got. For much of the month, away from the cameras, small protests were held in the favelas of Rio, effectively under occupation by the security forces for the duration. The feminist activist Sara Winter wandered through the hedonistic babble of Copacabana beach, her body smeared with the words, 'While your team is relaxing Brazilians are dying.' Protestors made a football field of Brasília's bus station on the day Colombia played Côte d'Ivoire, and asked the police to join in. They didn't. On the eve of the final, for good measure, the Rio police rounded up and detained many of the leading figures in the protest movements. Today, they have quietly corralled the small demonstration that dared to take to the streets and squeezed it down to nothing.

III

The players take up their positions. Germany are poised to take the kick-off, but Adidas have already won. In the preposterous marketing hype that has surrounded the World Cup since 1998, when Nike first entered the fray, the tournament has become synonymous with the struggle for market share in the global sportswear industry, which is worth $270 billion a year, and within which football is the most important segment. Between them, these companies control 70 per cent of the market: five billion dollars of football kit a year, around a fifth of their combined turnover. Nike, the bigger of the pair overall, are number two in football, while Adidas have been a World Cup sponsor and ball maker since 1970. Consequently, Nike have invested a lot of money in this World Cup, paying $8.35 million to Cristiano Ronaldo to wear their boots and a whole lot more to the ten national teams wearing their logo. Their marketing stars – Ronaldo, Brazil and England – have all been very disappointing, though. Adidas have just nine teams, but they have the pitch-side boards, both the finalists and the ball. Either way, everyone's earning a lot of money. Nike, which is valued at $17 billion (Mozambique's GDP, to give a sense of scale), pays its CEO $15 million; Adidas, worth $7.5 billion (more like Niger), pays its boss a parsimonious $2.5 million. Together, they will make more than $5.5 billion in profits in 2014.[18]

If you ask them what underwrites those profits, they will tell you, at some length, that it is their pursuit of high performance through technological innovation. Certainly, things have moved along in the world of sportswear: today, a player's kit, from head to foot, including shin guards, weighs less than 700 g, half of what it came in at just four years ago. Their boots are only a quarter as heavy as those worn by their peers four decades ago. Useful as this might be in the world of elite sport, where marginal gains matter, it is essentially irrelevant to the vast majority of the market. In this domain, the companies can rightly point to a long tradition of smart design, in which sportswear shades into street wear and high fashion, and where, amongst devotees, there is great attention to the micro-aesthetics of sneakers and hoodies. All this is important, but what is really driving sales, what makes the latest tweak in the shape of sole or the cut of a collar somehow matter, is branding and endorsement, or 'demand creation', as Nike likes to call it. Three billion dollars was spent on this in 2014: that's $100 a second, every second, all year, every year. Sponsorship by the two major brands, and in a precise reflection of wider patterns of income distribution and gains in a globalized economy, is concentrated on a very small number of individual players, club sides and countries. The Germans are getting more than $25 million a year from Adidas, while the Hondurans, for example, who were knocked out in the first round, get just $2 million from their sponsors Joma. Their whole squad's boot deals are worth less than that of Mezut Özil, who is on $5 million a year from Adidas. Having manufactured demand, all that remains is to arrange supply at a cost that ensures more than $5 billion profit per annum. It is at this that the companies excel: the creation and ruthless control of complex global supply chains, relentlessly seeking the cheapest labour.

Consider the shirts that the Germans are wearing, currently retailing at home for €85.[19] More than half of that goes to the taxman (€14) and the shops (€36), leaving just €35 for everyone else. Adidas, of course, have to cover the cost of sustaining the brand (€5) and take a whopping €25 profit, which leaves just €5 for the people who actually make the shirt. There are taxes and raw material costs, of course, and the subcontractors have got to get their cut, haven't they? Which, from your €85 shirt, leaves just €0.6 to pay the workers who made it – less than 1 per cent. The boots are not much different: workers may get more like €2 a pair.

The ball is one of 60 million manufactured in the Pakistani city of Sialkot, which has had a stitching industry since the 1890s. In the late 1990s, normal service was disrupted when it became known that child labour was widespread in the industry. For a decade or so, some of its business went to China and India, where the wages were even lower and subcontractors even further below the radar, but in recent years, Sialkot has regained its spot as the world's largest manufacturer of footballs. Child labour has primarily been displaced to the city's brick and metal working industries. Nonetheless, the ball will have required hours of eye-straining, carpal-scraping, back-breaking work.[20] In a case of commodity fetishization that would make Karl Marx's hair stand on end, Adidas have given the ball a name, a personality invented at a marketing weekend retreat, and its own Twitter account. A social conscience appears to have been harder to generate. Shirts, shorts, balls or boots, the wages of most workers in this industry are pitiful, and their living conditions and working conditions are worse. Trade unions are often banned, and where they are formed they are actively repressed.

In the first nine minutes of the game, Germany have had 82 per cent of the possession and completed 22 of their 30 passes in their final third. Argentina, by contrast, have had just 18 per cent of the ball and missed all their attacking passes. Nobody scores. The rest of the half plays out pretty much the same. The reason we know this, and a hundred other data points, is because across the world teams of young people are digitally coding every move and every moment of the match. In contrast to the more sedate, serial games of cricket and baseball, which had successfully constructed statistical recording devices for an era of pen and paper, football, being a game of flow, had proved a much more problematic sport to record. However, the arrival of plentiful video and digital recording devices has allowed companies like Opta and Prozone to note thousands of individual incidents in every game, in real time. This allows them to calculate everything from the average spatial position of a player during a game to the percentage of successful tackles a team makes in each third of the pitch, along with the average number, length and position of each player's dribbles. Combined with a huge volume of medical and psychological information on players, these databases have allowed elite football to become significantly more self-reflexive, in the ways both the players train and their teams play. Whatever happens in the second half of the game, as part of the growing store of information, it will reshape, in minute ways, the way each player will train and play in future.

While clubs and coaches are one part of the football data market, by far the largest and most lucrative collector of information is the digital games industry. Of all the video games on the market, one title stands above all: EA Sports' *FIFA* series. After signing up with the global godfathers themselves, the company's first outing was *FIFA 93*.[21] Annually updated, it has achieved global sales of over 50 million, and is regularly the best-selling game in dozens of markets. *FIFA*'s success is partly a function of its mechanics – the fluidity of movement it simulates, its positioning of players off the ball and the range of tricks that the control system can conjure – but what has given it the decisive edge over its main competitor, *Pro Evolution Soccer*, is not its fidelity to reality, but its fidelity to the simulacrum of the televised commercial spectacle. As one of the game's chief designers put it: 'The entire presentation aims for nothing less than an accurate rendering of the matchday experience, as seen on your TV.'[22] To this end, EA Sports have been signing up real teams for real money for image rights since the mid-1990s, squeezing out the competition. Alongside this they have replicated innumerable features of the televised version of the game – points of view that reproduce the camera angles of the spectacle, pre-match handshakes, sponsors' boards, club-specific chants, crowd abuse of the referee, leading commentators for each language and region and individual player celebrations. It has even offered players the option of tying their boots with rainbow laces in support of LGBT rights, a feature which made *FIFA* 17 a matter of debate in the Russian parliament, with

Communist deputies arguing that the game transgressed the country's anti-gay propaganda laws.

Deeper in the code, the game relies on a constantly updated set of player attributes and ratings, collected by the manufacturer's own huge scouting network. Consequently, professional footballers are amongst the most avid and addicted of *FIFA* players. Leyton Orient actually banned the game before real matches due to excessive late-night *FIFA* sessions. According to the German international Mats Hummels, 'some people use what they learn in *FIFA* when they find themselves on the pitch.' Others have claimed to scout opponents informally via the game, and Rio Ferdinand is just one of many to publicly rage over a poor rating awarded him by *FIFA*'s scouts. At least he got a rating; in 2013, Vero Boquete, captain of the Spanish women's national team, put up a petition on Change.org calling for EA Sports to add women to the game, and received more than 50,000 signatures. In *FIFA 16*, women's international teams were made available for the first time.[23]

Less popular than the *FIFA* series, but no less influential, is *Football Manager*, launched in 1992 as *Championship Manager*, with global sales of over 20 million. Fewer than *FIFA*, but more telling is the fact that each player is spending, on average, 240 hours a year on the game, a fact probably not unconnected to *Football Manager*'s regular citation in British divorce cases. The game, the interface of which is legendary for its dullness, allows players to take on the management of real football clubs: scouting, signing and selling players, arranging training sessions, tending to players' emotional needs, and taking or avoiding press conferences. With over two decades of updates, the game has become so sophisticated that its capacity to incorporate the consequences of Brexit (soft or hard) for Britain's football labour market was considerably in advance of the work done in Whitehall on this matter.[24]

The accuracy and intimacy of the gameplay is rooted in the game's global network of 1,500 scouts in 51 countries, compiling data on over half a million players. This resource has become so well thought of that professional clubs use it to scout players, and Ole Gunnar Solskjær claimed it to have been a key tool in his management education. The German lower-league team TC Freisenbruch turned over squad selection entirely to paid-up members, who monitored the players' progress and chose the team's formation through a shared *Football Manager* programme on the club website.[25] Comprehensive as the database is, it has not proved infallible, marking out certain cult players for greatness, like the Ghanaian Nii Lamptey and the Finn Mika Ääritalo, who in reality have proved deeply disappointing.

While *Football Manager* is, for the most part, a solitary activity without a lot of TV potential, *FIFA* is often played in groups, and visually offers rather more than *Manager*'s elaborated spreadsheets. Thus, across the world, in a bizarre inversion of the real and the digital, football clubs from PSG to Manchester City, from Wolfsburg to West Ham, are embracing eSports in general and *FIFA* in particular, fielding their own digital teams. Not yet the spectacular equivalent of today's game, eSports have nonetheless filled South Korea's World Cup stadium in Seoul.[26]

Goalless after ninety minutes, the game goes to extra time. Across the world, bookmakers re-evaluate their odds, offering bets on who will take penalties and in what order, and whether they will score or miss. This is amongst the biggest of days for the very big global gambling industry. Sports betting, over 80 per cent of it on football, has a turnover of at least $500 billion a year, though given that almost half of this is in illegal Asian markets it is impossible to really know.[27] In what has become a quadrennial ritual accompanying the World Cup since 2006, Interpol have helped orchestrate multi-country, multi-target raids on the illegal betting industry during the tournament.[28] Despite their claiming hundreds of arrests, and reporting the closure of many operations and the seizure of tens of millions of dollars, it is all a drop in the ocean. The great churning sea of money created by the world's insatiable desire to bet on football games rolls on, quietly diluting the streams of dirty money and narco-dollars that are laundered there.

Twenty-three minutes into extra time, André Schürrle takes the ball down the left wing and sends a looping pass into the area. Mario Götze, at high speed, cushions the ball on his chest and, as it drops towards the ground, volleys it into the net. Somewhere in the Adidas supply chain they ponder how many additional Götze shirts they will now need to make, whether they have enough umlauts in stock and, if not, how they can get more made at short notice. Götze's run into the box, Schürrle's sprint and assist, and the goal itself, are all being logged into a dozen digital databases. Götze's rating in *Football Manager* will surely soar, though his real form will sadly plunge. At EA Sports, and in a million bedrooms, they are checking whether *FIFA 14*'s controls are good enough to precisely mimic Götze's touch with his chest, and the exquisite angle of his outstretched leg; for, as the game's head of development said, 'Until *FIFA* is indistinguishable from football in real life and plays exactly like football, we'll always have more to do.'[29] And when that happens, will it then be the professionals aping the pro-gamers and their avatars? Either way, the bookies will still be in business. Just as now, they will be counting their winnings whatever the outcome.

IV

Hold your nerve: this is going to be excruciating. It's 10.36 pm; Germany have won the World Cup. We've been going for over three hours, and it's still going to take another twenty-five minutes to start the ceremonies; then it is going to get worse. Get out your phone so you and our ghostly companions can see how this thing worked back in 1986 when these sides, or rather Argentina and West Germany, met in the final of the Mexico World Cup.[30] On that occasion, Argentina were the winners, 3–2. Broadcast live on satellite relay, the television pictures have a watery chromatic quality that dates them, but are just about recognizable as part of the same football universe. The game has a global audience, but one restricted in number and reach by the absence of television sets and signals in much of the rural, global south, especially China and India. The presence of some of the usual corporate suspects on the tatty perimeter boards tells us that commercialization has arrived – indeed, FIFA and the World Cup, under then President João Havelange, were in the vanguard of the process – but compared to today the money is small change. Unlike the Maracanã, the Estadio Azteca, built in 1968 for that year's Olympic Games as well as the 1970 World Cup, is virtually unchanged for the occasion. The doves of peace icon, visible all around the stadium, is, like everything else, left over from the Mexico City Games. There is still space, with many standing, for 114,000 people and just a few VIP tribunes. Replica shirts are almost entirely absent amongst the crowd. In keeping with this stripped-down aesthetic, there has been no closing ceremony and the PA is, mercifully, so poor that the crowd can hear itself.

But what really separates this moment from our own is what happens when the final whistle blows. Within seconds, members of the crowd are negotiating the limited barriers and skirting the moat and blocks of police that edge the pitch. One by one, then in twos and threes or more, they vault the advertising boards and head out onto the green. Some of the bolder Argentinians throw their long-striped banners over the edge of the first tier of the stands, then abseil down to pitch level before running out onto the grass. A scrum of photographers, officials, substitutes, fans and men with banners coagulates around the Argentinian players. One man, sporting a foam World Cup attached to a white baseball cap, runs in a zig-zag, waving a Mexican flag.

That world is gone. It is hard, impossible perhaps, to imagine a World Cup in which the public spontaneously take to the field; impossible to think that a twenty-first-century Maradona could be carried aloft on the shoulders of the crowd, and that the authorities could be either slack enough or relaxed enough to handle it. The fabulously shambolic trophy ceremony that follows is even better. On that occasion, we cut straight to the chase: the West Germans receive their losers' medals in the shadow of Argentina's celebrations. FIFA President João Havelange, at least, knows what he is doing, sternly giving the cup to the Mexican president who passes it to Maradona. A very flustered Sepp Blatter, then General Secretary of FIFA, appears late with a tray of medals and has to haul Maradona back to give him his before the cup can be lifted and shared. The team descends with the trophy to the pitch, where there are now thousands upon thousands of people. One group, with a huge Argentinian blue-and-white-striped banner, is running an erratic, elliptical circuit of victory. The players and the cup are swept up alongside it, and Maradona himself is lifted onto the shoulders of a fan, balanced from behind by others so he can hold the cup aloft. People around strain to touch him and to kiss the cup. Framed by the TV cameras, there is not a member of the security forces or a commercial logo in shot.

Viewed from our own time, the 1986 World Cup final was the last in which the balance of forces, inside the stadium and beyond, was sufficiently in favour of the crowd that a real, spontaneous, chaotic carnival could take place – a world in which, if only for a moment, economic and political power and their needs were trumped by the numbers and the exuberance of the crowd, a proxy for the forces of global civil society.

Today's show is going to be very different and very soulless. The forces at work, which have transformed not merely the staging of World Cup finals but every single aspect of the game in every single nation on the earth, are two-fold. First, the agents of commercialization in football – the leading leagues, clubs, broadcasters, federations and advertisers – were already massing in the still-analogue environment of 1986, introducing advertising, marketing and sponsorship to sport when, even in its most advanced zones, the game was professional but barely commercial. They have gone on to shape and then dominate football in the era of the new global communications and digital technologies which have been the key to the economic globalization of football, multiplying the game's audience many times over, and forging the basis of the phenomenal income it now generates. In this they have been joined by the global super-rich, born of this era of extreme capital accumulation, from Russian oligarchs to US multi-billionaire financiers, from Gulf state sheikhdoms to the new Chinese industrialists who have been buying their way into the game. The money in football, in line with the patterns of the wider global economy, has been highly concentrated amongst the leading nations, the leading leagues and then amongst a handful of leading clubs and players.

Consequently, and already present in outline in 1986 and the early 1990s, twenty-first-century football has experienced a profound globalization of its player and coach labour markets, the ownership of clubs, and its patterns of consumption and fandom, and its integration with the global television industry and the huge global money-laundering, gambling, gaming and leisurewear markets. At its peak, this concentration of talent and capital has generated a football spectacle of an athleticism, sophistication and awe that is historically unparalleled, but the impact of globalization is not confined to the European core of commercial football. It has spread its tentacles across the globe, and directly and indirectly impoverished the football economies of much of the world. And that is only to count the cost in terms of its own logics of money. The insidious consequences of its preferred modes of anodyne consumerism have brought their own pathologies.

The arrival of so much money in football is at least a part of the explanation for the second force at work, for the twenty-first century has seen states and statesmen, politicians and political movements show an altogether greater interest in the game. Consider the former Honduran president Rafael Callejas, who financially secured his retirement by becoming the President of the Honduran Football Association, an institution even more corrupt and opaque than the office of head of state; or Faisal Saleh Hayat, a Pakistani cabinet minister who still found time to fleece the football federation he controlled and run the nation's game into the ground.

Football, however, offers many things more alluring to these men – and they are almost entirely men – than mere graft. At a minimum, association with the game appears to deliver profile and popularity. More substantially, it offers them established popular arenas for playing political theatre, ready-made and ritualized local identities to piggyback upon, and a source of explicable and malleable narratives to garnish their political progress with. Thus, under the unforgiving eye of television coverage, national team performances are treated by politicians, press and public as patriotic rituals, and as a gauge of the state of the nation. Some politicians have incorporated football fandom into their carefully constructed public personas and football metaphors into their language, like Brazil's President Lula, Iran's President Ahmadinejad, Zimbabwe's President Mugabe and Turkey's Recep Erdoğan. Others have actually played the game while in power, like Bolivia's Evo Morales or Hungary's Viktor Orbán.

The perceptible rise in politicians' engagement with the game has not been merely symbolic or an exercise in grandstanding – though there has been plenty of that – but has increasingly made football an object of state policy and intervention, from the government-ordained league of Myanmar's junta to Saudi Arabia's club privatization programme, to Argentina's nationalization of football's television rights. In China, where hosting and winning the World Cup have become national priorities, the game offers official markers of economic and social progress. In Qatar football has become the single most important instrument in the state's programme of economic and urban development and the most powerful plank in the nation's precarious foreign policy.

Governments, however, are not the only ones to have worked out the connection between football and power in the last twenty years. The game's capacity to lay bare the sinews of power, to serve as a goad to critical thinking, and as a reservoir of alternative and communitarian values, has proved strong enough that the new colonization of the game by commercial and political forces has created a small backlash: the eruption of a volcanic but fragile archipelago of resistance. The most significant of all has been the persistence and now rapid growth of women's football, as a grassroots mania, as a professional sport and increasingly as a national and global spectacle. After more than a century of almost unchallenged male domination of the game, on and off the pitch, and the saturation of its collective imagery and sense of self with masculinity, every women's game, every woman in the men's game, is an act of resistance, a reminder that another world is possible and necessary.

Resistance to power takes many forms, but listen hard and you can hear it. All over the world, crowd chants and collective performances have been challenging malign owners, intrusive policing and shameless profiteering. Self-serving TV networks and corrupt administrators have increasingly found themselves the subject of public ire in the stadium and beyond. More recently, organized groups and campaigns in football have multiplied. There are fan groups and football clubs that challenge sexism, violence, racism and homophobia, from the women of the Iranian diaspora demanding their sisters be allowed to attend football at home, to the brave anti-fascist start-up clubs of Eastern Europe. There are tournaments that seek to engage the marginalized and the dispossessed, ranging from the Homeless and Anti-Racist World Cups to refugee and amputee leagues. There are heralds of alternative politics like the teams of the Zapatistas of Southern Mexico, or Non-U FC, the club of the Vietnamese dissidents of Hanoi. The extent to which these new social actors have been able to challenge and mitigate the logics of their economic and political adversaries remains limited, yet their potential remains largely untapped. Progressive ideologies, however, have no monopoly on dissent. The new football has also driven the steady drift of Italian ultras towards fascism, the vast outbreak of neo-Nazi, white supremacist and ultra-nationalist football firms in Eastern Europe, and the mutation of Latin America's *barras bravas* into organized criminal operations.

The impact of economic globalization on football, the meaning and consequence of political interventions in the game, and the forms that resistance to the dominant order take, are at the heart of this book, but across the planet they vary wildly. As a result our examination of world football is geographically organized, primarily following football's own regional and continental structures. In Chapter 1, 'The Living and the Dead', we survey the state of sub-Saharan African football, where the game, in the shape of the 2010 South African World Cup, was meant to mark an African renaissance or rebirth. In the realm of football that has yet to arrive – indeed, in some ways it has undergone a slow death, for the negative consequences of economic globalization have been sharpest in Africa. Over the last two decades the affection of fans and the careers of players have been lost, en masse, to Europe and the rest of the football world. No continent has seen its domestic professional game hollowed out so comprehensively, a process Africa's football associations have often aided and abetted. It is a mercy, though by no means adequate compensation, that the continent can boast, as yet undimmed, the life, light and energy of its grassroots scene and its alternative football cultures.

North Africa, for the purposes of this book, is considered part of the wider Middle East, its football politics being more closely aligned with those of the Levant and West Asia than Sub-Saharan Africa. In Chapter 2, 'Regime vs Street vs Mosque', we explore the ways in which, in this three-way conflict between states, their societies and their religions, attempts have been made to interpret and mobilize football for political and ideological purposes. Issues of dress, participation and mixed-gender spectating and playing, for example, have become super-politicized, dividing not only men and women but also secular and religious, moderates and conservatives. At one end of the spectrum the stern and joyless versions of Wahhabist Islam abhor the game entirely: a theology that has led suicide bombers to blow themselves up in the football stadiums, cafes and tea rooms of the region. At the other end, amongst leftist secular Palestinians, the game is seen as an almost unique shared national project and a powerful instrument of women's inclusion.

In another part of the field, where the conflict has been between street and regime, the decrepit personal dictatorships of North Africa, from Ben Ali in Tunisia to Mubarak in Egypt, attempted to control the meaning of the game, but were symbolically challenged by the new football ultras of the region. Come the Arab Spring, in Egypt especially, these rulers were directly challenged by football fans. In the Gulf, where, despite the best efforts and deep pockets of the local ruling class, domestic football is barely worth dominating – not that they don't – international football is, as Qatar's purchase of PSG and Abu Dhabi's of Manchester City suggest, a more enticing arena, and a multi-faceted instrument of foreign policy.

In Chapter 3, 'From the Left Wing', we turn to football in South America, in an era characterized until recently by the advance of the region's Left. Traditionally wary of football as a political tool, the twenty-first-century South American Left embraced it, from Venezuela's and Bolivia's Left populists to Argentina's Peronists. There have been some successes and progressive advances along the way: in Chile, football was a small cultural catalyst for the phenomenal wave of youth, student and educational protest that the country underwent; in Colombia the game has been an important thread through the country's peace process; women's football is finding a toehold across the continent.

However, for the most part the game's main message has been to lay bare the seemingly insoluble economic problems of the continent, still so dependent on the global export of raw materials and agricultural produce. Locked into an unequal relationship with European football, the region has increasingly sold its best players on and, bereft of them, its domestic game cannot catch up with the competition. At the same time the disastrous local management of the game, the unchecked scale of corruption and the impact of the global drugs trade all hold back football and make it a microcosm of the continent's wider economic problems.

In Chapter 4, 'This Storm is What We Call Progress', we examine European football, the metropole of the global football empire. Here the game can be read as both an exemplar of the very best that the continent and its integration project can offer, and at the same time as a powerful indicator of the failures and inequities of its economic model. Here, at the centre of the globalized industry, the world's best players and coaches, equipped with finest support staff and infrastructure, have produced, at the pinnacle, the most extraordinary football ever played. Violence and disorder, aggressive nationalism and racism, while all still part of the game, appeared to

be on the decline, as carnival fans appeared at international tournaments and the first anti-racism campaigns in football flourished.
However, in the poorer peripheries of the continent, nurtured by a
new generation of nationalist and populist politicians, all these ills
are returning to the game with a vengeance. The politics of the continent's national teams and the diversity of their ethnic make-up,
have become a touchstone for the new and more viscous politics of
identity in Europe everywhere. Above all, despite the regulatory
efforts of UEFA and even the European Union, nothing is able to close
the great financial chasm between winners and losers in football, nor
halt the tax evasion, rule-bending and corruption of the powerful.

In Chapter 5, 'Continental Drift', we look at the many different
worlds of Asian football, in a survey that encompasses: the economically developed yet culturally marginal football cultures of Japan,
South Korea and Australia; the football madness of South East Asia,
where a combination of unchecked match-fixing and political conflict
helps keep the local game in a state of underdevelopment; and the
football vanity projects of Central Asia's post-Soviet ruling dynasties.
Yet Asia's place as a peripheral player in world football is changing.
Led by the Chinese, but by no means confined to them, the continent
has been on a global spending spree, buying players, clubs and influence. As the world tilts east on its economic axis, this is, the Chinese
seem to think, just the beginning of a longer power-play.

In Chapter 6, 'Trouble in Paradise', we survey the politics of football in CONCACAF – Confederation of North, Central America and
Caribbean Association Football – again which, in keeping with the loose
offshore banking regulations and tax regimes of the Caribbean, has
proved to be the most obviously corrupt of the regional federations
and a key node in the networks of global larceny that have engulfed
the game in recent years. Mexico, of course, reveals the deep metaphorical and narrative connections between football and public life,
nowhere more so than in the country's still unfulfilled longing to
make it to the fifth game at the World Cup. A close look at the game's
political economy reveals something of the nation's wider shortcom-
ings: its dependence on a narrow class of oligarchs and its prostration
before the drug lords. Across the border, the United States is acquiring a metaphorical relationship with football of hitherto unseen
intensity, but, as with so much in this deeply divided nation, it is just
one fraction of the nation, albeit a diverse coalition, that is doing so.

One common thread running through all these chapters is that corruption, in its many forms, is endemic, indeed systemic, in much of global football. In Africa, domestic football associations are the chief looters and embezzlers, though the same practices are widespread in South and West Asia. In Latin America, the same constituency has been assisted by corrupt media networks and football agents. Money-laundering and crossovers with the drug trade and organized crime are strongest here, but by no means unique. The building of football infrastructure, almost everywhere, is subject to rake-offs in the grey zone between public funds and private construction companies. Match-fixing and illegal betting, institutional conflicts of interest and fixed decision-making processes, can be found on every continent. There are deep structural reasons why there is so much more corruption in twenty-first-century football than ever before. In the first place there is more money around, and there are more ways to steal it. Most importantly, the wormholes of offshore finance have created more ways to hide it and eventually spend it without being caught. Secondly, the presence of so many powerful political figures within the game, and the influence they hold, mean that almost everywhere legal and police authorities are at best slow to investigate these crimes, and often simply complicit.

However, the fish rots from the head, and while even under the rule of Themis, Greek goddess of justice, corruption would have proliferated in modern football, it has been given the most magnificent lead from the summit. Sitting atop the football world through all of this has been FIFA, and in Chapter 7, 'The Game Beyond the Game', we explore the patronage politics operating at the highest levels of global football, and the corruption it allowed to proliferate. In its focus on Sepp Blatter, President of the organization between 1998 and 2015, it offers a case study of how football's ruling institutions have escaped scrutiny and regulation, and how the unvarnished and unchecked power that has enabled has deluded its office holders.

We conclude our global tour in Chapter 8, 'Back in the USSR?', in Vladimir Putin's Russia, where football has become an increasingly important tool in the regime's box of political technologies. Football clubs, like much of Russia's public realm, have been transferred into the hands of pliant oligarchs or the state's still huge public companies. Gazprom, the country's largest company, not only bankrolls Zenit St Petersburg, but also sponsors UEFA, Schalke 04 in Germany and a slew of smaller clubs in areas of foreign policy interest. The rich if unsavoury seam of hooliganism, right-wing ultra-nationalism and anti-migrant and anti-semitic sentiment that runs through Russian football was first co-opted by the regime and then, when inconvenient, suppressed. What began as a marriage of convenience between the state and football has proved so successful that Russia bid for, won and then hosted the 2018 World Cup, offering the regime a chance to build and show off its best and biggest Potemkin village. But let us deal with this World Cup first.

Ghosts, wake from your reverie!

The FIFA machine has finally got everything in place, and yet the agony is going to have to be extended. Before we get to Germany and the Cup, we are going to have to suffer the awards for the best player and the best goalkeeper of the tournament: Lionel Messi and Manuel Neuer respectively. Messi looks like death. Then, to ensure the world obtains its pound of pathos, the broken Argentinians have to do the whole loser's-medal routine. Finally, the German squad are given their medals, the cup held back until they have all assembled on a camera-friendly podium. The final handover of the trophy is the only moment of unrehearsed awkwardness, as it moves, like a ticking bomb, from Jérôme Valcke to Sepp Blatter to President Rousseff to German captain Philipp Lahm. He joins his team on their own separate Plexiglass plinth, the FIFA hierarchy and its allies as backdrop, all showered by golden foil confetti. Lahm raises the Cup to an emptying stadium and a vast phalanx of photographers assembled below on the pitch.

Here, at the very pinnacle of this global moment, this condensation of humanity's global networks and attention, we can, if we choose, see that after the football and the craziness that surrounds it, the real world has been present all along. The spectacle both dazzles and blinds us, but it has yet to seal itself off from challenge and critique, should we wish to engage with it. It is not obligatory to do so, but if we wish to retain some of the life and spontaneity of our game, if we want to preserve the real solidarities and collective identities we derive from it, if we think football should not be dominated by money and power alone, but by the logics of play, then it might be wise.

1

THE LIVING AND THE DEAD:
AFRO FOOTBALL FEVER

We want, on behalf of our continent, to stage an event that will send ripples of confidence from the Cape to Cairo – an event that will create social and economic opportunities throughout Africa. We want to ensure that, one day, historians will reflect upon the 2010 FIFA World Cup as a moment when Africa stood tall and resolutely turned the tide on centuries of poverty and conflict. We want to show that Africa's time has come.[1]

Thabo Mbeki, President of South Africa, 2009

Liberian football is dead. We are looking at ways of reviving it.

President of the Liberian Football Federation, 2015

1

Africa has been playing and following football for over a century and a half. Despite its British origins it became the dominant sport in the colonies of every European empire. Despite its imperial connotations it served, widely, as an instrument of the independence movements and, later, in the shape of CAF and the continental tournaments it created, a practical example of pan-African co-operation and identity. By the early 1990s Africa was considered the third continent in global football, its national sides way ahead of Asia and Central America at the World Cup, its best players finding their way to the top of European football, and its administrators a real power bloc in the politics of FIFA. Its domestic football was often erratic, but the biggest clubs, and the great derbies that had developed, were drawing enormous crowds, and the fever for playing and watching the game was palpable.

Thus, twenty years later, Africa's first World Cup was serving as a cipher for the rising status and immense potential of the world's youngest continent in an increasingly globalized world. Certainly the successful staging of the South African World Cup was a blow against the Afro-pessimists and their scaremongering. It was possible to discern something of the continent's intense relationship with football in its manufactured spaces, filled by the intense buzzing of ten thousand vuvuzelas, Pentecostal choirs in the stands, and every African uniting behind the Ghanaians.

African football has not, however, delivered on the promise of the late twentieth century. It has held a World Cup, but its national teams have not performed any better on the world stage, and are losing ground to the rapid development of Asian football. Its football administrators and politicians have ceded influence in the corridors of power to their richer Asian competitors. At the same time, the domestic game has been in decline across the continent, haemorrhaging fans and players to the rest of the world. It has not, across the board, fallen as far or as terminally as Liberian football, crushed by a decade of civil war and the devastating Ebola virus, but it can appear in many nations that the football dead outweigh the living. South Africa 2010 offered a few clues as to why this should be, but rather than try and gauge the state of the African game from the heart of the global spectacle, we might have done better by leaving the stadium and heading out into the city.

In Kampala, a low, long breeze-block building is rendered in the precise royal blue of a Chelsea shirt, the club's crest neatly painted on top. Manchester United's Red Devil, undulating on its corrugated iron canvas, stares back from a lean-to in Nairobi. Sitting amongst thousands in the agonizingly stationary go-slow on Lagos's Third Mainland Bridge, we can hear every radio tuned to 'It's Monday morning and it's a *huuuuuuuge* week in football. We got EPL. We got La Liga. We got Serie A . . .' Take a closer a look at the battered buses and the taxis and see the pennants, stickers and flags in foreign football colours on their dashboards. Step into a barber's shack, the key arena for the arbiters of taste and style in Africa's male urban social networks. Here, hand-painted signs offer the Essien, the Ronaldo and the Pienaar.[2] In Nigeria, Star Beer have partnered with five foreign football teams to produce dedicated club packaging and branding on their cans and bottles. From Lagos's main roads you can see the crests of Manchester City and Juventus, huge, high and back-lit, hanging over the rubbish dumps, slums and scrapyards that hug the hard shoulder. Above all, just stop and stare and see the football shirts. On a visit to a suburban police station in Kampala, my driver was in a Chelsea shirt, we passed an early morning jogger with an old Newcastle United top, saw that the man in charge of parking was in a Crystal Palace strip, and noted that the police detective I spoke to was wearing a belt with a large brassy clasp engraved with Manchester United's crest. In 2014, sportsdirect.com reported that almost 30 per cent of their sales of the new official Chelsea shirts were from Lagos alone. In the distant Omo Valley of Southern Ethiopia, lip plates and scarification are giving way to a new aesthetic of recycled European clothing, in which football shirts are prized for their blocks of intense colour.[3]

Like every other aspect of African society, football has been linked to global economic, technological and cultural networks that have put the continent at a disadvantage, and accentuated rather that narrowed existing inequalities between Africa and the world.

First, and most significantly, as our short tour through the African city suggests, African domestic football has been marginalized culturally and reduced to penury by the arrival of satellite television and the mass export of fans' affections and custom to European football in general, and the English Premier League in particular. Second, Africa continues to export its best and most highly skilled people, and football players are at the very head of the pack. Indeed, since the turn of the century the number of football migrants has risen, which has impoverished the local game as a spectacle, and has as yet to improve its finances, skills base or infrastructure. Third, Africa's stadiums were so neglected in the late twentieth century that they became increasingly deadly, prone to stampedes, riots and fires. In the absence of any investment from elsewhere, African football, along with much of the rest of the continent, has turned to China. As part of their vast soft-power initiative in Africa, the Chinese have built almost all of the continent's new stadiums – fit to stage televised spectaculars and presidential rallies. As with so many infrastructure projects in Africa, it is not clear that they are of any benefit to anyone else – not least the clubs who cannot afford to rent them, the fans who can't reach their distant locations, or the players, who might benefit more from some new boots and balls than secure underground car parks. Pharaonic in concept and execution, the staging of the African Cup of Nations (AFCON) in these new stadiums provides a powerful lens on the politics of Africa's oil states and the dynamics of contemporary African urban development. We begin this chapter by exploring these features of contemporary African football, before turning to Africa's regions and their more specific encounters with these global forces. In West Africa issues of governance, corruption and football violence are paramount; in East and Central Africa, football has had to survive gruelling civil and international wars; while in Southern Africa, in Zimbabwe in particular, the game has been used, consumed and diminished by Mugabe and ZANU-PF's unquenchable will to power.

Everywhere on the continent, however, and African football is by no means alone in this, the inequities and injustices of global networks have been multiplied by the corruption and incompetence of its ruling institutions. As we shall see throughout this chapter, national football federations have made their own special contribution to the often disastrous organizational state of their leagues and grassroots programmes, but they were given magnificent leadership by CAF and its long-serving president Issa Hayatou, the perfect incarnation of Africa's immovable presidents-for-life. When his twenty-eight years as president of the organization came to an end in 2017, his reign was exceeded by only those of Presidents Biya, Obiang, Dos Santos and Mugabe, of Cameroon, Equatorial Guinea, Angola and Zimbabwe respectively. Born in 1946 the son of a Muslim sultan in northern Cameroon, Issa Hayatou played basketball for his country, but football administration became his post-athletics career when he became the secretary of the Cameroonian football association in 1974. In 1988, he won the presidency of CAF.[4] Acquisitions of this kind of sinecure were not unusual in a family that remained very close to President Biya and boasted an ex-prime minister amongst its number. Challenges to his position in 2000 and 2004 were imperiously swept aside, and the vanquished were duly punished. For more than two decades, his rule in African football was absolute if comatose. He certainly entrenched his own and Africa's positions within FIFA, securing more World Cup places for the continent and committee roles for its tribunes. Under his rule, AFCON was expanded to sixteen teams and its slot in the middle of the European football season protected. TV deals and sponsorships for AFCON, as well as the CAF Champions League, inched up in value, but were worth less than 5 per cent of their European equivalents. What he did not do was address any of the long-standing structural problems in African football administration and governance.

On Hayatou's watch, and despite a rising stream of income to African football associations from FIFA, the cupboard was always bare amongst CAF's members, certainly when it came to paying football association staff, coaches and players. Money raised from government to invest in infrastructure and development, as well as cash from sponsorship and TV deals, rarely found its way out of African houses of football. The stand-offs and strikes that have affected African World Cup squads in the last decade are just the most visible consequences of a great mountain of late pay, cut pay and bonuses siphoned off into the bank accounts of directors and their front companies. In 2014, Ghana's players refused to go on until they received their World Cup pay in cash in Brazil, a transaction that required the personal intervention of President John Dramani Mahama. In 2016, after coming first and third respectively in the women's AFCON,

Nigeria's Super Falcons had to march on the national assembly in Abuja to receive their due, while Ghana's Black Queens had to stage a protest outside the Ministry of Sport in Accra to get their bonuses.[5]

Hayatou, predictably, saw none of this, exerted no pressure on Africa's national associations, demanded no reform. Was he so busy not looking that he did not glimpse his own fall coming? In 2012, the Ivorian Jacques Anouma had the temerity to mount a challenge. Hayatou dispatched him by having CAF's statutes changed so that only members of the executive committee could stand for the presidency. Anouma was not on the committee. In April 2015, the CAF statutes were changed again, this time removing the age limit of seventy for a president. This allowed Hayatou, due to be seventy a year before the next election, to put himself forward for yet another term. By now, his health and faculties were failing him. A man whose style was ambulatory at best, he survived a kidney transplant only to come to a complete halt. In 2015, when stand-in President of FIFA after Sepp Blatter's fall, he fell asleep at his own press conference. There was a gathering storm of accusations, too. He had survived revelations that he had received a payment of $100,000 from the marketing company ISL as part of its acquisition of World Cup rights from FIFA. Hayatou admitted receiving the money, but always said he used it to pay for a celebration of CAF's fortieth anniversary in 1997. We await the accounts. Suspicions were raised when CAF refused to announce the actual amount it was receiving from the oil company Total, one of its new sponsors. Simultaneously, the Egyptian public prosecutor announced that the deal Hayatou had done with French broadcaster Lagardère for the CAF Champions League had broken Egyptian law. In the fight to replace Blatter at FIFA, he backed Sheikh Salman, who turned out to be the wrong horse. The winner, Gianni Infantino, handed out a dose of Hayatou's own medicine and stripped him of his place on the powerful finance committee.

Thus, in 2017, already weakened, he faced a real challenge from the head of the Madagascan FA Ahmad Ahmad and his pugnacious Zimbabwean campaign manager Phillip Chiyangwa, a property developer with good ZANU-PF credentials who became president of the Zimbabwean FA in 2015 and was gunning for Hayatou from the off. The two had the votes of the Southern African region sewn up, and they found plenty of people who Hayatou had snubbed, excluded or overlooked in his ruthless allocation of patronage, especially in anglophone Africa. Hayatou responded by cancelling Madagascar's hosting of the U-17 African championships, and CAF sent intimidating if vacuous letters to Chiyangwa claiming he had transgressed all kinds of statutes. When the votes were counted, the king was dead, comprehensively beaten 34–20. It was hardly the herald of a new dawn in African football, or a real changing of the guard. The optimistic might argue that it was at least the end of the kind of endless torpor, decay and inertia over which Africa's morbid presidents have presided, but no one was counting on it. If there is life in African football we are unlikely to find it here.

II

The degree to which European football has entered everyday life in Africa is extraordinary. Step inside the fabulous art deco cinemas of Asmara, built when it was the capital of the Italian colony of Eritrea. Look beyond the exquisite period fittings and you will see that the list of show times is for European football games, not European art house films. As one cinema owner put it, 'You cannot find a place to sit when Arsenal play Manchester United. Some wear the team colours. The Italians would be surprised if they knew. The only thing they knew about was the movies.'[6] In Lomé, the capital of Togo, every Arsenal game was preceded by a city-wide cavalcade of fans on bikes and scooters, dressed in club colours and whipping up the atmosphere. In the small town of Lalibela in Ethiopia, Jonathan Wilson calculated that with every bar and viewing house in the town full, more than 20 per cent of the male adult population was watching the Premier League. It was no different in the capital, where one reporter saw 'Dozens of Arsenal fans gather around a bar in Addis Ababa's trendy Bole district . . . minibuses adorned with the club's crest speed through busy streets; teenagers selling cigarettes sport Arsenal's red home kit; and business executives tune in to watch the match at airport lounges.'[7]

African newspapers have kept track of English football since at least the 1950s, if only for the devoted followers of the pools. The BBC World Service has been broadcasting the scores on a Saturday afternoon for over half a century. Nigerians used to get a single weekly free-to-air highlights show of English football during the 1980s; many brought home prized video recordings of televised matches from their time in Britain. Enough to whet the appetite, but pretty meagre fare. The arrival in the mid-1990s of DSTV, Africa's main anglophone satellite broadcaster, and its francophone counterpart, Canalsat Afrique, changed everything. For the first time, live football from Europe was regularly and reliably available in Africa. Although costs kept the total number of paying subscribers down, a vast ecosystem of sharing screens in viewing houses, cinemas and sports bars allowed football to reach the majority of the population, even in rural areas.[8] Were we in Ouagadougou or Bamako, we might be watching French football, perhaps PSG or Olympique de Marseilles. In Luanda or Maputo, the bars would probably be showing Portuguese games, though only if one of the big clubs was playing. In Senegal, La Liga has acquired a fanbase, and El Clásico – the Barcelona/Real Madrid derby – is watched everywhere. Yet even in these franco- and lusophone nations, you would just as likely be watching Everton versus West Brom. A Sportmarkt survey of 2011 found that 72 per cent of Africans were interested in football, 55 per cent watched the EPL and 39 per cent followed an English team. No one can count the number of Africans in football bars, but the standard estimate was that 300 million Africans were regularly tuning into just the EPL. One suspects that the current numbers are much higher.[9]

English football may be the game of the people in Africa, but heads of state and prime ministers are equally engaged. Presidents Mugabe and Nkurunziza of Zimbabwe and Burundi respectively both publicly declared for Chelsea. Ian Khama, the President of Botswana, watched the national team play Togo wearing a vintage Manchester United jersey. The vice-presidents of Nigeria and Kenya declared for Arsenal on Twitter. The first tweet from Kenya's William Ruto read: 'DP @WilliamsRuto: I support #Arsenal. I just don't know where we are at the moment. #GOKInteracts.' Atiku Abubakar, Nigeria's Vice-President under Obasanjo in the 2000s, tweeted, in the midst of a particular fraught party conference, 'this was just what is needed an @Arsenal win to lift me up at a moment like this.'[10] President Paul Kagame of Rwanda was amongst many African Arsenal fans who joined the Wenger in/Wenger out debate. Less vocal on social media but no less supportive were Rupiah Banda, President of Zambia between 2008 and 2011, Prince Seeiso, the younger brother of the

King of Lesotho, Sierra Leone's President Ernest Bai Koroma, and President Adama Barrow of the Gambia, who acquired the Arsenal habit whilst working as a security guard at an Argos catalogue store in north London.[11] Both of Africa's richest individuals – the Nigerian king of concrete Aliko Dangote and Ethiopian-Saudi business magnate Mohammed Hussein Al Amoudi – support Arsenal and have both suggested that they would like to buy the club. The intersection of politicians and English football clubs has become so pervasive that African newspapers have begun to use the Premier League as a metaphor or analogy for their domestic political conflicts. In Kenya, for example, politicians were systematically compared to Premier League clubs.[12] William Ruto was Leicester City, who 'emerged from nowhere and took the position of the big boys', while Kalonzo Musyoka, an ex-vice-president whose own presidential ambitions had faded, was Manchester United, 'once the talk of the town . . . but slowly depreciating.'[13]

The preponderance of Arsenal fans amongst African leaders was broadly reflected on the ground. Measured by numbers of official African supporters' clubs – more than twenty compared to Manchester United's four – Arsenal was Africa's team, its fanbase reaching to the most unlikely corners of the continent, from South Sudan to Tunisia. Kenyans were the second most common visitors to the club's website, Nigerians the fifth. Africans were particularly prominent in the global 'Wenger Out' campaign, with banners noted and shared on social media at an anti-Zuma protest in South Africa, a big music gig in Nairobi and in the stands at a game in Ethiopia. Sharp-eyed visitors to the Emirates in recent years may have noted the large banner of Emeka Onyenuforo, founder of Arsenal Nigeria, hanging from one of the flagpoles outside the ground. The group had 10,000 members in 2017, while Onyenuforo was on the road establishing new supporters' clubs in Benin, Ghana, Togo and Niger. Research by Twitter on the geography of the clubs' online followers suggests that Arsenal has support all across Africa, especially in the east, but has conceded top spot to Chelsea in West Africa, where the presence of Didier Drogba, Michael Essien and Jon Obi Mikel at the club has won over many fans. More anecdotal evidence suggests that there are still plenty of Liverpool supporters out there but, as a young Nigerian and Ghanaian both said to me, 'Liverpool is for old guys.'[14] This may yet change.

While the embrace of European football is pan-African, it has reached its apogee in Nigeria. Amongst the most popular TV hits of recent years is *Celebrity Fan Challenge*, a game show performed in front of a live audience of 6,000, in which Nigerian celebrities – from rappers to Nollywood stars – face off against each other in competitive banter and games over whether Arsenal or Manchester United is the biggest club. Even the local radio traffic reports are peppered with Premier League updates, transfer rumours and details of contractual disputes. Thus at the pinnacle of Nigerian society, the rich, the famous and the powerful all flaunt their football affiliations and, in the case of Atiku Abubakar, actually attend the Arsenal home games on a regular basis. Below them in Nigeria's burgeoning cities, the emerging professional middle class are the mainstay of the country's many official supporters' clubs. In an evening spent with the Chelsea Official Supporters' Club, Lagos branch, I met Suliman, who founded the group and worked as an accounts officer for a second-division Nigerian football club; Adekunle, a banker; Kamal, in insurance; Funny Bone, one of Lagos's leading stand-up comics; and Henry, who ran his own import–export company. An evening spent with the Tottenham Hotspur Official Supporters' Club Lagos branch was equally instructive. A similar social mix, they highlighted the importance of the African diaspora and the longstanding interactions between ex-colonies and the imperium in creating these webs of footballing attraction. Here were Nigerians who had acquired Spurs while living in Britain, going to school in Cornwall, working in Mill Hill and going back and forth between Lagos and London on business.

Viewed from Lagos, the Premier League is not merely a great sporting spectacle and soap opera, it is also a slice of the global North that Nigerians can enter, if not freely then certainly with more ease than most international border posts. It is a realm of consumption and glamour that is tangible, and it is a world where things work. In fact, many Nigerians like the Premier League as a whole as much as their club. 'The EPL is like a religion,' one told me. 'It can really affect your mood. The thing with the Premier League is that I would watch Stoke v Leicester or Sunderland v Bournemouth. I would watch *El Clásico*, too, but Osasuna v Malaga? Forget it.' Another young Lagosian and Manchester United fan, when asked why he loved the whole of the Premier League – was it the style of play, the crowd? – replied, 'It's the branding . . . it's just so professional.'

Nigeria's love of the Premier League extends beyond watching and reading. In 2006, 27 December was deemed Arsenal day in the small city of Kogi in the east of the country. Eleven years later, hundreds of fans, all in club strip, were still gathering in the town square still bedecked with Arsenal banners. In 2008, Chelsea fans from the Lagos neighbourhood of Ebutte Meta gave out free jerseys and prepared a public feast, including a bull painted in team colours, in anticipation of their club's victory in the Champions League final. Chelsea lost but they ate the bull anyway. Love can breed hate. In the aftermath of Manchester United's defeat by Barcelona in the 2009 Champions League final, a United fan in the town of Ogbo in Nigeria drove his minibus past a group of celebrating Barcelona supporters. He then did a U-turn and drove straight at them, killing four people and injuring ten.[15]

Nigeria has no monopoly on this kind of violence. In 2010 in a bar in Lamu, Kenya, a Liverpool fan, Abibakar Bashie, was stabbed during their game with Manchester United after an explosive argument with opponents. Football suicides, though often related to gambling losses and debts, are disturbingly common. In Nairobi in 2009, Suleiman Omondi hanged himself wearing his Arsenal shirt after his side had lost 3–1 to United. Conversely, in 2013 a Manchester United fan plunged to his death from the seventh-floor balcony of an apartment block after his side had lost to Newcastle United.[16] The marital consequences of football have become a perennial of Africa's agony aunts who encourage women to accommodate their partners' obsession, not merely by timing meals and family events around the fixture list, but by embracing their club.[17]

A study of the impact of the Premier League on the small village of Bugamba in south-western Uganda in the late 2000s suggests much more than marital relations has changed.[18] The purchase of a satellite dish and a football subscription by one resident of the village led to the creation of a viewing house which proved phenomenally popular. Within a few months, the viewing house was the centre of village social life, a significant employer in its own right, while the owners rose significantly up the village's social pecking order. Over a two-to-three-year period, the villagers' conceptions of time and space changed too. While before the Premier League the basic distinctions were morning–afternoon–night, familiarity with its schedules meant locals began to use clock time. A quarter to eight meant nothing until it meant a midweek evening kick-off. Similarly, before the arrival of the EPL, the rest of the world was referred to as *burayeas*, which roughly translated as 'the global domain'. Familiarity with the cosmopolitan make-up of the Premier League meant that villagers – now arguing as to whether a player was a Croat, a Slovene or from the Ukraine – became acquainted with the basic geography of the world. Priorities shifted too, as dinner dates, previously unbreakable, could be shifted to accommodate the football schedules, so too marriages, baptisms and church services. Gambling, previously unknown in the village, became widespread, as did its malign social consequences. In 2009, the satellite broadcaster GTV went bust, and so too did the owner of the viewing house, who had extensive debts secured against his now football-less business and land. He lost both.

While the Premier League has been busy working North American and East Asian markets, Africa has only recently appeared on their commercial radar. Manchester United were the first to take note, playing Portsmouth in Abuja in 2008. Hordes of ticketless fans stormed the gates during the game, while the volleys of tear gas from the police blew back into the stadium. Undeterred, United have been back to Africa twice since, though not as yet to Nigeria.[19] By contrast, the Premier League is very much on African businesses' radar. Sunderland were the first club to have their shirt sponsored by an African operation. The oil company Tullow put the slogan 'Invest in Africa' on their shirts. The South African bank Bidvest succeeded them, and the club, in a very rare act of reciprocation, has established the league's strongest practical links with the continent, running coaching clinics and a supported grassroots facility. The Kenyan government has looked to sponsor a Premier League exhibition game or two, but the money initially allocated for 'the Magic Cup', as the project was fancifully known, evaporated. The private sector has proved more reliable. Everton, sponsored by the Kenyan online betting firm Sportpesa, played their first games in Africa in 2017 at a tournament in Dar es Salaam.[20]

African clubs don't keep the most comprehensive attendance records in the world, but casual observation of the stands and attention to the debate in the local press make it abundantly clear that the size of the crowds at the local game has, since the arrival of satellite television, plummeted almost everywhere on the continent. Writing of the national derby in the 1990s between Heart of Oaks and Asante

Kotoko, one Ghanaian recalled 'those days when football fans showed up at the then Kumasi Sports Stadium very early in the morning to stand in long queues to purchase tickets for a game that will kick off eight hours later. People outside Kumasi had to come a day before matches to sleep at the stadium.' Such was the demand that there was even a black market in tickets. Today, there are no queues and the stands are at best half full.[21] In Zimbabwe, the crowd at the country's biggest game, Highlanders v Dynamos, halved between 2012 and 2014. At just 13,000, it was easily the largest crowd of the season, when most clubs would be pleased with four-figure attendances of any kind.[22] In Uganda, where once Express v SC Villa could command crowds of 15,000, they now play in front of just a thousand people. In the provinces, the audiences are in the low hundreds.

The pull of European football in terms of both sporting spectacle and its encrusted cultural meanings are strong, but the parlous state of domestic football on television and in the stadium is equally important in pushing people away. Compared to the multiple cameras and microphones on European television coverage, and its slick editing and graphics, African football just can't compete. Many games, if they are shown at all, have been covered with just a couple of fixed cameras showing the whole pitch, with the occasional cut to a hand-held camera on the touchline. The stadium itself is often more unappetizing, with facilities of any kind thin on the ground. 'In our own stadium,' argued a Zambian fan of both beer and the Premier League, 'refreshments are not allowed. So why should I go to the stadium and be thirsty for ninety minutes when I can be watching in a bar with a big screen?'[23]

African leagues and federations have been considering change. Some have proposed shifting their entire seasons from the European, September-to-May, model to a summer league. Others have tried to shift their kick-off times. The general manager of FC Abuja was candid. 'Whenever we play at the same time as an Arsenal game, nobody shows up.'[24] As to the football itself? The cameras, however few of them there are, do not lie. The ball does not move sweetly, the pitches are, more often than not, in desperate condition. There is still talent in Africa, but more than 3,000 of its professionals are playing outside the continent. The top one hundred or so are concentrated at the biggest and richest leagues in Europe. They are on television almost every day, and they are not coming back.

III

In a series of paintings and collages, the Ghanaian artist Godfried
Donkor has cast the African footballer of the mid-to-late twentieth
century as a saint, and presented him like a Russian icon, head surrounded and illuminated by a halo of light.[25] In *Santo Eusebio*, the
Mozambican, who played his whole career for Benfica and Portugal,
is set against the share prices of the *Financial Times*. In *Santo Omam*,
we see François Omam-Biyik, the player who put Africa on the
world's football map when he scored Cameroon's winner against
Argentina in the opening game of the 1990 World Cup, with covers
of *Ebony* magazine, a style and political trend-setter amongst mid-
century African Americans and the wider African diaspora, floating
behind him in space. These works of art feature the heroes of decolonization, civil rights and black pride: Haile Selassie, Jackie Robinson
and Duke Ellington. Donkor's pictures capture the African stars of
another age: today's icons would have to put the African footballer
in the context of more contemporary models of success – TV stars
and rappers, the slick preachers of prosperity and the real-estate
hustlers – but the esteem in which they have been held in Africa has
not diminished. If anything it is much greater.

Wage slavery is long gone for those who play at the peak of European football. A backdrop of the *Financial Times*'s luxury-goods
supplement 'How to Spend It' might be more fitting. In either case,
the era of print is closing; for today's players, fame and presence has
been multiplied a thousand times by the arrival of the digital screen
in all its forms, and the ways in which the newly liberalized African
media has embraced the multi-faceted celebrity of these football
icons.

Of all the African players who have straddled these multiple
worlds and meanings, Didier Drogba is without peer.[26] Drogba's occupation of local media space was comprehensive – a survey of the
Ivorian sports press found that he featured in 80 per cent of player
photographs and nearly two-thirds of front pages. At his peak in
2009, his presence in the urban spaces of Côte d'Ivoire was pervasive.
The wooden walls of barbers' shops in the slums featured his carefully
painted image. A thousand shacks were enlivened by posters of him

in flight; so too the battered doors of Abidjan's *gbakas*, the vans that serve as the city's buses. A local brewery served up Drogba beer, and his name became a synonym in *nochui*, the local Franco-African slang, for 'strong' or 'tough'.

Another measure of players' popular celebrity is their occupation of musical space. Drogba had a major presence, but he was not alone. While at Olympique de Marseilles and Chelsea he became well known for celebrating his goals with a dance move that combined a horizontal swipe of the arm with a series of body jerks. This was part of the repertoire of *Coupé-Décalé* – a dance and music style invented by Ivorian migrants in the African nightclubs of Paris – which was hugely popular both in the diaspora and back in Côte d'Ivoire. A fan of the genre, Drogba was given its ultimate accolade by the invention of a dance move, the *Drogbacite*, based on his movements when playing. This in turn was referenced in dozens of popular songs, from 'Drogbacite' by Shanaka Yakuza and DJ Dream Team to DJ Arsenal's 'Shelobouka'. Ghanaian striker Asamoah Gyan, who rapped on three albums with hiplife star Castro, has a similar relationship to *Azonto*, an Accra dance craze. Originally called Appe or 'work', it mainly involved mimicking tasks and chores like driving, ironing, sweeping and washing. Gyan celebrated scoring the deciding goal against Nigeria in a 2010 Africa Cup of Nations qualifier with a hot routine that combined short hops and mime. It went viral online and triggered a craze on the dance floors. Samuel Eto'o and Alex Song have both featured in Cameroonian tunes. Maahlox's 'Alexandre Song Dans Ton Dos' celebrated the latter's red card that followed a sharp elbow on Croat Mario Mandzukic at the 2014 World Cup. Samuel Eto'o's old-man celebration – a creaking walk with an imaginary stick – was a riposte to José Mourinho's criticism of his decline, and became both a dance move and a song, 'La Danse du Grand Père', by Le Featurist.

Type the name of African football stars into Google and almost always you will be offered the popular search suffixes: net worth, mansion, cars, wedding. Many are remarkably generous in their donations to charitable foundations. Samuel Eto'o has built an entire hospital; Michael Essien has equipped his home town with functioning sanitation. But the African press knows what its public wants, and it is delivering: constructing footballing rich lists, and detailing Obafemi Martins's investments in the hotel industry; drooling over

Yaya Touré's neo-Georgian mansion in the Cheshire countryside and
the addition of a second Rolls Royce to his fleet of six cars; lionizing
El Hadji Diouf, the Senegalese striker, and his 'bling-tastic' glitter-gold
Cadillac Escalade; and covering players' visits home, their family lives
and their activities on social media with relish. In this celebrity space,
footballers have often played the 'big man': a patron, patriarch and
model of the conspicuous consumption that Africa's tiny but fabulously wealthy elites have made the essential cypher of success.
Didier Drogba played this game too on his visits to Abidjan, where he
was thronged by crowds outside his mansion, around his cavalcade of
cars and at the nightclubs he liked to frequent. The king of African
bling, though, was Emmanuel Adebayor, who in 2013 shared pictures
of his key assets on Snapchat. There were cars a-plenty, of course, but
a Miami mansion too, as well as a private jet and an Imelda Marcos-
scale collection of sneakers and sandals.

No one would accuse of Adebayor of mixing football and politics
too closely, but many of his peers do occupy political space in Africa.
Increasingly, the leading players have had the experience, the independence and the confidence to challenge the governance of their
own football associations: conflicts which are seen by African publics
as emblematic of their own struggles with failed and corrupt public
institutions. Footballers have begun to appear on the campaign trail
as a celebrity draw for politicians. Kanu worked the crowd for Goodluck Jonathan in the 2010 Nigerian presidential elections. El Hadji
Diouf serves at the call of Senegal's President Macky Sall. A few, like
George Weah, have crossed to the other side. Weah ran unsuccessfully for the presidency of Liberia in 2005, but has since been elected
as a national senator, and in 2018 in a second campaign actually won
the big prize. Drogba, while not holding any formal political post,
has been more engaged in public life than any other player of his
generation. Domestically, he has played important symbolic and
occasionally practical roles in the peace process that finally put an
end to Côte d'Ivoire's civil war, but in addition he has had an international political profile as a goodwill ambassador for UNDP.[27] Like
many other players, however, his brush with domestic politics has
proved less accommodating. Appointed, with much fanfare, to a
national reconciliation commission in 2011, he found himself a very
minor player in a report that many felt only scratched the surface of
the nation's problems.

Amongst players like these, at the top of the game, hardly anyone is playing at home or in the peripheral leagues of global football. Amongst the twelve sub-Saharan African squads at the World Cup between 2006 and 2014, two had no domestically based players at all (Côte d'Ivoire and Togo in 2006), and only two had more than four – the nine who played for Angola in 2006 and sixteen for South Africa in 2010. For some, the most direct route to European football has been to be born or grow up in the diaspora in Europe but choose an African football citizenship. Demba Ba, Frédérick Kanouté and Pierre-Emerick Aubameyang were all born in France but have opted to played for Senegal, Mali and Gabon respectively. Didier Drogba lived nearly all of his childhood there too, but chose Côte d'Ivoire. Another useful option is to keep it in the family. André Ayew's arrival at TSV 1860 München was eased by the pioneering Ghanaian star of the 1990s, Abedi Pele, who also happened to be his father. Rigobert Song was instrumental in getting his nephew Alex Song to Bastia. Older members of this generation, like Nigerians Nwankwo Kanu and Jay-Jay Okocha, actually had professional careers at home before ascending the club ladder in Europe, but this is increasingly rare.

While these routes to Europe remain open, and the old mechanisms of chain migration, informal connections and chance scouting are still in operation, the twenty-first century has seen a much more organized and systematic approach to the nurture and export of footballing talent.[28] The vast majority of Africa's stars have come through the complex cluster of football academies and schools that have emerged over the last twenty years. Some were entirely African operations, based at a few leading clubs like ASEC Mimosas' Abidjan academy, which produced Yaya Touré, or Ghana's Liberty Professionals, who nurtured Michael Essien and Asamoah Gyan. There were also Afro-European partnerships where the Europeans took a stake in the club, like Feyenoord Fetteh in Ghana, Aldo Gentina, originally Monaco's partner in Senegal, and Ajax Cape Town in South Africa, or more informal relationships like that between Generation Foot in Senegal and Metz – a link that took Sadio Mané north.

Outside the conventional club structures, private academies have sprouted up all over Africa, driven by a mixture of motives commercial and philanthropic. Some are the creation of high-profile ex-players like Abedi Pele in Ghana, Patrick Vieira in Senegal, or Salif Keita, whose Malian academy launched Seydou Keita. Others are more formal corporate entities, like the Pepsi Academy in Lagos, whose alumni include John Obi Mikel and Celestine Babayaro, and the Kadji Academy in Douala, Cameroon, which sent Samuel Eto'o to Real Madrid. Beyond these core institutions, there is a great periphery of small, undercapitalized academies, agents, middlemen, hucksters and scouts. They range from entrepreneurial ex-players with barely a squad's worth of talent in a Lagos flop house, through one-man bands working rural backwaters with a single European contact or connection up their sleeve, to the truly unscrupulous traffickers and tricksters.

While a tiny handful of players, families and academies will hit the jackpot, the reality for most is domestic football or a return to the insecurity and poverty of the informal economy. Sometimes it must be hard to tell the difference. The working conditions of most African football players are perilous.[29] In 2016, 40 per cent were playing without a written contract of any kind, a figure that rose to over 60 per cent in Côte d'Ivoire and Cameroon and almost 90 per cent in Congo. Rates of pay outside of South Africa's premier league and a few well-resourced clubs are meagre. More than half of all players in Africa are consistently paid late. In Ghana, 100 per cent of players reported that they were paid less than $1,000 a month, if they were paid at all. Paid holidays, insurance and medical care are very thin on the ground; so too is camaraderie. Ghanaian players reported a rate of attacks, verbal and physical, by club seniors ten times the global average. More African players (7.6 per cent) are forced to train alone as punishment than anywhere else.

If they survive their team mates and coaches, there is the public and the crowd to contend with. While hardly wealthy by comparison to their own elites, local footballers are visible, liquid and vulnerable. In 2014, the funeral of Senzo Meyiwa, goalkeeper for Orlando Pirates and South Africa, was held in Soccer City and attended by tens of thousands of fans, who mourned his passing and protested the epidemic of homicide and armed robberies in the country. Meyiwa had been shot dead in the course of a burglary of his apartment. Nigerian footballers seem at particular risk when travelling. On the first day of the same season, five Kano Pillars players were wounded by gunfire during an attack on the team bus travelling to Owerri. In 2016, Enyimba's bus was stopped by armed robbers in Kogi. The following season, lower-league Osun United had the misfortune to break down on their return from a game in Calabar, only to have the team bus stormed by an armed gang, who left machete cuts on most of the squad before departing with wallets, money and phones.[30]

The stadium itself offers little respite. One in four Congolese players has been attacked by fans on the pitch during their career. On the same weekend in Nigeria in April 2017, Kano Pillars fans attacked the players of Akwa United who had just beaten them 1–0, forcing them under police protection to barricade their dressing room, and Enyimba's players were pelted with stones and physically assaulted in Katsina by a crowd enraged by the away team's goalkeeper, who had, they thought, roughly handled a ball boy.[31] Match officials are perhaps even more vulnerable than players. Ghana's lower leagues seem particularly hazardous. Referee Kwame Kyei Andoh died from the beatings he received from fans of Dolphin Gold Stars, who objected to an offside call in their game against Najoo Royals. Repeated volleys of police gunshots above the crowd were required to save the beleaguered officials in a game between Tamale Utrecht and Berlin FC.[32] Fans of SC Villa of Kampala, Uganda's biggest club, have repeatedly stoned match officials and journalists.

Given the situation at home, it is hardly surprising that African players that can't make it to even the middling leagues in Europe have increasingly been heading to other countries and continents. In 2015, Africans made up just 2 per cent of the migrant players in Latin America, but they comprised 15 per cent of those in the United States, 23 per cent of almost 800 players in Europe and 27 per cent of the 2,000 foreigners playing in Asian professional leagues, making them the largest overseas contingent there.[33]

The life that awaits these global helots is closer to the experience of most poor African migrants than of those playing in the Bundesliga or Serie A. In Poland, for example, hundreds of Africans have played in the lower leagues, as far down as the semi-professional fourth and fifth levels. Here, in the margins of the margins, players have survived on free, if poor-quality, housing from their clubs, second and third jobs, and the hope that they might be able to move on up the footballing ladder. Very few do. In fact, only two Africans have been able to use Poland as a springboard to a place in the bigger leagues, and then only as far as Slovakia and Turkey. More often than not they head for Warsaw and the diaspora community that has gathered there. Many gravitate to PolBlack, an informal community club drawn from Africans in the city, many of them ex-footballers, who play in the park and survive on the margins of Warsaw's labour market.[34] They, and the many other park teams across the continent, include some of the thousands of football migrants who never made it to a trial or a club at all. Offered the promise of a shot at European football, they and their families were required to come up with the thousands of dollars necessary for passports, visas, airfares and fees, and then they found themselves abandoned on arrival. Others are not abandoned but imprisoned and moved sideways into the sex industry. Culture Foot Solidaire, an NGO created by the former Cameroonian international Jean-Claude Mbvoumin, has claimed that up to 7,000 young Africans have been tricked. While there are of course unwitting victims, there is complicity too. When compared to the cost and the dangers of the Sahel and Mediterranean crossings to Europe, some young Africans are ready to fly and take their chances on the streets of Lille, Ghent or Arnhem.[35]

Knowing that the margins of European football offer such thin pickings, other players have looked east to the emerging leagues of South and South East Asia.[36] Nigerians have been making their way to India since the 1980s. The Cameroonian star Roger Milla played in the Indonesian league in the early 1990s, and through word of mouth and personal connections opened up a steady flow of African players there. Now dozens of Africans can be found in the first-division squads of Malaysia, Singapore, Thailand and Vietnam, all of which offer salaries well in excess of African leagues. Even those that offer barely more money than at home – Cambodia, Bangladesh and Laos, for example – boast a significant African presence. As with their peers in Europe, many hope that a move to these leagues will be the first step to something better, but mobility is no greater in Asia than on the fringes of Europe, and the streets of the continent's cities are even tougher.

In all of this, as with so many of Africa's global linkages, the terms of trade are not equal, and there are just a few winners and many losers. Although African players, their agents and academies have become better and sharper business operators, transfer fees from Europe are not enormous. They are certainly enough to sustain the academies and enrich a few, but not enough to transform the wider economic fortunes of African football. Nor is the African game benefiting from the experience, skills and education its emigrés pick up. African football associations, often fearful of the high standards and expectations its star players acquire abroad, make their integration into the domestic game politically difficult, if not impossible. That same morbid preference for nurturing power rather than talent drives not only Africa's footballers to the four corners of the earth, but also millions and millions of its citizens.

IV

Africa's football stadiums were no strangers to tragedy, but the stench of death hung over them more heavily than ever at the turn of the century. In 2000, in Monrovia, at a game between Liberia and Chad, three fans died in a crush at a ludicrously over-full stadium. Shortly afterwards, during a World Cup qualifier between Zimbabwe and South Africa in Harare, thirteen people were killed in a stampede when police deliberately fired tear gas into the stadium exits. The Congolese police did the same in Lubumbashi the following year, leaving eight dead in their wake. Then in South Africa, an estimated crowd of over 80,000 was squeezed into the 62,000-capacity Ellis Park for the Kaizer Chiefs v Orlando Pirates Johannesburg derby. Panic in the crowd before the game, made worse by the police, turned into a stampede in which forty-three people died and 158 were injured; at kick-off the roar of the crowd smothered the screams of the dying.[37] Later in 2001, during the final seconds of the Ghanaian derby, with Hearts of Oak leading Asante Kotoko 2–1, police fired tear gas into the home crowd, many of whose members were already departing. The stampede that followed was jammed up against locked exit gates and left 126 fatalities.[38] The various post-mortems and inquiries into the state of African football and its stadiums that followed these events laid bare the shameless profiteering by officials who were over-selling tickets without any thought for safety considerations, and revealed stadium management, stewarding and policing all to be reactive and dire. As with so many other aspects of the African city, football's public infrastructure was antiquated, poorly maintained, and on occasion deadly.

These stadiums had been built in the immediate post-war era by colonial regimes who, just a decade or so later, would hand over power to newly independent African nations. Ghana, Nigeria, Zambia and Zaire were all symbolically born in football stadia. Architecturally unremarkable, these were at least functional and have served across the continent as venues for national celebrations, mass religious services, political rallies, temporary army bases and prisons, as well as football matches. However, despite their utility, no African state, Nigeria and South Africa aside, would prove able to build a significant post-independence stadium themselves, or even maintain their small inheritance, as these disasters demonstrated. In fact, for almost half a century now, the only new source of these uniquely important centres of African urban culture and politics has been China.

The Sino-African encounter began in earnest in the late 1960s and early 1970s, centring on Tanzania, whose politics of Afro-rural socialism and commitment to the non-aligned movement made it a natural partner for Mao's China. Alongside renovating the nation's railway network, the Chinese government initiated its programme of stadium diplomacy in Africa, building the national arena in Dar es Salaam in 1971.[39] Somalia acquired one in Mogadishu in 1978, and then through the 1980s and early 1990s the pace picked up, with gifts from the Chinese people popping up in the capital cities of Benin, Burkina Faso, Djibouti, Liberia, Mauritania, Mauritius, Niger and Rwanda. The Amahoro Stadium, completed just months before the outbreak of Rwanda's genocidal civil war, would serve as the headquarters of the UN peacekeeping force and a place of sanctuary for Tutsis fleeing their Hutu attackers. All these stadiums were small and offered very basic facilities, but the growing Chinese construction industry was soon able to build bigger and more architecturally brutal stadiums and associated multi-sports complexes for the dictatorships of Moi in Nairobi and Mobutu in Kinshasa.

Busy as the Chinese had been in the 1990s, the pace of their engagement quickened again. Since the turn of the century, they have paid for and built over thirty stadiums, with many more to come. It is not simply the scale of Chinese construction that has shifted: stadium diplomacy has become entwined with a much bigger economic and political project. In the 1980s, China had been content to foster solidarity in Africa and leverage it to diplomatically exclude and isolate Taiwan. After assessing the post-Cold

War landscape in the early 1990s, however, it became clear to the Chinese leadership that Africa offered rather more. China's burgeoning industrial economy and population would soon require new export markets, land for agricultural purposes and, above all, access to the full range of raw materials its factories consumed. Africa, particularly as its oil reserves grew, offered all of these in abundance and, given the United States' rapid withdrawal from the continent after the fall of the Berlin Wall, the price of entry looked very low. Since then, Sino-African trade, aid, investment and migration have all soared. China is now the continent's biggest single trading partner, and exports have risen since 2000 twenty-fold, to more than $150 billion a year. It is also Africa's largest external direct investor, with interests in dozens of countries in mining and manufacturing. Its state banks are responsible for the lion's share of infrastructure loans, and there is now a Chinese migrant population in Africa getting close to two million.[40]

Some of Africa's new stadiums, like Togo's and the Central African Republic's, have come entirely as gifts. In fact, the present list has extended to Sierra Leone's and Zimbabwe's parliaments, the offices of Mozambique's and Uganda's presidents, Ghana's national theatre and the new $200 million headquarters of the African Union in Addis Ababa: all facilities overwhelmingly enjoyed by the continent's elites, with whom the Chinese are also doing business over resources and trade. Other stadiums have been financed as package deals, in which one of China's state banks loans the money to the government, which then agrees to pay it back at a very low interest rate over a long period, if necessary with raw materials rather than just cash. At this point, public tendering goes out of the window, as China also supplies the contractors and subcontractors to build the things. They in turn bring much of the workforce required, especially highly skilled engineers. All this comes with a guaranteed 'no questions asked' policy on domestic politics, human rights or international law. As Sierra Leone's ambassador to Beijing tartly put it. 'If a G8 country had wanted to rebuild our stadium, we'd still be holding meetings.'[41]

The same model has been applied and scaled-up to fund the most important infrastructure projects ever built in Africa: six-lane motorways through the rainforests of Equatorial Guinea and Gabon, new railways and road networks right across East Africa, a colossal deep-water port for Tanzania, Ethiopia's biggest dam and Addis Ababa's light-rail system, giant solar farms in southern Africa, entire hi-tech neighbourhoods in Kenya. If the stadium programme is anything to go by, the scale and speed of Chinese investment have their costs. There is certainly an identikit feel to much of the stadium programme. For example, the arching roofs over the Levy Mwanawasa stadium in Zambia are identical to those of the Stade de l'Amitié in Libreville, Gabon, and both were the work of the Shanghai Construction Group. You would be hard pressed to tell the difference between Costa Rica's and Malawi's national stadiums, both built by the Anhui Foreign Economic Construction Group, a conglomerate with an interest in diamond mines in the DRC and Zimbabwe. Whatever the architectural merits of these buildings, their locations are often dismal and their scale unsustainable. Mozambique's Zimpeto Stadium, opened to host the All-Africa Games in 2011, has never been full since. Even for an important game, its crowds are dwarfed:

> Once inside, the Mambas fans sat stiffly together high up in one huge uncovered stand of plastic seating. The stands at either end of the pitch were completely empty. In the town centre, I'd seen motorists screaming their devotion to their team pounding their horns at one another and piling fellow supporters into their backseats. The atmosphere in Zimpeto was so subdued, drowned by the vastness of the place, that I could hear the players calling out at each other down on the field.[42]

Similar reports emanate from the new stadiums in Zambia, Ghana and Malawi, and it is not only the atmosphere that has been lost. For the previous generation of fans, the history embedded in the older stadiums has been swept aside. 'I am one of the many Zambians saddened that most of our national team matches are now staged in Ndola. This is not only because I live in Lusaka, where the team used to play its home games, but also because the move greatly diminishes, if not erases, the deeper significance of historic football venues.'[43]

Beyond these microscopic zones of hyper-development, the citizens of urban Africa continue to struggle with the daily grind of life in cities that have crumbling and inadequate infrastructure and threadbare levels of unreliable governance. The vast majority of football stadiums in Africa, the ones in which the sport is actually played, reveal the still perilous conditions and physical insecurity of the urban life this produces, and nothing, it seems, has been learnt from the disasters at the turn of the century. Faith is no barrier to calamity. Stampedes at religious ceremonies have claimed dozens of lives, like the thirty-six Malian fatalities at the Modibo Keita Stadium in Bamako, where 25,000 people had poured in to be blessed by an imam. A New Year's firework display claimed sixty-one people and injured 200 in a stampede in 2013 at the Stadium Houphouët-Boigny in Abidjan. Things have proved no different in football. The roll call of fatalities has been relentless: twelve dead in a stampede after Zambia beat Congo-Brazzaville in Chililabombwe; eight crushed to death in Liberia at a World Cup qualifier in 2009; twenty-two asphyxiated at the Stadium Houphouët-Boigny beneath a collapsed wall as Côte d'Ivoire played Mali. In the 2015 title decider between TP Mazembe and Vita Club at the Stade Tata Raphaël in Kinshasa, fifteen people died in the inevitable stampede that followed police firing tear gas into the stands. And still they come. Seventeen people lost their lives at a game in the provincial Angolan city of Uige in 2017, after fans, locked outside at the start of the game, broke into the stadium, triggering a stampede. President dos Santos ordered a report, but he could have just asked the main medical officer at the local hospital. Indeed, any observer of the cruelties of African urban life could have told him: 'Some people had to walk on top of other people.'[44]

V

History still counts for something in African football. The biennial African Cup of Nations (AFCON) remains the centrepiece of the continent's football.[45] Now over sixty years old, steeped in traditions of pan-African amity and pride, it is screened and closely followed across the continent and amongst the many African diasporas. Since 2000, every sub-Saharan tournament, with the exception of South Africa in 2013, has featured an array of Chinese-funded stadiums. Mali showed off six new ones in 2002. Ghana in 2008 and Angola in 2010 had four each. Equatorial Guinea and Gabon, the co-hosts in 2012, had two apiece and, as solo hosts in 2015 and 2017 respectively, they each added another couple. It is not entirely coincidental that Ghana's and Angola's biggest oil market is China, with

Angola selling five times as much oil to the PRC as it does to the USA. Gabon sent around 15 per cent of its oil and manganese to China, and Equatorial Guinea's biggest trading partner for oil was also Beijing. Intended as showcases and celebrations of the host regimes, the African Cup of Nations tournaments actually revealed more about how Africa's resource extraction states operate, and about their relationships with football and their own citizens.

In Angola, football, like everything else, had first to survive the long, harsh civil war that began in 1975 and only ended in 2002. For nearly three decades, football fields were laced with landmines and squads had to fly rather than traverse booby-trapped roads. The clubs – all run by state agencies, like the police at Interclube, the army at Primeiro de Maio, and the state oil company Sonanagol at Petro Atlético – had to play second fiddle to more pressing concerns. In 2005, to nationwide hysteria, Angola qualified for the first time for the World Cup. 'We had a lot of dreams when we were young, but they all disappeared as we grew up during the war. But everyone forgot about their troubles when the team qualified.'[46] Thomas Teixeira perhaps overstated things, but it was a seminal moment for Angola, tangible evidence of its post-war recovery driven by its enormous and now accessible oil reserves. More tangible, perhaps, than the team's performance in Germany in 2006, where they managed to draw with Iran and Mexico before going home. More tangible, perhaps, than the economic conditions of most Angolans who, despite living in one of Africa's fastest growing economies, continued to live in poverty. In the capital Luanda, where much of the population had gathered during the war, a monumental building boom in the new business districts sat alongside vast and growing shanty towns, unpaved roads and open sewers. AFCON 2010 made the contrast even sharper. Four new stadiums were built in Benguela, Luanda, Lubango and Cabinda, costing just over $500 million; $231 million alone for Estádio 11 de Novembro in the capital. Add to that the twelve new practice grounds built for visiting teams to train on, and that was a billion dollars just on football pitches. Foreign journalists were astonished to discover that Luanda was one of the most expensive cities in the world to live in.

Halfway through the second half of their opening game, Angola looked like they were going to win the whole show: 4–0 up and in control against Malawi. Inexplicably, they disintegrated, and finished the match 4–4. The team crawled their way to the quarter-finals, but Angola's primary celebration of itself remained its pharaonic architectural monuments rather than its football. A year later, all of the stadiums were either under-used or mothballed, the power disconnected. Vague plans for local clubs to play in them had failed to factor in their huge running costs, implausible rentals and distant locations from the popular districts, which remained without functioning transport systems.[47] The national team's only dalliance with success since then was a quarter-final place at AFCON 2013, where they were eviscerated by Cape Verde, a tiny cluster of lusophone islands in the Mid-Atlantic. The still highly censored and subservient press remained cautious in its criticisms, but Angola's Twittersphere was less reticent, exploding with complaint. Many decried the fact that there was enough money in Angolan football for the Luandan club Kabuscorp to sign the ageing but expensive Brazilian Rivaldo, but never any money for youth development. Cape Verde, it transpired, a considerably poorer country, was putting more money per capita into health and education, and by Angolan standards was a haven of democratic politics. As the Cape Verdean Prime Minister José Maria Neves put it in a newspaper interview on his team's performance, 'Our oil is good governance.'[48]

As might be expected, Gabon and Equatorial Guinea have leaned on the side of oil rather than good governance. These tiny coastal West African states, a French and Spanish colonial enclave respectively, were abandoned to their post-independence penury in the 1960s, and remained there until they hit the oil jackpot in the mid-1990s. In both cases, the cascade of cash that followed entrenched already long periods of personal and autocratic rule. In Gabon, President Omar Bongo had ruled from 1967 until his death in 2009. His son Ali Bongo has been running the family business ever since. In Equatorial Guinea, also a family affair, President Teodoro Obiang has been in power since 1979, when he overthrew his uncle Francisco Macías Nguema. Nguema had been in charge since independence from Spain in 1968 and was at best erratic, at worst sociopathic: he had 150 opponents hanged in the football stadium of the capital Malomo, their death throes drowned out by a recorded orchestral version of 'Those Were the Days (My Friend)' played on a loop. While this points to an extraordinary attention to detail, his failure to pay the army suggests otherwise. The troops mutinied and then

surrounded him and the national cash reserves in a bunker in Mon-
gomo. Obiang had him captured, tried and executed. Since oil was
discovered both nations' GDP per capita suggests they have become
middle-income-to-rich nations, easily able to afford the $1 billion
apiece they spent on staging AFCON in 2012, and similar sums on
individually hosting the 2015 and 2017 tournaments. On the ground,
however, both societies remained remarkably underdeveloped and
unequal, with more than a third of their populations living in extreme poverty.

Prior to AFCON 2012, Equatorial Guinea's football was equally
underdeveloped, with hapless facilities and an invisible international
presence. In preference to investing in local football, they experi-
mented with naturalizing foreign players, and in 2009 the women's
team became champions of Africa having recruited legions of Brazilians. Consequently, the men's national team went into the tournament
with twenty of the twenty-three-man squad naturalized citizens, who
had come via Mauritania, Rwanda and Niger. Wherever they came
from, the players were being offered extraordinary bonuses if they
could score goals and win games. Teodorin Obiang, oldest son of the
President and coincidentally Vice-President, offered a million dollars
to the team for each game they won. After they beat Libya and Senegal, ensuring a quarter-final place against Côte d'Ivoire, he was as
good as his word. Generous, but then this was a man who settled a
corruption case in the US courts by paying a monstrous fine and
funded it by selling off $30 million-worth of mere fripperies: a
Malibu mansion, a few Ferraris and a very respectable Michael Jackson memorabilia collection.[49]

The relationship between football and politics in both countries
has been less serene since AFCON 2012, for their ruling regimes
have been weakened by the tumbling global oil price and challenged
by re-energized opposition groups. President Obiang, alert to his
poor international standing, has courted friends by agreeing to stage
international events at short notice – a friendly football match
against Spain in 2013 and the African Union summit in 2014. Hopes
of maintaining a leading profile in African football were dashed by
CAF's decision to suspend the country after the national team had
illegally fielded a Cameroonian striker. Then, in late 2014, the
Moroccan government and football association, panicked by the outbreak of the Ebola virus in West Africa, withdrew their offer to host

AFCON 2015. Into the breach stepped the now unsuspended and much feted Equatorial Guinean football federation. With the kind of haste that only a gargantuan quantity of liquid petrodollars can deliver, three new stadiums were thrown up, teams were squeezed four to a hotel, and somehow the show got put on.[50]

The mood appeared very different from 2012. The opposition called for protest, and leading activist Professor Celestino-Nvo Okenve Ndo was arrested before the opening game for handing out flyers and T-shirts advocating a boycott of the tournament. He need not have worried. Apart from the home team's games, the stadiums were virtually empty. President Obiang may have bought 40,000 tickets to give away personally but, as the television pictures attest, he found very few takers. Those who did go did not offer a very positive version of the nation. In the quarter-final against Ghana, Equatorial Guinea found themselves 3–0 down. Fans began to rain down bottles on the Ghanaian bench, then onto the pitch and the police, and finally onto the small contingent of Ghanaian fans. An eyewitness reported finding on the pitch 'A piece of mirror, a broken plate, a broken-off handle, bottles filled with urine and stones.' The Ghanaians were forced to break through a pitch-side security fence to escape the assault, and then huddle behind one of the goals. Riot police fired tear gas to clear the stands, while a helicopter hovered menacingly above. Five hundred Ghanaians, too frightened to return to their lodgings, encamped at their embassy overnight.[51]

In Gabon, the 2012 tournament was a success for President Ali Bongo and his entourage. The national team had made it incident-free to the quarter-finals, where they narrowly lost to Mali on penalties. Over the next five years, however, Bongo's rule became increasingly fragile. Already limited health and education services were cut, and in Jean Ping, an ex-diplomat, Bongo faced a plausible challenger. Ping railed against the nearly $1 billion to be spent on a second AFCON tournament in 2017, and chose to make political points over Lionel Messi's appearance in the provincial city of Port Gentil, where he helped lay the foundation stone for one of the new stadiums.[52] In late 2016, in sharply contested national elections, Bongo was narrowly declared the winner. Ping's supporters, convinced the contest had been rigged, took to the streets and torched the national assembly. During the subsequent riots Ping's own HQ was burnt down, and five people were killed by the security forces.

Prime Minister Emmanuel Issoze-Ngondet, appointed by Bongo in the wake of this disorder, noted with refreshing candour, 'The tournament has come at the right time. It will help people forget.'[53]

It would have taken some act of footballing amnesia for AFCON 2017 to make the Gabonese forget the failures of their rulers. Indeed, it is likely to have made them all the more obvious. The Stade Omar Bongo, the new national stadium budgeted at $220 million, remained unfinished for the tournament, with games reallocated to an older stadium in the capital. The new stadium in Port Gentil was finished, but it sat in a sea of rubble, and next to it was a vast unfinished residential housing project intended for the locals displaced by the stadium's hasty construction. The new Stade d'Oyem, with its 20,000 seats, could have held more than half the adult population of this tiny market town deep in the rainforest. Notionally a new urban hub, it was unreachable for the vast majority of citizens.[54] In the capital, on striking black-and-red posters of the national team's players, the message read, 'You are not the team of the Gabonese people but the team of the dictator.' On the eve of the tournament, activists were rounded up or placed under house arrest. Almost alone, President Bongo and his entourage watched an opening ceremony that featured the cream of contemporary African pop, from Senegalese rappers Akon and Booba to Nigerian singer Davido. The opposition papers called it 'Le Grand Flop'. Jean Ping was contemptuous, deeming it 'a failure for the young man.'[55]

The government-backed media responded with a half-hearted campaign to sell cheap tickets, its slogan '*Tous au stade*', but with the exception of small Malian and Senegalese immigrant populations, no one seemed very interested at all. The organizers weren't helping. One observer reported that 'In a city covered in official signage, only a single hand-painted sign for a Fan Zone greeted supporters as they approached the stadium. Following the sign, we were directed on a circular tour of the stadium, bringing us back to the same sign without passing anything that might be recognized as a Fan Zone.'[56] Three dull draws were not enough for Gabon to progress from the group stage. In the final minutes of their decisive game with Cameroon, much of the crowd was already heading for the door before the inevitable elimination. Politics had certainly undermined the dressing room. 'It is clear that the political situation has affected our preparations for this championship,' thought goalkeeper Didier

Ovono, who led the Ping faction in the squad. By contrast, captain Pierre-Emerick Aubameyang had dedicated his 2016 African Player of the Year award to Bongo. On the final whistle, Aubameyang left the field alone.

The political, let alone the social, gains from staging AFCON are, on the evidence of the last decade or so, ambiguous to say the least. Yet still African elites are bound to the idea that stadiums and its spectacles will let them reimagine the future. The next three AFCONs were allocated to West Africa. Cameroon planned to stage the Cup in 2019 (but lost the tournament to Egypt when the level of internal conflicts proved too threatening for CAF's liking), Côte d'Ivoire in 2021 and Guinea in 2023. Once again, Beijing arranged the finance and the construction of all of the stadiums: three for Cameroon, four for both Côte d'Ivoire and Guinea. Ethiopia, which failed in its increasingly loud bids for all these tournaments, remains hopeful for 2025 and, with Chinese financial support, is doing the same in Addis Ababa. Unlike their predecessors, these new national stadiums will not be built as one-off projects or on land close to the traditional downtowns of these cities. Stadium Paul Biya is located a full ten miles from the centre of Yaoundé. Côte d'Ivoire's stadium will be just a small part of a gigantic array of sports facilities and accommodation in a suburb fourteen miles north of Abidjan's historic core. Ethiopia is building the future on its periphery, placing the stadium next to Addis Ababa's international airport.

They are all designed for elite consumption and television production, generously equipped with VIP boxes, private parking, media spaces and communication technologies. The African football stadium of the twenty-first century takes it cue from the new satellite cities and gated neighbourhoods that are emerging all over the continent: from Konza Technopolis outside Nairobi to King City near the booming oil port of Takoradi in Ghana, from Kalungulu in Dar es Salaam to La Cité du Fleuve outside Kinshasa, real-estate developers have abandoned the impossible chaos and poverty of Africa's megacities and established their own secure, offshore islands. In some ways Abuja, Nigeria's synthetic capital, is the mother of all these projects. Inconvenienced by the sprawling metropolis of Lagos, Nigeria's political class decamped to their very own purpose-built city. Declared the capital in 1991, it acquired the incredibly expensive Abuja national stadium in 2003. The political class have shown less interest in the fate of places like Surulere, the old national stadium in Lagos, now increasingly derelict and completely unusable, a temporary facility for the homeless, sex workers and drug dealing, and an indicator of the fate that awaits Africa's old urban cores.

VI

In the smaller nations of West Africa, football's association with death seemed systemic. In 2005, as Mali trailed Togo 2–1 in a World Cup qualifying game, thousands of furious spectators invaded the pitch and were met by tear gas. Pouring into the streets of the city, they gathered on African Unity Avenue, chanting, 'Give us Frederic Kanouté and Mamadou Bakayoko! We're going to kill them!' Others set up barricades of burning tyres across the main roads. Through the night, police and government buildings were attacked, shops were looted and Togolese restaurants and Chinese hotels were ransacked.[57] Conversely, in 2009, in the final days of President Dadis's violent rule, Guinean security forces stormed the national stadium in Conakry, where an opposition rally was being held. A gruesome and systematic massacre followed: 156 people were killed by bayonet and rifle butts, some were shot hiding beneath the seats in the stands, some were electrocuted on the live fence the soldiers had installed on the stadium's perimeter. Hundreds more were injured and subject to violent sexual assaults.[58]

The threat of death, in the guise of the Ebola virus, returned to the stadiums of Guinea, Sierra Leone and Liberia in 2014, where it was feared the highly contagious disease could easily spread. Domestic football, barely recovered from the grinding civil wars that had affected all three nations during the previous decade, came to a halt. CAF placed a ban on international football in these countries, forcing their national teams to play all their games away from home. At the height of the panic, the Seychelles simply refused to play Sierra Leone, home or away, and forfeited their tie. Opponents in Cameroon would not shake the players' hands. In the DRC, the team faced hostile chants from the crowd of 'Ebola! Ebola!' Living in virtual quarantine, players faced humiliating twice-daily screenings. One player despaired: 'I am a Sierra Leonean, not a virus.' In Liberia, where football had already been declared dead by the president of the football association, Ebola eradicated it. Monrovia's main stadium was converted to a treatment centre for over a year. Yet despite all this, Sierra Leoneans still flocked to their amateur neighbourhood championships in their thousands, and when the Guineans managed to make it all the way to the quarter-finals of the African Cup of Nations in 2015, although schools had been closed and large gatherings were banned, Conakry was engulfed with celebrations.[59]

There was no shortage of mortality then, but surely in West Africa, home to Senegal, Ghana, Nigeria, Côte d'Ivoire and Cameroon – the five major footballing nations of the continent and the main suppliers of African players to the global football market, who between them have taken the lion's share of the region's World Cup places – there was life left yet in African football? All of them have had their moments, but none of them have come anywhere near their potential. Senegal opened their World Cup account in 2002 with a stinging post-colonial rebuke to France, beating the reigning world champions 1–0, and then made the quarter-finals. It has all been downhill since. That team's final flourish was a dismal and indifferent departure from AFCON 2008, in which 'Kamara only broke into a run when strolling around in a daze became too boring and the entire defence could not even summon their will to communicate with each other.' Indeed, so vertiginous had been football's decline that by the late 2000s wrestling had, by some way, become more popular as a spectator sport in Senegal.[60] The country's return to the World Cup in 2018, after a long absence, saw them get a wisp away from qualifying for the knock-out stages, suggesting the fall has been long but not terminal. Cameroon, who have actually qualified for three World Cups since the millennium, have never made it out of the group stage. In 2010 and 2014, they were successively the worst and worst-but-one team at the tournament. Côte d'Ivoire, blessed with the most exceptional generation of players on the continent, failed to make it beyond the group stages of three consecutive World Cups. Nigeria actually made it to the last sixteen in Brazil in 2014, but their performance in 2010 was considered so lamentable that President Goodluck Jonathan tried to withdraw the Super Eagles from international competition.[61] Ghana's tumultuous passage to the quarter-finals of the South African World Cup in 2010 remains the pinnacle of the continent's achievement.

Explanations are not difficult to come by. The fundamental instability and short-termism that blights African football is reflected in the number of coaches each national side has had since 2000: twenty-one apiece for Ghana and Nigeria, seventeen for Cameroon, fifteen for Côte d'Ivoire and a mere nine for Senegal. Almost every one of their World Cup campaigns has been marked by a serious dispute between players, managers and often the government over bonuses and pay, an example of the wider and pervasive looting by officials, and the almost complete collapse of trust between squads and football associations. In Cameroon, the man in charge on each occasion was the President of FECAFOOT, Iya Mohammed, who in 2013 was arrested, tried and imprisoned for financial malpractice on the job, not to mention the CFA11 million diverted from his other job at the national Cotton Development Corporation. Nonetheless, he was able to win re-election while still in prison.[62]

The charge sheet is long, but totally representative of how business is done at most African football associations. In 2007, staff at FECAFOOT went on strike owed nearly four years' salary. FIFA bailed them out, but officials only passed on 40 per cent of the money, keeping the rest for themselves. They kept 100 per cent, as far as anyone can see, of the $24 million of public money allocated by the national parliament for stadium renovations. Monies from kit sponsor Puma, television companies and ticket receipts from home games were handled in a similar fashion.[63] Samuel Eto'o, Cameroon's greatest player, was banned from the national team after having the temerity to lead a strike over yet another set of missing bonuses. Things were little different in Côte d'Ivoire, where the Ivorian Petrol Refinery Company's $1.6 million annual sponsorship of the league was kept secret. The football association's reputation fell so low that companies preferred to make their payments via the Ministry of Sport. The misselling of World Cup tickets was so brazen that FIFA kindly offered to market Côte d'Ivoire's allocation themselves.[64] Ghana, while beset by less of this kind of corruption, has been rife with match-fixing. In fact, in 2016, Kwesi Nyantakyi, President of the Ghanaian FA, announced at a press conference, to nobody's amazement, that bribery and match-fixing, organized amongst club officials, players and match officials, was open and widespread in the country. Two years of complete inaction later, the GFA was actually dissolved in 2018 and domestic football ground to a complete halt, after the emergence of another round of damning evidence of match-fixing in the widely screened film *Number 12*, which featured most of the GFA hierarchy soliciting and receiving bribes.[65]

Nonetheless, football continues to be a magnet for many kinds of social hopes and aspirations, certainly in the guise of the national team. Although the case has been overstated, *Les Elephants*, as Côte d'Ivoire are nicknamed, and Didier Drogba in particular, can claim small roles in encouraging the end of the country's civil war and offering a symbol of diversity and reconciliation. In 2005, after the team's defeat of Sudan in Khartoum to qualify, for the first time, for the World Cup finals, TV cameras sent back pictures of wild dressing-room celebrations. The team decided to take the opportunity to send a message of unity home and passed the mic to Didier Drogba.

> Men and women of Ivory Coast, from the north, south, centre and west: we proved today that all Ivorians can co-exist and play together with a shared aim, to qualify for the World Cup. We promised that the celebration would unite the people. Today, we beg you, on our knees.[66]

The squad then dropped to their knees. 'Forgive. Forgive. Forgive . . . Please lay down your weapons. Hold elections. Everything will be better.' Then they sang, 'We want to have fun, so stop firing your guns.' It was hardly the only force at work in Ivorian politics, but a peace deal was eventually signed in 2007. The team responded with a gesture of reconciliation, Drogba calling for a game with Madagascar to be played in Bouaké, the rebel capital. The game went ahead with soldiers from both sides in the stadium. It was not enough, though, to deal with the intractable problem of President Laurent Gbagbo, who had been in power throughout the civil war and then the fragile peace. Many joked that Côte d'Ivoire's failure to win the African Cup of Nations despite such great players was 'the curse of Gbagbo.' Those who observed his authoritarianism, corruption and desperate attempts to avoid new elections might have thought the curse extended further than *Les Elephants*. After much prevarication, new presidential elections were held in 2010, which saw the opposition candidate Alassane Ouattara declared the winner. Gbagbo refused to accept the result, and was only removed from power after a second civil war, the intervention of French troops and his arrest. Some Ouattara supporters were so eager to confirm that the curse had been lifted that they gathered at Abidjan Airport to celebrate the team's return after losing the final of AFCON 2012 as if it were a victory. They finally got their wish in 2015. This time a million people gathered in Abidjan after the team had beaten Ghana in the final of the African Cup of Nations. President Ouattara, now often known by his initials, ADO, made it his business to greet them at the airport, lead them in his motorcade and officiate the ceremonies at the national stadium. Placards along the route read, 'The Ivory Coast is rising, thank you ADO.'[67]

In Ghana, the Black Stars had long been a symbol of national pride and development, and of the pan-African aspirations of Kwame Nkrumah, leader of the nation's independence movement and the first-post independence President. The former were to the fore when Ghana hosted the 2008 African Cup of Nations, the latter when it became Africa's representative at the 2010 World Cup. AFCON 2008, as far as the government was concerned, was a showcase for what a decade of political stability and economic growth could deliver, and a glimpse of what the arrival of oil promised. Alongside two new and two completely renovated stadiums, the government renovated airports and built some new roads. When Ghana scored a late winner against Nigeria in the quarter-finals, the commentator thought that 'The great courage and resilience of the Stars in fighting back from one goal down to win the game were glowing testimony that Ghanaians have what it takes to build a middle-income country.'[68] Christian evangelicals lent their own take on events, with a prominent Kumasi pastor calling on the faithful at a prayer meeting held on the day of the tournament, 'Let us pray that God will bring total victory to Ghana. God has chosen this nation for his own purposes.' Many had worked themselves up into a froth at the prospect of hordes of prostitutes and armed robbers coming to Ghana to service or fleece the fans. No hordes were sighted, but Ghanaian fans spontaneously broke into the hymn 'To God be the Glory' when Ghana made it to the semi-final. Their departure after defeat by Cameroon was met less rapturously.

In 2010, the best-selling posters on the streets of Accra read, 'Black Stars: Heroes of Africa' and 'Ghana. Africa. One love.' When Ghana found themselves the only African side left in the knock-out phase of the World Cup, they could have sold the posters all over the continent.[69] In South Africa, the ANC passed a resolution making them 'The Black Stars of Africa'. Provincial governments flew the

Ghanaian flag. Popular slang soon transformed the South African team's nickname Bafana Bafana into BaGhana BaGhana – a remarkable show of cosmopolitanism given the widespread wave of violent attacks on African migrants in the country in 2008. An extra-time victory over the United States took them to the quarter-finals and Uruguay. With the score at 1–1, Asamoah Gyan missed a late extra-time penalty, awarded after Luis Suarez had deliberately handballed to keep a shot out of the Uruguayan goal. Then Ghana lost the penalty shoot-out. Accra went silent once again.

> You could almost waltz with the ghosts of what might have been. You could feel the ghosts of what could have been because the real thing had been there all day. The build-up had started at noon, and then there had been all of this – dances, music, kissing, crashes, hope – here in Accra.[70]

The Ghanaians toured Johannesburg in an open-top bus and visited Winnie and Nelson Mandela in their homes, before returning to ecstatic crowds in the capital.

Given that Nigeria, by population at least, is larger than all of its West African peers put together, it is surprising that it has failed to match even the limited progress of Ghana and Côte d'Ivoire. It is even more surprising when one considers what a deep, entrenched football culture the country possessed in the 1980s and early 1990s, before the arrival of satellite television. Remembered now as a 'Golden Age' of Nigerian football, in this era teams like Lagos's Stationery Stores could draw crowds of 80,000, and send tens of thousands to away games. Outside the capital, Enugu Rangers, Shooting Stars, Enyimba and Kano Pillars could draw on comparable followings, and represented the aspirations of their regions or ethnic groups. National radio broadcasts by the much-loved and silver-tongued commentator Ernest Okonkwo brought the action to every corner of the country.

From such heights, domestic football has fallen further in Nigeria than anywhere else in Africa. The depth and scale of Nigeria's EPL obsession is part of the reason why, but the scale of the calamity is also homemade. Despite the end of military rule and even the peaceful handover of presidential power between the main parties in 2014, relative political stability and the aura of democracy have barely made Nigeria less dysfunctional. Indeed, the unchecked consequences of the nation's dependence on oil and the consequent hollowing out of its public realm to gossamer-thinness have meant that for most people the rule of law and basic security do not pertain, and certainly not in football. Just a few examples of the thousands of incidents of corruption, incompetence and violence that have blighted the Nigerian game will have to suffice.

In the four years that Sani Lulu was President of the Nigerian Football Federation between 2006 and 2010, he and other senior executives took a big slice of everything that came their way: FIFA World Cup money, players' World Cup bonuses, sponsors' money, not to mention the petty-cash drawer. One report suggested that less than 10 per cent of these income streams made their way out of the Glasshouse, as the NFF HQ is risibly known; a high tariff even in Nigeria. N1.5 billion allocated by the federal government to bail out the 2010 World Cup campaign evaporated. Some of it was siphoned off by the production of expensive invoices for cheap buses and hotels; some was given to the chairs of the NFF's state committees to secure their votes in future elections. Lulu and his accomplices are currently in the grip of the Nigerian legal system, on trial for corruption. The refusal of the Nigerian squad to train at the 2014 World Cup until their bonuses had been settled, and the fact that the wages and bonuses for the 2016 Rio Olympic team had to be paid for by a Japanese admirer of the Super Eagles, suggested that his successors proceeded in a similar manner.[71] It is a small advance of Nigeria's 2018 World Cup campaign that, though the team failed to progress from a tough group, there was no hint of the usual problems of bonuses and dissent.

The governance and probity of the domestic game has been of a similar calibre. In 2013, the NFF banned the chair of its own disciplinary committee, Olaleye Adepoju, for taking a bribe of $9,000 from Shooting Stars. The Ibadan club had hoped to avoid punishment for abandoning a game against Sunshine Stars, having refused to take the field after half-time as, they claimed, one of their officials had been attacked.[72] Eight years later, the Nigerian Court of Appeal would, on a technicality, dismiss the charges against Lulu.[73] That season was also an exceptional one in the top flight, where half the league went undefeated at home, and no one won away from home more than three times.[74] In an extreme case of a problem that wracks Nigerian football, the levels of violence and intimidation directed at match officials by home crowds reached a new pitch. Enugu Rangers,

Wikki Tourist and Kwara United had results overturned for such incidents, in a season where more than twenty punishments were handed out by the authorities, a fraction of the true number of episodes. The league's broadcaster SuperSport refused to send cameras to clubs in the north like Kano Pillars and Gombe United, fearing not just Boko Haram attacks but the volatility of the local crowds. Despite a great deal of sermonizing, nothing much changed. In 2014, referee Charles Ozigbo was beaten senseless after awarding a penalty to the Rancher Bees in their game against Kwara United, whose fans did the same in another match that season against Supreme Court FC.[75] The suspension of the league in 2015 and 2016, threatened by referee strikes, has yet to eradicate the problem.

Nigeria is nothing if not entrepreneurially energetic. Indeed, given the almost complete absence of public services, especially reliable electricity, Nigerians have to work three times as hard as anyone else just to stay still. No game can be watched it its entirety on television without experiencing a power outage that then requires five minutes of set-top box rebooting. Nigerians simply switch to illegal live streams on their phones and Facebook live broadcasts from their friends at Stamford Bridge. It is against these kinds of odds, but with a not dissimilar brio, that in 2012 a new independent professional league was established in Nigeria. First, the Nigerian Football Federation was forced to relinquish what semblance of control it had over the domestic game and cede power to the new league, owned by its clubs. This alone is progress. Nigeria has its first legally constituted professional league, and has even acquired a smaller women's equivalent. Television coverage from SuperSport brought a tiny bit of money and some coverage (until the collapse of the Nigerian currency in 2017 forced the company to depart). Nigeria's state governments have not proved to be better custodians of their clubs, but new private owners have emerged who are more promising; like Ifeanyi Ubah (the car spare-part king of West Africa), owner of the eponymous football club, and, most sensationally of all, the proprietors of MFM FC, Mountain of Fire and Miracles.

Founded in 2007 in Agege, a working class suburb of Lagos, by the Pentecostal church of the same name, MFM rose rapidly up the ladder of Nigeria's leagues. In 2015, they were the first team from Lagos to make it to the top level of Nigerian football for a decade. Once there, they challenged for the title in front of small but noisy crowds, with an evangelical band, dancing area boys – stoned off their heads – and Pentecostal ladies in their Sunday best. In part, their success was rooted in the kind of discipline maintained at the club. The squad lived in club accommodation with their own dedicated MFM pastor and had to accept ten cardinal rules, including keeping one's hair short, no saggy trousers, compulsory attendance at church events (allowing for the football schedule), and collective fasting and praying when required. As the director of sports at the club told me, 'When someone has an injury we all pray and fast for good healing. When someone has the possibility of an Adidas deal, we all pray for him to get the deal.'[76] The club also paid the players on time. Not very much, perhaps, but this was a real rarity in Nigeria. On such minor acts of trust and probity a football miracle is possible.

Such is the rapidity of the rise and fall of the country's football that nostalgia must move at the speed of light. Nigeria is already mourning the passing of its short-lived 'Golden Age'. What took England over a hundred years has been accomplished here in just decades. No one symbolizes that golden age and its passing better than Ernest Okonkwo, the nation's first great football commentator on radio and then on television.[77] Like Ghana's Jo Lartey and Harry Thompson or Zambia's Dennis Liwewe, he defined the standard of post-independence broadcasting and was beholden to no one. South Africa's Zama Masondo, who commentated in Zulu and coined the word 'Laduma!' as an alternative to 'Goooal!' is still with us. So too are the fabulous singing Swahili words of Kenya's Mohammed Juma Njuguna, but these two are amongst the last representatives of a tradition of African commentary that was something more than an echo of the bland clichés of contemporary satellite television. Okonkwo specialized in brilliant footballer nicknames – Idowu 'Slow Poison' Otubusin and Sylvanus 'Quicksilver' Okpala – and off-the-cuff eloquence: 'Okey Isima, with a short pass to Sylvanus Okpala, they both play in Portugal. They can communicate in Igbo, they can communicate in English, they can communicate in Portuguese and they just communicated with the ball.' Nigerians are scathing about his inarticulate successors in the satellite age. His name has been memorialized. The press box at a small stadium in Lagos was named after him but, unlike Okonkwo, no one will be commentating there on games in front of vast noisy crowds, swooning over the play. The players and the crowds, like Okonkwo himself, have long since departed.

VII

The shadow of war has hung over contemporary East and Central African football, but nowhere more than in Somalia. From the fall of the Siad Barré regime in 1991 until the formation of an interim federal government in 2005, Somalia had no effective central government. Two of the northern regions of the country, Somaliland and Puntland, seceded, and both attempted to assert their national sovereignty and acquire international recognition by fielding national football teams in non-FIFA competitions. The Somali national team, the Ocean Stars, had to play outside the country. A complex and shifting landscape of Islamist militias, traditional Somali clans and self-made warlords fought over the country, which descended into widespread famine and disorder. Twice, in 2006 and 2009–11, Islamist groups occupied the capital Mogadishu and much of the south, declaring Sharia law and banning the playing and watching of football. In 2006, it was the Union of Islamic Courts, who were then ejected by the Ethiopians, the African Union and Somalia's fragile transitional government. After this, it was the splinter group Al-Shabaab, by then an affiliate of Al-Qaeda, ejected by the Kenyans and their Somali allies.

They have, like the rest of Africa's twenty-first-century Islamists, had a torrid relationship with the game. The Union of Islamic Courts and Al-Shabaab both followed the conventional Wahhabist position on football: that it was immodest and sinful. In late 2008, armed Islamist militants stormed a cinema in Mogadishu and threw a grenade into the auditorium where a huge crowd had gathered to watch an FA Cup fifth-round tie between Manchester United and Arsenal; they left one dead and many injured. At the same time, in the city's hinterland, militants were busy destroying TV screens and projectors in other viewing houses. This kind of skirmishing turned into a full-scale military assault, and by 2010 Al-Shabaab were militarily and politically in charge of most of the country and began an active campaign to suppress the game. Beach football was banned; cinema and bar owners were warned to stop showing matches or be closed down. Leaflets handed out on the street told the populace much the same. The national stadium in Mogadishu became a military base criss-crossed by barbed wire and trenches. In 2011, when Al-Shabaab were ejected from the city by the Kenyan army and their Somali allies, the stadium was amongst their final strongholds. In retaliation for Uganda's contribution to the African Union's military presence in the country, Al-Shabaab extended the campaign beyond Somalia's border by planting bombs at a rugby club and an Ethiopian restaurant in Kampala, both packed with people watching the 2010 World Cup final. Sixty-four people were killed. They pulled the same trick in Kenya in 2014, killing nearly fifty people in Mpeketoni. However, once forced back into the countryside, Al-Shabaab has found that the hunger for football amongst its own ranks, let alone the general public, has been insatiable. Thus its militants were permitted to play the movement's own version of the game: no shorts, no swearing, and games to finish fifteen minutes before prayer whatever the score. Those who remained engaged with the EPL were shown less flexibility. In 2016, another thirty Somalis perished when a bomb exploded outside a restaurant in Baidoa, a city on the edge of Al-Shabaab's zone of influence. It was timed to go off during a game between Arsenal and Manchester United.[78]

Somehow, football survived this chaos, the Somali league only having been entirely abandoned for four seasons. In 2011, it was relaunched and, despite the enduringly difficult situation, it has proved one of the success stories of African football.[79] FIFA money was wisely spent renovating Mogadishu's stadiums and pitches. Sponsorship of the clubs has been provided by local oil companies and shipping firms, and the game was buoyant enough that a couple of dozen foreign players have come to Somalia in search of better wages. Tickets were incredibly cheap and, to avoid any clash with European football games on television, games were played on Monday to Friday. In late 2015 local football returned to Somalian television. Ratings were good throughout 2016, and crowds were at healthy levels of three to four thousand. In time, the Ocean Stars may actually play in Mogadishu rather than Djibouti.

Ethiopia, a founding member of CAF and once champion of Africa, saw its footballing inheritance destroyed, first by the long civil war that eventually deposed Colonel Mengistu and the afro-communist Derg regime in 1991, then by the internal turbulence and regional wars that characterized the rule of the EPRDF (Ethiopian People's Revolutionary Democratic Front) that replaced them. After

1982, the country failed to qualify for the African Cup of Nations. In 2008, with its chaotic football federation suspended, it did not even participate in AFCON or World Cup qualification. The country's clubs and facilities were in a parlous state but, as Meles Zenawi, Prime Minister for seventeen years, had always argued, 'Ethiopia needs fertilisers, not stadiums.' He died in 2012. Under his successor Hailemariam Desalegn, a football boom has been building. In part, this has been a function of the wider Ethiopian boom that saw almost a decade's worth of double-digit growth figures, a huge programme of construction in Addis Ababa and a massive transfer of state assets to the private sector. One of the biggest recipients of this largesse has been the country's richest man, Mohammed Hussein Al Amoudi, who, from his Saudi Arabian base, controlled huge swathes of the country's agriculture and industry: a pile big enough for him to throw a few crusts to the local game, sponsoring small international tournaments and building a new stadium for the big Addis Ababa club St George. This, however, was small change compared to the Chinese-funded, government-backed programmes that were building a 60,000-seat national stadium in Addis Ababa and seven others in the provinces of 30,000 capacity each.

The relative indifference of much of the population to domestic football shifted in 2012 when, for the first time in thirty years, the national team, under local coach Sewnet Bishaw, qualified for the African Cup of Nations, beating Sudan in a play-off. That evening, one local recorded:

> On the streets of Addis Ababa, people for a change were laughing, exchanging congratulatory messages and smiling to any stranger who passes by . . . even the federal police forgot their usual tough appearances and were dancing and singing with the people.[80]

The official media argued that the victory was part of the government's Growth and Development Strategy. Others took the opportunity to protest in the stands, flaunting the national flag with the government-ordained central emblem cut out. Later that year, amidst an even higher pitch of public excitement, Ethiopia faced Nigeria in a two-leg play-off, the winner of which would qualify for the 2014 World Cup. Addis Ababa was:

A carnival of the tricolour national team attire and every other conceivable artefact; people wearing and marking faces and bodies with the bright green, yellow and red national colours singing and chanting nationalistic songs on streets; even some government-owned FM radios – in an uncharacteristic move – playing the long-shelved nationalistic and patriotic music.[81]

Nigeria won the play-off, and the enormously popular Bishaw was sacked. The Ethiopian Football Federation claimed it was all about results, but everyone knew Bishaw's time was up after he went public with criticism of the government's failure to invest anything in grassroots football.

Since achieving independence in 1993 under President Isaias Afwerki and the EPLF, Eritrea has been in a state of almost permanent war. The country has clashed with Yemen, dabbled in the Somali civil war, skirmished with Djibouti and fought a short but bloody border war with Ethiopia. Despite the intervention of UN peacekeeping forces, the Eritreans maintained an unending state of enmity and insecurity in the region, until the fragile peace of 2018. The war economy built in this situation was one of enormous inequalities, with rationing of most goods for most people, the relentless mobilization of youth for the armed forces, and long periods of penal civilian national service required from everyone. At the same time, every avenue of alternative expression was closed down. Political parties were banned, Pentecostal churches have been sent into hiding. According to one observer,

people take refuge by watching European football and re-runs of Arabic-dubbed Turkish soap operas; the often-crowded cinema houses broadcast live football matches of Premier League or La Liga. The usual discussions and bets in public spaces are only about football. Most youth wear jerseys of the European clubs; even the President watches football and is a public Arsenal fan.[82]

In the absence of voice, there is exit. As of 2015, there were 350,000 Eritrean refugees outside the country from a population of six million, a ratio that puts the country second only to Syria in the scale of its exodus, despite a harshly implemented shoot-to-kill policy on the border. In this context, it is hardly surprising that international sporting events in general, and international football matches in particular, have offered the perfect opportunity to abscond. In 2006, four players from the regime's main club in Asmara, Red Sea FC, claimed asylum in Kenya after losing a Champion's League game. The following year, six players stayed behind after the national team was thumped 6–1 by Angola. The regime responded by temporarily withdrawing from international football and making every athlete who left the country leave a bond of $6,700, to be forfeited in the case of their failure to return. Undeterred, twelve members of the national team said goodbye to their bonds in 2009 after playing a regional tournament in Nairobi. Half the Red Sea FC squad of twenty-six did the same in Dar es Salaam in 2011, as did fifteen national squad players and their team doctor in Uganda the following year. Changing tack, the regime then decided to field a team made up of just overseas players (with no reason to abscond) and a few truly trusted regime loyalists. Even so, in 2015, after losing 3–1 to Botswana in a World Cup qualifier, ten more players sought asylum.[83]

In Central Africa, the genocidal wars of the 1990s brought two football-minded presidents to power. In Rwanda, President Kagame, his Arsenal tweets aside, has steered clear of grand populist footballing gestures. The capable if increasingly authoritarian calibre of the regime was reflected in its tough line on witchcraft and corruption in football. Its capacity for state-sponsored deception and rule-bending underwrote the national team's persistent and illegal use of foreign players. In Burundi, football was rather more centre stage in the nation's political theatre. Pierre Nkurunziza was a lecturer in physical education at the University of Burundi, and coach of both the army football team Muzinga and first-division side Union Sporting. Then came the civil war in the early 1990s, widespread genocidal attacks on Hutus, and a decade of conflict. By the end of the war, Nkurunziza was the leader of Hutu rebel group Forces for Defence of Democracy, and in 2005 he was elected the President of Burundi. Now a born-again Christian and a civilian politician, Nkurunziza created a presidential entourage that included his own football team Hallelujah FC – in which he invariably starred – and a large evangelical choir, allowing him to play matches and hold prayer meetings on his regal tours around the country. This kind of populism was sufficient to keep him in power until 2015, but after he orchestrated a constitutional fix allowing him to run for a third term as President, and with the prospect looming of him occupying the post for life, the opposition exploded into protest. This was only quelled after at least a hundred people had been killed on the streets. While riots, fires and gunshot wracked Burundi's cities, Nkurunziza was in his birth village of Vyerwa, playing practice games with Hallelujah FC inside his own private walled stadium, while shoeless kids stood outside its locked gates.[84] Fifty-four in 2018, the President was still in power and still playing, his increasingly repressive instincts seeing a string of arrests after a team from Kiremba, staffed by Congolese refugees, actually played the President and his team for real, regularly sending the head of state tumbling to the ground.

If Nkurunziza's insouciant kickabouts are one of African football's lowest points, Kenya and the DRC have offered two high points and two contrasting models of football development in Africa: one individual and rooted in the old politics of state patronage, the other collective, an expression of the new politics of African civil society. Congo took the former route, Kenya the latter. In the years since the death of President Mobutu, even during the long war in the DRC, powerful Congolese politicians have sought out the presidency of the country's biggest football clubs. The 2006 presidential hopeful Diomi Ndongala was also head of Kinshasa's most popular club, AS Vita. He was succeeded by André Kimbuta, the governor of Kinshasa state. General Gabriel Amisi Kumba, head of the army, created Maniema Union from scratch. But none of them lavished the attention or the money that Moses Katumbi, governor of Katanga province, lavished on TP Mazembe.[85]

Tout Puissant Mazembe, to give the club its full and magnificent title, was founded in the 1930s in Elizabethville, now Lubumbashi, the capital of Katanga. The most mineral-rich province in the country, it was also home to a secessionist political movement, crushed in the aftermath of independence by the CIA's point man, General, later President, Mobutu. Like both Asante Kotoko and Enugu Rangers, the teams of the losing sides in the post-independence struggles of Ghana and Nigeria, TP Mazembe carried and channelled some of Katanga's frustrated regionalist energies. All these teams went on to win continental trophies, in TP Mazembe's case the African Champions League twice. Like every other aspect of football in Zaire, as the DRC then was, TP Mazembe went into a two-decade hibernation after Zaire's humiliating exit from the 1974 World Cup. Mobutu simply abandoned the sport. When Katumbi, who had been in exile in Zambia, first returned to Katanga, he found the club he had supported as a child (and which his family had run) a wreck. With the fall of Mobutu soon after, Katumbi returned to Lubumbashi and the family businesses to stay. First, he was installed as the President of TP Mazembe, then he forged a close alliance with President Laurent Kabila, before being elected governor of Katanga in 2007. A decade of remarkably efficient governance by Congolese standards followed. Taxes and tolls were actually raised, government salaries were paid, and some infrastructure was built. TP Mazembe acquired a $35 million stadium with 12 VIP boxes, a huge football academy staffed by Ivorians, and two private jets to ferry its players to games. Estimates of the annual wage bill were around $10 million, making it the best paid squad in Africa. Consequently, for the first time in two generations, Congolese stars like Trésor Mputu stayed at home, while half of the Zambians who won the AFCON 2012 joined him. Alongside a raft of national championships, the club won the Champions League another three times, and in 2010 became the first African club to make the final of the World Club Cup, beating the champions of North and South America (Pachuca of Mexico and Internacional from Brazil) before losing to Milan's Internazionale.

In public, Katumbi's favourite look was a white jacket and a black Stetson, which matched nicely with Mazembe's black-and-white strip. Fans wore the shirt if they could, and painted the colours on their bodies if they couldn't. The 100 Per Cent Club, supported by Katumbi, filled the stadium with colour and their fabulous brass band filled it with music and praise for their patron. In 2015, Katumbi broke his political ties with President Kabila and warned of the problems ahead should he not step down from his final term as President and organize elections. Six months later, in an ominous herald of the wider political violence to come, a stampede was triggered by police tear gas at the end of the game between AS Vita and TP Mazembe, with the Kinshasa side 1–0 down. Fifteen people were killed. In early 2016, after TP Mazembe beat Etoile of Tunis in the African Super Cup, the chant 'Moise President' was heard amongst the celebrations in the streets of Lubumbashi.[86] In May, Katumbi announced his presidential candidacy. With no sign of Kabila actually being prepared to step down or organize elections for later in the year, huge street protests erupted. In September 2016, more than fifty demonstrators were killed. The continuing political violence forced the government to suspend the football league in late 2016, arguing that 'The general situation in the country risks spilling into the stadiums', but it had been there for a long time.[87] Throughout the autumn, the popular chant in the football stands was 'Kabila, your mandate is over.'[88] In fact it has taken more than two years of grinding and opaque negotiation to prise Kabila from the presidency, a path that proved too fraught and too expensive for Katumbi, however much adulation football had brought him.

At the turn of the century, Kenya and its football federation were a casebook study of everything that has gone wrong in African football. The culture and practice of corruption were so widespread that it is hard to describe the management style as anything other than looting. Not a penny was banked from dozens of national team games and their ticket receipts. FIFA monies were totally unaccounted for. Meetings, minutes, audits simply did not happen. Two thousand footballs were donated to the Kenya Football Federation, but not one made it onto the pitch.[89] Unable to effectively prosecute officials through the country's hapless court system, or to call on help from FIFA, whose interventions usually benefited the *ancien regime*, Kenya's clubs decided to break away altogether. The Kenyan Premier League (KPL) was founded in 2008 by sixteen clubs as a private company in which they were all equal shareholders and decision-makers, an arrangement that created the conditions for mutual accountability, transparency and fair play.[90] SuperSport agreed to screen the new league and, though it struggles with the European competition, the rot has stopped. Since 2009, crowds are much bigger, TV audiences have grown, match-fixing has been tackled, the clubs remain solvent and players' salaries have risen, though they remain pitifully low. The national team remains in the hands of the KFF. Hardly the October revolution, but in the context of African football, this was as close as it got.

VIII

In Southern Africa, football did offer one real moment of national unity and redemption when Zambia won the 2012 Africa Cup of Nations in Gabon. While every such victory in Africa is met with an outpouring of public celebrations and national pride, this one had a special edge.[91] In 1993, thirty people, including eighteen members of what was considered to be the most promising Zambian football team ever, died in a plane crash in Gabon on their way to a match in Senegal. Ten years later, the Zambian government finally admitted that the elderly air force plane that carried the team (there was no money for conventional flights) had serious mechanical problems and 'Gabon' had become Lusaka slang for a dangerously maintained vehicle. Almost twenty years later, a young, home-based squad went back to Gabon for AFCON 2012. Goalkeeper Kennedy Mweene spoke for the team and much of the nation when he said, 'We are going to this tournament to put the souls of our fallen heroes at rest.' They made it all the way to the final, where, against the much stronger Côte d'Ivoire, they took the match to penalties and won. Needless to say, the Zambian FA has returned to bitter political fighting, and the national team, which has been in steep decline ever since, failed to even qualify for a second AFCON in Gabon in 2017.

By contrast, football's unifying and redemptive power has been barely perceptible in Zimbabwe. Since taking power in 1980, Robert Mugabe and his ZANU-PF party have been alert to the political and symbolic power of the game: the country's knock-out tournament was renamed the Independence Cup, and celebrations of Unity Day and Heroes Day often included a game between Dynamos and Highlanders, the country's two biggest clubs, in an effort to bump up attendance. For the first twenty years of Zimbabwe's existence, ZANU-PF practically and rhetorically owned football like everything else. Then, at the turn of the century, as the country's economic crisis mounted, a new opposition emerged around Morgan Tsvangirai. The Movement for Democratic Change (MDC) challenged Mugabe over land and constitutional reform, and then went head-to-head with ZANU-PF in the 2000 parliamentary elections. Football was now contested political territory. In a speech at Rufaro stadium, characteristic of his whole campaign, Tsvangirai said, 'The people of Zimbabwe say to Robert Mugabe – we showed you the yellow card at the time of the referendum, and now today, Robert Mugabe, we are showing you the red card. Get off the field, Robert Mugabe. Your time is over.' The crowd responded with thousands of referees' whistles, but Mugabe still won the vote.[92]

Eight years of penury, crisis and repression followed, during which Mugabe and ZANU-PF maintained their precarious hold on power by the widespread use of violence and intimidation and the rigging of elections. In the muted and often metaphorical public conversation about the various parties' political tactics, the MDC played *bhora pasi* – playing the ball low – a reference to the movement's use of passive resistance and non-violence; ZANU-PF played *bhora rembabvu* – hardball – as members of the opposition who were relentlessly harried and intimidated for a decade would testify. And then there was the surreptitious stuff that everyone did, which was *bhora musango*: the ball you played in the bush. The strategy of *bhora pasi* seemed to pay off in the 2008 presidential election, in which, despite every kind of trickery, Tsvangirai won the first round with 47 per cent of the vote to Mugabe's 43, with every prospect of winning the second round outright. Over the next two months, *bhora rembabvu* triumphed as Mugabe and his party forced Tsvangirai and the MDC to withdraw from a run-off that Mugabe won. An uneasy power-sharing arrangement was then brokered by South Africa, in which Tsvangirai would serve as Prime Minister.

On the surface, football functioned as a balm. In 2010, on the eve of the South African World Cup, Zimbabwe hosted Brazil in Harare. It was considered to be the biggest day in the nation's sporting history. 'It's a big thing for the country,' said one member of the 60,000 crowd. 'In every corner, in every market, in every shop, people are speaking of this Brazil match.'[93] In a very rare show of unity, Mugabe and Tsvangirai took to the field together and shared the cheers of the crowd: a million dollars well spent. A better guide to the state of the nation was the football peace tournament played in 2011 in Bulawayo: a four-way league between ZANU-PF, both wings of the MDC and ZAPU. ZANU-PF won all three of their games at a canter, but it turned out that they had brought footballers rather than politicians, and had surreptitiously bussed in three separate teams to play just one match each, one of them a crack squad recruited from the local township.[94]

Between 2008 and 2013, ZANU-PF were in coalition, but they were planning for a future alone, a disposition indicated by their commissioning of the Mbare Chimurenga Choir to record the football-themed song 'Team', in which the only three members of Zimbabwe's team were Mugabe and his vice-presidents Joice Mujuru and John Nkomo. Similarly, at the behest of the party, Blessed Chari and the

Conscious People put out a whole album entitled *Bhora Mugehdi!* This time, there were not going to be any splits in the team or the need for a run-off with the opposition. 'Stand Up ZANU-PF team. Let's go forward with the ball. Let's score, boys. Kicking the ball out of play and not scoring will result in a replay. This time it's going to be a whitewash. Stick to the game plan of coach Mugabe.' Thus, for the campaign for the presidency in 2013, the party was actually rebranded as Team ZANU-PF. It fielded a long list of candidates with football credentials, campaigned on the slogan *Bhora Mugehdi!*, and launched it with a rally at a Harare stadium. 'This time we must score goals,' said Mugabe, and then told the crowd (mercifully unfamiliar with John Barnes's playing career): 'we need strong defenders like John Barnes who can pack powerful shots from the back straight into the net.' 'Team ZANU-PF plays samba football,' claimed Christopher Gwatidzo, a local candidate who in his stump speeches dropped into football commentary, in which his command of the midfield allowed him to set up the perfect ball for Mugabe to score a goal. The opposition responded in kind, calling themselves Team MDC-T and putting out adverts, placards and leaflets on football themes, with the usual red cards and whistles. *Bhora Musango!* Mugabe won an election that the opposition dismissed as profoundly compromised, and the country settled in for the long descent towards his death.

Zimbabwean football has moved in parallel. ZIFA was so broke that it auctioned off FIFA-funded training equipment to try to pay some of its many creditors – the office furniture and photocopiers had gone years before – including former employees and coaches, irate hoteliers and litigious airlines. To no avail: FIFA expelled Zimbabwe from the qualifiers for the 2018 World Cup. Mugabe and his clan have since been retired, but no signs of revival in Zimbabwean football have yet been seen.[95]

For football as a sign of an African renaissance, one was meant to look south to South Africa and the 2010 World Cup. The final cost of staging the tournament was around £3.3 billion. Compared to the money spent on its three successors (Brazil, Russia and Qatar), this was loose change, but in South Africa, where basic sanitation and housing were the privilege of a minority, the cost was not inconsiderable, and the beneficiaries were few. For its money, the country got some aviation upgrades, the Gautrain to deliver foreigners and financiers from Johannesburg's Oliver Tambo International Airport to the

Sandton City shopping and banking district, and a rapid bus route from downtown to Soweto. It also got five new stadiums and five major upgrades.

Most controversial, and emblematic of the whole process, was Green Point in Cape Town. Originally, the plan was to upgrade Athlone Stadium in the heart of the Cape Flats, where people actually watched football, but the rubbish-strewn sand dunes and barrack-like housing of this apartheid-era township couldn't compete with Table Mountain. At immense expense, land was bought and cleared in the Green Point district that sat at the foot of the city's number-one tourist cipher. The stadium was made even costlier by the insistence that the city should stage a semi-final game, necessitating the building of a whole additional tier of seats. In the absence of any money being spent on public transport, it remained unclear as to how the football public in the Cape Flats would ever make it there, but the wide-angle photographs were sensational.

In contrast to the anodyne business-district look of Green Point, the Mbombela in Nelspruit went cod-African, featuring seat patterns of zebra stripes and tubular towers like a giraffe in profile. Along with the Peter Mokaba Stadium in Polokwane, it was also the most obvious of the white elephants. Durban's ANC government was so insistent on getting its share of the cake that the Moses Mabhida stadium was built just 200 m from the perfectly serviceable but rugby-saturated Kings Park. The singular work of distinction produced for 2010 was the refashioned First National Bank Stadium in Soweto, re-clad and re-christened as Soccer City. A huge, undulating screen was erected on the apartheid-era concrete frame to produce an architectural take on the calabash, the traditional African cooking pot. During the tournament, it was brilliantly lit from inside, and gave Soweto a building of the grandeur the city's size and importance deserved. Seen in the cold light of day and set against the huge expanse of dense low-rise housing, it appeared more incongruous than iconic, and nowhere more so than in David Goldblatt's (no relation) brilliant photograph of the stadium. Shot before the tournament had begun and the final landscaping had been completed, it showed Soccer City in the background; in the foreground were the ruined brick stumps and archways of Shareworld, a theme park built in the final years of apartheid that went bankrupt.[96]

Street sellers and hawkers, hopeful of the tourist dollar, attempted to mobilize in advance of the tournament, seeking to claim a space inside FIFA's exclusion zones around stadiums and fan parks, which were to be stripped of non-sponsor advertising and traders. There were a lot of meetings, promises and discussion, and then the sharp reality that no one was getting in. In an otherwise supine relationship with FIFA, the South African government finally roused itself over the issue of ticket prices and the requirement for credit cards when buying them, for the simple reason that the majority of South Africans would not be able to afford them and, even if they could, credit card ownership remained very limited. A small number of tickets was set aside for cash purchase by locals. In actual fact the main opposition to the South African government and the tournament organizers was the global press, and the range of afro-pessimists and old-fashioned racists it gave voice too. In keeping with the coverage of all sporting mega-events, columnists fretted that stadiums would be hopelessly late, transport links would be inadequate and, in a special twist for the African World Cup, that personal security in public spaces would be a serious problem. None of these turned out to be true, but they were enough to send South Africa's reputation-anxiety complex into overdrive.

They needn't have bothered. With the 1995 Rugby World Cup and 2003 Cricket World Cup under its belt, South Africa's public was long acclimatized to the idea of performing from the stands and putting on the Rainbow Nation's best face for the international media. In the weeks leading up to the tournament, the country's roads were awash with car wing-mirror socks of the South African flag. The public actually responded to the official call to wear the national team shirt on 'Football Fridays'. First National Bank erected a *makarapa* – a football-themed construction helmet – seven stories high outside its Johannesburg offices. A huge ball was impaled on the tip of Hillbrow Telecom Tower, the city's highest building, while the world's widest football, 15m in diameter, was installed outside the equally oversized Emperor's Palace, Johannesburg's very own slice of Las Vegas. The official World Cup ball appeared everywhere: in the tourist shops made from Ndebele beads; moulded from chocolate in the windows of upscale confectioners; and at Shimansky's, South African jewellers to the rich and vulgar, who made their own $2.2 million, diamond-encrusted version.

Everywhere, that is, except the football fields of South Africa, where Adidas's *Jabulani* would have cost a week or two of a worker's wage. The Diski Dance, a series of dribble-style grooves, concocted by the South African tourist authority, gained currency amongst the nation's school children and TV variety shows. The South African public was even accommodating enough to hum along to the anodyne melodies of Coca-Cola's World Cup song, 'Wavin' Flag' by Somali-American rapper K'Naan, and the official FIFA tune by Colombian pop star Shakira. The former was a piece of glib anthemic advert music, the latter a sly piece of cultural appropriation, as Shakira rewrote and then murdered 'Waka Waka (This Time for Africa)' by the Cameroonian band Golden Sounds. Only a threatened strike by the South African musicians' union saved the nation from having to endure an eve-of-tournament concert dominated by foreign stars.[97]

FIFA and the South African legal authorities remained alert to the threat of intellectual property theft, banning the sale of the sweets '2010 Pops'. During the tournament itself, they would evict thirty-six Dutch women from a game for wearing orange dresses with the logo of Bavaria beer on their hems. South Africa responded magnificently. Widely circulating T-shirts bearing the slogans, 'MAFIFA: WE OWN THE GAME', and 'FICK FUFA'. Budget airline Kalua brazenly advertised itself as the 'Unofficial Carrier of You-Know-What', at 'The thing that is happening right now'. They still got taken to court. So too the 3,000 demonstrators who marched on the Moses Mabhida stadium in Durban, the only public protest against the tournament's immense cost. The police blocked the march and arrested activists handing out anti-World Cup leaflets on Durban beach and in the city's fan park.[98]

Spain won the World Cup, but 2010 will not be remembered for the football. It will be remembered, perhaps hazily, for the party. From the moment the opening ceremony began, South Africa drifted into a collective state of extended narcotic ecstasy. Observers thought that perhaps 'Prozac had been introduced to the water system.'[99] Like the heady days that followed Mandela's inauguration as President, the nation was high as a kite at actually pulling the thing off. Everywhere, across the old townships and the new slum cities, South Africa, as the locals would put it, put on the *braai*, cracked open a beer and parked off. Even the departure at the end of the group stage of the frequently timid South African side did not shift the mood. Foreign fans, in their hundreds of thousands, played their carnivalesque cameo roles. Rich Mexican-Americans from California dutifully appeared in joke sombreros and designer peasant blankets. The English and the Germans drank a lot. The Ghanaian government dispatched a thousand fans to put on a show in the stadiums, which they did until it turned out officials had sold their tickets for the later rounds on the black market.

Above all, the crowd blew the vuvuzela, a long plastic horn tuned to a single buzzing note somewhere in the vicinity of B flat.[100] A sporadic feature of football terraces in South Africa for a few years before 2010, it was given global exposure by the World Cup. Although virtually identical instruments, known by the rather more quotidian title of stadium horns, were circulating in the United States in the 1960s, the World Cup gave voice to three South African creation myths. The Nazareth Baptist Church, a Christian sect founded in the early twentieth century, had long used the *izimbomou*, a very similar trumpet fashioned from animal horn, in their services, and threatened legal action against the use of their invention. Freddie 'Saddam' Maake, a well-known fan of the Kaizer Chiefs, claimed to have made one from a metal bicycle horn in 1965 and coined the name, a compound of isiZulu words for welcome, unite and celebrate. Neil Van Schalkwyk first noticed these kinds of home-made vuvuzelas, often cobbled together from metal scraps, while playing semi-professional football in South Africa in the 1990s. In the early 2000s, he perfected a reliable plastic injection-moulded version, set up a manufacturing company and supplied the small South African market, including the winning World Cup bid team, who blew his vuvuzelas in Zurich at FIFA HQ when South Africa's victory was announced. Christian movement, black entrepreneur and small white business were all trumped at the World Cup by a flood of cheaper Chinese-manufactured variants.

The reaction to stadiums full of vuvuzelas, from Europeans in particular, was often negative, even hostile. Spain's Xabi Alonso and Dutch coach Bert van Marwijk were vocal in their dislike. Complaints flooded into television stations: 'It's just a nasty harsh noise and it does my head in.' While tinny television speakers did render the vuvuzela chorus as something close to a droning insect swarm, in the stadium it was a much more variegated aural experience. In the first place, it gave white South Africans, many of whom had never been to a football match before, something to do with themselves and a way of making noise at a game they were often indifferent to. Buzzing can be a little monotone, but try embarrassed silence. Second, the sound was not uniform. Tone, volume and rhythms all varied, often in keeping with the ebb and flow of the game. Most people could only produce a crude squawk or burp, but some could extract a range of notes. Set pieces and celebrations were punctuated with sharp, concentrated squeaking, and a degree of call and response could be heard between opposing sets of fans and their honking. FIFA President Sepp Blatter, to his credit, defended the vuvuzela: 'We should not try to Europeanize an African World Cup. That is what African and South African football is all about.'[101]

On the eve of the final, Danny Jordaan, the man in charge of the whole show, counselled, 'I think there will be huge post-World Cup blues on Monday. I hope South Africans go to work because there will be a great sense of loss. It's like you've had a huge party and then there's the morning after.' The morning after has turned into almost a decade.[102] Football remains an overwhelmingly black game in South Africa. In sport as in so many fields of everyday life, its citizens remain in their class and ethnic silos, tolerant but apart. By 2016, of the ten World Cup stadiums only Soccer City and Moses Mabhida had kept their heads above water. The rest were drowning in debt picked up by desperately underfunded local governments. Cape Town's Green Point was costing $7 million a year in maintenance alone. Ajax Cape Town's crowd was already small and felt pitiful in the oversized stands – they have since returned to Athlone – and no amount of conferences, wedding-photo shoots and church services could make the sums add up.

Outside of Cape Town only the Kaizer Chiefs and Orlando Pirates have attracted really significant crowds since the World Cup, while the rest of the teams in the top division have attendances in the low thousands. Indeed, many municipalities have been so desperate to fill their World Cup stadiums that they have invited the two big clubs to give exhibition games. A similar battle between two old giants that sucked up all the air in South African football was fought out at SAFA between Irving Khoza, owner of Kaizer Chiefs, and Danny Jordaan's factions, who became bogged down in endless accusations of match-fixing. As hosts, South Africa played AFCON 2013, but the national team has failed to qualify for anything since the World Cup, and few South Africans play in the top European leagues any more.

The singular triumph for the South African game since 2010 was Mamelodi Sundown's victory in the 2016 Champions League.[103] The club was owned by Patrice Motsepe, the first black South African to be included on *Forbes'* annual list of billionaires. He achieved this by his deft positioning between the ANC and the mining industry, allowing him to be the biggest beneficiary of South Africa's Black Economic Empowerment programme, which has transferred public and private assets into the hands of a new class of local oligarchs. That South Africa can mount this kind of continental competitive challenge is testament to both its enduring economic and cultural weight on the continent, and the still deeply unequal ways in which it distributes its wealth domestically.

IX

It can be hard to see how the real energies and possibilities of African football survive in the niches left by globalization. Sometimes one needs a sharper eye. Both visitors and the leading lights amongst a new generation of African photographers have that. Taking football as their subject matter, they have helped capture the game's deep historical meanings and living everyday presence.[104] The Senegalese, Omar Victor Diop, dressed as little-known but important figures from the African diaspora, took a series of self-portraits based on paintings from the fifteenth to the nineteenth century. Styled and posed like the African studio photography of the twentieth century, Diop made the twenty-first-century connection to these images by adding an object. Pedro Camejo, the only black officer in the army of Simon Bolívar, wearing goalkeeping gloves. Badin, first a slave, then butler and diarist to Princess Sophia of Sweden, holding a red card. The Belgian artist Jessica Hilltout offered no ironies or self-conscious intertextuality in *Amen: Grassroots Football*, a photo journal of a seven-month trip across rural and small-town Africa from Togo, Mali and Ghana to Mozambique, Lesotho and South Africa. If the many photographs of players, feet, home-made sandals and torn sneakers veer towards the gratingly pitiful, her photographs of their hand-made balls are quietly breath-taking. Constructed from twine, condoms, rags and tape (and each exchanged for a factory-made ball), in Hilltout's photographs they come to seem like finely cut jewels, testament to the exquisite ingenuity, craft and resourcefulness of Africa's poor.[105] The sharply dressed African women in portraits by Nigeria's Uche James-Iroha seem confident on the ball and, set against tattered football nets, put a face to the rising tide of women's football in Africa. More straightforward but emotionally richer is Andrew Esiebo's brilliant series *Grannys*, double portraits of African women as football players and as grandmothers with their grandchildren. His collection of street football, *For the Love of It*, shot in South Africa, Nigeria and Ghana, is the most exceptional of all, capturing in a blaze of chromatic brilliance the harsh environments and momentary joys of the game: teenagers playing three-a-side on a patch of concrete cleared of broken glass beneath the vast raised motorways of Lagos; a cross-legged game of disabled football on the hot tarmac of an Accra taxi rank.

Steered by such imagery one can see that that life is emerging in women's football in Africa, taking off with what looks like the same kind of energies that fired the men's game when it first arrived. Africa has acquired its first professional women's leagues in Nigeria and Burundi, and when Isha Johansen was elected to head the Sierra Leonean Football Federation in 2013, she became its first woman football president. Africa has also acquired its first openly gay male footballer when, in 2016, the second-division South African goalkeeper Phuti Lekoloane came out.[106] This was an act of uncommon bravery on a continent where football has become the site for some of the homophobic moral panics, nurtured by the evangelical churches and opportunist politicians, that have occupied the African media. In 2009, Uganda's FA went as far as to systemically outlaw sodomy in its statutes and conduct a witch hunt amongst coaches. In 2013 the Zambian authorities tried to do the same, though both were thwarted by FIFA's insistence that such statutes were not in accordance with their own. Nonetheless, a vice-president of the Nigerian football federation – a man hitherto silent on widespread accusations of heterosexual abuse in Nigerian football – thought 'Lesbianism kills teams. The coaches take advantage.' In South Africa, teams kill lesbians. In 2008, Eudy Simelane, a high-profile out player with the women's national team, was gang-raped, stabbed twenty-five times and left for dead in an act of calculated 'corrective rape'.[107] Yet the seeds of something else are stirring when, in Botswana, the football association starts supporting five-a-side tournaments for the nascent LGBT rights community.[108]

Life is also stirring in Africa's private and civic sectors. It remains the case that the vast majority of clubs in the continent (outside of South Africa) are controlled or funded by state organizations: armies and police forces, city and regional governments, ministries of state and national oil and mining companies. None of this is good for football governance. In the case of Nigeria's state governments, it is simply disastrous. In this context, the transformation of football clubs into conventional businesses has introduced a degree of transparency, shared decision-making and financial responsibility absent hitherto. It has also created a constituency in football with a direct interest in anti-corruption programmes. This kind of change has been most invigorating in Kenya, where real advances can be seen in the quality of local football and its governance, but the same process can also be seen at work in South Africa, Tanzania and even in Nigeria.

One African side has actually made it to a World Cup final: Angola's amputee football team, runners-up to the Russians in 2014. Their victory was the product of the devastating and widespread use of landmines in the country's brutal civil war. The same tragic conditions have made Liberia African champions. A transformative sport for the disabled, and the often traumatized and excluded veterans, amputee football has acquired huge public support. The opening match of the 2007 African Cup in Sierra Leone between the hosts and Ghana drew 10,000 people.[109] The same hunger for alternatives to poor-quality professional football can be seen in Senegal, where the neighbourhood-based amateur *navétanes* championships draw bigger crowds and stir infinitely more passions than the moribund official league. In Lagos, young professionals dissatisfied with both the grim conditions of local football and the passive consumerism of the Premier League have started their own amateur tournaments, the Twitter Premier League and Socialiga, as new kinds of social event for urban middle-class youth.[110]

For the hundreds of millions warehoused in the shacks and self-builds of Africa's slums, there is, before anything else, the problem of where to play. In the absence of public investment, the only options are the rare open spaces in these super-dense neighbourhoods and, given the complete absence of municipal refuse services, these are invariably piled high with rubbish and food waste. MYSA, the Mathare Youth Sports Association, was born of this dilemma in one of the largest slums in Nairobi. It now runs football coaching, leagues and boot libraries for 25,000 youths in Kenya, 5,000 of them young women. Teams score three points for a win, one for a draw, but six for doing their part in a now highly organized clean-up operation (and at least seven members of the squad need to show up). MYSA is also run by the youth of Mathare in a long-standing democratic framework, which has created a pipeline of educated, confident social entrepreneurs and local leaders, and made MYSA the backbone of civil society in the city and a key provider of health and education services. It has also won the World Street Football championships twice.[111] MYSA, though, is just one of a vast archipelago of NGOs that have emerged all across Africa, tapping into the game's extraordinary social potential. Alive and Kicking were Africa's first manufacturers of footballs. Based in Kenya, they crafted super-durable, low-cost leather balls designed to survive on the rough terrains of the continent, selling half and donating half of their output. The Tanzanian club Albino United provided a safe space and an educational tool for football players with the eponymous condition – one which carries a deep and pervasive taboo in much of Africa.[112]

But, perhaps more than anywhere, African football lives in the courtyard of Luzira prison on the south side of Kampala, where Barcelona play Manchester United, then Chelsea play Hannover 96.[113] Built in the 1920s by the British colonial authorities to house 500, Uganda's highest security prison now holds 3,000 inmates, yet none of the just 100 guards on duty carries a gun. Once a byword for the abuse of human rights and torture, it is now the most humane and successful prison in Africa, with an open-door policy to the world and a recidivism rate closer to Scandinavia's than Britain's or America's. Its hybrid prison culture draws on western concepts of human rights and individual rehabilitation, Christian notions of redemption and forgiveness, and African traditions of collectivism and restitutive justice. On a day-to-day basis the success of the prison depends on keeping the peace: the consent of the prisoners themselves to the rule of law. This is delivered by UPSA, the Upper Prison Sports Association, and the ten football clubs, Barcelona and Manchester United included, that have been established in Luzira since the mid-2000s. A democratic association with statutes drawn up by staff and prisoners,

UPSA elects all its officials, has open accounts, and under spartan conditions runs a player and club registration system, a transfer window and arbitration system, and provides match officials and sponsored tournaments – all with a degree of transparency and efficiency that would put most of the continent's football associations to shame. The reformers of the English public schools sought through sports to turn out muscular Christian gentleman who would go on to rule the empire. UPSA has attempted something much harder. It has tried to establish a space in which the rule of law is paramount, corruption is not tolerated, and transparency is king. At the same time, UPSA has kept the peace, relieved the boredom and in innumerable cases transformed the lives and outlook of its players and officers. African football is still alive, and it lives in Luzira.

2

REGIME VS STREET VS MOSQUE: THREE-SIDED FOOTBALL IN THE MIDDLE EAST

Agüero goes over! Oh God. Impossible! Impossible!
The dream has come true! The dream has come true!
In the final seconds: Agüero, Agüero, the Kun Agüero!
Hysteria. Madness. Drama. An incredible show.
Agüero did it.
On his right hand a tattoo, on his left hand a tattoo.
He put a tattoo of the championship in the goal, the title's tattoo.
City's scorer! City's falcon! City's falcon has appeared.
The blue moon is brightening up.
What a drama, what a madness!
The goal of the season. The goal that wins the title.
The goal to end the lost years, the dark years.
A dream come true.
Agüero said to the fans, 'Don't worry, what happened was
    just a nightmare.'
Now the dream can come true.

Faris Awad, 2012

Regime! Be very scared of us.
We are coming tonight with intent.
The supporters of Al Ahly will fire everything up.
God almighty will make us victorious. Go, hooligans!

Ultras Ahlawy, 2011

At home, in tea houses and coffee shops, from Fez to Basra, the Middle Eastern public's appetite for global football has been insatiable. In 2016, when the European Championships coincided with Ramadan and kick-off times coincided with *Itfar*, the meal that breaks the daily fast, football for the first time displaced soap operas as the public's choice of after-dinner relaxation.[1] In many of the region's cities, life stops for *El Clásico*, the game between Real Madrid and Barcelona. In Erbil, in Kurdish Iraq, the television schedules are cleared for hours in the build-up to the game. Afterwards, the winning side's fans parade loudly through the night in a motorized cavalcade of flags and horns.[2] In Gaza, Palestinians defied Hamas's order not to watch the game and turned on in their hundreds of thousands. On match day, the Qalandiya Israeli military checkpoint by Ramallah is a sea of fake Barça shirts for sale.[3] If Barcelona have the edge in the West Bank, Real are kings in Morocco, where local fans unveiled a banner at a World Club Cup game in 2014, 'Welcome to your second home.'[4] Real have reciprocated the love in the region by agreeing to remove the Christian cross from their club crest when they are in town.[5] Barcelona fans have beamed back their own message to the Kurds, with the banner 'Catalonia is not Spain, Kurdistan is not Iraq.'

This embrace of European football should not be read, however, as a simple form of neo-colonialism. The peoples of this region have long proved resistant and flexible enough to absorb and domesticate rather than merely mimic their temporary imperial overlords. Thus football, the game of the European colonizer, was, in North Africa and the Levant particularly, quickly embraced and then deployed as both a symbolic challenge to imperial rule, and a practical tool of organization and political self-education. In Egypt, Al-Ahly has always understood itself as the representative of the nation. In Algeria, football clubs served as clandestine cells for the growing nationalist movement, while matches against French settler sides offered perfect opportunities to challenge their rule. In the later stages of the War of Independence, the FLN would actually establish their own Algerian national team-in-waiting, touring the world to drum up support for the cause. The Arabic language has taken on and domesticated nearly all the English sporting terminology it inherited in the early twentieth century; converting 'penalty', for example, to *Darbat ul Jazaa*, the 'p' sound being impossible in Arabic. On the other hand, the language has remained open enough to employ the best of English football idioms: a player awarded a harsh yellow card for a fifty-fifty challenge is, like King Lear, 'more sinned against than sinning' in both Doha and Rabat, while Faris Awad's ecstatic poem celebrating Sergio Agüero's last-minute title-winning goal for Manchester City in 2012, composed on the spot, mingles Arabic and English.[6]

Forgive me, but there is no way in print to render the cadences and intensity of Awad's brilliant commentary for Al-Jazeera except through typological feint. Don't take my word for it, though: listen for yourself.[7] Or, like the rest of the Arabic speaking football world, tune in to the urbane but emotional Tunisian Issam Chawali, a graduate in French literature who peppers his work with cinematic and literary references and has become the leading commentator of the era, not least as the Arabic voice on the FIFA video game series. His high-intensity, percussive account of Lionel Messi's two goals against Bayern Munich in the semi-final of the Champions League in 2015 was the verbal equivalent of *craquage*, the simultaneous detonation of flares and fireworks beloved of North Africa's ultras.[8] Not that anyone should be surprised that Arabic should prove such a poetic medium in which to express the meanings of football, nor that its public should be so receptive to its rhythms. The language has a rich literary tradition of exaggeration and hyperbole, of tall tales that can render the everyday epic, an approach which retains a demotic, popular appeal. On the occasion of Palestine's first international game actually played in Palestine, the announcer began with the words of the nation's greatest poet, Mahmoud Darwish: 'Palestine will make the earth tremble! Football is more noble than war!', then read a series of his verses to the crowd before play commenced.[9] In this light, the Middle East's love of both poetry and European football suggest a civilization that is complex, playful, in parts refined, connected and cosmopolitan; all a welcome antidote to the stereotypes of closed and xenophobic Islamic republics and malign jihadi networks.

However, novelists writing in Arabic, no less entranced by the game than the poets, have touched on something darker. Naguib Mahfouz, in volume two of his *Cairo Trilogy*, sensed the unease that came from football's already intimate connection with politics. Set in inter-war Egypt, when the Liberal party was challenging the conservative and monarchical Wafds, Kamal, his own alter ego, 'wondered why he always found himself on the other side from Hasan Salim, whether they were discussing the Wafd Party and the Liberals or the Mukhtalat team and Ahly.'[10] Ahly, as we know, was the club of the republicans and modernizers; Al-Mokhtalat (later renamed Zamalek) was then the team of monarchists and reactionaries. More recently, in *Moon over Samarqand*, Mohamed Mansi Qandil explores a brutalizing dimension of the game. The main character, an Egyptian young man of privilege, must endure a grim rite of passage through football training in the military college he has been sent to; his lower class colleagues constantly remind him, verbally and physically, that on the pitch there is no privilege.[11] In the sly satire of Mohamed El-Bisatie's *Drumbeat*, an 'Emirates' nation qualifies for the World Cup and the ruling house decides to send everyone – everyone who is a citizen, that is – to France to support the team, all expenses paid. The team almost makes it to the knock-out stages, but the book's real concern is the new society being forged amongst the Filipinos, Egyptians, Indians and Pakistanis who make up the majority of the population and who have been left behind and alone to keep things ticking over. It turns out to be a much kinder society and a more benign life. However, the new solidarities that football can forge can also be malign.[12] In *Life is More Beautiful than Paradise*, the memoir of ex-Jihadi Khaled al-Berry, the author reveals the centrality of football in binding together a cell of suicide bombers.[13] Perhaps most telling of all and, uniquely, here told from a female perspective, is the movie *One-Zero*, directed by Kamla Abu Zekri. Set on the day of the final of the 2008 African Cup of Nations, in which Egypt are playing Cameroon, the film follows eight characters from morning till night against the backdrop of Cairo's mounting football fever. Egypt win the game 1–0, but all the characters are left alienated or distanced from the spectacle and the celebrations: at a moment of national sporting triumph an unmistakable hollowness pervades the city and its citizens.[14]

It was a hollowness perhaps at its most extreme in the dying years of the Mubarak regime in Egypt, but pervasive across the region in the early twenty-first century. It flowed from the relentlessly repressive politics of the region's variety of authoritarian polities: the unbendingly harsh Ba'athist and Socialist republics of Algeria, Egypt and Syria and their more personalized dictatorial variants in Saddam Hussein's Iraq and Gaddafi's Libya; conservative and impoverished monarchies conceding a modicum of representation in Jordan and Morocco; hydrocarbon billionaire sheikhdoms in the Gulf conceding nothing. Diverse as they were, all attempted to control and if possible obliterate all forms of serious political opposition and civil organization, relying heavily on the military, the police and security services for their rule. Only in Iran, Lebanon and Israel could some semblance of real democratic politics be seen, and even in those places it was compromised: in Lebanon by pervasive sectarianism; in Iran by theocratic and unaccountable centres of power; and in Israel by the predication of Israeli sovereignty on the absence of its Palestinian equivalent. In this political context, domestic football and the national team were treated as another zone of cultural life to be strictly controlled.

A brief examination of the names of clubs and their owners offers an instant tally of the region's football politics. Most straightforward in their meaning are the Al-Jaish's, the army teams of Iraq, Syria and Qatar, and their equivalents in Morocco and Iran, FAR Rabat and Niroye Zamini. In Iraq, Al-Quwa Al-Jawiya ('the Air Force') gets to play too. Al-Shortas are the teams of national police forces and they play in Syria and Iraq. Even Iran's revolutionary guards, once strongly opposed to the game, now have their own sporting tribune in Fajr Sepasi Shiraz FC. Qatar's Lekhwiya SC was a team just for the state internal security system, but the process of militarization has gone furthest in Egypt, where the top league boasts Tala'ea El-Gaish or 'Army Vanguard', Haras El Hodood ('the Border Guards') and El Entag El Harby, loosely translated as 'Military Production'. There they were joined by the two other wings of the regime: first its parastatals, like the state hydrocarbon companies that backed Petrojet FC and ENPPI; second, its chosen billionaire partners, like the club El Mokawloon, better known as 'Arab Contractors', the creation of the late construction magnate Osman Ahmed Osman. Across the Gulf, where the separation of the state and the ruling family has barely begun, either institutionally or financially, almost every team of significance has been owned by and presided over by a senior member of the ruling clan.

Hard as the state apparatus has tried to monopolize control over football, however, and despite its attempts to exclude its citizens from the game's operation, football needs crowds and a public and, as the most popular club names suggest, there is in the game a deep and latent aspiration for this to be recognized. The existence of so many Al-Ittihads ('United') and Al-Wahdas ('Union'), from Nablus in Palestine to Basra in Iraq, is testament to this. The most widely used name, Al-Ahly, which is found in Egypt, Bahrain, Jordan, Qatar and the UAE, can be translated as 'the nation', but with a sense of the nation as the people, not merely an institution. That there are two Al-Ahlys in Libya, two in Yemen and three in Sudan, and two Al-Wahdas in each of Yemen, Syria and Jordan, rightly suggests that who and what the nation consists of remain unresolved questions everywhere in the Middle East.

Thus the control of football, like the wider politics of these states, must still contend with alternative, if weaker centres of power. In almost every polity in the region there are two: the street, as shorthand for what little remains of civil society and public opinion, and which consequently expresses that opinion more by disorder than by argument; and the mosque, as shorthand for the complex web of cultural, political and judicial institutions and ideas that are rooted in Islamic theology and daily religious practice. The latter have a complex and variegated relationship to football that stretches back to the first appearance of the game in the Ottoman Empire at the turn of the twentieth century. Then, clerics argued that it was a worrying distraction from religious study and prayer and its dress codes were self-evidently too salacious. Some invoked the Karbala Event as the definitive case against the game. In 680 CE the would-be Caliph, Yazid, murdered the incumbent, Husayn, grandson of the Prophet Muhammad. It was claimed, subsequently, that the murderers severed his head and kicked it around. It wasn't much of a jump from here to the notion that football was unspeakable symbolic blasphemy. As late as 1969, the grand Mufti in Saudi Arabia, Abdul Aziz bin Abdullah ibn Baz, called for the sport to be banned, particularly in its organized competitive form, because 'the nature of the game sparks fanatical partisanship, trouble and the emergence of hate and malice.'[15] The immediate aftermath of the Islamic revolution in Iran saw a similar combination of arguments, made all the more urgent by the role that football had played under the Shah as an emblem of his version of Iranian modernity. In all these cases, however, the power of the theologians has been limited and football has prospered. In Turkey, the clerics were swept aside by the Ataturk revolution, their arguments and influence consigned to the margins of Turkish history for a century. In Saudi Arabia, the Royal House chose, as it often does, to turn a blind eye to those elements of Wahhabist theology that they found inconvenient, and invested heavily in football in the 1970s. In Iran, the regime, already overburdened by the desperate, attritional war with Iraq and conflicts with its own people, conceded football to its urban masses.

The reach of theological power, though, is such that even where these interpretations of Islamic theology have been rejected, they have been countered by others rather than met with secular indifference. Amongst mainstream Sunni and Shia thinkers, as well as more stringent Salafists, a clear alternative position has been offered. In particular, Muhammad's injunction to believers to maintain healthy bodies that they might better serve Allah provides the main foundation for both sport and football as permissible activities. It was under such Koranic cover that Osama bin Laden, Ismail Haniyeh, the leader of Hamas in Gaza, and Hezbollah's Hassan Nasrallah could all embrace playing football themselves and encourage it amongst their followers. Shaykh Mashoor Hasan Salmaan, a Palestinian Salafist, even went as far as to argue, in his 1998 treatise *Football: Its Benefits and Ills According to the Divine Legislation*, that the sport can actually be an exercise in 'unity rather than splitting, mutual love as opposed to hatred and animosity', and that its dependence on teamwork and the sublimation of the individual to the collective is praiseworthy.[16] But even such an apparent enthusiast, who reveals himself to be familiar with a scattering of global football history and mythology, had his doubts, and much of the treatise is an enumeration of all the ways in which the game can lead to distraction from prayer and immoral behaviour, the vice of gambling now being added to that checklist.

Notably, almost none of these debates specifically discusses women, gender and football, and no serious attempt has been made to excavate a theological argument that would exclude women from physical exercise. However, while Salafist clerics are gender-blind in their distaste for the game, the state and civil societies of the region continue to marginalize women's participation in most economic and cultural sectors, and football is no different. Thus in Iran and Saudi Arabia, where theological power is at its most conservative and influential, women have been excluded from the nation's football stadiums and cafes, and in Saudi Arabia prevented from playing football altogether. On the other hand, Jordan and Palestine are proving trailblazers in the region, the former the first in the Middle East to host and play in a Women's World Cup (the under-17 version, in 2016). Indeed, one of the biggest impediments to the growth of the women's game came from outside rather than within.[17] In 2007, in Toronto, a referee excluded a Canadian Muslim player, Asmahan Mansour, from a game for wearing a headscarf. Her team refused to play and the issue went all to the way to FIFA. Initially, it tried to support the decision on the grounds of 'No religious symbolism' but, when set against the signs of the cross and the prostrations made by male players, live on television, this was a level of hypocrisy even FIFA couldn't sustain. Instead, it went with a health and safety argument, on the grounds that headscarves in general and hijabs in particular were strangulation threats. It required six years of campaigning from a coalition led by the Jordanian FA to get it overturned, and for FIFA to agree an equitable policy for all forms of religious headwear.

Since the turn of the century, these kinds of arguments have been supercharged by the endless conflicts that wrack the region, the rise of jihadi networks, and the exponential growth in the region's obsession with and access to European and global football on television. Saudi Arabia, in particular, has seen a variety of clerics issuing explosive electronic fatwas on the game. In 2005, Sheikh Abdullah al Najdi issued a fifteen-point plan to Islamize the game. Alongside the usual calls for modest clothing and the rejection of western terminology, he argued, 'Do not set the number according to the number of players used by the non-believers, the Jews, the Christians, and especially the vile America. In other words, eleven players shall not play together. Make it a larger or a smaller number.'[18] Other innovations included playing one or three but not two halves, replacing the punishment of transgressions by red and yellow cards with more traditional instruments of Sharia, and celebratory hugging and kissing after scoring was to be sternly rebuked. Indeed, 'you should spit in the face of whoever puts the ball between the posts and then runs in order to get his friends to follow him and hug.' The Saudi Grand Mufti countered by arguing, 'All things that come from the West but are not unique to it are permitted. Soccer has become a world sport and does not only belong to non-believers,' and called for the fatwa's authors to be arrested.[19] A year later, with the entire region fixated on the 2006 World Cup, this kind of balm had little effect on the electronic jihadi community, which saw the tournament as 'a plot aiming to corrupt Muslim youth and distract them from Jihad.' 'It is illicit,' announced a Kuwaiti cleric, 'to watch these matches on corrupt television channels while our nation is decimated night and day by foreign armies.'[20] Even Shaykh Mashoor Hasan Salman, no ally of the jihadis, observed, writing in 2006, that many Muslims preferred to watch their team rather than attend prayers and that 'Football now has become one of the destructive hoes that our enemies are using in order to destroy the Ummah [community].'

The two-sided matches between regime and mosque, and the mainstream and the radicals, are complex enough, but in much of the region it is a three-sided game: enter the street. At times, this force has been aligned with the mosque in its opposition to the regime and its suffocating control of every feature of social life; at times it has sided with the regime, especially where the most radical clerics have sought to deprive the people of the game altogether. However, this complex and uneasy conflict of shifting allegiances and alliances took a more rigid form in the first decade of the twenty-first century.[21] In the stadiums of North Africa, in the stands behind the goals, a wave of football ultra groups emerged, first fighting for their place inside the grounds, then fighting the police on the way to the stadiums and outside them, where, as both individuals and collective actors, they became increasingly politicized. In 2010 and 2011, as the Arab Spring broke out across the region, they would in Egypt – the epicentre of the movement – take on the regime itself. It was not mere bravado amongst the fans of Cairo's Al Ahly, known as *Ultras Ahlawy*, when they sang the following on their way to Tahrir Square. They really meant it:

> Regime! Be very scared of us.
> We are coming tonight with intent.
> The supporters of Al Ahly will fire everything up.
> God almighty will make us victorious. Go, hooligans!

In the years since Tahrir Square, the ultra movement has been either destroyed or marginalized, the promise of democratization and reform halted almost everywhere, except in Tunisia. Governments have maintained their hold on power and the game, and for the most part have held off, at considerable cost, the challenge of Islamists and radical jihadis. As things stand, the street seems beaten, and reinforcements from the women's game – still crippled by neglect and control – have yet to arrive. Sometimes, as in Assad's war-torn Syria, football has been made to serve a facade of normality. In Lebanon, Libya and Iraq, the national teams have offered moments of unity in otherwise bitterly fragmented societies. In the Gulf, the game, as a staged spectacular, has become, more than ever, the crown jewel in programmes of hyper-accelerated modernization and public stupefaction. It in its original form, conceived by the Danish situationist Asger Jorn, no game of three-sided football is ever over.[22] There is no fixed time, or number of halves. There are no fixed patterns of alliance and co-operation. One does not win by scoring the most goals, but by waiting the longest and conceding the fewest. Middle Eastern politics, long in thrall to the power and potential of conventional football, has mutated into a violent and bitter form of the game's intractable and irresolvable variant.

II

Osama Bin Laden can be heard, in conversation on a shaky video recording, recalling the dream of one of his followers:

> Abu-Al-Hasan told me a year ago: 'I saw in a dream, we were playing a soccer game against the Americans. When our team showed up in the field, they were all pilots!' He said: 'So I wondered if that was a soccer game or a pilot game? Our players were pilots.' He said the game went on and we defeated them. That was a good omen for us.[23]

Another of his colleagues recalled seeing an Egyptian family watching the events of 9/11. 'They exploded with joy. Do you know when there is a soccer game and your team wins? It was the same expression of joy.' Familiar as the leading members of Al-Qaeda were with football, metaphorically and practically – Bin Laden was long thought to be an Arsenal fan – the Taliban, under whose rule they had established their secure Afghan bases, were less sympathetic. In power from the mid-1990s until 2001, when they were ejected from government, if not the country, by the US-backed Northern Alliance of Pashtun and allied tribes, the Taliban frowned upon all sports, banned many, including all women's participation in sport, and allowed, on sufferance, men's football to continue under restricted circumstances. The Taliban also developed a taste for staging executions in football stadiums as a form of pre-match entertainment: some victims, accused of theft, would have a hand removed, limbs would be hung from the goalposts, and murderers executed on the penalty spot.[24]

In the years after the fall of the Taliban, sporting life re-emerged in Afghanistan, and football continued to be the most popular grassroots sport. Money aside, it was, however, impossible to organize a national football league, given the vulnerability of travelling teams, who were regular targets for kidnapping and roadside IEDs. Despite this, grassroots football in Afghanistan endured, even prospered. Relieved of the baleful gaze of the Taliban, regional leagues, clubs supported by small businesses, and women's football, all grew. Khalida Popal, the captain of the first Afghan women's national team, was amongst a pioneering generation of players who started out training in hiding and endured public opprobrium and attacks when they played openly. The women's national team, created by the Afghanistan Football Federation, was only able to continue after a local NATO base offered them their protected pitch, but that it has played at all, and now competed internationally for six years, is considerable progress. Even then, Popal, like others, has headed into exile, unable to endure the death threats that came her way.[25]

By the time NATO began its military withdrawal in 2012, a men's national league had finally been launched. This did not betoken a real improvement in the security situation, but it was a reflection of how entrenched the nation's instability had become. 2012 had seen a significant reduction in civilian deaths and casualties from the war; nonetheless 2,769 deaths and 4,821 injuries were reported. The Afghan Premier League adapted accordingly. The league, which was actually a short tournament of mini-leagues followed by two knockout rounds, was invented by the AFF with the support of the MOBY

Group, the largest and most influential private media company in the country.[26] To circumvent the problem of travel, all the teams were based in Kabul and all the games were played in the city's main stadium. To circumvent sectarianism while maintaining regional appeal, the teams were invented concoctions, each allocated to one of the country's provinces. Players were initially recruited by means of a reality television show called *Maidan-e-Sabz* ('Green Field') and televised regional tournaments, with viewers' votes decisive in electing the squads. Subsequent seasons have given more weight to the views of coaches, and six women's teams with their own league were added to the roster, though the womens' game continues to be undermined by allegations of sexual abuse by officials.[27] The league has, given its geographical limits, proved hugely successful on television at home and in the diaspora. Games were scheduled to avoid clashes with European football, the league has attracted corporate sponsorship, and teams were able to pay their players small but living wages. Afghanistan even tasted international success, albeit at the lowest level of Asian football, when the men's team beat India to win the 2013 South Asian Football Federation Cup.

No one, least of all in Afghanistan, is confusing these developments with a return to normality or peace. The Taliban and its allies, far from being defeated, have maintained and even improved their military position since the departure of the main NATO forces. In 2016, a picture of a six-year-old boy called Murtaza Ahmadi went viral. He was wearing an improvised Argentinian national football shirt made from a blue-and-white-striped plastic bag on which his older brother had written 'Messi' and '10'. Later, he would receive a real signed shirt from Messi and even meet the player himself at a game in Qatar, but these were mixed blessings. After his family received repeated death threats from the Taliban they fled into exile in Pakistan.

Iraqi football had long laboured under the brutal and capricious rule of the Hussein family. Saddam's half-brothers, Barzan and Watban, ran their home club in Tikrit in the early 1980s, and miraculously acquired a winning team and a national championship. In the late 1980s Saddam's son Uday, perhaps the most brutal and psychotic of the entourage, was handed control of the National Olympic Committee and the Iraqi Football Association, and ruled by fear and violence.[28] Members of the Iraqi national team, like many other athletes, were punished and tortured for poor performances: the players who failed to qualify for the 1994 World Cup were made to kick concrete footballs until their bones broke. The IOC never worried much about any of this. FIFA, however, was unable to ignore the flood of reports of torture emerging from inside Iraqi football around 2000, and in 2001 sent an investigative delegation. They concluded that everything was just fine, a thought no doubt encouraged by the members of the Iraqi security services who were present at every interview they conducted.

Two years later, Uday was dead and his Olympic offices were a bombed-out shell. The American-led invasion was turning into an occupation. The Iraqi football league was, of course, abandoned, and would not resume as a completely national tournament rather than a regionally organized one for almost a decade. The US Army made itself at home in the national stadium in Baghdad, using the pitch as a car park for its tanks and specialist vehicles. The crude bleachers and concrete walls were pockmarked with bullet holes. The national team's kit and equipment were looted. FIFA, deeming anywhere in Iraq too dangerous for play, sent the national team into a decade-long exile of playing qualifying games in empty stadiums in Aleppo, Amman and Doha. Yet, in a pattern that other equally ravaged nations' football teams would follow – Syria and Libya, for example – the Iraqis performed miraculously, reaching the semi-finals of the Athens Olympics in 2004 under German coach Bernd Stange. At the time, the George W. Bush re-election campaign was running adverts showing the Iraqi and Afghan flags with the slogan 'At the Olympics there will be two more free nations and two fewer terrorist regimes.' 'The American army has killed so many people in Iraq,' responded the under-23s team coach, Adnan Hadad. 'What freedom is it when I go to the stadium and there are shootings on the road?'[29]

There are limits to fairy tales. Iraq lost the bronze medal play-off to the Italians and went home without laurels; but for a moment this transparently diverse team, featuring players of Sunni, Shia and Kurdish origin, offered a genuine and precious moment of national unity. It barely lasted the year. Stange quit, as many future coaches would, because of the death threats and the anonymous telephone calls. The occupation, already contested in 2004, turned into a gruelling and exceptionally bloody insurgency as ex-Ba'athists, jihadis of various shades, and Sunni and Shia militias fought each other and the Americans and British. No aspect of Iraqi life, no space in its cities, no social class or group, escaped its wrath. One player at the Baghdad club Al Zawra'a, Manar Mudhafar, was shot dead by a seemingly random burst of fire at a training session. Three mortar rounds would later explode on the same pitch, leaving shrapnel in the limbs of half the squad. The IED that exploded in 2007 at a match of Al Abara killed six spectators.

Worse was to come as the national team made its way through the closing stages of the 2007 Asian Cup, beating South Korea in a semi-final penalty shoot-out. That night, two car bombs were set off in Baghdad amidst celebrating crowds, killing 50 people and leaving over 130 injured. Manic celebratory gunfire across the city would take at least one more life. The team wondered whether it was worth carrying on in the face of this kind of violence, but in a televisual moment that seemed to reflect the mood of much of the country, a bereaved mother from the semi-final attacks insisted that they continue, for she would not bury her son till Iraq returned as champions.[30] Iraq went on to win the final against Saudi Arabia by a single goal, 2,000 miles away in Indonesia. The celebrations were so universal and happy that one journalist could report going out with a US troop patrol, which normally would at best be ignored, at worst shot at. 'That particular day, nobody cared. We were swarmed. There were floats. There were small little fireworks. There were people wearing wigs with these huge glasses on spraying us and the troops with silly string. It was absolutely surreal and completely spectacular.'[31] Visibility was not an asset in Iraq in 2007: the entire squad were the subject of threats and attacks, both from insurgents for supporting the government and from criminal gangs eyeing their new celebrity and wealth. Politicians and the public begged Brazilian coach Jorvan Vieira to stay on, but he quit, saying the job had made him 'crazy'.

Nothing in Iraqi football has come close since, for it has been rent by precisely the same conflicts and problems that have devastated the whole country: the Sunni–Shia conflict, the uneasy place of the Kurds and their secessionist tendencies, pervasive corruption and the rise of ISIS. The simmering Sunni–Shia conflict burst into view in 2008 and 2009, when the Shia Ministry of Youth Affairs dissolved the Iraqi FA and dismissed its Sunni President, Hussein Saeed.[32] Iraq, in turn, was suspended from international competition by FIFA for 'political interference in football', allowing Saeed to return to his post, where he remained for two long years of relentless in-fighting. For Shiite politicians, like the Minister of Youth Affairs in 2008 Jassim Jaafar, the Iraqi FA had always been seen as a Sunni organization and that had to change. This was certainly true under Saddam Hussein's regime, when Shias were excluded from most bureaucracies and positions of power, and it had remained so after his fall. Hussein Saeed, an ex-international player, had been deputy-president of the Iraqi FA under Uday Hussein, and was so close to the Ba'athist regime that the American occupying administration had tried to sideline him. He survived, with the active support of the FIFA hierarchy, and by making baseless accusations against his challengers, one of whom, Ahmed Rahdi, was conveniently arrested before new elections for the Iraqi FA were to take place in 2004. When the government dissolved the organization in 2008, the charge sheet was vast: failure to hold general meetings, failure to publish financial reports and failure to hold regular and fair elections for key posts, not to mention the usual acts of embezzlement, larceny and theft. Saeed has denied everything, but in his seven years in power the IFA was colloquially known as the Ministry of Tourism and Travel, and Saeed and his associates racked up gigantic global travel and hospitality bills on the lavish world football circuit. Meanwhile, the organization itself was so seemingly bankrupt that it could not pay its national team coaches, and constantly begged for freebie accommodation for its training camps in the Gulf. When Saeed's limpet-like grip on power was finally broken in 2011, he had taken Iraq from 44th to 110th in the FIFA world rankings.

Although Kurdish Iraq has suffered its share of deprivations and killings since the fall of Saddam Hussein, it has also acquired greater political autonomy and power than hitherto. Its football clubs benefited accordingly, with Erbil, the region's largest team, winning five championships, and its smaller rival Zakho one. This was in part because the relative security of the Kurdish cities made them attractive to players fleeing the sectarian chaos of Baghdad, in part because the Kurdish authorities helped sustain them financially. They were even more supportive of the formation and promotion of a national team, which, like other aspirant FIFA members, made its debut at the 2008 VIVA World Cup, coming third behind the Italian separatists of Padania and the team of the Aramean diaspora. In the realm of stateless nations and diasporas, the Iraqi Kurdistan team has proved reasonably strong, but there is only so much coverage that two successive quarter-finals in the ConIFA World Cups (the successor tournament to the VIVA Cup) of 2014 and 2016 will get you.[33]

Even so, there was a diminishing appetite for the Iraqi national team. Whereas the triumphs of 2004 and 2007 had been embraced in Erbil and Mosul, the passage of the under-20s to the semi-final of their World Cup and the victory of the under-22s in their Asian Cup – victories wildly celebrated in southern Iraq – were met with relative indifference.[34] Without a single Kurd in the team, there was nothing for those that had not already abandoned Iraqi football altogether to embrace. By 2016, with Iraq seemingly broken by the onslaught of IS, the Kurdish government swung between demands for more autonomy and full secession. Fans outside the region chanted at Erbil and Zakho games 'Peshmerga is ISIS' and 'Erbil is ISIS', and both withdrew themselves from the national league.[35] In 2017, President Barzani held a referendum on Kurdish independence within Iraq, winning over 90 per cent of the vote for 'yes'. The Iraqi and Iranian states, however, voted no, put troops on the borders, and precipitated Barzani's resignation. Erbil FC have returned to Iraq's lower leagues, Zakho have regressed to the Kurdish heartlands in their own small, penurious league and, for the moment, the idea of an independent Kurdish state and football team remains stillborn.

The success of the Iraqi youth teams in 2013 came at a moment of relative calm. The Americans had left, their combat units at any rate. Certainly, the level of civilian and military casualties in the ongoing civil war had been falling, although it was still measured in the hundreds every month. Finally, some of the nation's inaccessible but gargantuan oil wealth had begun to flow into rebuilding the infrastructure of the still-shattered country. Football got its cut.[36] Though many of the promised government-funded new stadiums in the provinces have yet to appear (even in design), the national stadium was refurbished, and in Basra there was, perhaps, a glimpse of the future. In a clear parallel if not emulation of Iraq Energy City, the gated enclave that served the hordes of international executives and technicians in Basra's hydrocarbon industries, half a billion dollars were poured into Basra Sports City. At its centre was a 65,000-seat state-of-the-art stadium, around it a smaller stadium, media facilities and the usual dull agglomeration of expensive retail space and gated apartment towers: a little slice of Dubai on the Tigris. An artificial lake in the shape of Iraq was promised, but mercifully has yet to be delivered. All this in a city where the wreckage of cruise missiles that fell in the first Gulf War had yet to be cleared, and where adequate sanitation was a rare privilege. Intended to host the 2013 Gulf Cup and the national team's first game back home for a decade, the complex did neither. The former was moved, for security reasons, to Bahrain; the latter honour went to Erbil. However, FIFA deemed the crowd trouble sufficiently scary there to send Iraq back into exile to play their subsequent qualifying games in Qatar, until, finally, in 2017 the men's national team took the field in Basra.

IS, the most active and organized of the Sunni jihadists in Iraq, made their move in 2014. First they took Ramadi, then they secured Anbar province, before overwhelming Iraq's hapless defence forces all over the country in June and July of that year. They took Mosul and a string of other cities, before Iranian and Kurdish forces halted their advance just short of Baghdad. In that vast swathe of Iraq, and the now conjoined zone of Syria that IS controlled, an often chaotic and inconsistent but invariably brutal form of Sharia law was imposed: satellite dishes, mixed conversation in public, dancing, watching foreign television, accessing the internet and football were amongst the many things banned and punishable. Abu Bakr al-Baghdadi, the leader of IS, had, in his youth, been a keen player. 'He was the Messi of our team,' an old friend recalled. 'He was our best player.'[37] Twenty years of radicalization and long sojourns in American prisons appeared to have eradicated whatever positive feelings he may have had about the game. Alongside the usual bans on playing and watching football, militants ripped down posters and adverts featuring footballers. In 2015, it was widely reported that IS had conducted a public execution of thirteen youths in Mosul, guilty of watching Iraq play Jordan in the Asian Cup. Four footballers from the then disbanded Raqqa club Al-Shabab were charged with being spies for the Kurdish YPG and publicly executed, while IS were happy to claim responsibility for the machine-gunning of a group of Real Madrid fans waiting to watch the game together in the Shia town of Balad. Nineteen were left dead.[38]

Under increasing military pressure, and finding it harder to attract supporters, IS developed a more opportunist and pragmatic football theology. In Mosul, in 2015, they gave permission for the population to watch *El Clásico*. However, when a minute's silence was held in the Bernabeu for the victims of the recent Paris terrorist attacks, militants rushed to the city's tea houses and cafes, turning off or breaking televisions.[39] In much of IS territory, the ban on playing was moderated. Children would be allowed to play, but not those above the age of 15. If needs be, that age limit could be raised. In Jordan, where mosques which had served as traditional recruiting grounds were ever more closely observed, IS switched to gathering up university students, who they thought had jihadi potential, at farms and rural retreats, lured in part by the promise of a football tournament in the country.[40] Foreign fighters were also exempt from the ban, and many appear to have had access to football on satellite television and *FIFA 15* on Xbox. If you can't beat them, join them? In the Syrian region of Deir ez-Zor, where IS was besieging government forces in the main city of the same name, local IS clerics ruled that referees rather than football were the problem. Following the law of FIFA rather than Sharia rendered them illegitimate. Football was henceforth permitted, but without referees. Instead, *Qisas* – the traditional Koranic system of restitutive justice and blood money – would be used to compensate injured players and resolve differences. Quite how differences over offsides and playing advantage were to be resolved was not revealed.[41] In Mosul, infidel logos and brands had to be hacked out of football shirts before play was permitted, and whistles were banned 'because the sound would make the devils gather.'[42] It would require three years of gruelling warfare to remove ISIS from Mosul and another year to get them out of Raqqa, where the liberation in 2018 was celebrated in the 'Black Stadium' – site of many executions – with a four-way football tournament, played under conventional, universal football rules.[43]

Football had served as an instrument of soft power and modernization under the Shah of Iran in the 1970s, and suffered accordingly during the 1980s, the first decade of the Islamic revolution. Deemed by the theocracy to be at best foreign and decadent, at worst blasphemous, football was frowned upon and virtually ground to a halt during the long war with Iraq. Popular pressure to play and watch the game was unquenchable, however, and a national league and team were steadily re-established. The game's revival and reformist credentials were clearly underlined during the 1997 presidential election that pitched the conservative Ali Akbar Nateq-Nouri against the more moderate Mohammad Khatami. Nateq-Nouri shared his platform with the leading wrestlers of the day, while the victorious Khatami included footballers in his political entourage. The opening months of his presidency coincided with the qualification campaign for the 1998 World Cup. When Iran lost to Qatar and then Japan, forcing them into a play-off against Australia, the new regime made a clear statement, moderating Tehran's revolutionary xenophobia by appointing a foreign coach, the Brazilian, Valdeir Vieira. Iran beat Australia, and on the final whistle the streets of Tehran and every provincial city filled with people – perhaps as many as six million nationwide. The crowds defied and taunted clerics and the *Basij* militias. Women and men openly mixed, some abandoned the veil, others danced on the roofs of the Toyota trucks used by the moral police. The crowd took flowers to the French embassy and cheered, 'See you in Paris.' When the national team returned to the city, 5,000 women – then as now excluded from the national team's games – stormed the Azadi stadium to honour the players. Next time the *Basij* were waiting. In late 2001, an Iranian victory over Iraq in a crucial World Cup qualifying match saw tens of thousands of youths celebrating in Tehran, only to be dispersed by tear gas and police baton charges. Ten days later Bahrain beat Iran, forcing them into a qualifying play-off against Ireland. A rumour on the streets that the regime had told the team to throw the match to prevent another outburst of public celebration prompted pitched battles in Tehran and Esfahan. Iran went on to lose to Ireland.

Three weeks before the 2005 presidential elections, between wealthy businessman and pragmatist Ali Akbar Hashemi Rafsanjani and conservative populist Mahmoud Ahmadinejad, Iran qualified for the 2006 World Cup, beating Bahrain 1–0. As ever, people took to the streets to dance, women removed their headscarves and, in the Resalat neighbourhood of Tehran, shopkeepers gave away flowers to the crowd. Iranian flags with Rafsanjani's face in the centre were handed out and flown, but there were reports of the same flag being flown with his face cut out. It wasn't enough for Rafsanjani. Ahmadinejad won the elections, but he was a different kind of conservative to his predecessors, with a strong base amongst the working class and the veterans of Iran's devastating war with Iraq – and a man who enjoyed football and grasped its political import. He took a close interest in the performance of the national team, was a regular visitor to their training camps, and is widely thought to have interfered in the business of the football association. After Ali Daei's team failed to make it to South Africa 2010, government supporters received a text reading, 'Due to the importance of national public opinion to Dr Ahmadinejad, Ali Daei has been forced out.'[44]

Ahmadinejad may have held sway over the football world, but he could not own its political soul. He was returned to office in the disputed election of 2009, in which the opposition accused his campaign of massive electoral irregularities. He then had to face down a gigantic series of protests by the Green Movement that had backed opposition candidate Mir Hossein Mousavi. Even after the protest movement had been crushed at home, Iran's final qualifying game against South Korea in Seoul offered an opportunity for resistance. Six players took to the field wearing green wristbands. Team officials initially tried to claim that these were Islamic symbols designed to help the players overcome the Koreans, but the meaning was clear to everyone else.[45]

Ahmadinejad's departure has, it appears, defused some of the emotional conflict around the national team. In 2013, the moderate Hassan Rouhani decisively beat his conservative opponents to become president of Iran. Less than a week later, the nation qualified for the 2014 World Cup, once again after playing South Korea in Seoul. The game was a draw, and that was enough for Iran (and, as it transpired later, for South Korea too). At home, hundreds of thousands partied peacefully. Clerical Supreme Leader Ayatollah Ali Khamenei even hailed the team for bringing national happiness. The only violence came in Seoul, where the Iranian players' wild celebrations on the pitch after the game prompted Korean fans to hurl abuse, bottles and cans at them. Thus Iran's national team appeared to be becoming a truly national institution, able to attract the support of the secular and the religious, and both moderate and conservative forces. In 2014, in anticipation of the World Cup, universities and schools changed their exam and holiday schedules to accommodate the tournament. Public viewing areas were set up in parks and squares. The religious authorities did their best to dissuade attendance, and the matches were still shown on delay to allow for censorship, but across the nation's cities, mixed crowds delighted in watching the team take just a point from their three games before going out, but that seemed victory enough.

A new front in the conflict was opened at the Asian Cup, held in Australia in 2015, where the majority of the small Iranian community showed up en masse at the national team's games. Out of around 35,000 people, 17,000 went to see Iran beat Bahrain in Melbourne, 22,000 to see them beat Qatar in Sydney, and a nationwide cavalcade travelled to Canberra to watch their nail-biting defeat to Iraq in a quarter-final penalty shoot-out. 'It was just like playing in Tehran,' remarked Iranian player Ashkan Dejagah, except that in Tehran there were still no women in the stands.[46] In Australia, Iranian women were a big part of the crowd and made their presence felt, dressed to impress, with hair and nails in the national colours. The Iranian FA was sufficiently rattled to instruct its players not to let themselves be photographed in selfies with women. One group came to every game with a banner of Ghoncheh Ghavami, an Iranian woman who had been arrested and sentenced to a year in jail for attending a volleyball game.[47]

Since then, the Open Stadiums group has been attending Iranian away games and displaying large banners calling for Iranian women to be allowed into stadiums. FIFA President Sepp Blatter, long an advocate, called again, in the strongest terms, for change to this 'intolerable' situation, and it was no coincidence that the AFC did not award the 2019 Asian Cup to Iran, which proposed that its usual rule should apply should they be hosts. There have been repeated statements from the governments of President Rouhani on the matter, most notably in late 2015, when it was announced that, with the exception of wrestling and swimming, women would be allowed into sporting events and that special women's or family sections would be created to facilitate this. No one, it seems, told the police or religious authorities. As of 2016, a young woman, known on Instagram as Shakiba, was posting pictures of herself at a Persepolis game in Tehran. She had dressed in five layers of clothing, added padding, and put on enough face paint to get past the police. Fans inside recognized her but actively hid her from the authorities.[48]

In 2017, it seemed that a breakthrough had finally occurred, as the Iranian FA's website announced that women could buy tickets for the upcoming World Cup qualifier against Syria. Thousands of tickets were bought in an instant, only for the Iran FA to rescind the offer and blame a technical glitch. Syrian women were allowed to attend. 'It was very bitter experience,' recalled one Iranian woman, who had queued up for her ticket but was kept outside. 'I was close to tears – never before have I felt so defeated and humiliated.'[49] Subsequent promises, including during the 2018 World Cup, that mixed viewing would be permitted and the Azadi open to all to watch Iran's games, were once again dashed by the authorities, leaving Iran, given Saudi Arabia's decision to permit women in stadiums, the only country to exclude half its population from the football nation they self-evidently believe to be theirs too.

III

Measured by titles and championships, the twenty-first century looked like becoming a golden era for North African football. Both Tunisia and Egypt would host the African Cup of Nations. Tunisia would win it in 2004, while Egypt would win an unprecedented hat-trick of titles in 2006, 2008 and 2010. All but Libya would qualify for a World Cup. Between 1999 and 2011 clubs from the region would win all but three African Champions League titles, and provide the losing finalist on nine occasions. Like the hollow dictatorships that had strangulated the region for over two decades – Mubarak in Egypt, Gaddafi in Libya, Ben Ali in Tunisia and Bouteflika in Algeria – outward displays of strength hid profound troubles and weaknesses.

At the turn of the century, after more than a decade of inter-national isolation following his regime's support for the 1987 Lockerbie bombing, and having abandoned his nuclear programme and support for jihadis, Muammar Gaddafi was erratically steering Libya back into the international community. No such relaxation was allowed in the realm of Libyan football, which in the mid-1990s had proved, on more than one occasion, a theatre for anti-regime protest – a Tripoli derby in 1996, for example, at which anti-Gaddafi chants were loud and clear, had turned into a riot during which the police killed eight civilians.[50] The presidency of the Libyan Football Federation, and thus total control of the game, was handed to the leader's third son, Saadi Gaddafi, who was also the owner, manager and captain of Al-Ahly Tripoli. Just in case anyone was unclear about Saadi's psychotic condition and status in the game, under his rule only his shirt actually bore the wearer's name, and his was the only one that commentators were allowed to utter. Everybody else was just allocated a number. Money flowed, if highly inequitably, as a bizarre array of advisers arrived: disgraced Canadian sprinter Ben Johnson, the ever-willing ex-England coach Terry Venables and, of course, Diego Maradona. They all took the Colonel's dollar and soon departed. Italian Franco Scoglio was brought in to coach the national team and then fired for not picking Saadi. Aiming higher still, the Libyan State Investment Corporation took a 7.5 per cent stake in Juventus and a place on the board, the kind of largesse and connections that would bring the Italian Super Cup, between Juventus and Parma, to Tripoli in 2002.

A better guide to the regime, however, was the fate of Al-Ahly Benghazi in 2000. The Gaddafis had long viewed both the city and the club with some distaste. The latter was a symbolic challenge to Al-Ahly Tripoli's claim on the nation, the former a long-standing alternative centre of power in the country. Saadi had been stealing the Benghazi club's best players for his own squad, and instructing officials to ensure their defeat. In what had already been a bitter season, full of absurd calls against Al-Ahly Benghazi, the team played their Tripoli namesakes at home in a cup game. Saadi was there with a selection of foreign dignitaries. The home side took a 1–0 lead, only to have two obviously fraudulent penalties given against them. The crowd went wild, booing Saadi personally, and the Benghazi players stormed off, only to be forced back onto the field at gunpoint by Saadi's armed retinue. The game finished 3–1 to the Tripoli team, but Saadi was not placated, and left saying, 'I will destroy your club. I will turn it into an owl's nest.'[51]

In the final game of the season, Benghazi needed a draw in their game against Al-Akhdar to avoid relegation. The inevitable award of a dubious penalty to the visitors with the score at 0–0 saw the crowd storm the pitch, its energy spilling out onto the streets of the city. There, it set fire to the headquarters of the local branch of the Libyan Football Federation, burnt photos and posters of a variety of Gaddafis, and dressed a donkey in a football shirt bearing Saadi's name. The first response was swift. The security services toppled and destroyed a statue of Omar Mukhtar, a hero of the anti-colonial struggle whose local supporters had founded Al-Ahly Benghazi. Then came the mass arrests: eighty people were taken in and interrogated, thirty-two were sentenced to a variety of harsh terms, and three were given a death sentence for 'colluding with foreign powers'. The coup de grace came on 1 September, the thirty-first anniversary of Gaddafi's revolution: an army battalion, equipped with three bull-dozers, destroyed Al-Ahly Benghazi's stadium and every last trace of its records, trophies and infrastructure except the rusty, broken stumps of the floodlight pylons. Despite all this, and a series of comic turns in Italian professional football, Saadi still found time to orches-trate the murder of Bashir al-Riani, once coach of the Libyan national team.[52]

In the rest of North Africa, this kind of treatment was reserved for more obvious threats to state security, like the Muslim Brother-hood in Egypt or the FIS in Algeria. Indeed, football, although of close interest to the regimes, was an almost unique area in which forms of public disorder and symbolic opposition were tolerated, monitored and controlled rather than extinguished. The opposition came from the ultras. Although there were differences in the timing of their emergence, and in their relationships with the local security forces, the sociology of these groups of organized football fans was almost identical. All took their cue from the Italian ultras of Serie A, well known to them from the satellite television coverage that began in the 1990s, and the increasingly widespread experience of young men who migrated to Southern Europe in search of work and escape. In Morocco in the late 1990s and early 2000s, the stands of Wydad AC were suddenly occupied by *The Winners*, Raja Casablanca's by *The Green Boys* and FAR Rabat's by *Ultras Askari*. In Algeria, *Verde Leone* appeared at MC Algiers, and across town *Ouled El Bahdj* were the ultras of USM Algiers. In Tunisia there were the *Ultras Lem-kachkhines* at Espérance and *African Winners* at Club African. Last, but certainly not least, the mid-2000s saw ultra groups emerge in Egypt, most notably *Ultras Ahlawy* at Ah-Ahly and *Ultras White Knights* at Zamalek.[53]

All these groups were overwhelmingly and often entirely mascu-line. A range of ages was represented, with young teenagers at one end and a few middle-aged veterans at the other, but the vast major-ity of the ultras were between eighteen and thirty. Socially, they were more mixed than one might imagine. Amongst the leaders of many groups, but also just present in the crowd, were students and univer-sity graduates, some even connected by family ties to important parts of the regime. In a survey of Moroccan ultras in 2008, members included film scouts, undergraduates, waiters and taxi drivers. None-theless, the majority were from poor and working-class families, and whatever strata they came from they were rarely part of the ruling complex or in secure government employment. They were almost all single, and they stood effective proxy for the vast majority of young men in marginal economic circumstances, unbound by family ties or commitments, with few or poor prospects, who were not merely impoverished but bored and deeply frustrated.

Initially, their activities focused on the construction and perform-ance of *tifos*. These choreographed, collective crowd displays combined huge banners with mosaic messages. Above all, the ultras performed *craquage*: the simultaneous detonation of coloured smoke bombs, flares, firecrackers and fireworks that began to spectacularly engulf entire stadiums. To this repertoire they then added organizing black-market ticket sales, transport for away trips, widespread graffiti campaigns and, at the margins, drug-dealing. In the Moroccan survey, to no one's surprise, the ultras also revealed themselves to be the most enthusiastic smokers of hashish and consumers of psy-chedelic drugs in the region. At first glance, and in their early pronouncements, the world of the ultras was a non-political realm of collective adrenaline, escapism and hedonism. However, under conditions of ailing autocracy, large, boisterous, protean crowds of marginal young men do not stay unpolitical for long.

Algerian crowds proved the most turbulent. Government figures, most likely considerable underestimates, suggest that the century began with 173 recorded incidents of football-related violence, 189 arrests, nearly 300 injuries and forty-five torched cars and vans. In 2002–3, the peak season for burning, Algerian ultras set 266 cars alight. The 2006–7 season saw 259 incidents, 710 arrests, 590 injuries and three deaths. One of those incidents occurred just after ES Sétif had beaten Al-Ahli of Jeddah in the semi-final of the Arab Champions League. The ultras of ES Sétif attacked the buses trans-porting players and fans of Al-Ahli en route to their hotel, causing dozens of Saudi injuries. The following year, when ES Sétif won the Arab Champions League against Wydad Casablanca, the ultras' cel-ebrations were so wild that three of them died after they brought a giant fence down onto themselves. Amongst the many games brought to a premature halt by fighting in the stands, or even on the pitch, the 2009 matches between Bordj Bou Arréridj and Mouloudia, and USM Annaba and ES Sétif were particularly bad, preceded, accompanied and followed by widespread knife fights.

Given the kind of coercive force that the Algerian state can bring to bear, should it choose, on its domestic opponents, it was remarkable how lightly many of those incidents were policed. It is hard not to reach the conclusion that the Algerian authorities, and their neighbours, had all taken a calculated decision that there was more to be gained from allowing some potentially threatening social energy to be flared off in the world of football than in trying to extinguish it. As long as it was visiting Saudis and the fans themselves taking the brunt of the damage, a certain number of police injuries were tolerable. The Tunisian star Tarak Dhiab was blunt about how the government of President Ben Ali operated. 'You saw the violence in our stadiums. Did they ever do anything to stop it? On the contrary, the violence worked in their favour. They made it that way to keep people away from the real problems in the country.'[54] As the 2009 riots in Algiers and Oran demonstrated, however, these incidents could serve as catalysts for something wider. During a final-day relegation battle between USM El Harrach and another Algiers team, ES Kouba, fighting in the stadium mutated into a three-day, city-wide series of riots requiring the deployment of 5,000 police. A few days later in Oran, the relegation of local team Mouloudia also ignited three days of rioting, as the authorities unsuccessfully attempted to put the city centre under lockdown.[55]

If there were limits to the degree of violence these regimes were prepared to rain down on football fans, it was partly because they sought to co-opt the game and the fervour it could generate for their own purposes. Algeria's President Bouteflika claimed to be the nation's number-one football fan. Presidents Ben Ali and Mubarak basked in the glory and nationwide celebrations from being hosts and champions of the 2004 and 2006 African Cup of Nations respectively. However, the games played between Algeria and Egypt in 2009, attempting to qualify for the 2010 World Cup, are indicative of something much darker lurking in the football nationalism of North Africa's dictatorships.[56] Precedents were not good: Algerian police had attacked Egyptian fans at a match at the All-Africa Games in 1978, and violence had accompanied Egypt's victory over Algeria in a 1989 qualifier for the 1990 World Cup. On that occasion, the Egyptian team's doctor lost an eye to a glassing, and the Algerians in the stands rioted. In an attempt to lower the temperature, the Algerian authorities compensated the injured Egyptian doctor, and welcomed the Egyptian team with flowers. Still, Algeria's coach Rabah Saâdane was a man on the verge of a nervous breakdown, openly weeping at press conferences, fearing for his and his family's well-being should the result go the wrong way. The government put 5,000 police on duty and Algeria won 3–1.

So far, so good. Except that in the run-up to the return match five months later, a distinctly different tone emerged. On the internet, bloggers and media outlets began to trade barbs over the game. Hackers, most likely from government agencies, crashed newspaper websites in both countries, as well as that of the Egyptian Presidency. Each nation's overwhelmingly government-controlled media indulged in a frenzy of hyper-nationalism, caricature and macho posturing. On the day before the game, the Algerian team bus was stoned en route to the squad's hotel, leaving a lot of broken glass and four players injured. The Egyptian press, masters of the cover-up and shameless diversionary argument, claimed the Algerians had done it to themselves or fabricated the incident altogether. The honour of Mubarak's Egypt seemed to hang like a thread. The Egyptians led 1–0 from the third minute, but this still left Algeria in qualifying position. A second Egyptian goal, five long minutes into injury time, levelled the teams on points and goal difference and necessitated a play-off in a neutral venue. Back in Algeria, crowds ransacked the offices of Egyptian companies and marched on the Egyptian embassy. In Cairo, fighting broke out in and around the stadium, and claim and counter-claim of knifings and beatings flew between Cairo and Algiers.

Both national FAs were allocated 9,000 tickets for the play-off in Khartoum in Sudan. Independent travelling fans bought tickets from the Sudanese, and the stadium was clearly holding a lot more than the official 36,000 maximum. It was a tense and bad-tempered game, decided by a single Algerian goal. Fifteen thousand Sudanese troops policed the match, but could not prevent a series of attacks across Khartoum, mainly against Egyptians, though it seems these were no more than scuffles leading to a dozen minor injuries, and nothing compared to the phantoms being conjured up on Egyptian state media. Old footage of knife-wielding Algerian ultras was offered as 'on-the-spot' reportage, while the Sudanese army frog-marched Egyptian fans to the airport. Mubarak's son Gamal, part of the large delegation of apoplectic Egyptian MPs, made wild claims and threats by cellphone to Egyptian television stations. A thousand-strong mob tried to storm the Algerian embassy in Cairo, and ambassadors were summoned and withdrawn across the region. Egypt threatened to withdraw from world football and President Hosni Mubarak told parliament that 'Egypt does not tolerate those who hurt the dignity of its sons.'

When Mubarak spoke those words in late 2009, I don't suppose he had himself in mind as one of those who had hurt the dignity of Egypt's youth, especially its football supporters. Irony was never his strong suit. In just over a year, those supporters would let him know. Egypt's ultra movement was the last to emerge in North Africa, but it made up for lost time. *Ultras Ahlawy* was formed in 2007 by disgruntled youth, drawn from amongst the Al-Ahly fans who had sought to break away from the suffocating control of the official fan groups effectively run by the club. Drawing on the Tunisian and Algerian examples, *Ultras Ahlawy* quickly established a reputation for brilliantly organized, large-scale *tifo* banners, fireworks and flares. Explicitly non-political in their few public statements and iconography, their displays featured a devil's trident and acid-yellow smiley faces. The Egyptian authorities were caught on the hop, unable to understand or comprehend a phenomenon that was now spreading to other clubs: the *Ultras White Knights* at Zamalek and *Ultras Yellow Dragons* at Al Ismaily. Unsure as to their real purpose and unable to prevent their emergence, the security complex was sufficiently befuddled that the ultras were able to occupy the country's *curvas*. Once there, they asserted that what happened in the *curva* would be determined by them and not by the state. Nothing, in late Mubarak Egypt, could be more political or threatening.

The first major conflict between ultras and the police occurred in 2008 during a game between Al-Ahly and the Police Union. Prevented from displaying their *tifos* by the police, the ultras attacked them with gusto. It was a psychological and emotional turning point; the police, they discovered, could actually be forced back. A rising tide of similar encounters inside and outside stadiums built through 2009 and 2010, and an increasingly anti-police militancy was palpable amongst the ultras. It was especially evident in their songs and their graffiti: 'ACAB: All Coppers Are Bastards' and 'Respect Existence or Expect Resistance'. The regime responded by treating them as a real political threat: a special ultras surveillance unit was established inside the secret service, banning orders on fans at games became more frequent, and those games that were played were policed more violently. The November 2010 parliamentary elections were amongst the most rigged in political history, with the promise of another decade of Hosni Mubarak and his hapless preening son Gamal. Still the ultras held the *curvas*, forcing the police into negotiations over match day protocol. Yet there remained nowhere for this energy to go.

The spark that lit the tinder came from Tunisia. There, as everywhere in North Africa, the pyre had long been stacked with deep structural grievances and problems: chronically high levels of youth unemployment, desperately poor economic development, massive concentration of wealth in a small number of hands, and escalating levels of surveillance and repression, behind the desperate facade of personal rule by men who had long turned into their own waxworks. On 17 December 2010, Mohamed Bouazizi, a vegetable seller harassed by the police in the small town of Sidi Bouzid, set himself aflame in protest. He would die from his burns just over a fortnight later. By then, a complex mosaic of resistance had been triggered: rural towns confronted their oppressive police, professionals protested, urban youth set fires and ran the security forces through the streets, high-school students cut classes and flooded Tunis en masse, and football ultras swelled the crowds, incited, directed and coordinated by a complex network of social media sites and digital activists. On 8 January Ben Ali played his last card and unleashed five days of killings and terror, care of the psychotic loyalist core of his security services. Snipers' bullets and night-time ambushes killed dozens of Tunisians, especially in the small towns. When, on 15 January, the march on the Presidential Palace reached the gates, Ben Ali had already fled to Saudi Arabia.

On 25 January 2011, National Police Day, a similar mosaic of social groups and protestors called by electronic media and word of mouth came together to converge on Tahrir Square in the heart of Cairo. As in Tunisia, the ultras were not operating as a conscious collective – the websites of *Ultras Ahlawy* and *Ultras White Knights* had declared their non-participation – but at the same time they also announced that any member of the group was free to do as they saw fit. Many heard the call. One member of *Ultras Ahlawy* recalled that on the way to Tahrir Square, 'When we saw the violent police reaction, we remembered the way the police used to treat us on our way into the stadium or even in the streets.'[57] As individuals and small bands of friends, later as self-organizing groups, the ultras were present alongside the secular youth movements, elements of the Muslim Brotherhood and radicalized professionals who occupied and then held the square for seventeen days against repeated attacks by the police and Mubarak's hired thugs. Here the ultras provided a degree of organization, tactical awareness and sheer front that no other members of the coalition possessed. Skilled, honed even, in the choreography of riots and police charges, they were a vital and at times heroic element in the mix. In the second week of the protest, there was an informal but real pattern of co-operation amongst the many Al-Ahly and Zamalek ultras who found themselves on the same side. On 11 February, unable to shift the people, and knowing that the army would not clear them for him, Mubarak stepped down.

The contagion and the hope spread. Given the football history of the Libyan regime, it was no surprise that the first acts of resistance broke out in Benghazi; within days volunteers were manning the barricades in Al-Ahly Benghazi shirts. As the Gaddafis fought to hold onto the nation, the national team kept playing. After Libya had beaten the Comoros Islands, Tariq Tayib, the team captain, told the press that 'the whole team is for Muammar Gaddafi', but others like Walid el Kahatroushi, Ahmed Al Sagir and Guma Mousa left to join the rebels.[58] In June, seventeen of the country's leading players and coaches, including four members of that squad, appeared in the rebel-held town of Jadu and announced their collective opposition to the regime. Hardly a decisive blow alone, but within a month Gaddafi had gone into hiding, his rule eclipsed. When the Libyan national team next met, in Egypt to play Mozambique, he had fled, and would soon be captured and executed. The pro-Gaddafi players were gone and a new kit had been created with the rebel flag stitched over the old coat of arms. There was enough post-revolutionary vim to get the team to the African Cup of Nations in 2012, and even snatch a victory from Senegal, but the chaos, indeed near civil war, into which the country has plunged has not been conducive to the game, or very much else: as of 2018, only three of the six league championships have been completed since the fall of

Gaddafi, and the national teams continue to play their home games across North Africa, but not in Libya.

In Tunisia, which moved from the fall of President Ben Ali to national elections in just eight months, over a hundred parties suddenly confronted the electorate. Football, rather more visible than politics over the previous couple of decades, was one way to get yourself noticed. The smaller of the two main Islamist parties, Justice and Development, recruited striker Yassine Bouchaal, while the Initiative Party, founded by an ex-foreign minister of Ben Ali, managed to get defender Saber Ben Frej onside. The Free National Party put forward Espérance's technical manager Chokri al-Ouaer, while Mehdi Ben Gharbia, a businessman and President of AC Bizerte, helped found the Progressive Democratic Party and became a member of Parliament. The joke in Tunis was that the new constitution would be drafted in Stade Rades rather than the chamber of deputies.

Tunisia's arc of democratization has not been easy. Yet despite violent Islamist terror attacks, enduringly poor economic performance and a desperately fragmented party system, the country has achieved a measure of political stability and openness unique in North Africa. The ultras remain active but politically indifferent: for those that want to, there are now better ways to voice one's discontent than in the football stands. Amongst the new rich, however, football remains a political project. Hamdi Meddeb, a youth footballer with Espérance in the 1960s, gave up the game to concentrate on building his Délice yoghurt and dairy products business, one of the largest in the country, and the kinds of personal and political links with the old regime that such an enterprise required. Installed as President of Espérance in 2007, he used his position to call on supporters of the club to vote for Ben Ali in the obviously rigged 2009 elections. Ali has gone, but Meddeb has not budged from Délice or Espérance. He has been challenged on and off the pitch by Slim Riahi, a wealthy businessman who established himself in exile in Libya and Britain, returned to Tunisia in 2011, bought himself a newspaper and founded a secular centrist party strong on neo-liberal economic medicine, the Union Patriotique Libre. He also made sure the public would know who he was by engineering his election as president of Club Africain. It was enough exposure for him to win sixteen seats in the 2015 general election and enter the cabinet as the junior member of a coalition government. The government responded to the enduring misdemeanours of Tunisian football by publishing the Black Books, a huge dossier of government and secret service documentation that made transparently clear just how compromised the football association, the national team, the football clubs and their owners had been under Ben Ali. No one had been punished, and many were still in the game. Thus the Tunisian national team went to the 2018 World Cup as surely the most unloved in its own nation: the local paper *Le Temps* reported that only 3.9 per cent of the population actually supported them.[59]

In Morocco and Algeria, where the ruling regimes were able to ride out 2011's wave of social protest, domestic football is a tangible reminder of the great simmering pool of discontent that lies beneath the surface of events. Both have sharpened the instruments of repression. Morocco, for example, passed a new law on stadium violence that required ultra groups to acquire permits for assembly. But the street was not ready to give in.[60] In early 2012, *The Winners* stormed the training grounds of their club Wydad Casablanca. Armed with knives, they threatened their own players and coaches, enraged by their poor form and rumours of corruption. In April 2013, the game between Raja Casablanca and FAR Rabat was preceded by wild fighting across the city, and followed by over 200 arrests. In 2016, the ultras of Raja Casablanca, by then fragmented into at least three separate organizations, fought amongst themselves in the stands of the Mohammed V stadium, ripping up seats and launching flares at each other, leaving three dead and fifty-four injured. The government responded by attempting to ban the use of flares; a casual check on the ultras' YouTube channels suggests this has been ineffective.

In Algeria, the level of violence and conflict has remained high, and has been increasingly accompanied by anti-government slogans and sentiments. At the 2012 Algerian Cup final between CRB and Sétif, the crowd called for a boycott of the general election ('One Two Three! Screw those who vote!') and for the resignation of the Prime Minister Ahmed Ouyahia.[61] As an old terrace favourite made clear, nothing had changed: 'The firms are all closed down. The generals are thieves.' Across the country ultras called out the corrupt: 'Chakib Khelil [a former minister accused of embezzlement] stole millions . . . and no one held him accountable.' The 2014 season saw 142 violent incidents, 600 injuries, 151 vehicles destroyed and one

dead footballer.[62] Albert Ebossé, a Cameroonian striker with JS Kabylie, had scored his side's only goal in a 2–1 home defeat to USM
Algiers. The Kabylie fans pelted their own players with stones as they
left the pitch. Ebossé was struck on the head and declared dead by
the time he got to hospital. There was much hand-wringing and no
change. The following season, an even higher level of fan intimidation of players and officials produced a league in which almost
nobody was losing at home.[63]

As ever, violence is borne of violence – the everyday hurts,
squalor and injustices of everyday life for much of urban Algeria.
Thus the repertoire of the ultras extends beyond narrow football
themes or even anti-regime chants. More often than not, you will
hear songs of migration and despair, like 'In Algeria we are Not
Alive':

Sardinia, we are coming. We are the true sons of Algiers.
There, we will have a better life . . .
We are not scared of the Marine Corps, and in God we seek refuge.
These fans left the country without a return.
You will see me one day in Canada.
There I will take control, dressed only in fashionable brands.[64]

And there are laments for the old neighbourhoods where fans once
lived close to their club, but, like so many of the Algerian working-
class, they have been summarily shipped out to peripheral slums and
alien new towns to make way for commercial developments:

We will live a better life and defect to Italy.
I will not come back.
I cannot live in my neighbourhood.
I cannot live.

Set against the emotional and political landscape of anger and
scorn in Algerian football, there is a great hinterland of pain and loss,
of melancholy and hopelessness. Yet there the fury remains, bottled
and contained, as this cameo of stark contrasts suggests:

In a 2014 video of Mouloudia fans lambasting the upcoming election, singing of the hospitalized President Bouteflika, 'Bouyahya
got dressed up and elected himself again', a policeman in uniform
stands a few feet behind the singing fans, unbothered, lazily

leaning against the wall. Quite literally at the same moment, in downtown Algiers, protesters peacefully calling for a boycott of the vote were being arrested and viciously beaten by the police.[65]

Egypt and its football ultras have charted a different course since the heady days of January 2011. Although the fall of Mubarak was greeted with delirium and gave the military government a modicum of credibility, the agonizingly slow move towards new elections and a new constitution, and its heavy-handed policing methods, soon erased it. Street protest persisted. Tahrir Square was cleared in August, but protest and occupations spread out across the other cities of Egypt. While ultras had remained involved, individually and in small groups, within the wider fabric of social protest through the summer of 2011, the widespread rioting and political violence of November 2011 on Cairo's Mohamed Mahmoud Street saw a step change in their engagement. The death of Muhammad Mustapha Kareeka, a member of the *Ultras Ahlawy*, was perceived as a direct and targeted attack on the ultras as organizations, and one that demanded a collective response. Ultra groups now became regular features of these battles, and when domestic football was finally allowed to recommence, the stands rang with the chant, 'SCAF [the Supreme Council of the Armed Forces] are dogs, like the police.'

In January 2012, the first post-Mubarak parliamentary elections were held, and delivered, as expected, an Islamist majority around the Muslim Brotherhood. SCAF would hold executive power for another five months, until Mohamed Morsi, the Brotherhood's candidate, beat Ahmed Shafik, Mubarak's last Prime Minister, for the Presidency. Before they departed, SCAF and the security forces had a goodbye present for the *Ultras Ahlawy*. On 1 February 2012, around 5,000 ultras had made the journey from Cairo to Port Said to see Al-Ahly lose 3–1 to Al-Masry. In retrospect, it was obvious something was up – why else would such a large game be so lightly policed inside the stadium? On the final whistle, and with a theatrical touch, the stadium lights went out. Thousands of people in the Al-Masry stands began to flow over the barriers and onto the pitch. Players, clearly terrified, ran for the dressing rooms as the small contingent of police that had been present melted into the darkness. Running the length of the pitch, the crowd stormed the Al-Ahly end, armed with bottles, rocks, clubs and knives. Most of the seventy-two Al-Ahly ultras who died were asphyxiated in an exit tunnel that led to a deliberately locked gate. A couple of dozen were stabbed and beaten. Some sought refuge in the Al-Ahly dressing room, where one died in the arms of team captain Mohamed Aboutrika. Live, by phone, on television, he shouted, 'This is not football. This is a war. People are dying in front of us. There is no security. There are no ambulances.' Days of protests in Cairo followed and an extraordinary array of martyrs' portraits were made by street artists the length of Mohamed Mahmoud Street.

Over the following year, the *Ultras Ahlawy* conducted their own boycott of football, refusing to attend games and calling for their players to join them. Enormous energy was devoted to returning, burying and memorializing the dead, raising money for the families of victims, recording testimony of the event from survivors and campaigning for justice. But while the ultras acquired the skills and methods of more conventional political forces, their connection to the wider movements for change was broken as they turned inward, concerned only with their own affairs. In January and early February 2013, as the government veered towards a more Islamist constitution, there had been a nationwide outbreak of anti-Morsi street protests, but on this occasion the ultras were not present. They were entirely focused on the court in Port Said where those supposedly responsible for the massacre were being tried. No one believed that those ultimately in charge were present, but the *Ultras Ahlawy* were expecting some measure of justice. The first verdicts announced found twenty-one people guilty and issued them with death sentences. Families and supporters of the accused, including many local ultras, responded by trying to storm the prison; two people were shot dead. Port Said erupted in a city-wide riot that was only controlled by the imposition of a thirty-day curfew and the deaths of another forty citizens, slaughtered by the police. A month later, the second verdict was announced: just two of the twenty-eight security service officers awaiting judgement were found guilty, and were given fifteen years in jail. Al-Ahly's training ground was engulfed in tear gas and angry rioting fans, but it made no difference.

President Morsi's vocal support for the police violence in Port Said won him few friends. Reduced to just the Islamists of the

Muslim Brotherhood, he had alienated both the Egyptian military and state machine, and burnt his bridges with secular and independent forces. In June 2013, the military moved against him in a straightforward coup. The Muslim Brotherhood was declared a terrorist organization, its facilities destroyed and membership repressed. Morsi was put on trial for his life, a new military constitution banned religious parties of any kind, and General Sisi finally took off his uniform, put on a suit and won a risible Presidential election in 2014. Having seen off the Islamists, the regime then came for the ultras. In truth, they were already falling apart. With Egyptian football still being played behind closed doors, the central purpose and energizing activity of the ultras – supporting the team and performing *tifos* in the stadium – was lost. The impact of Port Said and the political activism that followed had drained the already limited resources of the old leadership. Pressures of age, family and earning a living, suspendable for a time, began to cut into the activism and numbers of *Ultras Ahlawy*.

Over at Zamalek, where the *Ultras White Knights* had undergone a similar depletion, they found themselves in direct conflict with a supporter of the new regime. Mortada Mansour was an almost ever-present satrap of the Mubarak regime, both a high-court judge and an MP in the era's parliament of stooges. After lying low for a few years, he had managed to get himself elected President of Zamalek on the premise of spending money on the club's private member facilities and kicking out the ultras. Like the government, the first step was to demonize them. After a bottle of urine got lobbed at him by ultras, Mansour went on television. 'Last week they threw acid at me,' he said, 'but I continue because this is part of the nation's battle against terrorism.' A month later, on 8 February, Zamalek fans were trying to get into a game against the Police Union team, streaming down a narrow, barbed-wire-ringed alleyway. The latter's colleagues, captured on cellphone footage, repeatedly fired tear gas canisters and shotgun pellets into the crowd. In the stampede that followed, nineteen people were killed. One eyewitness was in no doubt as to what had happened: 'The massacre that took place today was revenge on those who took part in the revolution.'[66] The authorities' principal response to the tragedy was immediately to arrest the entire *Ultra White Knights* leadership. Three months later, the Cairo

Court for Urgent Affairs banned all forms of ultra activity and made the organizations themselves, in Egyptian law, terrorist groups, subject to the most penal and brutal legal instruments the state could offer.[67]

In 2016, though still denied access to the stadiums of Egypt, the ultras movement at least retained the capacity to mourn. *Ultras Ahlawy* held a public commemoration of the Port Said massacre. *Ultras White Knights* did the same on 8 February. President Sisi, in a very rare conciliatory gesture, invited the *Ultras Ahlawy* to put forward ten people to join a commission of investigation into the massacre. The ultras refused, arguing that this was a matter of justice, not debate, for the courts and the rule of law to determine. Whatever Sisi's real motivations and intentions, the Egyptian state reverted to its usual mode of engagement later in the year. Members of the Green Eagles, Al-Masry's ultras, were arrested in Port Said for singing anti-regime chants in the stadium and putting up complementary graffiti in the streets. Almost fifty members of *Ultras White Knights* were arrested for attending a Zamalek handball game. In July, both the big Cairo teams played African Champions League ties in the Borg al-Arab stadium in Alexandria, at CAF's insistence in front of a crowd. On both occasions, there were clashes between police and fans, and widespread arrests: 150 *Ultras Ahlawy* at their game with Espérance, and 500 *Ultras White Knights* at Zamalek's match, of whom almost half were charged and sent to a military court. Thus by early 2017, both groups were forced to cancel any commemoration of their stadium tragedies. As the *Ultras Ahlawy* Facebook page made clear, many leading members of the group were 'subjected to continuous raids on their homes and the arrest of their family members if they were not present.' Abdoul Aboutrika, a player who never left Egypt during his career despite innumerable European offers, has fled to Qatar. The courts have seized his Egyptian assets on a trumped-up charge of association with the Muslim Brotherhood. One wonders if Hosni Mubarak, now released from detention and comfortably dying, still thinks that 'Egypt does not tolerate those who hurt the dignity of its sons.'

IV

Israel, alone in the Middle East, plays its football in Europe. It was originally a member of the Asian Football Confederation, but high-level political opposition from across the continent in support of the Palestinian cause, from Indonesia to Iran, saw FIFA move the country, for football purposes, to Oceania, and then, in the 1990s, to Europe. Amongst the many paradoxes of that journey is the fact that Israel, over the same period, became less European, demographically at any rate. The core of the Jewish population that declared independence in 1948 was made up of European migrants. They were, of course, joined by a smaller component of Sephardic Jews from North Africa and West Asia. Since then, they have been joined by further waves of Jewish migration, above all from Russia, Yemen and Ethiopia. As a banner held by Hapoel Tel Aviv fans in 2015 in support of refugees read: 'Who isn't a migrant here?'[68] In the census of that year, only a third of the population had parents born in Israel. Everyone else is from somewhere else. Israeli football, if nothing else, reflects the extraordinary diversity of the country.

First and foremost, around 20 per cent of the population is neither Jewish nor European at all: they are Arabs, predominantly Muslims but with a small Christian minority and distinct Bedouin communities.[69] Their representatives in Israeli football have been Bnei Sakhnin. This is not the first nor the only Arab club in Israeli football, but they have become the community's 'senior side', regularly present in the premier league, and in 2004 winners of the Israeli Cup. Long the subject of terrace-level racism and abuse, they have, in Israel's ever more polarized politics, attracted the opprobrium of far-right politicians too. In 2014, Foreign Minister Avigdor Lieberman and Minister of Culture Limor Livnat called for the club to be banned from Israeli football, for taking $2million from Qatar to rebuild its dilapidated Doha Stadium and putting up commemorative plaques to the Emir of Qatar and Azmi Bishar, the Arab member of the Knesset who brokered the exchange. As the club chair tartly retorted, 'What do they want from us? The establishment doesn't give us any money, so why shouldn't we raise it overseas?'[70] Another 15 per cent of the country is made up of one variety or another of

Orthodox Jews, who, while they disagree about almost everything, are pretty united in their lack of interest in football. Their virtual non-participation in the sport at any level is a parallel to their non-participation in the nation's most important institution, the IDF (Israel Defence Forces). Amongst their political representatives, there have been sporadic calls to ban the playing of professional football on the sabbath. In 2015, they almost got their wish, when a case brought by observant but non-Orthodox players in the lower division challenging the requirement to play on shabbat escalated through the courts and took the country to the precipice of football-free Saturdays.[71]

The rest of the country, like its football teams, remains divided on political, ethnic and geographical lines, some drawn almost a century ago, though the once very close economic and administrative links between political movements and sports clubs have been modulated by the arrival of commercial forces and priorities in the 1990s.[72] Consider just the six teams that have won a national title since the turn of the century. Hapoel Tel Aviv and Hapoel Be'er Sheva have their roots in the Histadrut, the alliance of trade unions and the Labour Party that was the dominant political force from independence until the 1970s.[73] Fans of both retain elements of these older identities. *Ultras Hapoel* in Tel Aviv are amongst the most active anti-fascist, anti-racist groups in Israeli football, while Be'er Sheva and Ironi Kiryat Shmona are reminders, away from the cosmopolitan Mediterranean coast, of Israel's many small garrisons and border cities.[74] Maccabi Tel Aviv and Maccabi Haifa have their roots in the more centrist and conservative Zionism of the Maccabi movement, though, like the Hapoels, their original constituency was overwhelmingly Ashkenazim, whatever their politics. By contrast, Beitar Jerusalem drew on the nation's Sephardic/Mizrahim communities and the right-wing political movements that would later mutate into Likud.[75] As befitting a political landscape that has been increasingly dominated by Likud and a series of right-wing coalitions, Beitar, despite winning just two championships since the turn of the millennium, have been taking up nearly all the symbolic space in Israeli football.

The club was founded in 1936 but its fate, like that of all Jerusalem, changed with the 1967 Six-Day War. The Israelis captured the whole of eastern Jerusalem and expanded the municipal boundaries into the West Bank. Formerly a provincial town, Jerusalem now assumed the mantle of 'eternal capital' of Israel, with Beitar the national team of Likud and their predominantly Mizrahi constituency. On match days, a yellow convoy of cars and buses would throng the narrow road along the Jerusalem corridor, as fans streamed in from across the country. Another decade on, Beitar were established in the top flight, while Likud had come to power under Menachem Begin. The citadels of the football and political establishment had been breached. Members of Likud cabinets, from Benjamin Netanyahu to Ehud Olmert, could be seen in the stands. Yet Beitar still could not claim the top spot in Israeli football. What finally took them there was the arrival, in 2005, of Arcadi Gaydamak. A man of many passports, he generally travelled on his Angolan diplomatic one, carrying allegations of money laundering and arms dealing with him. In Israel, he bought into the media, food companies, supermarkets and Beitar. Sweeping up most of the Israeli national team and selected foreigners, Beitar stormed to victory in two consecutive championships.

Gaydamak then dipped his toes into the country's politics. During the second Lebanon war in 2006, he set up a tent city on a Mediterranean beach, to which residents of embattled border towns could flee. He did the same for Sderot in the south when the city came under persistent Qassam fire from Gaza. Then, in mid-2007, he created a political party, Social Justice, and stated his intention to run for the mayoralty of Jerusalem that year and the Knesset in 2009. However, neither he, nor any other owner or board of directors has been able to monopolize the meaning of Beitar. That has remained, ever more closely, the possession of La Familia, amongst the first of Israel's ultra groups, and their fellow travellers amongst the fanbase.

As one might expect, there was never much love between Beitar and Israel's Arabs and neighbours. The club certainly didn't field any Arab players, but its Mizrahim roots, not its racism, were the core of its identity. After the signing of the Oslo Accords in the early 1990s, however, Beitar's fans became ever more militantly anti-Arab and pro-settler. In 2002, this seething mass of discontent and anger was given organizational shape by the creation of La Familia, which imported techniques of support and protest perfected in Italian football. For a decade, under three different owners, they owned the curva at Teddy Stadium in Jerusalem, formed the largest and most aggressive travelling fan corps in the country, and increasingly allied themselves with extremist groups, most notably planting the club's flags alongside those of the settler movement on contested hilltops in east Jerusalem. Gaydamak was a chancer, an opportunist, and narcissist, but he wasn't signing up for this kind of politics. In trouble on both legal and financial fronts, he tried to sell the club in 2011 and walked away in 2012. In 2013 Beitar passed into the hands of another controversial businessman, Eli Tabib, who tried to change the club and its sporting fortunes by signing two Chechen Muslim players, Zaur Sadayev and Gabriel Kadiev. Despite some arrests of *La Familia* members and some tightening up at the stadium, the new recruits were under twenty-four-hour armed guard and subject to huge and vituperative abuse from *La Familia* at the club's training ground and in the stadium. When the two first played, the ultras displayed the banner 'Beitar. Pure Forever', and when Sadayev scored his first goal hundreds of fans walked out in protest. When that didn't work they went for the clubhouse, burning it and Beitar's entire collection of trophies and memorabilia to ash.[76] Remarkably, given the scale of the group's violence and its persistent association with street attacks on Palestinians, it remained largely untouched by the police, while remaining unchallengeable by the owners. In 2015, there was more despair than outrage in Tabib's voice when he castigated *La Familia* for the use of flares and racist banners, and an attack on Charleroi goalkeeper Nicolas Penneteau after a 5–1 thrashing in Belgium. 'I am ashamed and shocked by the behaviour of part of the crowd tonight. The whole world watched the horror, this embarrassing horror show, conducted by the same radical group who are not true Beitar fans in my eyes.'[77] Tabib has yet to find a buyer, but the Israeli police have at last swung into a modicum of action. In 2016, after Beitar fans had attacked a Hapoel Tel Aviv fan with an axe, police arrested fifty leading members of *La Familia*, sequestering the hundreds of military flares and grenades that they had accumulated.[78] While *La Familia* are in partial abeyance, no one should be fooled into thinking that Beitar has undergone any kind of transformation. In honour of his decision to recognize Jerusalem as the capital of Israel and to move the United States Embassy to the city, the club proposed renaming itself Beitar Trump.

Beneath the surface of these older and more conventional political projects of left and right, something else is stirring in Israeli civil society: the bottom-up demand for justice that motivated the 2011 mass occupations and protests. One footballing dimension to this wider mobilization has been the rise of Hapoel Katamon.[79] The club began life in 2007 as a breakaway from Hapoel Jerusalem, beginning in the fourth level of Israeli football and 3,000 members. Open to all, fielding Arab and Jewish players, fan-owned and self-consciously anti-racist, it is the last bastion of the secular left who, before the rise of the Orthodox and Likud, were the mainstay of the city. By 2018, the club was semi-professional and in the second division, its social arm running weekly neighbourhood tournaments at Arab and Jewish schools, and sporting rainbow corner flags on the weekend it sent a delegation to Jerusalem Pride. It has been followed by other fan-owned and breakaway initiatives, from Maccabi Kabilio to Beitar Nordia, an anti-racist breakaway from Beitar Jerusalem.[80]

After the devastating defeats of the 1967 Arab–Israeli war, and the occupation of the West Bank and Gaza, organized football barely existed amongst Palestinians, and what little progress that had been made was swept aside during the Intifada of the 1980s, when even street football was impossible. With the signing of the Oslo Peace Accords in 1993 and the abatement of fighting in the occupied territories, a revival of the sport became possible. Palestine grabbed it with both hands. In 1994, a Palestinian football association was created, and while Israel conceded the status of neither nation nor state to the Palestinians, FIFA did. Palestine joined the organization and the world of international football in 1998, fielding players from across its global diaspora. In the absence of UN membership, this football-based sovereignty has proved a potent political tool for the Palestinians.[81]

Palestine's very presence in World Cup qualifying campaigns and in the FIFA global rankings gives it the status of a nation of the world. Development money from FIFA has allowed the PFA to sustain its national teams, and to build a national stadium in Ramallah; prior to this nearly all home games had to be played outside the country in Jordan or Qatar. On innumerable occasions, the Israelis have refused to let the squad travel to tournaments, like the 2009 Arab Cup of Nations in Yemen and a 2010 World Cup qualifier in Singapore, but this has merely burnished the credentials of the team, who are vulnerable to the same kind of injustices and inconveniences that the rest of the nation suffers at its borders with Israel. So too the Palestine Football Association headquarters and facilities, which have been repeatedly bombed. The football world has also opened up new channels of support and solidarity. In Algeria, the first country to recognize Palestinian independence in 1988, there is a widespread culture of support for the team and nation. In 2014, after making the knock-out stages of the World Cup, the Algerian national team returned to Algiers in an open-top bus draped with the Palestine flag, and pledged their $9 million prize money to the people of Gaza. In 2015, Algerian fans filled the national stadium with Palestinian flags and actually cheered the Palestine team when they beat the home side in an Olympic qualifier. Pressure from allies at home and abroad saw the Argentine FA cancel a friendly in Israel in the run-up to the 2018 World Cup.[82] Celtic's supporter group, the Green Brigade, acknowledged and supported the Palestinian hunger strikes of 2012 with flags and the banner 'Dignity is more precious than food'. In 2014, during Israel's huge military attacks on Gaza that year, they unfurled Palestinian flags at a game in Iceland against KR Reykjavik, and did so again in Glasgow in 2016 during a Champions League game against Israeli club Hapoel Be'er Sheva. The club was fined just over £8,000 by UEFA. The Green Brigade responded by crowdfunding a £170,000 donation to Palestinian medical charities.[83]

Membership of FIFA also provided a brilliant forum in which to challenge the steady Israeli colonization of the West Bank with illegal and exclusive settlements. Six of these settlements included football facilities and a club that was allowed to play in the lower reaches of the Israeli league system. The Palestinian FA argued that this was contrary to FIFA statutes and put the suspension of Israel on the agenda of FIFA's 2015 congress. The Israelis were worried enough to mobilize most of their ambassadors in pursuit of support from FIFA delegates. Beset by the organization's own implosion and Sepp Blatter's resignation, FIFA pushed the issue back to its own Israel–Palestine monitoring committee, which in turn pushed it back to the UN, which was unambiguous. Wilfried Lemke, UN special advisor on Sport and Peace, wrote to FIFA that the Israeli settlements and by extension their clubs were 'Without validity and illegal under international law'. That was in 2016, yet in May 2017, two years after the issue had first been raised, FIFA, now under President Gianni Infantino, still thought it 'premature' to make a call on this one. As ever, the world awaits the right time to act on Israel–Palestine.[84]

In the decades before the creation of the Palestinian national team, the nation still had footballing representation. As Yasser Arafat said, 'One day when we had no voice, Al-Wehdat was our voice.' Except that the voice and the club were in Jordan.[85] Al-Wehdat was the team of the huge Palestinian population that flooded into refugee camps in Amman, making Palestinians close to 50 per cent of the Jordanian population. Jordan, essentially a creation of the British mandate, was ruled by the Hashemite king it had installed in loose alliance with the desert tribes, known as East Bankers, who feared becoming a minority in their own state, and having to cede their privileged positions in the military and state employment. Division and suspicion were entrenched in the early 1970s by a short and bitter conflict between the Jordanian state and the nascent PLO operating in the refugee camps as an armed militia.

The civil war, as it is known, remains the largest unspoken presence in Jordanian politics. Its footballing avatar is the game between Al-Wehdat and Al-Faisaly, which was originally the team of the Adwan tribe and was then named after an old King. Just in case anyone is in doubt as to the former's allegiance, Al-Wehdat play in the Palestinian national colours, and the club badge sports the Golden Dome in Jerusalem's Old City and the words *Allah, Wehdat, Al Quds Arabiya* ('God, Wehdat, Jerusalem for the Arabs'). Between them, the two clubs have won all but two of Jordan's league titles, and open antagonism between their fans stretches back into the 1970s.

In the early 2000s, during the second Palestinian intifada, the chanting took a much more pointed turn, with Al-Faisaly fans singing, for the first time, about the Palestinian roots of the royal family. This was a veiled warning to the Hashemites not to side with them: 'Divorce her, you father of Hussein, and we'll marry you to two of ours,' a reference to the King's marriage to Queen Alia, a Palestinian-American. So far the Hashemites have not switched sides. Indeed, they have maintained a gerrymandered electoral system that ensures that the Palestinian majority cannot be expressed in parliament. At the same time, the Royal House has justified its own autocratic powers on the basis that only it can stand between these competing forces, now including Islamists as well, and chaos, adding that to do away with the royals would be to invite back the days of civil war. What better way to remind everybody of its potency than to let some of those toxic energies flare up at football games, even if this comes at the price of a few anti-royal chants that would not be tolerated in any other context in Jordan? Consequently, on the final day of the 2008 season, when Al-Wehdat won the league, the Jordanian police were lax enough to allow outbreaks of fighting amongst the fans, then tough enough to give Al-Wehdat supporters a good beating. At the 2009 derby, Al-Faisaly fans stoned Al-Wehdat players while singing anti-Hashemite songs, forcing the game to be abandoned, but the press was silent. Only the clubs received fines, and light ones at that.

After more than three decades of turmoil, civil war and cancelled seasons, Lebanese football began the twentieth century in reasonable shape. Indeed, the hosting of the Asian Cup in 2000 was a remarkable achievement. First, because the extensive damage wrought by the civil war, including to most of the nation's stadiums, had been sufficiently repaired for the country to stage the show; and second, because the national team – a fictive presence for much of the 1980s and 1990s – received support from all quarters. This was no mean feat, for the civil war had literally obliterated the team. As its coach Theo Brucker said on his arrival in 2000, 'It was deeply underground. It was not existing at all.'

Moreover, Lebanon's sectarian divisions remained deeply etched into its football clubs. Al-Ansar was the team of the Sunni elite; the wealthy businessman Raffia Hariri was its president in the 1990s and the Prime Minister in the early twenty-first century. Nejmeh FC were the team of Lebanon's Shiites, Sagesse was the club of Christian Maronites and Safa played for the Druze. Christian Phalangists with Armenian roots had Homenetmen if they were on the right and Homenmen if they were on the left. Islamist group Hezbollah had Al-Ahed, sponsored by its own TV network. The club steadily rose up through the leagues to become, like its backers, a major player in the national championship. Domestic football was not entirely peaceable or civil, but, given the potential volatility of the situation, it remained within acceptable bounds.[86]

The fragile equilibrium in Lebanese politics disintegrated in 2005 after the assassination of ex-Prime Minister Hariri and twenty of his associates, an act later traced back to Hezbollah and its Syrian backers. It would take another four years for a stable government of national unity to emerge after another round of fighting, the departure of the Syrians, a lot of Israeli bombing and another national election. Once again, pitches were commandeered as marshalling yards. The Olympic stadium in Tripoli served as an army base for launching attacks on the restive Palestinian refugee camps nearby. In this context, the Lebanese Football Federation closed the nation's stadiums to fans, home and away. Every game was played behind closed doors. Even then, violence would break out as one club's fans would attack the team coaches of the visitors. It was surely with a profound sense of irony that the political class anointed the new government of national unity with a 'peace game' shown live on national television between mixed sides, one captained by the new PM Saad Hariri, the other by senior parliamentarian Ali Ammar, the political leader of Hezbollah.[87] Hariri's team won with a late goal, but it was the breathless incompetence of most of the politicians that caught the nation's attention.

In 2012, some fans were allowed back into some games, but the whole procedure remains fraught, minutely regulated and controlled by the army. 2013 was a year of match-fixing scandals, about which, given the long history of sectarian manipulation of games and the desperate wages of players, no one was very surprised. The national team's remarkably good run in the qualifying campaign for the 2014 World Cup, peaking with a victory over South Korea, was a rare shared experience for the nation. But it is a measure of Lebanon's fractured society that the World Cup itself, without the country's actual participation, is by far the greatest collective celebration the nation allows itself, with real support (and endless bunting and flags) for Brazil, Argentina, Germany and France. The land of a thousand proxy wars turns the world upside down during the World Cup carnival and chooses proxy teams for itself.[88]

For the first decade of the century, Syrian football was on the up. Although domestic football was inevitably dominated by the army team Al-Jaish, there was still room for other centres of footballing power and regional and ethnic identities. In 2006 Al-Karamah from Homs were good enough to lose an Asian Champions League final – the only time a Syrian club had progressed so far in a major club tournament. In 2011, on the eve of the civil war, the national team qualified for the Asian Cup for the first time in fifteen years. However, a better guide as to what was to come were the 2004 Al-Qamishli riots. Prior to a game played between the local Kurdish team Qamishli and Al-Fotuwa from the Sunni Arab city of Deir-ez Zor, away fans rode around the town centre brandishing posters of Saddam Hussein and verbally abusing Kurdish leaders. This continued at the game, where the locals responded with the chant, 'We will sacrifice our lives for Bush.' The police, at this point virtually absent, stood by while the Sunni fans piled into their opponents with sticks and knives, only then firing on the crowd and killing six locals. In the ensuing city-wide riot, the local headquarters of the Ba'ath party were burnt down. It would take another thirty deaths and a hundred people injured for the security services to retake the city.

In March 2011, the Arab Spring reached Syria. Simultaneously, protests and fighting broke out across the nation between the Assad government and its armed forces, and a variety of emerging militias, from the secular to the jihadi and from Sunni to Kurdish. Football, like everything else, just stopped. People chose sides, or left if they could. Football players, like the rest of the country, divided politically. Initially, some simply left the field and joined the rebels, like youth-team goalkeeper Abdul Basit Saroot, who became an icon of the uprising in Homs. Mosab Balhous shielded rebels in his house, for which he was later imprisoned. Firas Al-Khatib, the national team's star, refused to play for Syria and left the country to play in China and Kuwait. Jihad Kassab, once captain of Al-Karamah in Homs and a member of the national team, was arrested in 2014, held for two years and then executed.[89]

As of 2019, eight years later, and despite half a million deaths, four million refugees and seven million people internally displaced, the Assad regime has managed to cling on, its brutality towards its own people only matched by its resilience, exemplified by its capacity to maintain a semblance of a football league and a national team since 2012.[90] Given the military geography of the conflict, the league has been based in Damascus, where teams play out a much reduced fixture list in a stadium empty but for giant pictures of Assad. The Homs- and Aleppo-based teams have inevitably faded away. Enough money and players have been found to keep the men's national team going, and the regime was simply delighted that its scratch squad managed to win the West Asian Football Federation Cup in 2012. Not exactly a global triumph, but worth enough to Assad for him to shower the squad with apartments and bonuses. Many of the players who stayed found themselves caught between the two sides, pressured to play for the national team by the Assad government and accused of being accomplices by the rebel movements. Some allied themselves with a Free Syrian national team that trained in Turkey and Lebanon, which issued a call to their colleagues still at home: 'Leave such a criminal team. It is not Syria's team. It is the team of a criminal regime.' It is Assad and his team that have clung on, however, as first IS and then the rest of the opposition have been crushed with Russian support. Football confirmed the new dispensation. Despite playing all their games outside the country, the men's national team made it all the way to a play-off against Australia for a shot at the 2018 World Cup.[91] Firas Al-Khatib and Omar al Somar returned to the side from their self-imposed exiles and, despite losing to Australia, were with the squad in Damascus, welcomed by a smiling President Assad in a national team jersey.

V

At the turn of the twenty-first century, there was only one footballing power of any significance in the Gulf: Saudi Arabia. Dwarfing its neighbours – Kuwait, Bahrain, Qatar, UAE, Oman and Yemen – economically and demographically, Saudi Arabia had a national team who were in the midst of a run of four successive qualifications for the World Cup (1994–2006). In 1994, they had been the first team from the Arabic world to progress to the knock-out phases. Closer to home, the team made five consecutive finals of the Asian Cup between 1984 and 2000 and won three of them. These were the fruits of an investment programme in Saudi football started in the late 1970s by King Abdullah's regime. In a rare dismissal of the fatwas and arguments of Saudi Arabia's many anti-football Wahhabist theologians, the House of Saud drew on its new oil wealth to pay for the building of football stadiums and the employment of foreign coaches and players; many princes took a close and abiding interest in the clubs that they presided over. In a society with few alternative public pleasures, and still no satellite television, Saudi football drew big crowds in the 1980s and 1990s.

While this was sufficient to launch the Saudi game, its limits were becoming apparent a decade on. On the pitch, the 8–0 humiliation handed out to the national team by the Germans in their

opening game of the 2002 World Cup heralded a decline that has yet
to be arrested. While the King Abdullah Stadium was a remarkable
piece of architecture, its fine-filigree concrete and soaring Bedouin
tent roof unique in global football, it had almost no facilities for
anyone but the King. Lesser stadiums were even more basic, and by
the 2000s they were showing their age. Money had never trickled
down much beyond the top few clubs, leaving grassroots sides to
play on sand and tarmac, and the league was then importing cheap
African and Asian players. The arrival of European football on television accelerated an already sharp decline in stadium attendance.

The process of decline began to take on alarming proportions. In
2012, Prince Nawaf bin Faisal stepped down from the presidency of
the Saudi Football Federation, bowing to a torrent of public pressure
over the appalling state of the national team.[92] Not only was royal
power brought to heel by public opinion, but for the first time the
office of President of the football association was filled by a com-
moner, ex-player Ahmed Eid Al Harbi, also a known advocate of
women's football. An even more brazen assertion of the popular will
followed in 2013, when a fan campaign was mounted against Prince
Faisal, owner of Al-Nassr, who was subject to both online and physical attacks. At the same time, the league was beset by a match-fixing
scandal and a still unresolved financial crisis. The former was triggered by the case of Al-Monze, a small team that had achieved two
successive promotions in dubious circumstances, and above all had
no member of the House of Saud on the board. The financial crisis,
long in the making, lay in the huge and paralysing accumulated
debts of most of the top teams.

It was at this point that Deputy Crown Prince Mohammad Bin
Salman, the young and newly installed sheikh who had been given
effective control of the government machine, with a mandate for reform, launched, in 2013, the government's Vision 2030: the plan to
transform Saudi Arabia's moribund, state-centric and hydrocarbon-
dependent economy into a flexible, competitive and diverse post-
industrial success, at the same time ensuring, politically, that the
House of Saud remained firmly in control. In three areas in particular, football has paralleled the plan for the rest of the economy. First,
Vision 2030 has launched a vast programme of privatizations and the
sell-off of state assets. While hardly the flotation of Saudi Aramco,
all the leading football clubs were prepared for private ownership

and most have now been sold. At the same time, as the national government cut subsidies and price controls of many kinds, it has insisted that the clubs, albeit still with some help, put their balance sheets in order. In pursuit of opening more jobs up to Saudis, the recruitment of foreign players has been halted altogether. The new infrastructure, in football at any rate, has yet to come, but Jeddah Sports City is indicative of what awaits. First mooted in the 1990s, the complex opened in 2014 at the astronomical cost of over half a billion dollars. Unlike the earlier generation of Saudi stadiums, it has been equipped with the paraphernalia of the modern commercial stadium: expensive media facilities, executive boxes, concession stands and a family area, where women will be permitted to attend.

Good as all of this looks on paper, nothing has yet arrested the declining appeal of the local game. Stadiums are pitifully empty, yet at the same time one part of the population is banging on the door to get in: women. Pursuing the same theological logic as their Iranian counterparts, though of course on Sunni Wahhabist rather than Shia lines, the Saudi Arabians were implacable in their refusal to allow Saudi women into football stadiums where men are playing. While the authorities have not actually banned women from playing football or watching it on television, these activities have only been permissible under a complex series of Sharia-determined conditions (segregated viewing, etc.), and they did their best to marginalize and ignore the issue all together. In such a tightly controlled society it is hard to gauge public opinion, but there was certainly a huge online backlash when a Saudi woman fan appeared on television, in full niqab, supporting Saudi side Al-Hilal against Al Ain of the UAE in the away leg of their Asian Champions League clash.[93] Saudi women's exclusion appeared all the more unfair when, in 2014, female supporters of Western Sydney Wanderers were allowed inside the King Fahd Stadium to watch the second leg of their Asian Champions League final.[94] All of which makes it the more remarkable that, in late 2018, the policy of exclusion was finally reversed, though women will only be able to attend those new stadiums within demarcated zones. Their arrival may not save the Saudi Premier League but, as one young Saudi woman said, proxy for a huge body of hidden female fans, 'I don't know how to describe my feeling to you . . . it is such a pleasure.'[95]

Unsurprisingly, the state of women's sport in Saudi Arabia is more anaemic than anywhere else in the region. Following pressure from the IOC for the country to field a team of mixed genders, Saudi women have made their debut at the Olympics, but they were long-term expatriates. Closer to home, no provision of any kind existed for physical education for girls in school, or for adult women in the public realm. Under such constraints, Saudi women have not been waiting for permission to play, but have been forming their own private and sometimes clandestine fitness and sports clubs, playing basketball, badminton and football.

The rest of the Gulf is hardly female-friendly, but there has been change. Bahrain were the pioneers, their women's national team playing its first game in 2003. Women's teams from Qatar, UAE and Kuwait followed at the end of the decade. Even Yemen's women team made their debut in 2012, and Qatar and the UAE have established small women's leagues. Slowly and unevenly, women are making themselves an indispensable part of the football nation. In 2013, the government of the UAE flew women fans to Bahrain for the final of the Gulf Cup against Iraq.

Bahrain is the smallest and one of the poorest of the Gulf micro-states. As of 2017, the majority of its 700,000 citizens were Shias (only around 45 per cent of the inhabitants have citizenship), but they were ruled by the Sunni House of Al-Khalifa. A Shia uprising in the 1990s had been crushed, but a more open Bahrain had emerged. The Emir still picked the Prime Minister, but they both now faced a parliament elected on universal suffrage, in which political parties could organize, and which, constitutionally, held a modicum of power. Alongside this, Bahraini football was flourishing. As one national team coach observed, 'They are playing football every day, everywhere. It's a small place, but they play football.'[96] From this feverish grassroots culture of play that dotted the island with pitches and posts, a generation of stars emerged, including brothers A'ala and Mohamed Hubail, Salman Isa, and Sayed Mohamed Adnan. A semi-final place in the Asian Cup in 2004 was followed by a spectacular qualification campaign for the 2006 World Cup that led them to a two-game play-off with Trinidad and Tobago. Having managed a 1–1 draw in Port of Spain, they lost by a single goal at home. The qualification rounds for 2010 proved equally heartrending. Under Czech coach Milan Máčala – a man hired and fired by almost every Gulf state's football association – Bahrain crawled their way towards qualification. To give themselves a shot at the World Cup, in a play-off with New Zealand, they first needed a draw from their final game with Saudi Arabia. At ninety minutes, the score was 1–1 and Bahrain looked set, only for the Saudis to snatch an injury-time goal. Ten seconds from the final whistle, the ball was crossed into the Saudi box and glanced off the head of Ismail Abdul-Latif to give Bahrain the draw and the nation an ecstatic moment of imagined community, squeezing out their giant, overbearing neighbour. In the goalless home leg of the play-off, Bahrain had their chance: Salman Isa rounded the keeper only for his shot to fly off the post. They would lose the return game in New Zealand. In sombre mood afterwards, A'ala Hubail said, 'We don't know what will happen in the next four or five years, and it is difficult to know who will be playing for the national team at that time.'

The national team certainly wouldn't include Hubail or his brother, but not because their form had dropped. Inspired by the events of the Arab Spring in North Africa, on 14 February 2011 Bahrain saw its own outbreak of mass popular protest. Activists and youth, both Shia and Sunni, gathered on the Pearl Roundabout, a huge space in the financial district of the capital Manama. Once there, protestors established a camp and called for democratization and accountability. People from all walks of life, including sports professionals like the Hubail brothers, joined the throng. Sayed Adnan explained his own motivation for joining. 'My cousin is dead – he received one bullet in the head – I started thinking, "Why don't we do something to stop this killing?"'

In the Al-Qudaibiya Palace, the Al-Khalifas and their allies were barely listening, for they had already, without any real evidence, cast the movement as their own nightmare: another Shia uprising, with the rebels allied with Iran and intent on deposing them. Early attempts by the Bahraini authorities to move the protestors on, or at least to break their spirit, saw a number of deaths and many injuries but no end to the occupation. For this, the Al-Khalifas needed help. Almost a month after the protest had begun, this arrived in the shape of a column of tanks and troops from the Gulf Co-operation Council – primarily Saudis and Emiratees. The camp was destroyed. Thirty-two people were killed and thousands arrested. Amongst the latter were A'ala and Mohamed Hubail and Sayed Mohamed, all of whom were imprisoned and tortured for three months before being released.

'They said, "Captain A'ala, get your brother." They put me in the room for the beatings. One of the people who hit me said, "I'm going to break your legs." They knew who we were.'[97] It would later transpire that Sheikh Salman Al-Khalifa, then president of the Bahraini Football Federation (and later President of the Asian Football Federation and a member of FIFA's executive), had been head of the government committee assigned the task of identifying and punishing players who had been politically active. In 2013, the government obliterated the roundabout, removed all trace of the huge public sculpture that once dominated it and changed the road layout to make it seem as if it had never existed. A'ala Hubail left to play in Oman, Adnan went to Australia, the form of the Bahraini team has entirely collapsed and, after lying low and skipping a few IOC meetings, Sheikh Al-Khalifa is back on the global sports circuit.

The high point of Kuwaiti football remains the moment at the 1982 World Cup when Sheikh Fahad Al-Sabah, brother of the then Kuwaiti Emir and president of the Kuwaiti Football Association, stormed onto the pitch to remonstrate with the referee in their game against France. The Sheikh successfully disputed France's fourth goal, claiming that his players had been distracted by a whistle from the crowd. They still lost 4–1. In the years since, Kuwaiti football has never been quite the same, and nor has the country. The Iraqi invasion in 1990 and the first Gulf War triggered a series of political and social changes that have made the absolutist model pursued by other royal houses impossible for the Al-Sabahs. Over the last two decades, they were forced to accept a functioning parliament, political parties both secular and Islamist, women voters and parliamentarians, and even a constitutional court ruling that Islamic headdress was not mandatory. The ruling house responded to this new environment by breaking with the customs of succession. In 2003, the Emir appointed Sheikh Sabah as Prime Minister, a post hitherto reserved for the Crown Prince. Third in line to the throne, Sheikh Sabah brought a new kind of briskness to government operations, and when the Emir died the ailing crown prince was quickly out-manoeuvred by him. In opting for competency over rank, however, the Al-Sabahs unleashed political conflict amongst the many other wings of the royal family – for if the old model of succession was finished, then what other than power and position would determine one's place within the pecking order? Amongst the most active of the scheming princes was Sheikh Ahmad Al-Sabah.

Sheikh Ahmad served as government minister for a decade. He ran the vital oil ministry for five years, served as the national representative at OPEC, and at one point was both head of the national security agency and the national football team coach. Sport had always been an important part of his portfolio, and became increasingly so as he looked for ways to leverage his opposition to his domestic rivals. Already a long-standing member of the IOC and president of the Asian Olympic Association, his brother Sheikh Talal looked after things at home, running the Kuwaiti National Olympic Committee and the Kuwait Football Association. Sheikh Ahmad then got himself elected onto the FIFA executive committee, became vice-president of the International Handball Federation for good measure, and was instrumental in the successful election of Thomas Bach to the presidency of the IOC in 2012, and of Gianni Infantino to the presidency of FIFA in 2015.

Sheikh Ahmad's capacity to keep on the winning side in international sport politics seemed to desert him at home, as he flirted with opposition politicians, Salafists and tribal leaders, much to the annoyance of the Emir and his circle. He also made public accusations of support for Jihadi terrorism against senior members of the government, but they appeared baseless. He was then forced into a series of public humiliations, apologies and demotions. With him no longer at the centre of power, the government and its allies in parliament came for his sporting fiefdoms. Both the Ministry and parliament attacked him, and called for investigations into corrupt and unethical practice in Kuwaiti sports. They also passed legislation which gave the Minister of Youth and Sports the power to dissolve all the nation's sports organizations and establish new ones. For this transgression, the IOC and FIFA, as well as most other international sports federations, immediately suspended Kuwait from international competition. The Kuwaiti government took the case to the Court of Arbitration for Sport and lost, leaving the institutions and their officers intact. Sheikh Ahmad had managed to hang on.

Like so many other global sports barons, however, the fallout from the giant corruption scandals at FIFA would eventually seem to get him. In 2017, he was implicated in a range of corrupt practices in papers released after Richard Lai, a senior AFC official, had pleaded guilty to bribery to American investigators – a turn of events that saw Sheikh Ahmad both deny everything and withdraw from all his sporting sinecures, international and domestic. Withdrawal, however, is not the same as resignation, and after an indecent interval in which he skipped some IOC meetings and the limelight Sheikh Ahmad is, shamelessly, back on the global sports circuit. Needless to say, the state of Kuwaiti football hovers near an all-time low.[98]

The UAE, despite qualifying for the World Cup in 1990, began the century as a football backwater. The ruling houses in Abu Dhabi and Dubai, the Al-Nahyans and Al-Maktoums, had been the most sporting of the seven sheikhdoms that made up the UAE, but had traditionally preferred to invest in more reassuringly expensive sports like thoroughbred horse racing and powerboating. In the early twenty-first century, Dubai's government had added sports to the roster of post-industrial services – lightly regulated banking, tourism and logistics – that the enclave would specialize in. They built the first of the region's Sports Cities, and then Dubai persuaded the ICC (International Cricket Council) to move its headquarters from Lord's to the Gulf. Dubai also built one of the world's finest dedicated T20 cricket stadiums; it was amongst the busiest of the region's venues, regularly filled by the city's South Asian helots. The same could not be said for local football in Dubai, which struggled to attract crowds of four figures.

For the 1.4 million Emirate citizens (less than 20 per cent of the population), however, football and increasingly the European variety on television was the sport of choice. UAE president Sheikh Khalifa maintained an interest in Al Ain – both city and club – an ancient oasis city and ancestral home of the dynasty, but despite the team winning the Asian Champions League in 2003, both elite and popular interest in the domestic game remained minimal. The Gulf Cup of 2007, hosted by the UAE, would change this. For two weeks the stadiums were full and the nation was glued to its televisions, watching the progress of the team all the way to the final, in which they would beat Oman 1–0.

What followed was the single greatest public gathering and outburst of national emotion since the foundation of the state in 1971. Crowds, predominantly in cars, gathered on the roads around Abu Dhabi's World Trade Centre and proceeded in two vast caravans of dancing fans and honking horns to the Global Village shopping mall, where representatives of the Dubai Shopping Festival had extended opening hours and awaited the players. Received by the Emir in the royal palace the following day, the squad endured interminable speeches of praise and self-satisfaction, but at least they walked away with very substantial cash bonuses.[99] Recognizing the potential for a more sustainable local football, the government scrapped the old league and relaunched it in 2008 as a more professional operation, only to dissolve it and launch again in 2011. Either way, it has been a disappointing journey. The national team has come nowhere close to qualifying for anything. The league remains a very minor affair. Some of the younger princes took an interest – Al Jazira in Abu Dhabi was taken over by Sheikh Mansour and Al-Ahli in Dubai was the club of Sheikh Mohammed Maktoum – but in 2008, all these efforts were eclipsed when Abu Dhabi's Sheikh Mansour bought Manchester City for £200 million for the house of Al Nahyan.

As with other aspects of the UAE's engagement with the world, Dubai had set the pace. The city's airline Emirates first sponsored the Asian Football Confederation in 2002, added Arsenal's new stadium in 2004, and since then has picked up Olympiacos, AC Milan, Benfica, Hamburg and Real Madrid. However, they never took the step of actually buying the clubs. Abu Dhabi leapt ahead and so did Etihad, the airline of the UAE. Beginning of course with Manchester City and its stadium, the airline now sponsors the whole global network of clubs that City Football Group (Manchester City's holding company) has brought into the fold: big clubs in their leagues, like New York City FC, Melbourne FC and Yokohama Marinos, as well as small clubs in which to experiment with, train and loan players, like Spanish minnows Girona and the tiny Uruguayan outfit Club Atlético Torque.

If the UAE's football politics have a degree of opportunism and spontaneity to them, Qatar's approach has been very long planned and systematic. Sheikh Hamad bin Halifa Al Thani deposed his father as Emir in 1995 and for eighteen years, until his abdication in 2013, presided over a simply extraordinary accumulation of wealth. Smartly exploiting its gigantic gas reserves, by 2010 Qatar boasted the highest GDP per capita in the world. But as a tiny Gulf peninsula, geographically subaltern to Saudi Arabia and with just 200,000 citizens alongside 1.8 million foreign workers, money alone could never guarantee security. To this end, the Al Thanis have pursued a series of intersecting policies to raise Qatar's global profile. In 1991, during the First Gulf War, Qatar signed its first defence agreement with the United States, and liked it so much that a billion dollars was spent building a brand-new air base for them. Since 1996, Al Udeid Air Field Base has had up to 11,000 US personnel present and served as a major base during the Second Gulf War, as well as hosting a variety of bombing missions and other Western air forces fighting in Afghanistan and Syria. Alongside this, money has been poured into the media and arts: the Al-Jazeera news network, based in Doha but global in its reach, was generously funded, while Qatar's museums and galleries became amongst the leading purchasers of contemporary art.

Modern art works well for some audiences, but if you really want to put up some numbers, something else is required. For Qatar and Crown Prince Tamim Al Thani, Emir since 2013 but a key political player for more than a decade before, that something was sport in general and football in particular. As a first step, in 2003 the newly professionalized Q-League was launched, with $10 million allocated to each club. Not much in today's money, but enough at the time to attract the very best of the generation of players whose careers in Europe had come to an end: Argentine striker Gabriel Batistuta, World Cup winner Frank Leboeuf and the indefatigable German Stefan Effenberg. Where simple importation of foreign workers will not work, Qatar has actively explored all the options available for attracting and naturalizing sports people from elsewhere. This has proved particularly successful in athletics, where a couple of dozen leading Kenyan athletes were persuaded to take a Qatari passport. Football proved a harder environment, with FIFA long alert to this kind of dissimulation and reasonably active in policing it. An attempt to persuade three Brazilians, then playing in Germany, to sign up for the 2006 World Cup qualifying campaign was thwarted; not that the Qataris have given up, as the presence of numerous Algerian-Qataris in the national team in 2015 suggested.

Longer-term options have also been pursued. The scale of the operation is best grasped by just looking at the Aspire Academy in Doha. Opened in 2004, it is a multi-sport educational establishment, designed to nurture domestic and foreign sporting talent, the latter invariably qualifying for Qatari citizenship and international sporting duty by virtue of their length of stay in the country and the flexibility of the Qatari's own rules.[100] At its centre sits the Aspire tower, for a long time the tallest skyscraper in the country. Over 330m high, its flared conical form suggests a power station's cooling tower, topped with a neon torch, a combination that speaks to both the mass production of athletes and the sledgehammer aesthetics and ambition of the city. The Aspire dome next door is the largest indoor multi-sports venue in the world. Clustered around them are schools, sports science laboratories, exceptional medical facilities and practice fields of every kind, where the key work of the Academy happens. Since 2007, the national sporting agencies have reviewed the potential of every twelve-year-old Qatari for playing football; for those selected there is limitless support and resources.

However, given such a tiny population, the academy was always intended to be a global operation. Beginning in 2005, the Aspire Football Dreams programme has built a worldwide network of scouts and clubs, allowing it to find boys with potential across the developing world. The first trials were held in Africa, where the whole process was filmed and screened as a reality TV show on Al-Jazeera. The best players were offered generous scholarships in Qatar, with a view to naturalization at a later date. Since then, the academy claims to have reviewed over two million players in eighteen different countries.

The initial payback was nugatory. There was some progress shown by the national youth teams. The Q-League, or the Qatar Stars League as it is now known in brandspeak, is marginally better but no more popular. Women and therefore children do not attend. Qatari men remain indifferent to the point where one league game, live on television, really did appear to have just a single spectator in a stadium for 25,000. There is a huge reservoir of football fever amongst the expatriate workforce, evidenced by the crowds that showed up to watch Indonesia and Egypt play, but otherwise they are nowhere to be seen. Even the arrival of a player of the calibre of Xavi Hernandez in 2015 required migrant workers to be paid to go the stadium to welcome him. Indian workers were taught to chant songs in Arabic that they did not understand.[101] The only success on the field was the unlikely victory of Al-Sadd, which won the Asian Champions League in 2011, beating South Korean defending champions Jeonbuk Motors. It was a journey gilded by luck and hardly calculated to win friends. The team only entered the tournament after a Vietnamese club had been excluded for technical reasons. Their play was defensive and mean-spirited, and though they lost both legs of their quarter-final they still went through – the winning Iranian team Sepahan had a victory turned into a 3–0 defeat when it was revealed they had fielded an ineligible player, whereupon Al-Sadd went through on goal difference. The semi-final against Suwon Bluewings featured a great deal of time-wasting and gamesmanship. When the Qataris failed to return possession to the Koreans after the ball had been deliberately put out to attend to an Al-Sadd injury, the game descended into a brawl.[102] But as Qatar, recently awarded the 2022 World Cup, knew very well, an unpopular victory is still a victory.

All the attention lavished on the Q-League pales into insignificance compared to the resources devoted to the international wing of Qatar's football strategy. Slower off the mark than Emirates, and without a stable of clubs to back like the airline Etihad, the Qatar Foundation and then Qatar Airways have gone for quality, not quantity. In 2010, the former persuaded Barcelona to move on from UNICEF as their main shirt sponsors with a $30 million-a-season deal. More significantly, perhaps, 40 million viewers watched the Barcelona president announce the deal live on Al-Jazeera. The following year, Qatar Sports Investments bought the ailing Parisian club PSG, with which they have been conducting a steady and expensive assault on the heights of French and European football. When Emirates decided to end their relationship with FIFA at the end of 2014, it was Qatar Airways that took their spot.

Alongside sponsorship and overseas investments, Qatar has been the most active of the Gulf States in hosting international sporting events. There have been annual Qatari slots on the world tennis and European golf tours and the global volleyball, handball and motorbike racing circuits. Since 2000, Qatar has hosted world championships in table tennis, weightlifting, volleyball, indoor athletics, cycling road racing and, in 2015, the World Handball Championship, in which the hosts came second. Asian championships have included basketball and fencing, and the continent's major football tournament, the Asian Cup, in 2011. It is, in this context, hardly surprising that the country should have bid to host a football World Cup.

Hold off, if you can, on the bravado displayed by a nation of just 2.6 million, of whom only 300,000 are actually citizens, bidding to stage the world's greatest spectacular. Put to one side, for a moment, the audacity of a bid to host the World Cup in a Gulf summer, when daytime temperatures (in centigrade) are in the high forties, and the sheer front needed to suggest that this could be unproblematically accommodated by the application of air-cooling technologies as yet untested. Just consider the monumental scale of the preparations that Qatar promised. The price tag, impossible to really gauge, has been put at around $250 billion. It dwarfs the mere $40 billion spent by the Chinese on the 2008 Beijing Olympics, and even the $55 billion spent on Putin's Sochi Winter Olympics in 2014. The master plan envisages twelve World Cup stadiums, nine created from scratch plus three existing ones that will be entirely rebuilt. These, however, are just the televisual jewels sparkling atop an altogether bigger project.[103] The Lusail Iconic Stadium, enormous as it will be – a near 90,000-seat arena surrounded by a reflective circular pool of water and crossed by arching bridges – is merely the excuse for establishing an entirely new city in Qatar. Doha will not only receive four new stadiums, but also see the entirety of its downtown remodelled, its port rebuilt, and over a hundred hotels created. The Qataris are also embarking on a gigantic programme of transport investment to connect all of these new urban areas: a vastly expanded international airport in Doha has been completed, four-line underground metro systems for both Lusail and Doha are in progress, as is a countrywide high-speed rail network, linking every urban centre as well as planning to open a new route to Saudi Arabia and beyond.

The task of actually building these things has fallen to a vast army of migrant labourers, 40 per cent of whom come from Nepal, the rest from India, Sri Lanka, Pakistan and Bangladesh. Nearly all of them have been recruited by unscrupulous agents at home, to whom they incur huge debts at ruinous rates of interest, for the chance to go and die in Qatar on wages that turn out to be a fraction of what they have been promised. On arrival, they will have been introduced to the Emirate's *kafala* system, which binds them in legal vassalage to their sponsoring employer, without whose permission they can neither change job nor leave the country. Just to make sure their subservience is total, nearly all have had their passports and IDs illegally removed from them. This means that should they attempt to step out of the confines of their working lives, they will have to exist as illegal aliens in Qatar, a desperate prospect. Legal contracts, due process, legal representation and trade unions do not exist. Many workers have had wages deliberately withheld from them. As one desperate Bangladeshi put it, 'The company has kept two months' salary from each of us to stop us running away.'[104] Sometimes it appears to be done for the sake of sheer cruelty, as in the case of the French footballer Zahir Belounis who, after he had captained local team El-Jaish to a promotion, fell from favour and was marooned in Doha without wage or passports for two years.[105] He at least had a reasonable flat. The vast majority of workers have been surviving in the most appallingly squalid accommodation, living twelve to a room, all with a complete absence of adequate sanitation. Those that have tried to escape find themselves arrested or begging for food. As the Nepalese Ambassador to Qatar put it, the country was an 'open jail.'[106]

And this is before anyone has gone to work. There they are operating in temperatures of up to 50°C with only the most pathetic protective garments, and are regularly denied proper access to water and breaks, on shifts that can last twelve hours. And the world was worried about footballers playing for ninety minutes. Deaths are frequent, most often from strokes and heart attacks. In an effort to put some numbers on this carnage, the ITUC (International Trade Union Congress) asked the Nepali and Indian embassies, which count the returning corpses, how many Qatar had sent back over the previous three years. The answer was 1,239. Research commissioned by the Qataris themselves added another 600 Bangladeshis, bringing the total to more than 1,800, without including the other South Asians plus Filipinos and Egyptians also present in significant numbers. In high summer in 2015, with temperatures at extraordinary levels, the Nepalese Embassy was reporting a Nepali death almost every other day. Despite this avalanche of evidence, tangible human tragedy and international opprobrium, the response of the Qataris and FIFA has been a breathtaking combination of dissimulation, statistical quibbling and intransigence.

Neither the Qatari authorities nor their main foreign construction partners have been prepared to take a shred of responsibility for the situation, let alone display any degree of authentic contrition. All have sought to pass the buck downwards to the maze of subcontractors beneath them who organize the labour gangs, to whom the 'world-class' health-and-safety regulations that the Qatar authorities publish mean nothing. The Qataris have also responded by arguing that the rate of death is what would be expected at home, or might even represent an improvement, without acknowledging how the deaths are so obviously concentrated on the most intense and exposed World Cup projects.

Official promises to reform the *kafala* system proved laughable. The very worst of the insanitary accommodation has been improved upon. Simple wage theft has diminished, but otherwise nothing has changed. Given that FIFA exhausted what little leverage it had by shifting the date of the tournament to the winter of 2022, there was no pressure being exerted from Zurich, not that the organization has ever shown the remotest interest in or concern for the fate of the workers that build its global outposts. On these trends, we can expect the annual death toll of around 600 to remain unaltered. Indeed, in the frenzy to finish, it is likely to rise. Either way, and subject to how much extra time there is in 2022, there should be a death for every minute of football that is played.

In the summer of 2017, having seen off the human rights lobby and the international trade union movement, a threat to the 2022 World Cup came from a different direction. An alliance of eight countries led by Saudi Arabia (and including most of the Gulf states, as well as Egypt and Senegal) announced a series of boycotts and sanctions on Qatar, closed down border crossings and air space to its planes, and issued a series of political demands, including that it stop funding terrorism, close down Al-Jazeera, break its ties with Iran and in effect submit itself to perpetual Saudi suzerainty. The gargantuan hypocrisy of the Saudis telling anyone to stop funding terrorism need not detain us, for this was plainly a move in the wider struggle between Saudi Arabia and Iran for regional dominance, as well as an attempt to bring an upstart to heel. Amongst other indignities, the Saudis set up their own pirated national feed of the World Cup in 2018 and other international football, while closing down Qatar's beIN sports channel that actually owned the rights to these events. The Qataris, having negotiated alternative if expensive transport arrangements, made it clear that they would pay whatever price was necessary to complete the job. In Saudi Arabia and the UAE, wearing a Qatar national shirt or a Barcelona shirt with a Qatari sponsor became a criminal offence, punishable by both fines and long prison sentences.

Qatar responded with a global social media campaign fronted by friendly football stars – Xavi, Iker Casillas and the Dutch De Boer twins – tweeting for an end to the boycott. All of this was given a huge public airing in early 2019, when the Asian Cup was hosted by the UAE, who welcomed with gritted teeth amongst other guests both Saudi Arabia and Qatar. The Qataris had the delicious pleasure of not only breaking the boycott, for to have excluded them would have cost the UAE its place in global football, but also beating both the Saudis and Emirates on the way to the final, where they won the entire affair, beating Japan 3–1. An Englishman found wearing a Qatari shirt at one of their games was subsequently roughed up and arrested.

The boycott, at the time of writing, remains in place, and though Qatar's regional adversaries have been manoeuvring within FIFA to try to take at least some of the tournament away from the country, neither approach looks likely to dislodge its hold on the World Cup.[107] Indeed, one of the unintended consequences of the boycott was to decisively shift the calculus on workers' rights. More dependent than ever on global goodwill, the Qataris found themselves decrying the human rights abuses of Saudi Arabia and the UAE, while stalling on real reform of their own appalling labour regime. Thus, through late 2017 and early 2018, the Qataris committed, with the seal of approval of both the ITUC and the ILO (International Labour Organization), to an end to the *kafala* system and its replacement with transparent contractual and legal systems, a minimum wage, and improved healthcare and conditions of work and housing. As many human rights organizations noted, we have been here before, and seen bold declarations of change fail to materialize in Qatar, but there is now some hope that the annual rate of carnage might diminish. Sadly, in football, more often than not, hope will kill you too.

3

FROM THE LEFT WING: SOUTH AMERICAN *FÚTBOL* AND THE PINK TIDE

Let's Score a Goal for Twenty-First-Century Socialism!

Venezuelan government slogan for the
Copa América 2007

1

Pink has not, hitherto, been a football colour of the first rank. You can count on the fingers of one hand the clubs that play in shades of puce and peach. But then the South American left, whose recent advances have been referred to as a pink tide, have rarely put on the shirt, let alone scored a goal.[1] Argentina's Peronism, a unique amalgam of a progressive military junta and popular nationalism, was a generous sponsor of football and acclaimed in the stadiums of Buenos Aires in the 1940s and 1950s. São Paulo club Corinthians was, for a few years in the early 1980s, the epicentre of a democratization movement in Brazilian football and society. For the most part, however, and for most of the twentieth century, the left tended, and not without good reason, to see *fútbol* as mere bread and circuses. In doing so, of course, it left the field open to the right, who were only too happy to score a hatful of goals for their variety of unpleasant military dictatorships and post-junta governments. General Medici welcomed the Brazilian team that had won the 1970 World Cup to the Presidential Palace in Brasília, took hold of the trophy and began over a decade of direct government intervention in Brazilian football, from creating the first national league to militarizing coaching programmes and using national team games as rallies for its ersatz political party ARENA. The Argentinian generals revelled in staging and winning, by any means necessary, the 1978 World Cup. In a suitably Lilliputian version of this, Uruguay's beleaguered military rulers staged the 1980 *Mundialito* – the Little World Cup – ostensibly to celebrate Uruguay hosting and winning the first World Cup fifty years beforehand, but primarily to boost their chances of winning a referendum that would have legitimized their fragile hold on power. But in the twenty-first century, the right's long occupation of political office and the left's disdain for football have both come to an end.

The pink tide began in 1998, with Hugo Chávez's election to his first term as President of Venezuela, and swept across South

America, carrying leftists of one variety or another into power almost everywhere. In Uruguay, the Frente Amplio ('Broad Front') coalition won three consecutive presidencies – Tabaré Vázquez (twice) and Pepe Mujica – as well as controlling the legislature for over a decade. In Chile, socialist candidate Michelle Bachelet won two presidential terms. In Bolivia, Evo Morales and his MAS (Movement Towards Socialism) party have been in power since 2006, while in Ecuador, Rafael Correa's presidential election victory in 2007 inaugurated a decade of socialist rule. In Brazil, in 2002, at the fourth time of asking, Lula, founder and candidate of the PT (Partido Trabajdor or Workers' Party) finally came to power and, together with his hand-picked successor Dilma Rousseff, ruled the country until 2016. In Argentina, the Kirchners – a *Peronista* married-couple double-act, first Nestor, then Cristina – held the presidency from 2003 to 2015. Presidents Garcia and Humala brought a measure of Andean social democracy to Peru. Even in Paraguay, where historically the left has been at its weakest, President Lugo's term of office (2008–12) provided brief respite from the rule of the Colorados.[2] Only in Colombia was there no significant national victory for the left, though it acquired a significant presence in municipal government.

While there were considerable ideological and practical differences between these projects, they all sought to undo some of the damage wrought by a quarter-century of predominantly military rule, neo-liberal economics and austerity, and to shift the historical inequalities of power and status between men and women, and amongst the continent's diverse ethnic groups. There have been some considerable successes. Welfare reforms from Brazil's *Bolsa Familia*, Argentina's regularization of its huge informal labour market, Uruguay's multi-agency attack on extreme poverty and Bolivia's land reform have made real dents in the continent's staggering levels of inequality. The position of women and minorities has been advanced, from the introduction of same-sex marriages to the opening of Brazil's military to women. Indigenous rights and land reforms have been given constitutional and legal reality in Ecuador, Bolivia and Brazil. However, attempts to decisively shift the continent's position in the global economic order, and to reform the corrupt and clientelistic practices that had become the norms within and between government and big business, have proved harder nuts to crack.

Much of South America's new welfare state was funded by the

great commodities export boom of the era, driven by insatiable Chinese demand, and the taxes levied on the continent's hydrocarbon companies and industrial agriculture, like soya bean production. Nurturing domestic manufacturing and service industries that were nationally competitive, let alone globally, proved much harder, leaving 'pink tide' political projects vulnerable to the winds of global economic change, and the nations locked into unequal relationships with their buyers and creditors. South America's football has followed a very similar trajectory, in which the boom in European football has fed an insatiable demand for the continent's best players, reducing the domestic game to a state of subordination, where it has been kept by the incompetence and venality of its local economic and political masters. In this respect, football offers a masterclass in identifying the economic logics of globalization at work in South America and the local impediments to the progressive reforms that might take them on.

The continent's place in the global political economy of football is revealed by a few comparisons with Europe. In 2018, in by some way the best deal it had ever struck, CONMEBOL (the South American Football Confederation) sold the rights to the Copa Libertadores and its other club tournaments from 2019–22 for $350 million a year. That year, UEFA was already pulling in $2.75 billion a season for its competitions. Even allowing for Europe's larger population (740 million, including Russia, compared with South America's 420 million), this was four times per capita more than CONMEBOL could look forward to, and the gap is only going to widen. In the global market for football viewers and fans, Europe has long outstripped the continent. In the fifteen years of the Deloitte rich list, only one South American club, Flamengo, has appeared in its index of the top thirty richest teams in the world, and that was surely an error or an addition oblivious to the club's laughable balance sheets and galactic levels of debt. In 2005, Argentina's top twenty clubs shared around $320 million of income, just a shade less than Manchester United managed all by itself. In 2007, Chile's entire top league was turning over $40 million, enough that summer in the EPL to get you Darren Bent, an ageing Thierry Henry and change for the bus ride home, just about. As recently as 2015, Brazil's Campeonato secured a much improved $37 million a year for foreign TV rights to the league, yet just a single game in the EPL generates more income from overseas sales. Crudely put, if the European football industry is now worth something in the region of $25 billion, South America's is probably just 10 to 15 per cent of that.

Of course, the smaller and poorer domestic markets of South America account for the much lower incomes of its football clubs. There are, however, additional local circumstances that have made the gap even larger. In Europe, amongst big clubs, income broadly breaks down into three components: around half comes from media rights of one kind or another; a quarter from matchday revenues – tickets, banquets and booze; and a quarter from what are laughably called commercial revenues – as if the rest were acts of charity – that cover sponsorships and selling shirts and tat. Data from Latin America is more patchy, but overall it suggests that these three income streams, in about the same ratio to one another, account for just 60 per cent of a club's revenue; the rest comes from selling players.[3] Thus, as with the wider economy, Latin-American football is an export-driven business. In just the first six months of 2013, Latin America exported nearly 5,000 soccer players, in deals worth over $1.1 billion dollars. Argentina and Brazil alone accounted for 3,000 of them. To put this into some kind of economic perspective, the value of soccer exports from the region exceeds that from live animals. In Brazil, player sales bring in more than arms deals, in Ecuador more than tea and coffee exports, and in Peru more than cocoa. Uruguay, with a population of just three million people, exported over 1,400 players between 2000 and 2010.[4] The very best, and the majority from every national squad on the continent, are playing in Europe, but there are South Americans across the USA, in the Middle East and in East Asia. Brazilians can be found at clubs from the Faroe Islands to Australia.[5]

South American football is, at one level, exploiting its competitive advantages in the global football player market. It is wealthy and technologically sophisticated enough to possess global networks of scouts, agents and academies that facilitate the export of its players. Long-established historic links within key markets, especially Portugal and Spain, have provided important bridgeheads into the rest of the world. At home, the game continues to be utterly dominant in a virtually monocultural sportscape, and can draw on a deep pool of potential players from backgrounds sufficiently poor to ensure fearsome competition and dedication. Once they are found, there is sufficient human capital in the shape of a deep and sophisticated coaching culture to develop them for the global market, although no club or national association has facilities that can compare to Europe's best. In comparison with Africa, the world's other great exporting continent, South America is doing better, extracting better terms of trade in the market, and retaining a domestic football scene that, although diminished, is sufficient to retain the loyalty of local fans. But, given the many competitive disadvantages that South American football has acquired, it is hard to see the gap with Europe closing, or the level of dependence diminishing.

South American football has been underselling its media rights for decades. First, football associations and leagues have, hitherto, proved very poor negotiators, rarely aware of the real market value of their product. Globo in Brazil and TyC in Argentina have run rings around their sporting counterparts and worked hard to exclude potential competitors. Clubs have, at times, attempted to use their collective power to force better deals from the TV companies, but they have been picked off by the broadcasters, who have cut deals with the biggest clubs to the detriment of the small ones, and indeed the collective good. Second, even when administrators have been aware of the value of their organizations' rights, they have proved far more interested in the value of their kickbacks and commissions for allocating those rights to media companies, a direct and significant tithe on football's income. Third, despite having paid considerable bribes as well as actual fees to obtain the rights to local football, South American broadcasters have proved curiously indifferent to exploiting their real value. Globo virtually gave away the international rights to the Brazilian championship and continued to privilege its more lucrative telenovelas in its scheduling.[6]

While the top leagues in Europe are close to capacity, and even middling leagues can make significant money from their matchday receipts, attendances across South America have been falling, and the crowds that remain will not spend more money. In part, this is a consequence of the quality of football on offer declining each year, as the export industry drains all the talent away. In part, it is a consequence of the barras – the organized fan gangs – who have simultaneously saved local football from the ravages of globalization and locked it into a cycle of decline. On the one hand, they have provided an enduringly powerful spectacle in the stadium, whatever the quality of football, but their control of both the stadium space and many of its ancillary facilities (catering and parking for example) has made conventional European routes to gentrification, or at least rational commercialization, impossible. Even if it were possible, the region's clubs, with the exception of Boca Juniors, are very late to the game of global branding and cannot make the kind of money from shirt sales that Real Madrid or Bayern Munich can achieve in the world market. Meanwhile, at home, counterfeit goods are rife in markets in which very few can afford the official prices for official shirts. By contrast, the national associations of Brazil and Argentina, by virtue of their huge deals with Nike and Adidas respectively, have been able to sequester the contemporary profits generated from shirts made global icons by previous generations. They may not have spent very much of their cut on the grassroots of the game, but at least they held on to it. Much of the money that the continent's clubs have apparently earned from the vast exodus of players has gone elsewhere: to agents, of course, to family members under the table; to club officials taking their cut; in some clubs to the *barras bravas* who have similar arrangements; and to investors who have previously bought all or some of a player's transfer rights. Third-party ownership is the name given to this kind of modern-day indentured labour and, although banned by FIFA in 2015, it has proved particularly popular in South America, where desperately indebted clubs have been prepared to trade future profits for immediate liquidity, regularly underselling players. With elected presidents and boards offering access to immense local cultural and political capital, clubs are simply not run as profit-maximizing or even loss-minimizing utilities. As Julio Grondona, the late President of the Argentinian Football Association put it, 'Football is sport, economics and passion. Unfortunately, the passion comes first.' The consequences of that hierarchy of priorities is a permanent state of debt.[7]

Debt was surely the keynote of Argentinian football at the turn of the century. Racing Club was the first big club to be declared truly and irrevocably bankrupt, and was only saved by the passage of a specific law that allowed it to continue playing and in effect be taken over by a private company. Thanks to this kind of political and financial engineering, Racing actually won the title in 2001, at precisely the moment that the rest of the country was going to have to face the real consequences of Argentina's accumulated national debt. The government chose to default on its payments, leading to the country's exclusion from international capital markets, widespread capital flight and a massive devaluation of the peso. Much of the value of the country's savings was lost but borrowers, like football clubs, saw the ensuing inflation eat away at their debt. Better still, the government allowed the clubs to bank their transfer income in dollars, now worth considerably more at home. Even under these circumstances, they all lost money, and banks have steered clear of supporting them with overdrafts and loans. Consequently they, like clubs all over South America, have accumulated debt with either the government, by failing to pay income and employment taxes, or their own staff, who they have failed to pay. The scale and frequency of player strikes over unpaid wages in Peru, Bolivia and Ecuador, where they are virtually annual occurrences, is testament to the latter.[8] Despite the largesse accorded them in 2002, the $80 million owed in back social security taxes by Argentinian clubs to the government just seven years later is testament to the former. By 2015, the debt had grown to over $300 million. In Chile, the biggest clubs, Colo-Colo and Universidad de Chile, were declared bankrupt. By 2007, the situation was so out of hand in Brazil that the government created a new lottery, based on football results, with the clubs' payments for their image rights ring-fenced to pay off their social security back taxes. Despite this, in 2013, professional football owed the Brazilian treasury a staggering $2.1 billion.[9]

Thus the money that does come into football clubs, however many players they sell, has never been enough to put these already indebted institutions on a sustainable financial path. It is now not enough to attract and retain teams that are more than a combination of the young, the old and the going nowhere. In 2018, *Más Unidos Que Nunca* ('More United Than Ever'), a radical breakaway from the Uruguayan players' union, issued a manifesto in support of its strike for unpaid wages. It can stand proxy for the condition of most of the continent's football.

> Our football finds itself submerged in a perverse system that in general benefits and enriches a few, is not transparent, does not have adequate contracts, has a club infrastructure in dreadful conditions, does not carry out an audit of management, and continues to allow sporting institutions of dubious solvency to negotiate and receive money which does not always reach the players.[10]

Such clarity and honesty are rare, perhaps absent, amongst South America's football administrators and power-brokers. Thus we begin our survey of the continent amongst those who actually play the game, and who in their different ways have been mobilizing and organizing to challenge the status quo and its inequalities of class, gender and ethnicity. They range from players' unions fighting for a living wage to the feminist football leagues of Buenos Aires's *barrios* to the transformatory impact of Ecuador's now overwhelmingly Afro-Ecuadorian national team. The *barras bravas*, by contrast, have spent their time entrenching the status quo, apart from decisively linking the game to the global drugs industry (although in Colombia this relationship is longstanding). This has been a not-inconsiderable factor in explaining the unbelievable scale of homicides in South American football, and the difficulty of reforming its accounting practices and curbing its penumbra of violence and menace.

We then turn from these social movements to the state-led programmes of change in politics and football. First, to the new-left populists of Venezuela and Bolivia, who have materially and symbolically invested in the game in search of international recognition and domestic legitimacy. Second, to the Kirchners' contemporary version of Peronism, which went a stage further and actually nationalized professional football's media rights. Third, to Brazil, where the staging of the 2014 World Cup was meant to be a consecration of both Brazil's and the continent's successful leftist turn, but instead proved to be an autopsy. Fourth, we review the years since the 2014 World Cup and the turning of the pink tide. The impeachment of Dilma and presidential victories for the right in Argentina, Brazil, Ecuador and Chile have changed the continent's complexion. In Venezuela and Bolivia, Maduro and Morales have struggled to maintain their holds on power, Maduro, in particular, resorting to authoritarian measures to do so. In Argentina, the change in political climate has been accompanied by a serious programme of neo-liberal reform in football led by President Mauricio Macri. But the left and its relationship with South American football is not quite finished. Uruguay's Frente Amplio has maintained its hold on power and, miraculously, the country has retained its place amongst the leading international football nations. In Colombia, football has found a place in the nation's fitful movement towards peace, while in Chile, the bravado of the national team helped catalyse and sustain the Chilean youth uprising. Over a whole season, and given the strength and prolific scoring of the right, these developments might have not been anywhere near enough to sustain the pink tide indefinitely, but football has at least broken its streak and scored a few goals for twenty-first-century socialism.

II

The last decade has seen an unprecedented level of union organization and strike action by South American players. Driving much of the unions' work is the perennial problem of late and very late pay. Bolivian players, for example, struck on the eve of the 2010, 2012 and 2016 seasons to secure the previous season's wages.[11] Ecuadorian players did the same in 2015 and forced the federation to remove a statute that had enshrined the right of clubs to pay late.[12] In Argentina, the resolution of national player strikes in 2009 and 2017 over unpaid wages required government intervention. For every national strike there have been dozens of sit-downs, go-slows, refusals to train and walk-outs during games at individual clubs who have failed to pay up. In 2011, leading Colombian clubs Deportes Quindio and Once Caldas were forced to field their youth teams mid-season while their professional squads struck for their long-missing wage packets.[13] In 2013, with their salaries seven months in arrears, the players at Colón de Santa Fe refused to play their home game against Atlético Rafaela, resulting in a Molotov cocktail attack on the chairman's house, a small riot at the club's offices and the words 'piece of shit traitor' daubed all over the house of star player Iván Moreno.[14] A small but telling example of the degree to which football players are subject to threats of violence on the pitch, in the street and at their local grounds, from the police, vengeful fans and their opponents – a point made by Peru's players' union to their national federation in 2015, when Alianza Lima players were publicly beaten by their own fans after losing a Copa Libertadores game at home.[15]

As well as looking after their own interests, unions have been broadening their agendas.[16] In 2009, 500 players sent a letter of collective resignation to the Peruvian football federation, refusing to be called up for the national team unless a wide-ranging programme of reforms set out in the document was enacted. This included strict sanctions on clubs that failed to pay players and employment protection for coaches. In addition, noting the lamentable state of Peruvian football and the run of nine straight defeats suffered by the men's national team, the players called for investment in schools and youth football (non-existent outside Lima) and money for training youth coaches. The players came away with their wages and a ban on midday kick-offs in the blazing sun, but they were back striking again at the start of the 2012 season, when players were once again waiting three to six months for money at the majority of the leading clubs, campaigning for changes in the governance of the game. Despite resistance from the football federation, the players' union managed to persuade the Congress of the Republic to pass special legislation rewriting the federation's constitution and giving one-third of the votes in its decision-making assembly to players – a formal position of power that no other national body of footballers could claim.[17] A similar radicalization could be seen in Brazil, where towards the end of the 2013 season dozens and dozens of games began with acts of defiance – ten minutes of aimless passing or a sit-down in the centre circle – organized by FC Bom Senso ('FC Common Sense').[18] Founded by a few senior players in the league, this group quickly attracted 1,000 members and called for the insanity of the Brazilian football timetable to be reformed (the players were, at the time, being offered only a one-week holiday between the 2013 and 2014 seasons), clubs to pay wages still owing, and for the CBF (Brazilian Football Federation) to accept both financial transparency and a players' representative on the board. Initially rocked by the protests, the CBF and the clubs stalled and waited for the movement's energy to dissipate. By 2016, FC Bom Senso had closed down.

The greatest and most effective display of player power came in Uruguay, where the rule of Paco Casal was significantly checked, if not terminated, by the national team.[19] Casal made his first fortune as Uruguay's super-agent in the 1980s and 1990s, brokering the careers and the transfers of the leading players like Enzo Francescoli and Nelson Gutiérrez. Together with these two national stars, he founded the media company Tenfield in 1998 and made his second fortune. His opening move was to win the TV rights of the Uruguayan League, despite being outbid by more than $32 million. His key ally in making the 'case' for Tenfield and the kinds of 'added value' it would bring to the game was second-hand car salesman and President of the Uruguayan Football Association (AUF) Eugenio Figueredo. Tenfield would go on to pick up the national team's marketing rights too, for what was obviously a pittance. Casal's companies held those rights for almost two decades, helping lock Uruguayan domestic football into a permanent state of underdevelopment, while Tenfield whisked players to Europe and leached value from the national team and league.

Casal built his empire in an era dominated by Uruguay's old political parties and political methods. In 1999, for the first time, the left-wing coalition Frente Amplio took power. It has remained there ever since, growing in strength and confidence, and has begun an arduous process of reform. First, the government chased Figueredo out of Uruguayan football, though he merely decamped to the infinitely more profitable sinecure of a CONMEBOL vice-presidency. It also called for an end to third-party player ownership – a Tenfield favourite – and even initiated a major tax investigation into Casal. Initially, Casal saw the challenges off. He helped engineer the resignation of Figueredo's less pliant successor Sebastián Bauzá, the ministers who wanted to regulate player transfers lost their jobs, and in 2013 President Pepe Mujica called off the tax case against him.[20]

Perhaps he thought he was invulnerable? In 2016, the national team's marketing rights were up for auction. It was assumed that the pathetic offer of just three-quarters of a million dollars a year from Tenfield would be a shoo-in. Even the appearance of a bid from Nike worth at least four times as much did not seem to change the odds. Then Diego Godín, captain of the national team, posted an open letter on his personal website calling for AUF to do the right thing and take the Nike bid. He was soon joined in a massive chorus of live and online support from the rest of the squad.[21] In a board meeting as tense as a penalty shoot-out, the board of AUF voted 10–9 to forgo Casal's special 'added value' and take Nike's old-fashioned money. This defeat for Casal was underlined by Tenfield's loss of the team's broadcast rights later in the year.

If the balance between labour and capital has shifted marginally in favour of the former in twenty-first-century South American football, the balance between women and men has barely moved. As Dilma Rousseff, Cristina Kirchner and Michelle Bachelet demonstrated, it was easier for a woman to become the president of the country than the president of the national football federation. In 2016, there was not a single woman on the board of any CONME-BOL football association, let alone in the top job. Indeed, nowhere is the gap between men's and women's football so wide.[22] In 2016, Chile beat Argentina in the men's Copa América, and the two were placed fifth and first in the FIFA world rankings. At the same time, both their women's national teams were declared inactive, not having played official matches for over two years. Chile's newspapers failed to mention this fact, despite an inordinate amount of space devoted to the development of a sandwich named in honour of defender Gonzalo Jara. Even where teams were active, they were often short-lived and assembled only for tournament duty. If they did get it together, there was no guarantee that anyone would see them. The TV rights to Copa América Feminina 2014 were available for free, but not a single channel picked them up.

Despite widespread official indifference, women's football has, since the turn of the century, grown at the grassroots, and falteringly established itself at an elite level too. Brazil, Uruguay and Argentina were the first to establish women's leagues, while Ecuador, Colombia and Chile have all acquired national championships in the second decade of the century. Describing these leagues as professional, how-ever, requires some imagination. Many clubs with women's teams, even wealthy ones like River Plate, offer no medical insurance to their players. The players have to pay for this themselves, from earnings of around $40 a week, which is around 1/200th of the average wage in the men's team. In Chile, female players have complained of having to pay their own transfer fees and transport costs. Women's teams often eat separately from the men, and are given inferior fare or hand-me-down kits. At some clubs, boys' teams are given pitch-time precedence over adult women. The real state of affairs was laid bare at Brazilian club Santos, which closed down its women's team in 2011 to enable it to afford Neymar's wages.[23]

Against the odds, the continent, Brazil in particular, has pro-duced a steady stream of brilliant women's players, most notably Marta Vieira da Silva, who was FIFA player of the year for five con-secutive years (2006–10). But as with any other gifted Brazilian players, her career has been spent overseas. In 2016, Daniuska Rod-ríguez's sublime dribbling and curving shot at goal for Venezuela's under-17s in a game against Columbia was the first by a woman to be shortlisted for FIFA's goal of the year award.[24] Ecuador's Vanessa Arauz was the youngest coach ever at a World Cup. But the Ecuadorians, like the rest of the continent's teams, were out by the quarter-finals of the 2015 Women's World Cup. In part, this has been a matter of scant resources in already poor football cultures, though matters would have improved no end if any of the FIFA money earmarked for women's football on the continent had actually been spent on the game.

Things reached a new nadir in 2015, when most of South America's women teams had been removed from the FIFA rankings as their federations had stopped scheduling matches altogether. In Brazil, in 2017, the dismissal of Emily Lima, the first women's coach of the women's national team, triggered a series of high-profile protest retirements from the squad and the creation of a network of women players to pressure the CBF for reform. The CBF obliged, creating a committee of investigation but, as with the saga of the female head coach no sooner appointed than dismissed, they then disbanded the committee a few months later. In Argentina, the squad went on strike when even the paltry $10 day stipend the players had been promised failed to appear. Even when it did, it hardly covered their costs. As one of the team, a leading player at Boca Juniors on a monthly salary of $150, said, 'I have to get a gym membership to stay competitive, eat a decent breakfast, pay for boots and if my whole family didn't contribute to helping me live my dream, I would have had to quit years ago.'

Perhaps, as this generation of women players gets organized, a real shift in the status of the game has begun. In Chile, the new women's union contemplated going it alone, but found an active supporter in the men's players' union, with which it eventually merged, creating enough clout to get the Chilean FA to fund its women's teams and even to stage the Copa América Feminina in 2018.[25] The tournament was, finally, actually televised and, though it was banished from Santiago to the north-west, attendances were impressive. Even the general secretary of the Chilean federation had to admit, 'Despite assumptions that the Cup would generate little interest, the experience has proven quite the opposite.'[26]

As the fate of women referees in the men's game suggests, however, something more than just economic inequality is at work: good old-fashioned sexism is present too. In keeping with almost every football culture, the Latin American game has been a masculine space for over a century, but one inflected with its own regional version of patriarchy. *Machismo* is a blend of brutal swaggering misogyny and thinly disguised violence that frames all women with Catholicism's Madonna/whore complex, the combination of which has rendered the idea of women in football as unnatural, immoral and socially dangerous. Thus, in the late 1990s, the Argentinian football establishment was so implacable and indifferent to the demands of Florencia Romano that she was forced to go on hunger strike in her campaign to break into refereeing men's football in Argentina. She has been followed by just a handful of women in the last twenty years, all of whom have endured physical and verbal abuse from officials, fans and players along the way. Peruvian official Melany Bermejo reported being spat on, shoved and given a player's phone number when making a booking.[27] Her continuing presence at the highest level of the game is a standing rebuke to the institutional machismo of football, but she and other pioneers remain no more than that; after all, football is sufficiently tone-deaf to these issues that many people in the Brazilian game welcomed back goalkeeper Bruno after he had served just seven years of a twenty-two-year sentence for ordering the contract killing of his ex-partner and mother of his child.[28]

As might be expected with a continent whose demographics have been shaped by European conquest, the near genocide of the indigenous population, the massive importation of African slaves, and new waves of European migration during the industrialization of the late nineteenth and early twentieth centuries, issues of race, nation and citizenship have never been absent from South American football. In Brazil, for example, the white urban upper classes who first played the game initially refused to face Afro-Brazilians and teams that fielded them, while they were kept out of the national team by presidential fiat. After Brazil's dazzling display at the 1938 World Cup, led by Afro-Brazilian stars like Leonidas, football became a way of expressing a new Afro-European hybrid identity for the nation. But while football has offered a modicum of integration and a small presence in national life for minorities, the reality for South America's indigenous peoples and those of African descent has been systemic economic and social inequality, and almost complete absence from national narratives and dominant imagery, as well as everyday racism and exclusion. Football crowds have long racially abused dark-skinned players and officials, and football institutions have, for the most part, been entirely indifferent. The latter, at least, have begun to change as players, players' unions and anti-racist and human rights campaigners have begun to protest. Pressured by both the more racially sensitive governments of the pink tide and FIFA, local football associations have, since around 2014, finally begun to fine clubs for serious acts of racism.

Football, nonetheless, has offered a dispiriting tableau of popular attitudes to ethnicity. Grêmio, a club in southern Brazil, who ran a major anti-racism campaign with their old Afro-Brazilian star, Ze Roberto, were repeatedly fined when their fans racially abused Afro-Brazilian players at Internacional and Santos. Esportivo were forced to play five games away from home after their crowd made monkey chants at a black referee, vandalized his car and covered it with bananas. Tinga, a player with Cruzeiro, received similar treatment when playing away in the Copa Libertadores at Peru's Real Garcilaso.[29] Peruvian fans have proved vicious. When Real Garcilaso's striker Jhoel Herrera brought his mother to watch him play against Cienciano on Mother's Day, the away fans subjected him to ninety minutes of racial abuse. His already strained post-match interview was abruptly terminated as he headed off into the stands to try and protect his mother, then being abused by the same people. The same ones, presumably, who at home abused the Afro-Panamanian striker Luis Tejada until, seventy minutes into the game, he walked off. 'I couldn't take it any more,' he said. 'I could see that no one was doing anything.'[30] The Afro-Venezuelan Emilio Rentería, playing for San Marcos de Arica in Chile, was seen on television in tears leaving a game under similar circumstances.[31] Given its rich ethnic mix, Argentinian football can boast a long history of all kinds of ethnic prejudice. Black Brazilians and Afro-Uruguayans have been the subjects of racial epithets, in the press and in the stadiums, since the 1920s.[32] These kinds of attitudes are certainly not confined to the terraces. In 2014, Argentinian commentator Alberto Raimundi described the Colombian Teófilo Gutiérrez, on air, as a *negro de mierda* ('black shit'), while the Peruvian Phillip Butters said of Felipe Caicedo, an Afro-Ecuadorian player, that a DNA test would show he was 'not a human, but a monkey, a gorilla', and of Afro-Ecuadorians in general that 'if the players bite you, you'd get Ebola.'[33]

What you actually get from Afro-Ecuadorian footballers is talent, grit, skill and success, features sorely lacking from Ecuadorian football before their arrival. Indeed, the best that could be said of the game was that it wasn't as bad as Venezuela's, but only just. Politics wasn't much better: between 1996 and 2000, Ecuador went through a prolonged inflationary crisis and five presidents. The volatility of the situation was neatly illustrated by the shooting of national team coach Hernan Gomez after he refused to put an ex-president's son in the national junior team. Two more short-lived presidents would follow, before the election of Socialist candidate Rafael Correa in 2006. He would serve three terms before handing on the office to his deputy.

It was in this context that the increasingly good performances of the Ecuadorian national team, which qualified for the World Cup in 2002, 2006 and 2014, as well as those of its best clubs, like LDU Quito, which won the Copa Libertadores in 2008, were being celebrated as expressions of a new Ecuador. Quite what was being expressed has been a matter of debate. The singular most important fact about the Ecuadorian national team is the significant presence of Afro-Ecuadorians.[34] The descendants of slaves imported by the Jesuits in the sixteenth century, they constitute just 7 per cent of the population, but the players themselves are even more concentrated in two locations: the Chota Valley in northern Ecuador, which has just 0.2 per cent of the country's population, and the province of Esmeraldas in the north-east, which has 3 per cent. The former is a desperately poor collection of villages and sharecroppers eking out a living in the Andes, the latter the nation's only black majority province, in which three-quarters of the population are living in poverty and where the three million people and their thirty-seven football clubs share just five poorly maintained soccer fields. Yet seven of the twenty-three members of the 2002 World Cup squad came from El Chota, including stars like Agustín Delgado, Édison Méndez and Ulises de la Cruz. When LDU Quito won the Copa Libertadores in 2008, more than a third of the team came from the valley. At the 2014 World Cup, it was the turn of Esmeraldas, which supplied ten of the twenty-three players, all of them Afro-Ecuadorian. Even so, the Chota Valley supplied another seven members of the squad. By contrast, there was not one player from the overwhelmingly white and mestizo capital Quito.

Football has been played in these zones for almost a century, but their poverty, remoteness and blackness made them inaccessible or unappealing to Ecuadorian clubs and their white and mestizo coaches, and this only changed with the appointment of a Montenegrin, Dušan Drašković, as national team coach. In the late 1990s, he conducted a massive scouting sweep through every region of the country, including Esmeraldas and the Chota Valley. 'I drove myself with the aim of discovering new talents in every corner of the country: kids without clubs, playing on the streets, who had never stepped on a proper pitch with goalposts and referees.'[35]

Hitherto, Afro-Ecuadorians had been written out of the country's football history and national identity. Now their presence could not be avoided. White Ecuadorians swung between two poles. Some headed down the usual tracks of racialized biology, arguing that Afro-Ecuadorians were genetically predisposed to succeed in sport. A different tack was taken by commentators who tried to make the players' blackness invisible, arguing that the team was illustrative of a level playing field and a meritocratic society in which patronage and nepotism did not apply and categories and division like class or ethnicity were irrelevant. That must have gone down well in Esmeraldas and Chota, where the population, like Afro-Ecuadorians everywhere, endured lower wages, shorter lives, poorer health care, higher unemployment and less food than white, mestizo or indigenous Ecuadorians. It certainly would have been news to the players who had endured decades of monkey chanting in the stadiums, the perpetrators of which have never been properly held to account. As Alexandra Ocles, an Afro-Ecuadorian activist, argued amid the euphoria of the 2006 World Cup:

> Did you read the newspapers? There are news, shouts, commentaries: 'golden blacks'; 'Blacks are the best of the Tri'; 'Beautiful black men'; and others like this: 'how strong the black players are.' Everything is part of the euphoria of the moment. What would have happened if we had lost these two matches? Maybe racism would have emerged again and we could have heard calls for the whitening of the team, as was the case a few years ago. What doesn't change is the reality that Afro-descendants face in Ecuador: for many, we continue to be the thieves, the social predators, the prostitutes, or the simple domestic employees.

What doesn't change is that my daughter doesn't want to be black any more because it causes her too many problems in school.[36]

Despite a decade of leftist populism, and three appearances at the World Cup, white and mestizo Ecuador has yet to fully incorporate its indigenous or African populations into the national narrative, or to share the national wealth with them, but the challenges keep coming. Agustín Delgado, the top scorer for the national team, has acquired a post-football political career, having been elected to the national assembly for the Socialist Party, and has been the target of vicious racist cartoons for his troubles.[37] Indigenous Ecuadorians have staked their place in the football nation with the creation of their own team, Mushuc Runa SC, which has reached the top division. In Ecuador, football continues to offer the promise that on the right day, the world can be turned upside down. Independiente del Valle, a tiny team from the Quito suburbs with a stadium holding just 8,000, made it all the way to the final of the Copa Libertadores in 2016.[38] As Ecuador's fans chant to the national teams, knowing the odds are always against them, 'Si se suede'. Yes you can.

III

Uruguayans, even before the legalization of recreational marijuana, liked to describe the local vibe as 'Supertranqui', and the country's crime rates, though hardly Swedish, were amongst the lowest in Latin America. Yet, in the space of just one month in late 2016, Uruguayan football was the site of the most extraordinary acts of violence and disorder. First, Peñarol supporters shot three Nacional fans, in the provincial city of Canelones, in broad daylight. Then, mid-way through the first half of a game between Peñarol and Rampla Juniors, with Rampla one up, a man was repeatedly shot in the arms and legs in the toilets of the Estadio Centenario. A few weeks later, ticketless fans of Peñarol stormed the same stadium before their derby game with Nacional. They began by ransacking the food and beer stalls, before a massive brawl broke out with the police, who brought in horses, dogs and the riot squad. The Peñarol supporters responded with a fusillade of camping gas canisters hurled from the stadium's upper tiers. Outside the stadium, fans fought with the police all over downtown Montevideo, stoning cars and smashing windows.[39]

It was a miracle that no one was killed that day, but miracles are rare. These kinds of events, played out innumerable times across the continent's football stadiums, have, since the turn of the century, resulted in over 250 homicides: more than the rest of the football world put together.[40] Argentina, which saw seventy football-related homicides in the 1990s, has suffered more than a hundred since. Brazil adds another hundred or so. Colombia, despite the diminishing influence of the drug cartels, has seen thirty-two deaths, eleven in a spectacularly violent nine-month period in 2013. Ecuador, Uruguay and Peru together account for twenty murders between them. Since 2007, Ecuador has seen fans shot on their way to the stadium and while inside it, killed by flares, stab wounds or falling out of high tiers of the stands; so too in Peru where, in 2011, Walter Oyarce, a fan of Alianza Lima, was thrown from an upper terrace by Universitario fans and fell to his death.[41] Even Chile, with the lowest murder rate on the continent, saw a triple homicide in 2014, when Colo-Colo fans stabbed three supporters of Universidad de Chile.[42] Of course, these are just the most bloody specks in a huge canvas of violent acts that range from pitch invasions by supporters unhappy with their team's performance or the outcome of a match to attacks on police, players and officials during games and outside the stadium as well, not to mention fights between groups of supporters of different clubs, fights amongst supporters of the same club, as well as brawls, stabbings and shootings in bars and public places during or after games.

At one level, none of this should be too surprising, since Latin America has a pervasive problem with homicides. With just 8 per cent of the world's population, it is the site of one-third of its murders. The victims are, like the football crowds, overwhelmingly young urban men.[43] As with other countries with similar murder rates, massive inequalities, toxic forms of masculinity, the widespread availability of weapons and poor policing account for some of the region's problems, but what distinguishes Latin America and its football cultures and makes them so lethal is their intersection with the global drugs trade. Despite nearly half a century of the war on drugs, the concerted use of military and penal force has failed to eradicate the trade. Indeed, it is not clear that all this effort has even minimized its growth, let alone justified the devastating economic and social consequences of the region's militarization and abuse of human rights. In the last two decades, since the break-up of Colombia's main cartels, the industry has simply become more fragmented and more widespread. New routes from the main coca- and marijuana-growing zones in the Andes, Paraguay and Brazil are now flowing all across the continent, then heading north through Central America and the Caribbean to the United States, and through Argentina and Uruguay to Africa and Europe. Wherever it operates, the drug trade buys, shapes and corrupts the institutions that it touches, from the judiciary to the police to politics. Football is no different. Indeed, because of the global nature of the industry, and its fabulously opaque mode of operation, it has proved particularly attractive to *los narcotraficantes*. Cartel members have directly bought into clubs as a form of social prestige, but, above all, they are instruments of money-laundering.[44] The most pervasive connection between the drugs trade and football, however, are the *barras bravas* – the organized fans who have occupied the stands behind South America's goals for almost forty years, even longer in Brazil, where they are known as the *Torcidas Organizadas*.

The *barras* first emerged in Argentina in the 1950s and 1960s and have provided the model, institutionally and temperamentally, for organized football fandom across Latin America. At the core of the phenomenon are a series of hidden transactions between the *barras* and the directors of the clubs they support. The *barras* supply colour, atmosphere, flags, smoke bombs and *aguante* (backbone) in the stadiums. In return, they receive large numbers of tickets, some for themselves and many for lucrative re-sale. Directors have also found the *barras* useful when club election time has come around, as voters and more creatively as political muscle. Recalcitrant coaches and players have also been dealt with by visits from the *barras*. The quid pro quo for this kind of work has been an extension of their domain from the terraces to control of the parking business around the stadium on match day, a cut from the concession booths, drug sales in the stands, and shadow jobs and sinecures within the club itself. All these transactions are, of course, illegal, but the police and judiciaries have been indifferent to them at best, complicit at worst. Indeed, there is protection for the *barras* right the way up the political system. An already volatile and violent situation in the 1990s has been made steadily worse by the arrival of the international drugs trade in Argentina and Uruguay especially, and the role of the *barras bravas* in transporting and selling the products. Consequently, the looser gang structures of the twentieth century have given way to the conventional authoritarian pyramids of organized crime: street fights and knife fights are giving way to drive-by shootings.

Perhaps the clearest account of the internal structures of the *barras bravas* was given by Rafael Peña, head of security at the Uruguayan football association, who told the national parliament that the *barras* at Peñarol 'have transformed themselves into true cartels that even fight for control of territory and the criminal activity they are involved in.'[45] At the top was a small circle of around a dozen bosses, responsible for dealing with the club, the police and other narco-traffickers, as well as directing illegal operations. The fifty or so lieutenants below them were the core organizers of the group's criminal activities – drug running, selling and control of match day – and earned a small living from their work. Below them were 400 soldiers who, in exchange for tickets and weed, were responsible for the flags, singing, music and security operations inside the stadium. On the fringes, another few hundred candidate members were attached to the group, hoping to gain access to the core and its various privileges. The accounts of Peñarol's *barras* were not available, but Argentinian investigator Gustavo Grabia claimed that Boca's main *barra*, *La Doce*, could bring in $100,000 a game, and that was only a fraction of its income.[46] The most powerful of the groups were able to collect a 30 per cent levy on club transfer fees and 20 per cent on players' wages, as well as engaging in drug-running and money-laundering. For the small circle of leaders at the top of the organization, this amounted to a very handsome weekly salary, and with this kind of money at stake, and the intensely personal and charismatic character of authority within the *barras*, division and infighting has become more frequent and violent. Conflicts like these at River, Boca, Chacarita Juniors and Newell's Old Boys have added to the death toll.[47]

Now almost half a century old, many of these groups have undergone a kind of rationalization, not only in the sense that the system has become more obviously organized and hierarchical, but also that the emotional and identity-driven quality of football support that at first truly sustained the *barras* has become nothing but a convenient carapace for the rational accumulation of power and wealth. Jon Sistiaga, an Argentinian reporter, wrote of the upper echelons, 'I have not encountered a single member of a *barras bravas* who is capable of naming the complete line-up of their team.' Meanwhile, Monica Nizzardo argued that 'The *barra brava* is a mercenary who does not want to watch the game. He is attentive to the business that revolves around it.'[48]

Above all, they have become attentive to the dynamics of power, ensuring that the key relationships, transactions and protections that make the *barras bravas* possible have been left entirely untouched. The single attempt by a club president to take on the *barras* was at Independiente in 2012, when Javier Cantero tried to ban *Los Diablos Rojos* from the club's ground. It ended in comprehensive failure, with not a scintilla of support from government, police or the AFA.[49] An Argentine government official charged with dealing with security at football encapsulated the impossibility of the task. 'Corruption is endemic in Argentina, and it is what has allowed the *barras* to get so powerful. The problem is that everybody is taking a cut. It won't help just throwing the *barras*' bosses in jail: we've tried that. To break the *barras* you have to sever their political connections and root out those police complicit in their activities, and this is going to be hard. In fact, in the current climate I don't see how it's going to be done.'[50]

The incidence of violence in Brazilian football, already high in the 1990s, has taken another tick upwards. More than a hundred people died in football-related incidents in the decade that followed, though by comparison to Argentina and Uruguay the role of drugs and organized crime was relatively small. Brazil's *torcidas* are really much more interested in the fighting itself. Multiple incidents of disorder break out on most weekends, particularly towards the end of the season. In December 2004, for example, Botafogo fans stormed the pitch and attacked the referee as their team was defeated by Corinthians. The match was concluded while truncheon-wielding police fought their way into the stands and *torcidas* attempted to tear down the fences and netting behind the goals. At the same time, Guarani, relegated after being beaten by Paysandu, had its clubhouse stoned so badly that the last home game of the season was rescheduled to an out-of-town venue. Alongside these run-of-the-mill disturbances have been exceptional moments of mass disorder. In 2006, at the Porto Alegre derby between Grêmio and Internacional, fans threw dozens of portable toilets into the stadium moat, set them ablaze and pelted the firefighters attempting to put out the conflagration. In March 2012, about 500 Palmeiras and Corinthians fans took part in a pre-arranged brawl on São Paulo's Avenida Inajar de Souza, leaving two Palmeiras fans dead.

There have also been more provincial acts of barbarity. On 30 June 2013, in the small town of Pio XII in the state of Maranhão, referee Otávio Jordão da Silva, known as Cantanhede, gave player and sometime friend Josemir Santos Abreu a red card.[51] Abreu refused to leave the pitch, and in the ensuing argument Cantanhede pulled out a knife and stabbed him twice. Abreu died before reaching hospital. An angry and intoxicated mob then stormed the field, beat Cantanhede with a wooden pole, smashed a bottle of *cachaça* in his face, and drove a motorcycle repeatedly over his body, before he was finally decapitated and quartered. Football has provided the stage on which the desperate conditions and self-destructive energies of Brazil's poor can be played out. Accustomed to a world in which violence is pervasive, life is cheap and the public authorities – police and judiciary – cannot be relied upon to keep the peace or administer justice, many of Brazil's young men go armed and ready to use their weapons. Moreover, in a world that constantly strips them of economic dignity and offers them little but enduring marginality, humiliation in public becomes simply intolerable. It is the same rage and embarrassment that fuels pitch invasions when a team is losing or attacks on players who have let them down. From this act of grotesque rural revenge to the urban riots of the national championships, unchecked by the police and ignored by the sport's authorities, Brazilian football has been a holding room for the mental and emotional pathologies of a still brutalized society.

Time after time, South American football administrators and club directors have looked at the violence and looked away. National federation presidents have claimed that the violence is society's problem, not football's. National governments and city mayors have implored the football authorities to improve their miserable records of stadium maintenance and stewarding. In recent years, as the death toll has mounted, they have given up imploring and started passing legislation. Colombia was beset by a wave of football violence through 2013 and 2014. In just nine months, there were eleven homicides, from drunken bar-room stabbings for wearing the wrong shirt to huge post-match city-centre brawls. The situation was so febrile that no opposing fans were required to ignite a conflict. A street party to celebrate Millonarios's birthday turned into a riot that saw sixty people arrested.[52] Colombia's victory in the opening game of the 2014 World Cup ignited city-wide celebrations so out of control that nine deaths were recorded before order was restored. Consequently, the national government announced a ten-year plan to eradicate violence in football, with the intention of introducing ID card checks and CCTV cameras in the stadiums. Three years later, their introduction was still incomplete and violence had barely abated. Results have been equally mixed in Paraguay and Peru, both of which have adopted similar legislative programmes but are struggling to implement them. So to Chile, which in 2012 passed a raft of new legislation in anticipation of hosting the Copa América, making football-related violence at training grounds, on public transport, travelling to games and during celebrations in public space specific offences, as well as introducing laws governing racism and homophobia in the game.[53] That December, before an away game against Santiago Wanderers, Colo-Colo *barras* celebrated the championship they had won the previous week by storming the pitch and fighting their hosts with sticks. The game was abandoned.[54]

Argentina, in outline at least, has announced the most ambitious and draconian programme. In 2016, Minister of Security Patricia Bullrich set out new criminal legislation and new punitive sentences for *barras bravas* re-selling tickets, for those selling tickets to *barras bravas*, and for anyone charging for street car parking in the environs of a match.[55] The new Macri government also planned to give the federal government the power to regulate ticketing, manage admissions at stadiums and order the cancellation of any match that might not meet its standards. Should that and the new systems of ID checks designed to exclude blacklisted *barras* fail, there were increasingly harsh sentences for the possession of weapons at a game and the use of violence. It is too early to say whether these measures will turn the tide in Argentina. The equally draconian ban on away fans that began in 2013 has yet to do so. Nor has the government shown any real inclination for reforming the police who will actually have to implant these aspirations, or actively pursuing the *dirigente–barras bravas* nexus that animates the whole show. Indeed, in the absence of this kind of move, it is hard to imagine how these reforms will succeed.

IV

At first glance, Hugo Chávez's Venezuela seemed an unlikely candidate for scoring any kind of goal, let alone one that would hasten the arrival of twenty-first-century socialism. Venezuela had long cast itself as *El pais de béisbol*. Introduced by Americans working in the oil industry in the early twentieth century, baseball had claimed the mantle of national sport since the 1940s. Chávez himself played as a child, and then for the Caracas military academy team. His official biographies invariably tell us that he 'always dreamed of turning professional'. More pointedly, Venezuela was awful at football. In 1998, when Chávez won his first presidential election and inaugurated what he referred to as a Bolivarian revolution, Venezuela's FIFA ranking was 129th in the world. The country had barely won a game at the Copa América, and its clubs had never made it beyond the first stage of the Copa Libertadores. However, over the first decade of Chávez's rule, Venezuela's economy and football, like his popularity, moved in one direction: upwards.

Blessed with historically high oil prices, Venezuela boomed, and money was spent on food subsidies, income transfers and basic health and education services for the nearly 40 per cent of the country that had been living on less than two dollars a day. A lot of money also got blown on mega-projects, nationalized industries and foreign adventures. Under a new coach, Richard Paez, the Venezuelan team put in their best ever performance in a World Cup qualifying campaign, finishing off the bottom of the group for the first time. Money began to flow to the game from PSDVA, the state oil company, and other businesses, but football's place in the Bolivarian revolution was sealed by Venezuela's staging of the 2007 Copa América.

Official figures say the government spent $186 million on the tournament, but in the torrent of construction and public spending

1. Football is first. Then Turkish Prime Minister Erdoğan, and Bolivian President Morales, take to the field.

2. Germany 1, Argentina 0: Chancellor Angela Merkel and President Joachim Gauck celebrating the winning goal of the 2014 World Cup.

3. Finding space. Football beneath the motorway, Lagos, Nigeria.

4. Football and the rule of the gun. A helicopter disperses football fans during the Ghana and Equatorial Guinea game at AFCON 2017.

5. Football and the rule of law. The red card made for protests against the withholding of election results in Zimbabwe, 2013.

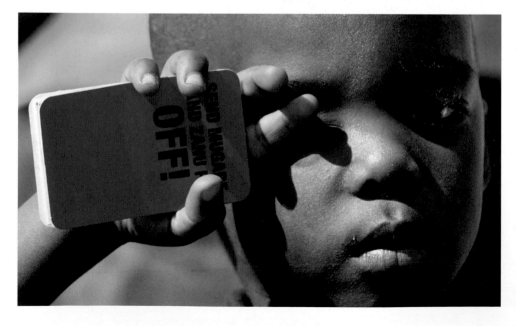

6. Starting from scratch. The Palestinian women's national football team training in Bethlehem.

7. Forbidden pleasures: Iranian women finally make it to the Azadi to watch the national team, 2018.

8. President Assad watches over a league game in Damascus played during the Syrian civil war.

9. Football's helots. Workers refurbish the Khalifa International Stadium in Doha, Qatar.

10. 'A teacher is worth more than Neymar.' Protestors march towards the Mineirão stadium in Belo Horizonte during the 2013 Confederations Cup.

11. We shall not be moved: Coritiba and Botafogo players take part in an FC Bom Senso protest, campaigning for improved conditions for players in Brazilian football.

12. FARC rebels play football in the mud at their camp following the ratification of the peace plan, bringing an end to the fifty-two-year guerrilla war against the Colombian state.

13. The Holy Grail: San Lorenzo win the Copa Libertadores and present it to one of their biggest fans, Pope Francis.

that had been unleashed, it was clearly considerably more.[56] For this, Venezuela acquired nine stadiums, three built from scratch and six entirely renovated. Chávez, despite the presence of Diego Maradona, took centre stage and made an absurdly long speech at the glitzy opening ceremony. Crowds filled the stadiums, the football was electric, with a cascade of goals (an average of nearly three-and-a-half a game), and the national team put in its best ever performance at a Copa América, losing to Uruguay in the quarter-finals. A measure of the team's importance was that Chávez's Sunday-night chat show *Aló Presidente*, which had never missed an episode, was cancelled for the big game. As the soft drink ads all over the country put it, '*En un pais de béisbol, también jugamos fútbol*' ('In the land of baseball, we also play football').

Even at this political high point, there were obvious murmurings of discontent. The crowd in Barquisimeto, where the opposition was in power, could be heard singing '*Y va a caer, y va a caer, este gobierno va a caer*' ('Going down, they're going down, the government's going down.') The national stadium in Caracas, due to stage three matches over the tournament, only hosted one, and when the Chavista mayor of the city, Juan Barreto, attended the game he was wildly booed, a reception he met by blowing kisses to the crowd and filming them before getting involved in a violent altercation.[57] But, for now, Chávez was on top of the world, bestowing the Order of Francisco De Miranda on Sepp Blatter, President of FIFA, and promising to bid for youth World Cups and perhaps even the real thing. *Aló Presidente* would now make way in the TV schedule for major football tournaments and games of the national team. At the Copa América 2011, the Venezuelans played their best yet, beating Chile 2–1 in the quarter finals and securing a place in the last four. Chávez was busy on his social networks exclaiming '*gloria al brave o pueblo*' ('Glory to the brave people' – the title and first line of the national anthem). Venezuela even beat Argentina in a World Cup qualifying game. Was there nothing the Bolivarian revolution could not accomplish?

In the aftermath of the Copa, the Venezuelan league was expanded from ten teams to eighteen, many of the country's leading players began to move to European sides, and the nation's clubs began to win a few games abroad. However, the most illuminating intervention in domestic football by the regime was the takeover of Zamora FC.[58] It was a small team in the state of Barinas – a Chavista stronghold in the west of the country – where Chávez's father and brother had been governors, but the club remained in the hands of opposition politician and local mayor Julio César Reyes. In 2008, as Chávez's brother Aden became the new state governor, Reyes was edged out and Chávez's youngest sibling Adelis (a football fanatic and an organizer at the Copa América) was installed as club president. Considerable sponsorship deals with PSDVA (the state petrochemical company), state banks and city hall then materialized, and in 2012 Zamora won their first ever league title; four more have followed. During this time, La Carolina stadium hosted many government rallies, appeared in PSUV election literature and even served as the set for an episode of *Aló Presidente*. Venezuela might not have become *el país de fútbol*, but the game was certainly now part of its domestic political repertoire.

On 5 March 2013, Chávez breathed his last. He was succeeded by his deputy Nicolás Maduro and Venezuelan football went into mourning. The league was cancelled to accommodate Chávez's funeral and when play did re-start, games were prefaced with acts of remembrance and garlanded with giant banners.[59] In the Chavista heartland of Zamora, they read, 'Chávez lives, the fight continues'. The crowd at Caracas FC's game against Grêmio in the Copa Libertadores held flags saying, 'The man is dead but the idea lives on: Eternal leader', while banners depicting just Chávez's eyes looked on. At Atlético San Martin in Tucumán, northern Argentina, a pitch-size flag showed Chávez in his red beret, with the slogan '100 per cent Commander'. Buenos Aires paid its respects with an immaculate minute's silence as Argentina played the Venezuelan national team at El Monumental. But when the team returned home to play Colombia in Puerto Ordaz, a new wave of anti-government banners and chants could be seen and heard amongst the Venezuelan crowd. There would be more to come.

In the presidential election later that year, Henrique Capriles, the otherwise sartorially conservative leader of the opposition, not only appeared at his big rallies in the red, yellow and blue national-flag track suits favoured by Chávez and Maduro, but also chose to wear the strip of the local football club wherever he was campaigning in the country. Not to be outdone, Maduro called on Diego Maradona to grace his closing rally in Caracas, a snip at one million dollars, according to the opposition. Despite widespread signs of economic decline and deep political discontent, Maduro and the PSUV squeaked home with a lead of just 1.5 per cent.

Venezuela never came anywhere near qualifying for the 2014 World Cup, but this did not save the tournament from national politics. The government, aware of the nationwide obsession with the Cup, chose to release the latest and once again awful inflation figures about an hour after the opening game kicked off. The opposition chose to run a 'red card' campaign on social media and on the streets, comparing the government's performance to those nations that had made it to the World Cup, and calling for it to be sent off. As one activist put it, 'We didn't make it to Brazil but we're representing Venezuela in the streets. We have to remind everyone that while they stay home watching the World Cup, things continue to get worse.'[60]

They would. As the global oil price continued its sharp decline, Venezuela was forced, for the first time since Chávez had come to power, to cut public expenditure. Inflation, already high, began to climb to unsustainable levels. The first shortages of foreign currency and imported goods began to appear. Key opposition leaders were put under arrest. At the 2015 Copa América in Chile, the Venezuelan crowds were full of hand-made placards calling for a recall referendum or for Maduro to just resign.[61] The team came bottom of the group and went home. At the 2016 tournament, held in the United States, a favoured destination for Venezuela's many exiles and asylum seekers, Maduro appeared on hand-made signs as a donkey, and fans chanted again for him to face a recall referendum. Venezuela made it to the quarter-finals, but it neither unified the country nor helped the Maduro government. On balance, football made the fragility and the weakness of the regime more evident than ever. In late 2016, in the seventy-fourth minute of a World Cup qualifying game in Merida, Venezuela trailed Brazil 2–0 when the floodlights completely blacked out, and no amount of editing by national television stations could disguise the fact.[62] Power rationing and sudden breaks in the electricity supply had become the new norms, as had the government's increasingly heavy-handed judicial and legal manoeuvres to keep the opposition at bay. Its control of the electoral commission, the REP, ensured that the opposition would never get the recall referendum they were demanding, a situation illustrated in the press by a cartoon of a football stadium in which the REP had hundreds of players to the opposition's eleven. It was also becoming impossible not to note the emptiness and decay of many of the stadiums built for the Copa América. The Pachencho in Maracaibo was so decrepit that, local unions thought, 'if the stadium is used to full capacity, it might not be able to support the weight and will most likely cave in.' Football reporter Guillermo Salas acidly described the rundown turf, seats and public areas of the Olimpico in Caracas as 'more a work of art than a sporting venue'.[63]

The opposition never got their referendum and held an unofficial one instead. The Maduro government, unable to reverse its decline in the polls or arrest the country's hyperinflation, opted to dismantle the opposition instead. The National Assembly, in which the right had a majority, was stripped of its legislative powers by the supreme court and the government announced elections for a new assembly which would re-write the constitution. Through the spring and summer of 2017, a huge and diverse series of protests against the election of the constitutional assembly was held. The army and the police were implacable and brutal, leaving over 200 people dead. Many members of the national team were recruited by the opposition to make a video called *Stop*, in which stars like Salomón Rondón and Oswaldo Vizcarrondo pleaded for the violence to end. 'Venezuela demands freedom, enough of so much repression and death,' said Nicolás Fedor, then at Rayo Vallecano in Spain.[64] In a game between Carabobo and Caracas, the teams held a minute's silence in solidarity with the victims of the country's political turmoil. State television edited it out, cutting straight to the kick-off. To avoid the same fate, the players of Lara and Anzoátegui kicked off and played one pass before all standing still, making the protest impossible to cut.[65] A few weeks before the vote, Rafael Dudamel, coach of the under-20 team, used his press conferences to beg for peace. 'Mr President, let's stop the weapons now. The only thing those kids going onto the streets want is a better Venezuela . . . the same as the Vinotinto kids.' (The national team is nicknamed 'vino tinto' because of its burgundy shirts). The videos were sweet and the pleas heartfelt, but they didn't really match up to the stack of state resources and voter enticements and voter-suppression strategies devoted to Maduro's victories in the 2017 referendum and the subsequent presidential election in 2018, not to mention another kick-about with Maradona.

Venezuelan football, like the rule of the PSUV, is formally in place, still ticking over, but it is a shadow of its former self and is being consumed by the economic consequences of its two decades in power. Uncontrollable hyperinflation, driven by the printing of money to cover the state's own finances, has sent the economy into a tailspin, and precipitated the desperate mass migration of three million Venezuelans to Brazil, Colombia and elsewhere. In football, like every facet of Venezuelan life, money is hard to come by and worth less every day, wages have been disappearing, crowds have shrunk, the official lifeline provided by PSDVA to the national teams and favoured clubs has dried up entirely. In late 2018, the nation's women's teams had been reduced to charitable donations to buy boots.

Carlos Mesa, Bolivia's president between 2003 and 2005, liked to make it known that he was an active member of the small La Paz amateur club Always Ready and had penned a sports history or two, but this was nothing compared to the role football has played in his successor's political career and charismatic form of rule. As Evo Morales put it, 'I would die fighting for people's rights, but if I don't get the chance, I would like to die playing football.'[66] Morales was born to poor herders in the Bolivian highlands. At the age of thirteen, he founded a club called Fraternidad and went on to star in it, captain it and coach it. He and his father sold the wool they sheared from their llama herds to buy balls and strips. Less unusual than it sounds, Fraternidad was one of many hundreds of football clubs established in the 1960s and 1970s by rural unions working with indigenous Indians, the game serving as a recruiting sergeant, an administrative training ground and a source of local pride. Forced by drought to migrate to the El Chape region, his family switched to growing coca, and Morales joined the local rural workers' union. He was elected local sports secretary, created and played in another team, and rapidly rose through the ranks, a trajectory that took him into electoral politics in the late 1990s and the leadership of the MAS (Movement for Socialism).[67]

In 2005, Morales was elected president, the first Bolivian of indigenous roots to hold the office. In 2008, in a wistful interview with Fox Sports, he claimed 'football makes us forget the politicians who are our problem.' His actions suggest he believes the reverse to be true. In over a decade in power, he has combined the presidency with signing and playing for three clubs: Litoral, a second division team in La Paz, San José of Oruro, and Sports Boys in Santa Cruz, the stronghold of the main political opposition, which he joined in 2014 on the minimum wage, with plans to play the occasional twenty-minute shift.[68]

There has also been time for friendlies, of a sort. In 2006, in the final seconds of an indoor game, Morales had his nose broken by the charging goalkeeper of Independence Warriors. At a match held in 2010 to inaugurate a redeveloped stadium in La Paz, Morales faced off against the team of city mayor and political opponent Luis Revilla, who had recently defected from his political party, MAS. A few minutes into the game, Daniel Gustavo Cartagena, a city hall official, put in an agricultural challenge on the President and gashed his leg. On getting up from the floor, Morales responded by showing Cartagena the wound and kneeing him in the groin. Morales played on. Cartagena got another knee from the president's bodyguards and was subsequently arrested.[69] Football has also formed part of Morales's diplomatic agenda. In 2005, at an EU–Latin America summit in Lima, he played for a team of Bolivians against some elderly Peruvian all-stars to promote the alternative Summit of the People.

In power, Morales's governments have sought, both symbolically and practically, to bring the indigenous poor of Bolivia's highlands, for whom serfdom was only abolished in 1952, into national political life. Externally, they sought a reassertion of Bolivian sovereignty vis-a-vis international companies and financial institutions, and challenged the United States on its war on drugs in the region and the legal status of the local coca leaf. Both agendas were admirably served by the renationalization of the country's natural resources, above all the hydrocarbon industries, which in turn has released enough resources to provide basic income and services for the poor. In the first eighteen months of Morales's rule, there was considerable domestic opposition from the right, and major disquiet in Brazil and Argentina, whose national oil companies held significant stakes in Bolivia's gas fields.

In a gift from the political gods, FIFA chose just this moment to announce a ban on the playing of international football matches at altitudes above 2,500 m, on the grounds that to do this was 'neither healthy nor fair'.[70] All Bolivia's highland stadiums, including the national arena in La Paz, would fall foul of this, not to mention grounds in Ecuador, Colombia and Peru. The ban was given added political piquancy by the fact that the Brazilians and Argentina were the loudest complainants when it came to playing matches in high-altitude stadiums in Bolivia, long arguing that it gave the home side an unfair advantage. Morales responded immediately, calling a cabinet meeting and issuing a strongly worded statement of protest: 'FIFA cannot make the historic mistake of discriminating against people who are born, live and practise sport at altitude.'[71] Plans were unveiled to send a million-signature petition to FIFA, and a call went out to the people of Bolivia to attend a huge demonstration with their footballs. Morales's office then staged a game in Bolivia's highest mountain range, 6,000 m above sea level, and put out pictures of the President scoring the winning goal on a snow-fringed pitch. The quote for the papers was, 'Wherever you can make love, you can play sports.' Even the constituent assembly, in which it had proved almost impossible to create unity since Morales's election, found common ground on the issue.

The following year, Morales brought Maradona to La Paz for a sell-out game, and Diego backed his host. 'All of us have to play where we are born, my brothers and sisters. Not even God can ban that, much less Blatter.'[72] Morales signed the match ball and sent it to Fidel Castro, asking for his backing too. In fact, international support was widely mobilized. Mayors from twenty cities in six Andean nations, all with stadiums well above the FIFA 2,500 m limit, were invited to a conference in La Paz to co-ordinate their actions. Both the Organization of American States (OAS) and the Andean Community of Nations trading block censured FIFA at Bolivia's behest. By contrast, South America's senior football administrators, many of them FIFA officials too, were reluctant to challenge their paymasters. Morales, uniquely for a head of state, went to CONMEBOL HQ and forced a statement of support out of its executive board. Bolivia then threatened to take FIFA to the Court of Arbitration of Sport. After much fulmination, the ban was rescinded in 2008.

Home advantage or not, high altitude hasn't been much help to Bolivian football itself, the country's long absence from the World Cup steadily lengthening. In 2009, after Bolivia failed to qualify for the South African World Cup, Morales told reporters, 'We're sorry about the performance of our team in the qualifiers. Until now football has been controlled by private autonomous entities, but they aren't getting results.'[73] Pressed as to the solution, he argued, 'What better thing than the intervention of the state?' State monies, at any rate, have not been forthcoming. Bolivian professional football remains in the hands of the wealthy, and perhaps Morales was content to leave them to it and the unrelenting debts and bankruptcies that follow. In 2015, as another poor qualifying campaign got underway, Bolivia's squad had to train at the nation's main military college and take rifle practice, and were told by Brigadier General Ponce that 'just as soldiers give their lives on the battlefield, we ask the players to give everything on the field of play.'[74] Needless to say, Bolivia stayed at home again in 2018 and Evo Morales was still in power.

V

As one might expect, two of the most viewed, most viral internet videos in contemporary Argentina concern football, but neither features goals or players. The first, released in 2011, is a seven-minute highlight reel of El 'Tano' Pasman, a middle-aged River Plate fan, secretly filmed by his family while watching football at home. The second is a comic sketch uploaded to YouTube of a young couple in a car arguing over a scheduling conflict: a wedding they have been invited to versus the opening weekend of the 2018 World Cup.[75] El Tano, who is, to be fair, watching the game that relegated River Plate to the second division for the first time in history, is little short of apoplectic. It is an extraordinary performance of living-room rage and despair: at the team, the fans who invade the pitch, the coach and the president, but also at himself for his insane fidelity to River, and to his family who passed on the affliction. It is also a masterclass in the flexible syntax of cursing in Argentinian Spanish, to which none of the various translations do justice. The World Cup couple's drive escalates into a titanic row, the humour of which rests on the man's completely unreflective, immovable assumption that the World Cup, indeed football, trumps everything. The quotidian obsessions of both men can stand proxy for much of the nation, and, during the World Cup final of 2014, for something genuinely close to the entire nation. Of course, similar sentiments could have been found before the advent of viral videos, but a brief survey of football in contemporary Argentinian music, literature and cinema suggests that the game is more central than ever.

Throughout the inter-war era and into the 1950s, Argentina interpreted its own way of playing football, *La Nuestra*, as an expression of its new urban cultures, its players part scrapping street kids, part sensuous tango dancers. In the 1970s and 1980s, the urchins and the vibes were still there, but the soundtrack had switched to *rock nacional*, the country's vernacular pop, which became an instrument of youth resistance to the junta. In the post-junta era, and especially under the grinding IMF austerity programmes of Menem's Argentina in the 1990s, the dominant note of both music and fan culture became *Aguante*. Loosely translated as endurance, fortitude and fixity, with a sense of putting one's body and soul on the line, *Aguante* captures the fidelity of the fan to the rock-and-roll lifestyle, and of the *hincha* (fan) to the club. In a world where there was no economic or political permanence, these things alone stayed true and made sense. In the years since Argentina's 2002 global financial default, and the chaos that ensued, this has appeared truer than ever.

Until the 1990s, with some exceptions, Argentinian literature steered clear of the game, living in the shadow of the grand old man, Jorge Luis Borges, and his famously acid remark that 'Football is popular because stupidity is popular.' Contemporaries like Juan Filloy, and successors like *avant garde* novelist Julio Cortázar, preferred boxing, the latter declaring that 'I hate football the way I love boxing.' All shared a certain reserve, if not distaste, for the mob, the collective mania that Argentinian football seems to induce and the game's potential for manipulation. Indeed, Borges, in his one considered piece on the subject, *Esse Est Percipi* (To Be is to Be Perceived), written in 1963 with Adolfo Bioy Casares, suggested that televised football was the ultimate illusion. In a Buenos Aires in which River Plate's huge El Monumental stadium has disappeared into thin air, a club president admits:

> The stadiums have long since been condemned and are falling to pieces. Nowadays everything is staged on television and radio. The bogus excitement of the commentator – hasn't it ever made you suspect everything is humbug? The last match of soccer was played in this city on 24 June 1937. From that precise moment, soccer, as the wide range of sports, is a dramatic

genre, in charge of one man in a cabin of actors with a T-shirt in front a cameraman.[76]

If electronic and popular mass culture was *terra incognito* to Borges, it was the natural home of the generation of writers and artists that followed him, who, growing up in the Sixties, had absorbed the interlinking cultures of commercialized football, television and popular music, and considered none of them inappropriate material for literary exploration. This was a not dissimilar trajectory to the English world of letters, which proved haughtily indifferent to football until, in the 1990s, it became obsessed. Roberto Jorge Santoro, the experimental poet, was amongst the first to take on the subject, editing the first literary compendium of football writing in Argentina, before being tragically killed at the age of just thirty-eight by the junta in 1977. In the years after the dictatorship, as many writers returned from abroad, a new wave of football writing appeared, the game serving as a cipher for home in the melancholy of exile, and a subject ripe for the exploration of addiction and conflict. The short story has been the format of choice, with collections from writers of the calibre of Roberto Fontanarrosa (*El Fútbol es Sagrado*), Rodolfo Braceli (*De Fútbol Somos* and *De Perfum de Gol*), and the most popular author of his generation, Osvaldo Soriano (*Cuentos de fútbol: Memorias del Míster Peregrino Fernández y otros relatos*).[77] In the last decade the Oscar-winning scriptwriter Eduardo Sacheri has picked up the baton with, most notably, the novel and film *Papeles en el Viento* (*Papers in the Wind*), which follows three grieving friends whose best friend bequeaths to them, on his death, the ownership rights of a young football player languishing in Argentina's minor leagues.

Sacheri's film is just one, though the most commercially successful, of a whole stream of football-themed works in twenty-first-century Argentinian cinema. Feature documentaries have included the sombre verité of *Argentina y su fábrica de fútbol*, the world of small-town football scouting and the profound emotions evoked by lower league provincial football clubs in *El Otro Fútbol*. Comedy drama has proved more light-hearted and commercially successful. In *En Fuera de Juego*, an unhappy shrink who hates football and a third-rate football agent reduced to staging kids' parties struggle over the right to represent a promising young football star; in *El Fútbol O Yo*, which was amongst the biggest hits in Argentinian cinema in 2017, a couple's relationship disintegrates around his football addictions and her ultimatum: football or me!

The biggest football movie of all, though, was the animated feature *Metagol*, released in the anglophone world as *Underdogs*. Indeed, it was and remains the most expensive Argentinian movie ever made. Based on a Fontanarrosa short story, it is a fairy tale in which our timid table-football-playing hero beats the local school bully and football star at the game. Years later, the latter returns, full of vengeance, buys up the village and builds a pharaonic football stadium in an effort to obliterate his shame and his nemesis. But our hero wins the day and the girl by way of his table-football players, who come to life and fearlessly take on the forces of evil. In the end, *Metagol* is a version of Argentina's relationship with football, bent to the norm of Hollywood's narrative and emotional arcs, with a version of *aguante* altogether too wholesome, neat and deracinated. Something closer to the profound nostalgia and the real melancholy of Argentina's version of itself can be found in the short *Un Santo Para Telmo* (*A Saint for Telmo*), in which a vulgar taxi driver and a Brazilian striker take a Homeric journey across Buenos Aires in an effort to make the last game of the season, and for the latter to save the day.

It is worth, for a moment, extending the earlier parallel with England. Imagine a world in which a Labour Prime Minister could have persuaded the Premier League to break its deal with Sky Sports and sign up instead, albeit for a considerably better offer, with the government itself, which would in turn make all the league's games (and that of the rest of professional football) free to air on television. Imagine too that the Murdoch press empire, despite using every last rhetorical trope and media outlet on hand to protest against this, lost the argument and the battle for public opinion. That, broadly speaking, was what happened in Argentina, making *Fútbol Para Todos* (Football for Everyone) one of the most emblematic policies of President Cristina Kirchner and her leftist *Peronista* governments, both in content and style of implementation.[78] The former, because under both Nestor and Cristina Kirchner's presidencies, state intervention of various kinds was used to advance the material interests of the poor, from the creation of the country's first universal social security system to the massive extension of workers' rights. The latter because, whatever the policy's social merits, it was also a political weapon and, characteristically of the Kirchners, one that was aggressively wielded.

The policy emerged in 2009 out of the confluence of two events: the government's long-term struggle with the Clarin media group and an economic crisis. The crisis, as usual, was in the finances of Argentinian football clubs. In mid-August of that year, with the new season due to begin in just a few weeks, nearly a dozen clubs had been suspended under new Argentinian Football Association (AFA) financial regulations because they could not demonstrate the capacity to pay their bills. The President of AFA, Julio Grondona, was looking for an escape route.

The Clarin group is the largest Argentinian media conglomerate, owns hundreds of newspapers, radio stations, television channels and digital outlets, and had totally controlled Argentinian football since 1992. It is, needless to say, on the right of the political spectrum. The long-standing antipathy between the group and the Kirchners had reached a new pitch in 2008 over the issue of Argentina's soya bean export industry. This had been enjoying exceptional profits on the back of China's long boom and insatiable demand for the product, so the government imposed a very stiff tax on the business. Clarin was amongst the most forceful in opposing the tax, in a conflict which deeply polarized the country. The government hit back, refusing to speak to the group's outlets, blocking its acquisition of a controlling stake in Telecom Argentina and, in 2009, passing an audio-visual media law. This gave the newly established Audio Visual Commission the authority to break up the largest media groups, forcing them to relinquish many of their channels and licences. All of this was aimed at Clarin.

It was in this context that Gabriel Mariotto, then the head of the Commission and later Deputy Governor of Buenos Aires Province, conceived the notion that the government might get into the football business. The debate inside the government over the audio-visual law first touched on football when it asked what, if any, sporting events should be reserved for free-to-air television. At the same time, the whole idea of rights to information and culture was being re-evaluated. 'We were paying millions of pesos to the Teatro Colón [the national theatre] for an audience of just 2,000,' Mariotto argued. 'Thinking about football just put on the table all of the issues around access and equity.' There was a strong case, he argued, for the state to invest in the football industry in some way, and free access to televised football was, if not a right, a basic precondition of the good life in Argentina.

Whatever the balance of motivations inside the government, and whatever one thought of Clarin's politics, its football coverage had been remarkably mean-spirited. The game was covered by its subsidiary Torneos y Competencias – slogan: 'We are the owners of football' – which for fifteen years had ensured a complete blackout on any images from the league's games until late on Sunday night, when the free-to-air highlights show *Fútbol De Primera* finally arrived. In the meantime, other channels and the viewing public were so desperate for snippets that they were tuning into hand-drawn and computer graphic recreations of goals, real-life simulations of contested incidents and cameras turned towards the fans for the entirety of matches.

Given this kind of mania for football, it was widely thought that Clarin was significantly underpaying AFA for its monopoly, a point that had been repeatedly made to the organization, but which it had hitherto chosen to ignore.[79] However, the state of the financial crisis in the game meant that AFA's President Julio Grondona could no longer stand by his comfortable deal with Clarin. First, Don Julio went to see Clarin and gave the company one last chance to up the money, which it declined. Then he headed for the *Casa Rosada*, where the President asked what the bill would be. Grondona wrote down the figure and the deal was informally agreed and signed on a napkin.

Fútbol Para Todos broadcast its first game on 21 August 2009. The government insisted that there would be no commercial advertising or sponsorship for the programme, and that was a condition that applied to any channel that wished to re-transmit the show. Instead, a huge slice of the government's own enormously expanded advertising budget was redirected towards football. The presenters and commentators came initially from outside the Clarin empire, many from radio and the provinces, and included a fair number whose *Peronista* sympathies were well known and often broadcast. Javier Vincente, known as 'El Militante', was particularly vocal in denouncing the then right-wing mayor of Buenos Aires, Mauricio Macri, running in the presidential elections, and warned of the consequences of him winning for the future of *Fútbol Para Todos*. Distasteful as this might have been to part of the audience, especially the Clarin group, which compared the operation to Chávez's Venezuela, the viewing public loved it. Ratings were immense for the biggest games, and in the country's interior, where there has been much more poverty and much less cable television, the service proved hugely popular. Not that the quality of play got any better, nor did the air of menace and disorder in the stadiums recede under *Fútbol Para Todos*, but Argentina's football continued to deliver an unending stream of narrative drama and variety.

The main guarantor of new storylines remained the mania of the two-short-leagues-a-season model.[80] Compressing the competitions down to just nineteen games apiece ensured that even the merest blip for any team became a crisis, triggering a lot of news and a merry-go-round of managerial intrigue and change. On the other hand, a short streak of great form could propel a small club to dizzy heights, and with enough grit and luck keep them there. Thus there were championships for the most unlikely teams. Lanus and Banfield, from the far southern industrial edges of Buenos Aires, won titles in 2007 and 2016, and 2009 respectively. Similarly, small neighbourhood clubs like Tigre and Huracán, even provincial minnows like Godoy Cruz from Mendoza, could finish high enough to play in continental competitions. In 2017, in a supreme act of giant-killing, Lanus beat River Plate in the semi-finals of the Copa Libertadores, before losing to Brazil's Grêmio in the final. None of these clubs, however, has been able to sustain its success. Indeed, the highs have often been followed by lows, as the hammer of permanent debt ensures successful teams are rapidly broken up and sold on, and, in the case of Banfield, relegated just three years after their unlikely triumph.

The good times have also come to San Lorenzo, one of the five giants of the league, who had been in melancholy exile since the military governments of the 1970s sold up their old stadium, the Gasómetro, to build a Carrefour supermarket, shipping them out to the always alien neighbourhood of Flores. Close to relegation and bankruptcy in 2011, they were renewed by a new board headed by lawyer Matías Lammens and Argentina's king of prime-time TV trash Marcello Tinelli, and reinforced by Argentina's biggest export of all, the new Pope Francis, a life-long supporter of the club. He welcomed them to the Vatican when they won the title in 2013 and gave them a Virgin Mary for the clubhouse. Something was working. In 2014, the club, at the fourth time of asking in a final, won the Copa Libertadores, went back to Rome to get the trophy blessed, and got ready to move back to Boedo, its original geographical and spiritual home, after buying up land for a *Nuevo Gasometro*.

Heart-warming as the victories and the homecomings have been, Argentinian football has also delivered plenty of *Schadenfreude*, for despite the creation of all manner of rules to make it almost impossible for big clubs to be relegated, they have been. Introduced in the 1980s, relegation in Argentina has been determined on the basis of average points over a three-year period, allowing big clubs who have single or even consecutive bad seasons to pull back from the brink. However, the incompetence and chaos of the nation's leading clubs have ingeniously outwitted the plan. In 2013, Independiente, then one of only two clubs to have never been relegated from the top division (Boca being the other) and winner of seven Copa Libertadores, played so poorly that their fate was pretty much sealed with half the season still to go.

Gleeful as this was for much of the football nation to watch, it was as nothing compared to the relegation of River Plate in 2011, the occasion of El Tano's bravura performance. The final descent had been preceded by three years of *telenovela*-scale intrigue and infighting, a titanic and vicious struggle for the presidency, a reversal of form so dramatic that they went from champions in 2008 to the bottom of the league in 2009, and a final stretch in 2011 that saw them go winless for two months, forcing a relegation play-off with Belgrano that they then contrived to lose. A year in the purgatorial ruins of Argentina's provincial football stadiums followed, but in a return that would never pass muster in fiction, for it would surely be considered too contrived, they returned to the top division in 2013, won the title in 2014, and in 2015 had the pleasure of beating Boca Juniors in the semi-finals of the Copa Libertadores – a clash far more electric than the gruelling two-leg final that they won against Tigres of Mexico.

There has been no such story of redemption for the Argentinian national team. Rather, the story of the five finals it has reached and then lost in the twenty-first century (four in the Copa América, plus the 2014 World Cup final) has been Sisyphean. In 2002, just months after the country defaulted on its international debts, triggering a cataclysmic collapse of the economy, political turmoil that saw four presidents in as many months, and nationwide demonstrations, occupations and riots, the team went to the World Cup carrying at least the hope of delivering some diversion at home and a modicum of international dignity. It managed neither, going out after the group stages.[81] The 2006 World Cup, played out against the relative stability of Nestor Kirchner's Peronist presidency, signalled an advance. The team scored perhaps the best collective goal in World Cup history – a twenty-six-pass move finished by Cambiasso against Serbia – but was squeezed out in the quarter-finals. Four years later, Argentina played the Germans again in the quarter-finals and this time were summarily dispatched 4–0. This marked the end of Maradona's two bad-tempered and chaotic years as national team coach.

Of course, his departure from the post gave him a lot more time to focus on what he was really good at, which was being Maradona. For much of the last decade, episodes of ill health and long sojourns in the tax haven that is Dubai aside, he has been an eternal presence in the Argentinian media and amongst the Latin American left, sharing public platforms and chat show studios, playing kickabouts, or appearing at rallies with Presidents Rafael Correa, Nestor Kirchner, Fidel Castro, Hugo Chávez, Nicolas Maduro and Evo Morales. There have been a lot of advertisements and endorsements too, including one featuring him as God in a white tuxedo, and, the dream of all narcissists, a church in his name.[82] Maradona's departure also left rather more space in the national soap opera for the real star: Lionel Messi.

Messi's story is first and foremost one of absence. Unable to obtain the expensive growth hormones and medical treatment that he required as a youth player, he left the penurious Newell's Old Boys and Argentina at the age of thirteen for Barcelona and Spain, where he has lived and played ever since. He is universally acknowledged at home as the greatest player since Maradona, and his extraordinary performances in Europe have been lauded. The country's relationship with him when playing for the national team, however, has been more problematic. Indeed, at times it has been vicious and vituperative. On the one hand, the country has put him on a pedestal and expected him to turn in the kind of displays that defined Maradona's career. On occasion he has, but it is a measure of the weakness of the rest of the team, and indeed the whole of the AFA, that these efforts, like his sensational hat-trick against Ecuador in 2018, have saved disastrous qualifying campaigns rather than winning trophies. On the other hand, when he has not, the pressure has been so great that Messi has announced his retirement from international football not once but twice, only to be drawn back by a national current of apologies and desperation.

Either way, the criticism that has then rained down upon him centres not on his real contribution, but his authenticity, questioning whether he is really Argentinian, whether he sings the national anthem, and whether he can play in an Argentinian way: all ciphers for the great unspoken question as to whether the globalization of Argentinian football and the export of its best talent have hollowed it out to the point of collapse, or at least to anonymity. Messi has said almost nothing on these topics or any other, other than to plead his unflinching Argentine identity and maintain his dignity in the face of impossible demands.

Maradona, on and off the pitch, has paraded a bombastic resistance to globalization, with his blustering patriotism, by his choice of political friends, and by his refusal not to accept international over Argentinian norms, as evidenced by his cigar-smoking in the VIP box at the Russia World Cup, but these pantomime performances of *aguante* are no answer to the realities of football's global political economy. In the absence of any practical model for reforming Argentina's subordinate position in the global economy, football or otherwise, silence may be the best that *aguante* can offer.

VI

In 2002, Luiz Inácio Lula da Silva, or Lula as he is known, won the Brazilian presidency at the fourth attempt with his Workers' Party (PT) and sought to establish Brazil's first social democratic government. Lula was also the first President to truly hail from Brazil's lower classes and establish a deep emotional bond with them while in office. Football was an important strand of Lula's popular persona. Certainly, his relationship to the game was far closer to that of the average Brazilian football fan than any of his predecessors'. He was a partisan supporter of Corinthians, often commenting on the team and its performances. When speaking to the Seleção by video link before the 2006 World Cup, he asked whether Ronaldo was still fat. The social kickabouts he held at the presidential palace were well attended and keenly contested, as evidenced by the finance minister Antonio Palocci entering Congress on crutches after a crunching game between the President's team and the Ministry of Fisheries. Innumerable state occasions and audiences involved the exchange of football shirts with diplomats, and meetings with players and coaches.

If football had helped define Lula's style of governance and public image, he did not begin his term of office focusing on the game. On the contrary, he came to power on the promise to measure the progress of the nation by how many Brazilians ate three square meals a day. Moreover, he knew that an easy intimacy with the Brazilian people and the game of football would only get one so far. Lula's success rested on the economic, social and political changes his governments helped bring about. First, Brazil experienced a decade of unbroken growth and increases in wages and living standards driven by the breakneck growth of China and the widespread industrialization of the global South, which together created a huge demand for Brazilian agricultural products. Lower interest rates and access to consumer credit saw the newly enriched working and lower-middle classes splash out on white goods and cars, in turn fuelling growth in Brazil's manufacturing centres. Second, the government introduced the *Bolsa Familia*, a nationwide welfare programme for poor families which did more than any single thing in the history of the country to alleviate poverty and hunger. Third, the government began spending serious money on desperately needed infrastructure. But, while being admirably focused on these kinds of policies, it was almost inevitable that Lula and the PT would be seduced by the allure of football. What they did not do, which would fatally undermine their wider political projects as well as their interventions in football, was effectively reform the Brazilian political and legal systems or tackle the endemic circuits of corruption between the political parties and the construction industry.

The PT began by attempting minor reforms. In 2002, the last year of the Cardoso government, and following the long Congressional investigations into the disastrous state of football governance in the country, the CBF were *personae non gratae* in Brasília. In their absence, the sports ministry crafted legislation that would force clubs to take the interests of their fans, or rather their customers, more seriously. Lula and his sports minister Agnelo Queiroz inherited the legislation that would become the Supporters' Charter and pushed it through Congress against the wishes of the football lobby. It had many components, but perhaps the most important was to give football fans the same legal rights as any other kind of consumer. While the most basic forms of consumer protection had been established in Brazilian law in 1990, they had hitherto not applied to people who bought match tickets. This in itself was an advance, as was the insistence that all football stadiums must be equipped with adequate numbers of functioning toilets for both genders, as well as drinking fountains and medical care, none of which had been the norm. More substantially, the law made the clubs themselves responsible for the health and safety of the fans, an obligation that had not occurred to most of them before. A Football Ombudsman was established, to whom fans could take their grievances. A week after the charter was signed into law, the flag of revolt was raised by the presidents of eight clubs, three state federations and the president of the CBF, Ricardo Teixeira, who, in an act of unabashed blackmail, suspended the national championship, claiming that the stadiums did not match up to the new requirements. The idea of the football establishment suddenly posing as the guardians of the public interest was so laughable that, after virulent nationwide criticism by President Lula and the press, they backed off.

Lula's Brazil proved better at passing reforming legislation than implementing it. In 2013, looking back on ten years of the Supporters' Charter, *Lance!* concluded that there had been real improvement for Brazilian football fans, but many elements of the original charter remained unrealized. Whether it was a consequence of political apathy or the widespread disregard in which judicial procedures were held, the Football Ombudsman was barely used over the ten years of the role's existence. Supporters continued to be treated with contempt by some clubs, especially away fans, who would continue to be deliberately delayed or denied entrance to grounds. Above all, the insistence of the charter that the relevant authorities draw up a plan of action covering security and safety for every game was simply not put into action, with the consequence that many games were blighted by chaotic logistics. The police continued to treat football more as an exercise in controlling public disorder than securing the safety of citizens in public spaces. Worse, what the charter and the other reforms of the Lula years did not do was halt the violence associated with Brazilian football, inside and outside the stadiums. Indeed, the problem became so serious that in 2010 the government updated and amended the charter with a whole series of highly draconian measures designed to crack down on the *torcidas organizadas*, with no noticeable effect.

Inevitably, if regrettably, the government reopened personal relationships with the CBF. In its early months, Lula's administration had persuaded many clubs to support its domestic policy programmes by wearing government-approved shirts, particularly in support of the *Fome Zero* (Zero Hunger) campaign that was a precursor to the *Bolsa Familia*. However, to make a really big impact at home and abroad the government needed access to the Seleção, and that access lay with the CBF. The CBF in turn needed access to the corridors of power in Brasília, made more urgent by the up-and-coming prospect of a bid to host the 2014 World Cup. A discreet dinner between the sports minister and João Havelange, the ex-president of FIFA, smoothed the way for a rapprochement, though in classic Brazilian style Lula and Teixeira never held a public audience, preferring informal Friday afternoon meetings over glasses of whisky. In early 2003, the Seleção played a friendly against China in shirts bearing the words 'Fome Zero', then against Ireland later in the year. The relationship between the government and the CBF was close enough that by the following year the PT Minister of Sport was able to grandstand with the team after they had won the Copa América 2004, while on visits to poorer nations the Brazilian squad handed out sports equipment manufactured as part of a rehabilitation programme in Brazilian prisons. Later, the team would play in Haiti, where the Brazilian armed forces comprised the majority of the UN Peacekeeping Mission, though one with a less than distinguished record.

The real undoing, though, of the PT and its football policies came with the sporting mega-events hosted under its rule. It began with the Pan-American Games, held in Rio in 2007. 'This is the chronicle of a mess foretold,' commented the sports columnist Juca Kfouri. Both the games and his epigram were prescient. No one ever quite worked how much they cost, but it was roughly six times the original budget, and that was after all the planned infrastructure improvements, and the clean-up of the toxic soup masquerading as Guanabara Bay that had been promised but never materialized. Instead, Rio was left with a lot of poorly sited, badly built stadiums, for most of which there was no post-games plan. The games did feature an open battle in the Complexo do Alemão on the northern edge of the city, where police, the army and drug gangs fought street to street, leaving forty-four dead. While this might have deterred some from staging further mega events, the city of Rio and the federal government were encouraged. Indeed, over the next couple of years they would pursue and win the hosting rights for both the 2014 World Cup and the 2016 summer Olympics. Both were seen, by the politicians at any rate, as wonderful branding opportunities and conclusive proof of Brazil's transformation and modernity. In fact, speaking after Brazil had been ejected from the quarter-finals of the 2010 World Cup, President Lula cast Brazil's World Cup journey as a kind of manifest destiny: 'I am amongst those who think that God has crooked handwriting. I think that if we could not win in 2010, it is because God knows that we cannot fail in 2014.' As the Pan-American games suggested, however, the journey was also going to provide a remarkable window on the corruption of Brazil's planning processes, the embezzlement that came with government contracting and infrastructural investment, and the flagrant brutality of its security forces.

Ricardo Teixeira may have been prepared to concede some space on the Seleção's shirts, but he certainly didn't intend to concede any power over Brazil's World Cup. He formed an organizing committee for the World Cup without a single government representative, elected or unelected.[83] However, while the organizing committee worried about FIFA protocol and ticketing, the real business of the tournament and the bulk of the $12 billion it cost was focused on building football stadiums. Sold as a sensible form of investment, funded by the long Brazilian boom which was still running despite the global financial crash of 2008, it all looked very different in the light of Brazil's subsequent economic meltdown. When the global cyclone finally hit Brazil, growth collapsed, the indebtedness of both public and private sectors squeezed it further, unemployment rose, and the government responded with the crudest of austerity programmes. As the new stadiums rose up, at a cost of nearly a billion dollars for the Estádio Mané Garrincha in Brasília alone, bellies emptied and schools closed.

Through the autumn of 2012 and into early 2013, there were small but visible signs of discontent. The *Comitê Popular da Copa e Olimpíadas*, an umbrella group for those opposed to Brazil's sporting mega-events, maintained their regular protests in Rio and other cities over the wastefulness and corruption of the World Cup infrastructure programme, attracting three to four thousand people to their anti-privatization marches on the Maracanã. At the same time, protests against increases in bus fares led by the *Movimento Passe Livre* were breaking out in Natal, Porto Alegre and Goiânia. Then, on 6 June 2013, just nine days before the Confederations Cup, the eight-team test tournament that precedes the World Cup, was due to begin, the *Movimento Passe Livre* began to demonstrate against bus-fare rises in São Paulo, blocking Avenida Paulista and other major thoroughfares. This could not be ignored. The police, as ever, reacted with the use of maximum force and, although the media were depicting the protest as an anti-social nuisance, the demonstrators' bravery in the face of police brutality began to bring more supporters onto the streets. Organized through a complex mixture of social movements, personal connections and massive use of social media, demonstrations took place every day in São Paulo and were supported by marches in Rio, Brasília and Belo Horizonte of between 1,000 and 5,000 people. Almost immediately, the protestors began to talk about more than just fare increases. Chants and placards soon made reference to the hopeless state of the nation's public education and healthcare systems, the pervasiveness of political corruption and the unaccountability and brutality of the police. Yet for all this, they remained small and only partially connected acts of defiance. What turned these smouldering embers into a conflagration was the football.

On 15 June, the Confederations Cup opened in Brasília with the host nation playing Japan. Riot police turned rubber bullets and pepper spray on a small demonstration close to the stadium, where protestors carried signs bearing slogans like 'Health? Education? No! Here everything is for the World Cup'. FIFA president Sepp Blatter stood to give his speech and was roundly booed. He attempted to respond by asking the audience, 'Where was the fair play in all of this?', but was booed even more loudly. President Rousseff, who had taken over from Lula in 2010, was next up, and she too was booed while protestors unfurled a variety of banners inside the stadium. The disparate demands of the street were suddenly given a theme around which its many concerns could crystallize. The protean spasm of activism acquired a focus and a rhythm. Two days later, major demonstrations were held in twenty cities, 65,000-strong in São Paulo and more than 100,000 in Rio. In Brasília, protestors climbed on the roof of the Congress. On 19 June, as Brazil faced Italy in Fortaleza, 25,000 people marched directly to the stadium, where they were met by the usual combination of armed brutality and incompetence. The following day was the occasion for the biggest demonstrations yet, as Brazilians took to the streets of 120 cities, including every state capital in the country. At least 300,000 people gathered in Rio alone, and were once again met by chaotic and violent policing. Everywhere the crowds carried thousands of handmade, hand-drawn placards and banners: from the crude 'Fuck International Football Association' and 'FIFA the bitch' to the entirely reasonable 'Brazil, wake up! A teacher is worth more than Neymar.' Everywhere, sprayed on the bus shelters and in the underpasses, one could read, 'The Cup kills the poor'.

On 21 June, President Rousseff made her move, going on television, accepting the right of the nation to protest and promising to address the people's concerns by holding down bus fares, importing extra doctors from Cuba to fill the gaping holes in Brazil's health service and reserving oil revenues for education, but defending spending on the World Cup. It wasn't much, but it was enough to take the sting out of the movement. Protest, though still widespread, thinned. In a final flourish, 120,000 people marched from the centre of Belo Horizonte to the Mineirão, as Brazil beat Uruguay in their semi-final. Activists occupied the state legislature and in the Sete de Setembro Square, the traditional place in which the Seleção's victories would be celebrated, the night ended with a fusillade of tear gas so vast that the huge obelisk in the centre, over thirty metres high, was completely obscured. Five days later, on the night of the final in Rio, a crowd of 5,000 marched on the Maracanã and was met by an enormous deployment of the Rio police department's riot squads. Brazil won the match 3–0 as the crowd outside was charged, gassed and dispersed.

Brazil 2014 just made it to the line. The stadiums were built, the two billion dollars allocated to security for the event was spent, and a fabulously well-equipped selection of army, police and riot police units steadily corralled what little of the protest movement lived on after the Confederations Cup. And once the party started, a wave of hope and expectation that the nation had been suppressing was unleashed. The CBF let it be known that it was employing sports psychologists just focused on getting the team to relax. If, as President Lula had suggested, God knew that Brazil was going to win the Cup, then the Lord had not seen fit to communicate that very clearly to the team, which, as the Brazilian commentator Paulo Vinicius Coelho wrote, appeared to be 'a sea of nerves and anxiety'. The CBF had brought back Phil Scolari, coach of the 2002 World Cup-winning side, and cast the tournament as 'Seven steps to heaven', while the Brazilian dressing room, never short of religious fervour and magical charms, overflowed with them in 2014. Scolari, a pious Catholic who had gone on a pilgrimage after winning the World Cup, prayed in hotel chapels before every game. Many of the squad, including Neymar, David Luiz, Fred and Fernando, were devout evangelicals. Almost everyone looked skyward and raised a finger to the heavens when they crossed the touchline or scored. The Lord's Prayer, theological common ground for the squad, was collectively recited in the dressing room, and David Luiz in particular, was forever sinking to the ground, looking up to the sky and giving thanks to Jesus.

Having scrambled their way through their opening group, Brazil were almost beaten by Chile, who took them to penalties in the round of sixteen. Captain Thiago Silva prayed alone on the touchline as the shoot-out took place, while goalkeeper Júlio César placed a magic charm in the goalmouth. In their quarter-final with Colombia, any semblance of the idea that this team was still playing the *jogo bonito* was abandoned. Their roughhouse tactics won the day, but at the cost of losing Neymar to a crunching and aggressive tackle. When the national anthem was played in São Paulo before their semi-final with Germany, David Luiz and Júlio César held up Neymar's shirt, perhaps as some magic totem to protect them, but here Brazil, both team and nation, came up against the limits of evangelical fervour, hysterical patriotism and blind faith.

In one of the most compelling acts of sporting destruction seen at a World Cup, indeed anywhere, the Germans eviscerated Brazil. The final score, 7–1, does justice to the utter domination of the Germans and the complete collapse and abdication of their opponents.

By the end of the match there were plenty of tears and even some burnt Neymar shirts, but reports from both stadium and the bars of São Paulo tell of Brazilians laughing at the comic farce, shouting '*Olé*' as the Germans dominated possession and standing to applaud the final goal. This at least salvaged something of the reputation of the Brazilian crowd in the stadium, which had insulted its own president, booed the Chilean national anthem and, despite its overwrought patriotism, remained somnolent for long periods of many games. President Dilma and the PT would still have a few more months before her impeachment, but the 7–1 served as a fitting full stop to their twelve years in power.

VII

The Seleção may not have won the *Copa de Copas*, but Brazil could at least claim to have hosted an extraordinary and intoxicating multilayered carnival of football. It soon became apparent that the party had been a wake for the pink tide. Within eighteen months of the final, and despite winning a second term of office in October 2014, President Dilma was facing impeachment proceedings and Lula was heading for trial on corruption charges. Argentina had shifted right, rejecting another term of *Peronista* government for the glib neoliberal promises of Mauricio Macri. By the time of the next World Cup final, the left remained in power only in Uruguay, Bolivia and Venezuela, where Maduro and the PSUV were heading down the path of hyperinflation and repression. In Brazil, the economy, long faltering, entered the deepest recession the country had ever experienced. Simultaneously, the *Lavo Jato* investigation ('Operation Car Wash'), initially a narrow but telling judicial probe into money-laundering, steadily exposed a vast national network of bribery and corruption. It centred on Brazil's biggest construction firms, which had been funding politicians' lifestyles and election expenses in return for innumerable favours and contracts. The anti-corruption protests returned to the street, but with a decidedly more upper-and middle-class crowd and right-wing voice, calling for Dilma's impeachment and the punishment of the ruling party.

Seeing their chance, Brazil's Congress impeached Dilma in early

2016 on the much lesser charge of fiddling the public accounts statistics before an election (an offence a number of her predecessors were surely guilty of too). Thus it was her vice-president, the reptilian conservative Michel Temer, who would open the Rio Olympics the following year, the culmination of Brazil's international branding by mega-events adventure. The new president was loudly booed, saved only by a swift switch to music on the stadium PA, and confined his involvement to Twitter, the media centre and a TV at the Presidential Palace in Brasília, where no doubt he saw the numerous protests at women's football games with banners in the crowd reading 'Temer Out' and 'Gold medal of hypocrisy'. More expensive, and more socially and environmentally disastrous than the World Cup, the Rio 2016 Games appeared as a giant party to which most of the city, which had paid for it, had not been invited. Brazil's men's team salvaged a measure of pride for the nation by beating the Germans, and for the first time winning the Olympic gold medal. Neymar, now fully recovered, scored the winning penalty in the inevitable shoot-out. But it all seemed like a very small return on Brazil's investments.

A better guide to the legacy of these sporting festivals than the Seleção's gold medal was the fate of the stadiums that hosted them.[84] As of 2018, of the twelve World Cup stadiums, eight featured in the ongoing corruption investigations and the testimonies of plea-bargaining construction industry executives. The ex-governor of Rio state, Sergio Cabral, was on trial for receiving kickbacks in connection with the reconstruction of the Maracanã. In time, Eduardo Paes, mayor of Rio, would be investigated for fraud in relation to the stadium's subsequent re-modelling for the Olympics. The governor of Minas Gerais, Fernando Pimentel, was alleged to have received $8 million worth of campaign funds via the building of the Estadio Mineirão, a method similar to that used by two previous governors of Brasília, and senior politicians in six other World Cup cities.[85] Arena Corinthians in São Paulo, paid for with public money, was, in the words of the chief executive of Odebrecht, the company that built it, 'a gift' to the club's most influential supporter, President Lula. And why not? That's the kind of largesse that comes from running a company whose turnover, under Lula's and Dilma's rule, had risen eight-fold to more than $130 billion a year. In the years since Corinthians, the in-house club of the PT, took possession of the stadium, the party has fallen from grace and government, and the new stadium has been assailed by landslides and flooded by water leaks beneath its underground car parks, and one of the stands was smashed by flying wall panels blown off their fixtures.

At least in São Paulo, and in Porto Alegre and Curitiba too, the stands were close to half-full. Most of the World Cup stadiums were virtually empty. In Manaus, Estadio Amazonas accommodated more local government workers in office space than fans in their seats; so too with Cuiba's stadium and the high-school students who studied there. In Brasília, a venue that cost not much short of half a billion dollars, the car park had been turned into a municipal bus garage. In Recife and Fortaleza, which at least have bigger, top-division clubs, the stadiums were located at such great distances from the cities' cores, and with virtually no official transport, that things were little better. In 2017 attendances at the Maracanã actually fell to zero. After an endless series of conflicts over who was responsible for its upkeep, and who should pay the huge outstanding bills for electricity and water, the stadium was closed, though with the kind of security detail that allowed thieves to loot its electronics and the kind of maintenance budget that allowed the turf to turn to dust.[86] There could be no more fitting monument to the hubris and waste of Brazil's sporting mega-events, and to the twenty years of unrelenting austerity that the new government had signed into law just a few months beforehand.

Stadiums are hardly full elsewhere in the country. Indeed, attendances at Brazilian football have plummeted since the 2014 World Cup, the average gate for the national championship falling below that of the USA, Japan and Australia. It is no coincidence that Brazil has also been charging amongst the highest ticket prices, relative to wages, anywhere in the world.[87] For those prepared to pay up, the football, while not without merit, is consistently undermined as a spectacle by the export of talent, the chaotic violence of the *torcidas*, the hapless policing of the game and its even poorer governance. The timetable remains full to bursting, with a third of the season taken up by the venerable state championships that pit the top-division clubs against regional minnows. Injuries, exhaustion and burn-out are common. However, as with the widely despised political class that continued to occupy state office and legislatures, the inner circles of the CBF proved implacable and immovable by domestic force alone. Their ejection would require international intervention, namely the 2015 FBI- and Swiss government-led investigations into FIFA's finances, the sale of South American football rights and vote-buying in the allocation of many World Cups, which accounted for the departure, and in one case imprisonment, of four previous presidents on the CBF.

Change, though, is what much of Brazil has been clamouring for, and in the 2018 presidential election the majority elected the ex-army officer and far-right politician, Jair Bolsonaro. It is not clear that they are going to get it this way either. Bolsonaro came to power on a campaign that mobilized public anger with corruption and fear of violent crime and robbery, at epidemic proportions but predominantly affecting the poor, and turned these emotions into a vote-winning but toxic cocktail of Amazonian hyper-development, more gun ownership and official shoot-to-kill policies. Footballers have been amongst his most prominent celebrity endorsers, including Rivaldo and Ronaldinho from an older generation, and Lucas Moura and Felipe Melo from the present one. In part this reflects the significant presence of evangelical Christians amongst Brazilian footballers, who in turn make up an important part of Bolsonaro's support. In part, it reflects the view of many of Brazil's more fortunate citizens that they are one step away from an urban uprising. In this Bolsonaro taps into the deep well of brutalized anger that characterizes the mood of much of Brazil's football, the anger that justifies any foul or foul play in order to win, that chooses conspiracy theory over reason for team purposes, that relentlessly repeats cycles of violence and disrespect. Given this, it is hard, in Brazilian football at any rate, to imagine that Bolsonaro will bring any meaningful change at all.

In Argentina change began with bereavement. One man in South American football had, with impeccable timing, eluded the reach of the US judicial system altogether. Indeed, truly nothing became him like his passing, for Don Julio went out on top: President of AFA for almost four decades, vice-president of FIFA and CONMEBOL. For a man who began with just a hardware store, he bequeathed a very considerable property estate, and was seen out with a funeral just short of a state occasion. AFA, astonishingly, declared a week of official mourning, cancelled all football, and placed Don Julio's body in state in the organization's downtown offices. The final send-off was graced by the governor of Buenos Aires province, the mayor of the city, Sepp Blatter and Lionel Messi, amongst others. All this just months before the FIFA scandals would unambiguously expose him as the corrupt, shameless rentier he had always been. But, venal as he was, he had brought a degree of order and purpose to the otherwise deeply and bitterly divided political words of Argentinian football. The election to succeed him pitted Marcelo Tinelli, vice-president of San Lorenzo, against Luis Segura, president of Argentinos Juniors. Segura was Grondona's anointed successor. Tinelli, an ally of the Kirchners and Argentina's most famous game-show and TV variety host, was the reform candidate, though many thought his candidature mainly a pitch to use football to enter politics. The vote was tied 38–38, which was bad enough, but given there were only 75 voters, not 76, there was a rogue vote to be accounted for; the whole show had to be cancelled.[88] A unity candidate could not be agreed, and Segura, as the incumbent, hung on until charges of corruption and embezzlement were levelled against him by the Buenos Aires prosecutor's office. It would take another year, under the jurisdiction of a FIFA normalization committee, before, in 2017, a successor to Don Julio could finally be elected.[89]

It was just this kind of bureaucratic incompetence that Mauricio Macri promised to tackle in his election campaign for the presidency in 2015, as part of his wider right-wing, new-broom assault on the political and economic woes of the Kirchners' Argentina. It was not the first time he had mobilized football in pursuit of political aims.[90] The scion of a rich industrial family, Macri worked in the family business under his father's beady eye until he established himself through the game. In 1995, he was elected president of Boca Juniors – the epitome of *porteño* working-class football – and at the turn of the century he presided over the club's most successful ever period, as national, continental and global trophies piled up. He was defeated in his first foray into politics, losing a run-off for the Buenos Aires mayoralty in 2003, but then won a term as a Congressman in 2005. In 2007, he triumphed in a second mayoral election, and ran the city for eight years until he was narrowly elected President in 2015. Along the way, Boca Juniors gave him visibility, a certain kind of authenticity, legions of Boca fans chanting club songs at his rallies and a story of entrepreneurial zeal. Under Macri's command, Boca Juniors acquired the nation's first executive boxes, had the first proper marketing department in the game, and turned itself into a global brand whose shirts and logos, while not as widespread as Barcelona or Manchester United, have a real global presence.

But this version of the Macri–Boca story, while all true, manages to miss a few vital details. Amongst other sly manoeuvres when in charge, Macri cut the money to the social side of the club and to sports other than football, in defiance of the club's membership. He also sharply raised the membership fee to try and exclude the hoi-poloi, and tried, unsuccessfully, to change Boca's constitution to drastically reduce the voting rights of those members. The VIP boxes came at the price of tearing down the stadium's famous and beautiful tower, and all these renovations were secured on what seemed to most to be eye-wateringly expensive building contracts. Above all, on his watch the leading *barras bravas* crew, *La Doce*, grew larger, richer and more permanently entrenched in the club's operations. Closer attention to these dimensions of Macri's football career would have given one a clearer indication of how he might operate when in government.

Macri's first move was an attempt to secure control at the still leaderless, rudderless AFA. The FIFA committee was actually headed by Armando Perez, a close ally of Macri, while the new statutes were drafted by the College of Lawyers, a known nest of Boca Juniors fans. Both were closely linked to Boca president Daniel Angelici, himself a friend and confidante of Macri. While Angelici would have been Macri's first choice as the new AFA president, it was too obvious a move. Moreover, two other cliques could command a significant bloc of votes within AFA: the group around Marco Tinelli, allied to the Kirchners, and the neo-Grondonists around Hugo Moyano, president of Independiente, whose real power rested on his presidency of the truckers' union. Moyano and Macri had been in sharp political conflict since the latter's election, disputing union laws, pay rates and public policy, but the two were united in their opposition to mainstream Peronists like Tinelli; Macri for obvious reasons, and Moyano because he had opportunistically broken from the Kirchners some years earlier. Tinelli, knowing he was outmanoeuvred, refused to contest the elections. Moyano put up his son-in-law Claudio 'Chiqui' Tapia, then president of the third-division minnows Barras Central, and a man whose demeanour said 'stooge' more clearly than most.[91] He got the job in an uncontested vote. Under this new coalition of the shameless, the AFA did finally manage to create a separate premier-league-style *Superleague*, abandoning the old two-tournaments-a-year format, and attempting to establish a more sustainable business model than hitherto. However, given the prior expansion of the top division to thirty teams – Don Julio's late 'gift' to the nation's small clubs – the league had to begin with an unmanageable number of teams and will spend its first four seasons relegating more clubs than it allows back in. Progress on the many other pressing items on its agenda, from the transparency of its own procedures to youth development, women's football and stadium security, has been ever more glacial.

If direct control of AFA was not possible, *Fútbol Para Todos* was another matter.[92] Despite campaigning with the promise of a hands-off approach to the programme, Macri began his term of office by appointing the showbusiness and TV impresario Fernando Marin to run it, who was also an ex-president of Racing Club. He began by changing the tone of the show, insisted on presenters wearing ties and jackets, stipulated no cursing and put an end to any political commentary. By this point the government was paying 1.5 billion pesos for the 2015 season and 1.85 billion pesos in 2016. At £72 million and £90 million respectively, that was small beer compared to the cost of European football rights, but in an era of very sharp reductions in public expenditure and public subsidies, *Fútbol Para Todos* was fiscally and ideologically unsustainable for the new government. Macri's election pledge not to privatize the show was steadily eroded. Government advertising was reduced and then withdrawn all together. Private advertising was permitted, as were re-broadcasts by private channels. The games of the second division were sold off to a re-born *Torneos y Competencias* and then, in spring 2017, the AFA announced that it had sold the rights of the newly constituted Argentinian Superleague to Fox and Turner. The *Fútbol Para Todos* experiment was over.

Macri began his term in office by doing easy things first. Argentina's government normalized its relations with international capital markets, gave farmers a $9 billion tax cut and conducted some simple privatizations, but the much more politically difficult reforms of taxation and the banking and energy sectors await. In the realm of football, he was bolder. Having divested himself of *Fútbol Para*

Todos, Macri then proposed doing something altogether more radical: seriously tackling Argentina's football violence problem and recommending that the nation's clubs should be converted from social organizations to private companies (a course he had tried to pursue when president of Boca Juniors). The anti-violence programme noted earlier has taken the easy option of increasing sentences and re-writing the law but, as with Macri's time at Boca, no action whatsoever has been taken to break the circuits of collusion between *barras bravas*, club directors and the police. The privatization plan has yet to make much headway either, as the club's themselves remain wary of the transparency and financial obligations that come with corporate status, and remain wedded to the idea of clubs as social rather than just economic institutions.

Fans, who have been keeping an eye on Boca under Macri's ally Daniel Angelici and seen just how private clubs might conduct themselves, are even more wary. In alliance with a Saudi Arabian property developer, Angelici proposed building a new *Bombonera* that was, in effect, a glorified shopping mall. Moreover, he proposed to build it on one of the only public parks in the Boca neighbourhood. There were large, vociferous and widespread protests that gave birth to a new fan activist group, *Boca Pueblo*, and forced the club to abandon the plan altogether, as well as destroying what remnants of trust existed between the management and much of the fanbase. *Boca Pueblo*, and like-minded groups at many other clubs, are part of a new wave of organizations in Argentina called *El Hincha Militante*, which seek to democratically organize fans around the running of their clubs. Macri's proposals have galvanized the movement further, leading to the creation of a national alliance of *hincha militante* united in their opposition to privatization. One might then be forgiven for thinking that the outbreak of anti-Macri chants across Argentinian football in 2017 and 2018, and the display of Macri coffins at Rosario Central, had been in opposition to his planned evisceration of Argentina's football economy, but they were, sadly, just a protest over Macri's and Boca's perceived control over referees and officiating, confirming the popular preference for conspiracy theory over political economy in the explanation of injustice. A situation that suited President Macri and his ilk just fine.[93]

VIII

If in Argentina football remains a deeply divided political and ideological battleground, in Colombia it has begun to make a small contribution to national unity and peace. In the 1980s and 1990s, after more than thirty years of anonymity, Colombian football burst back onto the international scene. In the late 1980s, América de Cali made it to and lost three consecutive finals of the Copa Libertadores, while in 1989, Atlético Nacional of Medellin actually won the thing. The national team, after a long absence, made three consecutive World Cups (1990–8) and at times dazzled with its innovative and intricate passing. In part it was the luck of having players of the calibre of Carlos Valderrama, and a brilliant coach in Francisco Maturana, but the fun was fuelled, above all, by cocaine. Both América and Atlético Nacional were teams of the cartel bosses, the Rodríguez Orejuela brothers and Pablo Escobar respectively, and Colombian football as a whole rose on the vast injections of money they shot into the game. This came, of course, at a cost: widespread corruption, money-laundering, assaults on referees, and thus, like the country as a whole, the steady collapse of the rule of law in favour of the use of the gun. A nadir was reached in 1994, when Andrés Escobar, the national team defender who had scored an own goal at the 1994 World Cup, was shot outside a bar by disgruntled low-level gangsters who had lost money gambling on the team.

While the 1990s saw the drug cartels checked and the leading bosses killed or imprisoned, neither a decline in the trade in cocaine or a rise in public safety were secured, for the long guerrilla war with FARC in the country's rural peripheries grew more intense. Intense enough for Colombia's plan to host the Copa América 2001 to be seriously questioned. In the months before the tournament, FARC kidnapped Hernan Campuzano, the vice-president of the football federation, while bombings killed twelve and injured over 200 people. CONMEBOL toyed with moving the show to Venezuela, until the TV companies told them not to. Argentina and the Canadians decided to stay at home. 'Let us root for peace,' implored President Andrés Pastrana, who made hosting the tournament a matter of vital national pride, before flooding the streets with army snipers and police bomb squads. Colombia, on a wave of euphoria and anxiety, won six games, conceded nothing and beat Mexico in the final 1–0.[94]

The Copa América was the last flourish for Colombian football for over a decade. The narco-induced highs of the 1990s finally ended, and the game shrivelled in the cold hard light of President Uribe's years in power (2002–10). Eight years more of a relentless US-funded war against both the cartels and the FARC guerrillas cost almost 200,000 deaths, nurtured a poisonous body-bag culture of extra-judicial killing in the military, left the drugs industry virtually unscathed and shielded the government from criticism and investigation of its appalling human rights and anti-corruption record. It did, however, transform the security situation in Colombia's main cities, and force FARC to the negotiating table. The national team failed to qualify for three successive World Cups and, like its once powerful clubs, performed dismally in South American competition. Under conditions of siege at home, attendances in the top division plummeted.

Uribe's hand-picked successor was the long serving defence minister Juan Manuel Santos, hardly a vector of reform, one might think, but his eight years in office proved otherwise. In the early days of his presidency, Argentinian police arrested members of the Norte Del Valle drug cartel, most of whom had decamped to Buenos Aires, from where they ran, amongst other things, a long-term $1.5 billion money-laundering operation through Santa Fe football club, the team of the President.[95] In response, Santos declared, 'Either we change football or it will be over for us.' His government then passed a body of legislation that pushed clubs towards more transparent public limited company status and required them to report to the government's money-laundering unit, while shareholders were henceforth required to demonstrate the probity of their money.[96] It also paid upward of $100 million to stage the under-20 World Cup, treated by government and public alike as something akin to the real thing. América de Cali, which had fallen into the lower divisions, returned to the top league and was finally removed from a US government blacklist for its past association with the narcotics industry.[97] Under the new dispensation, Millonarios contemplated relinquishing the 1987 and 1988 titles they had won when owned by the drug lure El Mexicano.[98] Nonetheless, just three years later, Colombia's public prosecutor was launching an investigation into money-laundering at eight professional football clubs.[99]

If there were limits to what brute force and punitive law could do in the face of Colombia's deep structural problems, the nation has shown considerable ingenuity in trying to just change behaviour directly. Antanas Mockus, the idiosyncratic Mayor of Bogotá, replaced corrupt traffic cops with clowns and mime artists in an effort to defuse the self-defeating anger and madness of the city's traffic jams, and issued red cards to car drivers as an alternative to more pugilistic forms of road rage. Colombia's most significant shift in attitudes and behaviours, however, came in 2012, with the revival of serious peace talks. Here, too, football had its cameo. Dag Nylander, the Norwegian diplomat and facilitator at the centre of the process, revealed that early antipathy between government and FARC delegations had melted in the face of an opportunity to watch Colombia versus Venezuela on television together.[100] As the talks progressed, and parts of Colombia's civil society began to support the peace talks' aims and methods of reconciliation, Carlos Valderrama and the rest of the nation's football royalty proposed that a 'game of peace' should be played in Cuba, where the talks were being conducted, amongst stars and politicians in support of the process. In response, FARC's negotiating team announced that they were 'fanatical about football', that they played amongst themselves in between talks, and even asked that a second game should be played in Colombia and a women's game arranged as well.[101] Like everything else in the peace process, it all took a lot longer than expected, and a single game was finally played in 2015 in Bogotá, alongside the high-profile national 'Peace Walk', by which time the real outlines of a deal were emerging.[102]

If the retreat of the narco-industry and the game's contribution to the peace process had detoxified Colombian football, its rebirth as a version of the nation's better self would await a team that could capture something of this changing nation. The arrival of Argentinian coach José Pékerman and a generation of football players whose careers had not been enmeshed with the drugs industry offered, if not a *tabula rasa*, a cleaner slate, and the attacking swagger of Radamel Falcao and James Rodríguez provided the goals to write a different story.

Thus, in 2014, for the first time in sixteen years, Colombia qualified for the World Cup finals.[103] Two weeks before the tournament began, Colombia held the first round of its presidential elections. The second, a run-off between the two leading candidates, the incumbent Santos and his right-wing challenger Óscar Zuluaga, was scheduled for the day after Colombia's opening game against Greece in Belo Horizonte. The campaign that ran alongside Colombia's preparation for the cup was ugly, polarized and bad-tempered, with Zuluaga incandescent over the compromises that Santos's peace plan would involve. 100,000 Colombians, many without tickets and all losing the opportunity to vote, opted for football and made the journey to Belo Horizonte in south-eastern Brazil for their opening game against Greece, where it was all Colombia, 'save for two small pockets of Greece supporters . . . The noise that greeted the "home" team was extraordinary. That was just for the warm-up.'[104] The *New York Times* reported that only 6 per cent of the country was uninterested in the fate of the team, the lowest football apathy rate in the world. Back home, Daniel Alarcón thought the nation equally entranced:

> It seems half the people on the streets are wearing the yellow national team jerseys, or trading Paninis in pop-up marketplaces across the city, or on the phone frantically trying to get their cable installed for the month. Colombia is back in the World Cup for the first time since 1998, with the kind of team . . . that makes you dream big.[105]

Dream big and drink big. In the nationwide bacchanalia that erupted after Colombia beat Greece, gunfire was widespread in urban areas and homicide rates climbed.[106] The following day, in a qualified victory for the peace process, Santos beat Zuluaga by 51 per cent to 45 per cent. A good chunk of the missing 4 per cent was spoilt ballots on which voters had written 'José Pékerman'.[107] Côte d'Ivoire, Japan and Uruguay were then all dispatched with some aplomb, taking team and nation to a quarter-final clash with hosts Brazil. Alcohol sales and drinking bans were in force across the nation while 'Half the population seems to be wearing the canary-yellow national jersey, even on days Colombia isn't playing.' The Brazilians would win 2–1, but Colombia took them all the way, and, when Juan Zúñiga's knee-first tackle struck Neymar's back and broke his vertebra, they made the Brazilians pay a very high price for their progress. The team returned to a parade in Bogotá to the acclaim of huge crowds.[108]

It would take another two years of gruelling negotiations and sporadic conflict for the fighting to finally stop. In June 2016, Colombia were making their way, by the skin of their teeth, through the Copa América; losing to Costa Rica, just getting through a quarter-final with Peru on penalties and crawling to a semi-final with Chile on the 23rd. That day, the government and FARC announced a definitive ceasefire, to begin in August, as a prelude to a complete peace deal. Colombia lost to Chile 2–0 but, as with the deal, just getting there had been a triumph. The deal would be rejected in a referendum and considerably rewritten in response, and Colombian football has yet to hit the same heights again, but across the country a kind of peace now reigns. FARC guerrillas have been forming teams, playing games of reconciliation with local communities they had previously disrupted or even preyed upon, and, in the shape of La Paz FC, they have created their own club in the lower reaches of the national leagues. Obscured by the great moments of the commercial spectacle, it is by such small measures that football is actually working for peace.[109]

IX

Uruguay remains a footballing miracle: a country of just over three million people which has, amongst many accomplishments, won the World Cup twice, and has, once again, become a real force in international football. Ever present at the World Cup, they made the semi-finals in 2010, and won the Copa América in 2011; their best players grace the squads of Europe's richest clubs. Like the leftist Frente Ampilo coalition which has presided over this and has found innovative ways for Uruguay to prosper from a globalization it cannot possibly control, Oscar Tabárez, the national coach since 2006, has reshaped Uruguayan football to cope with the weakness of its own domestic football and the endless export of players.[110] Recognizing that the best will all play in Europe, he has focused relentlessly on youth training and development, building team solidarities and allegiances before these young players inevitably depart and disperse. Clubs have been persuaded to release their best young players to the national squads two or three days a week. Unusually, for an international coach, Tabárez is also a trained history teacher, and has brought a deep sense of Uruguay's long and close relationship to football to his squads, one in which there is space for roughhouse tenaciousness but which privileges education and nurturing, modern precision and technique.

The connection between football and progressive politics in Uruguay is not surprising, but at the turn of the century the idea that football in Chile could be a catalyst of social change or an ally of progressive politics seemed fanciful. There was just too much baggage. In 1973, a week after the American-backed coup led by General Pinochet and the military had swept the democratically elected Allende government aside, the Estadio Nacional in Santiago was converted into a detention centre, torture chamber and morgue for 7,000 people. Over the next few months, it would process another 40,000, serving as a central node in a network of intimidation, violence and homicide – the Pinochet regime's *modus operandi* for the next seventeen years.[111] The detoxification of football began in 1988 when the Estadio Nacional was used as a polling station in the referenda that ended the military dictatorship. In 1990, the country's first elected head of state in seventeen years, Patricio Aylwin, and his supporters celebrated victory on the pitch. The stadium's place in the country's darkest historical moments was cemented by the release of Carmen Luz Perez's understated but devastating cinematic oral history *Estadio Nacional*. Since then, while the rest of the stadium has undergone extensive renovation, an area of wooden bleachers behind one of the goals has been preserved in its eerie 1970s form, accompanied by a plaque carrying the words '*Un pueblo sin memoir es en pueblo sin futuro*' – *A people without memory is a people without a future*.[112]

Whatever side of Chile's enduringly deep social and political divides you sat on, there was precious little to cheer from a national team that had not won a World Cup game since 1962. Consequently, draws were celebrated as if they were victories, aspirations were perennially low and regularly confirmed, encapsulated in the collective sigh that followed even the team's best performances, '*Jugamos common nuncio perdimos como siempre*' ('We played as never before, we lost as always'). The nadir came in 2007, on the eve of a Copa

América quarter-final in Venezuela, when six members of the squad were sent home for excessive partying – one in a long line of such incidents – leaving the rest to go down 6–1 in a humiliating defeat to Brazil. Change, though, was in the air. In the face of much domestic criticism, the new president of the Chilean Football Federation, Harold Mayne-Nicholls, appointed the Argentinian Marcelo Bielsa as national team coach.[113]

Running parallel with the first term of Socialist President Michelle Bachelet, Chile's first female head of state, Bielsa's term of office saw him ignite a minor cultural revolution in Chilean football that came to inspire and stand for a wider shift in the nation's political and emotional temperature. First, there was the love-in with the Chilean people, who were charmed by his down-to-earth humility, blunt sense of humour, personal frugality and phenomenal work rate. But it was the football he demanded of his teams that most eloquently expressed and nurtured a new mood in the nation.

Protagonismo, as Bielsa's style became known, was a game of relentless and fearless attack, underwritten by a willingness to take the initiative and make something happen, without fear of censure or failure. However, this stood in sharp contrast to the historic lessons learnt by the nation. As Armando Silva put it, 'The Chilean never protests, never complains and rarely makes demands. When Chileans have tried to rise up they've been brutally repressed.' Bielsa, working with a new generation of players born and brought up under Chilean democracy – like Arturo Vidal, Alexis Sánchez, Carlos Carmona, Gary Medel and Gonzalo Jara – began to challenge this. He encouraged the players to take charge of themselves and take risks, and many, with his encouragement, headed for Europe. In 2008, in the Estadio Nacional, Chile beat Argentina for the first time ever in a competitive fixture. 'He delivered a message to Chilean society. We can play as equals instead of living in constant fear of being thrashed.' The team was certainly listening, and the youngest squad at the World Cup 2010, despite going out in the round of sixteen to Brazil, were wildly celebrated for their attacking bravado.[114]

One telling subplot to South Africa 2010 was Bielsa's relationship with Chile's Presidents.[115] On meeting Sebastián Piñera, the newly elected conservative head of state, Bielsa barely deigned to greet him, evoking for many the spirit of Carlos Caszely, the one player in the Chilean 1974 World Cup squad who refused to shake Pinochet's hand. By contrast, Bielsa was regularly seen in close conversation with Piñera's socialist predecessor Michelle Bachelet, who visited the team while it was in South Africa. Piñera would get his revenge. First, Harold Mayne-Nicholls, head of the football association, attempted to introduce a new TV deal in which smaller clubs got a larger share of the revenue. In a direct parallel with the politics of inequality in the country as a whole, the largest and richest clubs, led by Colo-Colo, part-owned by Piñera, were implacably against.[116] Mayne-Nicholls was voted out of office by the leading club presidents, led ostensibly by Jorge Segovia, president of Union Española, owner of a chain of private universities and a close ally of Piñera. Bielsa had long made it clear that if Mayne-Nicholls went so would he, and thus just months after Chile's best World Cup performance in almost half a century he stood down. In a spontaneous display of support, there were demonstrations in central Santiago and at the Chilean FA headquarters. Armando Silva again: 'Bielsa signified a change in their mentality toward life; to be protagonists of their own lives.'[117]

It was precisely this shift, from despair to hope and from passivity to action, that animated Chilean youth, who just a few months later would initiate the country's greatest ever sustained outburst of social and political protest. The cowing of civil society was just one of the poisonous legacies of the Pinochet regime. Equally toxic was its economic performance, from which Chile emerged as one of the most unequal societies in the world, with an education system more deeply penetrated by market forces than any other on the continent. Indeed, the system had been constructed to channel what little state money was available to the rich, while facilitating grotesque levels of profiteering in higher and secondary education and reproducing already massive levels of inequality and tiny levels of social mobility. In 2011, driven by soaring levels of debt and the self-evident injustice of the system, a huge student movement took to the streets, reinforced by an unprecedented wave of activism amongst high school students, teachers and professors. Even the normally apolitical unemployed youth and flag-waving fans of Colo-Colo and Universidad de Chile were present at the biggest demonstrations. Jorge Sampaoli, the Argentinian coach of the latter and a disciple of Bielsa who had won three league titles and a Copa Sudamericana at Universidad with an even more aggressive, maniacal form of *protagonismo*, let it be known that he was with the youth too. 'Progressive people play offence,' he reflected, on his own and their style of operation. More directly, he invited key student leaders like Giorgio Jackson and Camila Vallejo to the club's training grounds. While the battle was far from over, the student movement forced the most fundamental re-think of public policy and spending since the end of Pinochet. The successive presidencies of Piñera and Bachelet were forced to seriously change tack, banning for-profit universities and public schools, and raising corporation tax to play for student grants and teachers' wages.

If the demonstrations of 2011 to 2013 were the high point of Chile's social *protagonismo*, the best of its footballing variant was yet to come. At the 2014 World Cup, now under Sampaoli, the new Chile were at their fearless, attacking best, mowing down the tiring *tiki taka* of Spain, the reigning champions, in a momentous 2–0 victory. The celebrations were uncontainable: '500 buses taken off the road, 6 hijacked; 40-plus bus drivers in accident and emergency; shops and supermarkets looted.'[118] Santiago's municipal authorities were, perhaps, quietly pleased that Chile did not make it past Brazil in the round of sixteen. The two variants of the new Chile both had their moment the following year, when the nation hosted and won the 2015 Copa América.[119]

The tournament was prefaced by a renewed wave of education protests, many of which had a footballing dimension.[120] Hundreds of thousands of students and professors marched through the capital under the banner 'The Copa América of Education' and splattered the city with painted footballs, while teachers gathered outside the national team's training camp and asked the squad to support their campaign for reduced contact hours and the payment of pensions and historic debts. Chile may not have been at peace, but it was galvanized. The team scored ten goals in its three group games, and the police expended more tear gas dispersing revellers in Santiago than they did dispersing the continuing wave of protests. They also worked overtime to make sure that Arturo Vidal, despite crashing his Ferrari while drunk, did not miss a game.[121] Then Chile dispatched Peru and Uruguay in the knock-out rounds and held their nerve in a penalty shoot-out with Argentina in the final. In 2016, they would win the tournament again.

Nothing is forever. In 2017, the same squad that won Copa

América twice underwent a precipitous collapse of form and failed
to qualify for the 2018 World Cup. Alongside this, Michelle Bachelet's government was beset by corruption scandals and an angry
students' and teachers' movement was still pressing for the reform of
the education system. Opinion polls suggested a majority of Chilean
voters perceived the team's decline as a clear symbol of the generally
poor state of the nation.[122] Later that year, the mood would be confirmed as Sebastián Piñera was elected for a second term as
President.

X

In late 2018, Boca Juniors, the club of Argentinian president Mauricio Macri, won a place in the final of that year's Copa Libertadores.
It was to be played over two legs against their great rivals River
Plate. Sensational as the prospect was for Argentinian football and
for CONMEBOL in trying to build the global profile of the competition, the omens were poor. The last time that the clubs had met in
the competition, in a semi-final in 2004, crowd trouble had meant it
was impossible to complete the tie. Football crowds remained fissipa-
rous enough that Macri's own government had banned away fans in
Argentinian football since 2013. Yet the next day Macri was calling
for away fans to be permitted on this occasion: 'I woke up this morning and said, we are going to make sure this final has the flavour of
Argentine football.'[123]

Be careful what you wish for. There were no away fans in Buenos
Aires, but there was trouble all the same. The first leg at Boca,
delayed by a day of thunderous anticipatory rain, was a 2–2 draw;
the second leg at River was never played. The Boca team bus, as it
approached El Monumental, was stoned, its windows shattered and
its interior pepper-sprayed. CONMEBOL, desperate not to lose its
TV monies, first tried to make the show go on, then abandoned
it, then called for the game to go ahead in Buenos Aires, and then,
finally, abandoned Argentina and its implausible promises of security
and moved the circus to Real Madrid's Santiago Bernabéu over 5,000
miles away. Under high-level policing by the Spanish, and in the
absence of the *barras*, fans of both clubs from Argentina and

across the world filled the stadium. River won 3–1, but this moment will be remembered as the occasion on which the Copa Libertadores – named after the generals that led the expulsion of the Spanish Empire from South America – returned as a supplicant to the metropole, unable to stage the spectacle itself. It was not the message that CONMEBOL would have chosen to send, but in clarifying the subordinate state of the continent's football, and the dismal condition of its governance, it could hardly have been more accurate.

4

THIS STORM IS WHAT WE CALL PROGRESS: FOOTBALL AND THE EUROPEAN PROJECT

Rendez-vous with history!

UEFA Euro 2016 corporate slogan

A Klee painting named 'Angelus Novus' shows an angel looking as though he is about to move away from something he is fixedly contemplating. His eyes are staring, his mouth is open, his wings are spread. This is how one pictures the angel of history. His face is turned toward the past. Where we perceive a chain of events, he sees one single catastrophe which keeps piling wreckage and hurls it in front of his feet. The angel would like to stay, awaken the dead, and make whole what has been smashed. But a storm is blowing in from Paradise; it has got caught in his wings with such a violence that the angel can no longer close them. The storm irresistibly propels him into the future to which his back is turned, while the pile of debris before him grows skyward. This storm is what we call progress.

Walter Benjamin, Theses on the Philosophy of History[1]

I

Imagine the excruciating polished blandness of a conference room in UEFA's headquarters in Nyon, on the shore of Lake Geneva. UEFA marketing executives and the 'guys' from the Portuguese branding agency that have been working up the 'concept' are sitting around a very large table. It's scattered with open bottles of mineral water, drained espresso cups and smart UEFA stationery. They are here to sign off on the official slogan for the 2016 European Championships. The big theme for the tournament that they've come up with so far is 'Celebrating the Art of Football', which Michel Platini, president of UEFA, loves and is fine as far it goes, but it's not the kind of dynamic injunction they have been searching for. So, as of today, they are going with *'Rendez-vous!'*, and that's good, as far as it goes. Think about it! The tournament is being hosted by France, it's just about the most well-known French idiom they can find, and they are liking the sense of appointment and gathering it evokes. But what are we actually *rendez-vousing* for? The brains trust, after much workshopping, has boiled it down to this: 'Twenty-four nations will meet over fifty-one matches during which the eyes of the world will be riveted on the best of European football', which is true, but both verbose and dull. So what else is in town? 'I know,' shouts one bright spark: 'History!'

Be careful what you wish for. Deep beneath the surface of official Czechoslovak communism, the Slovak-dominated team that won the 1976 championship stirred latent nationalist and irredentist emotions. The Danes seemed to make history when they won Euro 92 and rejected the Treaty of Maastricht, though they would be strong-armed and sent back to the polls to confirm it in a second referendum. Modern English nationalism showed its brightest and most appealing face in an unprecedented sea of St George's flags and self-deprecating nostalgia at Euro 96. Greece, in a sleight of hand every bit as good as the nation's accession to the Euro, snatched the prize in 2004, triggering ecstatic nationwide reveries which, along with the Athens

Olympics, constituted the last great party before the bitter reckoning to come. However, I'm not sure that any of the creatives in the room had these events in mind. Had they, and had they known the political context in which the 2016 tournament would occur, they might have been less blithe in their embrace of history.

Euro 2016 was the first European football championship to be held under a state of emergency. If, as Walter Benjamin, the lugubrious Marxist critic, suggested in his *Theses on the Philosophy of History*, written back in the 1930s, 'The state of emergency in which we live is not the exception but the rule', it is unlikely to be the last. Declared by President Hollande in the aftermath of the jihadi Paris attacks of November 2015, which included an attempted suicide bombing of a France–Germany match at Stade de France, the state of emergency was extended to cover the tournament.[2] The French police reported that Belgian militants were planning their own assault on the competition. The Ukrainian authorities announced that a French citizen, whom they suspected of planning terrorist attacks in France, was arrested with a huge cache of arms on the Polish border.[3] Consequently, nearly 80,000 state security personnel were mobilized, supplemented by 15,000 private security guards and a 10,000-strong military reserve, trained to deal with catastrophic bomb attacks on the fan zones and chemical warfare in the stadiums.

If jihadi-inspired attacks threatened to bring history to the party from beyond Europe, the most likely agent of disruption actually came from within. Just a few months before Michel Platini had initially announced Euro 2016's tryst with history, the British Conservative government had published its draft EU Referendum Bill, the first fateful legislative move towards holding the UK's EU referendum on 23 June 2016. This date, it would transpire, would fall halfway between England's final group game and, should they get there, a round-of-sixteen match. It did. On 20 June, a very fragile-looking England team scraped their way into the knock-out stages by way of a grinding scoreless draw with Slovenia. Three days later the UK voted to leave the European Union, then Iceland dispatched a shattered England team 2–1, and the rest, as they say, is history.

The place of football in European history wasn't always so central. Prior to the Second World War there were some international football games in Europe, especially amongst neighbours, but none of this made news beyond the back pages. For a brief inter-war moment the

Mittropa Cup – the forerunner of today's Champions League – blossomed amongst the cosmopolitan cities of northern Italy, Prague, Vienna and Budapest, but in a continent riven by war and the struggles between democracy, fascism and communism, there was little appetite for a European-wide football organization or tournament of any kind. Modern European football only began in 1954 with the foundation of UEFA, with French administrators in the lead displaying the same transnational ambitions and ideas that were shaping the parallel creation of the European Economic Community. In both cases, Britain stood aside. Successive Conservative governments dithered over whether to join the EEC, while in 1955 league champions Chelsea were offered the opportunity to participate in the first version of the European Cup – now the Champions League – but declined. Since then the status of the European game has changed entirely, even in Britain, the most Eurosceptic of nations. Once it was outside of Europe – both the EEC and the European Cup – entry became an obsession, for British governments and clubs alike. An exasperated Gordon Brown, campaigning for Remain in the EU referendum, wrote, 'a presence in the UEFA Champions league has become the epitome of footballing success: when Europe is the peak of ambition in football and we compete so ferociously to get there, why in other spheres of British life do so many seek to reject it?'[4] Janus-faced, the English have looked towards Europe at the same time as they have looked away. Either way, they are not alone in entwining their stories with European football. Franco's Spain re-engaged with the European mainstream through Real Madrid's domination of the European Cup in the 1950s; Salazaar's Portugal did the same through Benfica in the early 1960s. Silvio Berlusconi's political project at AC Milan in the 1980s and 1990s always prioritized the glamour and spectacle of European football, while Ceausescu's Romania took one last draught of legitimation from Steaua Bucharest's foreign adventures when they won the European Cup in 1986.

The idea that popular culture, let alone European football, should have come to occupy such a significant place in post-war national narratives is a notion the founders of the European project would have found hard to comprehend. Having survived the moral wasteland of two world wars, they had little truck with cultural definitions of Europe that made it the inheritor of classic antiquity or the Enlightenment. Overwhelmingly lawyers, diplomats and politicians, theirs was a Europe bound not by culture and belief, but by the rule of law, the practical compromises of pooled sovereignty, shared markets and institutions, and the powerful material forces of growth, technology and prosperity. When they did acknowledge the need for a European identity and shared mental space to give meaning and legitimacy to the institutions they had created, it was with a very narrow sense of the cultural. As Robert Schuman, French foreign minister and one of the architects of the EEC, argued: 'Before being a military alliance or an economic entity, Europe must be a cultural community in the most elevated sense of the term.'[5]

However, the elevated materials out of which to forge such a European culture have been very thin on the ground. Europe's reverence for the rule of law, liberal democracy and human rights has been articulated in universal rather than continental terms. Europe's national literary and cinematic canons remain irreversibly divided by language, and confined to a narrow stratum of readers and viewers. The de facto emergence of English as the language of international communication has made matters worse. Popular music, unencumbered by problems of literary translation, suggests more fertile soil and, indeed, as a televised European spectacular, football's only competitor is the Eurovision Song Contest. While it has done wonders in creating LGBTQ-heavy transnational networks of kitsch and subversion, and its judging has laid bare the power blocs and shameless horse-trading of European politics, it has done little to nurture any wider European musical style, taste or market, accurately reflecting the deeply parochial and perennially awful state of most European vernacular pop.

The European Commission's 1987 report *European Identity: Symbols to Sport* addressed itself to this vacuum, and on the basis of its recommendations the EU created networks of European universities and research institutes, popular and widespread student exchange schemes, and introduced the Union's twelve-star flag.[6] Its tentative suggestion that Europe might field sporting teams has only borne fruit in golf's Ryder Cup, where the continent faces off against the United States; testament to the sport's enduring place as the networking game of choice amongst the transatlantic business classes. All of this generated a modicum of *esprit de corps* amongst European elites, but singularly failed to generate a widespread, popular sense of Europe itself, or even a space in which it might be imagined. It is

Europe's loss that football was not on the agenda of the key protagonists in the forging of the European project, for at the turn of the twenty-first century the game was a rare cultural space in which a progressive, inclusive and popular idea of the continent could be elaborated.

At the turn of the century the European economy was still booming, and the newly expanded European Union – although still largely unloved by the public – appeared a model of regional co-operation and supranationalism, and European football appeared to reflect and nurture many of the best features of the continent: political, economic and cultural. Certainly, since the 1950s, European football has been able to offer a more expansive and inclusive vision than most other European projects, taking in, from the very beginning, not just the western European core of the EEC but everyone from Ireland and Iceland in the west to the Soviet Union and Turkey in the east. At the level of governance, and certainly when compared to FIFA and other continental football confederations – though this is hardly setting the bar very high – European football appeared relatively uncorrupt and sensibly regulated by UEFA, its commercial priorities tempered at least by some measure of social democratic redistribution from the richest to the poorest nations. Under the presidencies of Lennart Johannsen and Michel Platini, UEFA developed systems of economic redistribution and economic surveillance and control that would have been the envy of the European Commission. Its increasingly rigorous club-licensing system introduced a hitherto unknown level of transparency into European football finance, while the financial fair play regulations gave UEFA the power to investigate and punish spendthrifts, debtors, soft loans and over-generous sponsorship deals by companies linked to club owners.[7]

Football could certainly have been cast as an economic sector in which Europe was one of globalization's winners, able to use its huge internal market and technical edge to draw players, investment and audiences from around the world. In an era when growth rates in the core of the EU remained stubbornly around 2–3 per cent, football recorded the kind of double-digit growth more characteristic of the industrializing global south. By 2016, the European football market, narrowly defined as the turnover of the professional game and football associations, was €24.6 billion: just less than the entire European publishing industry, but larger than Europe's commercial music sector (both recorded and live markets combined).[8] The global audiences for the European Championships, the Champions League, and the leading national leagues of Europe, made it a much more successful exporter than its peers in the culture industry. Talent from every corner of the world, players and coaches, has flooded into the European game; and they come younger, stay longer and sometimes never go back home, and while in Europe they have been playing in the world's best football stadiums.[9] Primarily financed by the public sector, a huge wave of investment has been seen in Europe in the last two decades, driven by staging mega-events (these include France, Belgium, the Netherlands, Portugal, Germany, Austria, Switzerland, Ukraine and Poland), football-orientated populist projects (Hungary and Turkey), and the booming demand for new facilities in the continent's wealthiest leagues and amongst its biggest clubs.

Above all, football had showcased the dynamism and interconnectedness of European civil society at a level below the nation state, for most of the time the game was a contest between the cities and urban regions of the continent. Furiously competitive and technically brilliant, it benefited from Europe's high level of specialized education and training, the openness of its labour markets, and the ease and speed of knowledge and technology transfer. A glance at the state of European football's training complexes gives an indicator of the continent's competitive edge, indeed the gulf that exists with the rest of the world. AC Milan's Milanello complex, massively expanded by Silvio Berlusconi in the 1980s and 1990s, brought new standards of sports medicine and science to the game, and was renowned for preserving and implausibly extending the long playing careers of its stars. The French football federation's Clairfontaine operation was another early adopter of new, scientifically grounded nutrition, fitness and training regimes. Ajax, already famed for the rigour and sophistication of its youth development programme, acquired facilities to match in the early 1990s, creating at De Toekomst an infrastructural and training template for advanced football academies across the continent. Since then the leading clubs, and many national federations in Europe, have invested significant resources in duplicating these models. Liverpool's new Melrose complex cost £50 million, Real Madrid's Cibeles more than £70 million, while the bill for Manchester City's – more gated urban neighbourhood than football training ground – is over £200 million. Not just buildings and playing fields, these operations house psychologists, nutritionists, cross-training sports experts, analytics and video-analysis departments, ever more sophisticated in-house medical services, increasingly large and specialized coaching departments for all teams at all levels, and globally networked scouting operations.[10] All of this has delivered unqualified success at the apex of the game: European teams have won five of the six World Cups between 1998 and 2018, and provided more than three-quarters of the finalists; the World Club Cup, for what it is worth, has been a European monopoly since 2005; and in the shape of the UEFA Champions League in particular, Europe has created the sporting pinnacle of the commercial football spectacle. The football played by the leading dozen or so club sides that have monopolized the later stages of the competition has been without peer in the history of the game, and their narratives invariably compelling: *inter alia* the first iteration of Real Madrid's *Galacticos* at the start of the century; the imperious Real Madrid of Ronaldo a decade later; Barcelona in peak, mesmerizing *tiki taka* mode; Mourinho's post-modern *catenaccio* initiated at Porto and perfected at Internazionale; relentless, heart-stopping, last-minute turnovers and turnarounds from Manchester United and Liverpool.

Finally, while there was a long and unpleasant streak of ultra-nationalism and street violence running through the history of European football, the early 2000s – especially the 2004 European Championships in Portugal and the 2006 World Cup in Germany – were remarkable for their fabulous displays of benign and carnival nationalism.[11] If at Euro 96 football came home, at Portugal 2004 it was on holiday, a sun-drenched, beer-soaked, month-long jolly for the European football nation. Fabulously staged in some of the continent's most intriguing, inventive and colourful stadiums, it attracted more travelling fans than any of its predecessors: more than 150,000 English and 100,000 German fans made the journey, while the Dutch, the Danes and the Swedes were filling stands and squares, turning them orange, red and yellow respectively. Unlike Euro 2000, held in the Low Countries, the month was almost entirely without incidents of fans fighting, or even behaving terribly badly.

Certainly, racist chants were heard from the Croat contingent, but one could have been forgiven for thinking that, at this level at any rate, European football could become a platform for the continent's new tolerance and diversity rather than its atavism. English football, long possessing a squad of mixed heritage, had begun to truly tackle its stadium racism problems, France's multi-ethnic team had won the 1998 World Cup and the European Championship in 2000, creating a short-lived blaze of optimism that the country could make peace with its new demographic mix.

Nowhere was that hope more loudly expressed than in Germany at the 2006 World Cup. Gifted an approachable, young and multi-ethnic squad under Jürgen Klinsmann, who played with brio and above themselves, Germany fell back in love with its national team and itself. For perhaps the first time since unification, the German public felt at ease with its own flag and nationhood; happy to acknowledge its new diversity, and to celebrate it in a style that melded a Berlin nightclub suffused with MDMA love and the ambience of a vast Bavarian beer garden.

More than a decade since Germany's *Sommermärchen,* the continent looks very different. Indeed, it has been shaken to its core by three intersecting crises: economic, migratory and political. Given how accurate an avatar of the continent's successes and strengths European football has proved, it is no surprise to find that the game reflects and illuminates its travails too. In the decade since the global financial crisis of 2008, the European economy in general, and the Eurozone in particular, has undergone a period of contraction, in some states of historic proportions, and sluggish growth since. Almost everywhere this has been accompanied by austerity and deflation, imposed by the logic of the euro, the bond markets and the neo-liberal choices made by politicians. The pain has not, however, been equally shared. Indeed, the last ten years have seen some economic sectors and groups continue to prosper while the gap dividing them from those at the margins grows wider.

In this regard, at least, football continues to showcase the European project. At the core, European football appears to have entirely escaped from the conventional laws of economic gravity, and is perhaps best thought of as a variant of the financial sector. While almost every other economic indicator has been plummeting, the incomes of players and coaches – who, like bankers, are a tiny and highly internationalized pool of workers – climb relentlessly upward. The richest leagues have seen a step change in their incomes as they reap the benefits of a football-hungry, globally networked audience. At every level, already significant economic inequalities are widening and sharpening: between the biggest clubs in Europe and those in the second and third ranks; between the big countries and the increasingly marginal medium-size and small football nations; between the professional game and the grassroots. At the same time that the financial crisis has starkly revealed the engine of inequality at the heart of the European model of both capitalism and football, the last decade has also drawn attention to their large and enduring grey areas of criminality, from match-fixing to embezzlement to tax evasion, from money-laundering to the people trafficking of young players – and the seeming invulnerability of so many elites when caught out. Indeed, in much of European football it is hard to see whether there is anything but a grey area. In this regard football has been, across Europe, an accurate barometer of the pervasive capture and abuse of the public realm by private interests.

The migration crisis of 2015, and Germany's decision to accept large numbers of refugees, was just the most visible moment of almost two decades of change. A combination of legal and illegal movements, economic migrants, refugees and asylum seekers has transformed the ethnic make-up of many European societies, and evoked a fearsome populist, nativist and racist political backlash across the continent. While the spirit of civic nationalism and cultural cosmopolitanism that animated France 1998 and Germany 2006 has not disappeared, and the forces of anti-racism are, if anything, more organized than ever in European football, they have not gone uncontested. Indeed, racism, at the level of chants and abuse, is perhaps more prevalent than before in the Eastern half of the continent, and certainly not absent from the Western half. Right-wing gangs, neo-Nazis and ultra-nationalists have become an entrenched and very public presence on the terraces of European football. Thus the ethnic make-up of national teams has become an increasingly high-voltage lightning conductor for both sides of the divide, with players of migrant heritage, like the communities they spring from, relentlessly scrutinized for their allegiance and demeanour. As the striker Romelu Lukaku brilliantly put it, 'When things were going well, I was reading newspaper articles and they were calling me Romelu Lukaku, the Belgian striker. When things weren't going well, they were calling me Romelu Lukaku, the Belgian striker of Congolese descent.'[12]

Europe's heterogeneity and complexity means that no nation, no football culture, has been shaped by these economic and demo-graphic forces in the same way. However, they do provide a useful organizing principle for exploring the state of the game. In the open-ing sections of this chapter it is the economics of oligarchy and the politics of nation and ethnicity that figure most centrally. Against a backdrop of post-communist economic and political trauma, football in south-eastern Europe, the Balkans and Eastern and Central Europe has been colonized by the spectrum of organized criminals and pol-itically favoured oligarchs that pass for the regions' business class. While they have been able to extract both financial and political cap-ital from the game, they have proved unable to make it a popular commercial spectacular, leaving the stadiums and the wider meaning of the game to the ultras and hyper-nationalists for whom it has proved a fabulous platform for their toxic ethnic phobias.

By contrast, in the central sections of this chapter, covering West-ern and Northern Europe, the economics of globalization have been in the ascendant. Smaller and medium-sized nations, unable to com-pete in the new global markets for viewers, sponsors and players, have been squeezed. Some, like Scotland, have fallen further behind both economically and in sporting performance. Others, like the Netherlands and Portugal, keep their heads above water by dint of their phenomenal training and development programmes. The five largest European football economies – England, France, Germany, Italy and Spain – continue to operate in another world. At one level the fate of these football economies can be read as a comparative case study in dealing with globalization: a fabulously successful, commercial, hyper-globalized league and an often dire men's na-tional team in England; a still technically brilliant Italian league in seemingly irreversible decline as it struggles with its decaying infra-structure and volatile crowds; a regulated social-market model in Germany that has delivered both international success and a boom-ing vibrant domestic scene, though one troubled by conflict over commercialization; Spain's closed and protected duopoly that has virtually separated itself from the rest of the nation; a French model in which player development and player exports compensate for a weak domestic market and a brilliant national team compensates for a perennially weak national league.

The combination of endless austerity and a captured public realm might, by themselves, have been enough to trigger the populist surge, from Italy's 5SM to Hungary's Fidesz and Britain's UKIP, but what has given it urgency, weight and power has been the long-term political and cultural consequences of migration. Thus, at the intersection of Europe's economic and demographic woes there is a third, political, crisis. At the national level, the mainstream of social democrats, Christian democrats and centrists have been squeezed by nationalist and populist forces to both their right and left, producing ever more fragile and unstable coalitions, more toxic and polarized political environments. At a continental level, Britain's vote to leave the European Union in 2016 was just the leading edge of centrifugal forces at work in Europe, which, alongside the authoritarian turn and deepening resistance to Brussels' cosmopolitanism in Poland and Hungary, and the rise of deeply Eurosceptic parties in Italy and Austria, all threaten to unravel the European project. As we shall see, in many European countries football has become a route to political power and influence, and an increasing part of the rhetorical repertoire of populist politicians. Amenable to their model of politics as gameshow and voting as applause, the game has also offered a deep reservoir of nativist beliefs and racist anger to work with. However, in the two penultimate sections of this chapter, on Greece and Turkey, the process has gone so far that politics and political theatre have become an indispensable part of football. Greek football, in toto, has given us a dramatic performance which explores a public realm both endemically corrupt and utterly irreformable. Turkish football has perhaps been more operatic, its diva President Erdoğan, who has made football another battleground in his authoritarian remaking of the country.

For politics in a different key, we turn in the final section to the flowering of women's football in Europe, the growth of supporter activism, alternative football clubs and an anti-commercial culture, and the rise of Icelandic football, which offer a glimpse of what a communitarian but democratic riposte to the political crisis might look like. The European project, if it is to be saved, will require rather more than egalitarian sports programmes and reformed football associations, but it is a measure of European football's ascendant cultural status that it can make any contribution at all. Given, then, that football is now such an integral part of European history, it is a shame that UEFA, having made the rhetorical link, did not choose to explore the idea more imaginatively. In a parallel universe the conversation in the UEFA conference room would have gone something like this:

INT. UEFA CONFERENCE ROOM: DAY

UEFA EXECUTIVE 1: Sure. I'm with you on 'Rendez-Vous' . . . but 'Rendez-Vous' with what, exactly?

Portuguese consultant 1 and Portuguese consultant 2 exchange a knowing glance.

PORTUGUESE CONSULTANT 1: I know . . . History!

PORTUGUESE CONSULTANT 2: 'Rendez-Vous with History'? . . . That could work.

UEFA EXECUTIVE 2: Oh yes, Platini is going to love that.

UEFA EXECUTIVE 1: History? It's kind of abstract, isn't it? How does this thing work with the mascot? What's he called?

PORTUGUESE CONSULTANT 1: Super Victor.

UEFA EXECUTIVE 1: Oh yeah, Super Victor. Well, what is Super Victor going to be doing with History? Taking an exam?

PORTUGUESE CONSULTANT 2: Maybe Super Victor is the problem. Our colleague from the Frankfurt office, Walter Benjamin, wants to speak to this.

UEFA EXECUTIVE 2: Left back with Bayer Leverkusen, right?

WALTER BENJAMIN, who has been sitting to one side of the group, stands at the head of the table, a huge screen behind him, slowly bringing the Paul Klee painting Angelus Novus *into focus.*

WALTER BENJAMIN: A Klee painting named *Angelus Novus* shows an angel looking as though he is about to move away from something he is fixedly contemplating. His eyes are staring, his mouth is open, his wings are spread. This is how one pictures the angel of history.

PORTUGUESE CONSULTANT 2: OK, so that's our new mascot . . . Working nicely with the Art of Football Theme. No?

UEFA EXECUTIVE 2: Oh yes, Platini is going to love that.

As WALTER BENJAMIN speaks, he goes out of focus, and we bring the screen behind him into focus. The angel now occupies the right third of that screen. The rest is filled with the image of a football stadium seen from high in the stands behind one of the goals. The stand behind the opposite goal has been torn from the rest of the structure, leaving a gaping hole framed by concrete stumps and steel wires. Beginning on the horizon and accompanied by the rising roar of a cyclone, a great storm of wreckage – people, objects, lives, loves, footballs – comes hurtling into the stadium, flying past the camera and accumulating in the lower levels of the stand.

WALTER BENJAMIN: His face is turned toward the past. Where we perceive a chain of events, he sees one single catastrophe, which keeps piling wreckage and hurls it in front of his feet. The angel would like to stay, awaken the dead, and make whole what has been smashed.

UEFA EXECUTIVE 1: Awaken the dead . . . Make whole . . . OK.

PORTUGUESE CONSULTANT 2: Wait . . .

WALTER BENJAMIN: But a storm is blowing in from Paradise.

UEFA EXECUTIVE 1: Now you are talking . . .

WALTER BENJAMIN: It has got caught in his wings with such a violence that the angel can no longer close them. The storm irresistibly propels him into the future to which his back is turned, while the pile of debris before him grows skyward.

PORTUGUESE CONSULTANT 2: And this is the slogan to run on the pitch-side boards.

WALTER BENJAMIN: This storm is what we call progress.

UEFA EXECUTIVE 2: Oh yes, Platini is going to love that.

UEFA EXECUTIVE 1: Let me run this one past the President . . .

Dissolve to the closing seconds of the Russia v England game in Marseille in June 2016. We see the big screen, the score and the angel of history alongside them. We then cut to the stands and see the Russians charge the English crowd behind the goal, scattering them like ninepins. The camera pulls out to reveal, along the front of the stand, a shimmering LED board switching between the tournament's slogans, 'Rendez-vous With History', 'This storm is what we call progress'.

II

Late developers? One-off generations? The social energies released by the fall of communism? Whatever was at work in the late 1980s and early 1990s, football in south-east Europe's furthest reaches had its singular golden age. In 1993, a late equalizer against France by Emil Kostadinov took Bulgaria to the World Cup finals, a moment encapsulated by the much-quoted and always delirious line of commentary, 'God is Bulgarian.' The team was graced by the spiky talent of the nation's greatest player ever, Hristo Stoichkov, and once there they gave the country an American summer of love. After losing their opening game to Nigeria they beat Greece, Argentina, Mexico and then the Germans in the quarter-finals, before going out to the Italians in the semis and finishing fourth. The Romanians, led by the elegant Gheorghe Hagi, made the quarter-finals themselves at USA 1994, one in a run of three World Cup appearances in the 1990s. In both countries, the public took a brief break from the chaos and penury of the immediate post-communist transition to wildly party.[13] Football, popular but dowdy, and enmeshed with the institutions of communist rule, was suddenly the centre of attention, and wide open for occupation by the new political and economic forces that were emerging in both countries. It would not be a smooth or positive transition. Indeed, as a tearful Gheorghe Hagi, speaking after a particularly vicious crowd had booed the national team in a friendly in Bucharest in 1998, correctly warned, it would be awful:

For ten years we've hidden the dire conditions we have here in Romania. We have nothing, no football. Where are the performances produced by the clubs in Romania? We deserve for you to make us statues for what we have done considering the conditions in Romania. The results are now with us. Romanian football is gone. Gone. Zero. In two or three years, zero.[14]

In Bulgaria the quickest off the blocks in the race to sequester state assets were the country's notoriously steroid-hardened wrestlers, many of whom, in the 1990s, became gang leaders, then 'heads' of the first generation of security services, and then oligarchs. Their earliest purchases, in addition to compliant politicians and police officers, were football clubs which delivered the usual combination of local patronage and popularity, as well as ample opportunities for money-laundering and embezzlement. Iliya Pavlov, a wrestler who married into the family of the head of state security, followed precisely this trajectory.[15] In 1994, his gambling, prostitution and car-theft conglomerate, Multigrup, acquired the country's biggest club, CSKA Sofia, once the team of the Bulgarian People's Army. He would sell CSKA on in 1999, but kept his sporting hand in as president of the small provincial club PFC Cherno More Vanra until, in 2003, an assassin's bullet passed through his heart. His successor at CSKA was Vasil Bozhkov, then the country's richest man, who was riding high on the rentier's classic trio of gambling, real estate and government infrastructure projects. Always considered a secret Levski Sofia supporter by the CSKA fans, he won the club championships but no love for himself. Next up was the Indian steel tycoon Pramod Mittal, whose primary concern in Bulgaria was actually the state steelworks, Kermeitlovsti. Mittal killed two birds with one stone by first buying the club, and then installing Aleksandar Tomov as its president, a post that Tomov could neatly combine with being the boss of the said factory.

A similarly unsavoury selection of characters has been in charge of the nation's other clubs.[16] In the late 1990s a group of Pavlov's associates broke away to form their own operation, SIK, which then bought Slavia Sofia. Soon after this, police shot dead Milcho Bonev, the man in charge of the club's transfer policy, and five of his bodyguards, in Slavia's own restaurant garden. The club president, Mladen Mihalev, went into hiding, and the vice-president's son was kidnapped. In 1999 the nation's second club, Levski Sofia, was bought by Russian billionaire Michael Cherney. It says something for his reputation that the Bulgarians thought him such a security risk that he was expelled from the country in 2000, since when his legal representative, Todor Bakotov, has been in charge. More straightforwardly unpleasant are Nikolay Gigo, an arms dealer who bought Lokomotiv Sofia, and Ivan Slavkov, owner of Spartak Varan, who was arrested in 2008 for his extensive connections to drug and people trafficking, money-laundering and the sex industry. Grisha Ganchev, another wrestler turned oligarch who bought his local club, in this case Lovech in 1996, renamed it after his company as Litex Lovech, then won promotion, the Bulgarian league and the Bulgarian cup.

Bloodiest of all clubs, accounting for over a third of the fifteen homicides of Bulgarian football directors in the last twenty years, has been Lokomotiv Plovdiv.[17] This small provincial club was the team of another breakaway faction from the Pavlov empire, operating under the corporate umbrella VIS. The team was first purchased in 1993 by the wrestler Georgi Kalapatirov, and his associates, Nikolai Popov and Peter Pesho-Petrov, founders of the security firm, the *777 club*, and experts in blackmailing and racketeering. In 1995, the *777 club* merged with VIS, and a few months later Kalapatirov was shot through the heart. His successor at Lokomotiv, Georgi Prodanov, was a VIS specialist in pyramid schemes and financial scams, but not car mechanics; he died in a crash, in a vehicle whose brake hoses had been cut. Pesho-Petrov lasted three years in charge, until in 1998 he was gunned down outside his front door. Nikolai Popov, the last of the original trio, managed to leave the presidency alive in 2001, but in 2005 was shot and then bludgeoned to death. Meanwhile, Georgi Illiev, then the key figure in VIS, had taken on the job. In 2001 he merged Plovdiv with another club that he owned, Velbazhd Kyustendil, and bankrolled the team to its first Bulgarian title in 2004. However, in 2005, while celebrating a recent club victory at a bar by the Black Sea, he was taken out by a sniper's rifle. His widow, not surprisingly, decided to get out of the football business and sold the club to local businessman Aleksandar Tasev, whose seemingly innocent interests in cherries and the footwear industry did not keep him out of trouble. In 2007, Tasev too was assassinated.

In 2007 Bulgaria joined the European Union by the skin of its teeth. Almost immediately it was under pressure to mount a more serious programme of anti-corruption reform. Indeed, much of the promised funds from Brussels were withheld while the government struggled to drain the swamp, of which it was itself, inevitably, a large component. In football, the long-known and widespread practice of match-fixing, for both points and betting purposes, was finally made very public when four referees went on television to accuse the football association and its referees' committee of pressuring and blackmailing them; arrests and resignations followed.[18] Financial crimes have also received a modicum more attention, Aleksandar Tomov's crimes at CSKA Sofia in particular. Arrested and convicted of embezzling money from his steelworks and channelling it to CSKA, and with Mittal long gone, Tomov then passed the club into the hands of Dimitar Borisov and Ivo Ivanov, Bulgarian businessmen who would finally drive it completely into the ground.[19] Their four years in charge were the club's most dysfunctional. In 2010 alone they appointed ten coaches, while what little money was made from transfers and a short run in the Europa League was directed to their own personal accounts. Not long after the huge anti-corruption demonstrations that filled Sofia in the spring of 2013, the owners were driven out by a series of fan protests that included a storming of the Bulgarian Football Federation.[20] However, as if to clearly demonstrate that no progress would be made in this area, Aleksandar Tomov was put back in charge of the wreckage. By 2015, as CSKA's debts spiralled, the Bulgarian football authorities were withholding the club's licence. Despite a variety of efforts to pass the club on to someone, anyone, it was finally declared bankrupt and closed down only to live again. Grisha Ganchev, who, having passed his first team Litex Lovech to his son, took time off from fighting the tax evasion charges against him and acquired the legal remains of CSKA and has returned them to the top division.[21]

Given the disastrous state of Bulgarian football, and its laser-like capacity to focus one's attention on the country's political dysfunctionality, it is remarkable that Bulgarian politicians increasingly made it part of their populist rhetoric.[22] Both the right-wing mayor of Sofia, Boris Borisov, and then Socialist president Georgi Parvanov, organized kickabouts and more formal games with their aides, allies and visitors. The Bulgarian Socialist Party put out an election address claiming that they were 'the team with tradition and history. We are not a flash-in-the-pan phenomenon sponsored in a fixed game in a championship that has long been bought and sold.'[23] Borisov, who has described himself as 'the right's best striker', and is forever threatening to score against the left with his head and his boot, proved so enthusiastic about the game that, in between his two stints as Prime Minister in 2013, he very publicly signed a professional contract with the small club Vidima-Rakovski Sevlievo.

If in Bulgaria politicians have flirted rhetorically with football, leaving the everyday business of graft to the gangs and the oligarchs, in Romania the game has served as a launch pad for thugs into politics. The two men who ran the game for much of the post-communist era fit this pattern exactly: Mitica Dragomir, president of the national football league from 1996 to 2014, was elected for two terms as an MP for the Greater Romania Party – notable for its ultra-nationalism and anti-semitism – and was known, openly, as 'Corleone'; and Mircea Sandu, a former player who held the presidency of the FRF from 1990 to 2014, and also served, albeit in a regional chamber of deputies, again for the Greater Romania Party, and was known, openly, as 'The Godfather'. Brazen, and seemingly invulnerable, they were sufficiently powerful to terminate the old communist practice of mid-level teams exchanging home wins and points for a quiet life, and to keep any other match-fixing strictly under their control. This gave them more time to pursue their real interests: skimming money off of transfer deals, allowing them to amass small fortunes.

Where the transfer market couldn't deliver a decent rate of return Romanian club owners opted for taking the Champions League money and running. In 2002, real estate magnate Dumitru Bucsaru bought Unirea Urziceni, a third-division club from a town of just 18,000 people with one supermarket and one set of traffic lights.[24] Smart dealers in the transfer market, Bucsaru laid out less than half a million dollars a year but, with the team coached by national star Dan Petrescu and the experienced Mihai Stoica, they won promotion to the top division in 2005, and then won the league in 2008, qualifying for the 2009 Champions League. There they were good enough to beat Glasgow Rangers and Sevilla and earn over $20 million. Just as well for Bucsaru, for his real estate business was in turmoil. By 2011 all the money had been taken out of the club, the players sold, the premises gated and the club dissolved. A similar stunt was pulled at Otelul Galati, who qualified for the Champions League in 2012, their winless six games generating enough money for their owners to drain the bank account and move on. The club rapidly descended into the lower divisions and insolvency.[25]

While the Romanian authorities have proved unable to prevent this kind of legalized looting they did acquire the capacity to investigate the pressing problems of widespread tax evasion and embezzlement. Established in 2002, *Direcţia Naţională Anticorupţie* (DNA) – National Anti-Corruption Directorate has acquired a fearsome reputation for pursuing these kinds of cases. In 2007, in an early skirmish, it published a 20,000-page file covering almost a decade's worth of tax evasion in the football transfer market. Six gruelling years in court finally delivered eight convictions and prison sentences for coaches and agents, Cristi Borcea, former owner of Dinamo Bucharest, and George Kopos, the businessman, former Conservative Party MP and owner of Rapid Bucharest.[26] In a demonstration of the leniency with which white-collar thieves had been treated, hitherto, in the Romanian criminal justice system, these convictions helped catalyse a tidal wave of new scholarship and scientific investigations in the country's prisons. An obscure law allowed prisoners thirty days off their sentence for every scientific paper or monograph in the humanities they published while incarcerated. George Kopos turned his hand to 'Matrimonial Alliances as a Policy of Romanian Kings in the XIV–XVIth Centuries', a splendid if narrow work that, curiously, was almost identical to an American MA thesis of the same title, freely available online.[27] No doubt there will be plenty more work on the Romanian monarchy, or perhaps we can expect some ultranationalist revisionist essays on the Jewish question in Romania from Mitica Dragomir and Mircea Sandu. Charged by the DNA in 2014, and finally convicted in 2016, though the case remains pending, Dragomir was found guilty of tax evasion, money-laundering and embezzlement, Sandu of gross misconduct in office. Both have been sentenced to prison terms and, along with the organizations they used to run, fined a record $225 million. Whether after almost two decades of uninterrupted decline there is even a fraction of that figure left in Romanian football remains to be seen.[28] Either way, the Romanian court system, under pressure, is gradually rescinding their convictions under appeal.[29]

What does remain is Georgi Becali. He has served his time for attempted match-fixing, diminished by the pair of books he penned on his life at Steaua Bucharest, and he remains at large in Romanian football, and at the helm of at least one version of the nation's biggest club.[30] Born in 1958, Becali was a locksmith turned 'importer', earning money from duty-free jeans and cigarettes, but he really got his foot on the ladder when he exchanged a piece of land with the Romanian army for one that he didn't actually own, and then re-sold the army land to developers at an exorbitant profit. He has not been shy about spending the money that has come his way:

commissioning pictures of himself depicted as Jesus, bankrolling two very unsuccessful presidential campaigns, three more to get him into the European Parliament, and steadily buying up a majority share-holding in Steaua, a task he accomplished in 2003. When asked why he bought into football he was refreshingly blunt: 'I became rich, and when a man becomes rich, he wants to become famous. That is why I took over Steaua. And I became famous.' At Steaua he has provided non-stop entertainment. He responded to Arpad Paszkany, the owner of Cluj, 'You want in the ring, let's get in the ring, bastard. I'll break your arms and legs. Let's take guns too. Let us shoot with guns.' In an Easter message to Steaua fans he had abused he wrote, 'I'm sorry for offending them. Apart from the ones who called for me to die just before Easter. They are possessed by Satan.' He has also spouted some really toxic forms of racism, refusing to sign the Afro-French striker Florent Sinama Pongolle and declaring the club would never sign a gay player. In 2006 he was recorded on video chasing the Gloria Bistrita squad with a plastic bag full of money. In his defence he argued that 'offering money to another team in order to encourage them to beat another team is not a bribe, it's just a way of making things more competitive.' The courts were unconvinced by this line of reasoning when, in 2007, they tried the case of four men, the vice-president and one player from both Steaua Bucharest and Universitatea Cluj, who were arrested in possession of a suitcase containing $1.5 million of Becali's money. The DNA followed this up with an investigation into Becali and his land deal alongside dozens of other cases, resulting eventually in his imprisonment in 2013.

In his absence, a long legal case, initiated by the Romanian army, still smarting from the deal he scammed them on, worked its way through the courts. In 2014, their request to take control of Steaua's symbols, crest and colours was agreed.[31] Becali initially responded with bluster, planning to re-name the club after himself, but settled for FCSB. Nonetheless, he still had to change the club's kit, badge and every last logo, in what was soon a very empty stadium. Simultaneously, under the army's direction, CSA Steaua Bucharest started life in the fourth division, and attracted the vast majority of Steaua's ultras. Indeed, in 2017, a game against a similar phoenix version of the bankrupt Rapid Bucharest was attended by more than 36,000 people.[32] If Romanian football has managed, anywhere, to rise above the zero that Hagi predicted, it is here.

III

Football and politics had long been bedfellows in Yugoslavia. The national team, a genuinely federal institution in that still ethnically divided society, was the pride of Tito's Yugoslavia. At the same time, some leading clubs, like Dinamo Zagreb and Red Star Belgrade, proved hidden repositories of nationalist sentiment. It was against this background that a game played in Zagreb between Dinamo and Red Star in 1991, mythologically remembered as 'the Battle of the Maksimir', descended into a pitched battle between players, both sets of fans and the federal police, and became part of the concatenation of events that triggered the Yugoslavian civil war. In the wake of the match, the ultras from both sides, the Bad Blue Boys at Dinamo and the Delije at Red Star, departed for the new battlefronts and became the core of early nationalist militias, engaged in fighting and ethnic cleansing.

Franjo Tudjman, the Yugoslav general who became Croatia's first president, made sport a central element of his conservative nationalism, evoking Croatia's 'spirit' whenever its national teams played, and nowhere more than in football.[33] Croatia's international tournament debut at Euro 1996 was greeted at home as decisive proof of the state's existence. The teams' fabulous progress at World Cup 1998, where they beat the Germans in the quarter-finals, lost to France in the semi-finals and finished third overall, was taken as evidence of Croatia and Tudjman's greatness. The coach, Miroslav Blasevic, thought he had played an 'invaluable role', for 'without him all my young players would play for Yugoslavia and not for Croatia: without his bravery and that of his party we would not have experienced any of this.' The midfielder Zvonimir Boban thought him 'the father of all things we Croats love, also the father of the national team'. On the squad's return home, the press declared the national team's success a 'common holy interest'.[34] The father of the national team also found time to make himself president of Dinamo Zagreb, where he planned for the club to serve as a national champion in European competition.[35] To the dismay and fury of almost everyone he then re-named the club Croatia Zagreb.

It was this kind of high-level attention that ensured the team won almost every national title in the 1990s and, while the rest of the league was mired in poverty, stayed afloat on a cushion of UEFA television money, but it brought Tudjman nothing but contempt from the ultras at Dinamo and from fans and clubs across the nation. When news of his terminal illness spread, crowds began to chant, 'Tik-tak, tik-tak, Franjo ima rak' – 'Tick-tock, tick-tock, Franjo has cancer.' The gods of the football schedule bequeathed the dying Tudjman one last political spectacle: a qualifier for Euro 2000, played in Zagreb in the autumn of 1999, against Yugoslavia (the team of the still conjoined Serbia and Montenegro) for the first time since the end of the civil war. Hours of patriotic music were put on before the game began, wounded war veterans were paraded around the stadium, and a vast Croatian flag was unveiled on the pitch bearing the words 'Vukovar 91', a reminder of the siege of this Croat city by the Serbs. Before the game Tudjman was contemptuous of his opponents: 'We have a team that knows we are fighting for Croatia. The Yugoslav team will not be able to feature such homogeneity.' Perhaps, but both the sporting edge of such xenophobic nationalism, and the appeal of Tudjman and his HDZ governments, were waning. The game finished as a draw, but it was enough to send the Yugoslavs through to the finals. Just two months later Tudjman was dead, and soon the HDZ would, after a decade in power, be replaced by the more liberal and European-oriented Social Democrats.

Since then some progress has been made in Croatia in tackling its endemic cronyism and corruption, enough at least to squeeze into the European Union in 2012, albeit with regular admonitions from Brussels that these practices continued unabated. In the realm of football matters got worse, the game exchanging the imperious authoritarianism of Tudjman for the duplicity of the self-serving Zdravko Mamić. At one point in the 1980s he was a member of Dinamo Zagreb's Bad Blue Boys, but in 2003 he surfaced as the politically appointed chief executive of the now renamed Dinamo Zagreb. An active supporter of, and networker amongst, the politicians and officials of Tudjman's HDZ, Mamić asked fans to vote for the party in the 2007 election via the club's official website, had messages of support for the HDZ stitched into the club's shirts, and made considerable donations to both party and individual politicians. At the same time, and with no sense of any conflict of interest, he was made vice-president of the Croatian national football federation (HDS), from where he pulled the strings of every aspect of the game: who coached and played for the national team, who got be transferred and for how much, how referees were chosen and how much clubs were fined – and all in the service of Mamić first, Dinamo second, and then the scraps for everyone else. His demeanour was never anything less than unpleasant, his countenance rude, and his claims – that God spoke to him directly on team matters, and that he would give his liver for the club, risible.[36]

In all this he was a caricature of what passed for public life in Croatia and indeed much of the region. Under Mamić's rule Dinamo had a virtual monopoly on the title, and was run as a family business, with his brother taking a variety of senior roles, including head coach. Although, as a public official, he was notionally subject to elections and recall at Dinamo, Mamić proved a master of bureaucratic trickery, avoiding elections to the board of the club for more than a decade, allowing him to stuff it with HDS puppets, like football federation president Davor Suker, and HDZ politicians. In time this vast network of graft, tax evasion and embezzlement, conducted at Dinamo with nearly all of Croatia's leading players, would prove his undoing, while his systematic persecution of Dinamo's traditional rivals, Hajduk Split, would evoke sustained opposition.

In 2014 the Dinamo–Hajduk derby was played by just the home team and in front of an almost empty stadium in almost complete silence. Dinamo officials had refused many of the visiting Hajduk fans access to the stadium, so they decided to boycott the game en masse. The team then came out in support of the fans and returned to Split. 'We've been systematically set up for a long time,' argued the club chairman Marin Brbić, 'because Croatian football is set up to serve one club and one man – that club is Dinamo and that man is Zdravko Mamić.'[37] By this time Mamić had seen to it that Hajduk had no representation on the boards of the football federation or the professional league and received systematically harsher punishments for player and crowd misdemeanours. The following day more than 20,000 people gathered on the Riva, Split's main coastal promenade, to demonstrate against Mamić and the crony capitalism he had come to represent.

Such a huge display of resistance was not spontaneous, but the product of one of European football's most interesting experiments in fan power.[38] In 2011, the majority shareholder of Hajduk Split, the local city council, had run out of money and options, and offered the indebted club to its fans. A group of fans called 'Our Hajduk' took on the task, and conducted a revolution in administration, based on their own rule book, or codex as they call it, of good governance. This document commits the club to living entirely within its means, overwhelmingly relying on their youth academy; administrators were required to take courses in professionalism and sports ethics.

Dinamo's ultras, the Bad Blue Boys, have been in a long conflict with the club, dating from Tudjman's name change in the 1990s. Although a considerable presence in the early twenty-first century they have, under Mamić's rule, been diminished in number, influence and fervour. Indeed, in recent years they have been outflanked by a new body of fans with a new way of operating: *Zajedno za Dinamo*, Together for Dinamo, who, amongst other things, organized a 50,000-signature petition demanding new elections for the Dinamo board. Democracy can be catching. The White Angels have pursued a similar agenda at NK Zagreb, and from the more radical fringes of that club, the country's first explicitly fan-owned, anti-fascist side, Zagreb 041 has emerged, where the city's anarchists, environmentalists and refugees combine.[39]

If these initiatives suggest the emergence of a more progressive component to Croatian civil society and football, the behaviour of many players and supporters of the national team suggests they remain a minority. At the European Championships in Portugal in 2004, for example, Croatian fans gave black players the monkey-grunt treatment and displayed banners with neo-Nazi Celtic crosses. Even more ominously, perhaps, they could be heard chanting '*Za dom – spremni!* Ready for the homeland', a slogan intimately associated with the Croatian fascist movement, the Ustasha, who ruled the country as a Quisling regime for the Nazis between 1941 and 1945.[40] The phrase was banned in the former Yugoslavia, but in the post-communist era it had acquired popular currency. Just in case anyone was in any doubt about the kind of homeland these nationalists envisaged, it was made transparently clear by the eighty or so people who formed a human swastika in the stands during a match between Croatia and Italy in 2006. This kind of everyday historical amnesia and indifference to fascism that constituted public opinion was given its most visible outing in 2013, when Croatia sealed their qualification for the 2014 World Cup, beating Iceland in a play-off in Zagreb.

The Australian-born Croat player Josip Simunic took the opportunity to grab the microphone and addressed each of the four stands with the chant '*Za Dom*'. He received back a chillingly loud '*Spremni!*' Simunic pleaded ignorance of the historical meanings of the phrase, a few critics in the press lambasted him, but, as with the crowd in the stadium, the response online, at the HDS and in much of the media, was overwhelmingly supportive; thus the genuine shock and disbelief when FIFA deemed the gesture racist and banned Simunic from the World Cup, effectively terminating his international career.

While the ultra-nationalist constituency remains an important component of the Croatian football crowd, they have been joined, in recent years, by more radical forces, who have used the visibility of the national team's games to challenge and undermine the rule of Mamić and his HDS cronies. Starting in 2015, fans disrupted a game against Italy by throwing flares onto the pitch at the San Siro, with the result that the HDS was fined by UEFA and ordered that the national team play their next game behind closed doors.[41] The fans tackled this challenge by breaking into the stadium the night before and painting a huge swastika on the pitch in bleach, which became clearly visible on television the next day.[42] Then, at Euro 2016, during their game against the Czech Republic in Saint Etienne, and with the Croats 2–1 in the lead, fans threw dozens of lit flares onto the pitch, which stopped the game and started a fight amongst different factions in the crowd. Finally, in 2016, Mamić was arrested and charged with multiple counts of embezzlement and tax evasion. He held out through two years of courtroom drama, survived an attempted assassination, strong-armed Luka Modrić and Dejan Lovren to give testimony in his defence that was deemed sufficiently close to perjury to require their own trials, but in 2018 he was finally convicted and sentenced to six years in prison. He may even serve some of them.[43]

Football ultras may have provided the first shock troops of Serbia's wars with Croatia and Bosnia-Herzegovina, but they were no praetorian guard for President Slobodan Milošević who had initiated the conflict. Indeed, in 2000 they were amongst the leading forces on the street in the demonstrations that toppled him. In the decade and a half since they have mutated into organized criminal gangs, available as street muscle to far-right groups and leading politicians, and given a free pass by the police and the courts. As the Prime

Minister, Ivica Dačić, in a rare moment of candour, admitted, 'We have all courted those groups; even my party has pursued a benevolent policy towards chauvinism and anti-semitism.' Dobrivoje Tanasijević, once president of Red Star Belgrade, was blunter: 'The politicians use the hooligan fans for their own means and in exchange protect them from getting in trouble.'

Thus, in 2008, football ultras from a range of clubs appeared on the streets of Belgrade and began attacking the embassies of the United States, Germany and those of other states that had recognized the independence of Kosovo. The police, needless to say, looked on. This toxic mixture of organized violence and ultra-nationalism was the context in which, in 2009, Brice Taton, a supporter of the visiting French team Toulouse, was beaten to death by Partizan Belgrade ultras. In 2010 the Serbian press thought that acts like these were not driven by just spontaneous nihilism and xenophobia, but detected organized political power at work. First, football ultras were responsible for attacks on Belgrade's Gay Pride march, including stoning participants. This was followed by widespread disorder at Serbia's game against Italy in Genoa: flares were thrown onto the pitch, an Albanian flag was ostentatiously burnt, and chants of 'Kill a Shipatar', a colloquial slur for Albanians, rang out.

Much of the Serbian press considered this part of a plot by the far right to entrench Serbia's international isolation and slow or prevent its accession to the European Union. 'It is clear after everything that happened in Genoa that this was not spontaneous or happened by accident, that this precise stage-management is not aimed against football or an individual, but against Serbia.' Serbia won't be joining the European Union any time soon, and thus the ultras have been focusing on their core business: drug-smuggling and maintaining the country's poisonous levels of stadium menace and racism.[44]

Antediluvian as attitudes are in Serbia towards players of colour, they are progressive by comparison to popular attitudes to Albanians, and to both Kosovo and Albania itself. This was brilliantly highlighted by Serbia's Euro 2016 qualifying match against Albania scheduled for October 2015. Festivities opened with the stadium-wide booing of the Albanian national anthem and chants of 'Kill! Kill! Kill Albanians!', after which a torrent of bottles and stones rained down on the visiting team from the stands. Then a small drone appeared in the sky above the pitch, from which hung a flag emblazoned with the double-headed eagle of Greater Albania: as provocative a gesture as could be imagined, given that it stood for a nationalist project that envisaged incorporating Kosovo (and Serbia's most sacred nationalist sites) into Albania itself. After hovering above the players the drone descended to the pitch, where Serbian defender Stefan Mitrović grabbed the flag. The Albanians tried to grab the flag back, and a full-scale melee ensued. When Albanian striker Bekim Balaj tried to take the flag off the pitch he was attacked by a fan who had run onto the field, who then struck him with a flying plastic chair; the fighting that followed grew so bad that the visitors abandoned the field and the game was called off. The Serbian FA and foreign ministry tried to put the blame on the Albanian foreign minister, who was present at the game, but it seems to have been much more of a do-it-yourself prank.[45] It is notable that many of the ultras who invaded the pitch that night had also been present in Genoa in 2010, and had been supposedly banned from attending football since. As of 2019 they are still there.

Late that year the International Criminal Tribunal for the former Yugoslavia sentenced Bosnian Serb General Ratko Mladić to life imprisonment for crimes against humanity committed during the Bosnian civil war, not least of which was the slaughter of thousands of Bosniaks in Srebrenica. Knowing that his name, spoken or written, was banned from stadiums, Serbia's right-wing ultras still made their feelings known. Red Star fans, watching their team in Belarus, rolled out a banner: 'Even if you receive a hundred life sentences, you are still praised by honourable Serbs'; Partizan fans in Switzerland went with 'May your mother have our thanks', showing a symbol worn by Mladić during his trial.[46]

The Bosnian civil war was brought to a close in 1995 by the signing of the Dayton Accords but, as in Serbia and Croatia, the war and its consequences have been an ever-present component of the nation's footballing life. The state created by the treaty, Bosnia-Herzegovina, was complex to say the least. It housed three ethnic groups – Bosnian Muslims (Bosniaks), Catholic Croats and Orthodox Serbs – not to mention a whole bunch of folks who didn't or wouldn't subscribe to any of these categories, who were living across two political entities, Republika Srpska and the Federation of Bosnia and Herzegovina. Above them sat a federal government, staffed by a three-person rotating presidency, and above *them* sat the international institutions established by the Dayton Accords to oversee the new state. Below the entities, and testament to the still patchwork, ethnic geography that the war's brutality could not eradicate, were ten cantons and 149 municipalities.

No wonder, then, that the country began life with one national team, but three separate football associations and three football leagues.[47] No wonder, with so many administrations and jurisdictions to feed, that the Bosnian public sector was eating up over 50 per cent of the nation's GDP, to no great effect, thanks to the systemic levels of corruption that this fragmented polity nurtured: in 2005, the UN's High Representative for Bosnia actually removed the Croat third of the rotating presidency, Dragan Čović, for embezzlement.

The Bosnian football federation was no different. The game as a whole was plagued by endemic poverty and match-fixing, while the federation itself, riven by ethnic factions, was incapable of practical decision-making. It was, one imagines, hard to build a culture of trust and co-operation when the ethnic cleansing of the war retained such tangible footballing form. In Mostar, for example, prior to the war, the city's team Velez Mostar had played at the Bijeli Brijeg Stadium in the predominately Croat area of the city. The team, like nearly all Bosniaks, was evicted by force of arms in 1992 and re-located to the now overwhelmingly Muslim north of the city. The Bijeli Brijeg, however, has new occupants, in this case HSK Zrinjski Mostar, a team that disappeared in 1945, banned by the Yugoslav communists on the not-unreasonable grounds that they had served as the nationalist team in the city under the newly expanded Croatian Republic, which had been handed to Bosnia by the Nazis after they had invaded and dismembered Yugoslavia.

Given these kinds of divisions it is no surprise that for much of Bosnia's short history the national team has failed to attract a national following.[48] In the Republic Sprsaka state television did not bother to show most of their games. The most popular teams were Red Star Belgrade and Partizan Belgrade. Both were seen as more authentic carriers of the greater Serb nation than even the Serbian national team, let alone Bosnia-Herzegovina. The city of Banja Luka, the capital of Republic Sprsaka, housed many Red Star and Partizan fans, club graffiti was pervasive on the city's walls, and local ultras who travelled to Belgrade for games were given pride of place in the *curva*. Fifty miles north, in Nevesinje, ultras painted a sixty-metre-wide

Red Star crest on a strip of bare mountain. In the Croatian zones of western Herzegovina, the roads and kerbstones were painted in the colours of Hajduk Split. Although there have been players of all ethnicities in the Bosnian team, there have been far fewer from these communities, for promising players have invariably opted for Croatia or Serbia.

Pressure for change in Bosnia first came from the *BH Fanaticos*, the small ultra group that followed the national team, who in 2010 started boycotting and disrupting matches. Some national team players joined their campaign, refusing to play unless the football fedcration was reformed. In a well-attended public act of defiance the refuseniks played a game in Sarajevo against national veterans. Then, in 2011, UEFA, like the UN High Representative before them, lost patience with Bosnia's hapless football federation. Its rotating three-person presidency was proving as ineffective as the national government's. Its extra places on UEFA committees were proving unsustainable, and although it had finally created a top division that drew on clubs from both of the Bosnian entities, its lower divisions remained effectively ethnically segregated, and that was unacceptable.

The federation was dissolved and then reconstituted, and out of this reform a surprisingly different Bosnian football emerged. The new national coach, Ivica Osim, brought a kind of old-school Yugoslav pluralism to the job, stressing the virtues of diversity and calling out the self-destructive ethnic finger-pointing that had characterized the whole set-up for years. A new generation of players arrived, many of them from the migrant diaspora that fled the war, for whom the old ethnic and political divisions that had once plagued the national squad appeared antiquated. There was more diversity than ever before, with Bosnians like Edin Džeko and Miralem Pjanić, Bosnian Serbs like Sejid Salihović and Bosnian Croats like Toni Sunjić, and less internal division.[49] Defeat to Portugal in a Euro 2012 qualifying play-off signalled a major improvement in the nation's form, and in 2014 they beat Greece over two games to qualify for their first major tournament, the 2014 World Cup. It was a euphoric moment, above all in cosmopolitan Sarajevo, where the team's journey to Brazil had coincided with a spate of anti-government and anti-corruption protests uniting youths from across all ethnic groups against the now entrenched and still corrupt post-Dayton *nomenklatura*. For this generation, as Asmir Selimović put it, 'the pitch is the place where Bosnia really happens. It is the one glimmer of hope to show who you are.' [50]

IV

In the decade after the fall of communism, football in Poland, Hungary, the Czech Republic and Slovakia suffered from declining standards of play, and was watched by shrinking crowds in decaying communist-era stadiums, leaving more space than ever for the hooligan, nationalist and far-right ultra cultures, and that is not to mention the problems of match-fixing and corruption, and often indifferent and incompetent football administrations.[51]

Poland, in keeping with the region's strongest economic recovery, and its rising standing in European politics, saw the greatest turnaround in its sporting fortunes, its club sides creeping back into European competitions and its national team regularly qualifying for international tournaments since the turn of the century. In the mid-2000s, driven in part by the prospect of co-hosting the 2012 European Championships with Ukraine, serious attempts were made to reform the game. The police and legal authorities initiated an investigation into match-fixing which saw over 200 arrests, the suspects drawn from the upper echelons of the PZPN (Polish Football Association), senior players and coaches, and directors from seventy-five clubs. Most got away with it, a few were punished, and the 2007 champions, Zagłębie Lubin, were relegated for their part in the scandal.[52]

Having won the co-hosting rights, alongside Ukraine, to stage the 2012 European Championships, Poland invested public money in new and refurbished stadiums with better transport links, the whole apparatus of stewarding and policing was given a facelift, and the government ordered a crackdown on the hooligan gangs. What had begun as an afterthought for Poland and Polish football – for Ukraine had taken the initiative in bidding for the competition – was becoming a showcase for a nation enjoying a brief moment of success. Poland was one of the very few European countries to avoid a recession after the global financial crash, and had seen high levels of economic growth and investment under the stable centre-right governments of Prime Minister Donald Tusk and his Civic Platform.

However, Polish football continued to offer up an almost weekly diet of disorder and fighting.[53] In the FARE report into racism in Polish football, which covered most of the two seasons played between 2009 and 2011, fifty-six separate incidents, from chants to the use of ultra-nationalist symbols, were recorded in Poland, the majority of them anti-semitic.[54] In 2011, for example, the fans of Resovia, alongside a grotesque Jewish caricature, flew a banner saying, 'Death to those with curved noses, the aryan horde is coming!' Later that year, during a UEFA Cup game at Legia Warsaw, Israeli visitors Hapoel Tel Aviv were met by a huge flag saying, 'Jihad Legia' in Arabic-style font.[55] Considerable efforts were made in the run-up to Euro 2012 to counter Polish football's reputation for racism, and in particular the near-hysterical accounts of the country presented by the British tabloid press, the tournament giving over a lot of advertising space and pitch time to anti-racist messages.[56]

While all this was considered a success by the organizers, there were many voices, particularly on the far right and from the more extreme and conservative parts of the Catholic church, that deplored the clampdown and the exclusion of Poland's more traditional forms of football support. This unholy alliance of football ultras, the church and ultra-nationalists has been consecrated by the Fans' Patriotic Pilgrimage. The event, which began in 2008, brought together all of those constituencies at the fourteenth-century Jasna Góra Monastery, a renowned shrine to the Virgin Mary and a place of pilgrimage. There, up to 5,000 football supporters, most wearing club-branded clothing and hats, gathered to be blessed by Father Jaroslaw Wąsowicz, himself a Lechia Gdansk ultra.

Alongside priests in cassocks and Legia Warsaw scarves there have been displays of icons and slogans across the ultra-right spectrum, from Celtic crosses to demands for the return of Lithuania and Belarus to the Polish Empire, sermons that compared today's hooligans with the 'Cursed Soldiers' of 1939 – the tiny band of Polish troops destroyed by the German and Russian invasions – and calls to the ultras to 'Defend the continent against annihilation.'[57] More ominous than this kind of kitsch religious revivalism, football ultras provided a substantial part of the crowds of ultra-nationalists that have aggressively marched through Warsaw on Independence Day over the last five years.[58]

Given all of this, it is hardly surprising that anti-semitism is still very much alive and well in Polish football. In 2013, the fans of Lech Poznań chanted to their opponents from Widzew Łódź, 'Move on, Jews. Your Home is Auschwitz. Send you to the gas!': a statement that, remarkably enough, the local courts deemed not to be anti-semitic and therefore not prosecutable.[59] Three years later, suitably emboldened, the fans of Widzew Łódź publicly burnt two effigies of orthodox Jews, and displayed a banner referring to the foundation date of their cross-town rivals LKS Łódź that read, '1908, the day the Jews were named. Let them burn, motherfuckers.' The city of Łódź itself was plastered with similarly classy epigrams from both sides: 'LKS Jews' and 'Widzew Jewish Dogs' were ubiquitous. In the single most effective anti-fascist act in Polish football, an anonymous citizen, no doubt inspired by the surreal antics of the Orange Alternative under Communism, started painting alternative graffiti all over the city: 'LKS do not read books' and 'Widzew are cissies'. Within weeks anti-semitic epithets had given way to an ever more ludicrous selection of taunts: 'LKS wash their cars with pumice stones', and 'Widzew do not skin pineapples and are terribly light eaters.'[60]

One wonders quite what would have been the appropriate orange response to the wave of Islamophobia that has emerged in Eastern and Central European football, a trend sharply ratcheted up by reactions to the refugee crisis of 2015, and in Poland by the election of a more explicitly anti-migrant and Eurosceptic Law and Justice Party government, an event publicly supported and celebrated by Zbigniew Boniek, then president of the PZPN. Thus, in the immediate aftermath of Chancellor Merkel's decision to open Germany's borders to refugees in 2015, while the German football public responded by displaying huge 'Refugees welcome' banners in every Bundesliga ground, in Poland fans of Silesia Wrocław unveiled a 20 x 30-metre banner headed, 'While Europe is flooded with an Islamic plague'. Beneath this a crusading knight, the club's crest on his shield, wielded a broadsword against three boats aiming to land on the European continent: the USS *Bin Laden*, USS *Hussein* and USS *Isis*. A second banner unfurled below read, in medieval Polish script, 'Let us stand in defence of Christianity.'[61] The same weekend LKS Łódź went with 'No to Muslim immigrants', Lech Poznań with 'This is obvious and simple for us. We do not want refugees in Poland', while the Legia Warsaw banners read, 'The whole of Legia, shout it loud – "NO" to the Islamic hordes! Everybody on the march!'[62]

They were not alone in the region. In the Czech Republic, fans of Jablonec, playing Bohemians in Prague, hung up a banner that showed a cartoon Nordic female warrior carrying a shield inscribed with 'Europe', kicking a pig in a turban dropping a copy of the Koran.[63] In Budapest, after a match between Hungary and Romania, far-right ultras spilled out of the stadium and headed for Keleti train station where many stranded refugees were living, and attacked them there with fireworks and smoke bombs.[64] Later that season, after UEFA had asked clubs to donate a portion of their European match revenues to refugee charities, Sparta Prague and Lech Poznań fans simply boycotted their games, while the crowd at Legia Warsaw chanted 'Lost sheep. Welcome to hell.'[65] It was an atmosphere so toxic that when the national team captain, Robert Lewandowski, spoke out in favour of refugees' rights, Law and Justice MP Krystyna Pawłowicz questioned his 'national loyalty'.[66]

Toxic as Poland was becoming for migrants, it had nothing on the hysteria and vituperative, hostile tone of Viktor Orbán's Hungary. In the summer of 2016, in the run-up to a Hungarian referendum that rejected European demands that the country take in more migrants, state television filled the breaks between games from the European Championships in France with anti-migrant 'news', featuring the usual confection of fake refugees and welfare spongers. László Toroczkai, vice-president of the far-right Jobbik party, posted pictures on his Facebook page of handcuffed migrants on the border with Serbia with the caption, 'Violent invaders 0 – Citizen militia 1.'[67]

That football should be the space in which anti-migrant hatred has been expressed should come as no surprise in Viktor Orbán's Hungary, for the Prime Minister, in power now since 2010, has been a huge advocate of both.[68] In the late 1980s, when a law student and then an anti-communist activist, Orbán was a fearsome five-a-side player. In the early 1990s some of those team mates joined him as opposition politicians in the early days of post-communist Hungary when these young liberals began their mutation into today's Fidesz, a populist, conservative party of the nationalist right. They also kept playing football. Orbán's five-a-side team of the era, Fojikasor (*The beer . . . is flowing*), included the future Hungarian President János

Ader, and the House Speaker László Kövér. Elected for the first time as Prime Minister in 1998, he made his first official trip out of the country to the World Cup final in Paris. Indeed, Orbán has been to every World Cup and most Champions League finals over the last couple of decades. He dropped the five-a-side only to begin playing football in a semi-professional capacity for Felcsút FC in the Hungarian fourth division. Moreover, unlike other playing prime ministers and Presidents – Evo Morales, for example – Orbán really was playing full competitive games, away matches included, and, of course, training on a regular basis.

This continued for a couple of seasons when he was in opposition after losing the 2002 election, but with more time on his hands and less puff in his lungs Orbán then turned his attention to the club itself. In 2007 he inaugurated a football academy at Felcsút, co-opted the name of the nation's most venerated football player Ferenc Puskás to make Puskás Akadémia FC, and announced his aspirations to transform the Hungarian game.

Three years later, after the Socialist government had imploded around its internal divisions, rank corruption and disastrous economic response to the financial crisis, Orbán and Fidesz won the 2010 general election and took power. They have not relinquished a scintilla since, winning two further terms in 2014 and 2018, and vanquishing any serious opposition in both party politics and civil society. In their now near decade in power they have refined a range of right-wing populist political strategies and policies that Orbán himself has described as 'illiberal democracy'. Equipped with a massive parliamentary majority, the government has been able to rewrite the constitution almost at will, deliberately weakening the higher courts, making the judiciary more vulnerable to political pressure, and redesigning the electoral system to systematically favour Fidesz. State offices and institutions of all kinds have been made into personal and party fiefdoms. The state media has become an instrument of the government, opposition voices have been financially and legally harried, some have been bought up and then closed down. Domestic authoritarianism has been matched by an increasingly assertive tone abroad towards its neighbours with significant Hungarian speaking-populations, the European Union, especially over migration, as well as to the actual migrants and asylum seekers that have been crossing the country's southern borders.

Football has, inevitably, been part of Orbán's nationalist repertoire. He has quoted Puskás in election campaigns, and been ever
present at the national team's home games, declaring himself 'brain
damaged' after an 8–1 thrashing by the Netherlands in 2013 meant
that once again Hungary would not qualify for the World Cup. But
football really was more than just Orbán's hobby, and more than just
a useful ideological flourish or soft power advertising. It has been his
abiding obsession, and one that, refracted through the power structure of Hungary's illiberal democracy, makes it many other people's
abiding concern too. First, under Orbán all state companies have
significantly upped their support for the game: the size of the deal
between state television and the Hungarian FA seems particularly
generous; the national football pools return a much higher percentage of their profits to the sport than their European comparators;
while the national energy and utility companies have been encouraged to become big sponsors of clubs.

Second, since 2010 there has been a centrally funded and controlled programme of stadium redevelopment and new builds
intended to cover every first and second division club. The scheme,
which has cost more than £300 million, was generous to the point
of absurdity. Debrecen, with average gates of under 4,000, acquired
a stadium five times that size. Even Ferencváros, which has the largest fanbase of any Hungarian club, struggled to fill a third of 30,000
new seats. It was, however, very good business for construction companies and concrete manufacturers, many of whom had excellent
Fidesz credentials. It wasn't so good for the Roma communities of
Miskolc, whose long-established neighbourhoods were demolished
to make way for car parking at Diósgyőri's new stadium. Third, and
most importantly, the TAO – a specially devised tax loophole for
Hungary's largest firms, created under a special deal negotiated with
the European Union – was introduced. Hungarian companies were
able to get a matching tax credit in return for donations to the
nation's sports clubs, of which football predictably got the lion's
share. While the state's stadium funds were relatively transparent the
tax credit scheme was not. Although the total level of donations to
clubs was known – £210 million in the first five years of the scheme –
no one knew which companies had paid what to whom.[69]

Once in power Fidesz set about dismantling democratic checks
and balances, promoting its people to key positions in the judiciary,

the tax authority, cultural boards, state media and, above all, to the public prosecutor's office, thereby insulating itself from any difficult legal matters. Sports organizations were not ignored. Fidesz allies or officials took over the presidency of many of the most important sports federations: basketball, fencing and handball to name but three. In football, the party already held the presidency of two of the biggest provincial clubs, Videoton and Debrecen. To these they added three more first division teams: Ferencváros, the country's biggest club, whose president Gábor Kubatov is a Fidesz MP and its senior strategist; Mezőkövesd Zsóry, which is now presided over by András Tállai MP, the secretary of state for taxation; and MTK, Budapest's old Jewish club, which is now run by Fidesz MEP Tamas Deutsch, one of Orbán's oldest student friends and football team mates, and a founding member of the party.[70]

The hollow emptiness of Ferencváros's publicly funded stadium is one revealing legacy of Orbán's time in power. However, the most extraordinary architectural statement of this new renaissance of Hungarian football can be found in Felscút, Viktor Orbán's home village. In fact, Puskás Akadémia's stadium, the Pancho Arena, opened in 2013, sits right next to his country dacha. Sited on the edge of a community of just 1,800 people, it has seats for 4,000. At the apex, the roofs are perhaps seven storeys high. The stadium is officially said to have cost €10 million, but numbers alone cannot capture its grandeur. The design for the building was first sketched by the 'Hungarian Gaudí', Imre Makovecz, a noted aesthetic and political critic of the communists. Completed by his student Tamás Dobrosi, the great curves of the black, shingle-tiled roofs give the arena the feel of an art nouveau church or a great country mansion. Inside, the structure is held up by huge, breathtaking trusses of laminated mahogany set in the great fan patterns of a Gothic cathedral. Behind the main stand three fantastical turrets sheathed in beaten copper pierce the roof. Notionally in charge of the club is a man of few words or talents called Lőrinc Mészáros, once an impecunious local pipe fitter who became Fidesz mayor of Felscút in 2011, and whose companies have not only built the Pancho Arena but have acquired so many government contracts and favourable land deals that he is now thought to be amongst the richest men in the country.[71] Casual observation of the crowd at the Pancho Arena suggests there is only one king of the castle, and one game in town, for the handful of local football supporters is always dwarfed by a VIP stand overflowing with courtiers.

> Even if you hate football, you have to go to these matches. It is the only place that the elite are willing to socialise with anyone outside of their small circle. Big construction and infrastructure development projects and plans which require a lot of money are basically decided in the skybox.[72]

Here, surely, is the finest architectural monument to populism and politics' colonization of football. One can only hope, when Orbán is finally deposed and the money dries up, that it serves as well as a ruin.

V

For much of the post-war era, Scandinavia stood at one remove from the rest of Europe. Only Denmark joined the EU before 1994, and Norway has remained outside of it even now. Finland and Sweden, with their policies of neutrality, were late arrivals to NATO.[73] They were, however, enthusiastic participants in international organizations of all kinds, including international football: the Danes and the Swedes were amongst FIFA's founding members. In this realm they remained distinct by virtue of the Nordic sports model. While other European countries, with a similarly football-crazy urban working class, made the transition to professionalism and then commercialism between the 1920s and 1960s, Scandinavian football remained resolutely amateur and non-commercial, in its ethos and its structures. In both Europe and Latin America resistance to professionalism had come mainly from upper-class amateurs who, in the guise of keeping sport free from the perfidious impact of money, sought to maintain a social exclusiveness about the game. In Scandinavia, however, where the left either held power for long stretches, or were at least able to exert significant cultural influence, a 'popular' social democratic case against professionalism won the day. From this perspective football and its clubs were part of a broader social movement in which the priorities of sports institutions were the public good, recreation and well-being, rather than the commercial spectacle, an order of priorities starkly expressed by the Swedish and Danish FA's decision to ban players from the national team who had operated at a professional level anywhere, let alone at home. From the late 1950s through to the mid-1990s, the virtues of Scandinavian social democratic voluntarism, with its emphasis on player development and organizational solidarity, were enough to compete; for example, in 1979 Malmö, still an amateur side, was able to get to the final of the European Cup. An easing of the amateurism rules in the 1980s saw the emergence of the first generation of poorly remunerated semi-professionals and amongst the best a burst of player migration – like Denmark's Laudrup brothers – to the bigger clubs and leagues in Europe.

In the context of a still restrained professional game, a distinct and more plural football culture could emerge. It is hardly surprising, given the early adoption of feminist politics in Scandinavia, that women's football should have developed so rapidly there. Similarly, in contrast to Southern Europe, which nurtured the ultra movement in the 1970s and 1980s, and Northern Europe, which created hooligan firms, it was the Danes at the 1984 Euros and 1986 and 1990 World Cups who were amongst the earliest instances of carnival-style fandom at a major international tournament, expressing a benign, almost cartoonish nationalism. Christened 'rooligans' by the Danish press – the hooligans of fun – they brought face paint, replica strips, absurd head gear and entirely peaceful bacchanalia to the stadiums.[74] As late as the early 1990s, Scandinavian football could, at its best, hold its own in international competition: Denmark won the European championships in 1992, Sweden came third at the 1994 World Cup, and in the same year IFK Gothenburg were still good enough to win their Champions League group. Even Norway, where football had long played second fiddle to Nordic skiing, the game gripped the national imagination as the men qualified for two consecutive World Cups, and in 1998 made the knock-out stages after, sensationally, beating Brazil 2–1. However, these victories were the last triumphs of the Nordic system that was about to be devoured by football's globalization.

As fringe players in an increasingly integrated global and European football system, Scandinavian leagues and clubs, already small, have become microscopic, with budgets that are tiny fractions of their competitors', and are consequently unable to retain or attract sufficient talent to make an impact in European competition. Worse, the money once earned from player sales to the big leagues, especially the English Premier League in its early days, diminished as Scandinavia become a small part of what is now a global labour market for players. Scandinavia also struggled with the global market for fans. The long-established interest in English football, broadcast in Norway and Sweden since the 1970s, has been sharply increased by the new digital technologies, while a younger generation have acquired their foreign Champions League favourites.[75] First Denmark, and then Norway, adapted to the new order by vigorous commercialization. In the early 1990s the Danish league fought the national FA for more autonomy, re-formatted and re-launched, and re-named itself after a corporate sponsor. Its clubs became limited companies, ruthlessly merged where necessary to create more economically viable units. One of these, FC Copenhagen, was the most emblematic of the new football. Owned by a consortia of Danish businessmen, the club offered a self-consciously city-centre, metropolitan spectacle in Parken, the national stadium, which it owned and ran, in contrast to their main rivals, Brøndby, the team of the city's working-class suburbs.[76] These changes have kept professional football solvent, which in a small market is no mean feat, and so far the Danes have managed to avoid the stultifying rule of one or two clubs that has accompanied commercialization elsewhere. In Norway, however, where clubs' domestic finances are still pitifully low, access to the Champions League and its TV payments, even from just the qualifying rounds, gave Rosenborg from Trondheim such a built-in advantage every season that they won the league for a decade.[77]

Another consequence of the new inequalities in Scandinavian football is that in the lower leagues players' wages are low enough that match-fixing is a permanent temptation. In 2015, in its first match-fixing trial, Norway found three players guilty of throwing a game, while at the same time Denmark convicted one man of fixing three games in the second division on behalf of a Filipino betting syndicate.[78] Finland, where salaries are even lower, and where whole clubs can be bought by two-bit scam merchants, has been repeatedly stung by the match-fixers.[79] In 2005, a Chinese 'businessman', Zheyun Ye, fled Belgium, where he had bought a stake in Lierse, who had, most surprisingly, recently lost 4–0 to the worst team in the league, Germinal Beerschot. It was a game which had attracted, according to the police, an unusually large amount of betting. Ye made his way to Finland where, despite this paper trail, he was able, on a promise and a prayer, to purchase the small club Allianssi. Fortified by reliable players and coaches that Ze had first installed at Lierse, ably supported by a number of clearly injured players, and all equipped with short studs on a day of torrential rain, Allianssi went down, literally and metaphorically, 8–0 to Haka FC. Ze was gone the next day, no doubt departed to collect his winnings. Despite the promise of tighter due diligence and monitoring in Finnish football, in 2011 eleven players were put on trial alongside the notorious match-fixer, Wilson Raj Perumal, who had been in conversation with them over the outcome of Finnish league games.[80]

Sweden, in contrast to its smaller neighbours, was more reticent about commercializing the game.[81] Indeed, in 1998, after much grassroots pressure, the corporate route pursued in Denmark and Norway was closed when the Swedish FA instituted its own version of the fifty-plus-one rule, ensuring majority social ownership of all clubs. Consequently, domestic corporations and patrons, seeking media coverage and social influence, migrated to ice hockey, which has been much more nakedly commercial, and at times challenged football for the most popular sport in Sweden. Even where Swedish football has gone down the commercial route it has been at best a half-hearted effort: the size of domestic TV deals, and the calibre of TV coverage, remained somewhere in the early 1990s. Large Swedish corporations, invariably hyper-internationalized, have proved far more interested in golf and tennis than in sponsoring the domestic game. Thus, in the early 2000s, the turnover of the Danish league, with just 12 teams and half the domestic audience, was almost double that of its Swedish equivalent, the Allsvenskan. As before, the compensation for such economic modesty is a more diverse football culture. With less money at stake, and thus lower barriers to entry, it has been possible for recently established immigrant clubs like Assyriska FF, the team of Christian Assyrians in the Stockholm suburbs and now of much of the Assyrian global diaspora, and Dalkurd FF, a team founded in 2004 by Kurdish immigrants to the small city of Bolange, to make it all the way to the top level.[82] Indeed, most of the best things in Swedish football have come, overwhelmingly, from its new generation of migrants, none more so than the incomparable striker Zlatan Ibrahimović, whose demeanour and style has been defiantly un-Swedish: arrogant, self-centred and at times close to genius.

While the men's game has proved domestically ponderous and at club and national level internationally uncompetitive in the twenty-first century, Swedish women's football, indeed women's football in all Scandinavian countries, has blossomed.[83] Sweden and Norway have both made the semi-finals of the Women's World Cup twice, and a Scandinavian women's team has lost the last six finals of the European Championships. In the women's Champions League Umeå won two titles and Swedish clubs contested another seven finals, including tiny Tyresö, who in 2014 made it all the way to the final only to disintegrate under the weight of its debts immediately afterwards. By contrast, the peak performance in the men's game was somewhat humbler, when Östersund, a small town in the north of the country, beat Arsenal 2–1 in a Europa League game.[84]

Comparable in size, demographically or economically, to Sweden, but with considerably stronger football cultures, Belgium, the Netherlands and Portugal have fared better. While still economic minors by comparison with the big five of European football, they have, at the leading clubs at any rate, been able to stay in touch with the core by intensive and sophisticated player recruitment, development and transfer operations, and have as such helped produce national teams brimming with talent which have remained considerably more internationally competitive than their clubs. Portugal, although poorer than either of the Low Countries, has proved the most successful of the three. In the twenty-first century Porto, under José Mourinho, would win the UEFA Cup in 2003, and the Champions League the following year, the only winner from outside of the core nations since Ajax's win in 1995. In 2011, in an all-Portuguese UEFA Cup final, Porto would beat Braga to win it again. Benfica lost two consecutive heartbreaking finals of its successor, the Europa Cup, in 2013 and 2014. The national team, long absent from international tournaments, qualified for every European Championship and World Cup since 2000, was runner-up at the Euros it hosted in 2004, and won the thing in 2016, part of a run of national celebration that started with the election for a socialist government in 2015 and the end of the harsh austerity programmes of the previous seven years, and winning the Eurovision Song Contest. Its squads of this era could boast two exceptional stars, Luís Figo and Cristiano Ronaldo, and a platoon of players at Europe's biggest clubs, all testament to the exceptional scouting and coaching operations of Portugal's big three clubs, Porto, Benfica and Sporting Lisbon, and their academies.[85] Long accustomed to recruiting and developing African players from the remains of Portugal's empire, they have also proved adept at buying cheap, in the lusophone world especially but beyond it as well, and selling players dear.[86] Between 2010 and 2016, these three clubs sold players to the big five European leagues worth $1 billion. National and elite success has, as ever, come at the price of greater inequalities amongst domestic clubs, between those connected to global markets and those that are effectively excluded, which has in turn hollowed out aspects of the domestic game and helped nurture the conditions for widespread corruption.

Around the turn of the century Sporting Lisbon won the national championship twice, and Boavista, Porto's small second club, won it once. Since then it has been a Benfica-Porto duopoly. While the big three have always taken the lion's share of the public, perhaps 50 per cent of crowds in the 1980s and 1990s, they now account for more than 80 per cent of attendance at Portuguese football. Their domination of the huge Portuguese football media – the three sports dailies were consistently amongst the top five most read newspapers in the country – was even greater. Alongside unusually high ticket prices, and the draw of foreign and televised football, this kind of competitive imbalance is the main reason Portuguese football cannot fill its stadiums: even the big three, derbies and European matches aside, play to half-full grounds.[87] Both competition and coverage have been reduced to an endless merry-go-round of gossip and intrigue about this handful of clubs and their coaches and players, generating endless, recurring narratives of accusation and counter-accusation.

Concentrations of power and money in fierce competition with each other, covered by a pliant and distracted media, operating in an under-regulated grey zone, are in most spheres of life a recipe for corruption, and Portuguese football has not disappointed. Between 2004 and 2008, Porto, its President, Pinto Da Costa, and a slew of other clubs and their officials, were embroiled in the 'Golden Whistles' affair. The case, based on extensive phone taps and transcripts, focused on Porto allegedly offering prostitutes and money to referees, the former referred to as 'fruit' and now a term in vernacular use in Portugal. Porto and its president then performed a remarkable act of legal escapology and were ultimately cleared of criminal charges, mainly by getting the wiretaps ruled as inadmissible evidence. As usual, lesser figures and referees were successfully convicted and sentenced.

Benfica has its own sins to atone for. In 2017, one of Porto's directors claimed, on very substantial grounds, that their rivals were secretly monitoring the texts of Fernando Gómez, the chair of the Portuguese FA, and that club president Luis Viera had authorized payments of around €150,000 to a witch doctor resident in Guinea Bissau, Dr Armand Nhaga, in return for securing a good result in their upcoming Champions League game with Borussia Dortmund. Benfica lost the game 4–0 and when, in the ensuing email correspondence, Benfica complained, Dr Nhaga insisted there had been insufficient time for his magic to work. More substantially, in 2018, police repeatedly raided the club's premises, its president and vice-president suspected of tax evasion and money-laundering.[88] At the other end of the football hierarchy, the penurious lower leagues and smaller clubs have been prey to match-fixing by Malaysian syndicates, and money-laundering by Russian gangs who used donations to UD Leiria to clean their cash until their arrest in 2015.[89]

Portugal's shift to the left, the victory of Antonio Costa's Socialists in 2015, and the end to the worst of austerity economics have, so far, squeezed down the political space for right-wing populists and demagogues. However, Portuguese football, as the recent history of Sporting Lisbon demonstrates, remains fertile ground for their bitter and divisive politics. Clearly the third of the big three, without a league title for a decade, in a fabulous stadium it couldn't fill or pay for, Sporting was ripe for change. In 2013, in the pugnacious shape of Bruno de Carvalho, it arrived. Campaigning against the old grandees and elites, he was elected to the presidency of the club and again in 2017 with 86 per cent of the vote. Known in the press as Portuguese football's Donald Trump, he is undoubtedly as eloquent: 'They call me a populist, they say I'm an unethical demagogue. Well, I'll tell you something: if you're not with Sporting you're all shitheads.'[90] His popularity was built on a tirade of abuse against agents, not entirely unreasonably, and conspiracy theories about Benfica, Porto and the football association that chimed with the emotional logic of the terraces, all embellished by fist-pumping touchline antics.

However, as all kinds of populists are discovering, no amount of testosterone-driven fury can shift the structural realities of global capitalism: in Sporting's case a huge debt from building their stadium, the accumulated gap between them and Benfica and Porto due to their exclusion from Champions League money, and their low global profile. If you can't change reality, find scapegoats, in this case the players. After Sporting's defeat by Atlético Madrid in the Europa Cup Carvalho accused them of 'grotesque mistakes', and when at the end of the 2018 season they lost the Portuguese Cup final against Aves he threatened to suspend the team and posted 'Spoiled kids . . . let's resolve this, then.' Two months later a gang of around fifty hooded men, armed with sticks and belts, stormed the club's training ground, occupied the dressing room and attacked a number of players, which triggered mass resignations from the squad. As all of the players were well within their rights to abandon their contracts, the club also sustained a massive loss of transfer income, at least €100 million. Carvalho's response was to go on club television and derisively snort: 'This was annoying. Crime is everywhere these days.' Publicly admonished by the Prime Minister, he was voted out of office three months later, 71 to 29 per cent, just in time to avoid the inevitable bankruptcy proceedings coming Sporting's way.

The Dutch are also European champions, the women's national team winning the Euros in 2017, but it has been the fate of the men's team that has, so far, dramatized the mood of the nation. The twenty-first century began as the twentieth had finished: with glorious, self-immolating defeat. A Dutch team, still recognizably of the old school, collapsed in the penalty shoot-out of the semi-final of the European Championships, scoring just once against the Italians. This kind of defeat was comprehensible, but when the Dutch lost the long, gruelling final of the 2010 World Cup to Spain 1–0, Johan Cruyff was simply appalled: 'This ugly, hard, hermetic, hardly eye-catching football style. If with this they got satisfaction, fine, but they lost.'[91] The Dutch, to say the least, had not been easy on the eye, but then a similar squad had dazzled in their opening games at Euro 2008 and then been soundly beaten.

Under coach Bert van Marwijk, in a rare shift of emphasis, winning was prioritized. Given the resources at his disposal this meant a lot of defence and a lot of Nigel De Jong and Mark Van Bommel, whose physicality was reviled by Cruyff and part of the nation: 'It

hurts me that Holland should choose such an ugly path to the final.'
Nonetheless, 600,000 people welcomed the team home in Amster-
dam, and midfielder Wesley Sneijder spoke for the pragmatists,
sharply rebuking the romantics: 'Who is this Cruyff anyway?' But
Cruyff would not stop talking. Later that year, after Ajax were
trounced by Real Madrid in the Champions League, Cruyff wrote,
'This isn't even Ajax. Let me get to the point: this Ajax is even worse
than the team from before Rinus Michels' arrival in 1965.' It was a
tirade of sufficient weight to trigger a huge shift in control and management at Ajax itself, where an old boys' club of former players had
come to completely dominate the organization, but Cruyff's words,
on both his club and the Dutch national team, were part of a much
wider debate about Dutch identity.[92]

Both conversations, on the face of it, appeared to be about romanticism versus pragmatism, playing well and playing to win, though
Ajax had reached the point where they weren't even playing well.[93]
For Cruyff and many of his generation it was the technical brilliance
of past teams and their refusal to accept the playing/winning trade
off that defined the Dutch, and had brought them the glorious World
Cup defeats of 1974 and 1978 and four European Cups for Ajax and
Feyenoord in the early 1970s, all playing remarkable, modern,
innovative 'Total Football'. Seemingly uniquely Dutch in its perception and use of space, its veneration of communication and intellect,
and in its positional flexibility, this style or ethos of play chimed with
the Netherlands' declared policy of being a guiding light in international affairs, on the grounds that if you can't be big, be good.

The last rays of that golden era touched Ajax who, in 1995, won
their last, and probably final, Champions League. The following
year the squad had been entirely dismantled and sold off. Feyenoord
won the UEFA Cup in 2002 but since then a huge and widening
gap has emerged between the Dutch and the big countries' clubs
in income and in competitiveness at a European level. Cruyff and
his supporters in the football world still believe that the economic
logic of globalization can be resisted by a return to the purity and
authenticity of the unique Dutch football philosophies of the 1970s,
an argument given real urgency by the wider perception that Dutch-
ness, and the Dutch language especially, was being diluted, even
homogenized, by the incredible openness of Dutch society to global
networks.

However, as powerful a call to arms as this might be inside foot-ball and in the wider world, it is an emotional rather than a structural diagnosis of Dutch decline. First, as the game against Spain so obvi-ously demonstrated, all the innovations and ideas of the Dutch golden age have long since passed into the common sense of modern Euro-pean football. The Spanish side, many of them nurtured in an academy established by Cruyff, played Dutch-style football. Moreover, in such a networked world the Dutch are never going to be able to regain pole position by springing a surprise on the world as they did before. Second, while young Dutch players remain amongst the most technic-ally accomplished in terms of ball control, they increasingly appear to lack the tactical knowledge and sophistication of their European peers, whose academies have, again, taken the best of the Dutch model and then added a focus on other skills – psychological, tactical, etc. – that the Dutch, so certain of their own superiority, have neg-lected. The cosy and closed management circles of elite Dutch football, within which everyone knows everyone, suffer from not only compla-cency, but at times also a suffocating conformity. Arjen Robben, by some way the outstanding player of his generation, was a freak of Dutch football: armed with a dribble that no academy would have allowed him to perfect, he was saved by his isolation for many years in a peripheral village amongst German-speaking communities.

Ajax's bravura run to the semi-finals of the Champions League in 2019 suggested real progress, but the team was once again destined to be broken up and sold on the global market. Progress to the semi-finals of the 2014 World Cup, a final outing for the older generation of players like Sneijder, Van Persie and Robben, masked the decline that was to come. For the first time in almost three decades, the Netherlands failed to quality for successive tournaments: Euro 2016 and the 2018 World Cup. The Dutch were so bad in qualifying that it was not a question of what style they played and what it meant, but whether they could play at all. Cruyff, who died in the spring of 2016, did not live to see it. It is hard to believe, given his obdurate romanticism and the sepia-tinted spectacles of the exile, that he would have been any less strident in his calls for a return to the dis-tinctive Dutch football of his youth, but the Netherlands that forged him and his thinking are long gone.

While the style of play of the Dutch team and its leading clubs continues to offer a barometer of debates over Dutch identity,

Dutch football's attitudes to race have been equally if not more illu-minating.[94] Here, the call for purity and authenticity has come not from sporting aesthetes but from the populist and xenophobic right. Like Belgium, the Netherlands has experienced a series of post-war waves of migration, from Turkey and North Africa since the 1960s, from its old colonies Surinam and the Dutch Antilles since the 1970s, and more recently from the Balkans and the Middle East. Since the 1980s the national team has always featured a variety of non-white players, from Ruud Gullit to Frank Rijkaard and, though the national team has often been riven by conflicts, often reported as ethnically based, the players and the team were generally held up as an ex-ample of successful integration and multiculturalism.

However, attitudes to race in the Netherlands have been shifting, or, more accurately, bifurcating, with the rise of explicitly anti-migrant political parties. At the turn of the century the unlikely figure of Pym Fortune, a flamboyant gay businessman, made waves with the first electoral success for such a movement, though his political career was cut short by assassination in 2002. Since then, his mantle has been picked up by Geert Wilders and the PVV – Freedom Party. Wilders' engagement with football has for the most part been opportunistic. In 2013, after a lower-league match, three teenage players from Osdorp attacked the linesman from home side Alemre. The linesman was white and died. His assailants were Moroccan Dutch. The KNVB can-celled all amateur football for a week and Liberal Prime Minister Mark Rutte personally intervened, considering it an incidence of the wider problem of hooliganism and violence in Dutch sport. Wilders spoke for a considerable constituency in the Netherlands when he said, 'We don't have a sports violence problem: we have a Moroccan problem,' and called for the youths to be stripped of their citizenship and deported.[95]

Wilders and his ilk have also found a hearing and echo in the wider hooligan culture that, as Rutte pointed out, still persists in the Netherlands.[96] Although the widespread fighting and disorder of the late 1990s, especially between the organized firms of Ajax and Feyenoord, has been contained, and most hooligan groups have been reduced to out-of-town fight clubs, the atmosphere in the country's stadiums has proved less pliable. Certainly the long-standing anti-semitism that Ajax's self-assumed Jewish identity evoked in the 1970s and 1980s has persisted, as evidenced by, *inter alia*, the Groningen fans making Nazi salutes at Ajax in 2014. By the same token, Ajax ultras could sing to Kenneth Vermeer, Feyenoord's black goalkeeper, 'Kenneth NSB', a reference to the *Nationaal Socialistische Beweging* or National Social Movement that collaborated with the German occupation, and a comment on his transfer from Ajax to their rivals. At the same time, in the upper tier, one Ajax fan lynched a black doll wearing a Vermeer Feyenoord shirt.[97] Perhaps a better illustration of mainstream racism in the country were the responses to a selfie of a group of national team players (including Vermeer, Memphis Depay, Karim Rekik and Gregory van der Wiel) that went viral on social media. Many Dutch compared them to monkeys or *Zwarte Piet Black Pete* – the Netherland's version of Father Christmas, notionally a North African slave, invariably played as a buffoon by white people in blackface – and commented that the team simply weren't Dutch.[98]

While racism in Belgian football and society remains commonplace, particularly at grassroots and amateur level, it is, given Belgium's peculiar make-up, a secondary issue in the debates over the meaning of the national team.[99] Created in the early nineteenth century, Belgium has long been an uneasy federation of francophone Wallonia in the south and Flanders in the Flemish-speaking north. The long economic and political hegemony of the Walloons, blessed with the coalfields and factories of Belgium's industrial revolution, has been reversed in the last forty years. Wallonia has de-industrialized and become poorer, while the Flemish north has prospered. The fissures and conflicts produced by this shift have seen most of Belgium's national institutions divide into two (political parties for example), and the rise of a separatist Flemish nationalism represented by the NVA. This sharp division in the Belgian nation is made more complex by the fact that there are Flemish speakers in Wallonia, francophones in Flanders, and both in Brussels, the capital city, which is in effect the capital of Europe and a distinctive metropole in its own right. Under Belgium's fantastically complex constitutional arrangements, both language communities (and the German speakers), as well as Wallonia, Brussels and Flanders, have separate rights, political powers and institutions. As a consequence the federal state has very few powers, and Belgium and Belgianness few forms of public representation or reservoirs of affection.[100] Consequently, the Belgian national team had a rather thin following, and even when it had popular and successful moments like the semi-final appearance at the 1986 World

Cup, most of the conversation centred on the balance of Flemish and French speakers in the side, and antagonisms between them. A nadir was reached in 2000 when, as hosts, they ignominiously departed from the first round of the European Championships.

Since then, the Belgian football team has changed out of all recognition, and its place in Belgian society has been dramatically elevated. First, it has drawn on players born to the waves of migration that over the last thirty years have come to Belgium, and above all to Brussels. In addition to Walloonian and Flemish players of the calibre of Eden Hazard and Kevin De Bruyne, Belgium's line-ups have included Marouane Fellaini and Nacer Chadli (Moroccan descent), Vincent Kompany, Romelu Lukaku and Christian Benteke (Congolese descent), Mousa Dembélé (Malian) and Adnan Januzaj (Kosovan). All, however, have been schooled in the new system of training development instituted by the Belgian FA under technical director Michel Salon, created in direct response to the poor showing at Euro 2000, taking the best from the Dutch, but also incorporating the new systems of play and development emerging across Europe. While technique, given their proximity to the Dutch, is prized, Belgian football has increasingly noted and venerated the *football de la rue*, 'street football', that the new migrants have brought to Brussels and its suburbs: an addition to the mix that gives Belgian teams a physicality and guile they have previously lacked. With nearly all of its best players now at foreign clubs, the old domestic divisions between the francophones and the Flemish genuinely mean less to these squads. The arrival of multilingual coaches like Marc Wilmots, and foreign coaches like the Spaniard Roberto Martinez, has seen English emerge as the lingua franca of the squad. Wilmots as an ex-senator for the francophone and federalist party Mouvement Réformateur, has publicly linked the team's demeanour with the new hyper-diverse Belgium.[101]

In this regard, the Red Devils, as the team are ubiquitously known, and their red shirt have become the most important public emblem of Belgian identity and belonging, accessible to and supported by all parts of the community, the fringes of the Flemish independence movement aside, and infinitely more stable than the fractious federal governments the country's divided party system and super-proportional representation deliver. It is a protean field of meaning, by no means free of old-fashioned racism as players of African descent have attested, but there is no greater public theatre showing off Belgian's new and multi-layered diversity. The team, especially captain Vincent Kompany, have been well aware of this status, and its representation of what those who stand to one side of the old Flemish–Walloon division call *Belgique*: a more cosmopolitan, outward-looking version of Belgium. In 2012, Bart De Wever, the leader of the NVA, was elected Mayor of Antwerp and tweeted, 'Antwerp is for everybody, but this evening, it is for us.' When, a few months later, Belgium beat Scotland 2–0, Kompany responded by posting, 'Belgium belongs to everyone, but tonight primarily to us.' Thus it was particularly telling that, just a few weeks after the NVA had achieved its best electoral result ever, making it the second largest party in the country, the Belgian national team's run to the quarter-finals at the 2014 World Cup should provoke record-breaking levels of unity. As one Bruxellois remarked, 'It has also been good to see the Belgian flag hanging from balconies, and not the regional one.' Crowds in the fan parks of the capital were visibly very diverse. One bar owner reported that 'The fans chant alternately in French and Flemish, which is almost unheard of,' but, as Johan Vande Lanotte, deputy Prime Minister, put it, 'Yes, it's strange, but then we were the inventors of surrealism.'[102]

VI

There has been an air of the surreal about the game in Western Europe's Celtic periphery too. Here there was a version of those foggy isles in which Great Britain or the United Kingdom had barely ever existed, its constituent nations playing football since the last quarter of the nineteenth century as England, Scotland, Ireland and Wales; a fact recognized by FIFA since its own creation in 1904, and the only permitted exception to the 'one internationally recognized state – one team' rule. Ireland was the whole island until, in 1921, partition created Northern Ireland and the Irish Free State, sometimes Eire, later the Republic of Ireland, and confusingly the Football Association of Ireland (FAI) in Northern Ireland and the Irish Football Association in the Republic (IFA). Matters have been further confused by the question of anthems. The Irish sing '*Amhrán na bhFiann'*, 'The Soldier's Song', is the official anthem of the Republic, at football matches, but many other sports organized on an all-Ireland basis, like rugby union, have switched to the more consciously neutral if saccharine and sentimental 'Ireland's Call'. At Northern Ireland games they sing neither, opting for the British national anthem 'God Save the Queen', which is so controversial that much of the population will not only not sing it, but also refuse to attend the team's games on this account. The Welsh, whose national identity has been more closely aligned to song and language than the other nations, adopted *'Hen Wlad fy Nhadau'*, 'Land of my Fathers', as the unofficial national anthem in 1905, after it was sung by the crowd before the Welsh rugby team beat the mighty visiting All Black side. 'Flower of Scotland', written in the mid-1960s by folk group The Corries, was first sung before a Scottish national team match in 1993 and became the official anthem of the Scottish Football Association in 1997. It is a mournful dirge recalling the Scots' victory over the armies of Plantagenet King of England, Edward II, at the Battle of Bannockburn in 1314, but it is infinitely preferable to the prolonged booing that 'God Save the Queen' received through much of the 1980s. The English, inevitably, have remained very happily inside the carapace of Great Britain and, despite the adoption of the St George flag in preference to the Union Jack, the crowd is still belting out 'God Save the Queen', when it isn't singing 'Rule Britannia'.

Such is the confusion that, in 2012, British men's and women's teams appeared at the London Olympics, but they were England in disguise, the other nations' football associations all considering participation to be politically and culturally unacceptable; even, in the case of the Scots, treasonous. During the 2018 World Cup, polls suggested that over a third of Scotland actively wanted England to lose, while columnists in Wales and Ireland pondered whether there might be reason to support a new, more diverse and less entitled squad; the answer, overwhelmingly, remained no.[103] Yet however hard these football nations have tried to distinguish themselves from the English, and indeed set themselves in some sense in opposition to them, they have been and remain deeply bound, economically, culturally and emotionally, to English football. Indeed, in the past quarter of a century, as English football has boomed, their fate is more obviously determined by England than ever.

Ireland's intimate engagement with English football began the

moment the British state left the country, for one of the main consequences of Irish independence was a large wave of migration to
Britain, but especially England, in the inter-war and immediate post-
war eras. This established huge Irish communities in London,
Birmingham, Manchester and Liverpool. Many of them gravitated to
Arsenal (sometimes known as the 'London Irish'), Aston Villa (who
now sell more shirts in Dublin than any other city) and Manchester
United and Everton (in preference to their cross-city rivals who were
perceived to be Protestant and unionist in complexion), and brought
their allegiances and enthusiasms home. A steady stream of players,
many of whom, like Johnny Giles at Leeds United, had cut their teeth
in the Dublin youth leagues, helped build a following for English
football through the 1970s and 1980s, boosted by increasingly easy
access to English media and television.

Even so, the League of Ireland, all through the interminably grey
and dull Ireland of the 1950s and 1960s, could draw tens of thousands of people to its games, and its clubs could even make profits.
Yet in 2014 it managed average gates of less than 1,500, while
120,000 Irish fans a year were making the trip to England to see a
Premier League game, and they were just the tip of a great iceberg
of interest in English and European football. Even allowing for the
incompetence of the FAI and the Irish government, evidenced by
their disastrous, expensive and futile efforts to build a new national
sports complex in Dublin under Taoiseach Bertie Ahern, and their
inability to reform its youth development systems, Irish football
really never had a chance.[104] The explosive global growth and mag-
netic appeal of its giant and very accessible English neighbour was
unstoppable.

Northern Ireland, for similar reasons of migration, media and
proximity, has established fanbases for many English clubs –
Tottenham's popularity dating back to Danny Blanchflower's time at
Spurs, for example; but, in addition to this, Northern Ireland also has
a very considerable and more problematic Scottish football following. Inevitably, the long-standing ethno-national identities of Celtic
and Rangers, and the intimate economic and political connections
between Belfast and Glasgow, created significant support for the
clubs, and the enmity and conflict they generate in Scotland repro-
duced themselves across the water. Thus in 2009, when Rangers
pipped Celtic to the title, Coleraine loyalists celebrated the victory by

attacking Kevin McDaid, a Catholic, who was killed on his doorstep by a mob wielding hand-made weapons.[105]

Despite this long-term drain of sporting affection, Northern Ireland's domestic football has proved more resilient than that of either Ireland or Wales, even recording increased attendances and media coverage in the last few years. This is at least in part due to the enduring sectarian identities and conflicts played out through the game. Linfield and Glentoran, although bitterly opposed to one another, their games regularly the subject of disorder and violence, have remained unambiguous heralds of unionism and loyalism. Cliftonville, a north Belfast side founded in a once mixed area, has become the leading nationalist club in the league, as the ethnic segregation of the city saw the neighbourhood become almost exclusively Catholic. By the same token, their near neighbours Crusaders took on a much more aggressively Protestant demeanour: a member of their board recalled the era just after the signing of the Good Friday Agreement: 'If a Roman Catholic had walked into our bar just ten years ago he would have been shot dead.'[106] Earlier generations of football nationalists had abandoned the fight. Belfast City, subject to widespread sectarian violence in the 1940s, closed their doors. Derry City, experiencing the same in the 1970s, chose to commute and joined the League of Ireland over the border, where they remain. Cliftonville, like modern Northern Irish republicanism more generally, is staying put and contesting the ground: 'What's the alternative? Do we pack up and say we are going home? Playing in the League of Ireland isn't a viable option. And there's the thing, we're the oldest club in Ireland. We were founder members of the IFA . . . we were playing before any of the rest of them, fucking sure we're not going to be the ones that leave.'[107]

For much of the time an uneasy peace has held in the Northern Irish game, but sectarian spasms continue to break out. In 2011, for example, the final of the Belfast school cup culminated in a huge on-pitch fight between players and supporters of Belfast Boys Model Schools and St Mary's Christian Brothers Grammar. Later that year five Loughall fans, carrying Union Jacks, stormed the dug-out of their nationalist opponents, Lurgan Celtic.

Welsh domestic football was hollowed out long ago by the inclusion of its main professional clubs – Swansea City, Cardiff City, Newport Town and Wrexham – in the English football leagues. Consequently, as of 2017, the semi-professional Welsh Premier League clocked up average attendances of less than 400 people, which was considered progress on its predecessor the League of Wales. Its leading team, the New Saints (once Trans Network Solutions), is actually based across the border in Shropshire. Even with a foothold in English football Welsh teams are, if not beggars, paupers in their own home. By Facebook-based data at any rate, Liverpool and Manchester United are more popular in Wales than Cardiff and Swansea, both of whom had only just more fans in Wales than Chelsea and Arsenal. Swansea, then riding high in the Premier League, were probably unconcerned about their Welsh Facebook numbers, given that by then they had acquired more global followers than there appeared to be football fans in all of Wales.[108] Yet, while domestic football in Ireland, Northern Ireland and Wales has been relegated to a position of permanent under-development by their immediate neighbour, the place of football within their national cultures and in the complex hierarchy of sports and identities each possesses has, simultaneously, risen.

This shift in the status of the game and the national football team has been most evident in Ireland, where, in the immediate post-independence era, the GAA and Gaelic games assumed a political and cultural hegemony over Irish sport. Established as an instrument of cultural nationalism and resistance to the British, the GAA had invented and codified Gaelic games and established an island-wide network of clubs as redoubts of political nationalism, within which the playing of 'garrison' games like rugby and football was banned by statute, as was membership for employees of the British armed forces, police and government. The organization was a real player in the struggle for independence, and its national stadium in waiting, Croke Park, was in 1920 the site of a British army massacre conducted during a Gaelic football game. Thus the GAA and its sports emerged as national martyrs, heralds and keepers of the authentic Irish ludic soul. Football in Ireland certainly survived partition: indeed, as we noted, it prospered as a working-class preoccupation, but it was viewed with opprobrium by nationalist elites for both its alien origins and semi-professional skulduggery. The average fan, like the average Irish citizen, could live with that, paying deference to the hypocrisy of De Valera's sententious clerical nationalism while secretly enjoying the secular pleasures of the old masters: 'Readers who bought Dev's *Sunday Press* outside the church gates after Mass were not beyond slipping a copy of the *News of the World* beneath its folds.'[109] It was enough to sustain Irish football through to the 1980s, but at an ever lower level of attendance, and never enough to trouble international competition.

Ireland's re-entry into the world of global football began under the leadership of Jack Charlton, himself a quintessential English type, and a generation of players largely born and trained in England, with whom they qualified for two consecutive World Cups in 1990 and 1994. The teams' performances are perhaps best not dwelt on at great length, for they never offered much in the way of elegance, but the arrival of carnival fandom amongst the travelling fans was remarkable for its scale and bonhomie, and as a first indication of new, younger, more cosmopolitan Ireland emerging at the beginning of the long Celtic Tiger boom. Since then, football in all its forms, but especially English and European football, has gone mainstream. Even the GAA has been prepared to allow the game to be played on its grounds and to invite British civil servants into the fold. Thus, by 2012, Fintan O'Toole could write that playing football and rugby at Croke Park (during the construction of the new Aviva Stadium for those national teams) was entirely appropriate for the kind of country Ireland had become, and for the complex multi-layered sense of identity its citizens had come to possess.

> Irish sports fans have worked out a system of allegiances that is more complex, and more honest, than the old apartheid. At the level of the parish and of the county, the GAA teams are the standard-bearers. But rugby teams represent their provinces best, and the national soccer and rugby teams do battle in the international arena. And for the weekly fix of televised glamour, Manchester United, Liverpool and Glasgow Celtic provide both a globalized cosmopolitanism and (the darkest secret of all) a sense of belonging to what used to be called the British Isles. A single red jersey can cover the Cork hurlers, the Munster rugby team and Manchester United.[110]

Northern Ireland, which had hitherto seemed a place of the most singular, fixed and antagonistic identities, has, since the signing of the Good Friday Agreement, and under the sometimes tortuous experiment in self-government and cohabitation that has followed, begun to inch down the path the Republic had charted. Certainly in 1998 it would have been hard to imagine that Martin McGuinness, once head of the IRA Army Council and then Sinn Fein's Deputy First Minister at the newly devolved Stormont Assembly, should have revealed himself to have been such a football fan that, in 1989, he had personally defused an unexploded bomb near Derry City's Brandywell ground to permit a European fixture against Benfica to go ahead; or that in 2012 he would attend his first official football fixture at Windsor Park, home of both Linfield and the national team and widely perceived to be a redoubt of loyalism; or that both Irish national teams would qualify for Euro 2016, and that he would attend both games in an official capacity. Hardest of all to imagine is McGuinness exchanging football banter, as a Manchester United fan, with First Minister Peter Robinson, head of the DUP and, inevitably, a Chelsea supporter.[111] Yet they all happened. What made these kinds of symbolic political display, if not McGuinness's personal preferences, so hard to imagine, was that the atmosphere at Windsor Park, the Belfast home of the Northern Irish side, and the meanings associated with the team, were still, at the turn of the century, so poisonous.

Located in a staunchly loyalist part of Belfast, Windsor Park was the kind of place most Catholics would have avoided, whether there had been a football stadium there or not. As recently as 1982, when Northern Ireland miraculously qualified for the World Cup finals, there was still a smattering of cross-community support for a cross-community team. But in the bitter years marked by the hunger strikes of this era, and the gruelling armed struggle that followed, almost the entirety of nationalist football support in Northern Ireland switched to the Republic, leaving the team and Windsor Park itself an ever more concentrated bastion of loyalism; a fact underscored by the regular chant sung of 'No Surrender' between each line of the British national anthem. The degree of sectarianism in the national game, despite official blandishments, became impossible to ignore when in 2001 Neil Lennon, a Catholic from Lurgan, who had played largely without incident for Leicester City and the national side, moved to Celtic. There he received a torrent of hate mail and abuse, on and off the pitch, from Rangers supporters, that was then repeated and amplified back in Northern Ireland, where graffiti appeared in his home town saying 'RIP Neil Lennon', and the home crowd at Windsor Park booed him relentlessly. In 2002, now as captain of the national team, he received a bullet in the post, and announced his retirement from international football.

The IFA, under considerable political pressure, finally began to act, introducing a programme of anti-sectarian action around the national team, in the domestic leagues and in grassroots football. There have been, at the margins, some successes: grassroots schemes that bring children from both communities together have proliferated; Linfield finally started fielding Catholic players after a long informal religious ban; and at Windsor Park a part of the crowd started challenging sectarian behaviour, collectively drowning its songs with carnivalesque alternatives, like the sardonic 'It's just like watching Brazil.' Even better, at Euro 2016, was their adoption of Wigan Athletic's song for their in-form striker Will Griggs, pairing a 1990s dance hit with the crowd-pleasing chant, 'Will Grigg's on fire! Your defence is terrified!'[112] Coach Michael O'Neill refused to give him a single minute's play, which made the unrelenting singing and stadium-shaking dancing that accompanied it even better.

Yet, for all this, the Protestant unionist majority inside the IFA and Northern Irish football generally has struggled with the new dual identities available to the citizens of Northern Ireland and its players in particular. Used to calling players up from both north and south of the border, the IFA has been shocked to discover that many young players from Northern Ireland have been opting for the Republic,[113] while some of those that do play for the country are doing so with their heads, not their hearts. In late 2011 Niall McGinn played for a Northern Irish team that demolished the Republic 5–0, but tweeted afterwards, 'I'm a Republic of Ireland fan ... the only good thing to come out of tonight is that I got Robbie Keane's jersey.'[114] Most problematic of all has been the question of the national anthem, not only at international matches but also at major games in the domestic programme like the cup final. Cliftonville, the nationalist club from North Belfast, have twice, on playing the final, asked for the anthem not to be sung, but to no avail.[115] As with the wider politics of Northern Ireland, the matter remains at stalemate, but as the demography of the country steadily shifts in favour of the nationalist community, one wonders how long this kind of unionist intransigence can last.

Welsh football has had to compete for attention with English football across the border, and with rugby union at home. Its doubly subordinate position in Welsh cultural life seemed, at the turn of the century, to be a permanent condition. The men's national team had failed to qualify for an international tournament for more than four decades, and the Welsh game's handful of professional clubs were at the bottom of the English leagues.[116] At the same time, in 1999, the year Wales acquired the National Assembly, its first self-governing body for half a millennium, the nation hosted the Rugby Union World Cup. The opening ceremony was held in the Millennium Stadium, in the closest thing that the country got to, if not an independence day celebration, then a public affirmation of a new kind of Welsh nation. Shirley Bassey sang the official song in a Welsh-flag dress, and Cerys Matthews, of indypop band Catatonia, belted out 'Every day I wake up and thank the Lord I'm Welsh'. In the years since, the Welsh rugby team have had their moments of success, and the Millennium Stadium has never been less than full to bursting with well-oiled and well-drilled carnival nationalism: fantasy folk dress, daffodils and leeks, the nation as one big male voice choir from the mining valleys. However, the WRU and rugby union's self-appointed place as the essence, rather than as an element, of the sporting nation was always overstated.[117]

Beyond the national team, Welsh rugby union is a minority sport, overwhelmingly confined to the south of the country, played by fewer people than football and, at a professional level, the small fry of a bigger Celtic league. The game's reach has been particularly limited in the north of the country, which has looked to Manchester and Liverpool, both of which are far more easily accessible than Cardiff or Swansea, given Wales' hapless internal transport networks. Moreover, the core classes of the alliance that made and played rugby union – southern middle-class professionals and the working-class small industrial towns and mining villages, and in their incarnation as the Welsh Labour Party, the dominant social and political force in Wales – have been diminished, as the country's old industrial economy and non-conformist chapels have all but vaporized. In their place a post-industrial Wales has emerged that also accommodates a resurgent Welsh language movement and a growing Welsh-speaking population, which is the core of Plaid Cymru's nationalist and separatist vote: a more ethnically diverse population than ever before, and a more vibrant, distinctive Welsh popular culture. While the new Wales shares much of the cartoon anti-Englishness of the old, it has also expressed the desire to connect to the world independently of its neighbour. Football, especially the national team, offered a version of all of this that rugby could not approximate to.

In part, the rising status of football in Wales has followed on the coat tails of the world's obsession with the English Premier League. It was certainly that which had brought, first, Sam Hamman, the Lebanese ex-owner of Wimbledon, and then Vincent Tan, a Chinese-Malaysian operator, to Cardiff City. Hamman had tried to move Wimbledon FC to both Dublin and Belfast, but settled for selling their stadium to developers, and the club to Norwegian billionaires. He then transferred his ambitions to Cardiff, where he announced on purchasing the club that 'Wales and Welsh people are not an appendage, and it is through football and specifically Cardiff City FC that we are going to establish identity and pride.' Perhaps unaware there were already other sources of identity and pride at work, Hamman was, nonetheless, the first to try and consciously mobilize a Welsh football club in that direction. He changed the away kit to the red, white and green of the national flag, toyed with changing the club's venerable blue home strip to red, and planned to abandon the nickname 'Bluebirds' for 'Dragons', while building a new stadium with a Welsh name. Little of that came to pass, but he did institute 'Men of Harlech' as a pre-match song, recruited Welsh coaches and players, and created a wild media circus that got the club acres of coverage as it crept towards the top of the Championship. This carnival of ersatz nationalism was ultimately undermined by Hamman's wafer-thin knowledge of the country, and especially his attempt to diminish the club's rivalry with Swansea and even enlist Swansea fans' support. As one Cardiff fan said, 'We hate the Jacks more than we hate the English.'[118]

In the end, Hamman loved his money more than he loved Wales and, when the local council refused planning permission for his new stadium, he sold up, and the club passed into the hands of Vincent Tan, a Chinese-Malaysian monopolist who was brilliant at winning government contracts at home, but, by his own admission, knew nothing about football. At Cardiff he trod a similar path to Hamman but even more clumsily, actually changing the shirt to red, replacing the bluebird with a dragon on the crest – on the grounds that both were far more recognizable in the East Asian market – and triggering years of opprobrium and massive organized opposition from the fans. He eventually conceded, abandoning the 'Lucky Red' kit in 2015.

Unedifying as the antics of Cardiff City's owners have been, and precarious as Swansea's stay in the Premier League has sometimes appeared, they have helped make football part of everyday popular culture in Wales in the last fifteen years. Alongside this, a trio of dedicated national coaches – John Toshack, Gary Speed and Chris Coleman – with experience in top-level football in England and Europe, helped the FAW and the Welsh national team close the gap with their competitors. They immeasurably improved Wales's scouting methods, especially seeking out promising lower-division players in England with Welsh roots, raised the level of medical, psychological and scientific support to that which players would expect at their clubs, and made the learning and singing of the national anthem compulsory. Coleman's choice of *together stronger* as his unifying catchphrase may have been pedestrian, even cheesy, but it tapped a nerve with both his squad and the Welsh public, as the repetition of the hashtag on Twitter demonstrated. Add to this that the world's then most expensive player, Gareth Bale, was giving his all for the team, and Wales was able to finally cross the line, and for the first time in almost sixty years qualify for an international tournament.

At Euro 2016, Wales had a team that spoke to a country that had changed. It was certainly Wales's most diverse team, with both Welsh-born and diasporic members, English and Welsh speakers and, in Ashley Williams, Jazz Richardson and Hal Robson-Kanu, players with African and Caribbean roots too. The extent to which Wales's relationship with football had changed also became apparent. A much younger Wales, unencumbered by daffodils, filled the fan parks at home and the stadiums in France, up to 30,000 making the journey to the biggest games. The Welsh First Minister, Carwyn Jones, and as many members of his cabinet as could scramble on board, built their schedules around attendance at the games. Back home, BBC Wales and the rest of the national media were saturated: a BBC prime-time special, *C'mon Wales: Our Euro 2016 Singalong*, showcased the country's music scene and orchestrated versions of fans' chants: Eddie Grant's 'Give Me Hope, Joanna' for Joe Ledley, and the Human League's 'Don't You Want Me' became 'Aaron Ramsey, baby. Aaron Ramsey, oooooh.'[119]

At the opening game in France a banner referring to two mediaeval princes of independent welsh polities and an Arsenal midfielder flew in the crowd: 'Llewelyn 1258, Glyndwr 1404, Ramsey 2016.'[120]

It wasn't quite a bid for independence, but the Welsh team played with collective verve and purpose, got themselves to the knock-out stages and came alight, sweeping aside the much-fancied Belgians before finally going down to the eventual champions, Portugal, 2–0 in the semi-finals. At its most cosmopolitan and outward-looking, even flamboyant, there was the Wales of Hal Robson-Kanu, a black Welshman, then without a club, who executed the most technically perfect Cruyff turn for Wales's second goal against Belgium. Of course, old habits die hard. They may not have beaten England in their group stage game but there was, nonetheless, the delicious pleasure of doing immeasurably better than their neighbours, and scoring a sensational goal against them. As one long-suffering Welsh fan recalled, 'Gareth Bale has just delivered my message. He's interrupted the Queen's Christmas Day speech, snatched the microphone out of her hands, and told every man, woman and child in England to fuck off.'[121]

The ghost at the feast of Euro 2016 was Scotland. Indeed, since Morocco put three goals past a flailing Jim Leighton at the 1998 World Cup, Scotland have existed only in the netherworlds of desperate qualifying campaigns, having failed to make it to a single international tournament. Scotland, which should properly be understood as the co-creator of the modern game alongside England, whose football proselytizers and innovators have had a global reach, has taken a harder hit from contemporary globalization, and fallen further than any of the other nations of the British football isles.

As late as 1995 Paul Gascoigne's destination of choice after his Italian misadventures at Lazio was Rangers. Scottish football was certainly no less enthusiastic in its embrace of commercialization and pay-per-view television than England, though from the off the gap between them was huge. There was even a late flash of European success, though it was a pale shadow of the past. Celtic made it to the final of the UEFA Cup in 2003, its fans filling not only seven-eighths of the stadium in Seville but also much of the city's public spaces. In what was a historical recreation of the mythic, and much smaller, migration to Lisbon in 1967 where Celtic won the European Cup, somewhere in the region of a quarter of a million fans 'had to be there' to see, hear or feel the side dispatched by Porto.[122] In 2008, Rangers did much the same in Manchester, where they went down 2–0 to Zenit St Petersburg in that year's final, only with the twist that their fans rioted in Piccadilly Gardens when the big screen went down.[123]

Now there is no comparison and precious few linkages left between Scottish and English football. In the 2000s Scotland continued to supply a steady stream of players to the Premier League, not to mention up to a quarter of its managers, but those numbers have dwindled. It is hard to imagine that any Scottish club will be contesting the final of a European tournament any time soon. The Old Firm, who repeatedly explored different options for getting themselves into the English football ladder, have abandoned their efforts, for, legal impediments aside, the economic gap is now too large to bridge. Even Celtic, in a good year like 2016, and after you strip out the European money that they would be unlikely to get access to through the English leagues, were at best a strong Championship club.

In retrospect, 1998 was the end of a long sporting and political journey for the football nation, the final party for the now pacific Tartan Army, as the national team's travelling support had become known. Shorn of the country's youthful and sometimes violent football casuals, and self-policed to ensure that domestic rivalries and sectarian conflict did not rear their heads, the Tartan Army served through the late 1980s and 1990s as an ambassador for a rising but stateless nation. They distinguished themselves from the still bellicose English with their amity and drunken self-mockery, telling Italian fans, to the tune of 'Guatanamera', that they were 'gonna deep-fry your pizzas'. While never considered a complete proxy for the Scottish nation, they brought a measure of working-class bacchanalia and cheek to the otherwise more arid coalition of middle-class progressives, trade unionists, churches and professionals that had spearheaded and steered the long march to devolution. With the election of a Labour government in 1997, the recreation of the Scottish parliament, closed for almost 300 years, was almost a formality. The Tartan Army has had no more than near misses to relish in over two decades of defeat and disappointment. Results aside, with the arrival of the Scottish parliament and a slew of new Scottish civic and culture institutions, the place of football and the national team in representing the new Scotland shrank back. There were even those that worried the Tartan Army had become an embarrassing relic, 'our equivalent of Morris Dancers – grown men in ridiculous outfits, trying to conjure up enthusiasm for the good old days'.[124] However, if one wanted football that delivered a sharper and more acerbic account of the state of the nation since devolution, then domestic football provided just that.

The dominance of the Old Firm has loomed over Scottish football since the late nineteenth century, but since Aberdeen last won the league title in 1986 they have monopolized it. Already in a different income bracket from the other clubs before the years of hyper-commercialization, the two clubs, having failed to get out of Scottish football and into English football, have reverted to Plan B, which was extracting an even bigger share of Scottish football's turnover. Thus the league has been re-formatted and TV deals restructured to favour them, while their access to their respective global diasporas, to high-end corporate sponsorships and European football, has placed them in an entirely separate universe from the rest of the country. Consequently, the enduring sectarian identities and enmities that define the clubs' relationship have remained a huge element of Scottish football culture, crowding out the rest of the country both on and off the pitch.

At an official level, however, there was a remarkable complacency about the presence and acceptability of sectarianism. Scottish football had been telling itself since 1989, when Rangers signed Mo Johnston and broke the club's ban on Catholics, that the bad old days were over. Yet Old Firm games remained an occasion, in Glasgow and across Scotland and Ireland, for hundreds of incidents of violence, intimidation and social disorder. Between 1995 and 2001, at least five and possibly up to eleven homicides had their roots in Old Firm matches, played on days during which levels of domestic violence would rise sharply. Despite the Scottish government passing anti-sectarian hate crime legislation in 2003, the rate of incidents rose, reaching 700 in 2005 alone. Rangers fans persisted with celebrations of Loyalist victories, like 'Billy Boy' and the notorious 'Famine Song', the least unpleasant stanza of which went,

> They've all their Papists in Rome
> They have U2 and Bono
> Well the famine is over
> Why don't they go home?

Despite years of handwringing and summitry by the Scottish government and the Scottish FA, little had been achieved. Indeed, UEFA, who were keen to punish Rangers fans for sectarian chanting during Champions League games, had abandoned the effort on the grounds that 'we cannot demand an end to behaviour that has been tolerated for years.'[125] In early 2011, matters came to a head when a package full of bullets, addressed to Neil Lennon, now manager of Celtic, was intercepted on its way from Northern Ireland. Lennon was in fact no stranger to sectarian violence in Glasgow, having been personally assaulted on a number of occasions in the street. In April another viable parcel bomb addressed to him was stopped before delivery, as were the Hearts fans who invaded the pitch in May and, with menace, made a beeline for him in the technical area.[126] The newly elected SNP government at Holyrood responded by drafting and passing the ambiguous and draconian Offensive Behaviour at Football and Threatening Communications Bill. Impressive as its title might be, listening to the crowds at an Old Firm game suggests that the 'Famine Song' or republican iconography are not included in its remit. Unloved and unenforceable, the law was repealed in 2018. The tone of the crowd remains unchanged.

Beyond the Old Firm and its atavistic self-obsession, the new commercialism brought the usual selection of domestic and foreign patrons ready to squander their money, borrowed money and the clubs' money on success, a course often ending in bankruptcy and administration. For lovers of the romantic eccentric there was the English millionaire Brooks Mileson, who bankrolled tiny Gretna Green, a town of just 3,000 on the Scots–English border, and took them from the fourth tier to the Premier League in six seasons, not to mention a Scottish Cup final and a turn in the UEFA Cup. In 2008, as Mileson's health and fortune declined and the debts became unserviceable, the club was sent back down to the Third Division and bankrupted.[127] The club has subsequently been liquidated entirely. The reign of Vladimir Romanov, a Lithuanian businessman at Hearts, was more predatory and instrumental. Having acquired control between 2003 and 2005 when Hearts were in dire financial straits, he promised to invest in the side and prevent the proposed sale of the club's Tynecastle stadium for housing. Once installed he actually massively increased the club's debt, failed to invest in anything, sacked a manager who wouldn't play him in a friendly game against Barcelona, and ran the club into the ground, departing when it went into administration in 2013.[128] More prosaically, over-ambitious directors, bad management and the endless and unjustifiable optimism that fuels football everywhere took Motherwell, Livingstone and Dundee, twice, to the bankruptcy court. In every case, the money had been blown on player transfers and wages, and increasingly on players from overseas. In 1986, 97 per cent of players in the league were from Scotland; by 2016 they made up just half of the squads in the Scottish Premiership.[129] However, all of these financial basket cases and their demise pale into insignificance compared to the collapse of Rangers in 2012.[130]

In 2009 Rangers revealed that they owed the bank £18 million and, pending the outcome of legal challenge, had an outstanding tax bill of £49 million for monies not paid, indeed illegally evaded, through paying players by an exotic device with a prosaic name, an employee benefit trust: essentially accounts that received offshore loans to players, in lieu of wages, that would never be called in and were not, they all thought, taxable. David Murray, Rangers' long-term overlord and paragon of Scottish Thatcherism, ran for the hills, and sold the club and its debt to Craig Whyte, a venture capitalist of mixed fortunes and record, for a pound. Whyte then borrowed more money against season ticket receipts, failed the SFA's 'fit and proper person' test due to his undeclared bankruptcies, and put the club into administration. While rival factions of Glasgow businessmen fought over the corpse of Rangers, and attempted to revive it, the rest of Scottish football fought over where the rebirth should happen. Celtic, the leading clubs and the Football Association were all for re-installing them back in the top division, so as to maintain the already meagre values of everyone's TV rights. Everybody else thought that, given this kind of financial skulduggery and the preening self-importance and self-regard of Rangers, the rule of law ought to take priority and Rangers, like everyone else in this situation, should have to start again at the bottom.

It wasn't quite the 'Scottish Spring' that some thought at the time, but there was a substantial social media-led mobilization amongst lower league fans – the real paymasters of beleaguered small-time Scottish football – who pressured their clubs to vote against the pre-ferred option, and won. Thus in 2013 the new Rangers began the season in the fourth level, the start of their odyssey of humiliation and punishment through small-town Scotland – though along the way setting records for lower-league gates with their still huge travel-ling fanbase – before returning to the top flight in 2016.[131]

While some regretted their departure, it is clear that Rangers' absence, although it gave Celtic a monopoly of the league, opened up a more competitive space in the cups, allowing a whole series of other teams to actually win something, and created some room for a more diverse and complex Scottish football culture. Since 2012 the Scottish Cup has been won by Hearts, Hibernian for the first time in 114 years, and by Inverness Caledonian Thistle and St Johnstone for the first time ever. In this Scotland, nation and football appear less Glasgow-centric and less central-belt-centric than they have before. Although both Edinburgh clubs – Hibernian and Heart of Midlothian – have financially struggled through the twenty-first century, their recent prominence is in keeping with the city's growing importance as a real capital city and a centre of politics and power. Moreover, they have both consciously sought to distinguish themselves, despite their historical roots in the city's ethno-religious divides, from the sectarianism and focus on Irish issues that consumes the Old Firm. So too the long-suffering fans of Partick Thistle, Glasgow's third club, and proud possessors of the best mascot in world football: an angry, crumpled star called Kingsley, designed by fan and noted artist David Shrigley. Hearts, since Romanov's departure, have been transformed under the part-ownership and zero-bullshit managerial leadership of Ann Budge, the most powerful and important woman in Scottish football to date. The introduction of normal, responsible business and accounting practices has been a revolution by itself, but Budge, who is selling her share to the supporters' trust, and Hearts are pioneers of a new wave of social ownership in Scottish football.

The economic and demographic dynamism of the Highlands was represented by the arrival in top-level football of not just Inverness Caledonian Thistle – from the fastest growing city in the country – but its rural highland cousin, Ross County from the tiny market town of Dingwall. Indeed, Scotland could still claim to have the highest number of professional football clubs per capita in the world, and an attendance per capita exceeded only by Cyprus. These were just the most easily quantifiable signs of a still rich and deep football culture. Only Brazil could produce an anthology of national football poetry close to the size and literary quality of Alistair Findlay's stunning collection of Scottish football verse, while few literary scenes the size of Scotland's could boast the football-themed writings of Alan Bissett and Irvine Welsh, or sustain a quarterly of football writing of the depth and calibre of *Nutmeg*. And just in case anyone might think that Scotland was taking itself all too seriously, then the acerbic laughter and wit of BBC Scotland's eternal football phone-in *Off the Ball* would put them right.

In an increasingly febrile political atmosphere, punctuated by the independence referendum in 2014 and the European Union referendum in 2016, Scottish domestic football became more serious and more politicized in new ways. In 2006, the Green Brigade first appeared on the terraces of Celtic Park. A start-up ultra group of predominantly left-leaning republicans, their first priority was to create some atmosphere in the sometimes somnolent stadium. Having achieved this by the usual methods, they showed an increasing appetite for making political statements. These included protest over the wearing of poppies, their own treatment by UEFA, UEFA's marginalization of Scotland and other small nations, and shows of solidarity and support for Palestine. Not always popular with other fans, and especially with the Celtic management, there have been efforts to exclude them and to revoke season tickets, but their presence endures. In 2014, the campaigns and debates around the independence referendum called by the SNP Government touched and mobilized every corner of Scottish civil society, with football no exception. Rangers fans, as would be expected, unveiled a huge 'Vote NO' banner, while Celtic fans, despite their distaste for Alex Salmond's SNP government and their football legislation, were flying 'Yes' banners at their game against Dundee. As the 'No' campaign's early lead was eroded, in one poll actually exceeded, the unionists brought in the heavy artillery, Gordon Brown taking the lead amongst politicians, backed by a coalition of Scottish football figures, like Alex Ferguson, Ally McCoist and David Moyes, who had done so well down south.[132] It was just enough to keep the cautious Scots in the union, and just in time for them to watch the reckless English vote to remove them from Europe in 2016.

VII

Can we pinpoint the moment when modern European football began? One could make a case for 1992, the year the Premiership broke away from the English Football League and UEFA re-formatted and re-launched the European Cup as the Champions League, both igniting the vertiginous rise in the value of football's TV rights. Three years later, in 1995, a European Court ruling on the case of an obscure Belgian footballer, Jean-Marc Bosman, would end many of the restrictive practices in European football's labour market and open up the industry to a great flux of international migrants. Both dates have their virtues, and rightly make globalization and economics a marker of the modern game, but in so doing they obscure the enduring and pervasive importance of politics, populism and television in the transformation of European football, and in this field there is only one person, one place and one date to start with: Silvio Berlusconi, Italy, 1986.

Berlusconi had by then created Italy's largest private media group, by way of suburban housing developments, trashy cable television and fabulous connections to Bettino Craxi, Milanese scoundrel, leader of the Italian socialist party (PSI), and occasionally Prime Minister. Now he had purchased AC Milan. He announced his presence and his project by landing in a helicopter at Milan's training ground while the PA blared out Wagner's 'Flight of the Valkyries'.[133] In this he demonstrated his fidelity to the core truth of the modern game, and perhaps his only unwavering belief, other than in his own magnificence, that football is a televised spectacle.

In the first phase of the commercialization and globalization of European football, Serie A was the richest, most cosmopolitan and glamorous league, and Berlusconi's AC Milan epitomized it.[134] Insisting on attacking, entertaining football, securing wall-to-wall coverage of the team's every move, and rejecting the whole philosophy of Italian *catenaccio*, Berlusconi gave free rein to Arrigo Sacchi and his high-pressing, exuberant squads, paid the bills for the cream of Dutch football (Van Basten, Gullit and Rijkaard) and sat back and basked in the show as Milan won back-to-back European Cups. Even better, he got to watch much of it in a sensationally renovated San Siro stadium, paid for by the Italian public in anticipation of hosting the 1990 World Cup. Italia 90, thought at the time to be the most telegenic and spectacular World Cup yet, fused football and global advertising more fully than any previous tournament, and showcased Italy's high-tech *Dolce Vita*. It appears, in retrospect, as a last meal, and a very good one, for the *Pentapartito*: the five-party alliance, led by the Christian Democrats and Socialists and designed to exclude the Communists, that had run Italy for the previous twenty years, relentlessly feeding on bribes and kickbacks on government contracts diverted to party and personal coffers. Two years later the *Tagentopoli* scandal would erupt, led by local magistrates in Milan and elsewhere. The vast network of corruption and illegality that had consumed the Italian body politic was laid bare, and in months every member of the *Pentapartito* had been dissolved.

It was in this context that Berlusconi decided to launch himself into the world of politics, to occupy the political space vacated on the right by the collapse of the Christian Democrats: 'I heard that things were getting dangerous, and that it was all being played in the penalty area, with the midfield being left desolately empty.' Self-mythologized as *la discesa di campo* – the descent to the pitch – in 1993 Berlusconi created Forza Italia: a political party named after a national football team chant. His company Fininvest provided candidates, money, marketing and gloss; AC Milan fan clubs across the country provided an instant local infrastructure. The voters gave him 21 per cent of the vote, enough in alliance with the right-wing regional separatists of the Northern League and the neo-fascists of the Allianza Nationale based in the south to form a government. On the eve of the parliamentary vote that would confirm, or not, Berlusconi as Prime Minister, AC Milan played Barcelona in the Champions League. The next morning *Corriere della Sera* reported, '4–0 and 159–153, both Cruyff's Barcelona and Ochetto's centre-left were wiped out.'

Over the next near two decades, Berlusconi would serve as Prime Minister thrice (1994–5, 2001–6, 2008–11), and football would remain an important element of his armoury and furnish much of his admittedly narrow stock of analogy and metaphor. Certainly his return to active campaigning for the 2001 elections was framed by Milan's purchase of Filippo Inzaghi and Manuel Rui Costa for record sums, and was followed by a new run of success that included two more Champions League victories in 2003 and 2007. In 2011 he was actually using AC Milan's national network of fan clubs to explicitly tell their five million members to vote for his new political vehicle, the People of Freedom Party (PdL). Berlusconi's time in office was overwhelmingly dedicated to the task of preserving and if possible enhancing his corporate empire and, given the torrent of investigations and prosecutions into corporate fraud, money-laundering and tax evasion that came his way, keeping him out of prison. In this respect, if no other, we can consider his record in office to have been successful. In the realm of football, for example, his government oversaw the introduction of new tax loopholes that allowed Milan to write off huge quantities of debt and unpaid tax bills, while Mediaset, his main television company, was able to wrest the nation's favourite football highlights show from RAI, the public channel.

Good as Berlusconi proved at winning elections and championships, he was never a monopolist, losing on occasion to a variety of centre-left coalitions, and in Serie A to Juventus, 'the old lady', still the team of the Agnelli family and their main company FIAT. In 2006, they were politically and legally lithe enough to escape unscathed from a long-running investigation into doping at the club during the 1990s, and had just won their twenty-ninth Scudetto. No sooner had the celebrations died down than tapes and transcripts of conversations featuring their general manager, Luciano Moggi, began to circulate. It became very clear, very quickly, even to the president of the football federation and the Juventus board, that Moggi sat at the centre of a gigantic spider's web of connections between officials, clubs, players, referees and agents that allowed him to subtly manipulate the fortunes and careers of hundreds of actors, all designed to ensure micro-advantages for Juventus and disadvantages for their opponents: the theory of marginal gains applied to ghost goals, harsh red cards and extendable periods of injury time. As Innocenzo Mazzini, vice-president of the Italian football federation, said to Moggi, 'You're the boss of the Italian game. You own Serie A.' Juventus were stripped of their title, demoted to Serie B and their board resigned.

Yet *Calciopoli*, as the scandal became known, was no *Tangentopoli*. It would prove disruptive, but there would be no all-out judicial assault on the rest of Italian football's corruptions, let alone match-fixing and manipulation. Thus, in 2015, for example, the Cremona prosecutor, Roberto Di Martono, announced investigations into more than 100 people and sixty games, some of them in Serie A. Indeed, the scandal was buried almost as soon as it had erupted, for Italy's progress at the World Cup that summer demanded as many and bigger headlines.

No one expected Italy to win the 2006 World Cup, but there was, for the cynical, a fabulous precedent. The last time that Italy had

won, back in Spain in 1982, the tournament was prefaced by a betting and match-fixing scandal in the game. The final, and the party
that followed it, were Italy's single most intense moments of imagined community in the post-war era, given weight by the still record
television audience, and brilliantly condensed and focused by the
presence of President Pertini in the stadium: a dignified, but emotional, Italian everyman.[135] Needless to say, the great swamp of
corruption in Italian football was forgiven and forgotten. In this
trope at any rate, the 2006 World Cup was a worthy sequel, and one,
like the victories at Moggi's Juventus, built on the finest of margins.
In the round of sixteen against Switzerland they survived most of the
game with just ten men, and won with a last-minute penalty. In the
semi-final they played out 119 goalless minutes against the animated
and relentless Germans, before two goals in two minutes killed their
hosts dead in their tracks. In the final they held France 1–1 for three-
quarters of a game that went the full distance. The score sheet
records Trezeguet's miss in the penalty shoot-out as the decisive
moment, but it was Marco Materazzi's bitter words to Zinedine
Zidane, late in extra time, that really changed the balance of the
game. Enraged, Zidane head-butted Materazzi and knocked him to
the ground before departing the field. Italy celebrated like crazy.
'Campioni del mondo', set to the White Stripes' 'Seven Nation Army',
was ubiquitous.[136] Yet with Berlusconi such a divisive figure politically, and of course within the world of football, there was no one that
could play the Pertini role, no single point on which the Italian
nation could be focused. Certainly, in the years since 2006, on the
other side of the financial crisis which left the already anaemic Italian economy on something close to life support, there has been no
sign of any greater level of national unity, while Italian football
remains locked, peaks and troughs aside, in steady decline.

In the absence of Juventus, serving a purgatorial year in Serie B
and a good few more without a competitive squad, Internazionale,
their fans and their long-suffering president, Massimo Moratti, had
their moment. It was a glorious, operatic, swansong for the old
patronage model of Italian football. Moratti, a sentimental billionaire
who had inherited an oil fortune, had been spending money at Inter
like it was going out of fashion for two decades, and had almost
nothing to show for it but grief. Between 2006 and 2010 the club
lost more than $600 million of his money, but won five league titles

in a row, a roll culminating, in 2010, when they won the treble: the Scudetto, the Coppa Italia and, at last, more than forty years after *Il Grande Inter* had first won the European Cup under Moratti's father, they won the Champions League. Better still for the *interisiti*, they won it under coach José Mourinho, who constructed a team whose defensive solidity exceeded that of *Il Grande Inter*, once the byword for *catenaccio* and opportunistic counter-attacking and goal-poaching. In the years since, Inter, and indeed many of Italy's leading clubs, have been in turmoil or decline, and for the first time have been sold off to foreign investors. It was surely the end of an era when Moratti sold 70 per cent of Inter Milan to Erick Thohir, scion of one of Indonesia's biggest corporate empires. Berlusconi, who had held on to control of AC Milan through his long years of political office by every device and evasion, sold up in 2016 to Li Yonghong, supposedly a very rich Chinese businessman and mining magnate, but in fact another outrageous chancer who, having defaulted on all kinds of debts and payments, lost control of the club to the American hedge fund that had hitherto sustained him. Parma, bankrolled in the 1990s by the Parmalat global dairy goods empire, has gone bankrupt twice this century: first in 2004, and then again in 2015. In this vacuum, the new Juventus, just like the old Juventus, have been in control. Indeed, since 2011 they have won eight Scudettos, lost two Champions League finals and made their new financial strength and sporting ambition clear, by signing Cristiano Ronaldo from Real Madrid for his final flourish.

One of the reasons Juventus has had such feeble competition is that, Verona apart, they are the only Italian club that have managed to build their own stadium in the last twenty years and, with massively improved facilities, have been able to raise their matchday revenues to something close to their English or German competitors'. Other clubs have begun the process, but have yet to catch up. Italy's capacity to plan, fund and execute major infrastructure projects, indeed to maintain the infrastructure it does possess, has diminished. Its ports are now so antiquated that they are able to handle, in toto, less traffic than Rotterdam alone. The catastrophic collapse of the Morandi Bridge in Genoa in 2018 was just the most dramatic and visible example of the country's decaying roads.

Against this backlog of decay and inattention, the state of the nation's football stadiums is small change, but they are powerfully symbolic of Italy's desiccated public realm. Most stadiums are owned by local councils, and neither they nor the clubs have had an overwhelming interest in upgrading them. The municipalities, without much cash to play with anyway, could see no way of raising rents or attracting new business, while the clubs, who might have benefited from investments in new seating and other facilities, were reluctant to do so, as they would not own what was built. The resulting neglect has left many stadiums in the top division, and nearly all of those in lower leagues, in a state of decay. Toilet facilities are broken and notoriously unpleasant. The bucket seats – those that have not been removed and thrown on to the pitch or set alight with petrol – are dilapidated. Even where one can find a seat or a bathroom, the Italian football stadium is by now, by some way, the most volatile and intimidating of environments at the top of European football, and that is the responsibility of the ultras, the clubs and the police.

The Italian ultra movement, already three decades old at the turn of the century, remains one of global football's most extraordinary sociological phenomena. The new century saw ultra culture, the model for many fans in France, Spain and the former Yugoslavia in the 1990s, adopted across Eastern Europe and North Africa. At home, their occupation of the nation's *curvas* was uncontested and their choreographies, displays and performances, remained impressive and atmospheric. Taken at face value, they remained motivated by the same mixture of identities and aspirations: Italy's intense localism, notions of fidelity and authenticity, in contrast to the inconsistency and fakery of politics and power, a last refuge for warriors and masculine honour. Alongside this they have attempted to articulate both an anti-commercialism, resisting the processes of pacification and gentrification in football that have occurred elsewhere, and an anti-statism that resists the police and the increasingly intrusive Italian surveillance state.

While there is merit in both arguments, Italy's ultras have actually been making their point through violence, menace and chaos, as just a few examples from the turn of the century suggest. Liverpool's visit to Roma for a UEFA Cup game in 2001 saw widespread rioting around the stadium and an attack by Roma ultras on visiting fans, six of whom had their buttocks slashed with knives. The same year Inter's ultras raised the stupidity stakes when they stole a scooter from Atalanta fans, smuggled it into the *curva* and then threw it over the edge into the crowd below.[137] In 2005 they brought their Champions League semi-final against AC Milan to a halt by throwing dozens of flares onto the pitch. Perhaps the most emblematic moment of the ultras' power, though, and one that captures the entire nation's susceptibility to rumour, paranoia and conspiracy theory, was on show at what was morbidly named 'the Derby of the Dead Child'. The 2004 derby game between Roma and Lazio was preceded by fighting between fans and the police. On this occasion rumours spread through the *curva* that a young boy had been killed by the police, either hit by a vehicle or shot with a tear gas grenade, all of which proved to be completely fallacious. The volatile fans, however, appeared to find them plausible, lowered their banners and stayed silent, until they started hurling objects at the police. The latter, as usual, responded with volleys of tear gas into the stands. Four leaders of the Roma ultras then scaled the Plexiglas wall separating them from the pitch, walked onto the grass and held an impromptu meeting with Roma captain, Francesco Totti, and the Lazio captain, Siniša Mihaljović. The league, the TV people and the referee wanted to carry on but, as Totti put it, 'if we keep playing they will kill us.' The game was called off, and the stadium emptied while fires burnt in the Roma *curva* and tear gas filled the air.

Over the previous decade or so, Italian football had seen a dozen or so deaths, all of them ultras killed in clashes, by stabbing, falling off walls or jumping off trains. In early 2007, though, the victims were a coach, Ermanno Licursi, who had been killed while trying to break up a fight between opposing fans at a lower-league game in Sicily, and a police officer, Fillipo Raciti, who was bludgeoned during a riot by Catania fans. The deaths of Licursi and Raciti, as opposed to the deaths of ultras, evoked both an outpouring of despair and anger and a spasm of political action. This was underlined, later in the year, by the shooting of the Lazio ultra Gabriel Sandri at a motorway service station by a police officer: an act that triggered a weekend of ultra violence and protest all over the country. In the decade since, the Italian state has made a concerted legislative effort to tighten up the policing of football. Stewards became compulsory in 2005. In 2007, football banning orders were introduced, allowing police and clubs to exclude people from stadiums who had been convicted of any kind of football-related disorder, though without a way of checking fans when buying tickets or entering a ground, they were toothless. Thus in 2009 the government introduced the ID card scheme, the *tessera del tifoso*, which functioned as both a credit card and compulsory ID for the purchase of season tickets, allowing real-time connection with police databases.[138] The use of the card was then extended to away-game tickets, while intrusive, aggressive policing at the stadiums to check ID and tickets massively increased. All across Italy urban walls were sprayed with the words '*No alla tessera del tifoso*'. In 2009, 5,000 ultras from all over the country protested in Rome, cases were taken to the high courts challenging the scheme's constitutionality, and many ultra groups instituted away-game boycotts, all of which combined to account for the steady but perceptible emptying of the nation's stadiums.

Two events, however, suggested that the ultras' power over the *curva*, and on occasion the players and the whole stadium, remained tangible despite the efforts of the police and security services. The first, described by *Gazzetta dello Sport* as 'A chilling spectacle . . . right out of the dark ages', occurred in Genoa in 2013. Deep in the second half, with the home team 4–0 down to Sienna, the referee stopped the game when Genoa fans invaded the family section, threw fireworks onto the pitch, occupied the roof of the players' tunnel and demanded the teams' shirts. All but one complied.[139] The following year, prior to the final of the Coppa Italia between Napoli and Fiorentina in Rome, clashes outside the stadium saw a leader of Roma's ultras, Daniele De Santis, shoot a Napoli fan, Ciro Esposito, who would later die in hospital. Napoli ultras in the stadium then made it impossible for the match to begin, throwing innumerable flares onto the pitch and ultimately beckoning their midfielder Marek Hamšik and the officials to discuss the situation. They eventually agreed that the match could begin, and watched it in silence.[140]

The *tessera* has since been replaced by a new ID scheme (without the credit card and with a modicum of personal data protection). The Italian state continues to spend more than €30 million a year policing football. Neither strategy can work, though, for the enduring presence and power of the ultras rests in part on the incompetence and the collusion of the clubs and football authorities, and in part on the kind of money and connections that come from the ultras' increasing enmeshment with organized crime. Indeed, the Italian parliament's anti-mafia commission reported of the lower divisions that 'the ever greater desire of individuals linked to organized crime to become part of club boards, especially in the lower leagues, is worrying. For organized crime, the world of football represents a useful flywheel with which to attract electoral, economic and financial consensus.'[141] And the boards were not the only point of entry into football: the report also stated that at least 30 per cent of the ultras were either petty or major criminals. Gennaro de Tomasso, the leader of the Napoli ultras and a visible presence at the Coppa Italia 2014 final, has been repeatedly linked with the Neapolitan wing of the mafia, the Camorra, while the Calabrian 'Ndrangheta have a presence inside Juventus's ultra group with control over ticket sales.[142] The leader of Lazio's *Irreducabilli* was convicted in 2017 for industrial-scale cocaine distribution.

The ultras' political affiliations have become similarly unsavoury. Born of the same moment as the country's great wave of social mobilization and political protest from the late 1960s to the mid 1970s – an era of spontaneous strikes and occupations, radical cells and action groups, revolutionary chic and terror – ultras have emulated the language, clothing and structures of the country's innumerable new political movements. Through the 1970s and 1980s one could find left-wing, right-wing and regionalist ultras, but through the 1990s, and especially the twenty-first century, the overall balance of the movement has shifted sharply rightwards.[143] Indeed, the only remaining leftist ultras of any significance are the supporters of Livorno, the spiritual home of Italian communism.[144] Neo-fascism has long been the politics of choice at Lazio, Verona and Inter, but now predominates even at clubs like AC Milan and Roma, where there was once a left-wing or more neutral ultra presence. Inside the stadium, symbols, banners, flags and chants that reference Mussolini have been particularly popular, while Roma ultras attacked Spurs fans in 2012 on the grounds that they were 'Jewish'. By the same token, Lazio ultras have expressed their virulent Fascism by distributing fake Panini stickers showing Anne Frank as a Roma supporter, and by their antediluvian call for women to keep out: 'The Curva Nord represents for us a sacred space, an environment with an unwritten code to be respected. The first few rows, as always, have been experienced like the trenches. In the trenches, we do not allow women, wives and girlfriends, so we invite them to position themselves from the tenth row back.'[145]

There aren't many Jews left in Italy, maybe 40,000, but there are a lot of people of colour. In the twenty-first century, Italy's stock of foreign residents has risen from just over a million to more than five million people, over a million of them Africans. Though Italy had, after the war, been forced to confront at least some of its culpability in the deportation of Italian Jews to the concentration camps, and thus its deep seated anti-semitism (not least in the Vatican City), the same could not be said of its attitudes to race. Indeed, these remained pretty much intact from the era of Fascism and its disastrous African imperial adventures, preserved in aspic in much of what remained a deeply provincial and insular culture. It only remained for people of colour, footballers most prominent amongst them, to arrive for them to be reactivated. In 2005, for example, Messina's African forward Marco Zorro walked off the pitch, unable to endure the mass racist chanting from the Inter fans. This would barely make news in Italy's sporting press, and it certainly did not require the attention of the FIGC (Italian Football Federation).

The arrival of Mario Balotelli made this dimension of Italian culture impossible to ignore.[146] His personal story, while hardly representative of many immigrants' experience – most of whom are locked into the harshest and most precarious end of the Italian labour market – nonetheless traces an arc through the last two decades, during which Italy has acquired a substantial black population, and found it a deeply uncomfortable experience. Balotelli was born in Palermo in 1990 to Ghanaian immigrant parents. Two years later, having moved north to Brescia, Mario was taken in (but not adopted) by his foster parents Francisco and Silvia Balotelli, with whom he remained. He signed for Inter at sixteen, made his Serie A debut at seventeen, became the youngest player to score in the Champions League the following year and, in 2010, won his first national team cap.

He was, self-evidently, the first black Italian football star, and he would pay a price for it. Racist attacks of the most base and crude kind came at him from every direction: home fans and away fans, Italian fans and foreign fans, the football press and the football federation. 'There is no such thing as a black Italian' or more vulgar variants could be heard wherever he played. At Euro 2012 Croatian fans threw bananas and made monkey chants. To be expected, perhaps, but then *Gazzetta dello Sport* depicted him in a cartoon as King Kong. The following year Kevin Prince Boateng of AC Milan, in a friendly against Pro Patria, kicked the ball at the monkey chanters and, with the rest of the team, walked off.[147] A similar hail of abuse met Boateng and Balotelli when AC Milan played Roma later in the year, and that only ceased after the game had been suspended and Roma captain Francesco Totti had spoken with the Roma ultras.

Such acts of resistance and support are rare. While the football federation and the clubs have paid lip service to UEFA's dictums on racism, and the clubs are regularly fined for their fans' behaviour, it is no more than that. How could it be otherwise when the man leading the anti-racism campaign, FIGC president Carlo Tavecchio, could describe a foreign footballer in these terms: 'Here, on the other hand, let's say there's Opti Poba, who has come here, who previously was eating bananas and now is a first-team player for Lazio. In England he has to demonstrate his CV and his pedigree' – and then be shocked and outraged when his words were considered racist?[148] A similar incomprehension was expressed by the leaders of the Northern League, who had described Italy's first black minister, Cecile Kyenge, as an ape, and thrown bananas at her. And still the abuse came. Crowds at Italy's training centre before the 2014 World Cup could clearly be heard shouting 'Black piece of shit' and, 'Mario, you're really not Italian. Go away!' Despite scoring the winning goal in their game against England, Balotelli was made the scapegoat for Italy's subsequent defeats and early elimination. He was barely picked for the national team for the next four years. In his absence they did just fine: embarrassingly poor at Euro 2016 and then, in 2017, failing for the first time in more than half a century to qualify for the World Cup, an event described in the press as 'The End' and 'A National Shame'. Andrea Di Caro, the deputy editor-in-chief at *Gazzetta dello Sport*, thought, more reflectively, 'This is another blow, and not just in sports. Football reflects how the whole country is: it represents Italy's inability to look to the future, to employ young, well-prepared people.' As Di Caro must surely know, that is just the beginning of a long list of social pathologies exposed by Italian football. This is not 'The End', but there is plenty more national shame to come.

VIII

French football is paradoxical. Despite possessing the second-largest market of the big five, it has the football industry with the smallest turnover, and the lowest average attendances.[149] By 2016, its top division, Ligue 1, was bringing in less than half of the Bundesliga's revenue, and less than a third of the English Premier League's. Were it not for the purchase of PSG by the royal house of Qatar and its subsequent largesse, none of its clubs would make the top twenty in Europe. No French club has won a European competition since Marseilles in 1993. Yet, at the same time, the French national team has bookended the timespan of this volume with two World Cup triumphs in 1998 and 2018, not to mention one defeat in the final of 2006, and success in the European Championships in 2000.

The relative weakness of French domestic football has deep historical roots. The country's late and highly dispersed pattern of industrialization and urbanization produced one great, all consuming capital city, Paris, which proved uninterested in the game for much of the twentieth century, and many small cities that took to football, but without the financial or cultural capital to raise the national profile of the game. In Paris and the south west, especially, rugby union provided a sporting alternative and economic competitor. Neither, though, could match the national reach or cultural weight of cycling, whose appeal, as both a mode of transport and a test of endurance, had found a huge audience in the small towns and the countryside.

There were, in the 1980s and 1990s, during the first flush of modern football's commercialization, attempts to create a new kind of French football spectacle, but none has quite succeeded. Canal Plus, the media giants, invested in the newly created Paris super-club PSG. Claude Bez, an accountant-turned walrus-moustachioed-impresario, took charge at Bordeaux and revolutionized the club and the French football business, pioneering new forms of sponsorship, persuading the local council to build a new stadium, opening executive boxes and hammering French TV for more money. And when this wasn't enough, there were other strategies. As he himself said, 'Clubs will always find ways to break the rules. Me, I have three million ways.' When he was finally forced to stand down in 1991, the club's vast debts and unpaid tax bills were revealed, and Bez was convicted of fraud and sentenced to three years in prison. Bernard Tapie, a corporate raider and turnaround specialist who reinvented himself a charismatic left-wing populist, took over at Olympique Marseilles and bankrolled them till they were champions of France and Europe, before exploding in a mountain of debt and match-fixing escapades.[150] Jean Michel Aulas, owner of Olympique Lyonnais, who had made his fortune in the IT industry, was cut from very different cloth to Tapie and Bez, bringing a rare level of high-flown technocratic rationalism to the task of running a football club. It was enough to dominate French football, the club winning seven consecutive titles between 2001 and 2008, but not to crack the glass ceiling of high-level European success.

In the second decade of the twenty-first century, despite the rising tide of money coming into the game, French football has fallen further behind its obvious competitors. Neither its league nor its clubs have been able, despite the huge extent of the francophone world and the reach of its media channels, to attract a fragment of the interest accorded their English, Italian or Spanish peers. Neither has the domestic audience greatly expanded, in the stadiums or at home: the perennially low value of French football's TV rights does not lie. Many clubs play in municipally owned stadiums, which has made the route to commercialization through sponsorship, naming rights and hospitality packages more difficult. Whatever money the clubs do have, France's higher rates of personal taxation and employer contributions make it significantly more expensive for them to employ a player, on a given wage, than their competitors in England or Spain. The French tax authorities have also made the kinds of tax evasion and offshore payment systems that have flourished elsewhere more difficult to pursue. Consequently, there have been fewer foreign takers for French football clubs. Lyon cautiously sold 20 per cent of the club to a Chinese sports marketing agency. The House of Grimaldi, recognizing that even their fortune could not sustain AS Monaco, sold it on to Dmitry Rybolovlev, a Russian billionaire who had made his money by obtaining and selling the state potash industry and was looking for somewhere to comfortably park himself, his money and his reputation.

All have been eclipsed by the purchase, in 2011, of PSG by QSI

(Qatar Sports Investments), one of many corporate vehicles used by the Al-Thani family, aka the ruling house of Qatar. It was a move discussed in the highest diplomatic and political circles in France, right up to the Élysée Palace, and was followed, amongst other coincidences, by Qatar's beIN Sport's absurdly generous purchase of French football's TV rights. In a virtual replay of the Abu Dhabi transformation of Manchester City, QSI cleared the debts and spent a lot of money in the transfer market, helped by an implausibly large sponsorship deal with the Qatar Tourism Authority. Half a billion pounds' worth of players arrived in the first five years, followed by almost £400 million spent on just two more, Neymar and Kylian Mbappé. This has brought an unbroken string of French championships, and more French Cups and French League Cups than they know what to do with. European success, perhaps undermined by the complete lack of competition at home in a now one-club league, remains elusive.

Having effectively detached the club from the rest of French football, on the pitch at any rate, the Al-Thani regime has been doing its best to detach it from any remnant of its old fanbase. Certainly, in the years before they took over, some of PSG's ultras had acquired a well deserved reputation for violence and anti-semitism. In 2006, for example, one PSG ultra had died during an anti-semitic attack on visiting Israeli fans.[151] In 2011, after a fan died in a fight outside the stadium following a game against Marseilles, the last president before the Al-Thanis, Robin Leproux, banned 1,200 of the most notorious ultras from the Boulogne and Autiel stands that they had traditionally occupied at Parc des Princes. The Al-Thanis and their satrap, President Nasser Al-Khelaifi, have gone much further. First, they initiated a 70 per cent hike in ticket prices in an effort to see off the hoi-polloi. When this was insufficient, they have simply banned a lot of people – 13,000 in their first year – and got really close to France's security apparatus; Antoine Boutonnet, director of the Ministry of the Interior agency DLNH (Division for the Fight against Hooliganism), attended private parties and trophy celebrations at the club, while senior police officers moved seamlessly into security portfolios. Indeed, so willing were the French authorities to collude in this process that in 2013 they issued a list of 2,007 PSG fans to the club Evian, requesting that they deny them entry to their game against PSG. In 2015, it became clear that PSG and the Parisian police, in contravention of data protection laws, collaborated to create dossiers on troublesome fans. Perhaps the Al-Thanis will soon be changing PSG's club motto, currently 'Dream Bigger', to the words spoken by France's Minister of the Interior, who in 2013 told the Senate that they should be aiming for 'A football without football supporters'.

If the policies of the French state, certainly with regard to policing and taxation, have undermined French club football, they have been the making of the men's national team. All of the players who have won France's contemporary honours have passed through Clairfontaine, the shorthand for the FFF's (French Football Federation) national training academy. It can trace its institutional roots to the early 1970s, created as part of a wider Gaullist exercise in sporting *étatisme*, designed to both improve France's then dismal international sporting performance, and ensure central government control over sports federations and their policies, in an arrangement not dissimilar to the government's control of state utilities and companies. Clairfontaine created the template for national football centres everywhere, with its innovative use of age-specific training and its presence at the forefront of sports science. As one would expect of a child of French *dirigisme*, it then imposed its high standards in a uniform pattern across the clubs and the country. France's football institutions were hardly without their racist assumptions and biases, but their egalitarian and republican qualities were sufficiently strong that they could, through the 1980s and 1990s, draw on the rapidly expanding pool of talented kids from France's expanding migrant communities. The success of France's youth development programmes is there in the numbers. No European country exports more professional football players than France. Indeed, by 2018 only Brazil (a country with almost four times its population) exceeded it. Unlike Brazil, Argentina or Nigeria (the next most prolific exporters of players), the French domestic game has not been entirely hollowed out by this surge in exports. France's best players still tend to play a good part of their career at home. The national teams of the last couple of decades have been composed in equal numbers of domestic and foreign-based players, but the very best, from Zidane to Henry, from Ribéry to Griezmann, have played their best years at the leading clubs in England, Spain, Germany and Italy. This has made French domestic football significantly less competitive and compelling than it might otherwise have been. However, it has ensured a fabulous and deep pool of talent from which to construct a national team. Given the changing ethnic composition of the team and the nation, it has also ensured that Les Bleus have been a central feature of the nation's conversation about race and citizenship.

The ethnic composition of the national team has never been invisible, certainly since the 1950s, during which so many Algerian-French players defected to the team representing the nascent Algerian nation and its independence movement, the FLN. However, as issues of ethnicity and citizenship, driven by the rise of the far-right Front National under Jean-Marie Le Pen, came to occupy more political space, the national team has become a central part of that debate. In 1996, on the eve of the European Championships, Le Pen was contemptuous of the team – 'these players who come from else-where and who do not sing the "Marseillaise"' – and pointedly referred to individual players as 'the Armenian' or 'the Congolese'. Indeed, he thought the whole squad 'artificial'. Leading politicians of both left and right, from Gaullist President Chirac to Socialist Prime Minister Jospin, rejected Le Pen's ethnicized version of French iden-tity, and defended the republican tradition of assimilation. Christian Karembeu and Bernard Lama, while still maintaining their French-ness, reminded the country of its colonial past and explained their distance and disquiet. Karembeu, born and raised in France's Pacific island colony New Caledonia, said of Le Pen, 'From that day on I didn't sing the "Marseillaise". I know the history of my people.' Lama, from the World Cup bench, lifted his jersey on TV to reveal a T-shirt depicting Senegal's Gorée Island, the point of departure for many Africans sold into slavery under French rule. In the end, though, it was the response of the squad on the pitch, truly the most diverse that France had ever put out, and colloquially and affectionately referred to as 'Black-Blanc-Beur', that did the real talk-ing, their progress and play evoking an increasing level of national fascination at the 1998 World Cup, concluded by beating Brazil in the final.

France celebrated in what was, at the time, considered to be the greatest series of public gatherings and revelries since the liberations of 1944, and the biggest occupation of public space since *les événe-ments* of 1968, but concentrated into a single moment. One constant of the reports from across the country was a sense of collective car-nival and delirium, the kind of protean emotional plasma out of which real social change could be fashioned, and within which utopian interpretations of the moment predominated. Describing the scene in central Paris one observer was rhapsodic:

> There was no more hierarchy, or convention. No more disdain, no more bad mood. No more social classes, no more provincials or banlieusards. Nothing but the extraordinary, like the world turned upside down. No more landmarks! It was mad-Paris, uncontrollable-laughter Paris, delirium-Paris. Chaos-Paris, joyful-Paris, love-Paris. Paris the centre of the world, coloured and multi-coloured, fraternal.

Outside of Paris, kids from a provincial *banlieue* expressed their surprise and delight: 'People for once weren't racist any more. We went to the centre of town to celebrate, they smiled at you, they talked. Usually people are hostile.' In the true spirit of carnival a French Malian family could actually tease the police on the streets of Paris, waving from their double-parked car in the midst of the celebrations, 'No tickets tonight', and then, 'No tickets tonight! Tomorrow, the right to asylum!' Across the political spectrum writers and politicians revelled in the evident diversity of the nation: 'The crowd looked like its team,' one wrote: 'a resolutely plural France', while the following day President Jacques Chirac welcomed the squad to the Élysée Palace and declared them 'this simultaneously tricolour and multi-coloured team.' And yet, for all this, a poll conducted during the tournament for *Le Monde* found that 56 per cent of the country still thought there were too many Arabs in France. Even when they did show up with the tricolour, many of the right were patronizing at best. The notorious anti-migrant mayor Thierry Mariani, for example, found their presence 'surprising and agreeable'. Asked, just a year after the great triumph of 'black-blanc-beur', whether there were too many black players in the side, 31 per cent said yes, and the following year 36 per cent agreed with them. Thus, in a France that was not yet perceptibly changed, the team's victory at the European Championships in 2000, when they beat the Italians 2–1 in a compelling final that went to extra time, was greeted by smaller crowds – in Paris and Marseilles ultimately cleared by police firing tear gas – and less euphoric rhetoric. Françoise Giroud, writing in *Le Monde*, had retreated from the utopianism and high expectations of 1998 to the quieter hope that the team could serve as a kind of multicultural sporting avant garde who were 'prophets in their own land': currently a long way from the majority, but still 'scouts of the future'.

A rather better herald of the future, perhaps, was France's game against Algeria, played in Paris in late 2001, in the wake of 9/11. The game was never concluded as the Algerian-French youth in the crowd, many declaring open support for Osama Bin Laden, invaded the pitch. It was one of many incidents that contributed to the rising tide of Islamophobia and nativism in French society, and these forces of reaction would deliver their rebuke. In 2002, the voters sent a dilapidated French left packing, and put Le Pen and the Front National, for the first time ever, through to the second round of the presidential election. As Christine Taubiera, a French-Guinean representative in parliament, said, '1998 was an illusion, and a short one.' Chirac would, with the help of the left, beat Le Pen, but neither team or country were at peace. The defending champions were eviscerated in their opening game at the 2002 World Cup by their former colony Senegal. In 2005, the long-brewed discontents of the *banlieues* finally exploded, nationwide, in weeks of car-burning, police-taunting and rioting. The government's response, practically and lexically, was brutal, with then interior minister Nicolas Sarkozy promising to cleanse these neighbourhoods. As one of the residents said, 'We the *immigrés*, we are French when we help win the World Cup. But two weeks later, we are no longer French: Chirac, Sarko and all the rest forget us.' By the time of the 2006 World Cup, right-wing intellectuals like Alain Finkielkraut were labelling the team 'black-black-black', a fact, they thought, that made 'all Europe snigger.'[152]

In what was a final outing for many of the players who had won in 1998, the French team came alive in Germany, led by a revived Zidane. As we know from the Italian side of the story, Italy would win on penalties, the French psychologically shattered by Zidane's red card, given after he had head-butted Marco Materazzi late into extra time. Zidane then returned to France not, as one might have imagined, in disgrace or to a chorus of disapproval, but accompanied by a celebratory, number-one hit, 'Coup de Boule', which reflected, 'Zidane, he punched, but that punch has lost us everything, yet we still had a good laugh', while the nation as a whole accepted Zidane's claim that Materazzi had uttered some unspeakable slur on his family that had led to the incident.

'Coup de Boule', which also made it to number two in the Italian charts and topped the pile in Wallonia, is just one of dozens of songs, books, sculptures and other works of art that have taken Zidane as their subject; amongst football players, only Pele, and then only in Brazil, has been the subject of so much attention by artists. For example, prior to 2006, his legs were painted as fetishized commodities by Mexican Rodrigo De Florencia, while Douglas Gordon and Philippe Parreno's *Zidane: A Twenty-first Century Portrait*, was a ninety-minute, seventeen-camera focus on just Zidane during a game for Real Madrid in 2005. Since 2006, works have multiplied, including Harun Farocki's *Deep Play*, a twelve-channel reconstruction of the whole 2006 final, using TV coverage, security camera feeds from the day, animations and statistics, and Abdel Abdessemed's *Coup de Tête*, a five-metre-high bronze cast of the moment Zidane's head is in Materazzi's chest as he stumbles backwards. Amongst the most taciturn and enigmatic of football players, Zidane maintains virtual silence on everything, and certainly anything that hints of controversy beyond the world of football. This has made him, given the complexity of his own roots – French born and raised, to Algerian Berber migrants from Kabylie – an irresistible *tabula rasa* on which to project issues of identity, masculinity and secularity.[153]

The French team, under Raymond Domenech, was not a happy camp. Disastrously bad at the 2008 European Championships, they only qualified for the 2010 World Cup via a play-off against Ireland in which Thierry Henry's blatant handball provided the assist for the winning goal. In training, captain Patrice Evra had to hold back Florent Molouda from attacking Domenech, who then benched him. The team then disintegrated against Mexico: Domenech had an almighty row with Nicolas Anelka at half-time, and had him sent home afterwards. In Paris, a small, far-right protest at the FFF headquarters called for a 'White and Christian' team, and for the Federation to 'fire the blacks'. In South Africa the whole squad refused to train, and Anelka, like many, believed his harsh treatment was rooted in the FFF's racist bias. The following year *Mediasport* published an account of precisely that. Based on a series of recordings and transcripts from right inside the institution, it became clear that an unreflective racist discourse was the norm amongst the Clairfontaine elite.[154] Technical director François Blaquart and national team coach Laurent Blanc, amongst others, stereotyped black players as physical and uncultured, and were so troubled by the decision of some young French players of dual heritage to choose Algeria or Morocco as their national team (even though they had little chance of making it in France) that they began to wonder if the academy system could look for and weed out such faint hearts, and in so doing establish a new ethnic mix in the game.

If the plan really was to dissuade French players of colour from joining the national set-up, then it could claim some real successes. Sebastian Bassong, who had played for France's under-21s, was alienated from the FFF and the French team by these attitudes and opted for Cameroon. Benoît Assou-Ekotto, who did the same, was straight-talking on the matter: 'France has, at its heart, a problem where it has been unable or unwilling to accommodate the sons and daughters of former colonies, even though France benefited and enriched itself greatly from the relationship. That's hard to accept, and it's what is at the base of what is dysfunctional in France.' Despite all the public apologies and soul-searching that followed the quota affair, racism simply would not lie down in French football, the whole debate being reignited in 2014 when Willy Sagnol was reported as saying, 'As long as I remain coach of Bordeaux there will be far fewer African players coming to Girondins de Bordeaux.'[155] When Karim Benzema, then at Real Madrid, was not picked for the squad that would play at Euro 2016, he accused Didier Deschamps, the coach, of submitting to the 'racist part of France'. Benzema's collusion with some old friends who were attempting to blackmail the Lyon player Mathieu Valbuena (with a sex tape of his own making) may have been uppermost in Deschamps' mind. Either way, as Philippe Auclair put it, 'Benzema's real problem is that he ticks almost every single box in the list of what so-called home-grown French fear and detest, and even hate, the most.'[156] Perhaps above all, that he will not, and cannot, commit to a culture that continues to revile him and his peers: 'I quite like France but Algeria is my country, my heart; France, it's just the sports side of things.' It is a similar frame of mind that in 2014 saw France's *banlieues* erupt, not when *Les Bleus* lost a game at the World Cup, but when Algeria made the second round.

IX

The popularity of football in Spain, never in question, has, if the space it occupies on national television and in the press is anything to go by, steadily grown in the twenty-first century. On and offline, *MARCA* is easily the most popular newspaper in the country, easily eclipsing *El País*, *El Mundo* or *ABC*, and just one of four sports papers in the nation's top seven best sellers. Inside these papers football accounts for 60 per cent of their sporting coverage, while on the radio and television football accounts for over 80 per cent of their sports output. A football match has been the most viewed single programme on Spanish television every year between 1997 and 2010, culminating in a record audience of 14.5 million for the 2010 World Cup final. The 12 million-plus seats sold at football exceed attendance at theatre, ballet, dance and opera combined, and is 50 per cent more than that at classical and popular music concerts.[157] At the same time, La Liga has become the third richest league in Europe, with an annual income of over €2.5 billion, and this with the smallest population of the five core nations: just 46 million in Spain against France's 67 million and Germany's 83 million. The state of the women's game has been penurious, a long way behind northern Europe, but Spain's men's teams, at national and club level, have been magnificent. Since the turn of the century they have won: one World Cup, two European Championships, ten Champions League titles (and lost another four, two in all-Spanish finals), and ten UEFA Cup/Europa Leagues. There has, in all of this, been garlands for Atlético Madrid, the capital's second team and the self-appointed authentic soul of the city, in contrast to Real's shameless commercialism and global glory hunters. Valencia, the team of Spain's third city, at their peak in the early 2000s attracted huge crowds, and won two league titles. Sevilla, the UEFA Cup experts, have won the competition six times. However, the most obvious fact about Spanish football is the hegemony of Real Madrid and Barcelona. Between them they have, but for a single title for Atlético Madrid in 2014, monopolized the national championship since 2004, their players have pretty much monopolized the national team, and the day-to-day football conversation has been completely consumed by their rivalry. The teams of the Basque country (Athletic Bilbao, Oviedo, Racing Santander, Real Sociedad) continue to represent the region, its identities and strands of its political projects, but as the Basque independence movement has retreated and the long war with the Spanish state by its armed wing ETA has drawn to a close, both politics and football have been ever more dominated by the Spain/Catalonia, Real/Barça double act.

Yet the national question, important as it is, is not the only point of division in contemporary Spanish football and politics. Equally important has been the growing scale of economic inequality in the country.[158] Over the last two decades, under the alternating duopoly of the PP and the PSOE, Spain has reaped two harvests from the country's enmeshment with the European and the global economies. Before 2008, the country underwent a long consumer and property boom, fuelled by German-level interest rates. After 2008 it underwent a cataclysmic economic contraction, a financial crisis that stopped just short of a Greece-style bail-out, rocketing levels of unemployment, home repossessions and homelessness. The one constant during the years of both the boom and austerity was a steadily rising level of inequality that made Spain the third most unequal country in the whole of the European Union. A very similar story could be told of the fortunes of Real Madrid and Barcelona, who in the early part of the century had already corralled more than half of La Liga's total turnover for themselves and who, despite the economic collapse all around them after 2008, have continued to pull away from the rest. Both clubs have benefited for much of this era, like Italy's big three, from selling their own TV rights, rather than as part of La Liga as a whole. Already the largest clubs in Spain, their visibility and renown magnified by their long, real and bitter political history, they have by the usual multiplier effect made their sponsorship deals, kit deals and shirt sales worth ever more than their competitors'. Both have then multiplied this again by consciously pursuing a strategy of global branding and marketing that has made El Clásico the most watched game in the world's annual football calendar, and an object of popular and media obsession, not merely in the Spanish-speaking worlds of the Americas, but across Africa, the Middle East and Asia.

The domestic preconditions of this ascent were threefold. First, both clubs remained owned by their members or socios, who elected their boards and presidents. While this closed off foreign investment from the global super-rich, it opened up great channels of credit. The two clubs were able to clear their old debts by selling off city-centre land with rock-solid and politically delivered planning permission, massively increasing their value. Then, trading on their public significance and popular legitimacy, they have been consistently able to raise new capital from Spain's banks with the same kind of ease as the Spanish treasury. Secondly, the presidents elected around the turn of the century – Florentino Pérez at Real Madrid and Joan Laporta at Barcelona – completed the process of expelling their club's right-wing ultras – the *Ultra Sur* at Real and the *Noixos Boys* at Barcelona – from their stadiums, a trend in Spanish football that has seen ultra culture dwindle, with the strongest groups boasting no more than a few hundred members, primarily confined to Atlético Madrid, Galicia and the Basque country. Third, both have pursued a hyper-spending, zero-profit business model that really does measure success in terms of hype and heroism. Real under Pérez's *Galacticos* strategy repeatedly broke the world transfer record and brought a succession of the very best to the Bernabéu, amongst them Fígo, Zidane and Ronaldo, secure in the knowledge that the club's cut of their image rights would more than cover their costs. Real has also prioritized winning the Champions League, which they managed three times between 1998 and 2002. The team built around Cristiano Ronaldo a decade later followed the same logic, and delivered four further Champions League titles in the five years between 2014 and 2018.

Barcelona appeared to take a different tack, and although it has always featured foreign stars, the backbone of the teams of the twenty-first century have been nurtured in the club's own training academy, playing a high-intensity super-possession game, *tiki taka*, that appeared to be a distinctive Catalan contribution to world football. Of course, it had its roots in the Dutch football of the 1970s, carried across the decades by the club's relationship with Johan Cruyff as player, coach and elder, and with Ajax and its training styles, on which the club's own academy was modelled, with two more of the latter's graduates as team coach, Frank Rijkaard and Louis van Gaal, not to mention dozens more Dutch players. That said, the distinctive contributions of the club's Catalan coaches and staff, notably Pep Guardiola, brought this inheritance to fruition. This hybrid cosmopolitanism, combined with the club's long resistance to having a shirt sponsor, enhanced their already long-established place as the footballing tribune of Catalan cultural resistance, and built their global brand, especially amongst left-leaning fans and independence-minded nations, from Kurdistan to Scotland to Palestine. The addition of Lionel Messi, amongst others, and then the Qatar Foundation as its shirt sponsor, allowed Barcelona to match Real step by step, financially and on the pitch, where they won four Champions League titles between 2006 and 2015.

It has been an extraordinary two decades or so of magnificent, hyperbolic football,[159] the Mourinho–Guardiola years between 2010 and 2013 being a fantastical highpoint of intrigue and mania, peaking when the two sides played four *El Clásicos* in eighteen days in 2011: a league title decider won by Barcelona, a Copa del Rey final won by Madrid, and a Champions League semi-final that went to Barcelona. The duel between Lionel Messi and Cristiano Ronaldo, who together monopolized the Ballon d'Or between 2008 and 2017, has been spellbinding. However, as Spain's main political parties have discovered, such an unbroken concentration of wealth and power at the top has come at the price of the elite's own internal corruption and the casting of a penumbra of despair and discontent around them. Outside of important European games and *El Clásico*, and now in the absence of the ultras, the atmosphere at both the Bernabéu and the Nou Camp has often been somnolent and entitled. The presence of tourists at both stadiums is unmissable, and though both are capacious and reasonably full they are tiring architecturally, without the kind of money-making hospitality operations that the English in particular can boast, or the new sheen and high-tech flourishes of, for example, Germany's World Cup stadiums.

Struggling in the wake of the duopolists, most of Spain's clubs and their local patrons relied on debt as a way of keeping up: a strategy made all the easier in the years before the crash by the clubs' easy access to credit from Spain's deregulated and politically networked regional banks, and the then widespread Panglossian optimism that the boom in Spain would never end. As in the real economy, there were early warning signs of what was to come – Las Palmas, for example, went bankrupt in 2004 – but no one was really taking any notice. By the time the financial crisis had hit Spain's banks and the credit lines had dried up, more than twenty clubs had gone into bankruptcy proceedings.[160] By 2010, La Liga clubs owed €43 million in unpaid wages, more than half a billion in unpaid taxes to the Spanish state, and were carrying a total debt of around €3.5 billion. Seven of the clubs in the top division were technically insolvent, and still neither the government nor the football authorities intervened. Things were so out of control that the Spanish football federation was happy to issue RCD Mallorca with a playing licence, while UEFA, who looked at its debt of €85 million, three times the club's annual turnover, were so unhappy that they banned them from European competition. Then, in 2013, the European Parliament intervened, arguing that the failure of the clubs to pay tax, and of the state to collect it from them, was giving them an unfair advantage over their European peers, and denying the Spanish taxpayer their rightful dues.[161] Four years later, though the clubs have paid off some of their government debt, and the rash of bankruptcies has been staunched, yet the overhang from the boom years remains. Just four clubs, Valencia, Barcelona, Real Madrid and Atlético Madrid, still owe more than €1 billion between them.

This scale of structural debt makes for a buyer's market, and foreign buyers have come to pick the flesh off the bones of La Liga. Valencia, sustained by its own impecunious regional government, was sold to Peter Lim, Singapore's billionaire king of palm oil. Malaga was bought by the Qatari Sheik Abdullah Al-Thani, a minor member of the royal family, who spent enough money to get the team to fourth in La Liga and the quarter-finals of the Champions League before the inevitable consequences of overstretch saw the team's performance, the sheik's interest and the financial situation all sharply decline.[162] Espanyol were snapped up by Chen Yansheng, owner of the Hong Kong Rastar group, hitherto specialists in the manufacture of model cars; Granada was bought by Lizhan Jiang, who added the club to his eclectic sports marketing empire, which already included the Minnesota Timberwolves NBA franchise. Getafe, Madrid's third team, were bought up by the Royal Emirates Group, a vehicle for Dubai's ruling family the Maktoums who, risibly, added 'Team Dubai' to its crest. Atlético Madrid, already thick as thieves with the Azerbaijani government and its national oil company – both club sponsors – sold 20 per cent of the operation to China's largest real estate company, Dalian Wanda. Albacete were only saved from dissolution in 2011 and 2014 by home-town boy Andrés Iniesta, who covered more than half a million euros worth of back pay at the club from out of his own wages at Barcelona.

Given the depth of Spanish football's regional antipathies, the Spanish national team had rarely attracted universal support or affection. In 1964 when they won the European Championships, in much reduced form, the team and its style were monopolized by Franco's regime and its press, framed as an example of 'Spanish Fury': macho, masculine and proud, matadors and warriors. While such an explicit connection between the team and Spain's fascist past diminished during the first quarter of a century of democracy, the national question simply would not go away, and the national team became, increasingly, a place in which that conflict was expressed. At times, in its obsession with minutiae, it could border on the farcical, as in 2007 when the Madrid press railed at Barcelona's Carles Puyol and Xavi who, when lining up for the national team, appeared to have rearranged their socks so as to obscure their Spanish colours.[163] In 2017 a new strip was released which, to the sharp-eyed and politically minded, and because it included blue, could be read as a version of the flag of the Republic before and during the Spanish Civil War. 'It had been a long time,' said Pablo Iglesias, leader of the insurgent leftist party Podemos, 'since the Spanish football team had worn such a pretty jersey.' Alberto Garzón, the head of the Catalan nationalist party Izquierda Unida, commented on how much he liked the jersey too.

Players for the national team are spared the ordeal that many of their peers face – scrutinized to see how well and with what demeanour they sing the national anthem – because the Spanish national anthem has no words, and all efforts to craft some that have wide acceptance have been abandoned. However, as the Basque player Markel Susaeta found out when called up to the national team, the press and politicians are alert to any other words they might speak. Unable to bring himself to mention Spain, when asked how he felt about his first cap – 'I am very happy and proud to be here . . . here we are repressing . . . a thing . . . that we have to respect' – he was subject to a torrent of criticism. It has, therefore, been commonplace to attribute Spain's lack of international success – neither a trophy nor a final since 1964 – to the internal divisions in the nation and the team. Thus it was no surprise that Spanish centrists should read the amazing performances of Spain, winning the European

Championships in 2008 and 2012 and the World Cup in 2010, and the truly national bursts of celebration that followed, as a triumph for their vision of the nation and a rebuke to nationalists and separatists.

In 2008, as Spain made their way to the final of the European Championships in which they beat the Germans 1–0, a real shift in mood was noted. Polls indicated that 70 per cent of Catalans, an amazing proportion, were actually supporting the national team. 'The highest television audiences of the year in Catalonia and the Basque country,' reflected *El Mundo*, 'are when Spain plays an important football match. The chattering of some nationalist leaders at these times merely shows how distant they are from popular feeling.'[164] Some commentators thought the weakness of the Basque and Catalan separatist parties had made space for these shifts. Most reports from Catalonia suggested the overwhelming presence of Barcelona players in this and subsequent squads, most of them Catalans and many of them reared in Barça's own academy – including Carles Puyol, Cesc Fàbregas, Andrés Iniesta, Gerard Piqué, Sergio Busquets and Xavi Hernandez – and the team's adoption of Barcelona's *tiki taka* possession game, made embracing the side much easier. For the Basques there was Xabi Alonso, and Madrid was amply represented by coaches Luis Aragonés and Vincente del Bosque, the latter an avuncular figurehead, hard for anyone to dislike, who lectured the nation that 'Spain is not Barcelona, nor is it Real Madrid. Any victory belongs to Spanish soccer.' In 2010 Catalan TV was reporting that three-quarters of its audience, an unprecedented number, was tuning into the national team's games. When they beat Germany in the semi-final the streets of Madrid, Valencia and Seville were awash with red and gold flags, as one might have expected, but so too was the Ramblas in Barcelona. 'You will now find people out in the streets in *La Roja* shirts,' thought one local, 'or with Spanish flags that are normally considered taboo here.'[165] Josep-Lluís Carod-Rovira, a leader of the separatist Catalan Republican Left party, was incensed by his fellow Catalan's embrace of the team. 'This is ridiculous. We will end up with more Spanish flags being waved for the Spain–Holland match on Sunday than Catalan flags on the Saturday demonstration.'[166] Even in the Basque country, which had so far resisted public celebrations of the team, politicians were announcing their support. The 2012 European Championships, where they put Italy to the sword 4–0 in the final, marked the last triumph for this team, and a moment of relief for a country that had, in contrast to the balmy days of 2008, been rent by massive public spending cuts, rocketing unemployment and widespread social protest. Madrid erupted as ever, but there were far fewer reports of celebrations in Catalonia where, buoyed by the new PP government's inflexible attitude to its demands, the separatist movement was gathering strength again. By 2014 the romance was truly over. The recently elected Catalan government was holding another referendum on independence, and Spain, the world champions, were dismantled 5–1 by the Dutch in their opening game at the World Cup, a prelude to their early departure.

As early as 2008, one sober observer of Spain's national football fiesta had written, 'Beyond the outburst of pride and emotion that has seen cities and towns in Castile and Andalusia, as well as Catalonia and the Basque Country, festooned with red and gold, the dogged determination of separatist parties to keep chipping away at the remains of a unitary state and to prepare for eventual secession remains.'[167] The moments of imagined community evoked by *La Roja* aside, a cursory glance at the domestic game would have revealed that the national question in Spain was anything but resolved. In 2009 the Copa del Rey final was played in Valencia between Barcelona and Athletic Bilbao.[168] The national anthem and, by association, the royal family present in their VIP box were met by a wall of uninterrupted whistling and jeering. State television tried to turn down the crowd and turn up the band, which drove nationalists mad, but it made no difference. Even with the volume off the audience couldn't have missed the banners reading, 'We are nations of Europe' and 'Goodbye Spain'. The 2012 and 2015 finals were replays of 2009 but, with another few years of austerity and economic decline under Spain's belt, the noise and level of animosity had risen. Both main parties had, in effect, been split, as new insurgent forces of the left and right, Podemos and Ciutadans, grabbed almost half their vote, while in Catalonia independence parties flourished. In the 2014 advisory referendum on independence, 35 per cent of voters turned out and 81 per cent said yes. Not a conclusive mandate by any means, and one contemptuously dismissed on legal and political grounds by the Conservative PP government of Prime Minister Rajoy, but enough to sharply raise the temperature on the national question. Javier

Tebas, President of La Liga, thought it the moment to tell Barcelona, unequivocally, that if Catalonia left Spain they would be leaving La Liga, and could go and make their own arrangements in a new league so puny that Barcelona B would be the third or fourth biggest team. Undaunted, part of the crowd at Barcelona began singing chants for independence on seventeen minutes and fourteen seconds at every home game: 1714 being the date of the Battle of Barcelona, and the moment at which the principality of Catalonia was absorbed into the Spanish state. At the beginning of the 2015 Copa del Rey final around 90,000 people again drowned out the Spanish national anthem, in an atmosphere described in the press as 'monumental', 'stratospheric' and 'thunderous'.[169] The PP government thought it an example of a 'disease that part of society suffers', and considered criminalizing the defamation of Spain's symbols. One TV host responded with disgust: 'Where shall we put these 70,000 pigs, because pigs they are, these Basque and Catalan football fans who attend the King's Cup final to insult and profane the symbols of Spain?' A member of the public called in, adding, 'They are separatists, *separratas*, separatist rats.'[170] For all their fans' disdain for the symbols of Spain, Barcelona itself has fought shy of committing itself to this nationalist movement. In 2014 the club eventually endorsed the referendum, but was studiedly neutral about its outcome, and refused fans who wanted to display a banner in the Nou Camp stating, 'Catalonia: Europe's next state'. In part this has been a reflection of a divided city and divided fanbase, many of whom are against separation. In part it is an acknowledgement of the economic and sporting realities of leaving Spain. Barcelona, for all its commercialization, remains more than a club, for, win or lose, it reflects back to the Catalan nation its fissures, its options and its futures.

X

It had been a good run for conservative Germany. Helmut Kohl and the Christian Democrats had been in power since 1982, steering Germany through the final phase of the Cold War and the rapids of unification and into a greatly strengthened European Union. The German national team had won the World Cup in 1990, and the

European Championships in 1996, but at the 1998 World Cup they were, like Kohl, tired. The latter was replaced, in 1998, by a Red-Green coalition, the former were swept aside at the European Championships two years later, knocked out early, beaten by a mediocre England. Even making the final of the World Cup in 2002, felt to be almost a fluke by the Germans themselves, could not shift the sense that something was not right in the national game; a feeling reinforced by the collapse of the Bundesliga's then paymasters, the Kirsch media empire, in the same year. A result of the bursting of the dotcom bubble, Kirsch's demise cost German clubs over €300 million in lost rights payments, an experience which has helped temper their natural financial over-optimism.[171] While some, especially on the right, argued that German clubs had too many foreign players in their squads, and that the national team had lost touch with its authentic Teutonic self, other voices, particularly the venerable coach Ottmar Hitzfeld, thought the game needed to get in touch with Germany's new, more diverse self, and pay more attention to the regions and neighbourhoods, especially those with a large migrant population, that they had been ignoring. In the past Germany's largest migrant community, the Turks, although obsessed with football, had produced players that chose to make their careers in Turkey and even to play for the Turkish national team, because German football and its descent-based citizenship rules were both racist and exclusionary. However, at the turn of the century the new Social Democratic government of Chancellor Gerhard Schröder reformed those laws, allowing many more migrants to obtain German citizenship more easily.

Acquiring and using a bigger labour pool was one thing, but there was also a recognition that Germany's training and development structures, successful in the past but hardly altered for forty years, had fallen behind the best. Drawing on European best practice, the Bundesliga made it a requirement of any team's licence that they establish a high-level academy, regularly inspected by the league and playing in junior Bundesligas, which unleashed more than half a billion euros of investment. Thus at the 2010 World Cup the entire squad had passed through the academy system, the percentage of Germans playing in the Bundesliga had risen from 50 to 57 per cent and, most pleasingly for the traditionalists, 30 per cent of those players were with the team that had first nurtured them.

National team coach Jürgen Klinsmann and his then deputy, Joachim Löw, created the space in which such a young and diverse team could find themselves and flourish. In keeping with a more cosmopolitan, outward-looking and innovative Germany, Klinsmann broke up old cliques and refused to pick the previously unsackable but volatile and divisive goalkeeper Oliver Kahn. He also introduced sports science, big data, sports psychology, new training technologies and the theory of marginal gains to the DFB – mainstream in many sports and countries, but then rare in Germany. Above all, he began to change the culture: the very idea of what a German team was. At the 2006 World Cup, in particular, they played with an élan and refreshing boldness that was quite out of keeping with Germany's usual sense of its footballing self, while the nation appeared more relaxed about public displays of nationalism (the German flag) and hybridity (the German flag crossed with the flags of migrant home-lands) than ever before.[172] At the 2010 World Cup this became even more apparent. Sami Khedira thought, 'Up front, we exude a lot of Latin or Southern ease, but defensively we are incredibly disciplined, very German.' Mesut Özil found that, 'My technique and my feeling for the ball is the Turkish side of my game, and the always-give-your-all attitude is the German part.' It was precisely this combination of skill and temperament, honed by Löw at the 2012 European Championships, where they made the semi-finals, that allowed them to demolish Brazil 7–1 at the 2014 World Cup, and find the goal to beat an implacable Argentina in the final. Watched, in person, by the truly animated Angela Merkel, this was surely the cultural highpoint of her four terms and more than a decade as Chancellor.

The re-making and then the rise of the German national team has its obvious parallels with Germany's recent international economic success. While staying true to the best of German institutions and values, it has learnt from and adapted the best from elsewhere, and absorbed and integrated its older migrant communities while accepting new ones too. International success, be it winning the World Cup, or possessing the world's most competitive manufacturing sector, rests on a handful of truly global companies combined with the *Mittelstand*, the medium-sized, highly specialized and capitalized provincial firms that dominate the world's markets for everything from machine tools to printing presses. The Bundesliga, which is now second only to the English Premier League in its capacity to generate money, has precisely that structure. It has just two clubs of truly global reach and at the top of the European game: Bayern Munich and Borussia Dortmund. By some way the richest of Germany's clubs, they have dominated the Bundesliga, with Bayern some way ahead both financially and, given their recent run of seven titles, on the pitch too. Either way, the two clubs offer the spine of the national football soap opera. Portrayed as North v South, social-democratic Nord-Rhine Westphalia vs conservative Bavaria, old industrial coal and steel v BMW and high-tech, old-school working-class authenticity v the shameless narcissism and vulgar commercialism of the new rich, the rivalry captures one dimension of Germany's shifting social and cultural life, though of course neither club is a homogenous entity, Bayern boasting leftist ultras and Borussia a racist fringe. Below them there are more than half a dozen bigger clubs, like Schalke 04, Bayer Leverkusen, Wolfsburg, and Hamburg, that ensure the league is closely fought and competitive. Uniquely in Europe, the majority of the clubs, protected by the 50-plus-1 scheme that ensures that the original social and sports club, rather than any private corporation, controls the operation, are owned by their members, who elect the club's presidents and boards. This kind of governance structure, not unlike the regulatory boards of German companies that have reserved places for unions and their workforces, makes German clubs markedly more transparent to their fans, and mindful of their interests, than their European peers. They are also more closely regulated by their national authorities, who run a thoroughgoing annual financial and legal audit over every club before they can receive a playing licence, and have placed a break on football clubs' tendency to pay inflated fees and wages, sign self-harming and implausible contracts and accumulate unsustainable levels of debt. Thus, German teams have the smallest wages-to-turnover ratio of the big five leagues, and the lowest levels of bankruptcy and debt.[173]

All of this, alongside a good dose of German affluence, has combined to produce a football culture with the highest levels of attendance, and the fullest stadiums in Europe. Tickets are amongst the cheapest and not restricted to season ticket holders and, invariably, come with free public transport options. Inside the stadium, in sharp contrast to England, beer is available and can be drunk in view of the pitch, and sitting is not obligatory, given the retention of safe-standing terraces. Consequently the atmosphere, on a week-by-week basis, is the noisiest and most colourful in Europe: away fans are plentiful, choreographies, pyrotechnics and banners are pervasive, singing is relentless, and though there are incidents of drunken fighting and trouble outside the stadiums they are amongst the most peaceful and inclusive spaces in European football. Within this milieu there has still been room for arrivistes, and alternatives. TSG Hoffenheim were the team of a 3,000-population village in rural Baden-Württemberg who had never been higher than the fifth level of the league until Dietmar Hopp, an ex-youth player and resident, co-founder of the software giant SAP and multi-billionaire, took over. He built the club a stadium and, though hardly an Abramovich, provided sufficient financial backing for them to climb to the Bundesliga in 2008, attracting widespread opprobrium as a 'plastic club' from the traditionalists that dominate German football stadiums and commentary booths. St Pauli, Hamburg's second team, continued as the flagship of 'kult' football, as it is colloquially known, a mixture of punk aesthetics and social activism, and were led for a decade by Corny Littmann, Germany's first, and so far only, openly gay, transvestite president. On the football side there was a season in Bundesliga 1 and a good cup run, but that has hardly been the point, for the club has busied itself with anti-racist initiatives, social housing investments, and an awful lot of beer, techno and MDMA.[174] A similar DIY ethic has been at work at Union Berlin, a small club in the east of the city, who first acquired their alternative reputation in the 1980s as the team of resistance to the East German regime. Since unification its fans have kept it afloat by actually rebuilding the stadium themselves, and selling their own blood in the 'Bleed for Union' campaign in 2004 that averted yet another bankruptcy crisis.[175] It is argued, especially amongst the boards of the richer clubs, that there is a price to be paid for such restricted commercialism: at a European level, and in competition with the leading English clubs and their access to foreign capital and global audiences, or the Spanish giants with access to unlimited bank debt, German clubs are at a disadvantage. Clearly Bayern's two Champions League titles, 2001 and 2013, the latter won in an all-German final against Dortmund, are for some not enough; but this kind of reasoning has as yet proved insufficiently strong to shift the still essentially social-democratic disposition that frames the German game. Those present at Wembley in

2013 were treated to an exceptional game of football, accompanied by an exceptional crowd, whose level of noise and intensity has, on these staged televised occasions, become rarer and rarer. Maybe, as their compatriot Mies van der Rohe thought, less really is more.

The kind of show put on by the Bayern and Dortmund fans in 2013 doesn't happen without organization and a measure of power, and German football fans are without question the most organized and empowered in the world. The nature of club ownership and the election of club presidents gives them more leverage than most. However, in addition to this, every Bundesliga club has an entirely independent fans association which seeks to represent their interests at their club. The clubs themselves all have *Fanabteilungen* – fan departments – whose *raison d'être* is not fleecing their customers but incorporating fans and their representatives into the club's decision-making processes. German football fans have also organized themselves at a national level through the umbrella groups BAFF, *Unsere Kurve* and Profans, a lobby group that grew out of *Pro 15.30*, a campaign to maintain Saturday kick-off times. In one recent initiative FC Fair Play, a new NGO, has asked UNESCO to designate German football culture an 'intangible cultural heritage' in international law. Finally, behind the goals, and in the stands, a new generation of ultra groups has emerged. Taking their cue from Italy, the German ultra movement has copied their organized singing, displays of banners, love of pyrotechnics, and a culture of primarily masculine indefatigability, solidarity and authenticity. Unlike their Italian counterparts, they are not engaged in criminal activity, organized violence or a perpetual emotional war with either the police or their rivals, although increasingly they have sparred with both. Rather, the weight of the ultra's oppositional energies has been directed towards the football-industrial complex itself. From its inception, this new German ultra culture has nurtured a scepticism about the football authorities, the broadcasters and sponsors, and their plans for commercialization, particularly in respect of the direction taken in England, where, for example, the logic of commerce had led to the end of standing, expensive tickets and tourist fans, a drop in Saturday afternoon kick-offs and garish advertising. In 2008, these sentiments began to take active and organized form when fans at Bayern Munich repeatedly raised the banner '*Gegen den moderne Fussball* – Against Modern Football'. Here, more than anywhere, the new football had brought money and success, but with it came 'people dressing up as human sperm to form a white T, the letter of Bayern's main sponsor, in the stand; fair-weather fans waving plastic hands; empty VIP seats after half-time; an unbearably smug stadium MC whose every burp comes with a corporate endorsement; heavy-handed crowd control.'[176]

The ensuing conflict between ultras at all of Germany's clubs, supported by a substantial part of the rest of the crowd who were broadly in agreement with their arguments, and the authorities has been the political backdrop to the last decade of football. As the latter have attempted to assert their control over the spectacle more fully, the temperature of the conflict has been rising. In 2012, along-side a micro-moral panic over violent encounters in football, triggered by an attack by Cologne fans on a bus full of Borussia Mönchengladbach supporters, politicians and the football authorities announced proposals for much more draconian penalties for football-related offences, more intensive and intrusive policing of games, and another attempt to enforce another stiffer ban on the use of pyro-technics.[177] In a show of co-ordinated strength, unmatched anywhere in European football, fans organized the 12:12 silent protests that saw crowds impose an 'atmosphere ban' for the first twelve minutes and twelve seconds of games over three consecutive weekends.[178] Strictly observed by the crowd, it made it very clear, to the TV busi-ness especially, how vital they were to proceedings. As Frankfurt's coach Armin Veh thought, 'I found it horrible and strange.' By the same token German fans have also proved capable of national-level mobilization in defence of other people's interests. In 2015, after Chancellor Merkel announced that Germany would take the bulk of the refugees then streaming into Europe, Bundesliga games across the country were bedecked by signs announcing 'Refugees Welcome'; itself just the tip of an iceberg of efforts by clubs and fans to support and integrate Germany's new arrivals, from donations to migrant charities, to new host/migrant local leagues.[179]

A similarly warm welcome was not available, however, for RB Leipzig, who first joined German football's lower levels in 2009 and who, in 2016, after four promotions, joined the Bundesliga.[180] Back in 2009 they were just plain old SSV Markranstädt, a small-town team from Saxony in the fifth division. Enter absurd Austrian drinks manufacturer Red Bull, who had already taken over and re-named a team Red Bull Salzburg, but there is only so much coverage that an Austrian team can get you. Germany presented a challenge for this marketing strategy, as sponsors' names (of less than twenty years standing) were not allowed to be incorporated into a club's name. No problem. Red Bull bought the club, moved it, and renamed it RB Leipzig, the prefix notionally standing for *Rasenballsport* or 'lawn ball sports', but everyone got the point. They also made sure that there wouldn't be any irksome fan input into their marketing stunt by effectively circumventing the Bundesliga's rules on club membership: raising the cost of even non-voting membership to €1,000, ensuring that they had only seventeen actual members, all of whom were company employees. While many people in Leipzig were delighted, at last, to have a team worth seeing, the rest of the league was appalled by the club's structure, methods and purpose, seeing it as a Trojan horse for yet another round of privatization and commercialization. During RB Leipzig's years in Bundesliga 2, supporters of Union Berlin protested their presence by dressing, en masse, in black plastic ponchos and watching in silence. During a cup game in 2016 Dynamo Dresden fans threw a severed bull's head on the pitch. Even Hoffenheim, until then reviled for its own commercialism and ownership structure, saw fans display the banner 'We want our throne back: Germany's most hated club.' Borussia Dortmund's ultras refused to travel to their first away game against Leipzig, preferring to watch their own youth team.[181]

If RB Leipzig constituted a frontal assault on the German model, the DFB and the Bundesliga were quietly at work on its flanks. A decade of spectacularization had already brought crowd-drowning PA systems, lame half-time shows, rising ticket prices especially for away games, and the sponsorship of corners and substitute announcements. The DFB itself was increasingly mired in scandals dating back to the early 2000s and its campaign and slush fund that won the 2006 World Cup hosting rights. Meanwhile, pressure continued to come from some clubs to end the 50-plus-1 rule. Through 2017 and 2018 plans were hatched and confirmed to show more games on Sunday afternoons and Monday evenings, and to move away from free-to-air deals in Germany and towards pay-per-view. The first counter-blow came from the east where, in the spring of 2017, 2,000 ultras from Dynamo Dresden marched to their game against Karlsruhe wearing second-hand army camouflage, engulfed in grey and black smoke and with a banner that read 'War against the DFB'.[182] Everywhere that season Bundesliga grounds rang with 'Scheiss DFB'. The first wave of Monday-night games were met with opposition. Eintracht Frankfurt fans delayed their game against RB Leipzig for ten minutes by occupying the pitch and displaying along the touchline the banner 'Say no to Mondays'. At half-time they delayed proceedings further by showering the pitch with a thousand tennis balls and a great waterfall of unfurling toilet rolls.[183]

Although Dynamo Dresden's ultras were a catalyst for this wave of protest, most of the struggle against commercialization in the Bundesliga has been conducted in the west. The east of Germany, RB Leipzig aside, has been absent from the top level of German football for a decade. Indeed, Hansa Rostock and Dynamo Dresden only played in the league in the 1990s because, after unification, they were allocated two special places within it. Hertha Berlin has been a presence, but its West Berlin identity, consolidated during the Cold War, continues to differentiate it from the eastern *länder* it is surrounded by. More recently Energie Cottbus and VFB Leipzig have had a handful of seasons at the top between them, but both are long gone, the latter bankrupted by the western carpetbagger who took them over and embezzled them to the point of destruction. So too the flood of players that moved west after the fall of the Wall and staffed the national team or, like Michael Ballack, captained it. In 2014 only Toni Kroos, born in Greifswald, came from the former East Germany.[184] The demise of east German football has, since reunification, followed precisely the same tracks as the rest of its economy. Ill-equipped to survive in a new commercial environment, the clubs of the east lacked capital, management skills, and, to this day, a corps of local successful businesses from whom sponsorship deals could be obtained. While in the west of the country the consequences of a capitalist football economy have been challenged from the left, in the east they have helped stoke an ultra-nationalist right-wing reaction. Eastern Germany's ultras trace their roots back to the days of the GDR when football fandom, the skinhead subculture and right-wing, even neo-Nazi views, coalesced as a form of resistance to the communists. In recent years, smouldering resentment over the region's long term economic decline and political and cultural marginality has been ignited by issues of migration and identity, and football across the country, but especially in the east, where the right's hold on the game's imagination was never extinguished, has followed suit.

Thus, in 2014, just a few months after the victory of the nation's multicultural team at the World Cup, 5,000 right-wingers marched through Cologne, before conducting a pitched battle with police; at their core was a group called *Hooligans Gegen Salafistsen* (HoGeSa), the latest incarnation of a growing network of right-wing football fans, who then constituted the Cologne chapter of Pegida, the anti-Islamist political movement founded in Dresden.[185] The Leipzig chapter of the organization, known as Legida, was equally reliant on football ultra muscle at their demonstrations in the city in 2015 and 2016, the latter combining with a night of riot, arson and rampage by Lokomotiv Leipzig and Dynamo Dresden fans in the alternative neighbourhoods of the city.[186] In early 2017 fake Panini stickers that depicted Anne Frank as an FC Schalke 04 player began to circulate in the Ruhr. First used by the anti-semitic and Fascist ultras of Lazio as a way of taunting rivals Roma, the cards were attributed to neo-Nazi elements within Borussia Dortmund's support. Similar cards were seen in Leipzig, directed by supporters of Lokomotiv Leipzig against their rivals Chemie.[187] Fans of Energie Cottbus were less arcane in their symbolism when celebrating promotion back into the professional leagues in 2017. One fan, bare-chested, stormed the pitch in a huge public display of gargantuan Nazi tattoos, while fans at a big-screen viewing in the town centre wore Ku Klux Klan hoods embellished with Celtic crosses. The club distanced itself from all of these actions, but its claim not to be a neo-Nazi team was not buttressed by the coach and squad singing derogatory songs about gypsies after they had won their final game, or by the actions of their fans who made repeated Nazi salutes during their game against SV Babelsberg 03. A small group of anti-Fascist fans has emerged to challenge them, but their 'Energie Fans against Nazis' banner has been removed by the ultras on the few occasions on which they dared to show it.[188]

For some groups the stadium is too small a field of action. *Kaotic Chemnitz*, a neo-Nazi group supporting FC Chemnitzer and banned from games by the club in 2012, have lived on, online and in the streets. They were amongst the most active supporters of the huge and violent anti-migrant demonstrations in Chemnitz in 2017. The group posted on its Facebook page, 'Our city our rules', and 'Let's show together who has the say in this city,' and were seen in numbers on the march singing, '*Wir sind das Volk*.'[189]

Just who are 'the people' and what kind of 'people' they are remain very live and bitter questions in contemporary Germany. In 2018, in the aftermath of Germany's very poor defence of the World Cup, departing at the group stage, Mezut Özil announced his retirement from the international game, citing the barrage of 'racist' and 'disrespectful' treatment that came his way after appearing in a widely circulated photograph with the Turkish president Recip Erdoğan and the criticism he received in the media and the DFB for his part in Germany's disastrous campaign. In the case of the photograph, for which he had been booed during World Cup warm-up games by the German crowd, he wrote, 'it wasn't about politics or elections, it was about respecting the highest office of my family's country.' As for the World Cup, it was the same weary lament of all Europe's footballers of recent migrant descent: 'I am German when we win, but an immigrant when we lose.'[190]

XI

Britain's departure from the European Union has many causes, but amongst the most prominent were the uneven consequences of the country's brutally neo-liberal version of economic globalization, and the rise of an increasingly nativist English nationalism. The former was exemplified, in miniature, by the transformation and commercialization of English league football. The latter was forged, in part, in relation to the travails of the England national football team.

Timing can be everything, and the Premier League's was perfect. Established in 1992 when twenty-two clubs broke away from the Football League to establish their own competition, and keep all the money themselves, the Premier League was the beneficiary of a number of key changes in English football that preceded it. First, English football attendances had reached their nadir in 1985, before then, miraculously, rising for the seven years before the Premiership began. Thus the new commercial football was carried on a deep and powerful current in the country's relationship to football, one in which the game was read not as a post-industrial hulk to be avoided or forgotten, but as a newly burnished memory of what industrial working-class England had been. It remains the case that English players still earn wages, rather than salaries. And collectively they are still known as 'the lads', however venerable they might be. The coach is still 'the gaffer', the kind of rough-and-ready foreman that has disappeared from most of English working life. This nostalgic reconstruction of lost worlds – the old solidarities, geographies and identities of urban England – was accompanied and framed by an outpouring of writing on football in fanzines, novels and literary journals.

More practically, the Premier League began life when nearly all of the economic safeguards and regulations the League and FA had put in place a century beforehand had been dismantled. Whereas once club directors could not be paid, profits from dividends were strictly controlled, and clubs could not be floated on the stock market, all were now permitted. Lord Justice Taylor's report into the Hillsborough tragedy had already recommended that all top-division stadiums become all-seater, and lottery monies were soon diverted to allay the costs of stadium upgrades that should have been made twenty years earlier. Finally, the Premier League was lucky enough, in its first round of rights auctions, to have one bidder prepared to go to the wall over football. Sky TV, then haemorrhaging money and unable to persuade consumers to subscribe, saw the game, as Rupert Murdoch put it, as a 'battering ram' to get the channel into people's living rooms, and well worth paying over the odds for. He was correct on both counts.

Since then the EPL has become the richest football league in the world, with a more global audience than any other. It has certainly benefited from the global ubiquity of the English language, and its branding, marketing and communication operations are without peer. Ultimately, though, the league's success has rested on two things: the scale of its globalization, and the local cultural capital of its clubs and fans. In 1992, on the first day of the new league, there were only thirteen players from outside the United Kingdom in the day's starting elevens, just 5 per cent of the total. Since then the appetite for foreign players has risen vertiginously. In 1999 Chelsea fielded the first all-foreign eleven, while in 2005 Arsenal's entire team sheet, substitutes included, was without an Englishman. By 2018 the number of foreigners playing in the league had climbed to almost two-thirds of the total. The original mix of imports favoured Scandinavians, players from old imperial possessions in the Caribbean, and other Europeans from smaller countries and minor clubs. A quarter of a century later, fuelled by enormously greater resources, and superior access to global agents and scouting networks, the EPL's tastes are altogether more diverse, with more than sixty nationalities present amongst the most recent cohort of players. There are still a few Scandinavians but, facilitated by the EU's freedom-of-movement regulations, they have been overwhelmed by the arrival of players from all across Europe. To this have been added Africans, South Americans, Central Americans, Koreans and Japanese.

The market for coaches was not dissimilar. It remains the case that no English managers have won the Premier League, and their presence has often been reduced to less than half of the league's clubs. The bigger clubs have virtually abandoned English coaches altogether: Arsenal were last coached, full-time, by an Englishman in 1986, when Don Howe stepped down; no Englishman has coached Chelsea since Dutchman Ruud Gullit assumed the post in 1996; Alex Ferguson was succeeded by fellow Scot David Moyes, but since his disastrous year in charge the post has been held by a Dutchman, a Portuguese and a Norwegian. It is over a decade since Stuart Pearce was in charge at Manchester City. Exposure to new ideas and methods from across the world has allowed the Premier League's clubs to first catch up with best practice in the rest of the football world, and then in many cases to exceed it.

Most remarkable of all, and well in advance of any other big European league, the ownership of England's leading clubs has gone overseas. Mohammed Al Fayed, owner of Harrods and Fulham FC, both part of his desperate and doomed quest for a place amongst the British establishment, was the pioneer of foreign ownership in English football. Roman Abramovich's purchase of Chelsea in 2003, though, signalled a new era. American billionaires have followed, like Stan Kroenke at Arsenal, the Glazer family at Manchester United, Randy Lerner for a time at Aston Villa, and first the carpet-bagging Hicks and Gillette and then the New England consortium FSG at Liverpool. In 2007, Manchester City passed first to the exiled Prime Minister of Thailand, Thaksin Shinawatra, and then to the Royal House of Abu Dhabi, the ruling family of the UAE. South and South East Asian businessmen followed: Venky's, the Indian industrial chicken leviathan, bought Blackburn Rovers, Malaysia's Tony Fernandes and Vincent Tan bought QPR and Cardiff City respectively. Thais have taken control at Sheffield United, Reading and, most notably, with the Srivaddhanaprabha family at Leicester City. The global gallery of nationalities was completed when, in response to President Xi Jinping's football development programme, Chinese corporations bought Aston Villa, Southampton West Bromwich Albion and Wolverhampton Wanderers.

If the globalization of the English Premier League has created the money, the hype, the players and the coaching staff to stage the world's most popular football spectacle, it has relied upon the English crowd to animate it and bring it to life. In some ways it is remarkable that the English crowd has life in it at all. The steep increase in ticket prices since 1992 has driven out the poor and the young. Students, the unemployed and kids are rarer than ever, while the average age of the crowd has risen from around twenty-six in 1992 to over forty-eight in the 2010s and is heading for fifty. All-seater stadiums, the break-up of old terrace networks, over-attentive, even aggressive stewarding, and deafeningly loud public address systems that never stop, all diminished the noise and intensity of what remained. Yet for all that, the English football crowd remained a complex, living, protean creature, capable on its day of creating a deafening wall of white noise, songs of praise, comic turns, pantomime anger and anguish, tears and melodrama. This has shaped the pace and intensity of play in England and provided an aural and emotional chorus that has proved globally appealing and comprehensible. The fans' reward for such a contribution has been more expensive tickets at all levels, an ever greater occupation of the stadium by commercial paraphernalia, and schedules determined by the needs of television. There was, of course, a great deal of complaint amongst fans, but attendances rose year after year. As we shall see, there was even a small outbreak of anti-commercial resistance in English football, but for the most part the football nation seemed settled on the new dispensation.

Hidden beneath the carapace of the Empire, the English long pretended to themselves and the world that there was barely an English nationalism worth bothering about. The Empire was stripped away in the twenty years after the Second World War. The residual British nation, nurtured into life by the post-war consensus, was broken by

Thatcherism, whose Darwinian attitudes to declining regions revived Scottish and Welsh nationalism. By 1996, with devolution just around the corner, the English began to look at themselves. But how? The monarchy, armed forces, parliament and the BBC were all British institutions; the law was shared with the Welsh. The established church was English, but the country was secular. In this institutional vacuum the England football team was one of the very few popular civic organizations around which a sense of Englishness could be collectively imagined and performed. As late as the 1990 World Cup England fans would carry the Union Jack as their flag of preference, but at Euro 1996, at home, the St George cross overwhelmed every other symbol, and has since become the norm at England games. Though both the 1998 World Cup and Euro 2000 saw city-square scuffles with the police, the degree of drunken violence amongst the travelling support subsequently declined. Indeed, it was entirely absent amongst the much smaller and, one suspects, more cosmopolitan body of fans that congaed their way around Sapporo's stadium at the 2002 World Cup in Japan and South Korea. The 2004 Euros and the 2006 World Cup, both of which saw more than 150,000 fans make the journey, were huge beery but largely incident-free holidays. The nation filled its windows with St George crosses; flags flew from most vehicles.

The core of England support remained white and more working-class than many Premiership audiences. The innumerable St George flags were usually appended with the name of a club, mostly smaller northern and Midlands towns, from the lower leagues. The big clubs, from England's most globally connected big cities (London, Manchester and Liverpool), were conspicuous by their absence. At times the England crowd could put on a musical hall comedy – mass paper airplane-throwing at a game against Chile, or an old fashioned sing-song ('You're Not Getting On' to the tune of 'Knees Up, Mother Brown' on a packed Lisbon metro train) – but much of the crowd's repertoire dwelt on imperial pride ('Rule Britannia'), unfinished colonial conflict ('No Surrender to the IRA') or the Second World War (the 'Ten German Bombers' song and the music from the war movies *The Great Escape* and *The Dambusters*). Alongside this core, one could also find a more prominent business class constituency and a small strain of cosmopolitans behind grassroots efforts to organize *tifos*, fan embassies, and friendly games with fans overseas. There was also a small

but definite increase in the presence of ethnic minority fans at England games, and for the most part an end to open racist abuse of
players, English or otherwise. An end to overt racism did not mean
the end of xenophobia as Sven-Göran Eriksson, England's first foreign
manager, was about to find out. Despite having led the team to three
consecutive quarter-finals from 2002 to 2006, which could reasonably be considered par for the course, he was stung by the tabloids,
deemed a failure and squeezed out, denounced as a 'passionless
bungler'.

Sven's departure did not herald a new era. Under Steve McLaren
England failed to qualify for Euro 2008. The stern Italian authoritarianism of Fabio Capello took England to the 2010 World Cup, where
they put in, both on and off the pitch, a dismal, cramped performance. Dispatched by the Germans in the round of sixteen, and
sequestered away in their celebrity bubble, they barely interacted
with fans or with South Africa. At home the flags and the hype
declined, the former virtually invisible before the 2014 World Cup.
It was hard not to conclude that English football had bifurcated, and
that a chasm existed between the globalized and connected private
opulence of the Premier League and the public squalor of the England team, and the rest of football's common realm, its declining
playing fields and austerity-pinched facilities. In Brazil, England
were eliminated after just two games, and it felt like business as
usual rather than another glorious failure. The debacle of Euro 2016,
where England were eliminated by Iceland just two days after the
EU referendum, was a new kind of low. The bellicose chants of a
small minority – 'We're all leaving Europe' and 'Fuck off Europe, we
all voted Out' – were the loudest voices, as the rest of nation, in hor-
rified silence, watched its team freeze, completely unable to react to
what was going on around it.

Such a contradictory set of responses is to be expected, given that
football had continued to send the nation mixed messages about itself
in the years either side of the referendum. On the one hand, the sharp
increase in incidents of hate crime, racism and anti-semitism recorded
after the referendum have found their echo in football where, it
turned out, racism and xenophobia had not been eradicated: indeed,
it appeared they had been merely sleeping, while the rise of far-right
movements like the English Defence League and its successors have
found some football fans and firms a receptive constituency. On the

other hand, football's anti-racists and anti-fascists have, so far, challenged and resisted these developments, while the England team at the 2018 World Cup, if only for a moment, gave a glimpse of what an alternative version of the English nation might look and feel like.

The limits of English football's new tolerance was first exposed by Ellis Cashmore's online survey which, in 2014, revealed that more than half of all fans had witnessed or experienced some form of racism in football.[191] One of his respondents, while acknowledging the decline in the most vocal forms of hate speech, thought that 'anyone who attends football on a regular basis will confirm racist undertones are still there and very much alive.' Those racist undertones also lived on inside the professional game, as Malky Mackay's injudicious use of his mobile phone made clear. Then manager of Cardiff City, he was sacked in 2014 after text messages between himself and Iain Moody, the club's chief scout, were made public. They were at least diverse, ranging from the merely xenophobic to the unpleasantly racist, from the crudely homophobic and sexist to casually anti-semitic. In response to the arrival of a South Korean player and his representatives, Mackay replied, 'Fkn Chinkys', before warmheartedly reconsidering his position: 'Fk it. There's enough dogs in Cardiff for us all to go around.' Of Phil Smith, a football agent who, not for the first time in his career, was the subject of anti-semitic abuse, Mackay was contemptuous: 'Go on Fat Phil. Nothing like a jew that sees money slipping through his fingers.'[192] Somehow, the FA, on reviewing the case for eleven months, absolved Mackay and Moody, and took no further action. The following year, a video of four Chelsea fans on the Paris Metro went viral. They were pushing a black Frenchman back onto the platform while chanting 'We're racist, and that's the way we like it.' The number of official recorded incidents like this in English football had been in decline for over a decade, but in 2017 it began to rise again.

A similarly unsavoury combination of the everyday and deep institutional racism in football's governing institutions was exposed by the case of England player, Eni Aluko.[193] In 2017, it became public knowledge that she had accused Mark Sampson, the then manager of the England women's team, of racist comments in 2014. She would later reveal that other members of the coaching staff would speak to black and mixed-heritage players in mock Caribbean accents. A hapless FA internal inquiry then absolved Sampson and themselves, and paid Aluko hush money; the gruesome details of the FA's refusal to take players' complaints seriously, the attempts to reframe racism as harmless banter, the overweening self-regard and the culture of secrecy and bullying it traded in, were revealed when senior officials, including chief executive Martin Glenn, were traduced by a House of Commons select committee.[194] Racist undertones were not confined to the FA, as Raheem Sterling's treatment by sections of the press has demonstrated. In part he has been treated with the sneering condescension the tabloids reserve for the nouveau riche: a man with too much bling when he spends it, but not classy enough for the money he has when, Lord forbid, he should buy a pasty from Greggs. In part, he was constructed as the perennially suspicious, on-the-edge-of-gangsterism young black man of tabloid demonology. In 2018, playing at Stamford Bridge, Sterling was subject to very visible racist abuse from Chelsea fans just metres from him on the touchline. Pre-empting the usual handwringing from the tabloids, his post on Instagram the next day contrasted the way they reported on two players, one black, one white, buying their relatives a house. 'This young black kid is looked at in a bad light. Which helps fuel racism an aggressive behaviour, so for all the newspapers that don't understand why people are racist in this day and age all i have to say is have a second thought about fair publicity an give all players an equal chance.'[195]

These incidents might suggest that English football was ripe for the return of the far right. First the National Front in the 1970s and early 1980s, then the British National Party in the late 1990s, had made determined efforts to establish a presence on football terraces, and to recruit supporters as street muscle. As late as 1994 England's game against Ireland in Dublin was disrupted by a riot orchestrated by the neo-Nazi group Combat 18. All ultimately failed to establish a serious or enduring base of support amongst England fans, and over the next decade and a half the ineradicable presence of black and mixed-heritage players in the team made the equivalence of England and whiteness harder and harder to sustain. Instead, the far right found alternative targets: jihadis and Islamist terrorists, and by extension all Muslims. Thus in 2009 in Luton, in response to a local Salafist group's protest over a homecoming parade for troops that served in Afghanistan, the English Defence League (EDL) was founded. It drew to its banner a number of existing far-right micro groups, including

Casuals United, a loose network of far-right football fans with a taste for trouble, who provided much of the movement's street menace at marches and demonstrations. Without much ideology to bind these forces, beyond an unrelenting loathing of Islam, and regularly met by robust anti-fascist counter demonstrations, the movement splintered in 2013.

However, the air of everyday xenophobia and anger that descended on England after the referendum created a permissive environment in which some of the EDL's coalition could be reassembled. In June 2017, in response to the jihadi-inspired terrorist attacks at the Manchester Arena and London Bridge, the Football Lads Alliance (FLA) first took to the streets. At the inaugural march the FLA attracted a mix of football casuals and right-wing veterans, both enraged by Islamist terrorism, fearful of and aggressive towards the whole of Britain's Muslim population. They presented themselves as the non-violent end of anti-Islamist extremism but, as a casual glance at any of their social media platforms suggested, this soon leached out into the usual racist and violent tropes of right-wing ethnic nationalism. With the fissiparousness characteristic of the English far right, the original leadership stood down just a year after the group's formation and the organization collapsed, only for the network to be reborn as the Democratic Football Lads (DFLA) Alliance under new management. The Premier League and Football League had long banned any of these organizations and their insignia from the spectacle, but the DFLA was never really interested in the football anyway: their battleground was the street. Their first march in London in October 2018 had a very visible football presence, including Mark Phillips, the coach of West Ham United under-18s, but so too did the anti-fascist groups reinforced by the newly formed network, Football Lads and Lasses Against Fascism.[196]

In the two years between the referendum and England's appearance at the 2018 World Cup, the tenor of public conversation, consumed by the politics of Brexit, became angrier and more polarized, yet no more tethered to the real choices and trade-offs that it implied. By contrast, England under Gareth Southgate approached the World Cup with a remarkably clear-eyed view of what they might achieve, displayed knowledge and respect of their opponents and a notable humility – none of which could be said of most Brexiteers. The country, although yet to put out the flags, began to warm to

Southgate's thoughtful words and gentlemanly tailoring. They also warmed to a squad that was young, diverse and, unlike the recent predecessors, open and accessible. The squad's average age was twenty-six and, with just twenty caps a player, they were the second youngest and least experienced squad at the World Cup. Their training ground clowning and love of the *FIFA* video game confirmed this and endeared them to the public. Ethnically they were remarkably diverse. Harry Kane had Irish roots; Raheem Sterling's were in Jamaica. Dele Alli's father was Nigerian, Danny Welbeck's folks were Ghanaian, while Eric Dier grew up in Portugal and Trent Alexander-Arnold could have played for the USA. At the same time, they were indisputably English, with the players and their accents hailing from every corner of the country, and a solid core growing up in the game's traditional northern heartlands of the north-east, Lancashire and Yorkshire, with three of them – Kyle Walker, Jamie Vardy and Harry Maguire – from Sheffield alone.

Millionaires all, they nonetheless through their life stories spoke to some of their generation's difficulties: Dele Alli's absent or alcohol-dependent parents; Danny Rose's struggle with depression; Jamie Vardy's brushes with the law and his long journey, despite his talent, to be noticed in the lower leagues. These were and are not inconsequential matters in England, where high levels of economic inequality had driven equally high levels of drug dependency and mental ill health amongst the young, and where the almost complete collapse of social mobility saw the stifling and squandering of many of their peers' talents, and all this in a nation where the old had overwhelmingly voted to leave the European Union, and the young, who would live with that decision, overwhelmingly voted to remain.

The final ingredient required to ignite England's new love affair with its national team was for it to start winning games. England duly obliged, breezing through the group stages, winning a penalty shoot-out against Colombia, beating Sweden in the quarter-finals before meeting Croatia in their first World Cup semi-final for nearly thirty years. Accompanied by a long, glorious, endless summer, the English football nation reassembled in unprecedented numbers, in public spaces and parks, stadiums, gardens and streets. The song 'Football's Coming Home' underwent a revival, chanted at every game and fan park, but its currency multiplied a million times over through hashtags and memes. For a few idyllic days in July, this other England dreamt. Croatia abruptly woke them from their reveries, beating them 2–1 with a display of technically brilliant and psychologically relentless football. It was, perhaps, not yet time for this England, but it is young, knows that it can, as Southgate insisted, 'write its own history', and has yet to fully have its say.

June and July's glories soon gave way to the grind of the domestic season, and the excruciating endgame of the government's negotiations with the European Union began to take shape when, in January 2019, the House of Commons, by a vast majority, rejected the deal that had been agreed. Even the football world, long mute on the specifics of Brexit, began to speak and splutter. Boreham Wood, a semi-professional national league team on the northern fringes of London, posted a manifesto and a call to arms on its official website: 'Brexit means Brexit . . . so we implore MPs, please do your job – vote down the deal and please stop scaremongering us all about a No Deal.' Another week of dithering later, and Neil Warnock, septuagenarian manager of Cardiff City, seemed like many of his cohort to relish departure at any price, in any way. Responding to a journalist's question about player imports after Britain left the European Union, he snapped, 'I can't wait to get out of it, if I'm honest. I think we'll be far better out of the bloody thing. In every aspect. Football-wise as well, absolutely. To hell with the rest of the world.'[197] Amongst Premier League luminaries it was left to a foreigner, Jürgen Klopp, the German manager of Liverpool, to make the case against leaving altogether. Speaking to the BBC he argued with a clarity few on the official Remain campaign had ever managed:

> What do you want? A not-perfect situation alone or a not-perfect situation as a strong partner in a very strong unit? . . . history taught us that if you are alone you are weaker than the unit. I'm fifty-one years old so I have never experienced a war. We are really blessed in our generation, but the past showed us that as long as strong partners are together, Europe is a much safer place.[198]

Rather more quietly, and in keeping with much of the globally connected business sector, the Premier League lobbied for the best while planning for the worst. The central concern of the League has been what immigration regime would be established once the UK left the EU. In the absence of freedom of movement, all players of EU origin would become foreign players, and thus subject to quite different visa requirements. Under most scenarios the majority of teams would be able to retain their large core of foreign stars but, with the FA pushing for higher quotas of English players, and deep uncertainty over the final settlement, some diminution in the Premier League's foreign workforce seemed likely. Whatever the final balance between migrant and indigenous players the political economy of Brexit allows, there is no sign that the globalization of club ownership is about to change, or that the League will be any less commercial in its outlook. One can leave the European Union, but no one, as yet, has worked out how to leave global capitalism. Richard Scudamore, the Premier League's chief executive since its inception and, in truth, a colourless impresario, at least had the timing of a maestro, going out right at the top. He announced that he would retire in 2018, leaving the consequences of Brexit to his successor, and was venerated in the only way chairmen of the League's clubs could understand: a five-million-pound golden goodbye. A wave of social media outrage, contrasted this kind of munificence with the League's much more parsimonious attitude to the rest of the football world. Even so, he will still be getting his five million, while the nation's austerity-stricken councils abandon or sell off playing fields to pay for social care and social workers – not that Mr Scudamore is likely to be relying on either during his long and comfortable retirement.[199]

XII

Irony, tragedy, hubris: ancient Greece gave us the words, and at the turn of the twenty-first-century modern Greek football put them all to work. Irony traces its roots to εἰρωνεία: eirōneía, 'dissimulation' or 'feigned ignorance' to the ancient Greeks, and no better word could describe attitudes to either Greece's accession to the euro in 2001 or the parlous state of Greek football in 2002. The former had been reliant on everyone from the Greek government to the European Commission, from Goldman Sachs to the Bundesbank, turning a blind eye to the statistical sleights of hand required to bring the Greek economy in line with the tough criteria for joining the euro. Similarly, Greek football, never more popular or flush with cash, appeared to evade the laws of economics and jurisprudence, seemingly unaffected by a mountain of unsustainable debt and endemic problems of match-fixing. Stung by the dotcom bubble of 2002 and the collapse of its main TV rights partner, Greek football found itself suddenly impoverished and, having long ago spent the money that would never arrive, begged the government to fill the gap. In an almost unique display of rectitude, and despite a short-lived football strike organized by the club owners, they refused. Even so, with nearly €200 million of debt in Greek football, the long boom in salaries and transfer spending continued unabated. Greek TV aired tapes of Thomas Mitropolous, owner of Egaleo, a small Athenian club, and Yannis Spathas, the head of the Piraeus Referee's Union, discussing their preferred match results, during which the latter memorably thought, 'Only Olympiacos and Egaleo should win, and screw the rest of them!' The Greek judicial and football authorities declined the opportunity to follow those thoughts up.[200]

If this was all prelude, act one of the tragedy was Euro 2004. But for Latvia, Greece were the most unfancied team at the tournament. Coached by the stern German Otto Rehhagel, they were a side without stars, tenacious, and organized, with a fabulous knack for scoring from set pieces and scraps. It was enough to get them past the French and win their quarter-final, beat the Czechs in the semis, and then the hosts in a final that Greece won 1–0: now it was time for the hubris. Newly elected Prime Minister Konstantin Karamanlis announced that 'Greece is on the lips of everyone in the world who follows this mass and magical sport called football.' The Athens Olympics, to be held two months later, would be the five-star gala for the elite, the contractors and the Athenian great and good, but this was the people's party. Across the nation, in every mountain village, provincial town and tiny island chain, Greece celebrated. Huge crowds, estimated at more than three million, met the squad at the airport, and watched the fire engines provide a guard of honour all the way to the Panathenaic stadium in the centre of Athens. Along the way the crowd sang to Rehhagel, 'God is German'. Once inside the venerable arena, 120,000 people, including most of the Greek political caste, wildly acclaimed the champions. The Archbishop of Athens and All Greece Christodoulos blessed each of them. Once again Karamanlis hit the rhetorical booster button: 'These boys taught us a lesson as to what Greeks do when they really believe in something.'[201]

An equally good example of what Greek fervour can produce was the rise of the neo-fascist party Golden Dawn and its unpleasant violent brand of xenophobia and nationalism. The party was founded in 1985, and created its own football wing, *Galazia Stratia*, the Blue Army, in 2000. Their first public outing was at a game that year between Greece and Finland, where they unveiled a swastika banner and made a Nazi salute. In 2001, they protested at the Greek football federation offices in an effort to subvert their joint bid with Turkey to host the 2008 European Championships. A large and very aggressive crowd chanted 'Greeks above all', and 'Turks! Mongols! Killers!' Thus act two – the unwinding – opened in the aftermath of the final of Euro 2004, featuring the dozens of street celebrations orchestrated by the Blue Army which served to rally the troops and initiate hundreds of attacks on migrants.[202] They returned with a vengeance in September when Albania beat Greece in a World Cup qualifier, triggering dozens of attacks, and the stabbing and killing of an Albanian youth by a Greek supporter. This rightward drift in football was partly counterbalanced by the emergence of small leftist and anarchist fan groups, who found increasing purchase on the terraces amongst alienated youth. The government's 2007 package of reforms that attempted to try and regulate the stadiums through membership schemes, banning orders and higher police surveillance was met by widespread protest and resistance, made all the more emotional and confrontational after the police killed a young Panathinaikos fan, Alexandros Grigoropoulos, during a demonstration in Athens in 2008.[203]

Yet still the Greek bubble would not burst. The team played reasonably well through the qualifying stages of Euro 2008, rising to eighth in the FIFA world rankings, and arrived in Austria as reigning champions. The public pronouncements of the team and the columnists managed some bravado, claiming that Greece would show everyone that Euro 2004 was no fluke, but a better guide to the future was Rehhagel's earnest sign-off to the Greek press before they played Russia: 'Boys, pray for us.' Clearly neither the press corps nor Archbishop Christodoulos were praying hard enough. Greece played a dismal neo-*catenaccio* of unbending defence and caution. Their first-half performance against Sweden was so bad that it evoked spontaneous booing. They went on to suffer three defeats, and scored just one goal before their departure.

The national team traduced and exposed on the pitch, act three began the following year as, step by step, the real state of Greece's public finances became similarly clear. In a series of recalibrations by the Greek government and its many creditors, it became apparent that Greece's annual deficit was not 2 or 3 per cent of national income but somewhere nearer 13 or 14 per cent, and that cumulative debt had reached the stratospheric level of €300 billion. In the near-decade since, Greek political and economic life has been dominated by the endless, tortuous negotiations between the government and its creditors (the troika of the IMF, the EC and the ECB), and endless bailouts, that included only a small degree of debt writedown and rescheduling, have been exchanged for the retention of the euro and unending austerity. Greece's economy has contracted, unemployment has risen as high as 25 per cent and youth unemployment as high as 60 per cent. Needless to say, public services have been cut to the bone or have disappeared altogether. Savings have evaporated and poverty and hardship have been widespread.

Greek football has followed a similar trajectory. In the boom years, before 2009, attendance at football had almost quadrupled in a decade. Escalating and hidden debts aside, the turnover of Greek clubs soared: their collective transfer spending was the eleventh highest in the world. Since 2009 all the indicators have been precipitously down. Attendances, despite a late and begrudging drop in ticket prices by the clubs, have fallen by almost 50 per cent, with the majority of the clubs in the top division getting crowds of just 1,500. The value of TV rights, sponsorship and advertising has been equally affected, diminishing the quality of Greek football even further, and producing the same kind of negative spiral of decline that has engulfed the whole economy. Transfer budgets have collapsed, Greece falling to twenty-first place in the world's big-spender league. Most small clubs, unable to help themselves, have had transfer bans imposed upon them. Consequently, the majority of Greek footballers report going for long stretches unpaid and, beyond the very elite, have suffered a sharp drop in living standards; a fact not unconnected with the enduring allure of match-fixers who, according to FIFPro, have approached one in eight professional players.[204] The finances of AEK and Panathinaikos were so baroque that they were banned by UEFA from European competition. AEK and three other clubs actually put themselves into liquidation, discharging their debt and starting all over again two divisions down. Only Olympiacos, as ever, sailed above the misery, secure in their access to the title: a domination of Greek football that has seen them win nineteen of the league's twenty-two titles between 1997 and 2019, and thus regular access to Champions League money.

If it was European pressure that had forced the economic issues in Greece, so too in the realm of match-fixing. In 2009, UEFA sent three separate sets of detailed concerns about almost forty games involving Greek teams. The Greek football federation ignored them, until reports began to surface in the Greek media and UEFA suggesting that Greek clubs could be excluded from European competition. In 2010, a state prosecutor met UEFA officials at Athens Airport, who presented the former with a case so overwhelming that a public investigation was mounted. In 2011 its results were published, including many conversations recorded by the Greek national intelligence agency. In these we can hear club presidents, senior officials and referees discussing the allocation of officials and the outcome of games, many of them favouring Olympiacos: a sequence of events, perhaps, connected to their endless hegemony over the Greek league. In all, eighty-five people from the federation referees' committee and twenty-six clubs were cited in the prosecution, triggering four grinding years of legal action, resulting, sadly, in far fewer guilty verdicts and sentences.[205] While the owners and officials were working overtime to keep themselves out of court or prison, the rest of the country was facing up to the consequences of the greatest squeeze on living standards since the Second World War, and going out on the street to protest. Through 2011 and early 2012 football chat rooms and the radio phones-ins – normally politics-free zones – began to register the consequences of Greece's economic crisis. Ultras took their place amongst the many civic associations attending demonstrations against the troika and its bailouts. Banners began to appear in the stadiums that spoke to the moment. At PAOK there was straightforward political economy: 'Steal from the rich and give to the poor'. At Panathinaikos there was wry nihilism: 'In order to save the banks from their failure, they have led us into poverty and unemployment, they have sold our country out and whatever belongs to us, turn off the TV on the way to victory.' In Cyprus the ultras warned their own precarious government, 'Solidarity with the Greek people', and 'People should not be afraid of their governments. Governments should be afraid of their people.'[206]

Thus it was, with immaculate timing, that Greece would play in their third consecutive European Championships, but between two general elections. The first, held in early May, had deposed the previous incumbents New Democracy, and given Golden Dawn its first seats in parliament, but it singularly failed to create a workable coalition, forcing a second election in June. Midfielder Giorgos Karagounis tried to keep the meaning of the tournament simple, saying, 'Surely the Greeks are waiting for this joy and we hope to give it to them,' but with a quarter-final game against Germany played just days after a second election that would bring an unstable PASOK-led coalition to power, it was impossible not to see the contest through political lenses. The crowd exchanged taunts – 'Without Angie, you wouldn't be here!' was met with 'We'll never pay you back!' and 'This is how we fuck the ones we owe, take your bailout and shove it up your ass.' Ollie Rehn, then Euro Commissioner for Economic and Monetary Affairs, had his very own chant: 'You cannot take our Porsche Cayenne! Ollie Rehn! Ollie Rehhhhhn!' The Greeks booed Angela Merkel, present in the stadium, with gusto, but it was still Germany 4 Greece 2.[207]

These kinds of elision were becoming ever more common in Greece as personnel, groups and ideas moved, osmotically, across an ever more permeable football–politics membrane. Amongst the new parliamentary intake in 2012 were Theodoros Zagorakis, hero of Euro 2004 and now an MP for New Democracy; Tangelos Diamantopoulos, a founder of the Aris ultras and now a Syriza MP; and Ilias Panagiotaros, a key figure in Golden Dawn's Blue Army and amongst its first tranche of MPs. In 2014, Evangelos Marinakis, President of Olympiacos, launched a local political party, Victorious Piraeus, staffed by Olympiacos executives, dutifully supported by Olympiacos fans; Olympiacos's Vice-President Yannis Moralis now doubles up as Mayor of Piraeus, while Marinakis occasionally occupies a suitably large chair on the city council. Similarly, Axilleas Beos, president of Olympiakos Volou, leveraged his sporting profile into the local mayoralty. The Panathinaikos Movement, created from amongst some of the club ultras, actually stood in Athens' local elections and scored 3 per cent of the vote.[208]

Football politics was not, however, confined to elections. In 2012 Golden Dawn orchestrated a vicious attack on Syriza MP Dimitris Stratoulis as he watched AEK at the Olympic Stadium, and in 2013, on the seventieth anniversary of the beginning of the transportation of Greek Jews to the Nazi death camps, Giorgis Katidis celebrated his goal for AEK by stripping off his shirt and giving a full-frontal Nazi salute to the crowd. While Golden Dawn was strongly supportive of Katidis, criticism rained down on him from the game's anti-fascist groups. At PAOK they struck back. After widespread online threats were made against Kace, the club's Albanian striker, for wearing a Kosovo Liberation Army T-shirt, the fans countered by conducting a huge assault on the city's Golden Dawn headquarters, leaving it in ruins. A suitable point for an intermission, perhaps, while yet another three years of externally and ruthlessly imposed austerity take their course?

Act four began with the first general election of 2015, and a victory for the implacably anti-austerity, left party Syriza. In a change of course and voice, Alexei Tsipras's government attempted to renegotiate the terms of Greece's debt penury, and took the results to the people in a referendum that spring. Exhausted as Greece was from half a decade of decline and furious but ineffective protest, the 2015 referendum mobilized a level of civil engagement and organization that reached deep into Greek society. Football, already politicized, was a significant element of the mix. The leading ultra groups at AEK, PAOK, Iraklis, Atromitos and Panionios called for support for 'No' on their websites and encouraged their members to attend demonstrations. Panathinaikos fans proved particularly vociferous, displaying banners in the lead up to the vote that read 'No to the memorandum', 'The people do not kneel' and 'Greece wake up! Politicians, traitors, crooks. Greece is not for sale.' The club itself and its President, Giannis Alafouzos, were calling for a 'Yes' vote, but the president of the baseball section of the club was equally strongly for 'No'. Only at Olympiacos did the hierarchy and the main ultras, *Gate 7*, both support the 'Yes' campaign, though even here small local supporters' clubs made statements in support of 'No', one posting a banner from a 2011 game in Dortmund, 'Resist the 4th Reich', with the comment, 'More relevant than ever.'[209] The vote was a resounding victory for 'No', but rather than giving the Greek government more weight in its negotiations it seemed to diminish it, as they ended up signing a bailout package even more onerous than the one they had rejected.

While the Syriza government's main concern was external relations and debt, it had come to power on the promise of serious domestic reform: challenging the power of the country's oligarchs; closing the nation's vast tax loopholes; and tackling corruption in both the public and private sector. In April 2015, in an indicator of the scale of the problems they faced, yet another fabulously detailed report on match-fixing in Greek football appeared from the office of the Public Prosecutor, Aristidis Korreas, complete with another library of secret service wire taps.[210] These tapes made it clear that a cabal of owners and officials had conspired to stop the investigation into match-fixing first announced in 2011, and then went on to establish a new regime of control at the Hellenic Football Federation. As ever, this was one centred on the interests of Olympiacos and its new owner Evangelos Marinakis, who in 2011 had bought the club from Socrates Kokalis. Communicating by mobile phone, the conspirators arranged the refereeing lists of the Greek Super League, directed outcomes, and where necessary used threats of violence and actual violence to ensure their rule: most notably an arson attack on the bakery of Petros Konstantineas, who had refereed Olympiacos's defeat by Xanthi in 2012. Mariankis was ultimately cleared of forming a match-fixing ring, but a number of conspirators have been convicted.[211]

Act five has already begun, and the omens are not good. Syriza's efforts to regulate football have been about as effective as its efforts to diminish Greece's debt obligations.[212] In its first six months in charge the government suspended the Greek Super league three times: the first after a fan died in fights between two third-division teams; the second after yet another violent assault on a member of the HFF refereeing committee; and the third, in early 2016, after the Panathinaikos–Olympiacos derby descended into violence marked by multiple pitch invasions. On this occasion Syriza responded by suspending the league and passing a bill in the Greek parliament which gave the government the power to levy huge fines on clubs and associations, postpone or ban sporting events, and determine whether Greek teams of any kind would be allowed to play in international competitions. FIFA and UEFA, who have long arrogated the power to do all these things to themselves, were lightning fast in protecting their turf, and threatened to suspend Greece's football association and its national teams. A diluted version of the law was, after extensive negotiations with football's ruling bodies, allowed to stand, but it has barely made any difference. As the huge brawl that preceded the Greek Cup final in 2017, and the still unresolved case of match-fixing and conspiracy, attest, Greek football remains plagued by violence and barely subject to the rule of law.[213]

Troubling as these developments are, it is the failure of Syriza to really challenge Greece's oligarchs that is most disappointing. Ivan Savvidis, a Pontic Greek by ethnic heritage, made his fortune in post-Soviet Rostov, where he got his hands on a tobacco factory. After two stints in the Duma, from 2003 to 2011, as an MP for Putin's United Russia party, he emerged a billionaire. In 2015, he negotiated a €20 million tax amnesty for PAOK Thessaloniki with the Syriza government, and then bought the club. It is just one in a whole series of Greek assets he has acquired in the last few years, including extensive real estate, hotels and beach fronts, media companies, and the Port of Thessaloniki. In 2018, with just six games to go, and just a point off the lead, PAOK played top-of-the-table AEK at home. With the score 2–1 to the visitors, the referee disallowed a late PAOK equalizer, triggering a pitch invasion – but of just one man and his bodyguards, Ivan Savvidis, who, live on television, could be seen with a gun on his belt.[214] Savvidis was eventually banned from his own stadium for three years, but he has not been detached from the club, nor has he ceased to use it to his advantage.

His most recent move has been, according to OCCRP, funnelling money to nationalist groups in Macedonia, including the ultras around the club FK Vardar, a Macedonian club also owned by a Russian oligarch. Both they, and their equivalents back at PAOK, were amongst the most vociferous opponents of the planned name change of the country from Macedonia (unacceptable to the Greek state, which says it already has a province called Macedonia, thank you) to the Republic of North Macedonia (unacceptable to many Greeks, like those in Thessaloniki, who live in the province of North Macedonia, and to many Macedonian nationalists). It was a move that would have allowed the country to end its conflict with Greece and join NATO and the EU. PAOK fans displayed the banner 'Macedonia is one and only and here.' At Vardar the ultras have led anti-name-change protests inside and outside the stadiums. The referendum on the name change, when it came, did not attract enough voters to pass a minimum legal threshold, and so the stalemate persisted: a situation which must have suited Savvidis and his friends in Russia just fine.[215] The subsequent ratification of the new name in 2019, narrowly backed by the Greek parliament as well, suggests there are political limits to the reach of even such a potent alliance, but they are unlikely to be dissuaded from meddling in Greek domestic affairs. Indeed, PAOK's league title in 2019, suggests they are getting better and better at this. A moment on which to close act five: as Greece's own permanent state of austerity sees what is left of the public realm colonized by forces within and beyond its own borders.

XIII

In the two decades between Turkey's 1980 military coup and the election of the AKP government in 2002, the first Islamist administration since the founding of the republic, the Turkish economy began to industrialize, even boom, and football, already popular, became an unruly but compelling televised spectacle and commercial circus that reflected the new Turkey. As with the rest of political and cultural life, the game was entirely dominated by Istanbul and its three big clubs, Galatasaray, Fenerbahçe and Beşiktaş, all of them more or less republican in their outlook and fanbase. Anatolian clubs and cities were distinctly second rank. Satellite television brought foreign football and a window on Italy's ultras to Turkey, whose national variant of the subculture created extraordinary levels of noise and pyrotechnic displays. Finally, in a boom that had made a very narrow stratum of companies and families, all formidably connected to politicians, incredibly rich, ownership and control of football clubs became an obvious move for the liquid and ambitious.

Looking outward, the game became a place where the Turkish press and public expressed something of the nation's complex relationship with Europe. Obviously, games against Austria would evoke endless comparisons to the Siege of Vienna, while big defeats by England were framed with reference to the decline of the Ottomans and the First World War. At Champions League games in the 1990s fans would chant, 'Europe! Europe! hear our voice, this is the sound of the marching Turks!'[216] At a street level, though there were plenty of scuffles amongst Turkish fans through the 1990s, the game's most vituperative energies reserved for foreign visitors. Manchester United, famously, were met at the airport in Istanbul with the sign 'Welcome to Hell'. In 2000 two Leeds United fans, in the city for their UEFA Cup game against Galatasaray, were stabbed to death. Galatasaray fans then fought running battles with Arsenal supporters in Copenhagen, where they met in the final. One-third of the Turkish parliament were there, in person, to see Galatasaray win the country's first European trophy. The Minister of Sport thought it 'an important step to Turkey's accession to Europe'. The core of that side would, as the Turkish national team, go on make the semi-finals of the World Cup in 2002, returning to wild celebrations, a national holiday and a gift of half a million dollars' worth of gold sovereigns from Prime Minister Bülent Ecivit.

Whatever reflected glory he was getting, it was not enough. A few months later, the AKP (Justice and Development Party), led by Recep Tayyip Erdoğan, would win a landslide victory and a parliamentary majority, and sweep the Kemalist establishment, both left and right, aside. Erdoğan and the AKP were the latest in a long line of Islamist parties and movements who had challenged the political and cultural hegemony of the Turkish military, the republican political parties and secular Istanbul, but they were first to win and hold power. The challenge was mounted from their strongholds of conservatism and Islamic piety in Anatolia and the country's provincial cities. Their key political project was to dismantle the military's hold on the constitution, and more generally on political life which, through a combination of electoral success and relentless judicial prosecutions, they achieved. Erdoğan, who had made his political career as Mayor of Istanbul in the 1990s, had long cultivated a down-to-earth, roll-up-your-sleeves populism in which football made for easy small talk, and his own amateur playing career in the 1970s and early 1980s was depicted as an ever more golden epoch in his own recollections and the hands of his hagiographers. In power Erdoğan and the AKP flirted with football diplomacy. In 2008, for example, President Abdullah Gul was the first Turkish head of state to visit Armenia, albeit only for a World Cup qualifier between the two nations rather than a dialogue on the issues still outstanding from the Armenian Genocide. Still, this was a mere footnote in contemporary Turkish foreign policy. Domestic football, by comparison, has been a real and material concern.

In the first place, the government kept afloat what was, essentially, an entirely bankrupt industry, by endlessly rolling over the huge tax bills that most clubs had accumulated, and pressured Turk Telecom, a government-owned company, to compete against Digiturk, the Superliga's then rights holder, to artificially force up the final price of the deal. Yet as part of the sixth richest European league, not far short of France's Ligue 1, Turkish clubs are for the most part technically insolvent, and still spend the highest ratio of wages to turnover of any nation. Second, as part of the wider infrastructure bonanza of the last decade, the Turkish government has spent more than a billion dollars building twenty-six stadiums in twenty-four cities. Prior to the election of the AKP, most of Turkey's stadiums had been built in the 1960s and 1970s, and were tatty if functional. They also occupied prime real estate in the middle of what had become much-enlarged cities. The government, in the shape of TOKI, its public housing and construction arm, would, in many of these cases, demolish the old stadium and sell the land to private developers, find and purchase land on which to build a new stadium, pay the difference, and allocate the construction contracts to build it. The local municipality would then get the stadium, TOKI would get a cut off the top of the whole deal, and the football clubs would rent the stadium for a token amount. Of course, nothing is quite this simple in Erdoğan's Turkey.

First, the decision as to which cities and which clubs would receive this kind of largesse was dependent on your closeness to the AKP and to Erdoğan.[217] Amongst the first and most generously supported beneficiaries were Konya, home town of Prime Minister Ahmet Davutoğlu; Kayseri, home town of former President Abdullah Gul; and Trabzon, the base of the then Minister of Sport: all, needless to say, were bastions of the AKP vote. In Ankara, Osmanlispor and their honorary chairman, Melih Gökçek, AKP mayor of the city for two decades, got a brand new stadium, while the city's other three clubs, with other political affiliations, had to share one old one amongst themselves. Cities that were implacably opposed to the government, like the CHP-dominated city Izmir on Turkey's Mediterranean coast, would be ignored, while those the AKP thought it might tempt into their camp would be offered a gewgaw. However, as the names of the new stadiums suggest, this always came with strings attached. More than a dozen arenas previously named after Ataturk were given new honorifics, most of them from corporate sponsors. Thus Beşiktaş's Inonu stadium, named after the second president of the republic and a Kemalist stalwart, was reborn as the Vodafone Arena; Galatasaray exchanged Ali Sami Yen, their Albanian-Turkish founder, for Turk Telecom. Second, it is notable that nearly all of the companies receiving contracts from TOKI, and the developers buying up the old stadium land, have themselves been closely associated with the AKP. The same is broadly true of bigger infrastructure projects, from roads to bridges to airports, which have been part of a deliberate strategy by the party to create their own pliant oligarchs and commercial giants in one of the few areas of the Turkish economy that had not been monopolized by Kemalist families and their economic empires.

Third, almost all of the new stadiums have been built on cheap land at the edge of cities, with absolutely no thought given to context, landscaping, transport or atmosphere. 'Welcome to Hell' now refers to the traffic jams on the way to Galatasaray's new stadium, located in a no man's land of incomplete roadworks. Or perhaps this has been precisely the purpose of the exercise. The old stadiums were replaced by developments that took their architectural and social cues from Dubai and the other Gulf cities of the undead: eradicating public and unruly spaces and replacing them with air-conditioned, semi-gated shopping malls, in this case for the AKP-voting middle classes of provincial Turkey. Not everyone has been pleased with the exchange. When in 2011 Erdoğan attended the opening of the Turk Telecom stadium the crowd booed so much he left before kick-off. Rather more to his liking was the opening game at Başakeşhir's stadium in 2014. The neighbourhood was one of Istanbul's new peripheral, gated communities marketed to the pious wing of the middle classes. A group of local conservative businessmen, the backbone of the AKP, created the club and, with close connections to Erdoğan itself, got their new 18,000-seat arena paid for by the government. On the pitch, on the opening day, and surrounded by the faithful, all of whom had been vetted before they could attend, Erdoğan had his shooting boots on and scored a hat trick, live on prime-time television.[218]

That a football game should be so shamelessly manufactured would have come as no surprise to the television audience, who by then must have been sated with the coverage of Turkey's stupendous 2011 match-fixing scandal, and the long-running prosecutions that followed. Not that the country had not seen a great deal of match-fixing before, but 2011 was on a different scale.[219] In part it was the number of games, clubs, officials and players involved that marked the scandal out, but, above all, it was the quality of the case made by public investigators and prosecutors that made it unique: not merely wiretaps and transcripts, but photographic evidence of meetings and digital files of incriminating money transfers. The case centred on Fenerbahçe and their president Aziz Yildirim, a very rich Kemalist businessman with the usual portfolio of demagogic football skills: bluster, bullying and a fine line in sly threats to officials. In short, the evidence demonstrated, unambiguously, that Yildirim and his factotums had attempted to influence the outcome of numerous games to ensure that Fenerbahçe pipped Trabzonspor to the title in 2011. Yildirim and his associates were found guilty by a variety of Turkish courts, UEFA and the Court for the Arbitration of Sport, but dogged and expensive legal process saw them all cleared by the Turkish courts in 2015, who ruled that the original wiretap evidence was inadmissible on technical grounds. In football as in Turkish political life, the collapse of trust and the hollowing out of the justice system have bred frustration, paranoia and a febrile atmosphere in which conspiracy theories prosper.[220] That said, Turkish football fans were sufficiently cynical that even a match-fixing scandal of these proportions could not really dent their commitment to the game, for there was no decline in attendances and TV ratings after the story broke or while the investigation raged – indeed, both rose. However, the legacy of the Gezi Park occupation and the government's subsequent clampdown on football crowds may yet finally shrink if not eradicate them.

In 1921, the Ottoman-era Halil Pasha artillery barracks, located in downtown Istanbul, were demolished to build a football stadium, itself knocked down to create Taksim Gezi Park. It became a rare and much loved green space in a very dense part of the city, and was populated by a diverse cross-section of the city's population, favoured by yoga classes and football ultras, smokers and drinkers, bookworms and pickpockets alike. In his time as mayor, Erdoğan had wanted to replace this bastion of secular urbanism with a large mosque, but failed. In 2012, as Prime Minister, he backed the levelling of Gezi Park and the reconstruction of the Halil Pasha barracks in its place, but in a version that would accommodate more shopping malls, hotels and luxury apartments than the original. In May 2013 the first demolition of the park walls and the first uprooting of trees began. A small camp of environmental protestors had moved into the park and began to resist. They were met by an extreme display of violence by the police, who charged, beat and teargassed them on live television. The response was instantaneous and nationwide: people went out on the street. In Istanbul, they went to Gezi Park in their tens of thousands and, unarmed, faced the security forces. The next wave of police violence simply sent more of Turkey's citizens to the park, indeed every group the Erdoğan regime had excluded or ridden roughshod over showed up: republicans, liberals, socialists, communists, environmentalists, LGBT activists, Kurds, to name but a few. On the second and third day the crowds were noticeably swollen by the presence of football supporter groups, many in club strip. Although not as prominent as their peers had been in Egypt during the occupation of Tahrir Square, Turkey's ultras brought organization, solidarity and experience of confronting the police. Galatasaray fans, noting striker Didier Drogba's support for them on Instagram, sprayed 'Drogba is the answer' all over Taksim.[221] The biggest presence, though, were from the local team Beşiktaş, whose ultras Çarşı had long had an activist and left-wing streak to them, and took to the task of confronting the riot police with some alacrity.[222] When, two weeks later, the tear gas finally cleared, and the opposition had run out of energy, eleven people were dead, and the courts had put a halt to the proposed demolition of the park, but the politicization of football fans and the authoritarian drift of the government remained.[223]

In a piece of absurd political theatre thirty-five members of Çarşı were put on trial accused of staging a 'coup' against the government in Gezi Park. As one leading member of the group said, 'If we had the power to stage a coup, we would have made Beşiktaş champions.' The case was dismissed. The level of policing at games sharply rose, stewards were displaced by riot police, laws banning the drunk from games were tightened, attempts were made to actually enforce them through mass breathalysing outside stadiums, and the TFF (Turkish Football Federation) increasingly chose to ban away fans from games. Turkish football stadiums rang, relentlessly, with anti-government chanting, and taunts to the police – 'Spray, spray, spray your tear gas, take off your helmet and drop your baton, and then we'll see who is hardcore' – while the stands filled with political banners: 'Everywhere is Taksim. Everywhere is Resistance.'[224]

The government responded by passing new legislation to ban both but, unable to meaningfully police its own decrees, looked for other options to control the stands, and came up with the Passolig E ticket: a variant on the other ID card schemes in place across Europe, that allowed clubs and the police to refuse tickets to blacklisted supporters. Odious enough already to most fans, the Passolig scheme came with the additional twist that it could only be accessed if you were a customer of Aktif Bank, an institution that just happened to be run by Erdoğan's son-in-law Berat Albayrak. In the first couple of years of the scheme's operation there were organized boycotts, especially amongst left-wing ultra groups, amidst a more general ennui with the game: average attendances in the Superliga halved from 14,000 to around 7,000, marooned in the new government-backed 30,000 seat stadiums. Violent incidents within them had certainly dropped, but there seemed nothing the football authorities or security forces could do, in 2015, to prevent Fenerbahçe's team coach being peppered with gunshots as they drove home from their game with Rizespor.[225] Their attention, perhaps, had been diverted to the Kurdish regions of Turkey where, again, Erdoğan's government had shifted into much more authoritarian mode.

For the first decade of his rule Erdoğan's governments had been surprisingly conciliatory towards the Kurds and, though there had been bouts of armed conflict with the PKK, by 2013 the repression of the Kurdish language had been lifted, a nationwide ceasefire was in place, and the outlines of a political peace process were emerging. It was in this more relaxed context that Diyarbakirspor, a team from the majority Kurdish city of Diyarbakir in eastern Turkey, was allowed to rename itself Amedspor – for Amed was the old Kurdish name of the city – and take to the field in red, yellow and green, the national colours of the Kurdish people.[226] However, in 2015, the delicate balances of power that had helped make these developments possible was broken by the electoral breakthrough of the HDP (Kurdish People's Democratic Party), who, for the first time, entered parliament with 10 per cent of the vote, helping prevent a parliamentary majority for the AKP. Over the next year, the government abandoned the peace process and, in effect, reopened hostilities with the PKK, the army occupying much of eastern Turkey in 2016, causing immense urban damage and inflicting numerous casualties.

In this context Amedspor's amazing run to the quarter-finals of the Turkish Cup became a lightning rod for the emotions evoked by the war. At away games, the team were met by hostile nationalist crowds: 'Games became like a war mission – there were Turkish flags everywhere.'[227] At their game against Başakşehir, Amedspor's fans chanted, 'Children should not die: let them come to the match.' Afterwards the police attacked them, detaining over a hundred people. After defeating Bursaspor, the team's star Deniz Naki tweeted, 'Amedspor did not and will not lie down. We dedicate this victory to all that lost their lives or were left wounded in the atrocities going on for more than fifty days in our lands.' The TFF slapped a twelve-match ban on Naki (who has since gone into exile), the press branded him and the club as PKK terrorists, and their premises were raided by the police.

For all the blood spilt in Gezi Park and in the Kurdish parts of Turkey, the biggest threat to Erdoğan's rule actually came from within. Electorally, but above all institutionally and administratively, Erdoğan and the AKP have long been in an informal but close alliance with the exiled cleric Fethullah Gülen and his Gülenist movement. Notionally, a mere charitable and educational Islamist network preaching piety and good works, and creating the ideological and theological space in which pious Turkish capitalists could feel good about their money, Gülenists had an established presence in almost every field of Turkish life, but especially in the legal professions, and had been instrumental in supporting Erdoğan's jurisprudential assault on the military and their constitution. A sure sign that the alliance was over, indeed that an internal conflict had broken out, came in 2013 when the same prosecutors who had so ably supported Erdoğan in his battles with the military started using the same techniques to reveal corruption and embezzlement inside the government, including cases that involved Erdoğan and his family. Even so no one was really expecting the attempted coup of 2016 when, in typical fashion, with Erdoğan out of the country, military units occupied key strategic buildings and declared martial law. Erdoğan rallied his support, but what was decisive in defeating the coup before it had really got going was a massive outpouring of support on the street from the left, the Kurds and pretty much everyone. Erdoğan and the AKP's authoritarianism was bad, but almost nobody thought military rule was the answer.

Having re-established control, Erdoğan set about the most thorough purge of the Turkish state, and the most wide-ranging attacks on Turkish civil society since the 1980 coup, perhaps since the Kemalist revolution. Around 120,000 people lost their jobs, including civil servants, judges, lawyers, teachers and university professors, and another 50,000 have been detained in some way or another, on the grounds that they have been part of the Gülenist network and thus the coup. Critical journalists and their media organizations have been particularly sought out. It has, needless to say, functioned as an all-purpose attack on ideological and political opponents of many stripes, and bordered on a witch hunt, where opposition to the AKP's trampling of the rule of law has come to constitute treason. Turkish football did not escape, with nearly a hundred sackings at the TFF, including a number of referees with purported Gülenist connections. Galatasaray, under pressure from the ministry of sport, revoked the memberships of senior prosecutor Zekeriya Öz, former governors Şahabettin Harput and Hüseyin Avni Mutlu, and 2,700 others, most notably ex-players Arif Erdem and Hakan Sükür. Sükür, who had played with Galatasaray when they won the UEFA Cup, and Turkey when they made the semi-finals of the 2002 World Cup, was the country's most famous and decorated player. Known to be both pious and close to the Gülenists during his playing career, his much photographed marriage ceremony was performed by Erdoğan and witnessed by Gülen. Retired from the game, in 2011, he became an AKP member of parliament. The prosecutorial attack on corruption in the AKP saw him leave the party in 2013, and in 2015 Erdoğan and the AKP made sure he had no chance of getting back in as an independent. In the wake of the coup, they finished him off. Sükür was charged with insulting the President on social media and, taking his cue, has gone into exile.[228]

The football crowd and other opposition voices had been cowed. The Kurdish threat to Erdoğan had been checked by violence. The Gülenists had been traduced. Just the irksome problem of losing one's parliamentary majority, and the dire prospect of the opposition winning one, remained to be solved. The answer was to rewrite the constitution to create an all-powerful executive presidency and a much diminished legislature: Erdoğan, the AKP and their friends pulled out all the stops in a referendum to approve this. In the run-up to the vote Yıldırım Demirören, Erdoğan's appointee as President of the TFF, openly campaigned for a yes vote in direct contravention of FIFA and UEFA rules. Turkish cinemas were showing *Reis – The Chief* – a cinematic hagiography of Erdoğan which featured him in his amateur football days scoring a goal with a fabulous bicycle kick. He also drew on the support of Ridvan Dilmen, Fenerbahçe legend and the nation's leading football commentator, who initiated a social media chain letter amongst football players and other celebrities extolling the virtues of Erdoğan's plan. Dilmen kicked off with, 'The fatherland has been going through a very hard time, like a war of independence', and in a message to the Barcelona and national team defender Arda Turan, 'We want a strong Turkey. I am also in for "Yes" to a strong Turkey. Dear Arda, are you also in?' And what do you know? Arda responded: 'I have heeded the call from Ridvan. I am also in for a strong Turkey. Burak Yilmaz [a striker, then at Trabzonspor] my brother, are you also in?' Left-wing fan groups at Fenerbahçe announced Dilmen's death, to them at any rate, while opponents on Twitter, recalling his old nickname Seytan (the Devil), got the hashtag #SeytanaUymaHAYIRDe (Don't yield to the Devil) trending. Maybe that kind of ham acting was the difference, or maybe the systemic attempts to suppress the 'No' vote were decisive? Either way, the numbers went 51/49 to 'yes'. Erdoğan, looking at another decade in power, was content: 'It does not matter whether you win a match by 1–0 or 5–0; it only matters who wins the match.'

XIV

The density of European civil society, the richness of its associational life and cultural variety, is reflected in its football cultures. The eleven-a-side game is, increasingly, played alongside *futsal* and five-a-side leagues, and all are entwined with their digital video game avatars. The freestyle football scene is a growing presence, three-sided football has undergone a minor cult revival, and the many disabled versions of the game are acquiring more prominence. Disabled fans have acquired a Europe-wide voice, and have pressed for accessible, inclusive stadium design.[229] So too the LGBT community, who have been challenging football's deep and historic relationship with homophobia; Thomas Hitzlsperger, the German international who retired in 2013, is the highest profile footballer to come out, if only after retiring. Invisible on the pitch, the community has made its presence known in the stadium with the establishment of dozens of LGBT fan groups, from the Gay Gooners at Arsenal to Leipzig Pride in Germany, where an entire Queer Football federation of groups has emerged.[230] The anti-racist movement, already touched on in this chapter, has a presence in most of the continent. Alongside challenging the racism of crowds and institutions, it has been the backbone of European football's considerable efforts to support and integrate new migrants and refugees to Europe.[231] Berlin-based NGO, Street Football World, has been a key node in supporting and connecting up the rapidly developing global web of social and educational football projects. Its campaign to persuade leading football players to donate 1 per cent of their income to these causes has been laudable. While the digital revolution has, for the most part, killed off the DIY world of football fanzines, a new generation of more critical and considered football writing is thriving in magazine format across the continent, from *The Blizzard* in Britain to *So Foot* in France, from *Panenka* in Spain to *11 Freunde* in Germany and *Ballasterer* in Austria, while the continent can boast a vibrant circuit of football film and literary festivals. While all of these developments have challenged elements of the ruling football order, the most systemic challenges have come from the growth of women's football, and the new wave of supporter activism and anti-commercialism.

At the turn of the century, women's football in Europe, its Scandinavian and German strongholds aside, lagged a long way behind its American and East Asian peers.[232] In 2017, when UEFA announced that there were 1.27 million registered women players in Europe that year, the continent was catching up fast. A combination of pressure from below amongst the new wave of women players, coaches and activists, and pressure from above, as UEFA steadily demanded more action and commitment from national football associations, oversaw the creation of the basic sporting infrastructure of the women's game across the continent: national teams at all age levels, a senior-level national women's league, and a place in the governance structure of national associations. Though a drop in the ocean next to the budget for men's football, across the continent funding for the game from national associations doubled in the five years to 2017, to €100 mil-lion. A majority of Europe's FAs had created dedicated women's national academies, and the number of registered women officials more than doubled to over 10,000. A similar doubling boosted the pool of female UEFA-accredited coaches to more than 17,000.

Despite the boom in coaching education, it remained the case that almost everywhere the majority, indeed the vast majority, of coaching positions in the women's game were held by men. In a few countries, like Norway, Italy and Scotland, just two-thirds of coaches were men, but in most it was closer to a 90/10 male/female split. Remarkably, a few pioneers have made the move in the other direc-tion, coaching in the men's professional game. The first, in 2014, was the Portuguese Helena Costa, who was taken on by the French second division side Clermont Foot 63. Her disgust at the way in which she was treated on arrival, her authority quickly undermined by the President and board, caused her to resign. Undeterred, her successor, Corinne Diacre, successfully handled the board and the dressing room in her three years with the club before moving on to coach the French women's national team. In the Netherlands Sarina Wiegman coached the men's side Sparta Rotterdam B before, like Diacre, taking on the top women's job. In Ireland Lisa Fallon's appointment at Cork City in 2019 made her the first female coach in Irish men's football. All have had to field a lot of inane and sexist questions and keep their cool, but German coach Imke Wubben-horst delivered the kind of acid sarcasm they deserved. After taking charge at fifth-level men's side BV Cloppenburg, then teetering on the edge of relegation, she was asked whether she wore a siren to give the boys a chance to put their pants on as she approached. 'Of course not. I am a pro. I pick my team on penis size.'[233]

Professionalization of the women's elite game has also acceler-ated, the number of full-time players doubling between 2012 and 2017 to 3,000, but beyond the pinnacle of a few national leagues (England, Germany, France) most senior women footballers are eking out a living at best. Crowds for these leagues were small, no more than a couple of thousand for the most well-supported sides like Wolfsburg and Lyon, and television coverage is in its infancy. Yet on occasion remarkable crowds could be gathered. The women's national teams of Scandinavia and North West Europe saw a sharp increase in attendance at their games, in France averaging as much as 15,000. The Women's Champions League finals drew crowds in the 20,000s. In 2018 a new record was set for a women's club game in Europe when 42,121 people came to watch Athletic Bilbao v Atlético Madrid, in the Copa de La Reina, a crowd bigger than any seen at the men's game that season in Bilbao.[234] More significant has been the late arrival of some of the continent's leading clubs to the women's game. Manchester United and Juventus, originally uninterested in the women's game and without a women's team, have both created one. Barcelona and Bayern Munich have taken theirs much more seriously. In France Olympique Lyon's long-standing commitment to women's football has now been matched by PSG, with both clubs making the move to play their women's games in the main stadium rather than a satellite training ground. That said, the relative standing of the women's team with European clubs varies widely. In 2018 Manchester City decided to fuse the men's and women's teams' social media platforms into a single feed and give them real equivalence. The same year, at a dinner celebrating FC Basel's 125th anniversary, the men's team ate and mingled with fans and dignitaries, while the women's team sold raffle tickets and ate sandwiches in a side room.[235]

This kind of marginalization and, on occasion, humiliation continues to be repeated in European football's media rooms and club boardrooms, where women are either absent or a very small minority. Football associations are little better, with women board members few and far between. In fact there are probably a higher percentage of women in the crowd for men's football than in positions of authority. There is, of course, great variation in the female composition of Europe's football crowds, but the scattered evidence available suggests that women make up around 10 per cent of the regular crowd, but this can rise, under the right conditions, as at some English Premier League clubs for example, to something closer to a quarter.[236] Even then the majority of women fans in England report having to deal with aggressive exclusion – 'Shouldn't you be at home?' – and sexist stereotyping: 'Do you even know the offside rule?' Undaunted, they have not only been refusing to accept these norms, but they have also brought a sartorial pizzazz to football that the great unironed mass of English masculinity had lost, a blaze of colour captured by the fabulous photo project *Girlfans* and the football/fashion fanzine SEASON.[237]

Perhaps the best example of what a more feminine football spectacle might look and feel like was on show in Istanbul, in September 2011, when Fenerbahçe drew 1–1 with Manisaspor in front of a noisy and animated crowd composed entirely of women and children. The club had been punished, once again, for a pitch invasion by their fans at a pre-season friendly, and were due to play the game in an empty stadium. As an alternative the club suggested they allow only women and children under twelve to attend, and make the tickets free. The Turkish Football Federation agreed, and on the day more the 40,000 Fenerbahçe fans, predominantly in club shirts, filled the stands. Not everyone knew the words to all the usual chants, but a core of these women clearly did, and the rest were fast learners. It had an air of wondrous mayhem, but without a hint of menace; a herald of what a more gender-balanced football spectacle might look and feel like. As Manisaspors's midfielder Moer Aysan put it, 'It was such fun and altogether pleasant.'[238] They did it all over again in 2014 watching Fenerbahçe's 0–0 draw with Caykur Rizespor to win the championship, their male peers exiled to the surrounding streets for, as ever, violent behaviour and disorder. Emboldened perhaps by these scenes, and encouraged by the diminishing level of disorder in the country's stadiums since the introduction of the strict Passolig ticket system, women's presence has visibly increased, making up perhaps as much as 10 per cent of the crowd in 2018. By such small acts male hegemony is being slowly dismantled.

In the early twenty-first century, supporter movements, especially those of the left, were thin in the ground. There were a small number of clubs with long-standing left-wing identities and politics, like St Pauli in Hamburg and Livorno in northern Italy, birthplace of the Italian Communist Party, and the more developed German fan movement, in all its different forms, had acquired a clear anti-commercialism orientation. Over the last twenty years these groups have been reinforced from a number of directions.[239] First, new national networks of supporter organizations have emerged in Europe, giving fans for the first time a unified political voice. Denmark's was founded in 2003, Belgium's in 2005, and Sweden acquired a national supporters union in 2008, crystallizing around opposition to the plans then afoot to dispense with the country's model of socially owned clubs. More recently, aggressive policing and the securitization of stadiums have been the main motivation for the creation of fan networks in

France and Turkey. All have been strengthened by the creation of European-level organizations, like Supporters Direct Europe, networking these national forces together. They have been joined by the establishment of new grassroots clubs, beginning at the bottom of the national football pyramid, with an explicit commitment to communitarian and democratic values. Some have emerged as breakaways from established clubs like, AFC Wimbledon, who recreated themselves after their club Wimbledon was permitted to relocate to Milton Keynes, fifty miles away. FC United emerged as an alternative for Manchester United fans alienated by the new commercial atmosphere of Old Trafford, and bitterly opposed to the takeover of the club by the Glazer family. Austrian fans, appalled by the arrival of Red Bull at their club in Salzburg, abandoned ship and created their own Austria Salzburg. Anti-racist fans in Croatia have split from NK Zagreb to form Zagreb 041. Others have started from scratch with an explicit commitment to left-wing values, like the Easton Cowboys in Bristol, or emerged out of informal refugee football networks with a social and political agenda, like Afro Napoli United in Naples.[240] Lower-league clubs have acquired new, active and progressive fanbases like Dulwich Hamlet and Clapton in South and East London respectively, and Whitehawk on the south coast of England.

Another form the new fan activism took was the creation of supporters' trusts that financially rescued their own impecunious clubs. This has been particularly important in England, where so many clubs went into administration in the first decade of the twenty-first century. Clubs that have been saved, part-owned, and sometimes actually run by their supporters' trusts include Bury, Portsmouth, Swansea, Exeter and Cambridge. The movement, though, is not confined to England, and supporters' trusts and supporter-owned clubs have emerged in Scotland, Ireland, the Czech Republic, Croatia, Spain and especially in Poland, where long-standing teams like Legia Gdansk were rescued by their fans.[241] Finally, in response to more specific issues and complaints, new fan organizations and networks have emerged. The introduction of identity card schemes in Italy and Turkey produced, for the first time, sufficient unity amongst normally bitterly divided fans of different clubs that national forms of organization and protest emerged. In England, the actions of some ham-fisted foreign owners have provoked serious resistance. In

Liverpool, Spirit of Shankly was the leading force in challenging the ownership of Hicks and Gillette, and the club's ticket price policy. At Cardiff City, Vincent Tan's plan to replace the club's traditional blue shirts with more Asia-friendly red ones was also successfully opposed by the fans. English owners have proved equally cloth-eared, above all the Oyston family at Blackpool, whose mismanagement of the club and abuse of their own fans led to a four-year boycott by most of their supporters. Buoyed by this new influx of radical energy, England's Football Supporters Federation has been invigorated and become a more effective voice, leading campaigns for the introduction of safe standing, reduced away ticket prices and fan-friendly kick-off times.[242]

As with all new social movements, the use of digital technologies and social media has been amongst their vital tools, and all of the above have made ample use of them. However, three other digital interventions are worth noting. The first was the digital life of the hashtag #AMF – Against Modern Football. The phrase was born of a conversation on football and fashion websites amongst disgruntled English football fans disturbed by a game where, as Seb White put it, 'fans are priced out from attending, where the young generation can neither afford or are able to get tickets, where people that do turn up receive over-the-top regulation from police and stewards, where owners act with complete disregard of supporters' views.'[243] White and colleagues created the fanzine *Stand AMF*, and rapidly acquired a heterogeneous Twitter and Facebook following that connected many of the disparate anti-commercial forces in English football. The phrase itself has been taken up across Europe, either in its original English form, or translated as *Gegen modernen Fußball* or *Contro il calcio moderno*, appearing on protest banners and urban walls from Sweden to Greece, from Poland to Scotland. Second, a new generation of football consumers were not prepared to settle for the legal niceties of most pay-TV arrangements. Given that Europe's millennials watch television less and less, may well not possess a TV set anyway, and assume that any content can be found on the internet and watched on their smartphones, they are simply not buying cable and satellite subscriptions. Instead they are streaming and pirating and enjoying it on their phones and laptops. While football leagues and rights holders have already engaged in a protracted cat-and-mouse battle, legally and technologically, with streaming sites that facilitate this, they are in for a long war, and while it endures the business model that has made European football so rich remains under attack. A third front in the digital war opened in 2015 with the launch of the website Football Leaks which, over the next three years, released a torrent of legal and other documents from the otherwise secret heart of European commercial football.[244] In association with *Der Speigel* and a consortium of European newspapers, Football Leaks laid bare the scale of tax evasion in European football, and the systematic undermining of UEFA's financial fair play rules by Manchester City and PSG, with the connivance of senior UEFA officials. In the clearest testament to the power of neo-liberalism to commodify every last corner of the human soul, the site also revealed a clause in Neymar's contract with PSG that stated he was to receive an annual bonus of €375,000 for greeting and waving to fans.

Inevitably, given the balance of forces, AMF and the network of supporter activists were primarily a defensive movement, trying to carve out and preserve some space within commercial football. For a radical project that was transformatory, the rise of Icelandic football offers a stronger sense of what European societies could be on and off the pitch.[245] With a population of just 325,000, the country qualified for Euro 2016, their first international tournament, beating Turkey, which had 250 times its population. On the way they moved up the world football rankings from 131st to 34th. They went one better two years later, qualifying for the 2018 World Cup. On both occasions, a huge travelling support accompanied the team. In France, the Icelandic contingent was close to 5 per cent of the whole population. Back home, TV ratings data found that 99.8 per cent of the country was watching. The world was charmed by the winding tension of the co-ordinated slow clap-and-chant that accompanied their games. All this was accomplished in the wake of a catastrophic financial meltdown in 2006 that saw the country bankrupt and excluded from international capital markets.

The sources of Icelandic success are multiple. The real energies to invent a process of change and development came from below, amongst football players, coaches and fans perennially disappointed by the state of the game. In the era of easy credit, Iceland spent heavily and wisely on dozens of heated indoor football centres, making year-round training, playing and competition possible for the first time. Participation rates, for both genders and across all ages, became astronomical, yielding not only a bigger talent pool but also the powerful charismatic collective energies of a grassroots football mania. Above all, Iceland believed in education. In 2016 it had almost as many UEFA-accredited coaches as there were in the whole of England, and more than twenty times, per capita, the number of highly qualified coaches. Two of the things the EU was once meant to stand for were the strength of its social solidarities and the generosity of the welfare states that helped nurture its capacity to invent and sustain public projects for the public good. Iceland qualifying for Euro 2016 and the 2018 World Cup isn't going to write the manifesto we need for imagining an egalitarian, democratic, social Europe but, given the limits of what is currently on offer, it is good to be reminded that such projects are possible at all.

5

CONTINENTAL DRIFT: THE FRAGMENTED WORLDS OF ASIAN FOOTBALL

The Asian Football Confederation has signaled its intent to become the world's leading football confederation.

AFC Vision Statement: 'One Asia, One Goal'

I

In football as in geopolitics, Asia exists as a conceptual category. It may be embodied in continental institutions like the AFC and their excruciating vision statements, but they bear little correspondence to regional and local realities. The AFC and its football barons might imagine that their branding and their tournaments are the basis of a singular Asian 'vision', but Asia has neither political, economic nor cultural unity.[1] West Asia, the Levant and the Gulf (dealt with in Chapter 2 of this book), although notionally part of the continent, constitute an entirely separate geopolitical subsystem and, in addition to their Asian duties, play football in their own tournaments like the Gulf Cup. The AFC can rightly point to the fact that, almost universally in Asia, football has since the turn of the century become significantly more popular, often more remunerative, and an object of interest for political elites everywhere. In part this is a function of the wider process of breakneck urbanization and acquisition of satellite/cable television that has driven the spread and commercialization of football everywhere. Yet even without its Western reaches, Asia and Asian football contains multitudes, a diversity that reflects the different cultural histories and the multiple stages of development at which the states of the new Asia find themselves.

At Asia's sporting apex are the continent's three advanced capitalist nations, Japan, South Korea and Australia, hosting the richest and most organized professional leagues on the continent, and the most regular attenders at the World Cup. Japan and South Korea, expensively modernized with public money when they hosted the 2002 World Cup, have created a sustainable men's professional game, but in both cultural and demographic terms they are rather smaller than those envisaged by the scale of their tournament's architecture and hopes. In Australia an organizational and cultural revamp has served as the instrument of change, and here too football has struggled to acquire a truly central place in sporting popular culture. In South East Asia there is no ambiguity about football's position in the region's sporting and cultural hierarchies: it is the number one. Here the challenge to the game is not the popularity of other sports or the indifference of significant parts of the population, but the endemic problems of match-fixing and internal political conflict; these were respectively exemplified by the complete collapse of trust in the Vietnamese league and the bitter political conflict in Indonesia that saw, for a time, two football associations, two leagues and two national teams battle it out.

In South Asia, home to almost a third of humanity, football remains in the shadow of cricket, and has, despite great potential, been kept there by the world's most venal and ineffective football administrators. Yet even here, and especially in the globally connected cities of India, football's status is rising vertiginously, as foreign football on satellite television and the private sector razzmatazz of an alternative league find their way around the impediments India's public realm lays down. In Central Asia, made up of the ex-Soviet republics of the steppes, football has risen alongside their late and rapid urbanization. From Kazakhstan to Uzbekistan the new dynastic regimes that have monopolized power since 1991 and ransacked their own treasuries, have sought to legitimize and advertise themselves by spending some of their loot building their own football dynasties. Finally there is China, a world almost unto itself, where at the turn of the century football seemed irredeemably ruined by match-fixing. Basketball was poised to establish itself as the spectacular sport of the modern nation. A decade and a half later, despite NBA tours and Chinese stars playing in the United States, basketball has failed to secure the top spot. Indeed, the health of Chinese football has been made a national priority by Xi Jinping, the President of the People's Republic himself, and a national football development plan has been established that dwarfs its neighbours, and promises in short order that China will first qualify for the World Cup, then host it, and finally win it.

Given such diversity, no single trend encompasses the entire continent's football, but three are common enough to warrant closer examination before moving on to more local responses. First, there has been a small but discernible shift in the balance of power between Asia and the rest of the global football system: for example, the marketing efforts of foreign leagues have begun to evoke local resistance, while in the other direction Asian capital has been feverishly buying

European clubs. Second, while not entirely new, there has been a marked rise in the level of aggressive nationalism on display in Asian football, alongside a wider growth in social disorder and violence around the game. Finally, the intersecting problems of organized match-fixing, illegal gambling and money-laundering, present everywhere in world football, are at their worst in Asia. This has huge consequences, not only for the domestic game but, given the reach of Asia's gangs and gambling markets, for the integrity of football everywhere.

II

European football continues to be phenomenally popular in Asia. In the last twenty years the value of foreign leagues' TV rights, and the audiences they attract, have sharply risen. In China, for example, the $546 million paid for EPL rights from 2019–22 was a twelve-fold increase on the previous deal. East and South East Asia have continued to attract the leading dozen or so clubs on repeated tours to its major cities: Seoul, Tokyo, Hong Kong, Beijing and China's coastal mega-cities in the former; Kuala Lumpur, Bangkok, Singapore and Jakarta in the latter. However, such is the demand that in the last decade we have seen exotica like Bayern Munich in Kolkata, Arsenal in Hanoi, LA Galaxy in Manila, and West Ham in Wellington. The EPL has, since 2003, staged a pre-season friendly tournament every other year in east Asia. Initially, many of these forays were smash-and-grab raids, focused on extracting maximum revenue from minimum effort and engagement, often fielding reserve and experimental line-ups. More recently, however, there has been a recognition that 'brand building' requires visiting clubs to press the flesh a little more, while the demands of increasingly important Asian sponsors have begun to shape their itineraries and merchandizing. In 2014 Chelsea switched its shirt sponsorship from Korean giant Samsung to Japan's Yokohama Rubber, joining other Asian EPL sponsors like Hong Kong's insurance giant AIA at Spurs, and Thai brewers Chang at Leicester and Everton.[2] All have adjusted their touring schedules accordingly. Leagues and clubs have also been opening permanent commercial offices in the region; some, like Bayern and Barcelona, have opened branded academies. Manchester City has invested in a football reality TV show in Guangdong. Those who are nimble enough have made all their marketing available in local languages, put their apps into Mandarin, and their social media focus on Weibo rather than Twitter.[3] Asia is too big and too rich to be ignored, and increasingly it must be spoken to on its own terms and in its own vernaculars.

There has even been active resistance to European tours. In 2007, Manchester United were scheduled to play a game in Kuala Lumpur two days before the city hosted the Asian Cup final. Mohammed Bin Hammam, the AFC President, was appalled: 'It is a way of colonialism. It is not fair play at all. It's immoral, unethical, and disrespectful.'[4] More recently, *Ultras Malaya*, the organized fans of the Malaysian national team, have railed against their football association's penchant for pitting the team against visiting European club sides rather than scheduling international friendlies, a choice that has proved profitable for the Football Association of Malaysia (FAM) and disastrous for Malaysia's FIFA ranking. In fact, FAM has not proved averse to rescheduling the entire Malaysian league around such visits. In 2014, a boycott of Malaysia's match against Chelsea left the stadium part-empty, eerily quiet, and entirely blue. The following year, in the run-up to a Malaysia XI v Tottenham Hotspur game, a busy social media campaign said '#SayNoToCircusGame', and called to fans, 'Don't buy tickets. Don't go the stadium', and achieved a similar result.[5] That said, similar forms of organized resistance have been rare, for the real power in Asia football lies not with the crowd but with capital.

Asia's push into European football club ownership began with an act of outrageous opportunism. In 2007, Thaksin Shinawatra, the recently deposed Prime Minister of Thailand, found himself in exile and in need of a project, particularly one that would allow him to maintain a dialogue with his public at home. As luck would have it, Manchester City, then haemorrhaging money from its consortium of British owners, was up for sale. Shinawatra bought himself a glorious season in the sun, grandstanding from the director's box, displaying messages in Thai for the King, and waving home to millions of football fans and voters. It did not, however, cut much ice with the military junta that had exiled him. His assets were frozen, and he was thus forced to sell the club (at a very handsome profit) to the Royal House of Abu Dhabi. Fellow billionaires and business people, attempting to navigate the eddies and rapids of Thailand's unstable politics, were taking note. Vichai Raksriaksorn, chairman of Thailand's duty-free monopolists King Power, and an ally of Thaksin when in power, moved fast. First, he disowned Thaksin and made his peace with the new regime, and then in 2010 bought himself and his company some very reasonably priced global visibility with the acquisition of Leicester City for £39 million. Later known as Vichai Srivaddhanaprabha, a honorific awarded him by the King, he would reap inestimable political capital from the club's miraculous Premier League championship in 2015. Vichai and the entire squad visited the royal Grand Palace, the Premier League trophy displayed on an altar bedecked by flowers where visitors could pray for the health of the ailing King. Later they would enjoy a victory parade through the streets of Bangkok. His death in a helicopter accident at the ground in 2018 unleashed a wave of mawkish collective mourning in Leicester and Thailand. Others have followed suit. In 2016, the sons of the founders of Thai Union Frozen, the world's largest producer of canned tuna, bought themselves into the English Championship: Dejphon Chansiri acquiring Sheffield Wednesday, and Narin Niruttinanon half of Reading. Billionaire Sumrith Thanakarnjanasuth plumped for Oxford United.[6]

In Malaysia, where conglomerates' hold on monopoly profits and government contracts can be as fragile as in Thailand, business people have proved equally enthusiastic in their pursuit of foreign football. Tony Fernandes, the founder of Malaysia's leading low-cost airline, has, despite his long-held love for West Ham, thrown money at QPR since he bought part of it in 2011. Vincent Tan, whose billion-dollar fortune began in the 1980s with Malaysia's first McDonalds franchise and the acquisition (without competition) of the government's new lottery, has a stable of clubs including Cardiff City, FK Sarajevo and the lower-league Belgian outfit, KV Kortrijk. Now they have been joined by Datuk Noordin Ahmad who, in 2016, paid €12 million for half of Bari, and claimed it was just a sentimental journey: 'I suffered my second heart attack in Rome. I thought I was going to die, but the doctors in Italy took care of me and they saved me. I feel I should do something for Italy.' His purchase will no doubt make for interesting small talk amongst the executives of the Italian and Malaysian aerospace and defence companies he works with. Quite what corporate small talk Venky's – the Indian industrial chicken producers – have garnered from their purchase of Blackburn Rovers in 2010 is another matter. Given their unmitigated incompetence in managing coaches and players and handling the fans as they have taken the club from the middle of the Premiership to the third level, it is unlikely to have been complimentary.

While these South and South East Asian entrepreneurs have been buying themselves and their brands some combination of global exposure, political insulation and domestic popularity through European football, some had other motives. When, in 2010, Hong Kong financier Carson Yeung bought Birmingham City for £81 million, his meteoric rise was generally attributed to smart dealing on the stock exchange and his chain of high-end hairdressing salons. The truth was more prosaic. Arrested by the Hong Kong authorities soon after Birmingham had been relegated from the Premier League, Carson tried to run the club from his cell for three years. He finally stepped down on the eve of receiving a six-year sentence for massive amounts of money-laundering. That said, Yeung's mendacity and bravado was totally outstripped by the Indian con artist Ahsan Ali Syed, who in 2010 appeared as if by magic to rescue the deeply indebted Spanish club Racing Santander. He may have described himself as the CEO of Western Gulf Advisory, a multi-billion-dollar investment fund based in the Gulf, but his arrival and performance in northern Spain was a circus.[7] He paid just €3 million to the Motavalo family for the club and its €50 million debts, and suggested they conclude the deal by swapping watches; the Spaniards, with embarrassingly cheaper timepieces, declined. Syed was celebrated in the sports press as 'a saviour', appeared with the fawning Miguel Angel Revillia, president of the Cantabrian regional government, and swept through the town with his ostentatious entourage in dark glasses and a green cravat. He immediately fired the coach Miguel Angel Portugal, and then three more before the club was relegated for the first time in a decade. By then Syed was long gone. Never in town, never answering phone calls, he disappeared without a trace. The board he left behind resigned; so did the coach and then much of the squad as their salaries entirely evaporated. Syed, now wanted by Interpol, was sighted in Bahrain in 2011, where Western Gulf Advisory was going to sponsor a motorsport event, but that was that. Syed remains wanted in a number of jurisdictions where he offered large loans to failing and desperate business people. They, of course, had to pay a million-dollar up-front fee for the loan to be arranged, and by the time they realized the latter was never coming, Syed was gone. Racing Santander can at least console itself that in his short tenure Syed never managed to arrange the loans and investments he had promised.

This already significant set of investments in European football has been expanded by more recent purchases of much bigger and more expensive clubs. Erick Thohir, the son of Teddy Thohir, one of Indonesia's richest industrialists, moved out of the barbecue chain he had been running for his father and into Indonesia's rapidly growing media markets and their consumers' insatiable desire for sport, buying the local football club Persib Bandung, DC United in MLS, before really pulling out some money, spending €250 million for 70 per cent of Italian giants Internazionale.[8] Singapore financier and palm oil king Peter Lim seemed to break the habits of a very profitable lifetime when in 2014 he bought Valencia and its considerable debts for €420 million.[9]

However, nothing quite compares to the torrent of capital unleashed since Chinese President Xi Jinping made his interest in football a central element of national politics and committed the country to a course of hectic football development. As ever, attempting to manage upwards, and build political favour at home, Chinese businesses and tycoons responded with alacrity. Wang Jianlin, the nation's richest man and owner of the real estate company Dalian Wanda, was quickest off the mark, taking a 20 per cent stake in Atlético Madrid. In Spain he has been followed by Rastar Group, a toy and model maker, now the proud owners of Real Espanyol. In France, hitherto a football economy that was difficult for foreigners to invest in, and where the economic prospects seemed poor, the Chinese have been undeterred: a Chinese consortium has purchased a majority stake in OCG Nice, while IDG European Sports Investment paid €100 million for 20 per cent of Olympique Lyon. Chinese companies were leaving few stones unturned, hoovering up clubs in even more marginal leagues, like CEFC Energy's acquisition of Slavia Prague in 2015, bought at the same time as they were concluding major deals in the Czech Republic.

In England, in 2016, in a mirror image of Chinese companies' purchase of what was left of the car industry in the region, three of the oldest West Midlands clubs were snapped up: Tony Xia, owner of the Reco group, bought Aston Villa for £76 million; conglomerate Bosun International bought Wolverhampton Wanderers for just £45 million; and West Bromwich Albion went to Shanghai-based Yunyi Guoakai Sports Development for £150 million. Since then Lander Sport Development have taken a majority stake in Southampton and the first summits have been conquered. In 2015, two Chinese consortia, CMC and CITIC, paid £400 million for a 13 per cent stake in the Abu Dhabi-owned City Group, itself owner of Manchester City and its global network of clubs. Suning Commerce, a sprawling retail conglomerate based in Nanjing, paid €270 million for 70 per cent of Internazionale (leaving the Indonesian Erick Thohir as a minority shareholder), and in 2016 Haixa Capital bought AC Milan and its huge debts for €740 million. The collapse of the latter just two years later, and the loss of the club to an American hedge fund, suggests that, for all its mighty tidal power, Chinese capital possesses its own weakness and aporias.

Globalist in Europe, Asian football has been increasingly nativist at home. National team games have increasingly become the focus of both spontaneous and organized nationalist politics. South East Asia leans to the former. Crowds in Myanmar have proved particularly volatile in defeat. After losing to Oman in a World Cup qualifier in 2011, they unleashed a hail of bottles and stones on the away bench and their own police force.[10] When in 2013 the team lost to Indonesia in the semi-finals of the South East Asian Games the rioting was of a scale to require the widespread use of water cannon.[11] Malaysia's fans, especially the wilder fringes of the organized *Ultras Malaya*, have been boiling over. The team's victory over Vietnam at the 2014 AFF Suzuki Cup was accompanied by widespread attacks on the away fans. When Malaysia hosted the 2015 SEA Games the home fans roundly abused opponents – 'Singapore are dogs' being a favourite – and beat up two Myanmar fans during the final. Thai fans at the final of 2015 AFF U-19 Championships in Laos rioted while their team beat Vietnam 6–0. Laotian police had attempted to enter their part of the stands and take control of the area where hundreds of flares had been lit.[12]

East Asia, by contrast, has seen more organized interventions. In China, particularly, popular sentiments have been inflamed and directed at football games by the government and the small nationalist campaigns that are given official encouragement or toleration. This combination of forces made its first outing at the 2004 Asian Cup hosted by China. The home team, backed by near hysterical crowds and ultra-nationalist media support, made their way to the final. At the same time, their eventual opponents, the Japanese, were treated to a rising crescendo of whistling and booing. During the final itself this reached fever pitch as the Japanese won 3–1. When the visitors tried to celebrate, the stadium ignited. Japanese flags were set alight, Japanese cars around the stadium were smashed.[13] Things have not improved. In 2007 the Japanese under-23 team were fiercely abused during a youth tournament in Shenyang. But worse was to come for the Japanese at the Women's World Cup played in China later that year. Tension over the disputed Diaoyu Islands, claimed by both nations, was running high, and the Japanese game against Germany had to be rescheduled. The original date, 18 September, was also the seventy-fifth anniversary of the Japanese invasion of Manchuria. When they did play the game, the Chinese crowd was distinctly unfriendly. The Japanese anthem was booed, the team were intimidated and the Germans warmly applauded. After the game, the Japanese reappeared with a banner saying 'Thank You China', and bowed to the crowd. The icy response of one Chinese nationalist, present at the game, can probably stand for many of his compatriots: 'Its a heart-warming display of kindness. I don't think it will do much to end the heckling.' It certainly didn't help the men's team at the 2008 East Asian Games, also held in China, when the locals again booed their anthem and jeered them, this time during their game against North Korea, and burnt their flag during their game with China itself.[14]

The ire of aggressive Chinese nationalists is not confined to Japanese opponents. After a South Korean TV station leaked advance footage of the opening ceremony of the Beijing Olympics, anti-Korean chants, boos and even street demonstrations peppered the games, and engulfed the archery events. More recently, in 2017, relations were under strain after South Korea installed a number of anti-ballistic missile batteries in response to North Korea's ICBM launches and hydrogen bomb tests. The Chinese interpreted this as a threat to their own security, where security means the right to be able to devastate your neighbours, and so the authorities nurtured a vast consumer boycott of Korean goods, while introducing harsh trade barriers to Korean firms. The atmosphere was so toxic that, by the time China were due to face South Korea in a World Cup qualifier in Changsha in Hunan province, the Korean embassy issued warnings to their fans not to travel, and if they did, then to keep schtum. In Changsha, the Chinese authorities surrounded the Korean squad and the stadium with thousands of troops. On the night, the Chinese crowd drowned the Korean anthem, roundly insulted the team and their relatives and, despite seeing their team win 1–0, burnt the South Korean flag in the streets. The security forces looked on while the pyrrhic victory was played out, for China would not be qualifying for the World Cup and South Korea would. Similarly, the democracy protests in Hong Kong, and the simmering resentment towards the mainland amongst local youth, evoked a football backlash. In the group stages of the 2017 Asian Champions League, during a game between Chinese champions Guangzhou Evergrande and Hong Kong champions Eastern Sports Club, the travelling mainland fans unveiled the banner, 'Annihilate British Dogs, Wipe out Hong Kong independence.' Locals responded with the old epithet, 'China dogs' and booed the Chinese national anthem when the Guangzhou fans sang up. Witnesses reported scuffling and punching beneath the banner for much of the game as Guangzhou slaughtered Eastern Sports 6–0.

Anti-Japanese sentiment remains as strong in South Korea as in China, and has been an ineradicable element of their sporting encounters for decades. When, for example, during the 1994 Asian Games held in Hiroshima, the South Koreans won a hat-trick of key gold medals against the Japanese in judo, volleyball and the marathon, the media announced, 'the third sweeping victory': a direct reference to a decisive battle in the sixteenth century when the Koreans repulsed a Japanese colonial invasion. Since the tight-lipped and short-lived rhetorical peace of their jointly hosted 2002 World Cup, these kinds of sentiments have returned to football. When South Korea beat Japan for the bronze medal in men's football at the London 2012 Olympics, their star Park Ji Sung celebrated by ripping off his shirt and holding up a hand-painted sign, 'Dokdo is our land', a reference to the small island chain over which both nations claimed sovereignty, and which had recently been visited by the South Korean president. The following year, at the East Asian Cup held in South Korea, the teams met again; the main body of organized Japanese fans, the *Ultra Nippon*, had a benign banner sympathizing with the victims of a recent earthquake in Korea. However, no one was looking at it, because they were all focused on the one fan who held aloft the infamous sixteen-ray sun flag, considered as good a symbol of Japanese fascism and imperial aggression in Asia as the swastika is of its German variety in Europe. The South Korean Red Devils had come prepared. At the beginning of the game they unfolded their own message, 'For a nation that forgets its history, there is no future,' and displayed portraits of Admiral Yi Sun-Shin and An Jung-Guen. The former was a sixteenth-century naval commander, remembered and celebrated for his heroic victories over the invading Japanese navy, all conducted at a massive numerical disadvantage. The latter was a turn-of-the-century Korean nationalist who, in 1909, on the verge of Japan's colonial annexation of the nation, assassinated the Japanese Prime Minister Ito Hirofumi. He was, of course, hanged by the Japanese. The stadium authorities forced them to take the banners down at half-time, with the result that the Red Devils refused to cheer for the rest of the game.[15]

IV

Important as these developments are, the place of ultra-nationalism and xenophobia in international football in Asia is no greater, and in some ways much smaller, than on other continents, while Asia's European buying spree has yet to yield anything more than a wall of slightly forlorn trophy purchases. Indeed, Asian professional football's growing appetite for migrant players, now almost 20 per cent of the workforce, from star players in the richest leagues like China's and Japan's to jobbing Cameroonians in Laos, may ultimately prove more consequential. For the moment, however, the linked phenomena of systemic match-fixing and illegal gambling are the way in which the region wields the most significant influence over global football. Zhang Jilong, when interim president of the AFC, argued that 'No continent is now left untouched by this disease. Match-fixing is now a pandemic in world football.'[16] He was right, but the plague's heartland, where it rages most fearsomely, and from where it has spread to many other parts of the world, is East Asia. A short tour of the region (China aside, which we will return to later), and touching on only the most notorious of cases, illustrates this.

Malaysia's M-League has never been able to rebuild the trust that was shattered by the huge match-fixing scandal of 1994, when twenty-one players and coaches were sacked and fifty-eight more suspended, for the problem will not go away. Indeed, the problem seemed more endemic than ever. In 2011, in what had become an annual ritual in Malaysian football, eighteen youth players and their coach were banned from football for match-fixing, while in 2013 five players from Kuala Lumpur were banned for life. In South Korea in 2011, President Lee Ayung Bak declared that 'The entire nation is rotten.' Mass arrests of players took place and three players, including Yoon Ki-Won, goalkeeper at Incheon United, committed suicide, all part of a vast match-fixing scandal that ultimately saw thirty-nine people convicted. In Vietnam in 2005, with fourteen people including some referees and coaches already accused of fixing during that season's V-League championship, police arrested national team stars Pham Van Quyen and Le Quoc Vuong, charging them with trying to fix Vietnam's semi-final against Myanmar in the South East Asian Games. All were found guilty and sentenced in 2007, but deterrence simply doesn't work. In 2014 nine players and a bookmaker were imprisoned for fixing Vissai Ninh Binh's AFC Cup match against Malaysia Kelantan, while six Dong Nai players were arrested after their 'soft' 5–3 defeat by Quang Ninh; again, all were found guilty and banned from football in 2016. In Indonesia, match-fixing has assumed comically transparent proportions. The final minutes of a cup game between PSS Sleman and PSIS Semarang, in which the winners could look forward to a match against Sleman Pusamania, a team from Borneo with known connections to organized crime, saw both sides competing to score own goals in an attempt to avoid that fate.

Thailand has struggled with players, bookies, referees and officials colluding together. So much so that in 2014 the Football Association of Thailand (FAT) took more than 100 officials to swear an oath of honesty before the venerated Emerald Buddha in Bangkok. Thai referees Thanom Borikut and Chaiya Mahapab must have been absent or kept their fingers crossed, because in 2016 they were banned from football for life by the AFC for a slew of games they had manipulated at the time. In 2017, officials and six players from the Thai Navy club were arrested for fixing, while the chairman of Nakhon Ratchasima, Tewan Liptapanlop, tested even the most credulous when he feigned surprise at his team's extraordinary run of defeats. 'I really wondered why my team lost 3 to 5 goals in the last minute during the last five games.'[17] The same year Laotian football, already in a perilous state, entirely collapsed as yet another slew of player arrests saw sponsors withdraw their money, eight teams leave the league and referees go on strike, with the consequence that the 2017 national championship was abandoned.[18]

Some of those fixes will have been for points, ensuring promotion and avoiding relegation. The vast majority, however, will have been about betting and money, and in this realm Asia has no peer. While some of the world's fixes are conducted through the legal betting industry, both onshore and offshore, the vast majority of business is done on the huge and unregulated and usually illegal betting markets of East Asia. Tentative estimates put the size of the sports betting market between $200 and $500 billion a year, of which 80 per cent is gambled in grey or illegal markets, and more than half of that is in Asia. Similarly, while there is plenty of locally organized match-fixing in Europe and the Americas, it is in East Asia, especially Singapore and China, that many of the world's most audacious and costly match-fixing operations have been organized. The continuing existence of these markets rests on the widespread illegality of betting, based on the same kind of prohibitionary logic that has been working so well in the war on drugs, and their practical utility to many elites, economic, political and criminal, who, rather than legalize and regulate the industry, prefer to launder huge amounts of cash through it. Thus the fabulous and sententious hypocrisy of Cambodia's Prime Minister, Hun Sen, who in a widely reported speech in 2010 said, 'On Friday, the World Cup will start. I would like to appeal to the people not to bet on football . . . Both secret and open football betting must finish. Just watch it and clap your hands.'[19] The legal prohibition of gambling and this kind of moral exhortation sits side by side with the tolerated casino strips, notionally for foreigners only, that have grown up in the no man's land between Cambodia's border posts and those of some of its neighbours': Poipet and O Smach on the Thai border and, most notoriously, Bavet on the Vietnamese border.[20]

While East Asia hosts these essential back-office functions for the business, it still requires a front office, overseas and in the field, for doing the actual fixing. The most important of the individuals involved, and since he put out an autobiography the most forthcoming on how the system works, is the Singaporean Tamil Wilson Raj Perumal. He was arrested in Finland in 2011 and has been spilling the beans ever since. His earliest brush with the game was a conviction in 1995 for attempted match-fixing in Singapore, followed up in 2000 by a violent attack on a player whose co-operation was required in another fix. He is still wanted in Singapore for skipping bail after driving his car over the feet of an airport police officer. Amongst the confirmed cases he was responsible for were Zimbabwe's comical tours of Asia between 2007 and 2009 that saw them go down to Thailand, Malaysia and Syria; an entirely fake Togo team that played in Bahrain; and a raft of friendly and exhibition games played in the run-up to the 2010 World Cup.[21] The key to the latter was the Singapore-based company Football 4U, which not only arranged games for national football associations but also relieved them of the irksome task of having to find officials by supplying handpicked staff themselves. The kind of officials who could guarantee wins for South Africa against Thailand, Bulgaria and Colombia and, in the shape of Football 4U's own star, Niger referee Ibrahim Chaibou, three penalties from three handballs in Bafana Bafana's 5–0 demolition of Guatemala.[22] After the World Cup Perumal based himself in Europe where, in addition to his work on internationals, he was busy in the Italian, Hungarian, Greek and Finnish leagues. When he was finally apprehended, his mobile phone made for interesting reading: innumerable football federation officials, international referees and players, and Dan Tan, once a director of Football 4U and a Singaporean businessman, who Perumal alleged placed all the operation's bets on Asian markets. When Interpol reported on the matter in 2013 they listed, in Europe alone, 380 matches suspected of interference, and 300 elsewhere, most notably World Cup qualifying matches involving the Nigerian and Honduran national teams, and the

Champions League game in 2009 between Liverpool and Hungarian club Debrecen.[23]

Perumal has since been released from jail and is doing the media rounds. Dan Tan remains in the charge of the Singaporean legal authorities, but Asia's football gambling problems have not gone away. In what has become a now biennial event that accompanies either the European Championships or the World Cup, Interpol coordinates raids in multiple East Asian countries, targeting the illegal betting markets, their physical premises, their websites and their call centres. In 2016 operations in eleven countries, including China, Malaysia, Singapore, Thailand and Vietnam, saw 4,100 arrests and Interpol trumpeting a cash haul of over ten million dollars. The markets and the bookies barely noticed the hit and are all still very much in business. In South East Asia alone, Euro 2016 attracted more than half a billion dollars' worth of bets. If the AFC really does imagine the continent has one vision, it is surely seen from a blind eye. The rest of the football world cannot afford such complacency.

V

The 2002 World Cup, jointly hosted by Japan and South Korea, did not launch football in either country: rather it was intended to raise and then cement the place of the game in their national sporting cultures. Japan progressed to the knock-out rounds for the first time, and managed a restrained level of low-key carnivalesque nationalism, but South Korea had the better tournament. The team made it to the semi-finals, and the crowds that gathered to watch them on big screens were simply unprecedented, rising to 7.5 million people for their game against Germany.

Time, however, has been much kinder to the Japanese game. Now over a quarter of a century old, professional football has established itself as a permanent fixture in Japanese popular culture. The J. League, launched in 1992 as a single closed league, has successfully expanded to include three divisions, and is now linked with local football pyramids, ensuring the smallest of clubs can dream of promotion. The clubs themselves have made the transition from amateur corporate, almost factory teams, to city-based clubs, actively

nurturing an urban or regional fanbase. This was particularly important in economically more marginal cities and regions, where clubs
like Kashima Antlers (an anonymous, centre-less, satellite city of
Tokyo) or Albirex Niigata (from Japan's epitome of a corrupt rural
backwater) have been the focus of both economic development and
reinvented local identities. These clubs were steered from above by
local corporations, politicians and bureaucracies, but the J. League
has also made space for new community initiatives and amateur
clubs from below like Mito Hollyhock and Thespakusatsu; the former
using a European-style socio-membership system to sustain itself, the
latter surviving by embedding players in local businesses. Although
there have been a few cases of bankruptcy, its leading clubs are
financially sustainable and closely regulated, and the value of the
league's TV rights, though modest by global standards, has risen. At
the same time its initial reliance on a host of foreign stars has passed.
J. League clubs are now restricted to three foreigners, one extra
player from Asia and a fifth, if they choose, from South East Asia,
though few take up their whole allocation, and most of the players
are either Brazilian or Korean. Japan's youth academies turn out a
steady stream of players, and at any one time around two to three
dozen have been good enough to play in Europe, a handful at the
biggest clubs. These patterns of development and migration have
helped produce a strong national team – qualifying for every World
Cup since 1998, and winning the Asian Cup in 2002, 2004 and
2011 – but a domestic league that lacks glamour, is relatively weak
in Asian competition and, so far, unattractive in foreign markets.

This is just one of the conundrums and trade-offs that Japan's
encounter with football has produced. As a society that continues to
understand itself, whatever the contrary evidence, as biologically
and socially unique, by virtue of its gene pool, its history and its long,
misremembered periods of global isolation, Japan was always going
have a complex relationship with a game invented in Victorian Britain but which claims to be universal. Baseball, which arrived in the
late nineteenth century, and was easily the most popular sport for
much of the twentieth, prospered because it could be reinterpreted
as a Japanese game. Its combination of omnipotent coaches and
managers instructing hyper-focused and disciplined players, bound
by a deep team harmony, or *wa*, perfectly matched the vertical hierarchies and deference to authority of Japanese working life. Football

proved much harder to domesticate. Indeed, part of its attraction in the early 1990s was that it might provide the mindset and the skills that Japan so sorely lacked. While the strict hierarchies of baseball mirrored the arrangements that had made industrial Japan such a success, it was the flexibility, spontaneity and networked individualism of football that seemed to offer a clearer path to the post-industrial future. However, as the first generation of foreign coaches in the J. League discovered, Japan has not proved fertile soil for this kind of thinking. Arsène Wenger, who coached Nagoya Grampus Eight in the 1990s, said of Japanese players, 'They wanted specific instructions from me . . . But the player with the ball should be in charge of the game. I had to teach them to think for themselves.' Hidetoshi Nakata, who would go on to play in Serie A and the EPL, shocked Japan when as a teenager he refused to address his footballing seniors with the appropriate honorifics, arguing that the logic of football knew no such hierarchies. While Japanese players no longer pass the ball on the basis of seniority, once commonplace, they have yet to truly break from this stifling inheritance.

Japanese football crowds are surely unique. Since the inception of the J. League Japan has had the most feminine football crowds in men's professional football, and has sustained a ratio of around 60 per cent men to 40 per cent women, though at many clubs the crowd could be almost half and half. This fact, combined with Japan's elaborate systems of etiquette, produced, to European or Latin American eyes, quite unprecedented forms of behaviour. Crowds would cheer both home and away teams, and cheered louder for the video replays than for the goals themselves. No referee or official was ever subject to barracking, however poor their decisions, and games would conclude with applause for both teams, who would then take a solemn bow on the goal line. When the crowd did sing, it was karaoke-style: led by the big screens, and saccharine in tone.[24] However, some fans, predominantly men, often those familiar with European ultra culture and, like Nakata, sensing that football's logics stood in opposition to so many Japanese norms, yearned for something else. As one ultra from Gamba Osaka, comparing the stands to the suffocating formality of his working life, put it, 'Here I can let myself go. I can shout for ninety minutes, tell the players what I think if they're rubbish, or call the referee a wanker . . . this is the one place I can be open.'[25] The first group to form, at Urawa Red Diamonds in 1993, were the

Crazy Calls. From the Italian ultras they borrowed collective chanting and the co-ordinated display of banners, and combined this with the mordant wit and knowing pop culture of the English. The team's precipitous decline in form was met by the crowd humming the Elvis tune, 'Can't Help Falling in Love'. Like fans everywhere they began to boo the opposition and the referee. However deviant this behaviour might have been, they reverted to Japanese type when the leading member of the group began assaulting the team's players in the street: the sense of collective shame was such that the entire organization disbanded. It is a fate shared by a number of ultra groups whose aggressive or violent behaviour has overstepped the mark.

Despite Japanese football's assiduous cultivation of women as consumers of the game, it has been altogether less diligent in cultivating women as players of football. In 2010 there were 870,000 registered male players and just 30,000 women. Yet in recent years the women's national team has proved more successful than the men, not only winning the women's Asian Cup and World Cup in 2011, but making a far deeper imprint on the collective imagination. On 25 March that year a huge earthquake occurred, its epicentre located just off the eastern coast of Japan. The tsunami created by the quake washed up on the coast of the Tohoku region and devastated it, including the Fukushima nuclear plant, which was close to meltdown for the next couple of months. The day after the disaster, in an image that went viral through Japan, national team player Atsuto Uchida, playing for Schalke 04, finished a game with a T-shirt that read, 'To all Japanese people, I pray for the survival of as many lives as possible. Let's keep on loving together.' Over the next three months many Japanese football clubs organized exhibition games, fans of Cerezo Osaka and Kyoto Sanga agreed to watch their derby match in silence, and football players were prominent in raising money for relief efforts. Japanese football, above all its national teams, became entwined with the wider public mood of resilience and solidarity. A few months later at the 2011 women's World Cup in Germany, the coach of the Japanese squad, Norio Sasaki, showed the team footage of the disaster before their quarter-final with Germany and their semi-final with Sweden. In the final against the United States, who they had failed to beat in over twenty previous

outings, they took the game to 2–2 in extra time and won it on penalties. As Hope Solo, the US goalkeeper, put it, 'I truly believe that
something bigger was pulling for Japan.'[26]

In the wake of this victory, Japanese sponsors, advertisers and
media companies have given more prominence to football and football players as celebrities and endorsers. By 2013, all five major
national television channels had acquired a football-lifestyle-celebrity
show. Japanese magazine publishers, aping the model used for music
stars, produced dozens of new titles focusing on single players. Yet
within this body of material there was remarkably little diversity in
the ways in which both male and female football players were
framed. The men's national team, known as the Blue Samurai,
offered the football player as noble disciplined warrior. At a finer
grain the media divided the squad into hardworking older salarymen
and younger single *tarentos* (celebrities). The women's team, rather
than Samurai, are known as the *Nadeshiko*: a frilly pink carnation
that encapsulates traditional conceptions of Japanese femininity.
While the idea of *Nadeshiko* carried notions of women's toughness
and resilience, characteristics which chime with a sporting identity,
its main connotations of submissiveness, frail beauty and poise, do
not. Consequently much of the media struggled with who or what
these new specimens of Japanese femininity were.[27] Indeed, the coverage of the players often turned on the question of whether they
were women at all. In an interview with five members of the World
Cup-winning squad on Fuji TV's *New Junk Sports*, players recounted
stories of being mistaken for husbands and brothers, and upbraided
one of their colleagues who had dressed up for the occasion as
'trying too hard'. The JFA itself seemed to find it hard to imagine
that their women's team was staffed by women, issuing them all with
official dark masculine suits and flat caps. On the other hand, in
Akimi Yoshida's clear-eyed and incredibly popular manga comic *Umi-
machi Diary*, the hero is a brilliant young girl who plays football with
the boys, and has to work her way through the obstacles and the
stereotypes that block her path. In 2015, the *Nadeshiko* made a
second consecutive World Cup final, but this time the US were too
strong, thrashing them 5–2. While both the public and the media
were disappointed, there was no sense of shame: indeed, as the star
of the men's team, Shinji Okazaki, argued, 'They always provide a

dream . . . the fact that they got to the final shows how strong they are. We, the men, must learn from them.'[28]

After losing the third place play-off game in the 2002 World Cup, and saying their final goodbyes to the fans, South Korea's players unveiled a banner: 'CU@K-League'. For almost a decade they did. While never attaining anything close to the football fever of the World Cup, domestic football saw average attendances steadily rise, peaking at around 15,000 in 2010; though even then most crowds were dwarfed by the inappropriately large World Cup stadiums bequeathed to them. Since then the league's decline has been precipitous: attendances fell to an average of less than 8,000 per game, TV ratings plummeted, while the league's new TV deal was worth just $5 million a year – less than the value of a single EPL game. In the second tier of the K League average attendance fell below 1,000, in stadiums that could accommodate forty and fifty times as many.[29] Teams, especially in poorer regions, backed by cash-strapped local governments, like Incheon United for example, could barely keep going. The largest clubs, supported by the country's industrial conglomerates or *chaebols*, like Jeonbuk Motors (Hyundai), FC Seoul (LG) and Suwong Bluewings (Samsung), continued to be solvent, sometimes able to attract near full houses, and were even competitive at an Asian level, where South Korean sides won four Champions League titles between 2009 and 2016. However, as government tax breaks and corporate budgets were squeezed at these clubs the league as a whole has been impoverished. In addition to the long-standing loss of the very best players to Europe, the increasing wages available in China and Japan saw another tranche of talent depart. Although South Korea has been an ever present at the World Cup since 2002, nothing had come close to that on or off the field. The country's indifferent performance at the 2014 World Cup was no worse than the other Asian qualifiers (Japan, Iran and Australia), all of whom failed to win a single game and finished bottom of their respective groups, but only the Koreans had to return home and face a fusillade of toffees at the airport. (In Korea the expression 'Go eat a toffee' broadly translates as 'Screw you'. The public's mood swings with regard to the national team are surely a version of the country's deeply pathological relationship with competitiveness and success.[30]

What, beyond the ups and downs of the national team, explains Korea's lukewarm relationship with the game? Certainly, in terms of media coverage and TV ratings, baseball and taekwondo remain ahead and, on an annual basis, baseball seats outsell football five to one. The K League's huge match-fixing scandal in 2011 did not help, feeding into the same widespread cynicism and disillusion that repeated corruption scandals at the highest levels of Korean politics and business had produced.[31] The presence of a small and aggressive ultra culture, and the occasional outbreak of fisticuffs at some derbies and bigger games, likewise. However, seen in a longer-term perspective, the nation's football problems are rooted in its original conditions of production, and its subsequent failure to adapt. South Korean football was first professionalized in 1986 under the auspices of an authoritarian, militarized regime. From its inception it has been supported by the state, nationally and locally, and its allied network of huge industrial conglomerates, the *chaebols*. Chung Mong Joon, son of the founder of Hyundai and majority shareowner in its heavy industrial wing, found time alongside his political and industrial careers to serve as the president of the South Korean football association from 1993 to 2013. He handed the post on to his younger cousin Chung Mong Gyu, president of the Hyundai development corporation. These kinds of networks proved invaluable in persuading the government to back the World Cup, embark on a vast stadium building programme and support penurious teams. For the biggest five or six clubs the *chaebols*, or rather their money, have delivered success. However, the model of development that this cadre of administrators has pursued has proved indifferent to or ineffective in the more subtle arts of building grassroots support and marketing the game to new audiences. Japan, in the men's game at any rate, has excelled at these tasks. In multiple, contradictory and fractured ways, playing, following and consuming football in Japan remains a route to the future. In South Korea this mantle has been claimed by football's two most serious cultural competitors: K-pop and eSports.

It is telling that the most global impact of Korean culture on the world of football has not been Park Ji Sung, or any other player, but Psy's 2012 K-pop hit 'Gangnam Style', a manic satire on Seoul's nouveau riche accompanied by an irrepressibly funny horseriding dance. Gangnam-Style goal celebrations have been recorded in professional, even international football from Malaysia, Canada and Italy to Scotland, Bolivia and Brazil; Paul Pogba, on Manchester United's training pitch, and Neymar, in the *Seleção*'s dressing room, have joined in.[32]

K-pop is just the most successful element of the broader K-wave that has seen the emergence of a huge Korean popular cultural industry, proving phenomenally successful in much of Asia and increasingly beyond: a mix that includes boy bands and girl groups, TV dramas and movies, and online gaming, overwhelmingly consumed by the young. This matters for football, because, first, the youth market is shrinking. South Korea is going through an accelerated demographic shift that is projected to see the population decline from 50 to 34 million, with half the country over sixty. Second, K-pop has colonized celebrity culture in Korea, whose neurotic individualism is a great driver of compensatory consumption but a poor gateway to the imagined collective solidarities of football fandom.

If K-pop has trumped the K League in the imaginary realm of fandom and celebrity, then in the realm of sport proper football is up against eSports. In the 1990s South Korea's economic planning agencies decided to shift the country away from its reliance on heavy industries and engineering, successful as those had proved, and towards to the new digital industries. Consequently, at the turn of the century, South Korea had the fastest broadband service in the world, the highest percentage of the population online, and a huge gaming culture nurtured in the thousands of PC bangs – gaming cafes – that sprung up everywhere. The government founded the Korean eSports Association KeSPA in 2000, made it a member of the Korean national Olympic committee, and helped create the environment in which commercial tournaments could flourish and a generation of pro-gamers emerge. In 2014, the League of Legends World Championships were held at the Seoul World Cup stadium and pulled in more than 40,000 paying spectators, better than the vast majority of crowds at FC Seoul, who were the usual occupants.

It is one small measure of the gap between South Korea and North Korea that the DPRK, as it likes to be known, only acquired its first digital football game in 2017. 'Soccer Fierce Battle' was a version of the *FIFA* series configured for the regime's own tablets and smartphones, but few beyond Supreme Leader Kim Jong-un had ever been seen with such a device. Despite this kind of connection, there has been precious little real opening of the country to the world under the third Kim, who was installed in power after the death of his father Kim Jong-il in 2011. Indeed, in the realm of power politics, the country's acquisition of thermonuclear technologies has seen an ever greater closure of economic and diplomatic relations. However, in the realm of football there was, under both leaders, a flicker of openness and engagement. The men's national team managed to qualify for the 2010 World Cup, and proved so good in their opening game, a narrow defeat against Brazil, that the government permitted, extraordinarily, live coverage of their next game against Portugal, who thrashed them 7–0. The women's national team, in a very rare reversal of priorities, has been accorded at least equal if not greater importance than the men's team, and has duly won three Asian Cups, appeared in two Olympics, won three gold medals at the Asian Games and qualified for the 2011 World Cup. Kim Jong-un has gone so far as to publish a book on the subject (originally a phenomenally long letter to a party sports congress), *Let us Usher in a New Golden Age of Building a Sports Power in the Revolutionary Spirit of Paeltu*, in which he extolled the nation to prioritize football and put it into the service of all manner of revolutionary aims. It might not constitute quite the agenda he outlined, but North Korea under Kim Jong-un has hired its first foreign coaches, and put a lot of world football on its digital TV channels (albeit with a delay of a few days and available to just the elite). He has also permitted a number of promising footballers to play in the lower leagues of Italy, with the usual proviso that the government takes most of their salaries. Little wonder, then, that South Korean President Moon Jae-in, seeking to open new channels of conversation with his recalcitrant neighbour, should propose that they make a joint bid for the 2030 World Cup.[33]

In the 1990s, while other Australian sports professionalized and commercialized, growing richer on the new television technologies and media deals, Australian football, or soccer as it continued to be known, remained their poor relation. Its ruling bodies, Soccer Australia and the National Soccer League (NSL), were a byword for bad governance and political in-fighting. Although the game was steadily becoming the most popular participation sport in the country, this surge of interest could not be converted into a successful commercial spectacle or a successful national team. The NSL struggled to attract mainstream Australian interest, especially in the media, and the Socceroos, as the men's national team were known, had failed to qualify for the World Cup since 1974. For mainstream, read the old Anglo-hegemony that had, since the end of the Second World War, cast the game as 'wogball', the preserve of unstable and unsavoury migrant groups: Italians, Serbs, Croats, Jews and Greeks. In the late 1980s and 1990s there was a concerted but unsuccessful effort within Australian soccer to de-ethnicize the game, by requiring clubs like Sydney's Olympic and Hakoah, and Melbourne's Hellas and Croatia, to change their names, and eradicate other tell-tale symbols of their roots from shirts, crests and branding, but it was met by widespread resistance.

The short-lived multiculturalism of the Australian Labour Party governments of this era, and their acknowledgement to indigenous people of the nation's colonial and genocidal roots, might have begun to change the conversation, but electorally they were soundly defeated. Australian soccer would transmute into its new form under John Howard and the Liberal Party, who would rule Australia for the next decade with a combination of cookie-cutter neo-liberalism and cultural conservatism. The latter rejected multiculturalism in favour of a singular Australian national identity that was a barely updated version of the historically amnesiac, stultifying Anglo-hegemony that had served as the national culture for much of the previous century. In the realm of sport, Howard's presence at the Sydney Olympics sat uneasily with its symbolic messages of aboriginal-Australian reconciliation, and football was simply not on his radar. However, his relationship with both the men's national cricket and rugby teams was close and personal: he was heard to say that the very pinnacle of success for an Australian was to captain the former.

None of this boded well for the old football order in Australia. Indeed, in the long struggle over the governance and marketing of Australian soccer, the government and its agencies could be counted upon to side with the forces of the new commercialism. In 2001, the Ministry of Sport and the Australian Sport Commission (ASC) announced the formation of an inquiry into Australian soccer, led by the reliably commercial accountant David Crawford, whose 1992 report had transformed the governance of Australian rules football.[34] Two years later, the 2003 Crawford Report provided the blueprint for fundamental change in football, and was then imposed, in part, by the ASC's threat of withholding government support from the game. The Socceroos would stay as they were, but Soccer Australia was to be dissolved and reconstituted along global norms as Football Federation Australia. Its internal structure was designed to remove the influence of the old clubs and their political cabals by reserving most power for the executive, and diluting the old opposition by allocating some degree of representation to players and minorities. The NSL was to be dissolved too, and replaced by an eight-franchise A-League, allocated and closely supervised by the FFA. The old ethnic clubs would remain marooned in the suburbs and semi-professional football. Frank Lowy, the billionaire owner of the global chain of Westgate shopping malls, took charge at the new FFA. As the president of one of the few NSL clubs to actually abandon its ethnic name, and long the leading voice in the campaign to transform Australian football, he was the natural political choice, but the aesthetics of his malls – the global gold standard for the commercially anodyne and the upscale bland – was a perfect fit too. The A-League and its franchises' initial names, colours, branding and crests were all centrally supervised and controlled, and designed to appeal to a youthful urban demographic.[35]

Some of the clubs were initially owned by the league, others by rich local business people like Tony Di Pietro at Melbourne Victory or Tony Sage at Perth Glory, who were meant to bring a degree of commercial savvy and probity to the game. However, entrepreneurial success in one realm is no guarantee of competence in football, as Con Constantine, the Greek-Australian retail magnate, so ably demonstrated. In 2008 he added the Newcastle Jets to his roster of local malls, papers and businesses and oversaw a precipitous decline in the club's form, crowned by his championing of an ageing and disinterested Mario Jardel, the much-travelled Brazilian striker, who brought nothing but lassitude to the side. Fan group the Squadron displayed their club banners upside down in protest. Once the security had removed those banners they were replaced with ones saying 'We've been CONned' and, in reference to the team's league position, two-metre-high high wooden spoons. Con invited the leaders into his skybox to discuss the situation and then threatened to throw them over the balcony; the FFA and the A-League revoked his licence. Into the breach stepped Nathan Tinkler, then the youngest billionaire in Australia.

Tinkler's improbable story had begun in 2006 with him scraping together a half-million-dollar loan to get himself a piece of a coalfield. He would sell that coalfield on to McArthur Coal for cash and shares, which by the magic of a stock market asset bubble would turn into a billion-dollar paper fortune. Tinkler's style was to go big.

He did the mansions, the yachts and above all the horses – AUS$150 million blown on thoroughbreds. In this context, his purchase of the Newcastle Jets and the local rugby league team was a mere bagatelle. Two years later Tinkler was running for his natural territory, the bankruptcy courts, as his always speculative empire disintegrated amidst the global downturn. The Jets stopped paying wages and admitted to their debts. The A-League revoked Tinkler's licence while the club played out its worst ever season, rooted to the bottom of the table.

If these kinds of old-school patriarchs and delusional hucksters are a core part of Australia's business class, they have been joined in recent years by a flood of foreign carpetbaggers. David Traktovenko made his money in the wild banking world of Yeltsin's post-Communist Russia, ascending from the *nomenklatura* to the boards of Vyborg-Bank, Promstroy Bank and Zenit St Petersburg FC. When Gazprom decided to take the club over in 2003, he accepted their generous offer and appears to have relocated himself, his reputation and his fortune out of Putin's Russia and headed south, where he bought a big chunk of Sydney FC. In 2008, the Indonesian Bakrie Group, amongst the nation's largest corporations, bought Brisbane Roar. In the usual manner, they promised to make them the biggest and the best. There were flashes of this on the pitch as a well-stocked squad actually challenged for the title in 2015 and 2016. Regular wage payments were rather less frequent. In fact, in 2015 the management were forced to admit, as they once again failed to pay the squad, that the club was AUS$9 million in debt. In early 2018 just 1,279 people showed up to see the biggest and best club in the A-League lose 3–2 to Filipino minnows Ceres-Negro in an AFC Champions League play-off. In 2018 Robert Gerrard, Liberal Party insider and the aged scion of a long-established Australian industrial group, sold Adelaide United to a consortium of anonymous European and Chinese investors improbably fronted by Dutchman Piet van der Pol, also the chair of a tiny Chinese amateur club, Qingdao Red Lions. And to complete the set, the owners without which no league can truly be said to have been sold off to the global super-rich, the Royal House of Abu Dhabi, through their footballing amanuensis City Group, bought Melbourne FC.

The A-League, in its own terms, has been a success. Although it has struggled to find the right balance and distribution of clubs and owners, attendance and television ratings have been respectable and rising, without seriously challenging the country's other professional sports leagues. The 'ethnic' connotations of the NSL and the old soccer have by and large been eradicated from the A-League, though 'ethnic' clubs and fanbases continue to exist in the lower leagues. However, the efforts of the A-League and its brand managers to wholly mould the crowd and the spectacle into the very narrowest of confines has been resisted. Indeed, one of the most successful elements of the A-League has been its capacity to nurture organized singing and chanting groups, in contrast to the atomized tedium of most rugby and cricket games. The Melbourne and Sydney derbies have proved particularly volatile and, for the broadcasters, ratings gold dust. This has never sat easily with the grandees of the Australian sporting press, most of whom, in 2015, applauded the publication in the *Sunday Telegraph*, Rupert Murdoch's local foghorn, of the leaked names and photos of 198 fans banned from A-League grounds. Indeed, it was an opportunity to re-work all the old tropes about football and its fans, the paper describing them as 'grubby pack animals'. The conservative rugby bore and radio host Alan Jones, with his usual nuance, compared their actions to the contemporary Paris jihadi attacks, while the Murdoch press thought them 'suburban terrorists'. This in turn evoked a nationwide boycott of games initiated by the North Terrace, the organized fans at Melbourne Victory, protesting above all about the absence of any appeal system, and the harsh decisions meted out by the A-League. The league was forced to concede at least an appeals procedure.[36]

The viciousness of conservative Australia's attacks on football was driven, at least in part, by the game and its new constituencies proving hard, perhaps impossible, to ideologically co-opt to their agendas.[37] Prior to November 2005 this was a matter of little concern. Cricket, rugby and Olympic gold medals continued to deliver a steady stream of mainstream sporting nationalism on which they could feed. The Socceroos' performances on the global stage were so bad as to be invisible. Then came the final play-off for a place at the 2006 World Cup. Tied 1–1 against Uruguay after extra time, it came down to a penalty shoot-out, won by John Aloisi's strike. For the first time, in an era of global communications, Australia experienced football fever, and Peter Costello, Deputy Leader of the Liberal Party, was keen to stamp his own interpretation on it. In a widely reported speech he claimed:

> A television commentator was moving amongst the crowd. He came across an elderly woman with a heavy accent. He asked her where she came from, and she replied, 'I come from Uruguay to Australia twenty years ago.' The reporter said, 'So you're barracking for Uruguay.' The woman was outraged. 'No!" she yelled back at him, 'I go for Australia!' and looked incensed that he would think otherwise. Whether she went on to say, 'Australia is my country,' I can't be sure, but that is what she meant.[38]

Come the World Cup itself, John Howard got up at 5 a.m. and put on his Socceroos tracksuit to be on television watching television. Crowds near 10,000-strong watched big screens in Sydney and Melbourne. Australia, nearly all of its squad playing outside the country, opened with a 3–1 win over Japan. A draw with Croatia was enough to see them into the last sixteen. There they held out against the Italians for 95 minutes, until finally undone by a bit of old-world trickery: Fabio Grosso's masterly dive delivered a penalty in the fifth minute of added time, scored by Francisco Totti.

However, the Liberal Party's late bid to co-opt football has not been uncontested. Their defeat at the polls in 2007 heralded eight years of Labour governments who would champion the cause of diversity in Australia, and shift the country's entire foreign policy orientation away from the global North and wholeheartedly toward Asia. Football was already heading in that direction. In 2006, anticipating the Gillard Labour government's white paper *Australia in the Asian Century* by some way, the FFA joined the Asian Football Confederation, its clubs made their debut in that year's Asian Champions League, and the men's national team would play their first Asian Cup in 2007.[39] Adelaide United would go on to lose a final of the Champions League in 2008 and Western Sydney Wanderers would win it in 2015. The Socceroos also appeared to find Asia a convivial environment, qualifying for the 2010 and 2014 World Cups; the global environment has proved harsher. In South Africa they didn't make it to the knock-out rounds, and in Brazil they conceded nine goals and lost three games.

Whatever kind of Australia can be gleaned from these experiences it was still an overwhelmingly white, male one. Indigenous

Australians make up around 3 per cent of the country's population, 9 per cent of professional players in Australian Rules Football, and 12 per cent in Rugby League, but less than 1 per cent in football. Jade North, who successfully played in the J. League and the K League as well as for the Socceroos, was the only aboriginal player in the A-League in 2017, in a career that has signalled indigenous Australia's exclusion and potential.[40] The same could be said of the Matildas, the women's national team, who, unlike their male counterparts, and with considerably less support, made the quarter-finals of a World Cup in 2015.[41] Their reward was working conditions and pay rates so poor – including no maternity leave or health care cover – that later that year the squad went on strike before a lucrative US tour. These strands of Australian football culture, of course, have deep historical roots, from the enduring political and cultural invisibility of indigenous Australians to the white majority and football scouts, to the ban on women's football that killed the nascent game dead in the 1920s. The Asian Cup, hosted by Australia in 2015, was perhaps the future.

Almost nothing was spent on infrastructure and, freed from FIFA's Croesian demands, small grounds, even the grass-banked Hunter Stadium in Newcastle, could play host. Ticket prices were kept low. Crowds, even for the most esoteric of encounters, were good. Australia's many Asian migrant communities, from the Japanese to the Palestinians, from the Chinese to Uzbeks, showed up in force, above all the Iranians, whose female-heavy following was dazzlingly attired and very noisy.[42] By contrast, Tony Abbott, the then Liberal Party Prime Minister, and a man who still appeared to believe that Australians were inexorably white and Christian, was booed by the crowd.[43] Australia played South Korea in the final and won 2–1 in extra time. Abbott was toppled from within his own party by Malcolm Turnbull just a few months later.

VI

In the great arc of nations that runs south of China from Burma in the west to the Philippines in the east, football, long popular, has become a much more central component of both popular culture and popular politics. Its relatively slow development can in part be explained by the region's particular pattern of colonial rule. American influence in the Philippines made basketball the leading sport. In Indonesia, the anti-colonial elites of the 1920s and 1930s found badminton more convivial, both socially and ideologically: given the region's long history of shuttlecock games, the sport could be read as indigenous rather than a colonial imposition. The French, holed up in their vast rural tropical plantations rather than in the cities, were late to introduce the game to their Indo-Chinese colony and its peoples. Only in imperial Burma and the Malay States was the British presence sufficient to ignite a significant football culture amongst the locals in the colonial era. Now, half a century since decolonization, and after a near quarter-century of what is nearing saturation satellite television coverage of football, foreign and domestic, the game, amongst the new urban masses and elites alike, has no peer. South East Asian football has not, however, become very much more competitive. It remains the case that, the 1934 Dutch East Indies side apart, not a single nation in the region has qualified for the World Cup or contested an Asian Cup final. Indeed, the two fourth places achieved by the now defunct South Vietnam in 1956 and 1960 remain South East Asia's greatest local success. If the region's football reflects its breakneck encounter with globalization and urbanization, it is also a reasonable pointer to its political pathologies and sometimes vicious internal conflicts.

In Malaysia this colonial legacy was strong enough to make its football team one of the strongest in Asia in the 1970s; the nation's nostalgia dwells on qualifying for the 1972 Olympics, and taking a bronze medal at the 1974 Asian Games. Small beer, perhaps, but, compared to the subsequent decades, during which Malaysia has, except as host, failed to even qualify for the AFC Asian Cup, a golden age. It is the memory of those years, in part, that underlies the nation's fractious relationship with the team, which continues to serve as a barometer of the national mood. Malaysia's victory at the 2010 AFF championship, a biennial tournament for South East Asia alone, saw a very public outpouring of pleasure and celebration.[44] By the same token, when the national team lost 10–0 to the UAE in a World Cup qualifier in 2015, one opinion column thought it a national disaster aligned with the then precipitous collapse in the value of the national currency: 'This is a new all-time low in our football history. We don't need another new low, because that news angle has become repetitive through the updates of our *ringgit*'s value these days.'[45] Similar angst had accompanied a 1–1 draw with the micro-state of Timor Leste and a 6–0 thrashing by Palestine, but the *Ultras Malaya* responded to the UAE game even more directly than the press. At the next qualifying game, played against Saudi Arabia, *Ultras Malaya* displayed a banner saying, 'FAM: Sleeping for 31 years', a reference to the thirty-one years that members of the Royal House of Penang had been running the national football association, and then rioted, throwing dozens of flares and bucket seats onto the pitch and roughing up a few visiting fans.[46]

An even greater level of disorder has broken out in domestic football, where most of the leading clubs have acquired their own ultra groups: the *Elephant Army* at Padang, the *Bos Gaurus Mob* at Perak, *Ultras Kelata* at Kelatan, and *GB 13* in Sarawak in Borneo.[47] Recent fights that have made the news include the league game between Johnor Darul Ta'zim (JDT) and Padang MSL in 2014 and the Kuala Lumpur–Perak quarter-final of the 2016 Cup, both notable for large-scale brawling inside and outside the stadiums.[48] However, perhaps more illustrative of the mood on the terraces, and their almost ubiquitous disorder, is a 2015 survey of fans from four of the largest clubs. Not unusually, 68 per cent admitted to making obscene gestures during the game but, indicative of the scale and frequency of disorder in Malaysian football, over half said they had damaged public property during a game, nearly 40 per cent had been involved in fighting, and one in ten had lit flares or fireworks.[49]

If Malaysia's claim to a golden football age was never more than gilding, Burma really could look back on a period of strong school- and youth-level football and reasonable international sporting achievement: two golds in the Asian Games in 1966 and 1970, runners-up in the 1968 Asian Cup, and the fondly remembered fair play award at the 1972 Munich Olympics. However, as the country's economic and social fabric unravelled, strained by the long-term impact of harsh military rule and international isolation, results went the same way. In fact, they went so far in that direction that, to save embarrassment, the national team was withdrawn from even trying to qualify for the Asian Cup until the mid-1990s. Even then, the regime were taking no chances in friendlies and local tournaments, ordering national television to pull the plug on live coverage of a 5–0 slaughter by Indonesia in 1999.

If the military regime was sensitive to the negative political consequences of football, it remained eager to reap its potential benefits, all the more so in the twenty-first century as, under increasing domestic and international political pressure, it contemplated a shift in governance that relied less on force and more on quiescence if not consent, however it might be manufactured. Domestic football, long neglected by the government, and played by miserably funded parastatal clubs like Forestry, Central Supply and Transport, and Finance and Revenue, didn't appear to offer much potential, but foreign football looked intriguing. In 2009, General Than Shwe, head of the junta, at the insistence of his grandson, explored the possibility of the Burmese state purchasing Manchester United, but concluded that in the devastating wake of Cyclone Nargis, the billion dollars it was going to cost might 'look bad'.[50] Thus the junta, instead of reviving and reshaping the old or buying into a global brand, chose to launch an entirely new league. In keeping with its broader mode of governance, it did so with the collaboration of the leading magnates and businessmen who depended on them for contracts and concessions. Each was required to pay $200,000 for the privilege of running a new club, and expected to cover its costs with wage bills that attracted not only the best local players but also Cameroonians, Argentinians and Ivorians.

Zaw Zaw, head of the Myanmar Football Federation (MFF) and the new Myanmar National League (MNL), also ran Max Myanmar, a company with extensive interests in jade mining and rubber plantations. Yangon United were allocated to Tay Za, head of the Htoo Group, whose logging divisions were responsible for vast swathes of deforestation in Karan state, and whose construction arm was building much of the junta's new capital city, Naypyidaw. Magway FC went to the conglomerate Asia World, founded by the late heroin lord Lo Hsing Han, and currently in the hands of Tun Myint Naing. Both he and Za were on the US sanctions lists for suspected narcotics trading and money-laundering.[51] Eden Group, the nation's leading operator of hotels and international resorts, found room for Delta United in a portfolio that also included golf courses and uranium prospecting. South Myanmar United was backed by the Yuzana corporation and its owner Htay Myint, a real estate tycoon with a taste for illegal land grabs, facilitated by close personal ties to the regime's second-in-command General Maung Aye.[52]

In its first season, the MNL appeared to be a success. It was sponsored by the Japanese firm Canon, it certainly boasted the biggest crowds domestic football had seen in a long time, and that with ticket prices set at half a day's average wage. While some were prepared to pay up, much of the crowd was there on free tickets given away by the companies, some of which also gave their staff time off to go to games. By 2012 the numbers had already halved as the curious gave up, and then they dropped again. This left crowds as small as 1,000 people in cavernous stadiums, matched if not outnumbered by soldiers and assorted policing personnel. Matters were not helped by the precarious security situation in much of the country as the military pursued its long and bitter conflicts with the nation's ethnic minorities in Rakhine, Shan and Kachin states, restricting most clubs and matches to stadiums in Yangon. Listen hard enough and a hint of dissent could be registered as crowds there told Yangon United's owner, Tay Za, what a shitty airline he ran.

The transition to a civilian and democratic regime began in late 2011, when the National League for Democracy (NLD), winners of the 2010 elections under Aung San Suu Kyi, finally assumed power. It has not proved a convivial environment for the general's footballing project. In the first place, the kinds of insider influence and natural resources concessions that came with backing a club have now evaporated. Secondly, the previous regime's generous allocation of public grounds and stadiums to their teams has been challenged by newly assertive local governments, which have insisted on the clubs either paying some rent, allowing access to their facilities to other clubs or, best of all, just leaving. As one campaigner trying to eject Nay Pyi Taw FC from their city put it, 'Paung Laung Stadium was not built by a government: it was built in 1973 by the people of Pyinmana with their own money. Since the government seized the stadium and gave it to the club, residents have not had a stadium.'[53] The owner of Manwmyay FC, U Zahkung Ting Ying, a general in the notoriously corrupt border guard force, closed his team in a fit of pique after local people failed to support him in national elections. Or, as the club manager put it, albeit less candidly, 'the owners were disappointed when the people spoke ill of them.'

While the NLD governments have presided over a marginally

more plural and less repressive Myanmar, this has not applied to the country's peripheries, especially to the Muslim Rohingya communities of Rakhine state. In response to raids on border posts by Rohingya insurgents, many based over the border in Bangladesh in the already large refugee camps, the military unleashed a long campaign of ethnic cleansing, driving hundreds of thousands of people from their homes. The Malaysian national team initially refused to play Myanmar in protest, only relenting under threat of suspension from international football.[54] Kyrgyzstan did actually cancel a game in protest, and the nation's Iranian *futsal* coach resigned. The genocidal campaign continued nonetheless.

Although Thailand's billionaires have hitherto concentrated their footballing energies overseas, both Thaksin Shiniwatra's dalliance with Manchester City and Vichai Srivaddhanaprabha's occupation of Leicester City were ultimately directed towards domestic audiences and domestic politics. However, for those with smaller fortunes, Thai domestic football has retained sufficient public interest to remain attractive. Bangkok's biggest club, Muangthong United, rose to prominence on the money of Rawi Lohtong, owner of the huge media corporation Siam Sport Syndicate.[55] Yet the most successful team in contemporary Thai football, Buriram United, is from one of the country's poorest regions, 500 miles north of Bangkok near the Cambodian border. Created in 2010, they won their first national title in 2012, then beat the Japanese and Chinese champions in their first stab at the Asian Champions League, made the quarter-finals of the competition in 2014, and have won four out of the last five Thai titles. They are the invention of owner, chairman and all-round impresario Newin Chidchob, who bought a little-known club called PEA (Provincial Electrical Authority) and then relocated it to his political stronghold, the provincial city of Buriram. Previously a local MP, he was a close ally of Thaksin, but on his patron's demise was agile enough to switch sides and survive. He was then excluded from parliament having been convicted of electoral malpractice, but remained the de facto leader of the Bhumjaithai Party and its thirty-four MPs. Even so, this left him more time for football and local politics; as one candidate said, 'Eighty per cent of the 70,000 fans in the town would vote for Newin's party.'[56] Chidchob not only invested in the squad but also built a new stadium, known as 'Thunder Castle', and, though there are plenty of free tickets and noodles, they are the best supported side in the country. Maybe Chidchob is moving on from politics? His personal team talks to the squad on the pitch before every match suggest a taste for coaching. The addition of a Buriram United-themed hotel and Castle Mall motorsport track to the city suggest a chain of theme parks awaits.

Chidchob, whatever his ulterior motives, actually put something into Thai football. The same cannot be said for Worawi Makudi, who, until his demise in 2015, had ruled Thai football for almost two decades, and with whom the traffic was all one way. His larceny was an open secret in Thailand. When in 2014 a petition of 10,000 signatures was presented to the Thai junta asking for his removal as president of the Football Association of Thailand (FAT) they were minded to do so, but for FIFA's threat of suspension for 'government interference'. The charge sheet was long: the FIFA money intended to develop women's football, for example, never made it to the women's game. Indeed, the Thai women's national team only survived on subventions from the well-connected and well-heeled Democratic Party politician Nualphan 'Madam Pang' Lamsan. When FIFA gave FAT the money to build a new football development centre it transpired that the land it would be built on was owned by Worawi's family. FIFA made him transfer the land to FAT, but he remained a director of the company contracted to build the centre. When Malaysia played Thailand in the 2014 AFF Cup, FAT sold around 45,000 tickets at 100–500 bahts a piece, not to mention collecting TV rights and sponsorship money, but only declared an income of just 46,000 bahts from the game. Do the maths! Worawi Makudi certainly did; like the time he assigned 60 per cent of the shares in Thai Premier League to himself and 13 per cent to his general secretary. Sometimes he was less generous. When discussing his vote for the 2018 World Cup hosting rights with the then FA chairman, Lord Triesman, he is said to have requested the TV rights for an England–Thailand friendly all for himself. He was finally removed from office in 2015 when a court in Bangkok found him guilty of forging documents during his presidential re-election campaign, and gave him a sixteen-month suspended jail sentence. FIFA, as ever trailing in the wake of others, suspended him and the rest of the FAT executive committee later in the year.[57]

In the ensuing and bitterly contested elections to replace them, the still active Worawi camp put up Charnwit Polcheewin against the candidate of the junta, the media, Newin Chidchob, Vichai Srivaddhanaprabha and pretty much everybody else, retired police chief Somyot Poompanmoung. If there was any doubt about Polcheewin's status as a mere proxy, this ended when it was revealed that he had had a 'chance' meeting with Worawi (banned from any football activity by FIFA) during the campaign. By the same token, if there was any doubt that Poompanmoung was there on the basis of his political rather than his football credentials, this ended when it became clear his main experience in sports administration was a two-year presidency of the Thai bowls association. Poompanmoung won the vote 64–4, and has so far presided over a Thai league and a men's national team that are beginning to achieve their potential; a turn of events that suggests, for the moment, that the poorer an administrator's 'football credentials', the better their governance.

Given how endemic corruption had been within the Vietnamese Communist Party and its state agencies, it would take a really exceptional scandal for a member of the politburo to actually step down, even when transparently exposed. In 2006, football delivered precisely that when the Minister of Transport Dao Dinh Binh resigned and his deputy Nguyen Viet Tien was arrested, both accepting responsibility for endemic corruption in their own department: in particular, the fact that over 200 civil servants had embezzled $4 million-worth of aid money from Japan and the World Bank and blown the lot gambling on European football.[58] The scandal broke when a senior manager in the ministry, But Tien Dung, confessed to the police after he had gone on a catastrophic losing streak, burning $1 million in total, including a losing $180,000 bet on a Manchester United–Arsenal game and $150,000 blown on Barcelona v Real Betis. He was not alone in raiding the aid kitty for these purposes, but he was the most senior, responsible for 70 per cent of Vietnam's transport budget, little of which seemed to be finding its way to the country's pot-hole-ridden highways. Much of it ended up in the hands of illegal bookmakers who did not resign. Indeed, they have become ever richer and, according to the local police, were taking tens of millions of dollars' worth of bets a day during the 2014 World Cup, making it a multi-billion-dollar business.

The nationwide compulsion to bet on international football has not been matched by any compulsion to bet on, attend or even take note of domestic football. The V. League, professionalized and re-organized in 2000, has struggled to attract crowds, loyalty and interest. The arrival of corporate sponsorship, both foreign and from within Vietnam's new class of connected business people, has not invigorated the league. Perhaps more than in any other nation in the region, the lure of the EPL has significantly dented local football's appeal. As one visitor reported,

> When I tell a friend I'm going to watch Hanoi T&T FC play he offers up a derisory snort. A local mechanic shakes his head and mutters something in a tone that suggests derision, a bartender laughs at me. Vietnam is a football-mad nation, but ask a Viet-namese person if they follow a team here and they blush.[59]

For those who did make it to Hanoi T&T FC, there was no short-age of Premier League replica shirts for sale. In 2011, Nguyen Du'c Kien, a billionaire banker and owner of Hanoi ACB FC, went public with the criticism that everybody knew, but did not voice: the V. League was a disaster characterized by dismal levels of play, very poor refereeing, insultingly obvious forms of match-fixing and a stitch-up of a TV deal that had given the state broadcaster carte blanche for two decades.[60] The following year, eight of the leading clubs, under Nguyen's leadership, broke away to create a new league independent of the Vietnamese Football Federation. Initially success-ful, the league has since been effectively reincorporated into the VFF and placed back under state control. No coincidence then that Nguyen Du'c Kien, despite all his money, is now sitting in jail con-victed of fraud and tax evasion.[61]

Vietnam's problems with match-fixing predate the V. League. In 1997, for example, seven players at Ho Chi Minh City Customs, then Vietnam's national champions, were arrested, charged and eventu-ally found guilty of match-fixing. The investigation was triggered by the sight of the goalkeeper running full pelt for the halfway line, while one of his defenders, by then twenty metres behind him, belted the ball into his own net. Since then, and despite repeated investiga-tions, prosecutions and harsh jail sentences, the fixers have been busy, and have found no shortage of accomplices: from the national team players who threw matches at the 2005 South East Asian games to almost an entire club's worth at Vissai Binh Minh, who consequently actually withdrew from the V. League in 2014. Since the turn of the century not a season has passed without obvious cases of corruption and another squad in court. It has all been to no avail. In 2016, during a game between Ho Chi Minh and Long An, with the score at 2–2, late in the match, Nguyen Minh Nhut, the goalkeeper of Long An, responded to yet another obviously fallacious penalty call by turning his back on the spot and allowing Ho Chi Minh a free shot. Another goal followed from the restart as the rest of the squad stood still while Ho Chi Minh moved the ball forward. In a theatrical twist, Nguyen somersaulted over the ball as it headed for the net.[62] Inevitably both the Ministry of Sport and the VFF thought to punish Long An; the referee, who had effectively gifted Ho Chi Minh's first two goals as well, was left untouched.

The same cannot be said for Non-U FC, the one club in Vietnamese football the authorities do not seem able to break or bend to their will.[63] Not that Non-U FC are playing in the V. League: indeed, they are not in any league at all, and struggle to finish a ninety-minute game. The team was formed in 2011 amongst a small group of dissidents who had attempted to protest over what they saw as the government's supine attitude to China's aggressive territorial claims in the South China Sea. The small protests they conducted were broken up, and attempts to re-group in cafes or restaurants were met with refusals from worried staff, or harassment from the police. For many of the dissidents the football pitch seemed a better alternative and the club was launched on Facebook, announcing its games, often just practices, at obscure locations and at the last minute. Non-U, emblazoned on their black-and-white shirts, referred to the U-shaped line the Chinese have drawn in the South China Sea demarcating their territorial waters, a line much contested by all of its maritime neighbours. FC, testament to the globalization of English, stands for both 'Football Club' and the team's favourite chant, 'Fuck China'.

Relentlessly pursued by the police and the secret services, the club has engaged in an elaborate game of cat and mouse with the authorities. A team from Petrovietnam, a state company that was challenging China by drilling for oil in the South China Sea, were initially prepared to play them, but the offer evaporated when pressure was applied. Some sanctuary has been available at the football grounds of the military, an organization considerably more anti-Chinese than the party, but for the most part the club has constantly had to find new pitches on which to play after owners have been

pressed into refusing them access and, when they do find somewhere, playing just part of a game before the uniformed cops storm
the pitch. Undaunted, team members, which include poets, bankers,
bloggers, students and folk musicians, have endured losing their
jobs, divorce and imprisonment for their football politics, but, as
blogger Le Gia Khannh argued, 'The team exists to prove that the fire
in our hearts is still alive.'[64] It has also offered a working model
of dissent, and provided practical support to dozens of new citizen
initiatives in Vietnam, from rural farmers illegally displaced by development to urban preservationists protesting the destruction of
ancient trees on the city's boulevards: the sort of political and social
projects that are becoming the backbone of the country's emergent
civil society. As Non-U FC's captain put it, 'People don't feel scared
playing soccer.'[65]

Across the vast oceanic archipelago of Indonesia, the fourth most
populous nation on the planet, football mania rages through its over
a quarter of a billion people: 'Football is everywhere in Indonesia: in
the streets, in the bars, in narrow alleys, in grand and packed stadiums, and in the shabby empty lots of urban decay.'[66] The national
team's televised games, despite often pitiful performances, have
attracted audiences of up to 100 million. The fever is so hot that,
despite an almost universal interest in European football bordering
on the obsessive, the domestic game attracts the largest crowds in
the region and has spawned Asia's most intense ultra fan culture. At
the same time the actual level of play is dismal, a level of underperformance only exceeded by the self-serving incompetence of the
people running Indonesian football. At the turn of the century, the
dream team at Indonesia's football association, the PSSI (Perserika-
tan Sepak Bola Indonesia), was President Nurdin Halid and Vice-
President Nirwan Bakrie. Both were prominent members of Golkar,
the party that had served President Suharto's murderous regime so
faithfully, and that since his downfall had carried the flag for those
that had benefited most from the era's corruption and clientelism.
Halid spent most of his presidency running the PSSI from a prison
cell, having been convicted on a variety of charges of corruption; a
fate that would also befall his brother for illegally streaming World
Cup games on his cable channel network, and his PSSI treasurer
buddy Joseph Revo, who beat his wife to death with a laptop computer.[67] Not that this prevented Halid from syphoning off PSSI funds,

decimating what few football development programmes were in place, and running a league beset by administrative and financial incompetence.

In 2011, the Ministry of Sport, despite FIFA's best efforts, forced Halid out, only for Indonesian football to then descend into civil war. The first salvo came from the camp of Vice-President Nirwan Bakrie and his brother Abruzial Bakrie who, amongst his many roles, was the chairman of the Golkar party and a likely candidate for the presidential election in 2014. Through careful husbandry of the industrial estate bequeathed to him by his father, one of Suharto's leading cronies, he was also the richest businessman in Indonesia. In an effort to take charge of Indonesian football, financially and politically, the Bakries backed a breakaway. For two years there were two football associations (PSSI and KSSI), two football leagues (the Indonesian Super League and the Indonesian Premier League), two national teams and, in the case of the Yogyakarta club, Persebaya, there were two teams (Persebaya Surabaya and Persebaya 1927) in the two different leagues, supported by two, now bitterly opposed, sets of ultras (*Bonek* and *Bonek 1927*). As with all civil wars, the consequences were disastrous, audiences plummeted and sponsorship deals collapsed. In 2013, when it became apparent that Bakrie's run for the presidency was clearly doomed, agreement was reached to merge the leagues. In 2014 they actually played a whole uninterrupted season. In 2015 they managed two weeks of play before the sports ministry brought it to a grinding halt, on the grounds that many of the clubs were financially incapable of surviving the year or paying their staff.

A few weeks later, matters came to an extraordinary head at an extraordinary congress of the PSSI held in the East Javanese city of Surabaya.[68] 1,500 riot police were deployed around the Marriott Hotel, where they were met by 10,000 football ultras, led by the *Bonek*. They called for the resignation of the association president La Nyalla Mattalitti, who was also the part owner of the other Persebaya club, the integration of their own club into the new league, and for national president Joko Widodo to extend his programme of reform – what he often called 'an end to the old ways' – to one of the old way's greatest redoubts, Indonesian football. Inside the hotel, La Nyalla's coronation as chair of the PSSI suggested business as usual, and he blithely announced that the league would resume.

However, before the high court in Jakarta could resolve the Ministry v PSSI dispute, FIFA finally stepped in, banned the nation from international football, and gave them another year to sort it all out. The league finally resumed in 2017, and the PSSI acquired a new president, Lieutenant General Edy Rahmayadi, previously commander of the army reserves, and an ally of President Widodo. He at least has brought a note of realism to the post, announcing on election that 'The PSSI will start not from zero, but even less than that.'[69]

One of the many things in the general's in-tray was Indonesian football's growing reputation for protest, disorder and violence. The small NGO, Save our Soccer Indonesia, has recorded sixty-five football-related deaths since 1994, eleven in 2017 alone.[70] The list consists of the usual gruesome mixture of manslaughters and homicides, resulting from tear-gas-catalysed crushes and stampedes, vicious bar and roadside knife fights, stone-throwing and concussions; all the product of the interaction of unhinged ultra cultures and semi-militarized police forces, in a context of pervasive urban discontent and political manipulation.[71] Ultra culture can be traced back to the 1980s in Persebaya, where the *Bonek* first emerged. There an existing network of small fan clubs called *laskars* had begun to fuse. Already adept at hitching rides en masse to away games, or jumping trains and riding rooftop if necessary, and storming turnstiles, they were named by the papers the *Bonek*, loosely translated as 'the lawless'. The groups, in touch with global football culture, began to take on the characteristic features of European ultra groups: the claiming of specific stadium space, a wild outbreak of football graffiti and street art in the city, the emergence of a hierarchy of organizers, and the execution of choreographed displays and relentless chanting. To this they added the local political practice of occupying urban space and advertising one's presence by arriving at games in a cavalcade of motorbikes and flags.

The *Bonek* were almost exclusively male and, although the group included students and activists, the mania and the numbers came from the urban poor. Indonesia's pattern of industrialization has increased their number and housed them, in city after city, in vast informal settlements and poor peripheries. The same demographic that swelled the ranks of *Boneks* have become the *Ultras Persib* in Bandung, *Ultras 1950* in Medan and the *Brajamusti* supporters of

Yogyakarta's PSIM, whose name refers to the chosen, pike-like weapon of Ghatotkaca, a warrior with super-hero powers of invisibility and size-changing who featured in the Hindu epic the *Mahabharata*. Amongst the most notorious of the groups have been *Jakmania*, the ultras of Persiaj, Jakarta's biggest club. In 2016, for example, sixteen-year-old fan Muhammed Fahreza died outside the stadium during Persiaj's game against Persela Lamonga. He was one of the thousands who gather close to the locked gates waiting for *jebolan*: the moment, normally at the end of half-time, when the police open the gates again and allow the ticketless a slice of time inside. The authorities believed he died in the stampede, but social media blazed with rumours of police brutality. The club's next home game against Sriwijaya was abandoned after a late goal for the visitors ignited a fusillade of firecrackers from the ultras in protest. The police responded with tear gas, and many fans, led by *Jakmania*, headed over the advertising boards and onto the pitch.

In all of this, the Indonesian ultras movement is a complex collective act of resistance and a challenge to the exercise of authority in Indonesia, particularly the authority of the police, the army and the football federation, all of which, since the fall of Suharto, have been amongst the most unreformed of Indonesia's institutions. Driven by an intoxicating mix of nihilism, adrenaline and hyper-masculinity, it is closer to an act of self-harm than a real threat to the dominant order. However, in Surabaya, amongst the ultras of *Bonek 27*, a different kind of football politics has been nurtured. Forced into real political action by the division of the national leagues and then the club itself, many found themselves debating, networking and organizing in Warkop Pitulikur, a cheap noodle bar with a very big television permanently tuned to the football. Here, in the closest thing Indonesia has to the coffee bars of Red Vienna, food, football and politics have enriched each other. In opposition they have begun to forge alliances with other ultra groups, arguing successfully that the PSSI is the main problem in everyone's lives, and to take real political action, petitioning and pressing President Jokowi to make good on his promise of reform.[72] However, as with the president's attempt to reform the Indonesian state, there has been plenty of push back. In 2017 the ultras' leading spokesperson Saleh Ismail Mukadar was making the groups' case live on local television, when he was verbally and then physically assaulted by members of Pemuda

Pancasila, the nationalist boy scout movement that, back in the day, provided Suharto with so much thuggery. The assailants remain at large. There will be more of this to come.

VII

The isolated islands of Polynesia and Micronesia are perhaps weaker football nations but, per capita head, nowhere underperforms like South Asia. In 2018 the region's minnows – Bhutan, Nepal, the Maldive Islands and Sri Lanka – stood at 196th, 174th, 156th and 198th respectively in the FIFA men's world rankings. India, nearly a fifth of humanity, had crawled its way to 105th, though its average ranking over the last two decades has been 133rd. Some of this can be explained by the popularity of cricket which, since the arrival of the short-format one-day game and satellite television, has become the uncontested national sport and commercial spectacle of modern South Asia. However, football has been a significant presence within the sporting landscape of the region since the late nineteenth century. In regional and urban enclaves the game, both amateur and semi-professional, remained popular throughout the twentieth century and, while the digital media spaces of the twenty-first were saturated with cricket, they also opened up the worlds of European and global football to a new audience that has been growing rapidly. Not enough to win the World Cup, perhaps, but surely more than enough for Pakistan (201st in the FIFA rankings; population 193 million) to do better than Monserrat (200th in the FIFA rankings; population 4,900). The region has no monopoly, inside or outside football, on systemic corruption in dysfunctional public institutions, but it has been making a serious bid for the top end of the league.

Football in the Maldives, for the four years between 2012 and 2016, was entirely consumed by political infighting. Internal conflict had delayed new presidential elections for two years, after which FIFA installed a 'normalization committee' to run the association instead, and to redraft its statutes and hold elections. Stability at the top was not, as the Sri Lankan experience suggests, a guarantee of good governance. The man in charge of the Football Federation of Sri Lanka (FFSL) for almost three decades was Vernon Manilal

Fernando, who graduated from local graft to executive positions at both AFC and FIFA. In 2011, two of the country's leading investigative journalists argued that, despite the $7 million received by the FFSL from FIFA for football development, and the $3.5 million given in the aftermath of the 2004 tsunami, the organization had failed to produce any tangible football initiatives or relief efforts, and that not incidentally the actual destination of those monies could not be traced. Indeed, despite this largesse, Sri Lanka's world ranking had continued to decline. Only a single player was good enough to play outside of the country, and then only in the Maldives, while the national team remained without a national stadium of international standards. Fernando was banned from football by FIFA in 2013 for taking AFC President Mohammed Bin Hammam's dollars in the run-up to the 2011 FIFA presidential election. His departure appears to have made little difference. Sri Lanka's world ranking dropped as low as 194th. In 2015, a series of investigations by Sri Lanka's sports ministry revealed that another half million dollars given by various other charities to the victims of the tsunami had been misappropriated by the FFSL; so too a quarter of a million dollars given by the AFC to Sri Lanka for staging tournaments.

A similar script played itself out in Nepal. When asked how the devastating 2015 earthquake would affect the country's football, the vice-president of the All Nepali Football Association (ANFA), Karma Tsering Sherpa, tartly replied, 'Nepali football is more impacted by corruption than the earthquake.'[73] In a series of letters written to FIFA in 2013 and 2014, Sherpa had alerted the organization to the ANFA's recently failed financial audit, the swarm of unaccountable cash movements flying through its bank accounts, and the failure of the president, Ganesh Thapa, to call a general assembly of the organization since 2012. FIFA conspicuously failed to act on any of these warnings, leaving it to the Nepali public accounts committee to force Thepa out in 2013, having accused him of embezzling $5.8 million from ANFA. FIFA's ethics committee eventually banned him from the game in 2015 for having 'committed various acts of misconduct over several years, including the solicitation and acceptance of cash payments from another football official, for both personal and family gain.' Or in layperson's terms, for taking bribes from Mohammed Bin Hammam in the run-up to the 2009 AFC and 2011 FIFA presidential elections.[74] The local press reported that Thapa had, nonetheless, retained his parking spot at the ANFA headquarters, where the current president Narenda Shesthra is considered a straw man. Whatever his influence now, Thapa's magnificent legacy, after almost two decades in charge of the game, remains undiminished: the grassroots of Nepali football was so impoverished that in 2015 one district football association staged a tournament, but announced they were doing it with their last functioning ball.

In Bangladesh, Kazi Salahuddin has been running the national football federation for a decade. An ex-player, elected in 2008 on an anti-corruption ticket, he proved adept at securing himself further sinecures within the web of regional and global football governance. The development of Bangladeshi football proved less of a priority. In 2016, on the eve of a new round of presidential elections at the Bangladeshi Football Federation (BFF), an organization called Save Football, backed by dozens of retired international players and administrators, campaigned for Salahuddin's removal. Amongst the long list of complaints were his failure to have a development plan of any kind, let alone implement one, and widespread financial irregularities in the running of the BFF. Needless to say, Salahuddin denied everything, and then won a third term in office. Six months later Bangladesh lost to Bhutan 3–1 in a qualifying play-off for the Asian Cup, a defeat so humiliating that fans gathered at the BFF headquarters with placards like 'BFF is rotten, football is dead' and, in reference to the country's vertiginous fall down the FIFA world rankings, 'Congratulations Salahuddin, we are heading towards 200.'[75]

Pakistan had made it there before them, and no one is more responsible for this than Faisal Saleh Hayat.[76] President of the Pakistan Football Federation (PFF) since 2003, he was also the *Saijad Nasheen*, a hereditary aristocratic title that made him the custodian of a Sufi shrine in the Punjab. While this continues to generate a steady stream of tax-free cash from pilgrims and the pious, and a solid local vote bank, shrines ain't what they used to be. Thus, in addition to his occasional ritual duties, Hayat has devoted most of his energies to politics, a considerably more profitable line of business for those like himself nimble enough to survive: in 1999, his support for the new military junta would earn him a decade's worth of senior ministerial posts. Somehow, along the way, he found the time to run Pakistani football and, since being ousted from the cabinet, has appeared more eager than ever to retain this sinecure. His political enemies had other ideas and, with the tacit support of the government sports ministry and sports board, an anti-Hayat faction began to coalesce in Pakistani football.

In 2015, in an opening strike, Ali Haider Noor Khan Niazi, an MP from the governing party, filed papers to stand for the presidency of the Punjabi regional FA. Given the support offered by other government loyalists and the Pakistan sports board to his candidacy he was an obvious challenger to Hayat and his candidate Saradar Naveed. In a move typical of Hayat's mode of rule, the PFF rejected Niazi's application on the grounds that he could not 'establish his football credentials': a criterion that, had it been systematically applied to the PFF, would have emptied its upper echelons entirely. Undeterred, the pro-government faction then found new challengers to Saradar Naveed, but lost the election when eight of their number had their votes discounted for having participated in a short-lived occupation of the PFF's offices after Niazi's candidature had been rejected. Both factions then held separate congresses, both claimed they had a quorum, and both elected a President of the PFF. After a dozen visits by all sides to the Lahore High Court, the elections were declared null and void, and a senior judge was installed as the administrator in temporary charge of the PFF. FIFA, eager as ever to support an incumbent, however incompetent or venal, accepted the high court's administrator but, rather than installing a normalization committee with more neutral figures in place to establish some semblance of governance, they gave Hayat and his friends a two-year deadline to sort out the PFF's constitution and hold fresh elections.

If nothing else, the delay has provided time for the scale of the organization's larceny to be revealed in a series of reports on the fate of the projects funded by FIFA's Goal development programme.[77] Of these, the only one that had actually been completed was the PFF's own headquarters in Lahore, and half of that had been rented out to a foreign corporation. The Hawkes Bay technical centre, funded by FIFA in 2006 and a decade in the making, was designed to house and train the national teams, but by 2016 all that could be found was an incomplete concrete hexagon topped by a stone football. Grass, water, pitches and people were thinner on the ground. No national team has ever trained there. At Quetta, lodgings and a canteen had been completed, but there was no playing field of any kind;

at the Abbottabad training facility there was a football pitch, but not, however, any water or electrical supply. The $650,000 given by the AFC in 2010 to build a training centre in Punjab had produced precisely nothing. Burdened, no doubt, by the Herculean task of holding clean elections, the PFF and organized football have effectively ground to a halt. The national team ceased to play international matches of any kind in early 2016, the national league was cancelled and has yet to recommence. Hayat has since survived a car crash, government pressure and a devastating majority vote by his board to remove him from his post. FIFA finally suspended Pakistan from international football, but Hayat, although unlikely to recover, has yet to be run out of town.

Cricket is king in India, the biggest matches, especially against Pakistan, attracting audiences close to half a billion people. However, in the new India Bihari sharecroppers, even Dalits can watch the national team in the Cricket World Cup on a flat-screen television and feel part of the imagined community. Thus, amongst the new and status-conscious elites of its exploding global cities, Delhi, Mumbai and Chennai, the embrace of foreign football in general, and the English Premier League in particular, has become a new marker of aspiration and differentiation. They are, however, just a small part of a hitherto subterranean, but extensive Indian football culture.

Competitive football, even professional competition, has a long history in India, stretching back to late nineteenth-century Calcutta, but both before and after independence it was a regionally concentrated phenomenon, confined primarily to Bengal, Goa and Kerala. National-level governance and competition in football was dogged by the political infighting and antiquated transport infrastructure of Congress's India. It was as late as 1996 that the All India Football Federation (AIFF) created a national league, and only in 2007 when it rebranded the hapless competition as the I-League that it acquired even a modicum of regular TV coverage. However, the state of the league's pitches, and thus the quality of much of the play, was dismal. Games were increasingly scheduled during the day and mid-week, so as not to clash with the best of European football, ensuring impossible conditions, small crowds and bankrupt clubs: a combination that drove the venerable sides of Maharashtra, JCT and Mahindra United to close down altogether. By 2013 the league's own broadcasters had decided it wasn't worth showing the opening games of the season, and the *Economic Times* wrote of the I-League, 'it might as well be happening on Mars.'

In a reprise of much of India's recent pattern of economic development, in which a sclerotic state was regularly bypassed by an altogether more dynamic private sector, it responded to the dilemmas of professionalizing and commercializing league football not by reforming the old, but by outflanking it. Thus, in 2013, the AIFF, the global sports marketing group IMG, and Indian industrial conglomerate Reliance – all previously supporters of the I-League – created the Indian Super League (ISL). Lexically and institutionally modelled on cricket's phenomenally successful Indian Premier League (IPL), the ISL was a made for television spectacle: an eight-team competition maniacally played at TV prime time night after night through the last quarter of the year, the I-League's off season.[78]

Not that any I-League clubs were going to be allowed in: rather the ISL offered its teams as ten-year franchises for $25 million a pop, and cultivated three constituencies that would ensure, if not the league's success, then a few years of blanket media coverage. Cricketers have been prominent, including three ex-captains of the national team: Sachin Tendulkar taking part ownership of the Kerala Blasters, Sourav Ganguly at Atletico Kolkata, and MS Dhoni at Chennaiyan. They have been joined by a raft of Bollywood stars, producers and fixers: heart-throb John Abraham took on North East United himself, actor Hrithki Roshan bought into Pune City, while Chiranjeevi, an old-school screen idol and regional politician, bought into Kerala. Money came in the shape of companies like GMS Shipping, owners of Delhi Dynamos, and industrialists like Nimmagadda Prasd at Kerala, and Jaydev Modi, the casino king of Goa. Wages by global standards were modest, but enough to bring in an eclectic if elderly selection of stars like Alessandro Del Piero, Nicolas Anelka, Robert Pires, Freddie Ljungberg, David Trezeguet and Diego Forlan. In an opening ceremony, unique to Indian football, the ISL was launched with the presentation of owners and coaches, to a crowd that cheered wildly at the improbable sight of Sachin Tendulkar and David James jogging out together in the kit of the Kerala Blasters. In its first week in 2014 the ISL pulled in over 50 million viewers, within sight of the figures recorded by cricket's IPL, and more than fifteen times the size of the best I-League audiences ever. The numbers fell and settled around 11 million, but that, alongside average crowds of 27,000 – albeit considerably padded out by the widespread release of free tickets – was considered an enormous success.

Intended, at least according to its sponsors, as a complement to the I-League, and a way of raising the profile of the game as a whole in India, the ISL has merely made the inadequacies of the old order clear: poor infrastructure, very poor marketing, and no televisual appeal. The debate has now become how the two can be merged, and on what terms. What the I-League does have, at least at some clubs, is an entrenched local following that doesn't need cricket stars or fireworks to show up to a game. In Kolkata, both Mohun Bagan and Mohammedan Sporting East still draw large crowds, and remain closely bound to their respective Hindu and Muslim communities. With less history but more attitude were the Yellow Brigade, a singing fan group that emerged at Mumbai FC, and whose repertoire included Indian variants on English staples like 'When Mumbai goes Marching In' as well as their own compositions. Visiting teams would always have their regional snacks unfavourably compared to the local speciality: 'What is better than *rasgulla*?' they called to fans from Bengal where the syrupy dumplings are prized. The answer: '*Vada paav*', Maharashtra's own spicy fried potatoes.[79]

However, the most vital of India's new fan cultures emerged in Karnataka at Bengaluru FC, a club founded in 2013 by local firm JSW. The club won the title in its first season in the I-League, the All-India Cup after that, and then another title in 2015. The club has also acquired India's largest and noisiest organized supporters group, the *West Block Blues*. As one member of the group explained,

> I always found it very hard to connect with a European club. When I heard that a new club was being formed, it was like the answer to my prayers, because for a long time I wished there were a professional football club that was local to me, which I could go and watch every week.[80]

For perhaps the first time Indian football generated that precious resource, away fans. In 2016 Bengaluru fans went in numbers to Goa and Mumbai, while one female fan travelled over 3,000 miles to see the team in Shillong.[81] Whether the AIFF manages to combine the best of the Super League and the I-League into a single entity that, unlike the current ISL, is connected to Asian football above and grassroots football below, remains to be seen. Either way, football will find an audience. In 2017 India hosted and played in its first World Cup – the men's under-17s – easily the best attended and most widely reported of its kind. Prime Minister Narendra Modi appeared surgically attached to Twitter for the duration of the competition, meeting and praising the Indian national team, and declaring that 'We want to encourage football in the entire country. There is no life without sports. And those who are a part of the sports lifestyle, their development is of a different level. It is very important for overall development as well.'

Although football was played in Bhutan in the 1970s and 1980s, it could only be seen live. Not only was the game not televised, but there was no television of any kind. It was only the overwhelming public pressure to be allowed to watch the 1998 World Cup that saw the long-standing royal prohibition on television lifted. Bhutan's sub-sequent relationship with both football and television, harbingers of modernity for this isolated mountain kingdom, have been mixed at best. The screen has certainly offered Bhutanese football its singular moment of global coverage, featuring in the Dutch movie *The Other Final*, which followed the two lowest-FIFA-ranked teams, Bhutan and Montserrat, as they played a game against each other on the morning of the 2002 World Cup final. Bhutan won 4–0, but there have not been many more victories. Indeed, at the beginning of 2015 Bhutan could claim to have won only four games in thirty-three years, none of them competitive. Things had picked up since the 20–0 drubbing handled out by Kuwait in 2000 but, on the eve of their World Cup qualification campaign for Russia 2018, their most recent perfor-mances were a 3–0 defeat by Afghanistan, and an 8–2 thrashing from the Maldives. Yet, with an entirely amateur squad, no facilities to speak of, and just forty days to train, Bhutan beat Sri Lanka, twice, in a two-leg play-off, 1–0 away and 2–1 at home, amidst a sea of orange and yellow flags, Bhutanese drumming, 25,000-person Mexican waves, and a clanging chorus of cymbals and chants.[82] In their next three games against Hong Kong, China and Qatar they shipped seven, six and fifteen goals respectively. Whether this is adequate recom-pense for the costs of introducing television to the kingdom – widely thought to have nurtured new patterns of inequality, dissatisfaction and mental ill health – remains to be seen.[83]

VIII

The central Asian republics that were created within the Soviet Union – Kazakhstan, Uzbekistan, Tajikistan and Kyrgyzstan – were, in both political and sporting terms, peripheral colonies. Football, while popular in the region's small cities, was hardly the object of political intrigue or an instrument of political power in what were still overwhelmingly rural societies. In the twenty-first century, under conditions of accelerating urbanization, football has become both, and thus offers a histological slice through the diseased tissue of central Asia's body politic. At the centre of any such autopsy are the group of autocrats, all senior members of the Soviet *nomenklatura* who, on the break-up of the empire in the early 1990s, rose to their nation's respective presidencies and have barely moved since. President Nursultan Nazarbayev stood down after almost thirty years in power in Kazakhstan. Emomali Rahmon in Kyrgyzstan is still in post. Uzbekistan's Islam Karimov made it to 2016 before succumbing to his second heart attack. Tajikistan's first President, Asakar Asaev, survived a mere fifteen years before he was ousted by a popular uprising in 2005, a fate that awaited his successor, Kurmanbek Bakiyev, deposed in 2010. The presidents that have followed all of them have not proved any more democratic. Indeed, they, like their peers, have concentrated and consolidated political power, and established systems of rule characterized by high levels of nepotism and corruption. High political and administrative office has been lavished on family members. State assets are under the control of a tiny court clustered around the presidency. Constitutions have been rewritten repeatedly to allow ever more terms of office for incumbents. Elections have been rigged with a shamelessness that ranges from the mere 91 per cent Islam Karimov managed in Uzbekistan's 2007 presidential election, to the 97 per cent that voted for Kyrgyz President Emomali Rahmon in 1999. Opposition parties have been harassed and infiltrated, and their leaders imprisoned and tortured. The media, what little there is of it, is tightly censored and controlled. Increasingly, football is what has been filling its pages and the political agendas of its elites.

Kazakhstan, blessed with huge hydrocarbon reserves, began the century in Asia but, seeking markets, visibility and kudos, applied to join Europe in the shape of UEFA in 2002, and was accepted in 2004. It was not a move that paid any immediate dividends, as the national team struggled to make any impression on even the qualifying rounds of continental and global tournaments. On failing to make it to the 2010 World Cup Kazakh Football Federation secretary-general Sayan Khamitzhanov fumed on television, 'How long must we endure it? We are ashamed of the results.'[84] As usual, the national coach, in this case Dutchman Arno Pijpers, was unceremoniously fired. At least Pijpers was just fired. A rather harsher fate awaited Rakhat Aliyev, president of the national football federation in the early 2000s and son-in-law of President Nazarbayev. In a sudden fall from grace worthy of the best political noir thriller, Aliyev found himself relieved of all of his many official positions, including control of football, and divorced by his wife at a distance without any direct contact. Punished at the very least for his ambition, and perhaps for his active conspiracy against the president, he would flee the country, but die in an Austrian prison cell awaiting trial.[85]

Since then, the regime's football strategy has been focused on Astana, the country's new capital city. Funded by the nation's immense oil wealth, the transformation of the small town of Akmola into Astana has been Nazarbayev's greatest physical legacy. A Doha of the steppes, it boasts, albeit on a slightly smaller scale, the same mirror glass skyscrapers and vast inhumane plazas of the Gulf, designed by the same galaxy of starchitects, but in a desert of snow and scrub. It was also gifted a team. Two clubs based in other cities, Almaty Megasport and Alma-Ata, were forcibly merged, re-named Lokomotiv Astana, and re-located to the new capital. Then the real business began. Initially backed by the national rail company, they upgraded to Samruk-Kazyna, the national welfare fund, which is in effect a vast state holding company that controls much of the public sector. They were then renamed FC Astana, given kit that matched the colours of the national flag – pale blue with yellow stars – and folded into a portfolio of sports organizations in the city, including ice hockey, basketball and the cycling team that raced on the European circuit, known as the Astana Presidential sports clubs. Now explicitly backed by the national government and the president, these clubs were always intended to globally brand the city, and represent the nation in international competition. Consequently FC

Astana moved out of the grim municipal ground they had been using and into a brand new $185 million stadium.[86]

For a few seasons the city actually had two clubs.[87] FC Astana 1964 was located across the river from its better-funded rival, in what had been the Soviet-era city, and remained virtually disconnected from the wealth and power of the new metropolis rising on the other side of the water. There was enough resentment generated by these contrasts that fights and scuffles broke out between fans during cup games. Despite repeated financial crises, FC Astana 1964 had been kept alive by fans and the local mayor. However, in 2014, the club went into bankruptcy once again, and this time folded altogether, and there was clearly less room for sentiment in the new Kazakhstan. Mayor Adilbek Zhaksybekov could see which way the wind was blowing. He called for the city to get behind the new team and the President. It's not clear that they were listening. Despite having the highest budget in the league, foreign players and domestic success, FC Astana have struggled to draw more than 5,000 people to their domestic games. However, as the only Kazakh team to make it to the UEFA Champions League, and the group stages at that, an event accompanied by total media saturation, it must make its sponsor, the national welfare fund, think it all money well spent.

Kyrgyzstan and Tajikistan lie south of Kazakhstan on China's western borders. Both did poorly in the post-Soviet resource lottery, ending up with a lot of mountains but few of the hydrocarbons and minerals found in Kazakhstan and Uzbekistan, but then the Soviet Union had hardly been an economic or sporting golden age for either. The peak moment for Kyrgyzstan's FC Alga Bishkek, the nation's footballing tribune under Soviet rule, was to finish third in the second division once in the 1960s. Tajikistan's footballing zenith came too late, when Pamir Dushanbe finished tenth in 1991 in the final year of the Soviet first division. Since then neither's economy nor football has prospered. In 2015 Kyrgyzstan's national team games were still being played in the afternoon, as the cost of floodlighting them was prohibitive. The previous year the team, with no back-up shirts available, were unable to swap jerseys after playing Moldova. It was only in 2015 that a game played at home by the Tajik national team was televised, and that required funds and assistance from FIFA to make it possible. Nonetheless, politicians have thought it worth their while to dabble in the game.

In Tajikistan in 2008, football acquired a new political importance when Rustam Emomali, the twenty-one-year-old son of the
president, founded a new club in the capital called Istiqlol
Dushanbe.[88] He also played as their main striker and captained the
team. The presidency of the club was passed to Shohruh Saidzoda,
a man with even less football and administrative experience then
Rustam, but as an old school friend, and the son of the head of the
nation's customs service, he was impeccably qualified. Under this
youthful leadership the club have won all but two of the league titles
contested since their creation. In 2010, with Rustam up front, Istiqlol
were virtually unbeatable in the league and won the AFC President's
Cup, a tournament for the winners of poorly performing Asian
leagues. In 2011 Emomali was elected president of the Tajik Football
Federation (TFF), and gave up his playing career. To this sinecure he
added membership of the Asian Olympic Council, FIFA's development committee and, conveniently for all, the running of the state's
anti-corruption and anti-smuggling agencies. Istiqlol managed without him on the field: indeed, they seemed to be doing better than
ever. In 2011, fans of their main rivals, Ravshan Kulob, rioted after
Istiqlol were awarded a very late and very dubious winning goal. The
crowd made for the referee, then the police and then the away team
buses, before the tear gas drove them back and forty people were
arrested by the police.[89] Similarly, in 2015, having beaten Istiqlol
1–0, Ravshan players were inexplicably and heavily penalized by the
referee at the end of the game, resulting in multiple cards and suspensions. On social media fans raged that Emomali used his power
to 'crush teams that defeat Istiqlol on the pitch'.[90] However, Rustam's
elevation, at the age of twenty-seven, to mayoralty of the capital
Dushanbe, and the simultaneous lowering of the minimum age for
the presidency to thirty, suggests that he might be moving on from
the TFF to bigger things. As and when that happens, Ravshan and
everybody else will have to deal with Shohruh Saidzoda who, alongside running Istiqlol, became a vice-president of the TFF and is
Emomali's natural successor. I wish them luck.[91]

Football and the question of political succession were even more
closely linked in Uzbekistan, where there was enough Soviet footballing heritage and post-Soviet loose money to make a real splash.
In the country's first international tournament Uzbekistan were good
enough to win a gold medal at the 1994 Asian Games, while their

leading club, Pakhtakor Tashkent, had been an occasional member of the Soviet top tier in the 1970s and 1980s. The leading club of the post-Soviet era, Pakhtakor – literally, the cotton growers – were a team, economically and politically, of the old agrarian, Soviet Uzbekistan. FC Bunyodkor, formed in 2005, were the future.[92] Created from scratch, the club was a subsidiary of the Swiss-based conglomerate Zeromax. Despite its legal location, it was the largest private company in the country, with interests in oil, gas, mining and telecommunications. Bunyodkor won the amateur league in 2005, and their first professional league title in 2006, the first of another five over the next seven seasons. From out of nowhere, large crowds in Tashkent were conjured up, and caravans of travelling fans, hitherto unknown in Uzbekistan, appeared. A co-operation deal was signed with Barcelona, and their then president, Joan Laporta, laid a ceremonial brick at what was to become the club's brand new modern stadium. In 2008 Brazilian star Zico arrived as coach, and huge wage offers were made to Barcelona's Samuel Eto'o, Carles Puyol and Andrés Iniesta: at $25 million a year, big enough for Samuel Eto'o to actually think about it. Big enough to convince Brazilian Rivaldo, then in his late thirties, to come onboard, and to take the club all the way to the semi-finals of the Asian Champions League.[93] The arrival the following season of Brazil's World Cup winning coach, Phil Scolari, on an $18 million two-year contract, suggested they were aiming even higher. More players arrived, and Bunyodkor won their league at a canter, dropping just four points all season. Even a defeat by South Korea's Pohang Steelers in the quarter-finals of the Asian Champions League did not seem to dent their ambition: they just bought two of Pohang's best players.

What made all of this possible was that Zeromax and Bunyodkor were actually controlled by Gulnara Karimova, the eldest daughter of the Uzbek president Islam Karimov. Seen in the mid-2000s as a possible successor to the old man, Karimova had a few, short, gilded years. Considered a billionaire in her own right, she not only reaped a considerable income through Zeromax, but was also a conduit for huge bribes being paid by telecommunication companies seeking concessions and contracts in Uzbekistan. At the same time she played cosmopolitan IT girl, a singing society hostess, with her own high-end clothing and jewellery lines. Then, in a shift of fortune whose real determinants remain opaque, Zeromax was declared bankrupt by the Uzbek courts with debts of $500 million. Karimova was appointed ambassador to Spain and sent into exile. Rivaldo would later report in court that the wages had dried up in mid-2009, and that he had been putting up other players in his home when their hotel bills weren't being paid by the club. He never got the $14 million he claimed he was owed, and Bunyodkor, now tied to a local natural gas company, shrank back into insignificance.[94]

Karimova may have been taken down a peg or two, and Bunyodkor's continental, even national, ambitions truncated, but President Karimov and his government seemed to have acquired a taste for football victories, however small. In 2010, when Uzbek official Ravshan Irmatov was selected to referee the opening game of the South African World Cup, his image, in full kit, appeared on prominent urban advertising hoardings, and on the noticeboards of every government office. The following year Uzbek club Nasaf Qarshi won the AFC Cup, a tournament for minor leagues, and its players were rewarded with salary increases and housing from the regional government. Similarly, when the Uzbek under-17's made the quarter-finals of their World Cup they were excused all university fees and entrance exams. Tax breaks for clubs and government edicts requiring new stadiums and academies have been issued, and new rules forbidding face-painting by fans have been published, if not yet acted upon. A deal this time has been struck between Tashkent and Real Madrid, and a new football school is promised. Meantime the reports are of lamentably small crowds and dire local finances, even the beginning of dissent: a game between Nasaf and Shurtan in the city of Guzar ignited a two-day city-wide conflict, reminiscent of the dynamics of North African football riots that mutate into wider social protests. It is a shame that if there is more to come, Karimov, now in his mausoleum, won't be there to see it.

IX

It has been a long way back for football in China. Between 1966 and 1972, as the Cultural Revolution raged, all forms of formal competition were abandoned, the Chinese Football Association (CFA) virtually ceased to exist, and dozens of coaches, players and administrators, suspect for their allegiance to such a foreign game, were publicly humiliated by the Red Guards and sent for re-education in the rice-bowl gulag. In 1972 Mao Zedong finally ordered the army to stop the madness he had unleashed, and a small, fragmented football culture re-emerged. With Mao's death in 1976 the new leadership re-engaged with the world and China rejoined the international sporting bodies, like FIFA, it had left, and then began to play in international competitions, with pitiful results.

The nadir for the national team was a defeat to Hong Kong in a World Cup qualifier played in Beijing in 1985. China actually conceded a lead, going on to lose 2–1, igniting a riot in the streets afterwards that saw hundreds arrested. It was, perhaps, an early indicator of the gap between the expectations unleashed by Deng Xiaoping's 1980s market reforms and the reality of economic and political life for most of China: the same gap that would fuel the Tiananmen Square democracy protests of 1989. After the latter had been dispatched by force and the spilling of blood, Deng set the country on an unambiguous course of change: authoritarian party control in politics and market-steered hyper-industrialization in economics. It was only in this context that Chinese football could take the first steps towards basic professionalization and commercialization.

While the Communist Party retained considerable control over the football association, it permitted a variety of new kinds of private and semi-private club ownership, encouraged the CFA to establish the basic infrastructure of the country's first nationwide football league, and permitted the importation of foreign players and coaches. These clubs were expected to live by their own means, acquire sponsors and run balanced budgets. The CFA responded to the new mood by creating the first fully professional national league pyramid in 1994 and, in the first flush of China's extraordinary double-digit growth, it proved quietly popular, introducing China's new urban population to football as a spectacle, and clubs as urban symbols. The very fact that so many people could gather in one place at one time and not be policed to death and moved on, as the innumerable laws against public assembly and association required, was a rare breath of collective freedom. While ostensibly in good financial health, and enjoying rising incomes, the clubs were not the most generous or reliable payers of their players: many, especially in the lower divisions, subsisted on a worker's wage, and often faced being paid late. This, combined with the relentless pressure on the businessmen and local politicians that ran most clubs not to lose face, was a recipe for corruption. As one coach from the first division recalled, 'By 1998, bribery and match-fixing had become a common phenomenon in the league. Sometimes we bribe the referees not for match-fixing, but for a clean game. Many clubs bribe the referees annually. We call that an "annual salary".' The state of the game was becoming obvious to everyone at the turn of the century as goalkeepers dived over shots, referees seemed to have forgotten the offside rule, and whole teams would abandon their posts.

Two episodes finally blew the roof off of China's football: the 'Five Rats of Division One incident' of 2001, and the 'Black Whistle Riots' of 2002. The former referred to a series of games played over the final two weekends of the Jia B season in 2001. Shanghai Zhongyuan had been promoted after scoring a goal in the final seconds of injury time with their striker Mark Williams in a position that would have appeared offside even if viewed from a geostationary satellite. Chengdu, chasing the second spot, had rather miraculously improved their chances by winning 11–2 that weekend against Sichuan Minyang. On the final day, Chengdu's 4–2 win left their competitors, Changchun, needing to score four goals in their own game to take the promotion spot. The final five minutes of that match were duly extended until this had been achieved. Even the corrupt CFA couldn't stomach this level of mendacity, and fined just about everyone involved, cancelled Changchun's promotion and demoted Sichuan for leaking eleven goals so nakedly. Public trust, despite all this, had evaporated. The following season, in the game between Shaanxi Guoiuli Haus and Qingdao Beer, the score at 3–2, Qingdao were awarded and scored a last-minute penalty. The stadium exploded, chants of 'Black whistles' turned to a hail of coins and mobile phones rained down on the Qingdao players, the plastic seats followed, and then the stadium was set on fire in China's first football stadium riot.

In an attempt to deal with the game's rapidly declining probity and popularity the CFA reorganized and relaunched the national league in 2004 as the Chinese Super League. However, Pepsi had already jumped ship as sponsors, to be replaced for a lot less money by Siemens. The Germans, whose capacity for tolerating corrupt clients is legendary, would also bail out. With no change of personnel at the top of the CFA, and with a sharp decline in the game's crowds and income, problems of match-fixing and gambling simply multiplied. Football, increasingly in the shadow of the country's Olympic triumphs and its infatuation with Yao Ming, the NBA and basketball, looked doomed to occupy a marginal and rather unsavoury place in the Chinese sports landscape. That, however, was to calculate the future without the presence of Xi Jinping.

Born in 1953 to a family of senior communist cadres, Xi Jinping joined the party after the Cultural Revolution and, through a series of regional political positions, worked his way up to the governorship of Shanghai, and then in 2007 became a member of the politburo and vice-president. He is reported to have been an enthusiastic player at school amongst the other Red Princelings of the era, and there are tales, perhaps apocryphal, of him returning to Beijing from his provincial political work in Hebei to watch the football. Similarly, he is reported to have been deeply moved and angered after attending the national team's humiliation in a 1983 match against an England select team. Biding his time, perhaps, it was only in 2009, on a state visit to Germany, at Bayer Leverkusen's training ground, that he made his first serious public pronouncement on matters, declaring that China was in the business of 'improving its football'.

Later in the year, at Xi's behest, a major anti-corruption programme in football was launched under a new CFA vice-president, Wei Be. It was a measure of Xi's already significant political influence, and his obsession with football, that the programme was both wide-ranging and successful. It began with the arrest of hundreds of players, officials, and match-fixers in the lower leagues. In 2010, in a move upwards, two CSL clubs, Chengdu Blades and Guangzhou Pharmaceutical, were relegated for match-fixing. Then they got really serious. In 2012, two previous heads of the CFA, Nan Yong and Xie Yalong, were jailed for ten years.[95] Four former players in the national team were sentenced to six years for match-fixing, and the infamous 'golden whistle' referee Lu Jun went down as well.[96] All had taken bribes to swing games, but Yong had also accepted payments from players in return for being selected for the national team (with extra payments required if you wanted to get on the bench or actually play a few minutes). The campaign peaked in 2013 when Shanghai Shenhua were stripped of their 2003 national title, fined, and given a six-point penalty for the next season.[97] The state anti-corruption agency was confident enough in the success of its mission that, when China won its opening three games at the 2015 Asian Cup in Australia, its website boasted of the contribution it had made to the victories: 'A level playing field is vital for the sector's healthy development; the same with economic and social development, which could be destroyed by corruption, the social tumour.' Australia may have knocked China out 2–0 in the quarter-finals, but the team came home in glory: 'The football field no longer shelters filth.'[98]

While eradicating this kind of graft – being surreptitiously paid to do your job well or badly, depending on the situation – has been the most public and frequent target of Xi Jinping's anti-corruption campaigns, in football and across Chinese society it is actually only the junior element of a much more political strategy. Of far greater concern to Xi and his allies in the party had been the emergence of self-enriching economic and political factions, whose writ, including questions of corruption and embezzlement, seemed to be running further than that of the central government. While under the presidency of Jiang Zemin (1993–2003) the party had kept corruption in check, under his successor Hu Jintao (2003–13) a combination of massive and multifaceted private economic growth and hugely more complex administrative systems created spiralling levels of graft and kickbacks, and the formation of intersecting cliques whose connections and power were built around provincial governments and state economic giants: for example, those cliques built around Bo Xilai, party chief of Chongqing, and the petroleum faction centred on Zhou Yongkang, a member of the Politburo, head of the nation's security agencies and formerly head of the Sichuan government and the nation's oil industry. Destroying these groups would, amongst other things, require the destruction of Dalian Shide, the leading club of the first era of commercial football in China.[99]

Dalian, in the far north-east of China, has traditionally been one of the strongholds of football, and between 1994 and 2005 its leading club Dalian Shide won eight national titles, supported by the Blue Wave, the noisiest fan group in the country. In 2000 the club was sold to the billionaire Xu Ming, under whose ownership the team continued to win national leagues and cups. However, in 2005, something began to change: Xu Ming switched his philanthropic attention from Dalian Shide to the Guanghua Foundation, a device for channelling funds to the Chongqing Public Society Bureau, and from there to the pet protects of Chongqing's party chief Bo Xilai. Indeed, it later transpired that Xu Ming and Bo Xilai's henchman Wang Lijun had signed an agreement to create a new and mighty CSL team in Chongqing, backed by hundreds of millions of Xu Ming's dollars. In 2011, with the club adrift and up for sale, and the arrest of Bo Xilai and many of his associates as part of the anti-corruption campaign, Xu Ming first disappeared from public view and then reappeared in 2012, in court and under arrest. In his absence Dalian Shide were only able to struggle to the end of the season via a subvention from the CFA. Efforts to sell the club came to nothing. Xu Ming's subsequent testimony not only contributed to Bo Xilai's demise, but was also significant in the downfall of Zhou Yongkang, who was arrested in 2013 and subsequently convicted and imprisoned. In 2014, convicted of a range of bribery and corruption offences, Xu died in his jail cell. Xinhua reported that 'he continued to have a high degree of interest in football,' and that, with the decline and then disappearance of Dalian Shide, he had fallen into irreconcilable 'despair'.

Breaking the power of other factions through the anti-corruption campaign was in turn just one aspect of a wider political strategy to reassert the party's control over the state, and the state's control over political factions, the military and economic interest groups. This centralization of power was cemented by Xi's acquisition of all of the highest offices in the state, party and the military, and then a rewriting of the constitution, allowing him an unlimited number of terms of office rather than the two five-year terms that the old model had prescribed. From such a position of strength he has pursued a more assertive foreign policy, launched the Silk Road infrastructural initiative to bring most of Eurasia and Africa within the ambit of the Chinese economy, and is attempting to begin the environmental and financial reforms that China's economy and society require, all while trying to politically and ideologically control a rapidly mutating society.

Given such a Herculean agenda it is remarkable just how much time President Xi has found for football. In 2012 he checked in with the LA Galaxy, where he got himself a David Beckham shirt, and did a little besuited keepy-uppy at Croke Park on a trip to Dublin. The following year the highlight of his visit to the UK was not the open-air carriage ride with the Queen but a selfie taken at Manchester City's training ground with Sergio Agüero and David Cameron. In 2014, he declined a box seat for the World Cup final, but did hang out with goalkeeper Edwin van der Sar in the Netherlands, and while in Buenos Aires received an Argentina shirt from the vice-president with Messi's number but his name on the back. It was these events, in part, that stimulated the great rush of Chinese capital into European football between 2013 and the present.

However, when it came to reforming Chinese football something more than hints and photo opportunities was required. In 2015 this came in the form of a fifty-point reform programme, issued by the Central Committee of the Communist Party and the State Council but overwhelmingly the work of a small reform committee chaired by Xi. Making the case for such a grand intervention, the document argued, 'Revitalizing soccer is a must to build China into a sports powerhouse as part of the Chinese dream. It is also what the people desire.'[100] Laid out in the opaque codes and injunctions of the Chinese Communist Party, there is, nonetheless, a clear sense in these documents that China's status and success as a modern nation can only be tangibly realized and demonstrated if it has a football economy, culture and men's national football team to match. The fate of the women's teams and their tournament is a distantly second-rank concern. Alongside building a successful sports industry and commercial football economy, the plan prioritizes what Xi Jinping has referred to as his 'three wishes': that China should qualify for another World Cup; that it should host the World Cup; and that, of course, it should win the World Cup – and all by 2050. Alongside the usual injunctions and exhortations to follow Xi Jinping's thinking and come into harmony with various declarations of the Central Committee, the heart of the plan is, first, to give the football authorities and industry more autonomy from the government, making the CFA a genuinely independent organization; second, to invest massively in school and youth football, hitherto almost entirely ignored by the nascent professional game and the CFA; and, third, to make football part of the national curriculum. The impact of the 50,000 soccer schools Xi has promised to build has yet to come.

Meantime, Chinese football is still focusing where the money is, re-organizing and re-launching the Chinese Super League and turbocharging it with a simply torrential wave of investment from companies who want a piece of the action, and the kind of *guanxi* required to make things happen in Xi's China. The media conglomerate CMC, for example, outbid the state flagship CCTV for the rights to the CSL, paying $1.2 billion over six years, almost tripling the value of the previous deal.[101] No one, least of all CMC, thought they were going to turn a profit from this, but then no one thought that they could afford not to get into football. Every one of the sixteen teams in the Super League has a major corporate backer – half private, half state-owned enterprises – whose names grace the clubs, and whose logos increasingly appear inside their crests. Beijing Guoan and Guangzhou R and F are big in real estate; Shanghai SIPG are the team of Shanghai International Ports Group; Tianjin Quanjian of the herbal medicines company. The most successful of modern China's clubs, winning five CSL titles in a row and the Asian Champions League twice, in 2013 and 2015, has been Guangzhou Evergrande, bought in 2011 by the Evergrande property conglomerate, and now part owned by Jack Ma, himself the owner of China's largest online retailer, Alibaba. To accommodate dual ownership the club is now known by the even more unappealing name Guangzhou Evergrande Taobao, the latter a subsidiary of the Alibaba online retail empire. While the clubs had been raising their spending on transfers and wages for a few years, Shanghai Shenhua bringing in Nicolas Anelka and Didier Drogba in 2012 for example, 2015 and 2016 saw an altogether different level of expenditure; indeed, in both those seasons net spend in the Chinese Super League was greater than in any other league in world football. As well as the usual selection of older stars at the end of their careers, like Carlos Tevez, Chinese clubs started buying players at the peak of their form, and taking them from established European clubs. Jiangsu Suning, for example, paid Shakhtar Donetsk £37.5 million for Brazilian Alex Teixeira, while Guangzhou Evergrande forked out £31.5 million for his compatriot Jackson Martinez, then at Atlético Madrid.

Better players, better stadiums, more hype and marketing have seen the Chinese Super League recover from its early twenty-first-century collapse, and in 2017 it could boast average gates of more than 25,000. Quite what those 25,000 people were doing and thinking is another matter. Certainly China is not a conventional football culture. For many the game remains a novelty, and one brought to them first and foremost by advertising, sponsors and television, rather than via playing the game, neighbourhood or family tradition. Consequently, market research regularly reports with some glee that nearly three-quarters of fans' affiliation is, first and foremost, to their favourite player rather than a club. Most follow at least two clubs, and the vast majority prefer official club social media and websites to any other source of information. Clubs have created official supporters groups but their stadium presence is regimented and rather dull.

Such pliant consumers – two-thirds apparently intend to buy their club's sponsor's products – may be the stuff of marketing department's dreams, but there is some grit on the terraces of Chinese football. Certainly, as we saw earlier in the chapter, crude and bellicose nationalism is capable of firing up China's crowd, but in the domestic game it cannot function as a similar emotional catalyst. Instead there has been a wave of new 'independent' fan groups and the emergence of real regional and urban identities amongst the crowds. While many of these new groups amount to no more than a few dozen young men, claiming their small patch of the stands and producing their own T-shirts and banners, such organizational autonomy remains a rare and precious psychic space in contemporary China. Larger, and with more presence, are groups like Beijing Guoan's *Yulinjun*, which loosely translates as 'Royal Army', and refers to the forts that used to encircle and protect the imperial capital.[102] Amongst these fans there is a tangible sense that the team, and the group, represent the 'Real Beijing' or 'South Beijing', as many of them refer to it: home to most of the capital's citizens, and a very long way from the closed compounds of the Forbidden City and the party elite's homes.

Perhaps the clearest show of defiance from this new fan culture was seen in 2014, when the huge real estate developers Greenland bought Shanghai Shenhua and, to the dismay of the clubs' fans, planned to rename it simply Greenland FC. At the opening game of the season they certainly looked like they were intent on this act of vandalism, as they filled a wedge of the stadium with their employees dressed in corporate green T-shirts, and smothered the area around the stadium with Greenland branding. The main fan groups, led by the *Blue Devils*, kept schtum for the first nineteen minutes of the match, ensuring effective silence, and then unveiled a banner with a saying of Xi Jinping's: 'Abandoning tradition is tantamount to severing your spiritual lifeline.' As the security forces grabbed it from them they chanted 'Give us our Shenhua back.' In a rare victory for such protest, the owners agreed to call the club Shanghai Greenland Shenhua. As one member of the *Blue Devils* put it,

> In Shanghai we have a lot of foreign people living beside us, so we come into contact with things from Europe or even the world quickly. Our open-mindedness is the most important thing to understand in all of this – take a look at Hongkou Stadium and you can see – we are way ahead of most other fans in the rest of China.[103]

Perhaps the most remarkable thing about the fans of Shanghai has been their relationship with the Japanese club Urawa Red Diamonds, who played an Asian Champions League tie against Shenhua in 2007.[104] With the tie bizarrely scheduled during a working day, the stadium was empty but for 1,500 Urawa ultras. The local fan group, the *Blue Devils*, were so blown away by their dedication that they sought the Japanese out and spent the night with them in drunken reverie in the city centre. Given the scale of anti-Japanese sentiment in China, which, as we saw earlier, regularly rears its head in footballing contexts, this amity is strange enough, but the *Blue Devils* have taken it a stage further by showing up at Urawa's Champions League games and abusing their Chinese opponents. After doing so against Beijing Guoan in 2015 they were denounced in the Chinese press and social media as 'traitors' and 'Japanese dogs', but this only seems to have emboldened them. The following season they gate-crashed local rivals Shanghai SIPG's game against Melbourne Victory and unveiled a flag saying 'Only Shenhua Rep Shanghai'.

The twin threats of organization from below, and the reckless spending of private capital, have of course provoked a reaction, and not from the CFA but from above. In 2017, the party released its latest 'firm' policy advice to the CFA and CSL, snappily entitled: 'Strengthen Management and Guidance. Promote the Healthy and Stable Development of the Professional League.' In an effort to limit the flood of imported talent, which had led to the exclusion of local players, clubs were limited to just three foreign signings, and required to select at least two Chinese under-23s in every game. In an effort to damp down the arms race of spending amongst the clubs, a tax was introduced on transfers and its proceeds allocated to youth development. Perhaps most important of all, clubs will be required to use a united accounting system and submit themselves to third party auditing, a degree of financial transparency unknown in most of Chinese business, let alone football. Whether the irrepressible ingenuity of Chinese companies will allow them to circumvent these restrictions, or whether the rule of law, albeit merely company law, will pertain, will be just one of the indicators of China's wider trajectory that Chinese football is going to deliver.

6

TROUBLE IN PARADISE:
FOOTBALL IN THE AMERICAS

Before I came here this morning to explain to you, I saw a few of you rush to the office in New York, the CONCACAF office in New York, to talk of business before we had even talked of it among ourselves. You rush off to New York, I imagine by now it is in Reuters and DPA. I know there are some people here who believe they are more pious than thou. If you are pious, go to a church, friends, but the fact is, our business is our business.

Jack Warner, President of CONCACAF, at an extraordinary meeting of the Caribbean Football Union, Trinidad, 2011

I

FIFA, at least as an acronym, has something going for it. Short, memorable, with an uplifting vowel sound at the end, it is almost like a word, but not quite. CONCACAF cannot even claim these small virtues. It was created in 1961 from the merger of NAFU (North American Football Union) and the CCCF (Confederación Centroamericana y del Caribe de Fútbol). In the years since, the organization has picked up dozens of new post-colonial members in the Caribbean as well as Belize and Guyana. Its name remains as cumbersome as its geography. Depending on your definitions, it spans two continents and at least three regions, brings together one superpower (USA), one large state (Mexico), one medium-sized one (Canada), a dozen small ones, and another dozen or so micro-states, dependencies and island chains. The Confederation of North American, Caribbean and Central American Football, to give it its full name, was thus originally best understood as the rump of the sport in the Americas: the continent minus the southern cone and the Andean nations, who long ago created their own federation (CONMEBOL, in 1916) and never had any intention of letting in the rest of the hemisphere. Fifty years later, in 2011, when Jack Warner spoke those words, CONCACAF might still have had an ugly name and a complex geography, but it was no longer a mere rump. Indeed, under the Trinidadian's presidency, ably supported by his accomplice in crime, the American general secretary Chuck Blazer, CONCACAF had become a key player in the global politics of football, headquartered in Trump Tower on Manhattan's Fifth Avenue, where 'business is our business.'[1]

Warner and Blazer's actual business record need not detain us, for their personal contribution to the development of the game in the Americas is virtually zero, and, seen in a wider perspective, probably negative. However, they remain a superb case study of the endemic corruption and incompetence in football administration. Chuck, from lower-middle-class Jewish stock in Queen's, New York, made his first foray in business by illegally manufacturing and selling the original yellow smiley badges of the late 1960s, and then rose through the ranks of US football administration by taking any post going. Jack Warner climbed out of poverty by becoming a history teacher but, with a fearsome interest in money and power, he was always aiming higher. The two met when Jack, then President of the Trinidad and Tobago Football Federation, was making a bid for the CONCACAF presidency, and both realized they were just what the other had been looking for. Chuck ran Jack's campaign, Jack won and then made Chuck his general secretary. In the years running up to 2011, both men proved adept at taking and hiding substantial kickbacks from the allocation of CONCACAF tournament TV rights, extracting huge and entirely bogus commissions, payments and expenses from the organization, and diverting funds that came from FIFA or other con-federations to their personal, offshore bank accounts. Whatever was left after they had taken their tithe was ruthlessly apportioned to ensure the political support of the region's many small football asso-ciations, which were dependent on this kind of largesse. At the same time, they were both riding the FIFA gravy train as members of its cosseted executive committee. Warner, and his family travel agency, illicitly sold World Cup tickets obtained by the Trinidadian FA and created a small property empire from FIFA grants. Blazer preferred to spend his money on himself and his cats, who got their own Trump Tower duplex, and to eat himself to death at New York's finest restaurants. Warner parlayed his money and status into Trinidadian politics, founding his own ersatz political party, and managing, for a short period, to bag himself a cabinet ministry. For almost two dec-ades both men, with the exception of Andrew Jennings' FIFA reporting, got a free pass from the football press, the law and their own organizations. In the case of Chuck Blazer, who had long ago stopped filing tax returns, the IRS should be added to the list. In retrospect, their methods of deception were crude, and their money-laundering efforts pitifully amateurish. However, they were protected by the collusion of the people they bullied in their own offices, the national football administrators who sat on the CONCACAF board and pretended not to see anything amiss, FIFA's own cankerous levels of corruption which made them feel untouchable, the media executives who bribed and kept their misdeeds out of the press, and their own shameless combination of front and bombast.

Blazer and Warner were also helped by the fact that, when they came to power, much of the region still appeared unpromising soil for football, a backwater with which no global or judicial agency would bother itself. Soccer was the dominant sport in only Mexico, Suriname and Guyana, and only Mexico could claim any kind of professional league or global footballing presence. In the United States, the collapse of the NASL in the early 1980s had again left the country without a professional men's league. Grassroots and women's football, with their respective footholds in middle-class-suburbia and higher education, were flourishing, but the place of the game in wider American popular culture was marginal at best. Canada remained wedded to ice hockey and, in a few cities, baseball and basketball. The former had a significant presence in the Caribbean and Central America. Baseball was easily the most popular game in Cuba, the Dominican Republic, Puerto Rico and Nicaragua, with a presence in Haiti, Mexico and on the isthmus from Panama to El Salvador. In much of the anglophone Caribbean, cricket, especially on the international stage, with the various nations competing as the West Indies, remained the most obvious sporting tribune and popular pastime. Since then, baseball, outside of its Cuban and Dominican strongholds, has struggled to retain the public's interest: even in the United States, MLB, flush with money, has been relegated to the number three spot behind the NFL and the NBA. In Cuba baseball is dependent on the practical and ideological support of the Communist Party, which has long preferred it to the suspiciously globalist game of football. However, in the streets and parks of Havana, the young have voted with their feet and turned to soccer and, despite the desperate economic conditions of the local game, sufficient talent has emerged for the state to permit, for the first time since the revolution, professionalization and even the migration of leading players to Mexico.[2] Despite its allure, and the global reach of the NBA, basketball remains at best the second-rank sport everywhere else in the region. Caribbean cricket has been eclipsed. The West Indies have never come close to replicating their successes of the 1970s and 1980s, while the centre of the game's financial and sporting gravity has decisively shifted to India.

By contrast, over the last two decades, football's popular appeal and cultural weight have risen everywhere in the region, and CONCACAF, Blazer and Warner just rode the wave. The shift has been greatest in the United States, where the twenty-first century has seen the consolidation of a successful men's professional league, the biggest and most vibrant women's football culture in the world, the relentless demographic expansion of Latino football, and the emergence of a huge subculture of cosmopolitan football fans. Together, they constitute a profound, perhaps structural transformation in the place of football in American cultural life. In Mexico, football's significance was never in doubt, but its meanings and uses were predominantly controlled by the PRI–Televisa alliance that had run the country since the 1950s. In the twenty-first century, they have lost their respective monopolies of the presidency and television, and the meaning of football. In particular, the national team – once, like the PRI, primarily a symbol of national unity and developmental possibility – has become part of a never-ending saga of disappointment, underperformance and unfulfilled promise.

In Central America, still beset by bitter internal conflicts and the unfinished business of its long civil wars and insurgencies, the region's national football teams have offered rare moments of unity, even euphoria. In 2013, Honduran President Juan Orlando Hernández declared a national holiday to celebrate merely qualifying for the 2014 World Cup; his Panamanian peer, Juan Carlos Varela, did the same in 2017. Varela's tweet, in response to the wild public parties that followed Panama's first qualification for the World Cup, made clear that he didn't have much choice: 'The voice of the people has been heard. Tomorrow will be a national holiday.'[3] Hernández's predecessor, the leftist President Manuel Zelaya, would probably have done the same back in 2009 when Honduras qualified for the 2010 World Cup, but by then he had been deposed in a military coup. Under Roberto Micheletti, installed temporarily as president in his place by the armed forces, football remained important enough that the nightly curfew was temporarily lifted when the national team was playing. Yet with Zelaya still holed up in the Brazilian embassy and his supporters active on the streets, even a semi-final place at the 2009 Gold Cup did not produce a burst of public ebullience. As one observer put it, 'Rallying in the streets is reserved for politics and violence.'[4] The return to civilian rule under President Porfiro Loba Sosa and then Hernández saw the curfew lifted, but precious little progress elsewhere. Honduras remains engulfed in corruption and drug-related violence, often targeted on the press and judiciary. Both men presided over Honduran World Cup campaigns during which the government and the public told themselves that the squad's journey, aside from being a glorious distraction, might be a force for unity and peace. But for all the hysterical optimism, there has only been a 0–0 draw against a fractured French team to celebrate. Given the bleak state of Honduran politics under both these presidents, and the enduring brutalities of everyday life in the country, one could be forgiven for thinking that the dream rose to the occasion.[5]

World Cup qualification has had similar effects in the Caribbean. Jamaica's and Trinidad and Tobago's successful World Cup qualifying campaigns were marked by their respective Prime Ministers, PJ Patterson and Patrick Manning, declaring national holidays; in both cases these accommodated island-wide public celebrations. On their debuts, in 1998 and 2006, Jamaica (population: 2.6 million) and Trinidad and Tobago (population: 1.3 million) were the smallest nations ever to have made it to the finals. No one thought they were going to win very much, but they were sure going to let the world know they were there. As Maximus Dan, the Trinidadian singer, put it in his wildly popular calypso for the tournament,

> I'm ah soca warrior I come to shine meh nationality brighter
> And any opposition dat we meet, hear me now
> We go defeat dem by we feet
> We go shine with all we might.[6]

In Haiti, the game had long served as a sporting tribune. In the popular football memory, the nation had claimed Joe Gaetjens, the American of Haitian descent who scored the winning goal for the USA in their victory over England at the 1950 World Cup. In 1974, Haiti lost every game and conceded fourteen goals, but the island's outing at the West German World Cup is still revered for Emmanuel Sanon's brilliant goal in the opening game against Italy, when, for just a brief moment, Haiti looked like winners.[7] In the aftermath of the catastrophic earthquake that hit the nation in January 2010, the game has again been pressed into service, in this case as a symbol of national survival. The quake left 300,000 dead, the capital Port-au-Prince in ruins, and millions homeless. The Haitian Football Federation's offices were completely destroyed, and all but two of its thirty-two staff were killed. Inevitably, many players and coaches at every level of the game were amongst the dead. The national stadium was badly damaged and for over a year served as an impromptu refugee camp. Football, barely functioning at any level, ground to a halt when, during a vicious outbreak of cholera, the U-17 national team was banned from a tournament by their panicky Jamaican hosts, lest they spread the disease.[8]

In this context, it was a minor miracle that Brazilian coach Edson Tavares should have been able to assemble any kind of team, but he found surprisingly rich pickings amongst the Haitian diaspora and its sons: players like Jean-Eudes Maurice at PSG, and Steward Ceus at Colorado Rapids. Equally, given the desperate state of the Stade Sylvio Cator, it was incredible that the nation could stage any kind of match, yet in 2011 Haiti played their opening game for qualification to the 2014 World Cup at home against the US Virgin Islands. The recently elected President Michel Martelly, who evidently believed in miracles, told the squad that,

> Haiti is ready to show that new face. In the past we talked about our problems and issues. But today is a chance to prove that Haiti can be a great nation and can be victorious. I couldn't express in words what Haiti would be like if . . . when, not if, we qualify for the 2014 World Cup in Brazil.

Despite being scheduled in blisteringly hot weather, as the absence of mains electricity made a night game impossible, so many people showed up that around 10,000 didn't make it into the stadium at all. At times they were fought off by baton-wielding police and only the arrival of a tropical rainstorm prevented more serious fighting. At the same time, President Martelly, in national team strip, led out the squad, put a shot into the back of one of the nets, and settled down to watch Haiti carve up the opposition 6–0. It was, perhaps, the high point for both President and team. The former certainly came up short when measured against his campaign promises of cracking down on corruption and rebuilding the shattered infrastructure of the country, while his prediction for the national team was even wider of the mark. Only with Martelly's departure from the political stage, and a return to his musical career, did the Haitian squad offer some measure of real progress, qualifying for the Copa América in 2016. But all things are relative, progress included. Once at the tournament, Haiti were very publicly thrashed, losing three games, the worst a 7–1 rout against Brazil.

It is not only the national team and World Cup qualification that draw Caribbean politicians to football: the domestic game and neighbourhood clubs have their appeal too. The template was struck in Jamaica in the 1970s by Edward Seaga, the leader of the right-wing JLP (Jamaican Labour Party). He organized the demolition of part of Kingston's burgeoning slums and their replacement by Tivoli Gardens – tens of thousands of public housing units, which were stuffed with rock-solid JLP voters. Matters of local justice and patronage were steadily handed over to the gangs that emerged in these neo-slums, and entertainment and visibility were provided by a new football club – Tivoli Gardens FC – which played, lest anyone should forget whose show this was, at the Edward Seaga stadium. The then governing party, the PNP (People's National Party), countered by repeating the trick in Arnett Gardens next door, which has been Tivoli's political and sporting rival ever since.[9]

More recently, in Barbados, there has been a minor football arms race amongst politicians. In 2008, David Thompson, leader of the Democratic Labour Party, conducted much of his election campaign in association with community-based football tournaments, heartily endorsed and supported by the Barbados Football Association and its President Ronald Jones. When Thompson was elected Prime Minister, he made Jones Minister of Education. The opposition Barbados Labour Party countered by staging its own alternative tournament, publicly launched by party leader Mia Motely. The Democratic Labour Party, now in government but without the recently deceased Thompson, hit back with their very own David Thompson memorial football tournament.[10] Football has also provided a route back into public life for retired and disgraced politicians like Patrick John, once the President and the Prime Minister of Dominica. John had been forced from power by popular protest in 1978, but attempted a comeback in 1981 with a motley alliance of American neo-Nazis and South African white supremacists. In a ludicrous private version of the Bay of Pigs, they planned to land a force on Dominica and install John as their figurehead while they looted the island. The plot was uncovered and thwarted, and John served five years of a twelve-year prison sentence: enough to debar him from domestic politics, but not from the world of football. On his release, he parlayed what was left of his reputation and his background as an amateur player to take command of the national football federation, which he then milked for a decade, until his sudden resignation in 2011.[11]

John was just one of many Caribbean football federation presidents and executives who resigned that year. He, like many of the others, listened to President Warner's 'our business is our business' speech at the Royal Hyatt Hotel in Port of Spain, Trinidad, earlier that year. The business to which Warner referred, and the real basis of CONCACAF's rise, was the impending election for the FIFA presidency, pitting incumbent Sepp Blatter against the Qatari businessman and president of the Asian Football Confederation, Mohammed Bin Hammam. The task at hand was co-ordinating the votes of the Caribbean Football Union (a sub-region of CONCACAF but one that accounted for 25 of its 35 members) in that election, which hitherto Warner had masterfully corralled, ensuring a powerful and expensive block vote in FIFA decision-making. As we shall see in detail in Chapter 7, Warner and Bin Hammam's clumsy but generally well received efforts to bribe the CFU – $40,000 a head in brown paper envelopes! – triggered a series of events that would result in Warner's and Bin Hammam's resignations and expulsion from football, multiple resignations amongst and punishments for Caribbean football officials, Chuck Blazer turning FBI snitch, and the whole show snowballing into a gigantic US federal investigation into corruption in global football that became public in 2015.[12] It is testament to Warner and Blazer's twenty years in power that this, without question, has been the region's greatest contribution to world football.

II

In a region that has been wracked by wars – border, civil and narco variants – widespread political violence and extrajudicial killings, it is fitting, if regrettable, that its most famous football moment remains the 'Soccer War' of 1969, as brilliantly if unreliably chronicled by Ryszard Kapuściński.[13] A three-game play-off to qualify for the 1970 World Cup began when Honduras won their home leg in Tegucigalpa. The Salvadorans then won their home leg 3–0, after the subjection of the Honduran squad to sleepless nights, attacks on their hotel and the burning of their flag in a stadium full of screaming

Salvadorans and very scary soldiers. The victory was followed by attacks on Hondurans in the capital, San Salvador, and across the country. Honduras responded by attacking and then expelling the hundreds of thousands of poor Salvadorans who, in search of land and work, had been crossing their border over the previous six months. Diplomatic relations were severed, and two weeks later El Salvador actually invaded Honduras. Six days into the conflict the Organization of American States enforced a ceasefire, after which El Salvador won the final game in Mexico City. A World Cup place was secured, and around 6,000 people were left dead.

In the years since the Soccer War, Central America has had plenty more of the real thing. El Salvador's civil war ran from 1971 until the early 1990s, during which period state-backed death squads killed tens of thousands of civilians. Guatemala's civil war, already almost a decade old in 1969, dragged on until 1996. Honduras, long ruled as a military dictatorship, was wracked by right- and left-wing guerrilla forces through the 1980s, the conflict exacerbated by the presence of US-backed Contras in the country, fighting the Sandinista regime in Nicaragua. In the twenty-first century, those wars finally appear to be coming to an end, but they have left the region with the most fragile of states, plagued by unaccountable militaries, unreformed police forces, weak judicial institutions, deeply corrupt traditional elites and the same desperate inequalities and poverty that generated the conflicts in the first place. The drug trade, long present in the region, has become even more influential over the last two decades, corrupting politics, the police and the judicial system from above, while nurturing the already considerable presence of urban gangs from below. Civil rule has returned, but the war appears to have moved to the bulging cities of these nations, where the army, the police and the gangs have been fighting it out for control of urban territory. It is a combination that has left the region with the highest rate of homicides in the world. However, the forces of anti-corruption have been fighting back and scoring some victories.

Across the region, nearly a third of the presidents elected since 1990 are either in prison, or have been or are under investigation for corruption and embezzlement of one kind or another. El Salvador's president between 1999 and 2004, Francisco Flores Pérez, fled the country, charged with embezzling a $10 million donation from the Taiwanese government before it reached the victims of an earthquake. Costa Rica has imprisoned former heads of state Presidents Fournier and Figueres, while their successor President Echeverría exiled himself to Spain to avoid similar treatment. Guatemala is leading the way, though. In 2006 the Guatemalan government and the United Nations established the CICIG (*Comisión Internacional contra la Impunidad en Guatemala*, or in English *The International Commission against Impunity in Guatemala*). It is a national investigative and prosecuting agency, independent of the then deeply corrupted Guatemalan judicial system, its autonomy guaranteed by international treaty, resources and oversight, which has allowed it to expose systematic corruption and human rights abuses in the police, the armed forces and municipal government. Most impressive of all, in 2015, its investigations into the network of organized graft at the heart of President Oscar Molina's administration forced his resignation and that of his vice-president.

It is not surprising then, that, amongst the haul of football and television executives brought into the American judicial system in 2015 by the FBI's investigation into corruption in the global game, Central Americans should figure so prominently. Indeed, every football association but Belize could boast at least one guilty party. Eduardo Li, president of the Costa Rican football federation, pleaded guilty to a variety of charges of bribery, corruption and racketeering, and is doing his time in the United States. Julio Rocha López, the president of the Nicaraguan federation, also pleaded guilty, but died of cancer before sentencing. Reynaldo Vasquez, once head of football in El Salvador, has yet to stand trial, but only because the Salvadoran authorities imprisoned him first, sentencing him to eight years on a variety of counts of embezzlement, mainly from the workers at his own bed manufacturing company.[14] Ariel Alvarado, president of the Panamanian football association, stayed at home, where the Americans have been unable to extradite him. A laughable domestic court case was brought against him and he was cleared of all but the money-laundering charges he faced, but it is hard to imagine, in a country where almost no one is ever convicted of the felony, that he will be brought to justice over this.[15]

The three Guatemalans imprisoned were: Héctor Trujillo, general secretary of the national football federation but also a former judge of the Guatemalan constitutional court, the organization's president Brayan Jiménez, and his predecessor Rafael Salguero, who had graduated to the school of advanced graft on the FIFA executive committee. Their departure did not immediately herald a cleansing of the stables. Indeed, Jiménez was initially replaced by Milton Mendoza, brother of the head of the Mendoza drug cartel based in the Northern province of Peta. As with the wider struggle against corruption, however, Guatemala has proved more tenacious than most. Mendoza was dismissed and replaced by an interim committee led by Adela de Torrebiarte, previously a commissioner for police reforms as well as president of the national league. Under Torrebiarte, and the steely eye of the auditors she invited in, the previous senior management was removed, most contracts reopened for bidding, and provision made for players, referees and the lower divisions, hitherto excluded from power, to have a say in the running of the federation. There has, inevitably, been a considerable backlash from many of the club owners and power brokers in the game, making agreement over a new set of transparent and democratic statutes for the national federation impossible to agree, and thus elections for a new president remain in abeyance.[16]

If Guatemala suggests the possibility of reform in Central America, Honduras, and its intimate connections between football, politics and corruption, graphically demonstrate how hard the task is. The two Hondurans pursued by the Americans were Alfredo Hawit, a player then lawyer who climbed his way to the presidency of CONCACAF, and Rafael Callejas, who was actually Honduran President between 1990 and 1994 and had acquired the Honduran Football Federation as a useful sinecure in his retirement. Both pleaded guilty to charges of racketeering and are awaiting sentence. Domestic football has gone the same way.[17] Yankel Rosenthal, scion of one of the nation's most connected families, at various times a congressman, a government minister and twice a presidential candidate, also owned Marathon, one of the country's most popular teams. In 2018 he was sentenced to nearly two and a half years in prison on charges of laundering drug money through real estate deals and the football club, including the new stadium he had purportedly built for it.[18] Julio Gutiérrez, businessman and president of their rivals, Motagua, was forced to resign and then placed under house arrest following innumerable accusations of fraud. The joint owners of Atlético Choloma, Melvin Sanders and Javier Hernandez, have also moved on. The former was murdered in his own home by the local drug cartel, the latter arrested with a lot of cash at the Guatemalan–Salvadoran border. Perhaps Ramon Sarmie was just protecting himself, but he also had to stand down from the presidency of his club, Juticalpa, when arrested for possessing a vast armoury of military-grade weapons at his home in Sarmiento. Thus, when in 2015 police arrested members of the drug gang *Los Gaidos*, they were probably not surprised to find that their leader was one Alex Ramires, owner of the local football club Sula FC.[19]

Costa Rica, by contrast, has been by some way the most stable, rich and peaceful of the Central American nations, while its recent World Cup record is far better than those of its neighbours. *Los Ticos* made the second round on their debut in 1990 and qualified for both the 2002 and 2006 tournaments. In 2014, drawn in an impossible group with England, Italy and Uruguay, Costa Rica were unstoppable. First, they beat the South Americans 3–1, then the Italians 1–0, in doing so qualifying for the next round with a game to spare, effectively ejecting a dismal England team from the tournament before they had even met. The nation had been given two hours off for both games by recently elected President Luis Guillermo Solís, but no one went back to work after them. The President himself, in a national team jersey, could be seen amongst tens of thousands running around the monumental fountain – La Fuente de la Hispanic – in the centre of the capital San José. In one report, from the barrio of San Rafael Abajo on the outskirts of the capital, a local shopkeeper spoke with the defiant pride of small nations everywhere: 'They all said that Costa Rica was an easy three points in the Group of Death, but we showed them . . . Our *muchachos* showed them who we really are.' And who were the *Ticos* at that moment? With half an eye to their neighbours on the isthmus, he continued, 'The truth is that we are better. We don't have an army, everybody knows how to read and write and all that makes us feel good. And when we get into the final sixteen in the World Cup we know the world knows we are great too.'[20] On the field, in Brazil, they certainly were, taking the Netherlands to extra time, only to lose 4–3 on penalties. Closer to home, in San José's Independence Square, where a large crowd had gathered to watch the game on a big screen, defeat turned into a brawl amongst two groups of supporters and three people were stabbed to death in broad daylight.[21]

Despite Costa Rica's long history of demilitarization and relative social peace, this incident was not entirely out of keeping with a new mood in the country. Over the previous ten years, the arrival of both the Mexican and the Jamaican drug cartels, who used Costa Rica as a transit station and local gangs as both dealers and muscle, had produced a very sharp spike in homicides and robberies. The *barra bravas* of the larger clubs were on the fringes of this kind of work, and had clearly begun to absorb its culture of easy violence, hitherto absent from the Costa Rican game. In early 2014 the game between Alajuelense and Cartaginés was brought to a halt as fans from both clubs fought each other and the police in the stands. Just after the World Cup had finished, the derby match between Saprissa and Alajuelense saw widespread fighting between their *barras, La Ultra Morada* and *La Doce* respectively; sixty-nine people were arrested including a fourteen-year-old who had punched a police horse.[22] A similar story can be told in Honduras, where, in 2016, a Deportivo Olimpia supporter, stoned by rival Motagua fans, died on his way to hospital and was recorded as the twenty-third death in Honduran football since 2000. The following year, the entire league was suspended after Marathon fans disrupted their game at Real España before a disputed penalty for the home side could be taken; repeated volleys of police tear gas were required to clear the pitch.[23]

In El Salvador, crowds can also be violent, but the single most salient fact about football in the country is that nearly all clubs have stopped using the numbers 13 and 18 on their squad shirts; fixture lists released by the league are similarly allergic to these integers. The presidents of the leading teams agreed on the measure when they found themselves besieged by players begging not to be given those shirts and the attention they attracted.[24] The two numbers refer to the two dominant gangs in the country – the 13th Street and 18th Street gangs – named after the places in Los Angeles where they were founded in the 1970s. Now they have extended their reach back to the home country, though they are subservient to the more powerful Mexican cartels who ship drugs through the country. El Salvador's homicide rate stands at around 65 per 100,000 people; the World Health Organization considers a rate of 10 per 100,000 to be a state of emergency. Estimates vary, but perhaps around 90 per cent of those deaths are gang-related. One can understand why number 13s and 18s have been nervous. In Panama, whatever your squad number, you had better look out. In 2011, Javier De La Rosa, a young striker with Chorrillo FC, was shot by a stranger outside the Estadio Javier Cruz in Panama City, just after a match in which the team had qualified for the final of the Clausura championship. In 2013, Miguelito Lasso, a national team player, was shot dead leaving a nightclub. Extraordinarily, they are just two of more than twenty players and coaches who have been murdered in Panama since 2000. No one is secure, even in retirement, even Alfredo Pacheco, El Salvador's most capped player. In 2015, he was shot dead at a petrol station. In 2015 Arnold Peralta, the captain of the Honduran national team, while on holiday in his home town, was gunned down by a man on a motorbike. Motives are rarely uncovered in these cases; suspects are rarely found, let alone tried. They could be robberies, cases of mistaken identity, debt collection gone mean, or score-settling of some other kind. This has become the norm for young men in the region.[25]

III

The World Cup, held every four years, coincides precisely with the campaigning season for Mexico's federal legislative elections. Every twelve years it overlaps with the country's presidential elections. Either way, football always wins. Even the production lines of the *maquiladora* factories come to a halt when 'El Tri', as the national team is colloquially known, plays at the World Cup, although the hours will be made up later. If the team wins, every town square will be packed with flag-waving fans, and traffic jams of honking cars in numbers that no politician could hope to call upon. Yet, if football appears, at first glance, to overwhelm politics in Mexico, politics has a way of reclaiming the ground. Candidates of all parties go out of their way to appear as super-fans, and, now equipped with Twitter accounts, act as almost constant cheerleaders, pictured at home in the national shirt or taking time out from a diplomatic encounter to watch the games. The story of *El Tri*, however, offers richer metaphorical and political pickings than can be expressed in 140 or even 280 characters.

The novelist and commentator Juan Villoro, reflecting on Mexico's desperate route to the 2014 World Cup – saved from elimination by a US victory over Panama, their place then secured by the humiliating necessity of a play-off against New Zealand – thought of the team as 'a combination of the nation that has been promised a lot, but the promises have never been fulfilled and there is a feeling like maybe they never will be. It is a very Mexican team in that regard.'[26]

The national narrative of unfulfilled promise began in the 1970s. After almost thirty years of sustained development under the authoritarian PRI, symbolically peaking with the staging of the 1968 summer Olympics and the 1970 World Cup, Mexican growth began to falter. The economic and technological gap between it and richer capitalist nations widened rather than narrowed. In the late 1970s and early 1980s, the PRI sought to reinvigorate the economy through newly acquired oil money and foreign loans, but global recession and a collapse in oil prices brought the economy to its knees. In the 1990s, under President Salinas, the PRI took a neo-liberal turn, signing NAFTA – the North American Free Trade Agreement – opening the hitherto closed and protected domestic economy, and promising sustained prosperity. This has, as widely predicted, created millions of poorly paid industrial jobs and destroyed just as many in the countryside, while at the same time massively enriching a narrow stratum of conglomerates and their political allies. Inequality and poverty, already high in Mexico, have become steadily worse through the twenty-first century.

These cycles of optimism and disappointment, extravagant promise and hapless execution have found a near perfect resonance in the performance of *El Tri* at the World Cup. In 1986, at home, to national acclaim and near hysteria, the first golden generation of players like Hugo Sanchez and Javier Aguirre took Mexico to the quarter-finals of the tournament, the country's best ever performance. Poised, it seemed, to go one better next time around, the team was banned from the 1990 World Cup after the national federation had been found fielding over-age players in youth tournaments; once again, it seemed, that Mexican promise was undercut by the incompetence and corruption of its political and administrative classes. Since then, Mexico has never failed to qualify for the World Cup, nor to get eliminated in the first knock-out round. Playing the *quinto partido* – the fifth game – which would mean Mexico had acquired a quarter-final place again, has become a national obsession, the key marker of sporting and social progress. Every time Mexico has fallen short.

Certainly, each of the twenty-first-century's *sexienos* – the single six-year terms allocated to Mexico's presidents – have begun with promise of change and reform but ended in a deepening sense of disappointment. In 2000, Vincente Fox, candidate of the PAN, broke the monopoly of the PRI on the presidency, which, as the victors of the Mexican revolution, they had held for over eighty years. A telegenic business executive, previously head of Coca-Cola Mexico and governor of Guanajuato state, Fox offered himself as a new broom: promising an end to the clientelism, torpor and corruption of the PRI and the now creaking corporatist state it had built, and of course the usual neo-liberal snake oil. Previously seemingly indifferent to football, he declared himself a supporter of León, publicly supported *El Tri*, and asked George Bush whether he would like to join him somewhere near the border to watch the USA–Mexico clash in the round of sixteen at the 2002 World Cup. Bush's office, with its characteristic indifference to Mexican affairs, let Fox know that as the game was being played in East Asia, the president would be asleep when it was on. Fox stayed up for the game and watched Mexico go out of the cup, beaten 2–0. Afterwards, he did his best to rescue the situation and extravagantly praised *El Tri*, but for a nation that has told itself that, in football at least, it has the beating of its bullying northern neighbour, this was cold comfort. In this, as in much of his presidency, Fox proved better on television and making gestures than at governing. Corruption and the drug trade went unchecked. Indeed, in the absence of the PRI's frayed but functioning paternalism and the party's loose control of the narcos, Fox presided over an era in which poverty rose, while the cartels, unhinged from the formal political system, effectively became the political and judicial arbiters in much of the country.

In the 2006 elections to replace Fox, held alongside the World Cup in Germany, Felipe Calderón, the PAN candidate, made football a central theme of his campaign. In speeches, he compared himself to Mexico's World Cup-winning under-17 team, and he staged games where he could show off his ball skills to the media. Roberto Madrazo, the PRI's man, planned a series of rallies in football stadiums where the crowd could listen to him before watching the national team play on big screens. When, in the opening game, Mexico swept Iran aside 3–1, President Fox compared the high scoring élan of *El Tri* to the high number of houses built during his six years in power. Calderón, who had predicted a 2–1 victory, took it as a sign that he and Mexico were going to win in July. Even Andrés Manuel López Obrador, his main challenger from the left and a man normally wary of football talk, recalled that he had predicted a 3–0 win, and was thus closer to hitting the mark. Perhaps the only political force that summer in Mexico to refrain from making symbolic capital of football were the Zapatistas and their allies. And they had certainly done so in the past.

The Zapatistas, or the EZLN (*Ejército Zapatista de Liberación Nacional*) as they are formally known, had emerged out of the forests of the southern state of Chiapas in 1994 to announce their opposition to the neo-liberal globalized order inaugurated by the signing of the NAFTA treaty, and their intention to defend the interests of the state's marginalized indigenous peoples. Although there were, and have continued to be, armed and violent encounters, the Zapatistas have proved to be a much more complex, imaginative and successful movement than more conventional leftist guerrillas in the region. First, they have sought to build autonomous enclaves in Chiapas rather than overthrow the Mexican state; second, their absolute insistence on participatory democracy has deeply and successfully rooted them in their communities; third, they have actively sought allies at home and abroad, utilizing digital technologies to spread the word and build international alliances that have stayed the most violent hand of the Mexican authorities. In this realm, in particular, football has proved an invaluable tool. The central figure in this has been Subcomandante Marcos, the masked public persona assumed by the EZLN leader. Widely believed to be former university lecturer Rafael Guillén Vicente, he has impishly claimed a multiplicity of alternative past lives, including being a member of the youth team at Monterrey. More concrete evidence of his relationship to football emerged in a widely circulated exchange with the Uruguayan writer Eduardo Galeano. In the course of a long letter, in which he described watching local kid Olivio play football with Zapatista commander Major Moises, he revealed, 'I am a discreet, serious and analytical fan. One of those that reviews the percentages and histories.'[27]

A year later, in 1995, the EZLN, having secured their base in Chiapas where they had created a network of self-governing communities, took the struggle to Mexico City, where they were campaigning for a rewrite of the Mexican constitution to enshrine the rights of indigenous peoples. The signing of the San Andrés Agreements that emerged from this process was marked by a game of football staged between a team of veteran Mexican internationals and an EZLN team. The veterans had to supply the Zapatistas, who had arrived in their combat gear, with old football boots. Despite the heat, the insurgents played in their usual masks and balaclavas. The Mexicans won 5–3, but Subcomandante Marcos praised the playful, vivacious spirit of the Zapatistas, arguing that 'we did not lose because we did not have time to win, as Napoleon put it. The boys were affected by height, climate, smog, the pitch, the Asian crisis, Popocatepetl, the Clinton–Lewinsky affair and those jerseys that fit two into one.'[28] Alerted to the football politics of the EZLN, the most adventurous of Europe's radical football clubs came to play. In 2000, Bristol's Easton Cowboys toured Chiapas, accompanied by street artist Banksy, whose early murals can still be seen there.[29] Italian fans came afterwards and helped fund a community stadium in the rebel enclave of Guadalupe Tepeyac.

The more cordial relations established with the Mexican state were short-lived, as the EZLN deemed that new legislation had broken the terms of the San Andrés Agreements and the two sides returned to a state of low-intensity warfare in Chiapas. It was under those conditions that the EZLN received one of its most unusual offers of support. Javier Zanetti, Argentinian captain of Inter Milan, had persuaded the club to allow him to collect changing-room fines and donate them to the EZLN to rebuild a damaged medical centre in Zinacantán. In an open letter to the movement, Zanetti wrote, 'We believe in a better world, an unglobalized world, enriched by cultural difference and the customs of all the people.' Inter coach Bruno Bartolozzi delivered money and supplies later in the year. Subcomandante Marcos appeared in an Inter shirt and sent an open letter to the club president, the Milanese oil billionaire Massimo Moratti.[30] Announcing that he had been appointed both coach and 'Head of Intergalactic Relations' for the EZLN football team, Marcos proposed a home-and-away tie against Inter. The home match would raise money for legal aid for political prisoners in Mexico. Maradona would be the referee, the Uruguayan writers Eduardo Galeano and Mario Bendetti would call the play-by-play, and Mexico's LGBT community would be invited to do the half-time show. Then he really got going: a game in Los Angeles to support the undocumented in

California? A game in Cuba to protest the US blockade? On their way to Milan they could make a detour to the Basque country to support the separatists? 'We might, perhaps, revolutionize world football, and then, perhaps, football would no longer be just a business and once again be a game of true feelings.'[31] Moratti replied with considerable enthusiasm, but though the EZLN–Inter relationship has persisted, there has, as yet, been no game.

In 2005 and 2006 the EZLN were too busy with the Other Campaign – a riposte to the 2006 presidential election campaign, rejecting the electoral system for a national tour of alliance-building, protest and solidarity with the marginal and poor across Mexico – to be considering an international football tournament or even Mexico's progress at the World Cup. Andrés Manuel López Obrador of the PRD, the left's candidate again and this time the favourite for the presidency, also steered clear of football, refused to appear in televised debates, and took his message on the road too. However, Felipe Calderón, candidate of the PAN, did keep focused on the sport and, despite trailing López Obrador for much of the campaign, won the election on a razor-thin margin of 243,000 votes out of 41 million. Challenged on the streets and in the courts, the federal election commission ratified Calderón's victory and his *sexieno* began.

A few weeks into his presidency, Calderón made the decision that defined the next six years. He ordered Mexican military units into the north of the country to close down the cartels. Over the next six years, at least 80,000 deaths could be attributed to the war and a million people were internally displaced. In the cities of the north, bodies were hung from motorway overpasses, corpses were left on the street, and beheading became widespread. The drug trade itself was almost entirely unaffected, but Mexican civil society paid the price for the complex series of conflicts unleashed. The cartels divided, and fought each other and the army, all in a context where the local police forces, judiciary and municipal governments were often in their hands to begin with. Their reach now extended to the military and intelligence services. At the murderous height of the war he had unleashed, President Calderón was unrepentant, happy to find inspiration from any source to support the reckless course he had set for the nation. When *El Tri* beat Italy, albeit in a friendly before the 2010 World Cup, he was ecstatic, saying, 'the National Team is showing something that Mexicans need to exercise more often, which is character, determination, a vision determined not to give up, not to be overwhelmed by fatality or criticism.'

Calderón bowed out of the presidency in 2012, and was succeeded by Enrique Peña Nieto, candidate of the PRI, whose policy-free centrism and vague promise to rein in the madness of the drug war saw him easily beat the opposition. In power, he proved as uninspiring and predictable as his slick campaign had promised. Even Mexico's unexpected gold medal at the London 2012 Olympics men's football tournament, in which they beat Brazil 2–1 in the final, could only evoke the anodyne. In his state of the union address, given a month later, Peña Nieto argued that

> The Mexican team gave us the gold medal against Brazil, what better testimony to demonstrate to Mexicans that if we put on the shirt and sweat we can show that Mexico is a country that can be a power, that Mexico can face any challenge.[32]

Well, maybe. Peña Nieto suffered cripplingly low levels of public support, and presided over a *sexieno* of unparalleled torpor, unable to enact any of the key reforms on corruption, taxation, monopolies and infrastructure that Mexico required. A better guide to the meaning of the victory in 2012 was the lower-key note struck by the winning coach, Luis Fernando Tena, who told TV Azteca, 'We know this isn't going to change the problems of anybody, much less the country, but the win is a proud moment for a country so in need of happiness.'[33]

Mexico followed up this triumph with their worst qualification campaign for a World Cup in two generations, and at one point in 2013 had four coaches in a month. The last of these was Miguel Herrera, known as *El Piojo* (The Louse), whose touchline mania, berserk responses to referees and hyperactive social media accounts got *El Tri* through their qualifying play-off with New Zealand and into the round of sixteen in Brazil. Up against the Netherlands, Giovanni dos Santos gave them a 1–0 lead. For almost forty-five minutes, the prospect of the *quinto partido* lay before team and nation. Then the Dutch scored two goals in six minutes and it was all over, all over again. The following year Herrera would lead the team to victory in the 2015 Gold Cup, but he was fired after punching Christian Martinoli, a journalist with TV Azteca, while queuing for the return flight home. The national team has been mediocre, at best, since his departure, and though it qualified for the 2018 World Cup, no one was expecting any *quinto partido* any time soon. Juan Virollo, reflecting on all the tribulations of *El Tri*, was mordant. 'Crimes can be redeemed, but nothing saves you from mediocrity.'[34]

What explains this mediocrity? What accounts for the pervasive sense of permanent underperformance in Mexico? One constant is that Mexican football, like the nation's economy, is owned and run by a very narrow circle of the country's richest men and their factotums, for whom neither football nor the public good is a high priority. The relationships between football, politics and business were first established in the 1960s by Emilio Azcarraga, owner of Mexico's dominant, indeed hegemonic, media company, Televisa. Closely linked politically and personally with the PRI, Televisa delivered ideologically supportive news and, where that didn't work, the fabulous distractions of its soap operas, comedies, endless variety shows and spectacular, relentless coverage of football. Above all, it covered Club América, and made it the PRI's team. In the twenty-first century, both the PRI and Televisa have lost their monopolies and, although América has been able to win the occasional title, this triumvirate is no longer the dominant force it was in the 1970s and 1980s.[35] The long-term challenger to Televisa's control of both football and the media has come from TV Azteca, itself part of the vast Grupo Salinas amassed by Ricardo Salinas, Mexico's fourth richest man and owner of the football clubs Atlas and Morelia. The Televisa–Azteca duopoly, established in the first decade of the twenty-first century, was challenged both technologically and financially by Carlos Slim, Mexico's richest man and owner of Grupo America and Movil, the telecoms company with the vast majority of the nation's fixed lines and mobile business. Initially unconcerned with football, Slim was looking to break into the TV and cable market, while protecting himself from existing cable operators challenging his telecom business. Purchasing the clubs León and Pachuca gave him content for a media business and a seat at the football politics table, though his recent sale of both signals a rare retreat.[36]

Others are not to be moved. Cruz Azul, the working-class team of Mexico City, remained the proud possession of the industrial conglomerate CemMex. Valentin Díez Morodo, the fabulously connected banker and businessman, whose portfolio of directorships encompasses most of the Mexican economy, held onto Deportivo Toluca.

Jorge Vergara, the vitamin king of the Spanish-speaking world, has owned Guadalajara since 2002, turning the team of nativist Mexican nationalism – still yet to sign a non-Mexican player – into a billboard for his oft-questioned global pyramid-selling herbal remedy scheme.[37] More conventionally, old-fashioned patrician politics has been at work in Tijuana, where the billionaire scion of an old PRI family, Jorge Hank Rohn, then mayor of the city, founded a new team in 2007. Tijuana FC, known locally as Xolos, were quickly promoted to the top division on the back of his huge online gambling fortune. Rohn had served as the city's mayor between 2004 and 2007 and held aspirations for higher office. Speaking in 2011, he boasted, 'Xolos are obviously the team of Baja California but also the team of the PRI. The rise of the Xolos brings votes for the party and for me in the race for governor.' Perhaps the electorate paid more attention to the murder of a journalist carried out by Rohn's bodyguards, or the police raid on his home that uncovered hundreds of illegal firearms, for his run at the governorship of Baja California faltered and he remains, for the moment, without political office.[38]

If there are still some limits on the purchase of power in Mexico, the same cannot be said of a place in the top division. Mexico, almost uniquely in world football, combines promotion and relegation with a club franchise system, which means that any big club that gets relegated can buy its way back to the top by purchasing the franchise of another club and moving it; thus small and medium-sized towns are forever losing their teams, particularly on the rare occasions that they manage to make it to the top division. Irapuato, for example, after decades of lower-division football, finally won promotion in 2001, only to be immediately closed down, the club having been bought by richer business people in Veracruz, whose own franchise had inconveniently been relegated. A second incarnation of the club was closed down in 2004 for drug-related financial irregularities, then a third version was established in 2010, but lasted just three years before being relocated to Zacatepec. A fourth Irapuato has emerged, but only on the basis of the purchase of the franchise of an even smaller club from an even smaller city.[39]

The atmosphere in Mexico's stadiums is not entirely helping the game's development. In the late twentieth century, Mexican football was a little rough around the edges. Like everywhere, it proved a catalyst for the formation of groups of young men poised between supporters' club and gangs, but it was, by and large, peaceful. This began to change in the late 1990s, after the fans of Pachuca brought in Argentinian and Chilean advisers and began to transform themselves into a more conventional Latin American *barra bravas*, both in terms of their mode of support (drums, organized chanting, etc.) and in their use of violence and intimidation to obtain kudos, tickets and money. By 2003, every first division team had acquired such a group.[40] In 2007, the authorities responded by bringing in new and stronger legislation to control crowds and police football. It has been no surprise to anyone that this has made not the slightest difference; indeed, the situation has worsened. Emboldened and empowered, the new *barra bravas* have been flagrant. For example, in 2013 the *barras* of Cruz Azul, then losing their game to Toluca, tore down the internal fencing of the stadium and invaded the pitch, some making it as far as the players' tunnel, to which the objects of their ire had retreated.[41] Guadalajara has, perhaps, seen the worst of the violence and disorder. In 2012, the city derby between Atlas and Chivas – as Guadalaraja are colloquially known – was played out while the Chivas *barras* and the police viciously fought each other in the stands. Three years later, when Chivas knocked Atlas out of the quarter-finals of the national championships, the Atlas fans invaded the pitch looking to attack their own players. Out-of-towners beware! When Atlas played Monterrey in 2014, again losing a quarter-final of the national championship, their fans set upon both the police, who were beaten with their own batons, and the away fans, who, under cover of tear gas, were forced to reconvene on the pitch for their own safety.[42] Things are no better in the lower leagues: the final of the second division championship in 2016 between Necaxa and San Luis was finished off with a huge parking lot brawl accompanied by gunshots. More recently, Veracruz fans, when their team was 3–0 down at home to Tigres, broke through a security cordon and attacked the away fans on live television.[43]

If Mexican football suffers from many of the same problems as the economic system it operates within, it also reflects the consequences of the nation's unending war against its own drug cartels. The game's involvement with the drug trade first surfaced in the 1990s, when the banker and businessman Jorge Lankenau bought Monterrey and began the garish commercial transformation of Mexican football. He introduced the characteristic multi-brand mobile billboard look of the country's club shirts, shorts and socks, put advertising into the stadiums and painted it onto the pitch itself. Lankenau was arrested in 1997 on a variety of charges, mainly money-laundering and tax evasion via his own Banco Confina, with cash linked to the local Juárez cartel and their Colombian partner in Cali. In 2003, Carlos Alvarez, a Colombian defender who had played for Necaxa, was arrested at Mexico City airport heading to Medellín with a million dollars in his luggage. Under questioning he revealed that someone, whose name he had forgotten, had offered him $50,000 on delivery of the cash to a mysterious person in Colombia called 'El Negro'. He stayed silent and served five years. The US State Department and Drug Enforcement Agency have been more vocal, identifying Jorge Mario Rios Laverde, an active football agent in Mexico, as a member of a Colombian cartel. They also noted that José Tirso Martinez, then owner of two club franchises – Queretaro and Irapuato – transported seventy-six tonnes of cocaine to the USA between 2000 and 2003. The authorities eventually revoked Martinez's licence, dissolved the clubs and then pretended that this kind of issue would disappear.[44]

All this occurred before Calderón's fateful decision in 2006 to militarize the conflict with the cartels. In the years since, the cities of the north of Mexico and their football clubs have had to operate in what has, in effect, been a war zone. At the same time, the corrupting influence of drug money, already pervasive, has become ubiquitous. In the northern border town of Ciudad Juárez, where at the height of the killing in 2010 over 3,000 homicides were recorded, the decline and then collapse of the local club Indios was a measure of the city's own desperate situation. The team's youth coach was shot dead in a mobile phone shop, and the goalkeeper left town after a thief held a gun to his head. A record twenty-seven consecutive winless games followed, the anteroom to relegation, bankruptcy and, in 2012, dissolution.[45] The return of some kind of normality since the end of Calderón's *sexieno* has also seen the return of football to the city. Los Bravos de FC Juárez, backed by a consortium of PRI-linked business people, entered the second division in 2015 and immediately won promotion. An obvious vehicle for political advancement, the club's change of name and shirt colour to the green of the PRI have met with considerable fan resistance. This battle is, so far, merely rhetorical. In 2011, in Torreón in northern Mexico, the game between local club Santos Laguna and Morelia was interrupted when a huge and very real gun battle began between the Los Zetas drug cartel and city police directly outside the stadium. The match was abandoned and much of the crowd remained on the pitch, unable and unwilling to enter the killing fields outside.[46]

At least in Torreón the cartels remained outside the stadium. The rest of Mexican football has been colonized in innumerable ways. As relatively wealthy individuals, footballers have long been a target for the gangs and micro-cartels who supplement their narcotics income with ransoms and kidnapping. In 2005, for example, Cruz Azul's coach Romano Ruben was held for over two months, while in 2016, Alan Pulido, a national team forward, was kidnapped in his home state of Tamaulipas. Footballers are not so wealthy, though, that they cannot be enticed to change sides. In 2012 the goalkeeper Omar Ortiz, then suspended from his club Monterrey for steroid use, was arrested and charged with aiding a gang of kidnappers. Ortiz's role was, it was said, to pick out suitable victims from amongst his wealthy circle for members of the Gulf cartel to abduct and ransom. Footballers are also prized by the cartels as friends and associates. Jared Borgetti, one of the national team's most prolific strikers, was close enough to ex-Tijuana cartel boss Francisco Arellano Felix to see him assassinated at his birthday party by a man in a clown outfit.[47] More insidious, and suggestive of much more extensive financial links between the cartels and football, was the murder, in Aguascalientes, of Paola Portillo, a twenty-seven-year-old woman with known connections to the cartels but none to football. On her person was found a folder with the original contracts of the Colombian players Eisner Loboa and Hernan Burban, who had been with León for a couple of seasons. There was, needless to say, no investigation into this bizarre connection by the Mexican football authorities. The federal authorities in the United States were less accommodating. In 2017, after a long investigation into the operation of Raul Flores Hernandez – a mid-level drug trader and money-laundering expert – the US State Department announced that forty-three individuals and institutions were to have their US assets frozen. This included Rafael Marquez, captain of the national team at four World Cups, who the Americans claimed had acted as a front for one of Hernandez's many money-laundering operations. Marquez, who denies everything, remains connected and beyond the reach of the US authorities. Daniel Gomez, a young defender at Tijuana, was not so lucky. Arrested at the US–Mexico border with forty-eight pounds of methamphetamine in his car, he can look forward to a long period of incarceration.[48]

The country has been trying to look forward to a different kind of Mexico. The 2018 World Cup, for which *El Tri* had qualified with some ease, was accompanied by not so much the election of Andrés Manuel López Obrador, by then known as AMLO, the left's defeated candidate for more than a decade, as his stately progress towards a coronation. Up to thirty points ahead of all his competitors for much of the campaign, he promised a real assault on the nation's endemic corruption and structural inequalities. Mexico's elite could see what was coming. For the first time the Azcarragas and Televisa, normally AMLO's sworn nemesis, rented the Estadio Azteca to him for his final campaign rally. Hope, for once, was palpable. *El Tri* had opened their campaign by defeating the reigning champions Germany, and scrapped their way to the round of sixteen. *El Quinto Partido* and an AMLO presidency awaited. 'Just as we dreamed for Mexico to be the World Champions,' said one fan, exhilarated by the team's progress, 'we want our country to be free, filled with peace and prosperity.' Brazil put paid to the first half of this plan, dispatching *El Tri* 2–0, but AMLO won the election by a landslide. If his administration can make it anywhere close to delivering on the second half of the statement, it will, even in Mexico, be a bigger triumph than winning any football game, anywhere.

IV

Lansing is a small and forlorn rust-belt city in Michigan in the Midwest of the United States. In 2012, I spent an evening at the indoor football centre, a piece of miniature 1970s brutalism. Outside, a backlit, lozenge-shaped sign still announced 'Indoor Baseball'. That was then: in 2012 it was buzzing with football. Just finishing up were a group of white middle-class high school students. Back in the 1970s, they would have been doing softball practice at best, but more likely cheerleading. Now they were warming down and goofing about after an hour of five-a-side. One young woman held the ball between her toes and, keeping it there, executed a front flip. At the apex of the turn, she let the ball go and it looped over to her friend, who cushioned it on her chest. Warming up on the second pitch, with pleasingly undue seriousness, were a bunch of guys, old enough to be their fathers, and perhaps they played baseball here as kids, but now football is the game, and from the look of the assorted replica shirts, the Premier League is the thing. The team I was with were a bunch of hyphenated professionals and recent arrivals: an Italian-American historian, a German philosopher, a Lebanese restaurant owner whose collection of shirts – 1970s' Juventus, Bayer Leverkusen – was much more obscure and cosmopolitan. The opposition arrived as they warmed up: a team of blue-collar Latinos, decked out in a range of Chivas Guadalajara shirts that accounted for most of the last twenty years. They had also brought friends, their families, a picnic and some atmosphere to proceedings. The whippet-thin referee, in austere black, called the captains to the coin toss and, with thin flanks of hair either side of his pate and round gold spectacles, he appeared the spitting image of the fork-wielding farmer in Grant Wood's painting *American Gothic*.

My evening in Lansing was hardly conclusive proof of the transformation in football's popularity in the United States. Neither Lansing's indoor football, nor football culture as a whole, is a demographic Xerox of the nation. African and Asian Americans, absent on that occasion, are generally under-represented in the game. The evening was, however, tangible evidence of the geographical reach and depth of the game in the United States and its three core constituencies: women, middle-class urban white men and Latinos. By comparison to the other major leagues, the rosters and audiences of MLS are the most ethnically diverse in the United States.[49] The NHL, and ice hockey in general, is almost exclusively white. The NBA, WNBA and the NFL have a majority of African American athletes and precious few Latinos. MLB is closer to America's demographic mix right now – its players are around 60 per cent white, 30 per cent Latino and 10 per cent African American – but the future is MLS, where there are no majorities. In 2017 its players were 48 per cent white, 25 per cent Latino, 10 per cent African American, and 20 per cent other, many of them black players from overseas. Whatever the precise ethnic breakdown of the men's professional game, football, as the Lansing 'dads' team suggests, has finally found a sustainable place in the mainstream of American sports culture.

On television, at any rate, this meant that foreign football's viewing figures and advertising rates were good enough, in 2015, for NBC sports to pay a billion dollars for the US rights to the English Premier League. Alongside this, America's cosmopolitan football fans and recent arrivals, still wedded to the game at 'home', have easy access to the UEFA Champions League, La Liga, the Bundesliga and Serie A, not to mention much of Latin America's football season and the soccer-dominated sports channels of the Middle East and the Gulf. It is noticeable that this has nurtured a huge outpouring of writing on foreign football in the United States. ESPN and *Sports Illustrated* have taken note and expanded their coverage, while once virtually football-free zones, like the *New York Times*, the *Wall Street Journal*, the *New Yorker* and even *Vanity Fair*, have started covering the game.

Despite this kind of competition, MLS, just six years old at the turn of the century, when it was losing franchises and bleeding money, has now been going for two decades and has expanded from just ten teams in 1996 to twenty-three in 2017, with more in the pipeline. Its TV audiences remain small, but the league is now played in soccer-specific stadiums rather than the cavernous arenas built for American football, and crowd numbers are good. Average attendance has almost doubled from a low of 13,000 in 2000 to over 22,000 in 2017, while the addition of many franchises has seen total attendance rise from just over 2 million in 1996 to more than 8 million a year today. Inevitably, the collision of such a globally conscious cosmopolitan football culture with crowds of this size has nurtured all kinds of new fan cultures. Broadly speaking, MLS's organized fans take their lead from the *tifo* and song-driven repertoire of Italian ultras, minus the organized crime connection, while there is plenty of ahistorical affection for the blue-collar machismo of an imaginary England of the 1970s and 1980s: thus the many dire Hollywood hooligan movies of recent years, *Green Street* being the most typical. In a strange pantomime reinterpretation of that era's particular version of toxic masculinity, fist fights have not been unknown in MLS, and are a presence amongst the American Outlaws, the men's national team's organized fans.[50] At the other end of the gender spectrum, fans of women's club the Portland Thorns have created fearsomely loud and intimidating atmospheres without a hint of machismo.[51]

In toto, soccer in the United States remains some way short of the big three, but it is certainly challenging ice hockey for number four. However, if we were to see all of these sports not merely as men's games but women's as well, then football's position would be higher. American soccer draws on only part of the ethnic, regional and class spectrum in the United States, but in the realm of gender it is the nation's most telling sporting avatar. Lansing's new freestyle footballers are just one tiny indication of the biggest and most developed women's football culture in the world. The United States began the twenty-first century with 7 million registered women football players, more than the rest of the world put together and, although the rest of the world is catching up, it remains the power in the women's game. The US won the inaugural FIFA Women's World Cup in 1991, came third in 1995, won the gold medal at the Atlanta Olympics in 1996, then rounded things off by hosting and winning the 1999 World Cup. Mia Hamm was the most accomplished female player of the era. Brandi Chastain delivered the team's most iconic visual moment, though it required her to remove her shirt and reveal her sports bra when celebrating after the 1999 World Cup final penalty shoot-out to get on the front page of *Sports Illustrated*. Since then, the United States has been one of the few countries in the world where the press and public routinely differentiate between the men's and women's national teams by name, referring to them by the ungainly but egalitarian acronyms USMNT and USWNT.

Yet, despite the obvious strengths of women's football in the USA – a huge grassroots pool of players and clubs, very strong women's soccer programmes in higher education boosted by Title IX monies, high levels of technical ability, regular success for the national team, and at least some media coverage – it has taken three attempts to create a sustainable women's professional league. The first, the Women's United Soccer Association (WUSA), launched with much fanfare in 2001, lasted just three seasons. Its successor, the Women's Professional Soccer League (WPSL), tried to operate on a more modest scale in smaller stadiums, but still managed to burn out financially in three years, overspending on expensive imported stars. The third model, the National Women's Soccer League (NWSL), launched in 2012, has so far steered a steadier course and lasted longer. The US women's national team, by their own high standards, have faltered, only making the semi-final of the next two World Cups, ceding top spot in the world rankings to the Germans and losing the 2011 World Cup final to the Japanese. However, in 2015, the Women's World Cup held in Canada demonstrated just how popular the women's game had become in North America, and how good the USA national team could be.

The 2011 edition had broken records for attendance and media coverage, but the 2015 World Cup exceeded it in every way.[52] A record 1.4 million tickets were sold, many of them to Americans, who formed a significant presence at a lot of games. In the United States, where Fox had been given the rights for free by FIFA, ratings were unprecedented. The final saw the USA blow the Japanese away, taking a 4–0 lead in just sixteen minutes, including a whirl-wind hat-trick from Carli Lloyd, and finishing as 5–2 victors. It attracted 25 million viewers, and was the most watched game of football in US television history. The squad was accorded that pecu-liar, but special accolade of Americana: a New York City ticker tape parade.[53] In the wake of this triumph, attendances at NWSL games rose, and the team's stars acquired serious sponsorship deals.

Money and fame have not so far blunted the squad's critical edge or its capacity to make waves. The USWNT was amongst the most voluble of FIFA's critics when it announced that the 2015 World Cup would be played on artificial turf – a decision that it is impossible to imagine them applying to the men's game – and has been a noisy advocate for equal pay. Five World Cup winners, Megan Rapinoe, Hope Solo, Becky Sauerbrunn, Carli Lloyd and Alex Morgan, filed a legal complaint against the USSF with the US Equal Opportunities Commission. Solo has gone on to contest the presidency of the USSF and has called out Sepp Blatter, who she claimed 'grab[bed] my ass' before the 2014 Ballon d'Or ceremony. Rapinoe, in particular, has been an outspoken supporter of LGBT rights, and in 2017, in sup-port of the NFL's Colin Kaepernick, took a knee during the playing of the national anthem before two USA games. All have been critics of the Trump presidency.[54]

This kind of political edge is certainly one reason why women's football in particular, and football in general, appear alien and sus-picious to the nationalist right and its constituencies. In 2014, the political performance artiste Ann Coulter took to the internet and the chat shows to lambast football with the same tropes that nativists and preachers of American exceptionalism have been deploying for almost a century: 'a sport for girls and Third World peasants'. More politically pointedly, she argued:

> If more 'Americans' are watching soccer today, it's only because of the demographic switch effected by Teddy Kennedy's 1965 immigration law. I promise you: no American whose great-grandfather was born here is watching soccer. One can only hope that, in addition to learning English, these new Americans will drop their soccer fetish with time.[55]

Not only are they not going to drop their soccer fetish, they are also watching other people's soccer. In fact, the most popular and bankable team in US soccer is *El Tri*, the Mexican national side. Once considered an irrelevant Yankee backwater, the Mexicans started playing friendlies in the US in the early 1990s, and when, in 1995, a game against Chile in Los Angeles drew 60,000 people it was clear there was money to be made. Since 2003, in a deal with the US football authorities' murky commercial arm SUM, *El Tri* have played the majority of their friendlies in the USA, where at $2 million a game they are bringing in more than triple what they would at home. Chicanos cannot get enough of them. Between 2007 and 2017, sixty-two of the ninety-three games played by *El Tri* in the United States, more than half of them friendlies, attracted more than 50,000 people.[56] Many of these games are concentrated in Latino strongholds like Southern California, where a midweek friendly against lowly New Zealand could still bring 90,000 to the Rose Bowl. However, as America's Latino population has grown and spread geographically, *El Tri*'s appeal has widened, with huge crowds attending matches in Atlanta, Charlotte and Nashville. Everywhere they play, games are prefaced by a sea of tricolours in green, white and red, the sound-track is provided by mariachi bands, and nostalgia for home is widely available at the taco stands, the stalls selling *pinatas* and Liga MX shirts. Games have a double-sized camera crew, one half filming to feature Spanish-language advertising, the other, working from the reverse position, to feature English-language brands; together they are bringing in around $50 million a year to the Mexican Football Federation. For the older generation of Mexican-Americans, their enthusiasm and allegiance are unproblematic: 'I will root for Michael Phelps or Gabby Douglas or other American athletes, but I unapologetically will never root for American soccer. I root exclusively for Mexico, it's not even an issue I struggle with.'[57] Indeed, they not only root for Mexico but they wish their hosts ill: 'If the United States gets better than Mexico at soccer then what do we have over you guys?'[58] More recently, second- and third-generation Chicanos and Chicanas are finding the choice more complex: some parents are going to games in Mexican green, but with their kids in tow in red, white and blue, but they are a minority.[59]

While *El Tri* is the most popular team, the United States' most popular league, by television ratings at any rate, is neither MLS or even the EPL, but Liga MX. Once just the Mexican *Primera*, the re-branded Liga MX opened its 2016 season with a double-header at the StubHub Centre in Carson, south Los Angeles, and is looking to replicate the annual visits of *El Tri*.[60] The call of home is strong enough in Southern California that one quarter of the crowd that watches the Xolos of Tijuana will have crossed the border and driven south from the United States. There they have been able to see Mexican-American players like Joe Corona, who commutes to the Xolos from San Diego. As one supporter put it, 'We're not a Mexican club, we're not an American club. We're a border club.' Another imagined the region without the borders at all, the old *El Norte* of the Spanish empire: 'Xolos represent both Baja California and Southern California.'[61]

In this context, it is hardly surprising that MLS and professional football in the United States has struggled to attract the unambiguous interest of its potential Latino audience. Indeed, it has, on occasion, gone out of its way to alienate them: for example, the naming of Houston 1836, the date of Texan independence and the defeat of the Mexican empire, in a city with a huge Latino population. More promising was the establishment of a second Los Angeles MLS franchise, Chivas USA, owned and branded by the Mexican giants Guadalajara FC – more often known by their nickname *Chivas* or 'Goats'. The most self-consciously Mexican of the country's football teams, with a bar on fielding foreign players, Guadalajara obviously hoped to parlay their Mexican nativism into a big homesick audience in Southern California. The task was made easier by the fact that LA Galaxy, the city's first franchise, were obviously closer in style and demographic to the white Westside and the Hollywood Hills than to East LA or Boyle Heights. Launched in 2005, in a kit and with a badge near identical to Guadalajara's, Chivas USA never quite delivered on their promise on or off the pitch. After a reasonable first few years, with a second-place finish and crowds averaging around 17,000, Jorge Vergara, owner of Guadalajara, bought out his local Mexican business partners in Chivas USA and then really drove the club into the ground before dissolving it altogether.[62]

If MLS and the professional spectacle have had little success in attracting and retaining Latino support, they have at least not tried to exclude it. The same cannot be said of organized grassroots youth soccer in the United States. Unlike in much of the football world, American grassroots football has not been the provenance of either the official football authorities and the pyramid of professional and amateur clubs that train and develop players in Europe and Latin America, or, as in Africa, a network of private academies that scout talent on the street and export it to the world. The penury of the USSF, the instability of professional football and the absence of the street game from the nation's cities closed off all of these options. Instead, the single most important actor in shaping youth football has been the American Youth Soccer Organization (AYSO), whose clubs and classes have been ubiquitous in American suburbia since the 1970s. As one sharp observer of the organization wrote, 'The leaders of AYSO sought to redefine the sport so that it would not be seen as a foreign game, but instead the perfect game for the newly ascendant suburbs. These leaders were explicit in seeing the ethnic nature of soccer as a problem,'[63] and in achieving these aims they have proved very successful.

It is worth reminding ourselves of the depth of the problem AYSO faced. Although football had been part of American sports culture since the third quarter of the nineteenth century, and had been able to sustain small professional leagues at the turn of the twentieth and in the 1920s, it was predominantly played and followed by working-class and recent migrant communities. Baseball had long claimed the mantle of national game, and American football was the nativist's code. Football, by contrast, was enduringly foreign: the preserve of recalcitrant minorities who would not or could not integrate. The closer the rest of the world cleaved to the game, the more American disinterest could be read as a proud emblem of American exceptionalism. AYSO countered this discourse by working with the grain of white American middle-class parenting,

which, shaped by both Dr Spock and the ripples of the countercul-
ture, found traditional American sports like baseball and gridiron
either too confrontational and violent or too authoritarian. In time,
as basketball became the sport of the African-American inner city, it
would also prove to be too black. Thus in the 1960s and 1970s, the
centre of gravity of grassroots football completely switched from
mainly migrant enclaves, including the new Latino arrivals, to the
white middle-class suburbs, where AYSO ruled in alliance with the
'soccer moms' of America.

While AYSO has the recreational and community end of the game
all sewn up, the space for more competitive football has been occupied by private clubs, or 'travel teams' as they are known. This system,
known as pay-to-play, means annual fees from $3,000 to $6,000 a
year for participants, sums out of reach for most working-class and
minority households. Even then, there are the additional hidden costs
of time, extra training camps, transport and hotels for any family
hoping to support their child's football career. A few of these clubs
will have the odd bursary, but even these are prized by middle-class
families looking to get their offspring, if not to the big leagues, then
to one of the increasing number of soccer scholarships at state and
private universities. Even without these kinds of structural and economic barriers to participation, Latino players, coaches and parents
have to deal with the inevitable micro-aggressions of everyday life in
America: the invariable assumption by opponents that their players
will be uncouth or untrainable, and disrespect for their accent and
language.

If football in the United States is so divided, it is hardly surprising
that the men's national team did not, unlike most places, attract
much attention or function as a space in which any kind of nation
could be imagined. Even a game against Iran at the 1998 World Cup
went unnoticed by most. It also helps if you are any good. It is a measure of the injustice of the world that the US Women's National Team
has had to win the World Cup three times to start getting really
noticed. The US men's team surfaced in the wider popular culture
after making it to just the knock-out rounds of the men's World Cup.
In 2002, a series of gutsy performances peaked when they beat Portugal in the round of sixteen and then went on to lose to Germany in the
quarter-final. What would have, in almost any other nation, brought
life to a momentary halt barely flickered on the collective radar. Even

victory in the CONCACAF Gold Cup in 2013, recording the USA's first win over Mexico in the Azteca stadium, failed to penetrate far beyond the small core of football fans. The 2014 World Cup would be different. For the third time in a row, Americans would be the most enthusiastic ticket buyers for a World Cup, travelling in large numbers to Brazil. The team, under California-based German Jürgen Klinsmann, had sharply improved. While there was some disquiet over the number of German-Americans he had discovered and brought into the team, the squad was actually the most ethnically diverse to go to a World Cup. It included players with Latino roots (Alejandro Bedoya, Omar Gonzalez, Nick Rimando), African-American heritage (Jozy Altidore, Tim Howard, Jermaine Jones, DaMarcus Beasley), plus DeAndre Yedlin, who could claim African-American, Native American and Dominican ancestry, while at the same time being celebrated for being the first player to come into the team who had been developed by MLS and its home player policies.

Their second match, against Portugal, drew around 24 million viewers, and was, at the time, the most watched game of football in US history. To put that in perspective, the final game of that year's NBA finals had attracted only 18 million viewers and the best rated game of MLB's World series the previous year had been watched by just 15 million people. The team was good, but for television purposes, the travelling crowd was even better. In addition to the American Outlaws, a noisy, boisterous American crowd gathered, peppered with fanzine superhero costumes (Captain America) and historical figures (General Patton), belting out 'U-S-A', 'When the Yanks go marching in', and, in defiance of all analysis, the old US Navy chant 'I believe that we will win'. However, when the cameras found 'Teddy Goalsevelt' celebrating the US equalizer in the first-round game against Portugal in Manaus, they had found their man. Mike D'Amico had taken a month off from his Chicago advertising job, blown his savings and headed for the Brazilian World Cup. There, in a safari suit and droopy moustache, he appeared as the living incarnation of US President Theodore 'Teddy' Roosevelt. In minutes, Goalsevelt had gone viral. The next day he was on *Good Morning America* and the front page of the *Wall Street Journal*. A crowdfunding effort to keep him in Brazil as long as the US were playing was completed in days. Jürgen Klinsmann tweeted a standard letter for fans to give their employees, asking for a day off to back the USA. Public spaces and parks in US cities saw unprecedented crowds gather for the games. The US would lose their third game against Germany 1–0, but it was enough to take them through on goal difference to a round of sixteen clash with the Belgians, which they then lost in extra time. On the squad's return, Clint Dempsey made it all the way to the Letterman show, not an honour accorded to previous returnees. Teddy Goalsevelt spoke for some when he tried to present this new spasm of sporting patriotism in a depoliticized light.

> US soccer gives people an outlet to be patriotic in a way that doesn't feel like there's so much at stake. You're not proving that your political ideology is better, you're not proving that you support the troops more than someone else. It's a way to show your love and your pride in our country through a way that is purely about joy.[64]

But one blogger was much sharper in his analysis.

> For a generation who have watched over-confidence in American power lead to disaster, cheering for the US in a contest that we knew we wouldn't win offers a similar existential thrill. Soccer fandom in America is speculative fiction: What if the US was just a country among countries?[65]

Certainly the form of the USMNT since 2014 suggests a kind of normality, with the team proving so infuriatingly inconsistent that, despite very weak competition, it actually failed to qualify for World Cup 2018. Of course, this is a fiction for just one part of the American nation, the current football coalition of the urban middle-classes, women and Latinos. It may be that this narrative, like its political corollaries, has reached an upper limit of support.

7

THE GAME BEYOND THE GAME:
THE FALL OF THE HOUSE OF BLATTER

There's games beyond the fucking game.

Stringer Bell

I

In movies, comedy and politics, timing is everything. In spring 2015, Sepp Blatter may just have combined all three to perfection. In May that year, after four decades as an employee of FIFA and seventeen years as its president, Blatter announced that, pending new elections for the post, he was standing down. It had been an extraordinary long weekend, beginning with the mass arrest of football and television executives in FIFA's favoured Zurich hotel, followed by a FIFA congress in which Blatter retained his post in a contested election. It finished, two days later, with him announcing his resignation. Just three weeks after this, a thirty-million-dollar movie, financed almost entirely by FIFA, made its debut at the US box office. Entitled *United Passions*, it purported to tell the story of football's ruling body, with a sizeable role in the story for Sepp himself.[1]

The omens were not good. Completed in 2014, the film's only written review came from Jérôme Valcke, general secretary of FIFA, who had sent a DVD to all 209 member football associations, assuring them that the movie was 'open, self-critical and enjoyable to all'.[2] At best, the attached note indicated that he had failed to watch the film; at worst, it underlined his reputation for combining the oleaginous with the mendacious. The film had premiered at the Cannes film festival where, of its actors, only Gérard Depardieu, cast as mid-century FIFA president Jules Rimet, had had the front to show up on the red carpet. The rest of the cast – Jemima West as Rimet's daughter, Martin Jarvis and Sam Neill as Rimet's successors, Sir Stanley Rous and João Havelange, Tim Roth as Blatter himself – had maintained a suitable *omertà* over the whole proceedings. Louisa Maurin, chief executive of one of the film's production companies, claimed, 'We consider the film excellent, but in the cinema it is sometimes difficult for a film to find its audience.'[3] No kidding. There are reports of the film being screened in India, Portugal, Hungary, Serbia, Azerbaijan and Russia. There are even claims that someone, somewhere, actually paid to go and watch the movie in these territories, but they are uncorroborated. By the time the film made its sorry way to the United States, director Frédéric Auburtin was running for cover, telling the *Hollywood Reporter* that he thought he was going to make a cross between a 'Disney propaganda movie and a Costa-Gavras/Michael Moore movie', and imploring the industry to forgive him. 'My name is all over this mess,' he begged: 'don't remember me as the guy making propaganda movies for corrupt guys.'[4] His wish is unlikely to be granted. It is just as well for all concerned that they weren't on percentage deals. On the first and only weekend of its US theatrical release, *United Passions* took less than a thousand dollars. Some movies have lost more, some have taken even less, but none can claim a ratio of costs to box office so appallingly bad.

The anglophone press had a field day: 'Less a movie than a preposterous self-hagiography more appropriate for Scientology or the Rev. Sun Myung Moon. As cinema it is excrement.'[5] The *New York Times* rightly thought it 'one of the most unwatchable films in recent memory'.[6] All of which is absolutely true, yet, viewed from the right angle, *United Passions* reveals itself as a flawed but deeply illuminating gem. Consider its conditions of composition and production. The initial pitch to FIFA appears to have been made by producer Louisa Maurin in 2012 and was warmly received; so much so that over $10 million was immediately allocated to the project and the Azerbaijani film council came on board as well. Maurin then signed up Auburtin as the director. The ever-biddable Depardieu was recruited as the lead. The question of the script, however, remained. Auburtin and his colleague Jean-Paul Delfino received the final credit, but it has Blatter's hands all over it. Indeed, it is impossible to imagine that such a deranged and ludicrous rewriting of FIFA's history could have been accomplished without the very closest attention to the President's own unique interpretation of events.

In this regard, it's best to think of Blatter as your insufferably self-centred uncle. He's married to your increasingly miserable Auntie Lili, and he dotes on his bone-achingly dull daughter, Corinne. This is a man you have had to put up with for a lifetime of Sunday lunches and family dinners, sucking up all the oxygen; all the more so when lubricated by his seemingly inexhaustible supply of expensive single malts. It's a blur of stale, conservative homilies delivered as epigrams, along with the endless retelling of misremembered and reconstructed self-serving accounts of family life and his own career. It was bad enough when you were younger and had to endure the relish with which he told you about his sleazy sales tricks in the stockings trade and his glory years as an amateur footballer. Later, it became harder to take and impossible to process. Somehow, inexplicably, Uncle Sepp had ascended to a position of global visibility, status and power (not to mention acquiring a very comfortable bank balance). We're talking Uncle Sepp here.

The man was born in Visp in 1936, then a small village in francophone southern Switzerland, now a small town. In recent elections, nearly 70 per cent of voters chose the achingly conservative Catholic Christian Democrats, as they always have. The majority of the rest go with the right-wing anti-immigrant populists. Then, as now, the main employer was a chemicals plant where Blatter's own father worked. That was not for Uncle Sepp, who got himself to university, waited tables in the ski resorts and sang at weddings to help pay his way, and took his cues from Eddie Constantine, the louche American actor who had reinvented himself as a French B-movie detective and ladies' man. He may have stayed in Visp and married Liliane, the girl next door, but Uncle Sepp always had a roving eye. In the sixties, our family man tried his hand in the new worlds of marketing, corporate PR and promotion at Visp's own mighty tourist board, then the Swiss pantyhose manufacturers' association. Equipped with ever more garish checked suits, wide lapels and aviator glasses, Uncle Sepp moved up in the world, bringing his glad-handing and crooner's charm to the Swiss Ice Hockey Federation and to luxury watch peddlers Longines.

Then something happened: something he's never been terribly clear about. All of a sudden, Uncle Sepp is working for FIFA, except that he's really at Adidas, and, no, not the bit that deals with sports kit, but some weird 'political' unit. Before you know it, he's the general secretary of FIFA, and has divorced your Auntie Lili, marrying the daughter of the man he's displaced (not that this ends well, but that's another story). Fast forward another two decades and he ends up the president of the whole thing: king of the world, the man who runs football. Uncle Sepp? President Blatter? WTF? What the fuck, indeed. How could it be that a man of such mediocre talents, intellectual incuriosity and narrow cultural horizons should rise to the top of one of the twenty-first century's most important international cultural organizations?

Like many successful and powerful people, Uncle Sepp is prey to two illusions: first, that he, rather than some vast set of structural and institutional changes, decisively shapes the world he participates in; second, that his rise to the top is self-evidently meritocratic rather than a composite of multi-layered and unacknowledged privilege, audacious good luck, and a judicious measure of deception and/or criminality. It's not the stuff of after-dinner anecdotes, though: for that you need a different story. But Uncle Sepp can't tell a story, not one that anybody who isn't a captive audience is going to be able to stomach. Enter our French producers and script writers, who know nothing about FIFA, football, or their histories, and who have just four months to come up with something that's going to work for the President. For Uncle Sepp, they must have been the mother of all captive audiences: eager to please and, once he has found another $15 million of FIFA's money to finish the job, equipped with the wherewithal to make that 'other story' he had been concocting for the last twenty years into a real 'Hollywood movie'. It wasn't quite Eddie Constantine but, as you can hear Uncle Sepp say, poised to take a well-deserved dram, 'Hey, not bad for the boy from Visp?'

Seen in this light, even the most incomprehensible elements of the diseased psychic collage that is *United Passions* make sense. Take the 'poor kids playing on the wrong side of the tracks' sequences that punctuate the entire movie. This is the filmmakers' clumsy but sincere attempt to reproduce cinematically the kind of patronizing and sanctimonious cant that passes for FIFA's and Blatter's commitment to grassroots and youth football, a topic on which Uncle Sepp must have endlessly sermonized on. The result is part Benetton advert, part creepy football coach's fairy tale. The protagonists in these scenes are, at first glance, global and diverse, but they are utterly unplaceable. The location – notionally war-torn and rubble-strewn – is somehow so staged and clean that we are closer to the theme park than the battlefield. The kids themselves, though their costumes signify dignified poverty, are all unfeasibly healthy and scrubbed. The light is crystalline, the sky is blue and the sun is warm. Goals are scored against the odds, outsiders are included, a young woman takes on the boys and wins, and everything is just too good to be true. Nevertheless, Blatter's personal and political interventions are even more tangible in each of the four blocks that pass for the rest of the film's dramatic structure. Examination of them reveals his personal delusions, but correcting them can form the basis of a real history of FIFA, from which we can then approach its contemporary pathologies.

Beneath that very thin veneer of salesman charm, Uncle Sepp had toughened up a lot and learned to get his retaliation in first. The opening half hour of the movie is thus devoted to a cartoon demonization of the English/British, whose newspapers' investigations had been his main opposition while in power, and whose Executive Committee members had proved pathetically naive but nonetheless incorruptible. In particular, the British are depicted as spluttering imperial racists who believed that women and Africans could never play football. There were, of course, plenty of those kinds of characters around, but the idea that the British had a monopoly on this is absurd. It was, after all, the Brazilians who made women's football a federal offence, and the French who banned their Congo-Brazzaville subjects from playing football with boots. This is not to say that the British in general, and the English in particular, were usually anything other than sceptical, condescending and dismissive towards FIFA for most of its first forty years of existence. But this version of the story manages to miss out the fact that FIFA has actually had three English presidents in its time, and that in 1947 the English FA effectively saved the organization from bankruptcy. The second sequence, which covers the presidency of Jules Rimet from the 1920s until the 1950s, should not be understood as a reliable account of the origins of the World Cup and its most culturally significant moments over the first thirty years of its existence. On this, and much more, it is relentlessly inaccurate, wrong, hackneyed, uncritical and unread. Instead, in its anachronistic sanctification of Rimet as a resolute anti-fascist, anti-racist and proto-feminist, it should be read as Blatter's attempt to root FIFA's current, dismally insincere commitments to these causes in a fantasy past, one which is remarkably like the present in being populated by pot-bellied, gentlemanly francophone administrators.

The third sequence covers the presidency of Brazilian João Havelange from 1974 until 1998, and the arrival of one Josep Blatter onto the global football scene. In this version of the tale, Havelange is depicted as shifty, without this quality being entirely explicated, and as a noisy bully around the boardroom table. He is allowed a bit of visionary twaddle on the global power of football but, like Sancho Panza in flares to Havelange's linen-suited Quixote, it is Blatter that is there to save the day. Quiet, selfless and unassuming – Tim Roth seems to mutter so low sometimes that one could be forgiven for thinking he was trying to efface himself from both script and film – it is Uncle Sepp who secures extraordinary sponsorship deals for FIFA from Coca-Cola and Adidas. The late João Havelange would not have wanted our pity, nor is he worthy of it, but, as the singularly most influential person in steering the history of FIFA and international football, he commands our clear-eyed attention. Render unto Caesar what is Caesar's. In the case of Havelange, that is our respect for his mastery of the arts of institutional and charismatic power. In his pathetically insecure and clumsy attempt to deny Havelange his due and claim his triumphs as his own, Blatter reveals just how far short he falls of the master's high patrician standards.

In fact, Sepp Blatter was entirely absent from the initial deals that were done between FIFA, Coca-Cola and Adidas. Nor was he responsible for establishing the new TV rights model for the World Cup, or for the creation of FIFA's in-house marketers and TV rights seller ISL, which made the organization so wealthy. These were the creations of Havelange, Horst Dassler – then the boss of Adidas – and marketing consultant Patrick Nally. In the late 1970s Blatter was notionally FIFA's technical director, but was actually seconded to Dassler's extensive political and lobbying operations, learning the dark arts of international sports politics. Suitably straightened out, Havelange considered Blatter a servile replacement for Helmut Käser, the increasingly inflexible general secretary at FIFA. Havelange's Brazilian-style clientelism and patronage politics never sat easily with the bureaucratic and legally-minded German. The breaking point came on FIFA's seventy-fifth anniversary, when Havelange arranged for everyone attending the grand jamboree to receive an expensive Longines watch. He deposited the bill on Käser's desk and told him to get on with it. A few months later, Havelange would bully him out of the organization and give Blatter his job. In a bitterly cruel masterstroke, Havelange gave his blessing to Uncle Sepp's second marriage to Käser's daughter. The old general secretary is said to have wept and did not attend the nuptials. For eighteen years, Blatter faithfully did Havelange's bidding and got a world-class education in football politics. Above all, he knew how to sign the cheques, move the money and stay silent. As has become clear, the bribes received by Havelange and other members of the FIFA executive committee for allocating World Cup TV rights to ISL were dutifully facilitated by our Uncle Sepp.

By the time we get to the final part of the film, which covers Blatter's election as FIFA President in 1998 and his early years in office, the script sessions must have been conducted in the wee small hours of the morning. The whisky bottle must have been close to empty too, because the already gossamer-thin connection between reality and the movie's narrative entirely disintegrates. This is given stylistic form, for the film now hurtles desperately towards an end that cannot come soon enough and is reduced to an incomprehensible high-speed montage. Blatter, running as a force for reform and change, wins the 1998 FIFA presidential election, succeeding Havelange. On assuming office, he appears to confront his executive committee with the news that a new sheriff is in town and he's-a-gonna clean up. A flinty-eyed and unappealing investigative journalist appears on the scene, making coded accusations against all and sundry – except Blatter, of course – but then disappears altogether. Blatter's aides worry that he works too hard, someone accuses him of something bad in the run-up to the next presidential election, he tries to sleep on executive jets, and suddenly we are in Seoul in 2002: he's won re-election. With a universal sigh of relief, the closing credits roll: we see a beaming Roth-Blatter announce that South Africa will host the 2010 World Cup, and Madiba himself celebrating.

Back in the real world, the 1998 election for the FIFA presidency was a fight between the old order and forces proposing a modicum of reform. In sharp contradistinction to the plotline of the movie, Blatter was unambiguously the candidate of the old order, and his challenger, the Swedish president of UEFA, Lennart Johansson, was the man promising transparency and democracy. Havelange mobilized his old coalition of Latin America, Asia and Central America for Blatter. Mohammed Bin Hammam, the then rising Qatari star of Asian football politics, rode shotgun and made himself and his jets available to Blatter, while retired French star and titular organizer of the 1998 World Cup, Michel Platini, provided supportive football glamour. Johansson, and any threats to the established way of doing business at FIFA, were dispatched. The journalist scene is worth an entire psychoanalytical paper on Uncle Sepp. It is surely a fantasy version of his relationship with the investigative journalists who pursued him through the years, perhaps a sanitized version of Andrew Jennings, the most systematic, informed and ruthless of FIFA's critics. The idea, however, that Jennings or anyone else would have briefed Blatter against the 'bad guys' inside FIFA while offering him a free pass, is pure wish-fulfilment.

The strange mélange that passes for FIFA's internal politics in this era is, not surprisingly, fabulously confusing and imprecise, because the truth is so damning. In May 2002, Blatter's successor as FIFA general secretary, Michel Zen-Ruffinen, turned whistle-blower, distributing amongst the executive committee long and detailed reports of financial mismanagement in the organization, inexplicable missing payments for World Cup rights and the culpability of Blatter for much of this.

> The President, against the statutes, took over the management and administration of FIFA, combining both, thereby working with a few persons of trust only and manipulating the network through the material and administrative power he gained to the benefit of third persons and his personal interest. FIFA today is run like a dictatorship.[7]

Blatter hustled Zen-Ruffinen out of the organization. Opponents, primarily a mix of European and African football associations, then mounted a last-minute challenge, fielding the Cameroonian head of CAF, Issa Hayatou, as a presidential challenger at the FIFA congress to be held in Seoul a couple of months later. Blatter ran that meeting so as to ensure that none of his critics were allowed to speak. His core constituency, led by Al-Saadi Gaddafi, son of the Libyan dictator, sporting a 'revolutionary' beret, spent the whole day filibustering. His opponent was soundly beaten in a secret ballot. As for South Africa's World Cup, they were meant to get it in 2006 but were outmanoeuvred by the Germans. Uncle Sepp made sure they got it next time around by, amongst other things, restricting the competition to African hosts, and allowing FIFA's finance department to funnel bribes from the South African Football Association to CONCACAF in return for their votes. The truth is all very well, but even for Uncle Sepp it is not exactly the stuff out of which cinematic drama can be constructed, but then neither were his own delusions. There was, however – and this is where the production company missed a trick – a third option. Thirty million dollars buys a lot of high-end television, enough at least to make series one with the promise of three or four more; and the template had already been struck. *United Passions'* problem wasn't that it was based on the unchecked self-serving ravings of your drunken uncle, or that the world of football politics and power does not have dramatic potential: the problem was that it was trying to be a Hollywood biopic when it should have been *The Wire*.

II

Some writers, not unreasonably, have suggested that *The Godfather* or *Goodfellas* are the most suitable cinematic models for retelling the story of FIFA. The institution's creepy self-reference as 'the football family', or even 'the FIFA family', makes irresistible comparison with the organized criminal gangs built around kinship networks that both films depicted. But the Corleones and the Luccheses, and their mode of operation, are the product of another era. Organized corruption, racketeering and embezzlement can no longer be depicted, if they are to be fully comprehended, in such a narrow frame of reference, or be shown to be reliant on the crude, antiquated forms of power and threat available to Don Corleone. Moreover, their parochial charm fails to capture the depth to which contemporary societies have been penetrated and reshaped by global organized crime, how the fragility of the rule of law corrupts multiple spheres of life, and how the lines between criminal gangs and a multitude of other social actors and networks have been blurred. In all these realms *The Wire* has no peer.

First shown on HBO between 2002 and 2008, *The Wire* was a five-series drama set in contemporary Baltimore. It remains the most important, complex and enduring product of twenty-first-century America's new, long-form television. In its capacity to render a city in all its personal, social and physical complexity, it is the match of Dickens's London, but with a political economy closer to his contemporaries Marx and Engels. The range of its sociological landscape is huge. Beginning with the struggle between the local police force and one drug gang, the Barksdale clan, it opens out into the policing

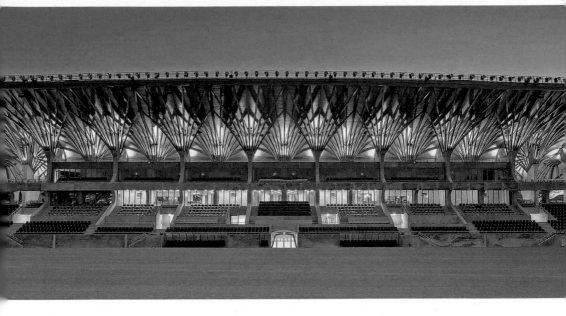

14. The king in his castle. The Pancho Arena in Felcsút, Hungary. Prime Minister Viktor Orbán's skybox is in the centre of the stand, his dacha is next door.

15. Football as salvation. The Patriotic Pilgrimage of ultranationalist Polish football ultras to the Jasna Góra shrine.

16. Afro Napoli. The Italian club was formed in 2009 to welcome migrants.

17. Women and children only: fans watch Fenerbahçe against Manisaspor in Turkey, after men were banned for yet another bout of rioting.

18. Rendez-vous with history? Russian fans charge English supporters in Marseilles during Euro 2016.

19. No to Monday-night football: Eintracht Frankfurt fans throw tennis balls and streamers onto the pitch.

20. The shirt and road initiative: Brazilian President Michel Temer presents Chinese President Xi Jinping with a Brazilian football jersey.

21. Workers in China make footballs ahead of the 2018 World Cup.

22. The football nation. Gigantic crowds gather in South Korea to watch
the host's games during the 2002 World Cup.

23. In the shadow of Fukushima: Japan's women win the 2011 World Cup.

24. New York state of mind. Football fever in Brooklyn Heights.

25. AMLO takes the Azteca. Supporters of presidential candidate Andrés Manuel López Obrador fill the Azteca stadium during the 2018 presidential elections.

26. The game beyond the game: FIFA President Sepp Blatter pranked at a press conference.

27. Putin's umbrella: World Cup trophy ceremony, 2018.

and politics of the city's docklands, where organized crime, unions and the judiciary collide, before moving through the interlinked worlds of education, municipal politics and the local media. In all of them, the insidious impact of extreme inequalities, and the disastrous course of the war on drugs, combine to produce urban decline and widespread corruption. As Stringer Bell, in effect the chief financial officer of the Barksdale gang, put it, 'There's games beyond the fucking game.' It might have proved a hard sell to the TV companies, but it would have been a better strapline for FIFA's corporate branding and pitch-side advertising boards than the manufactured vacuity of 'For the Game: For the World.' *The Wire,* though, offers FIFA more than mere slogans. While a shifting cast of police officers, politicians, informers and gang members provides some long narrative arcs through *The Wire*, most prove expandable. What persists across the whole show is a lasting and three-dimensional sense of the deep, structural and institutionalized forms of power that shape this world. FIFA deserves no less.

In a perfect scenario, we would go back and make one, maybe two, whole series on João Havelange and Latin America. This, after all, is where the model of clientelistic political relationships was first forged in football, and Havelange proved a master of its arts during his near two decades in charge of the Brazilian game. While he initially lacked the financial largesse available to Blatter for these kinds of machinations, he proved adept at trading more World Cup places, more committee memberships and better expenses for unwavering political loyalty. Blatter, reaping the financial gains of Havelange's work, would inherit and then bureaucratize this system. Looking at this era would also give us a chance to explore the role of Horst Dassler, head of Adidas, in shaping the new FIFA. If he was not quite Mephistopheles to Havelange's Faust – the latter's soul having long departed – he offered him an unparalleled level of expertise in, and connections to, international sports politics, plus a model of rights marketing and sponsorship in which commissions and secret payments were the norm, and for which he and Adidas would be richly rewarded. Looking to the future, both Russia and the Gulf, where football and high politics have become intimately intertwined, promise equally strong storylines. Geography has its virtues as an organizing principle but, as *The Wire* demonstrates, there is something to be said for examining each of the separate but intersecting social worlds that have helped make FIFA and football so profoundly corrupt.

The global epidemic of elite corruption and embezzlement, of which FIFA's sins are just a small, local outbreak, has a complex aetiology, but three factors seem particularly important: the capacity to find, create and use the offshore legal and financial loopholes of the global economic system; the ways in which massive inequalities of wealth and power are used to undermine the rule of law in general and judicial, policing and regulatory institutions in particular; and the failure of most of the media, both sports and other, to pursue these transgressions. Even where they have any interest in doing so, they are often stymied. Perhaps we could set one series in the realm of international institutions, many of which, like FIFA, have sheltered under the light-touch jurisdiction of Swiss law: the kind of legal off-shoring that the world's elites have relentlessly explored as they send their companies and capital to tax havens. It would be interesting to spend an episode really following the money: it begins, digitally, in a TV company's slush fund registered in the Bahamas, is then moved to a series of shell operations in the Caribbean, before popping up in Zurich in a FIFA account. There it is smartly transferred to a num-bered account in Luxembourg, where a uniformed chauffeur withdraws tens of thousands of euros in cash from an ATM, stuffs them into an old leather suitcase and drives to Paris, where we see the money spent by his bosses in the city's perfumeries, brothels and bou-tiques. Alternatively, we could build a series that looks at matters from the bottom up, starting in the realm of national politics proper, exploring the ways in which the power inequalities and corrupt prac-tices of many countries' polities and judiciaries are simply transferred to their football associations by the powerful politicians, civil servants and tycoons who control them and who turn them into private assets and personal sinecures. Readers of this book will be depressingly familiar with this narrative trope everywhere from Pakistan to Trini-dad to Russia. Perhaps we could consider a series that focused on FIFA's broadcasters and sponsors. The former, as we now know, are the people who do most of the actual bribing, usually in pursuit of TV rights. Hardly surprising, then, that, although the global football media has often been contemptuous of Blatter and the gang, the investigative work that has helped topple them is the work of a few key individual and media groups. FIFA's shameless and expensive use of legal bullying tactics against journalists should make for some great sub-plots. So too the discussions going on inside the boardrooms of FIFA's main corporate sponsors – Coca-Cola, McDonald's, Continental, Sony and Emirates for starters – about the organization's innumerable scandals. It would be a welcome addition to the wall of complicit silence that they maintained in public.

First things first, though. We need a series that focuses on FIFA itself. Perhaps it could begin where *United Passions* left off in 2002. Despite having seen off the legal threat of Zen-Ruffinen's and the Executive Committee's evidence-driven allegations, and then Issa Hayatou's electoral challenge, Uncle Sepp remained vulnerable. However, in a series of sharp political and legal moves, each of which could form the backbone of an episode, he secured his position. First, the dangerous allegations from Zen-Ruffinen, and the documents which revealed, in a very transparent fashion, that in the 1990s ISL had paid a variety of bribes to FIFA's executive committee (some of them expedited by Blatter himself when general secretary), were brilliantly parked. In the absence, in Swiss law, of a criminal definition of bribery and corruption in international organizations, the prosecution of the case was stymied. Then FIFA paid to ensure that the list of ISL's beneficiaries remained securely locked in a vault in Zug, the jurisdiction outside of Zurich where the case had been investigated. Second, in an effort to quell the growing chorus of criticism levelled at FIFA's appalling record of governance, Uncle Sepp established an 'ethics committee'. Then he appointed the British Conservative politician and sports administrator, Sebastian Coe, to chair it: a man so alert to corruption, so finely tuned to the nuances of international sporting politics, that he could serve for years on the board of the IAAF and claim to know nothing of the multiple indiscretions and corruptions of its president, Lamine Diack.[8] Third, just as Havelange before him had to dispense with the services of an over-punctilious and legally minded general secretary for someone more flexible, so did Blatter. First, he fired Zen-Ruffinen. Then, when his successor, Urs Linsi, proved irksome, he too was let go, and awarded a gigantic pay-off that has secured his silence. Third time lucky, Blatter finally found the kind of man he had been looking for. Jérôme Valcke cut his teeth at FIFA as marketing director between 2003 and 2006, during which period a New York judge stated that Valcke had lied to two groups, Mastercard and VISA, during their competition to be a FIFA sponsor. The judgment was vacated and remanded on appeal and FIFA and Mastercard ultimately settled. Mastercard, who had lost the sponsorship deal, were paid off to the tune of $90 million and, suitably laundered, Valcke was now able to step up as Blatter's new general secretary.[9] It was a marriage consecrated by Mammon. In 2011, together with FIFA's acting deputy general secretary and former finance director Markus Kattner, they would write and approve secret employment contracts for themselves that, over the next four years, awarded pay rises and bonuses to the troika exceeding $55 million, $23 million for Blatter alone.

Of course, we will need some more personal and intimate stories to wind through Uncle Sepp's power plays, and there is rich material here. Poor Barbara Käser, his second wife, was dispensed with in 1995, replaced by a younger model. Uncle Sepp started dating Ilona Boguska, the Polish tennis player, a friend of his daughter and around thirty years his junior. In 2002, in a plotline so fabulously left-field that it would never have survived a script meeting, Uncle Sepp got married, for the third time, to Graziella Bianca, a dolphin whisperer and aquatic therapist. He actually asked Pope John Paul II, given his divorces, for a special dispensation to be blessed in a Catholic church. His Holiness was not inclined, which was just as well, really, given that the relationship was over the following year. This, of course, could also prove a good moment to feature Uncle Sepp's wincingly old-fashioned sexism: from his thoughts on kit – 'Let the women play in feminine clothes like they do in volleyball. They could for example have tighter shorts' – to his humiliating condescension towards the first women to serve on the FIFA executive committee: 'Say something, ladies. You are always speaking at home: now you can speak here.' This, of course, would be just the tease for storylines that exposed the institutional sexism at work in the organization, and the systematic diversion of FIFA funds, earmarked for women's football in Latin America or Africa, into personal accounts.

But we are getting ahead of ourselves. For the first decade of the twenty-first century, Uncle Sepp just let the good times roll. The global boom and the insatiable demand from broadcasters and multinational companies for the eyeballs that the World Cup attracted saw FIFA's income sharply rise. Between 2003 and 2006 the organization brought in $3.3 billion. Over the next four years, this would rise to $3.9 billion and, in defiance of the global slowdown that followed the financial crisis of 2008, FIFA's income hit $4.8 billion for the period 2011 to 2014. While much of this, of course, was consumed by the cost of staging the World Cup and the many other tournaments the organization was responsible for, profits were also up. This left plenty of room for FIFA to extend its largesse to its member associations through the FAP (Financial Assistance Programme), and Blatter's own baby, the GOAL project. The former provided block grants to every football association, and in the case of many of the smaller nations was effectively their only source of income; a fact that irrevocably bound them to the ruling order in a clientelistic relationship that Blatter was adept at cultivating at a personal level. He would also add an increasing number of appointments of administrators to FIFA committees to his armoury of patronage: a gift that not only bestowed status, but from the per diems alone also constituted a considerable personal financial injection.

Where this was insufficient to secure loyalty and votes, there was the more targeted option of the GOAL programme, which provided grants for specific projects, particularly new football association headquarters and grassroots support. That was the theory, anyway. As Michael Zen-Ruffinen had outlined in great detail, between 1998 and 2002 the programme was driven by other agendas: primarily allocating grants to allies, nations on the president's travel schedule, and, where necessary, to waverers. 'The president has used and abused GOAL for his personal interests as a vehicle to retain the services of various personal advisers to the president and for campaigning.' Now, secure in his post, Blatter was able to delegate the business of the GOAL programme to his two eager princelings Mohammed Bin Hammam and Michel Platini, chairman and deputy chairman of the GOAL committee, and by then presidents of the AFC and UEFA respectively. Between 2003 and 2007 alone they doled out $100 million. While some things were built, some pitches were laid, and some programmes actually benefited some football players somewhere, the record of corruption and plain theft of GOAL funds was staggering. Amongst the various methods deployed, we have examples of GOAL money being used by football administrators to buy land for themselves, their families or their shell companies; then to buy that land back from themselves on behalf of the football association; and to employ contractors owned by or controlled by themselves, who then over-billed and under-built, if they built at all.

However, when it came to FIFA itself, there was no hint of any cost-cutting. In 2007, Uncle Sepp opened the organization's new headquarters in the upmarket neighbourhood of Zurichberg. Designed by Swiss architect Tilla Theus, 'The House of FIFA' came in at around $200 million. For that they got a street named after them, FIFAstrasse, care of Zurich city council, two really classy football pitches, a large football confederation-themed botanical park, and a long, low office building with internal courtyards and gardens, all wrapped in a huge high-tech steel-mesh facade. Inside, you could see there had been no skimping: high walls of hand-finished Brazilian granite, gorgeously polished American walnut staircases, chrome fittings and hammered aluminium screens, and the kind of floral display in the foyer that says 'We're not even counting.' Uncle Sepp played it nauseatingly coy: 'The house we were in before was much prettier, of course. There I had a view of the lake, but on the other hand, we're not out to look impressive.'[10] If this comment on by far the biggest and most straightforward expression of the era's bombastic opulence suggested plain old self-deception-cum-bare-faced lying, Uncle Sepp's thoughts on the huge panels of glass that made up much of the ground floor suggested real delusion, the kind that only unchecked power can deliver: 'This allows light to shine through the building and create the transparency we all stand for.' In fact, two-thirds of the structure's volume was invisible and below ground, including two floors of parking and the boardroom reserved for meetings of FIFA's executive committee. In a building that spoke volumes, this was the Library of Congress.

The FIFA congress, meanwhile, made up of delegates from each of FIFA's more than 200 member associations, was the ultimate sovereign body, and responsible for electing the president. It met just once a year, and was both toothless and pliable. The executive committee, however, was another matter. Its members owed their position not to FIFA itself, but to elections and power games in their own regional confederations. Once at FIFA they retained real power independently of the president, above all as the committee that decided where to allocate World Cups. Uncle Sepp merely held the casting vote in the event of a tie. Even after a decade in power, he was no more than the first amongst equals within this unstable band of collaborators and competitors. While the congress was a public if staged affair, the meetings of the executive committee were closed, held twenty metres below the earth's surface, without wi-fi or mobile reception. The executives' boardroom was a windowless black box with a floor of lapis lazuli, furnished with stark and very expensive high-modernist furniture and the most luxurious and deeply upholstered black leather chairs: an aesthetic that was part Bond-villain lair, part *Dr Strangelove* crisis committee. The bathrooms sheathed in floor-to-ceiling black marble, setting off their golden fittings, were straight out of a seven-star Gulf hotel; the prayer room, a cave of lustrous onyx, offered an ecumenical space for reflection and meditation.

Prayers are good, but they don't pay the rent. For that you needed the kind of deal the executive committee were awarding to themselves, with Uncle Sepp's encouragement, and the kind of governance structure that let this kind of conflict of interest just sail on through. FIFA's 2010 financial report stated that £20.3 million was spent on salaries and expenses for the executive committee and the four most senior managers in the organization. Evenly distributed, that amounted to £700,000 over the year in the bank, and that's not to mention the average of nearly half a million each in pension contributions. Then there were the perks. In the months leading up the executive committee's decision to allocate the hosting rights to the 2018 and 2022 World Cups, these were coming thick and fast. At the grand dinner laid on by the Australia 2022 bid committee, there were pearl earrings for everyone. The Japanese gave each member of the committee, and their spouse, ten thousand dollars' worth of trinkets: carved *yakusugi* cedar wood balls, top-of-the-range digital cameras and high-fashion clutch bags and pendants. One can imagine the disdain with which the United States' bid bag and its Christmas cracker-standard offerings would have been met: a USA Soccer pen and badge, a USA bid badge and sticker, and a book written and signed by former president Bill Clinton. No one, though, could match the largesse of the Qatar 2022 committee, which, in November 2010, in just one of innumerable examples of excess, flew Ricardo Teixeira (President of the Brazilian CBF and executive committee voter), his wife and daughter to Doha, for a friendly between Brazil and Argentina. Teixeira's room alone cost $25,000, twenty times more than the room deemed suitable for Lionel Messi, and forty times the price of the berth allotted to Teixeira's compatriot Robinho.

This was the peak of the boom for Uncle Sepp, the days of wine and roses. The 2010 World Cup in South Africa had been a great success. Brazil 2014 was on the horizon, and still looked like it was going to be a sure-fire hit. FIFA was looking forward to having a billion dollars in its reserve fund alone. It only remained to allocate the 2018 and the 2022 World Cups. The first was going to Europe, and was a fight between the English, the Russians, a Belgium-Netherlands joint bid and the Spanish. Uncle Sepp knows the English have got no chance, and like the Low Countries are playing it all way too straight. The Spanish don't have the resources to back up their guile, so the Russians are a shoo-in. The second is more open, for the Americans, Japanese, South Koreans and Australians have all been working the room hard. Surely one of them is going to take the prize, rather than tiny Qatar, which is proposing playing games in air-conditioned stadiums in the full microwave heat of a Gulf summer? Surely, even this motley crew of football princelings and ambitious barons won't vote for *that*?

INT. – FIFA EXCO BOARDROOM – DAY

The camera, looking directly upwards from the centre of the room, frames the huge circular chandelier that sits above the FIFA executive committee.

As THE PRESIDENT begins to speak, the camera tilts downwards through 90 degrees, framing him and THE GENERAL SECRETARY at the square conference table. A black, unmarked ballot box sits between them.

THE PRESIDENT: Places where people make a decision should only contain indirect light, because the light should come from the people themselves who are assembled there.

We cut to an empty seat bathed in a cone of dirty grey light. Thin wisps of acrid black smoke linger in the air. A tarnished name plate reads 'AMOS ADAMU – Nigeria'. Next to this, in a second grey cone, we see the nameplate 'REYNALD TAMARII – Tahiti'. Both men have lost their seats on the executive, and both have been temporarily banned from football by the FIFA ethics committee, after a Sunday Times *sting operation, published a few months earlier, found them soliciting bribes for votes.*

We then cycle through five anaemically lit figures. Their sallow skin gives off just enough illumination to show their wrinkled features: GEOFF THOMPSON – England; MICHEL D'HOOGHE – Belgium; JUNJI OGURA – Japan; ŞENES ERZIK – Turkey. When we reach MARIOS LEFKARITIS – Cyprus, the light, already pale, dims again, and the outline of the man appears to dissolve into the dark.

Now, looking from above, from far higher than the real ceiling of the room would allow, we see the two grey smoky cones and the five small pools of light around the conference table. The other seventeen seats are occupied by different shades of black. As the camera descends we realize that within each pool of gloom there are dark but distinct figures, sitting upright in their leather chairs.

The camera, like the wire-controlled robots strung above stadiums, swoops down and focuses in front of one figure. On the screen the caption reads, 'CHUCK BLAZER – USA'. The dark, obese shadow of the General Secretary of CONCACAF is elongating towards breaking point.

Tracking left across the Latin American contingent: RICARDO TEIXEIRA – Brazil; NICOLAS LEOZ – Paraguay, and RAFAEL SALGUERO – Ecuador. The dark figures are, unmistakably, versions of Francis Bacon's screaming popes. Flames lick their crooks and robes.

The camera swiftly moves along a cosmopolitan conveyor belt of exploding bureaucrats: WORAWI MAKUDI – Thailand; JACQUES ANOUMA – Côte d'Ivoire; HANY ABO RIDA – Egypt; FRANZ BECKENBAUER – Germany, ANGEL MARIA VILLAR – Spain; VITALY MUTKO – Russia.

Zooming out, the camera frames one whole side of the conference table. The six darkest figures are in front of us. These are FIFA's vice-presidents: the Cameroonian ISSA HAYATOU, the South Korean CHUNG MONG-JOON, and our old friends JACK WARNER, MICHEL PLATINI and MOHAMMED BIN HAMMAM. We see them elongating behind Bacon's painterly bars, beginning to be ripped apart by their own terrible wailing. Their bodies are now so completely dissolved into the gloom that envelops them that only their freakishly white jaws and teeth remain. Finally, we focus on DON JULIO GRONDONA – Argentina, darkest of all, his mitre in flames.

The camera swings sharply away from DON JULIO and momentarily fixes on THE PRESIDENT and THE GENERAL SECRETARY on the other side of the room, both still sitting at the conference table, the ballot box between them.

We zoom, telescopically, towards them, stopping when both their heads fill the frame against an entirely black background. The harsh light from above catches the beads of perspiration on both men's brows.

THE GENERAL SECRETARY: (Whispering) You know, if it is Qatar, we are all finished.[11]

THE PRESIDENT: You know football – people are mad. Football makes people mad.[12]

The camera zooms out to reveal the executive committee, its members rising to carry their ballot papers to the box.

FADE OUT

III

Watch the official announcement: it's a whole lot more telling than the South African World Cup scene in *United Passions*. 'The 2022 World Cup will be held in Qatar.' Uncle Sepp holds it together, but this was definitely not part of his plan.[13] Russia? Well, that he could handle. Did the British really think that the beaming Davids, Cameron and Beckham, were going to swing any votes? But Qatar? Now Uncle Sepp realized that he had lost control of his barons, and that the reach and finances of bid committees like the Qataris were even greater and more enticing than his own. Redressing that issue could come later, but first the backlash. The anglophone press was in predictable uproar. The Americans and Australians railed against the money they had wasted and wondered if a democracy could win a competition like this again. Lord Triesman, previously chair of the FA and England's 2018 bid, speaking under parliamentary privilege, spilled the beans: Nicolas Leoz, apparently sated by his immense wealth, was asking around for a knighthood; Jack Warner's 'centre of football excellence' had received an all-dancing, all-paying visit from Beckham's football academy. But it was all to no avail: the die was cast.[14]

Of course, what appeared to be the main story and the main threat to our hero – the fall-out from the Russia and Qatar decisions – turned out to be just a sideshow. The real threat to Uncle Sepp in the short term, and the source of his ultimate demise further down the line, was the FIFA presidential election of 2011 and the challenge of his erstwhile friend and ally Mohammed Bin Hammam; and to tell that story is to tell the story of Jack, Chuck and Mo.

Jack Warner and Chuck Blazer were, respectively, the president and the general secretary of CONCACAF, and notorious even within FIFA for the nakedness of their venality. Enter Mo – Mohammed Bin Hammam – the Qatari businessman who bankrolled Uncle Sepp's first presidential campaign, and who in addition to his presidency of the AFC has been lording it at FIFA as a member of the executive committee, a vice-president, and chairman of the GOAL Programme. He, like his closest competitor Michel Platini, President of UEFA, believes that Uncle Sepp, with a nod, a wink and a twinkle in his eye, has anointed him his preferred successor. Both have been restless for some time and, with Blatter's third term coming to an end in 2011, both must have considered regicidal options. Mo, emboldened no doubt by the recent successes of Qatari lobbying and the part he secretly played in its World Cup bid, and with his own fortune to play with, decides to launch a presidential campaign. Asian votes will have been taken for granted. South America and Africa, the key axis of Havelange and Blatter's constituency, will have to be chipped away at. However, at CONCACAF, there are thirty-five reliably organized votes available care of Jack.

So Mo's people call Jack's people, and Jack suggests that they start with the praetorian guard of CONCACAF's electoral army: the Caribbean Football Union (CFU). Jack calls a meeting of the CFU at the Royal Hyatt Hotel in Port of Spain, Trinidad, all care of Mo, who is covering everyone's expenses. In addition, there are the brown envelopes – actual brown manila envelopes – each stuffed with $40,000 cash. At this point, reality exceeds fiction, for the speech

Jack gives to the CFU – preserved in audio and transcript versions – could not be bettered.[15] He calls the meeting to order, reminding the Caribbean football family of the facts of the matter: 'If you are coming in this room here with cuss and disagree and rave and rant but when we leave here our business is our business. And that is what solidarity is about.' For those delegates whose consciences were delicate enough to require a modicum of self-deception, he offered this: 'So I am making the point here, folks, that it was given to you because he could not bring the silver tray and a silver, some silver trinkets and so on, and something with Qatari sand.'

Needless to say, there were plenty of takers, but not everyone bought into Jack's *omertà* speech. Officials from eight Caribbean federations declined Mo's generous offer, and some of them decided to call Chuck. A couple of days of frantic telephone calls between Chuck and Jack followed. Any illusions Chuck might have had that this was not a great big vote bazaar, and that Jack and Mo were going to get him busted, were disabused. He panicked, cracked and called Uncle Sepp at FIFA HQ. When the story was made public, Mo and Jack denied everything, but there the similarities ended. Mo stood down, abandoned his campaign, beat a retreat and stayed schtum. Jack went ballistic, threatening a fusillade of revelations and revenge. 'I tell you something, in the next couple of days you will see a football tsunami that will hit FIFA and the world that will shock you.' Despite subsequent promises of such retribution, they have yet to materialize. In the meantime, FIFA's ethics committee, acting with hitherto unknown haste, relieved both men of their official positions and banned them from football, and all just before the FIFA congress was due to meet. In this sudden power vacuum a more ruthless player would have now seen their chance, perhaps. Yet, with Mo out of the way, and Uncle Sepp still mired in the fall-out from the hosting of the World Cup, Michel Platini was nowhere to be seen. We now know that he must have been busy attending to the SFr2 million back-payment he had recently received from FIFA, authorized by Uncle Sepp, for services rendered more than a decade previously.

Thus, once again, Uncle Sepp presided over his own coronation. Indeed, the whole 2011 FIFA congress was cast in his image. The opening ceremony took the form of a Saturday-night variety show on Swiss TV, featuring a virtuoso dulcimer player, Grace Jones lured out of retirement for a ten-minute medley of her greatest hits, and

Melanie Winter, a former Miss Switzerland, doing the pleasantries. At the congress proper, most of which was conducted in the realm of the narcoleptic, a rare highlight was the shameless grandstanding of Don Julio Grondona, telling the British press where it could go with its accusations of systematic corruption:

> We always have attacks from England, which are mostly lies, with the support of journalism which is more busy lying than telling the truth. This upsets and disturbs the FIFA family. I see it at every congress. They have specific privileges with four countries having one vice-president. It looks like England is always complaining, so please, I say, will you leave the FIFA family alone, and when you speak, speak with truth.[16]

The dirty work done, Blatter was free to try and calm the storm of criticism raining down on FIFA, promising once again a programme of reform and transparency. His speech ended with a series of impromptu thoughts as to who amongst the world's great and good could help FIFA in its great reform endeavours: 'Placido Domingo . . . Henry Kissinger . . . There could be a woman?'[17]

Chuck Blazer, still publicly basking in the glory of his whistle-blowing act, and capable of immense personal duplicity, might well have thought himself just the person to join these luminaries, but he never got the chance. In late 2011, he left his Trump Tower apartment and set off along 56th Street on the mobility scooter his now impossible bulk required for even the shortest journey. He never made it to Uncle Jack's Steakhouse, which was good for his diabetes but otherwise a sub-optimal outcome from his perspective. He was stopped and detained by IRS agents, acting on information passed to them by investigators working for the new president at CONCACAF. They had managed to follow all kinds of dubious payments and commissions from CONCACAF to Blazer's network of offshore Caribbean companies and bank accounts, none of which had been declared to the IRS. They all returned to Trump Tower and, after two days of 'conversation', Chuck agreed to plead guilty to everything and help the FBI with what was obviously a gigantic and multi-tentacled investigation into not just CONCACAF and Chuck and Jack's little games, but the entirety of the football world.

For the next twelve months Blazer worked for the FBI, carrying an elaborately hidden wire, and arranging and conducting meetings

of their choice with a huge number of FIFA and football confederation officials, as well as television business executives, many of
whom would later be indicted by the US attorney general. For the
moment he retained his Trump Tower duplex, as did his cats, which
had one all to themselves. He also held onto his CONCACAF credit
card. He wined and dined in style at the London 2012 Olympics, but
the vultures were circling. At CONCACAF, the new president and
board began by taking a good long look at what little paperwork
Chuck and Jack had left in their wake: the bogus contracts, the personal commissions, the ever-giving credit cards, the absurd expense
accounts, and the questionable appointments of an alcoholic financial
controller in New York and Jack's personal accountant from Trinidad
as bookkeeper and external auditor respectively. Time was up.

In November 2012, no amount of oxygen or New York eateries
was going keep Chuck from his appointment with intensive care.
First, he came down with pneumonia, then he was diagnosed with
colorectal cancer and underwent a long and arduous course of
chemotherapy, though not so arduous that he could not find time to
open a lawsuit against his now former employers CONCACAF for the
$7 million he claimed they still owed him. While Chuck, confined to
hospital on the east coast of the United States, waited for the Feds to
start arresting people, Uncle Sepp was oblivious, still living the life.

Say what you like about him, laugh if you must, but on the way
to the top Sepp stayed true to some part of his old self. Sure, he
didn't have the icy hauteur of Havelange, the effortless sense of
superiority that comes from a life of unambiguous privilege and
power, but he had developed his own presidential style; even presidents need to let their hair down, however little of it they may have
left. Watch him at the opening ceremony of FIFA's 2014 congress in
São Paulo, sharing the stage with Brazilian supermodel Fernanda
Lima.[18] The wedding singer took a crafty ogle of her cleavage,
dropped his shoulders, clicked his fingers and showed her a few
moves while CONMEBOL's then President, the surely bemused Eugenio Figueredo, was called to the stage. At the following year's
congress, he showed up with his latest companion, Linda Barras, a
wealthy and very married Swiss socialite, nearly thirty years his
junior. Eddie Constantine-style, Uncle Sepp matched her ravishing
red evening dress with black tie and a dashing casual cashmere scarf.
Not quite the aura of papal infallibility and otherworldly gravitas that

Havelange pulled off, but Uncle Sepp had become Havelange's equal in the mastery of institutional power, and nowhere more so than in his capacity to co-opt, dilute and then bury the reform of FIFA's governance he had promised in response to the scandals of 2010 and 2011. As Alexandra Wrage, president of Transparency International – the global anti-corruption NGO, and at the time an appointed part of the reform process – remarked, 'It has been the least productive project I have ever been involved in.'[19] Which is exactly how it was meant to be.

In the immediate aftermath of the 2011 congress and Blatter's call for reform, two reports were produced on reforming FIFA. The first came from Transparency International; the second was a FIFA-commissioned report from Mark Pieth, a Professor at the University of Basel Institute of Governance. FIFA then created a third Independent Governance Commission, headed by Pieth but picked by themselves, to play for time, muddy the waters and dilute the programme.[20] While the three reports differed on details, and the Transparency International report was more thoroughgoing in the range and depth of reforms it proposed, there was a clear consensus around a few key areas: the introduction of term and age limits for the presidency and executive; the establishment of a compensation committee that was transparent and had outside representation; more figures on the executive committee, some of them even independent; and adoption of best practice in international organizations' auditing, anti-corruption policies and conflict-of-interest resolution mechanisms. Typical of the organization's response to these policies was the introduction of term and age limits, which would have debarred Blatter from standing at the next congress in 2015, only for them to be adroitly removed, by a massive majority vote, at the 2014 congress. On the most generous estimate, only half of the recommendations of the much more lenient IGC were implemented under Blatter.

While the process of institutional reform was expertly guided into the void, what remained of FIFA's internal governance system, the ethics committee, still had two outstanding and dangerous issues to address: the unresolved ISL bribery allegations of the 1990s, and the long and tortuous investigations into the allocation of the 2018 and 2022 World Cups. In 2012, seemingly in keeping with the new spirit of reform, Blatter appointed two new chairs of the two chambers of the committee. Investigations were to be run by Michael Garcia, the American lawyer and former New York district attorney with a hot track record in money-laundering and corruption cases. The adjudicatory chamber, which decided what to do about the findings of those investigations, was headed by the German judge Hans-Joachim Eckert, equally experienced in the realm of organized crime. In 2013, they reported on the ISL case, which had been forced back into the public domain by relentless pressure from British journalists. The legal authorities in Zug finally published the documents from the case that they, at FIFA's behest, had been holding back. Above all, they published a list of 'commissions' paid by ISL to the FIFA executive committee in the 1990s and outlined their mode of transfer, including one handled by Blatter for Havelange. Clearly there was going to be blood on the carpet after this one.

The worst offenders from the old guard, Havelange, Leoz and Teixeira, all claimed ill health and retired from their remaining positions in world sport before they were stripped of them. Blatter, however, managed to survive. Indeed, the most that Eckert could bring himself to say was he had been clumsy, but there was no evidence of any criminal or ethical misconduct. How it is to handpick your own judges. Uncle Sepp, who had worked tirelessly to prevent the publication of these documents and spent tens of millions of dollars of FIFA's money in doing so, including the settlement of Ricardo Teixeira's outstanding legal fees and fines, was, once again, scot-free. The Garcia report into the bidding process for the 2018 and 2022 World Cups, eventually published in redacted form in 2014 (and finally in toto in 2017), was even more of a damp squib. Bereft of any serious investigatory powers, the most it could do was grumpily accept the integrity of the outcome and fine Franz Beckenbauer and Vitaly Mutko for not showing up to talk to them. Finally, there was still the matter of the Qatar 2022 World Cup and the prospect – if you didn't believe the implausible and extravagant claims being made for air-conditioned stadiums – of playing in temperatures above 45 degrees centigrade. However, by comparison to the acts of escapology Blatter had already performed, reconstructing the global football calendar to accommodate this was child's play. Despite much huffing and puffing from the leagues and clubs who would have to take a long winter break, the 2022 World Cup was duly moved to the more clement months of November and

December. At the 2013 FIFA congress, where he announced the 'end' of FIFA's anaemic reform process, Uncle Sepp allowed himself a moment of supreme public self-satisfaction. 'We have been through a difficult time. It has been a test for football and those who lead it. As your captain, I can say we have weathered the storm.'

What is the point at which the lies we tell ourselves assume their own life as permanent delusions? When is the moment that the carapace of power becomes impermeable, when your ears close and you can no longer hear the world? Whenever that moment came, Uncle Sepp had by now long passed it by. At the final of the women's football tournament at the London 2012 Olympics, Blatter's presence was met with booing from almost the entire stadium. While this could be written off as the usual sour grapes from the British, the reception he met in Brazil at the Confederations Cup the following year could not be dismissed in the same manner. With the tournament serving as a lightning rod for a gigantic spontaneous public protest over Brazil's wasteful and corrupt state, President Dilma was booed into silence at the opening game. When Uncle Sepp tried to come to her rescue – to give him his due, in very serviceable Portuguese – he was booed even more. Both tried to keep a low profile at the World Cup, both begged the protestors, with straight faces, not to mix politics and football, but there was no escaping the public's contempt. At the final of the Asian Cup in Sydney in 2015, Blatter got the same treatment all over again.[21] He was equally oblivious to the rising chorus of disapproval from international institutions, individual politicians and digital campaigns like Change FIFA and NewFIFANow. Transparency International's reports on FIFA's governance process regularly described it as amongst the worst in the world.

Yet Uncle Sepp seemed impervious, indefatigable, still capable of imagining that the world thought of himself and of FIFA as highly as he did. One skin-crawlingly sanctimonious project that sprang from Uncle Sepp's late and unchecked megalomania was the 'Handshake of Peace'. This absurd project, which smacked of the small-town Masonic lodge, was cooked up between Blatter's office and the Nobel Foundation, and was intended to be the compulsory gesture of greeting for players and officials in all FIFA matches. Notionally a signifier of peace, anti-racism and respect, its introduction would, Uncle Sepp would later admit, hopefully lead to a nomination for the Nobel Peace

Prize, for FIFA the institution, of course.[22] But you know who would have been in Stockholm to pick up the gong. It is one of the small mercies of Blatter's downfall that this project has been abandoned.

The handshake, at least, had the virtue of being cheap. The same cannot be said of the woefully under-visited FIFA Football Museum in Zurich, which Blatter saw as part of his legacy, and which came in at a cool $140 million.[23] And then, as we know, there was *United Passions*. Think of Uncle Sepp again, poised at the end of the telling of the tale to take a well-deserved shot: 'Hey, not bad for the boy from Visp?' For once, just for once, you know you can trump his homily with another of his very own making. You sigh, a melancholy note in your voice, but you keep a twinkle in your eye. 'You know football – people are mad. Football makes people mad.'

IV

The final episode of series one would be set in Zurich in May 2015. The FIFA congress, due to take place on the Friday, had brought the whole 'family' to town, and many of them had settled in for a very comfortable stay at one of FIFA's favourite hotels, the Baur au Lac. At dawn on the Wednesday, Swiss police, acting at the behest of the US Department of Justice, raided the hotel and arrested seven of the delegates. Later that day, in a globally broadcast press conference, the Attorney General, Loretta Lynch, outlined the huge case it was pursuing against these men, and another seven not yet in custody, for decades of fraud, money-laundering and racketeering in the football TV rights business. At the same time, it was announced that the Swiss attorney general had launched a criminal investigation into the decisions to award the 2018 and 2022 World Cups to Russia and Qatar. The initial tranche of arrests rounded up mostly television executives and administrators from South America, Central America and the Caribbean. Over the next year, the number of people on the indictment sheet would rise to almost fifty, and they hailed from every continent.

The first trials and judgments took place in late 2017, resulting in multiple convictions. The guilty parties included two former presidents of CONMEBOL, its general secretary and treasurer, and half a dozen other presidents of South and Central American football federations, including the plum prizes of Brazil's José Maria Marin, and Guatemalan Rafael Salguero, also a member of the 2010 executive committee that gave the World Cups to Russia and Qatar. As of 2019, the US case is far from over, and the Swiss legal authorities have yet to begin their process of indictment and trial. Even so, the fates of the rest of that committee are worth dwelling on.[24]

Three key members of that executive, listed on the indictment, remained at home, either avoiding – Leoz in Paraguay, Teixeira in Brazil – or fighting – Warner in Trinidad – extradition to the United States. Two of them are no longer with us. Don Julio Grondona, with impeccable timing, died in 2014, though eerily he lived on in the depositions of the American investigation as co-conspirator #10, a central figure in almost all of the frauds and rackets they looked into. Chuck Blazer, now retired from special agent duties, rotted in New Jersey and died in July 2017, robbing the courts of their chance to convict him. It is worth noting that his immediate successor as general secretary of CONCACAF, Enrique Sanz, was investigated by the Americans and in 2015 banned from football for life by FIFA, while Jeffrey Webb, successor to Jack Warner as President, has since been indicted, tried and convicted by the American authorities for wire fraud and racketeering. Mohammed Bin Hammam, barred from football for life, has retreated to Qatar and his fortune. South Korean Chung Mong Joon, scion of the Hyundai *chaebol*, lost his seat on the executive in an Asian Football Confederation vote to Blatter's then ally, Prince Ali of Jordan, not that this would last. Chung has proved no more popular with the Korean public, who showed little appetite for his failed run at the country's presidency in 2012. Two of the executive committee's African members, neither of whom remain at FIFA, fought out their own revengers' tragedies. In 2012, Jacques Anouma had the temerity to mount a challenge to the old man, planning to stand against Issa Hayatou for the presidency of the African confederation, CAF. Hayatou countered by getting the CAF executive to debar him from standing on technical grounds, then orchestrated Anouma's defeat in the elections for the CAF executive committee the following year; an act which removed him from football altogether. However, after a quarter of a century in power at CAF, Hayatou finally made enough enemies and snubbed enough aspirants that in 2016 he was himself deposed, losing an election to a

coalition of the angry and the excluded led by a cabal of Madagas-
cans and anglophone Southern Africans.

Worawi Makudi lasted longer on the executive committee than
he did as President of the Thai Football Association, losing the post
after having been found guilty of forgery and malpractice during his
re-election in 2013. FIFA's ethics committee, reviewing the evidence
in the Garcia report and claims that Makudi had requested personal
ownership of the TV rights to the Thai national team, finally banned
him from football in 2015. Franz Beckenbauer has also left the committee. First he stepped around the slush fund that the German DFB
used to support its 2006 World Cup bid, then he refused to speak to
the Garcia investigation into the 2018/2022 World Cups. Perhaps
he will be more forthcoming with the Swiss attorney general, on
whose orders Beckenbauer's house has been raided and searched,
and a case against him opened. Angel Maria Villar resigned all of his
football positions in 2017 after he was arrested in Spain, charged
alongside three others with illicitly funnelling national development
funds to the Spanish football regions in return for the votes that kept
him in power as head of the Spanish football federation for eight
consecutive terms. Vitaly Mutko rose, first, to become the Russian
minister of sport, then Deputy Prime Minister, a key figure in the
organizing of the Sochi 2014 Olympics, the 2018 World Cup bid and,
once it was won, the chair of the tournament's organizing committee. He was also, it transpired, at the centre of Russia's state-backed
athletics doping programme. Although he denies the charges against
him, he has resigned all of his sporting positions.

There may have been a few empty seats at the FIFA congress,
held just two days after the swoop on the Baur au Lac, but there was
no shortage of interest. What had seemed, a few days earlier, the
formality of electing Uncle Sepp for his fifth term as FIFA president,
with him facing a mere stalking horse in the shape of Prince Ali of
Jordan, suddenly appeared to have become a real contest. Initially,
never a serious contender for power, given Uncle Sepp's iron hold on
the congress, Prince Ali had received lukewarm support from his
allies within UEFA and Asia, and the distant blessing of Platini, still
unable to bring himself to mount a plausible attack on the old man.
Surely, with the reputation of FIFA and the whole football world in
tatters, a voice of reform, even one that owed his position to the
Hashemite hereditary monarchy, was now a better bet than Uncle

Sepp? In perhaps the performance of his life, Uncle Sepp danced in the final shaft of light left available to him. In that parallel universe, he and FIFA were the victims of a terrible betrayal of trust. The football barons from Latin America and the Caribbean were the problem, not him; and he was still the man to clean out the stables. I doubt that anyone, even his allies, was buying this stuff, but they were listening to his parting shot. Spoken in French and aimed at the delegates from francophone Africa and the Caribbean, he made sure they knew his order of priorities: 'The World Cup is the goose of the golden eggs. We must protect that. We have the obligation not only to fight against corruption.'[25]

While other votes at the congress were cast electronically, the US Soccer Federation had, not unreasonably, insisted on old-fashioned pen and paper for the presidential vote, because there was no guarantee that FIFA would not be able to track what was supposed to be a secret ballot. Blatter, for the fifth time, was the winner, 133 to 79. In his valedictory address, he kept working the nautical metaphors that had served him so well. 'I thank you, you have accepted me for the next four years. I will be in command of this boat of FIFA. We will bring it back off shore.'[26] And then he was just freewheeling, telling congress that 'We need in this committee women. We need ladies.' And just in case anyone was worried that he might have it in for Qatar 2022: 'We won't touch the World Cup. I am a faithful man. God, Allah, whoever, they will help us to bring back this FIFA.' His first sign-off was pure showbiz: 'I like you. I like my job. I am not perfect. Nobody is perfect. Together we go. Let's go FIFA! Let's go FIFA!' He should have left it there and gone out at the top of his game, but clearly something was eating Uncle Sepp, and he came back for a second bite at the cherry. 'It is my congress, I have the right to make the closing remarks. You see I am in a good mood. I was a little bit nervous today, but now I am the president of everybody, I am the president of the whole FIFA. This game is important, but more important, enjoy life!'

It makes you think. Maybe Uncle Sepp wasn't enjoying life? Maybe the prospect of another four years of global disdain and relentless political escapology was just too much for a man approaching his eightieth year? Maybe he knew where the paper trails were going to take the FBI and the Swiss attorney general? Whatever ate away at him that weekend, he returned to FIFA HQ on the Monday, the world's press having departed, and announced, in perhaps his lowest-key press conference to date, that he would, on the election of a successor the following year, resign his post. He would not, however, be allowed to walk out of the front door.

First, they came for Jérôme Valcke. The ethics committee must have been spoilt for choice as to what charges to investigate, but they settled on Valcke's habit of using FIFA jets for private purposes, and the favours he had shown the sports marketing company MATCH in the allocation of World Cup tickets. He would eventually be banned from football for twelve years. In September 2015, the Swiss authorities announced that they were investigating Uncle Sepp and Platini in connection with the SFr 2 million payment made by FIFA to the Frenchman in 2011 that we encountered earlier in the series. FIFA's ethics committee moved faster and, after reviewing the evidence in October, banned both men from football, a judgement confirmed when the two appealed against the ban at the Court for the Arbitration of Sport.

Blatter, still riding in a black Mercedes, and still hiding out in all his old FIFA haunts, remains unrepentant and deluded. Platini all but disappeared from public life, until his arrest in 2019, in connection with Qatar's World Cup bid, brought him back into the spotlight. Their names, once recorded in stone in the foyer of the House of FIFA alongside those of so many others from amongst the guilty, in commemoration of the building's opening, have been stripped from the wall. It would, perhaps, have been better to have left them there and added a new roll call of dishonour, in which their crimes and punishments were, like Olympia's Zanes, displayed for subsequent generations of administrators to ponder.

Three months later, in February 2016, there were five names on the ballot paper at FIFA's extraordinary congress to elect Blatter's successor: Prince Ali, once again; the serious, if quixotic, reform candidate Jérôme Champagne, previously FIFA deputy general secretary; Tokyo Sexwale, an opportunist South African politician who pulled out at the last moment; and the contenders Gianni Infantino, Swiss general secretary of UEFA, and Sheikh Salman, the Bahraini President of the Asian Football Confederation. Monied and connected Sheikh Salman was the favourite going into the congress. The Western press drew attention to his role in the suppression of dissent and abuse of human rights in Bahrain during the Arab Spring of 2011, but few thought it would make him unelectable. Infantino, who had served as Platini's general secretary at UEFA for a decade, stepped into his boss's shoes and inherited his political support after the Frenchman was banned from football. While he was pleased to assume the role of modernizer and reformer in the race, one that Salman's record made it impossible for him to play, most of what he had to say in his manifesto concerned money. At the congress itself Sheikh Salman signed off with the conspiratorial warmth of, 'At the end . . . I am one of you.' Infantino got down to brass tacks, almost shouting while at the podium, and promised the congress a significant increase in their travel expenses and direct grants: 'The money of FIFA is your money. It is not the money of the FIFA president, it is your money.'[27] For the first time there was a round of spontaneous applause. In the first round of voting he pipped Sheikh Salman 88 to 85. Prince Ali, a long way behind in third, withdrew, and on the second vote nearly all of his votes went to Infantino.

Infantino's term of office began inauspiciously. There was an ugly spat over the size of his very generous salary, a series of ethics committee investigations into his use of private jets, and a simmering row with Dominic Scala, the man in charge of FIFA's still incomplete reform process, that resulted in the latter's departure. Infantino's removal of the chairs of both parts of FIFA's ethics committee in 2016 was equally brusque, while the newly reformed executive committee, the FIFA Council, retained the right to hire and fire their notionally independent replacements. On issues of human rights, FIFA has proved no more robust under Infantino than under Uncle Sepp: the appalling fate of North Korean workers on Russia's World Cup building sites has been noted and passed over. The conditions of their South Asian peers in Qatar have improved, but this has been due to pressure from labour unions and NGOs as well as Qatar's soft-power response to the Saudi-led boycott it has faced, not FIFA's doing. Some of FIFA's fainter-hearted sponsors have departed, to be replaced by more clear-eyed operations like Russia's state energy giant Gazprom and the Chinese conglomerate Wanda. While Infantino has proved less clumsy and gaffe-prone than Uncle Sepp and has, for the moment, staunched the daily revelations of corruption in the organization, he has yet to redeem its image. Indeed, that this may now be impossible is surely one of Uncle Sepp's greatest legacies.

If history repeats itself first time as tragedy, second time as farce, what is it third time around? In 1982, João Havelange presided over the first twenty-four-team World Cup, part of the payback to the global south for its political support. In 1998, Blatter took power as the World Cup was expanded again to thirty-two teams. Infantino's single biggest innovation since becoming president has been to announce, for 2026, a forty-eight-team World Cup. While Infantino made the case for change in terms of inclusivity and a more globally balanced competition, the political logic of the model is overwhelming: the same dynamic of clientelism and the exchange of patronage for votes and loyalty persists. While the vast majority of national football federations are themselves profoundly dysfunctional, captured, corrupt and unaccountable, this is unlikely to change, whatever tinkering FIFA makes with its own processes of internal governance. Perhaps, after tragedy and farce, the third iteration is stalemate and ennui?

8

BACK IN THE USSR?
FOOTBALL IN PUTIN'S RUSSIA

All the ulcers of Putinism that plague the modern Russian state – thievery, incompetence, and corruption – affect Russian football too.

Boris Nemtsov

What I enjoy watching most is when Russia wins.

Vladimir Putin

I

Boris Nemtsov, then de facto leader of Russia's opposition, did not mince his words when, in 2010, the country won the right to host the 2018 World Cup; though he might have added racism, violence, ultra-nationalism and disinformation for good measure.[1] Nemtsov, who had served as deputy prime minister under Yeltsin, and was then leader of the Solidarnost forces in the Duma, was well aware of the widespread corruption in Russian institutions, and his foundation's work on the preparations for the 2014 Sochi Winter Olympics must have made him acutely aware of the pathologies of sporting mega-events.[2] Eventually billed at $55 billion, the games were, the military budget aside, the single biggest government programme of the century and, by Nemtsov's informed estimates, around $20 billion was skimmed off the budgets and into private hands. The World Cup was going to cost less, but it would no doubt operate in a similar fashion. Nemtsov never got the opportunity to tackle the issue. In February 2015 he was shot as he walked away from Red Square and the Kremlin. During the inconclusive investigation that followed it was revealed that, on the night of his death, the cameras that honeycomb this high-security zone were not working.

Surprisingly, perhaps, his nemesis, President Putin, did not show much more enthusiasm for football. Indeed, for a politician who made manly recreations and populist photo opportunities the mainstays of his public profile, he proved almost allergic to the sport. While we have been graced with Putin playing with professional ice hockey teams; fighting a judoka half his age; riding horses bareback and submerging himself in ice water in just his Y-fronts; fishing in vast Siberian rivers; and shooting, albeit with tranquillizers, tigers and polar bears – we have yet to see him in a national team football jersey or orchestrating a compliant midfield. He was present at many games of the national team, and attended the 2014 World Cup final, but there were no histrionics, no social media 'super-fan' antics. His comments at the many meetings and stadium openings connected to the World Cup, by comparison with his evident enthusiasm for the Sochi Olympics, were bland.

Nor did football obviously warm to Putin. A few players and ex-players, like Roman Pavlyuchenko, were candidates for his ersatz political party United Russia.[3] In 2017, at a match between Lokomotiv Moscow and the Istanbul side Fenerbahçe, played in the wake of the Turks shooting down a Russian plane in disputed airspace near Syria, Dimitri Tarasov displayed a Putin T-shirt and supported him in interviews.[4] He did, as we shall see, dip his toes in the world of football fandom, and made the occasional gnomic pronouncements on the problem of too many foreign players in Russia's top division, but football, at first glance, appeared a very minor component of his and his government's political technologies.

It is not as if the football they inherited offered much political capital to work with. In the Yeltsin years the game tracked the chaotic and tumultuous changes going on around it.[5] First, it was diminished, geographically and psychologically, by the break-up of the Soviet Union. The Baltic states, who had an independent political and footballing existence in the inter-war era, were the first to leave the football federation of the Soviet Union, their top clubs withdrawing from the Soviet leagues in preference to their own. Georgia followed and, with the announcement that Ukraine would do the same, it was clear that the transnational Soviet football empire was finished. It was given a final outing at the 1992 European Championships where, as the CIS (Commonwealth of Independent States), the rump of the soccer union took the place of the Soviet Union that had qualified the previous year. They managed to draw with the Germans and the Dutch but, thrashed 3–0 by Scotland, they were going home and into historic oblivion. Second, the now shrunken core of Russian football inherited sclerotic Communist institutions that had failed to commercialize or professionalize in the late Soviet era, playing in dilapidated stadiums to a shrinking fanbase that was ceding ground to the first flowering of hooligan firms in the game. A shadow of its former self, the Russian league was sponsored by a brand of Danish chewing gum, shown on television but virtually for free, and played in stadiums that were eerily empty. The best of that generation's players headed west if they possibly could. The now Russian national team was thrashed by Brazil and Sweden at the 1994 World Cup, then failed to qualify for the next in 1998.

It is in response to precisely this arc of decline and humiliation that Putin's political project has unfolded. At the core of his now almost two decades in power has been the salvation of the Russian state and its transformation into a real instrument of power at home and abroad. The first prerequisite of the project has been staying in power. Putin has never quite entirely dispensed with the trappings of liberal democracy – contested elections and the rule of law – but he has never let them stand in his way. Alongside the traditional tools of authoritarian rule – closing down or buying up the opposition's media, stuffing ballots and controlling the judiciary – has been added more subtle forms of manipulation, known as political technologies: creating front political parties and social movements to undermine opponents; shaping rather than explicitly censoring the media landscape; infiltrating and undermining organizations in civil society. Where all else fails, potential presidential candidates have been debarred from standing. It has proved remarkably successful and, on the face of it, football-free. However, in four important areas, the game illustrates an important component of the regime's political strategies.

First, almost immediately on assuming office, Putin reset the relationship of the Russian state with the class of oligarchs it had created in the 1990s. In short, and in blunt language, they were told that they could keep their economic empires on the condition that they stayed out of politics and paid up when required. Those that did, like Roman Abramovich, who dutifully served as a governor and paymaster of a Siberian province, and paid for most of Russia's 2018 World Cup bid as well as the extravagant salaries of a number of Russian national team coaches, were allowed to keep and indeed offshore their wealth. Those that didn't, like Boris Berezovsky, Mikhail Khodorkovsky and Vladimir Gusinsky, were driven into exile or imprisoned, and had their prize assets taken away from them, which were then turned into state corporations or passed on to more pliant allies. Alongside this changing of the economic guard, Putin's government has taken much more systematic control over state banks, state infrastructure companies and the petrochemical and mining sectors, nurturing huge corporations that serve both political and economic, domestic and international ends, most notably the country's largest business Gazprom. Buoyed in the mid-2000s by record high oil and gas prices, this also allowed the Russian state to direct generous levels of support to its political allies. All of these elements of the project have their footballing corollaries: the initial beneficiaries of the privatization of Russian football clubs in the Yeltsin era have been displaced; state banks, Russian Railways and Gazprom have all become club owners; and in the North Caucasus government reconstruction money was allocated to football clubs and football stadiums run by the Kremlin's local clients. Russian football, at the top level at any rate, was transformed. It did, on occasion, bring real success, as CSKA Moscow's and Zenit St Petersburg's victories in the UEFA Cup made clear. Whether this was economically sustainable, let alone whether it constituted a wise use of public money, was rather less obvious.

Second, while regional governors could be directly appointed, political opponents intimidated and assassinated, political parties invented and controlled, forces from below were another matter. Acutely aware of the fragile legitimacy of their own rule, Putin's governments have been peculiarly alert to the potential threat of independent social movements of all kinds: environmentalists and human rights activists, of course, but biker gangs, orthodox revivalists, ultra-nationalists, neo-Nazi groups and football fans too. Indeed, the regime's relationship with the hooligan firms in Russian football was a case study of its wider policies of managed nationalism. Far right, neo-Nazi, anti-migrant groups and football firms have all been kept under close surveillance, but allowed to operate within bounds set by the Kremlin. Sometimes they have been actively co-opted, the use of football fans as muscle for the Kremlin's invented youth movements an obvious example. At the same time, the government has also shown that, should they pose a threat or prove inconvenient, they can be closed down, as the fate of Russia's itinerant hooligans and their semi-official travel agency, the All-Russia Football Supporters Federation, demonstrates.

Third, Putin's regime paid a great deal more attention than its predecessor to the countries that once constituted the Soviet Union, and which the Kremlin considers its legitimate sphere of influence. In the world of football there remains considerable nostalgia for the Soviet-era league in which Russia's biggest teams were arrayed against the best from the provincial capitals: Dynamos Minsk, Kiev and Tbilisi, for example. As late as 2013, the CEO of Gazprom and the chief executive of Zenit St Petersburg were proposing, with

$1 billion-worth of backing, the integration of Russian and Ukrainian teams into a new transnational league. In the absence of such a league, resisted by UEFA and FIFA, the Russian model has been both emulated and rejected. In Azerbaijan oil money has been funnelled to grand sporting projects. On the other hand in Ukraine, in 2014, the pro-Russian president Viktor Yanukovych was overthrown by public protest, strongly supported by football ultras.

Finally, the wider foreign policy of Putin's Russia had its sporting component too. After exploring a more European, even Western-oriented approach in the early years of his presidency, the expansion of NATO, American support for the Kremlin's opponents in Georgia and Ukraine and the wider tacit humiliations heaped on the still imperial-minded Russia, saw Putin shift decisively. In this more aggressive posture, Russia has engaged in multi-level, multi-front conflict with the West, targeting its domestic political systems and challenging it in Syria, Crimea and Ukraine. Even the sports media could see what was up: at a press conference in Zurich that followed Russia's award of the 2018 World Cup, a journalist asked Putin whether the Cold War was back. 'You know,' he replied, 'a great many clichés survive since the Cold War. They roam Europe like so many flies, buzzing above one's head to frighten people. Things are really quite different.'[6]

Putin is of course right: this is not the Cold War, one driven at least in part by ideology, nor do today's conflicts herald a return to a bipolar international order. Despite its oil wealth, and even after a massive refurbishment of its armed forces, recently tested out in Syria, Russia is in a very much weaker position than was the USSR: the rise of China alone has diminished its position in the world order; its military possesses a tiny fraction of the American's armoury; it has very few allies and even fewer admirers; its population has been shrinking, and its economy, so dependent on mining and energy, is curiously vulnerable. Nonetheless, there is a real and multifaceted conflict going on. Given these weaknesses, Putin's foreign policy has made the most of the few strengths that Russia possesses: a willingness to use military force, state economic power and diplomatic duplicity without many of the domestic constraints that face its opponents; and a world-class intelligence, counter-intelligence and cyber-warfare operation refined by its own domestic political technologists of disinformation and discord. Just what you need to orchestrate semi-official athlete-doping programmes, hooligan sprees on the French Riviera, and, in a deeply corrupt and cut-throat world, the capacity to win the rights to host global sporting mega-events. These, surely, were the kinds of games that Putin liked to watch Russia play: games in which, unlike football, they were at least competitive.

II

For almost all of its existence, private ownership of football clubs, let alone that of any other business operation, was not legally possible in the Soviet Union. State ministries and agency's sports and social clubs were the effective custodians of football teams. In 1988 the first company law was passed, making joint stock ownership a possibility. While a few private companies were created before the fall of the Soviet Union in 1991, the decade afterward saw a whirlwind of privatization as a vast chunk of public assets made their way into private hands. While there was much talk of a transfer to the population as a whole, the vast majority of functioning state enterprises ended up in the hands of either the narrow cabal with access to finance to buy them up (at a snip), or those who were just there, in place and in charge, when it happened – the old *nomenklatura* transformed into twenty-first-century capitalists.

The first team to emerge from the chaos, as a sporting and an economic force, was Spartak Moscow.[7] For nearly seventy years the club, without a fixed home in Moscow, had survived and thrived as the team of quiet opposition and resistance to the Soviet leviathan. In the immediate post-Soviet era, it was the only club whose past identity resonated with the new times, and the only one that could attract fans and money. Under their coach Oleg Romantsev they won all but one league title between 1991 and 2001. Romantsev's extensive scouting network across the former Soviet Union helped, as did a steady stream of player sales to Europe. Thus, in 1993, when the Spartak board voted to make the club a joint stock enterprise, the entire operation was handed over to him. Once in charge he and Spartak gained first-mover advantage as their presence in the Champions League for a decade gave them access to a revenue stream that dwarfed other Russian clubs. The club also built a property portfolio based on the apartments that the Communist Moscow city government had made available to the squad, and which, after the fall, somehow became part of the informal Spartak economic empire. There they joined a roaring trade in tax-free imported cigarettes and alcohol, a bizarre concession made by the Yeltsin government in an effort to support the football industry.[8]

Toward the turn of the century both Spartak and Romantsev began to unravel. Always a committed smoker and a very serious drinker, Romantsev seemed to do more of both as the nineties wore on. His stress levels, long apparent, rose as he took on the additional and unenviable role of Russian national team coach. Spartak's financial edge was steadily eroded as new oligarchs, with unmatchable financial resources, began to engage with Russian football. In 2001, sponsorship money from LUKoil, the largest private and second largest fossil fuel company in the country, arrived via Spartak fan and LUKoil executive Andrei Cherbichenko, a man described as, '100 per cent incompetent in football.'[9] Cherbichenko was made vice-president and, over the next three years, as Romantsev and his team maintained a steady decline, he squeezed the coach's shares out of him, just in time to sell the club on to one of his bosses, the billionaire Leonid Fedun, a vice-president of LUKoil and owner of around 10 per cent of the company. Since then Fedun has spent somewhere in the region of a billion dollars of his and LUKoil's money on Spartak, covering losses, salaries and finally a home stadium. The returns were remarkably poor. Fourteen years without a championship, until finally they won the league title in 2017.

In Spartak's absence Russian football was dominated by two clubs, CSKA Moscow and Zenit St Petersburg. The first move on CSKA, the team of the Soviet armed forces, was made in 1996 by the then President Aleksandr Tarkhanov, who announced that he was the majority shareowner of the club. The army disagreed and forced him out but, alert to the possibility of a minority shareholder with cash, turned the venerable institution into a joint stock company and promptly sold 49 per cent of it to a Chechen consortium headed by businessman Shakhrudi Dadakhanov. The military, it seems, soon realized that they had hugely underpriced their asset, and so began a campaign to regain the club so they could sell it all over again. Dadakhanov was accused in the press of smuggling arms and money back to Chechnya. Then his nephew was arrested in his Moscow flat, where the police 'found' $25,000 of counterfeit money and videos of Chechen rebels killing Russian soldiers. Dadakhanov got the message, cut his losses, and gave his shares back. A year later they were sold on again, this time notionally to businessman Evgeniy Giner, but in actual fact to two very obscure companies, the UK-registered Blue Castle Enterprises (which owns 49 per cent) and a Russian company AVO capital (which owns 26 per cent), whose ultimate owners have proven untraceable. An investigation by UEFA dismissed the persistent rumours that Roman Abramovich held a controlling stake in both Chelsea and CSKA, but Giner, who has been the president of the club ever since, had been a very regular visitor to Stamford Bridge. More tellingly, Abramovich's oil company, Sibneft, signed a sponsorship deal with the club more than twenty times larger than its previous deal: a steady flow of cash big enough to deliver six league titles since 2003 and the UEFA Cup in 2005.

Zenit St Petersburg, the only big club in Russia's second city, were actually relegated in 1992 and spent three years in the second division. Twenty years later they were certainly the richest, and amongst the most successful, of Russian clubs, winning the league four times and the UEFA Cup in 2008. It was a transformation made possible by the company, headquartered in the city, that alone constitutes 8 per cent of Russian GDP: Gazprom. It was carved out of the Soviet Ministry for Natural Gas, and retains a monopoly on the nations' vast reserves. Privatized in the 1990s, it was, under Putin, brought firmly under the control of the Russian state, its board staffed by reliable political allies. As well as generating huge resources for the Russian treasury, the company has also been used to serve a variety of other political ends, especially in foreign policy, and its engagement with football has been central to that. Zenit itself was converted into a joint stock company by the Deputy Mayor of St Petersburg, Vitaly Mutko. Gazprom arrived initially as sponsors, but steadily took a greater share of the club, until in 2003 they bought the last of the other investors out.

Dynamo Moscow, the team of the KGB during the Soviet era, found it harder than most to attract fans and sponsors in the Yeltsin era, but under Putin they did make a short-lived comeback.[10] Help came from two directions. First, the bank VTB bought a slice of the club, gave them an implausibly huge sponsorship deal, and, in exchange for permission to erect a vast shopping mall on club land, started rebuilding Dynamo's dilapidated stadium. Then, in 2013, a second tranche of shares was sold to Boris Rotenberg, a twenty-first-century billionaire and, most importantly, in his youth a judo training partner of Vladimir Putin. After a sojourn in Helsinki as a personal trainer, Rotenberg washed up in St Petersburg, renewed his acquaintance with Putin, with whom he has remained close friends, and co-founded a bank, SMP, that built its fortune on its close association with Gazprom. A decade later his companies, including the once state-owned VTB bank, were involved in twenty construction projects for the Sochi Olympics. A good example of his management style was the football career of his son, a defender of confirmed mediocrity. He had been on the books of Gazprom's team Zenit St Petersburg, but in actual fact was always out on loan to minor clubs who still didn't play him. In 2013, he arrived at Dynamo and actually got a game. The avalanche of VTB money was enough to win two fourth places in the league and a spot in the Europa Cup in 2015, but then the party stopped. When Uefa's Financial Fair Play auditors came to town they reckoned that VTB's sponsorship deal was valued at ten times the going rate, and that all told the club was a quarter of a billion dollars in debt. Consequently Dynamo lost their Europa League spot, and everyone – sponsors, owners, players and coaches – bailed out. In 2016, for the first time in its history, Dynamo were relegated to the second division, and the club was sold back to the original sports society for a single rouble. The threat of a similar fate has hung over Lokomotiv Moscow who, despite having been the club of RZHD (Russian Railways), and thus the recipients of considerable state largesse, had considerable debts and inflated sponsorship deals with four of the organization's subsidiaries.[11]

UEFA's auditors will not, however, be visiting Torpedo, Moscow's fifth grand club, any time soon.[12] From its foundation in the 1920s, Torpedo was the club of Zil, the state vehicle manufacturer, and the people of the neighbourhood who worked in Zil's factory and filled the Eduard Streltsov Stadium. In the late 1950s and mid 60s they were fabulous, the rest of the time not so good, but either way they had a lot of soul. In 1996 Zil was in economic meltdown and no longer able to sustain the club, which was sold to the newly emerged Luzhniki company who had taken control of the national stadium, and were now looking for someone or something to fill it. What they got was a team that played to crowds of less than 5,000 in a stadium that could accommodate over 80,000. Meantime Zil had sufficiently recovered to create a new Torpedo team playing for the old crowd back in the old stadium. Starting in the lower leagues, they actually made the top league in 2003, before they were sold off to the conglomerate Norilsk Nickel and renamed FC Moscow. The remaining Torpedo got itself relegated in 2006 and 2008, at which point Zil stepped in again, bought the club back from the Luzhniki group and returned it to the Eduard Streltsov. Here, miraculously, they managed to get themselves promoted in 2014, before once again imploding and going bankrupt.

Beyond Moscow and St Petersburg, the leading clubs have not come from middling provincial cities, but from the capitals of the troubled republics of the North Caucuses and of Tartarstan. Here regional leaders, closely allied to the Kremlin, have been allowed to use state funds to build sporting tribunes. Alania Vladikavkaz was founded in 1991 by Akhsarbek Galazov, President of North Ossetia. As with Spartak, the club was permitted to profit from cigarette and alcohol smuggling, in this case across the Georgian border, but also received government funding and attracted huge local crowds to see a primarily home-grown team. In contemporary Russia the team's budget would barely pass muster in the second level, but in 1995 it was enough to win the league, and in 1996 to force a final championship play-off game with Spartak. Since Galazov's death in 1998, local government revenues have not been able to match the kind of money metropolitan teams have been showered with. Relegation and bankruptcy have followed. A final attempt by Russian Hydro, a state energy company, to revive the club ended in its dissolution.[13]

The trajectory of Anzhi Makhachkala, based in the capital of the republic of Dagestan, is similar if more compressed. In 2011 the businessman Suleiman Kerimov bought the club from the president of the Republic, or rather he received it and its debts, free of charge, for the promise of investment. Not that he was, as the owner of Russia's main potash producer Uralkali, short of money. Whatever Kerimov's precise intentions, there was no ambiguity about the scale of his ambition. He immediately spent $50 million on players, and $200 million on building a new stadium. Roberto Carlos, albeit at the age of thirty-seven, was unveiled as the club's new star, and was joined by Yuri Zhirkov from Chelsea. Both were exceeded by the arrival of Samuel Eto'o, in a personal jet, and signed for $21 million a year. Dutch coach Guus Hiddink took his $10 million too but, match day aside, no one was living in Dagestan. The whole squad lived and trained in Moscow. Dagestan, as it had been for some time, was rife with chronic low-level warfare between jihadis, separatists, local security forces and the Russian state. In the first year of Kerimov's project Dagestan, with 378 fatalities, was more than twice as dangerous as Chechnya. Nonetheless, large crowds gathered to see the team in Makhachkala, even Jean Claude van Damme was persuaded to put in an appearance, and in 2013 they managed to come third in the league. Another bout of wild spending on players followed but, just two years after the circus had begun, Kerimov suddenly upped sticks. Budgets were slashed, a fire sale of players ensued and Anzhi, as fast as they had risen, disappeared into the lower leagues. There they passed into the hands of Osman Kadiev, previously president of their cross-town rivals Dynamo Makhachkala, where he got the club relegated and himself banned from football for issuing death threats to opponents and visiting referees mid-match with machine gun-wielding guards. At Anzhi he cut down on the theatricals and concentrated on leading the club into bankruptcy.[14]

Rubin Kazan and Terek Grozny have proved more resilient. The former, based in the capital of the Muslim-majority Republic of Tartarstan, was owned and backed by both the president of the republic and the mayor of Kazan itself.[15] It spent the 1990s and early 2000s in the second division but, generously sponsored by TAIF, Tartarstan's petrochemical monopoly (of course owned and run by the president's family), the club began its ascent. Rubin went on to win the Russian league in 2008 and 2009, but on a budget considerably smaller than its metropolitan opponents'. Coach Kurban Berdyev, a pious and taciturn Muslim from Turkmenistan, reinforced the club's outsider and underdog status with his own demeanour and style. Even the sceptics were charmed, for it was obvious that the club didn't have the resources to 'buy' a championship, they actually won it. TAIF would eventually take the club over entirely, but by 2017 its attempts to get back to the top of the Russian game had mainly produced debts and a player exodus.

Terek Grozny, the team of the capital of Chechnya, has, like the republic and the city, survived two brutal and destructive wars between local rebel forces and Russia.[16] Since the early 2000s the club has been the effective property of the Kadyrov family who, after fighting the Russians in the 1990s, took their side in the 2000s and have made the republic's presidency their effective property too. Akhmat Kadyrov who, with Kremlin support, became president in 2003, was assassinated in 2004 and passed the club to his son Ramzan Kadyrov. Ramzan would ascend to the presidency in 2007 and found the resources, from the largesse bestowed upon him by the Kremlin, to get the club promoted to the Russian Premier League in 2008. The Kadyrovs also found the money to rebuild the centre of the city that they had previously helped flatten, including, in 2011, a new stadium for the team; though curiously the money was not found to pay many of the workers on the project. Kadyrov celebrated by playing, himself, in the opening game for Team Caucus against a Team World that included Luis Fígo and Diego Maradona. For Putin's sixty-third birthday in 2015 Kadyrov put out a team called Leader-63 to beat a selection of old Italian all-stars including Dino Baggio and Salvatore Schillaci.

Indebted as Ramzan is to the Kremlin, he remains intent on securing his local dynasty. In 2017, after naming mosques, martial arts clubs, towers and public spaces after his father, he changed the club's name to Akhmat Grozny FC. On his Instagram post he noted, 'A club bearing the name of Great Akhmat-Hadji, a man of legend, a man who saved our people and Russia from international terrorists, MUST PLAY A HUNDRED TIMES BETTER THAN IN PREVIOUS YEARS!' One wonders if the ninth place the team secured in the 2018 season was a sufficient response from the squad, and what their fate will be if it was not.

III

In 1990, in the dying days of the Soviet Union, the sports writer Gennardi Larchikov described Spartak Moscow as 'the team of intellectuals and hooligans.' Spartak had long attracted writers, scientists, artists and professionals, wooed by their attacking play and relative independence from the Soviet State; they were the only club with a measure of self-management rather than being bound to a ministry or security agency, and attracted a crowd that understood their support as a quiet 'no' to the system. From the late 1970s, taking their cue from Western European, but especially English football, Spartak attracted a new generation seeking autonomy and a theatre of resistance, but who preferred the skinhead aesthetic and the thrill of disorder to the earnest kitchen table politics and private salons of the older generation. Dismissed by the party youth movement Komsomol as 'degenerates', they made their point in streets and the stadium with graffiti, disorder and the occasional fight with the police.

In the chaotic, brutal years of Yeltsin's first presidency, attendances at football plummeted. In part, it was a matter of economics: with so many citizens pushed to and below the poverty line football was beyond their means. For those who had a choice there were so many new options available. At most games, even in the top division, the gates would be opened at half-time to let in for free those who had waited. The decaying, half-empty stadiums of the 1990s, barely staffed by security of any kind, proved fertile soil for the kind of fandom pioneered at Spartak in the late Soviet era. Now exposed to the ultra cultures of southern Europe, new groups emerged at almost every leading club, adding *tifos*, pyro and chants to the repertoire of the English hooligan. Menace, scuffles and provocations became the norm at games in Moscow, but increasingly in provincial cities too. In 1995 a huge fight broke out at a Champions League game between Spartak Moscow and Legia Warsaw, who were supported by members of the recently founded firm at CSKA, *Red Blue Warriors*. Fighting spilled outside of the stadium, where the traffic was brought to a halt on Arbat Street as hundreds fought out an ugly brawl. In 1999, in the Moscow satellite town of Ramenskoe, all hell broke loose when, after wild Spartak goal celebrations, the police began to attack the crowd. They responded by tearing out the seats, throwing them at the police and then charging them. For the first time, a league match was abandoned due to fan violence, only halted by the arrival of a detachment of specialist riot police.[17]

Football ultras and firms were not the only place in Russia for nihilistic and alienated young men to gather. The skinhead cultures that had given birth to the first firms endured, and mutated into a great archipelago of ultra-nationalist, white supremacist and neo-Nazi organizations. As hundreds of thousands of Caucasians fled the wars in their own republics and headed for the informal labour markets of Moscow, the same groups began to coalesce around new anti-migrant organizations; all of these micro-groups and gangs drew on the football firms for at least part of their membership. Effectively ignored under Yeltsin, they were a matter of some concern for President Putin and his government, who saw them as a threat to both public order and perhaps even their own political power. The capacity of mass publics, given a core of determined activists, to overthrow governments – as they had in the Rose and Orange revolutions in Georgia and Ukraine in 2003 and 2004 respectively – worried them a lot. Consequently, the government attempted to manage this nationalist upsurge, creating their own front nationalist organizations and youth movements, and bringing some of the football firms into its orbit. As Vasily Yakemenko, the founder of Walking Together and Nashi, two such operations, said, 'Skinheads are sincere patriots.' Walking Together drew on ultras from CSKA as their in-house heavies, while Nashi directly employed the Spartak firm Gladiators, a group whose leader, Roman Verbitsy, was also listed as the man in charge of Nashi's 'volunteer youth brigade'. The brigade's main work appears to have been intimidating the government's opponents, including armed attacks on the National Bolshevik Party in 2005 and 2006, and environmentalists blocking a road in the Khimki forest in 2009.[18]

In 2010, the authorities appeared for a moment to be losing control of the movement they had helped nurture. In Moscow in early December, a Spartak fan, Egor Sviridov, was killed by a Dagestani gang, and the police let the main suspects go after questioning. Spartak's largest fan group, the *Frataria*, called for a protest, and 2,000 people blocked Leningrad Prospekt at rush hour. The suspects were rearrested, but by then a call had gone out to assemble at Manzeh Square. More than 6,000 attended, the core of them Spartak fans, but alongside them the whole panoply of intersecting ultra-nationalists and provocateurs. The crowd, without an obvious opponent, beat up some handy Armenians, the police, and anyone who looked Caucasian. The mob screamed 'Russia for Russians!', spray-painted swastikas, and threw flares, bottles, and metal guardrails. Then some of the thugs descended into the Metro, and, screaming 'White car!' dragged Caucasians and Central Asians from the trains and beat them unconscious as policemen looked on helplessly. In a rare concession to the street Putin held talks with Spartak ultras and visited

Sviridov's grave. The following year, for the first time, his presidential campaign included a stop with football fans in St Petersburg, where they chewed the fat over beer and snacks, while football ultras could be seen bulking up crowds for the cameras. After the election in 2012, an anti-Putin flash mob in Revolution Square was broken up by a hooded mob of Spartak ultras.

Whatever arrangements had been made, the football firms seemed a law unto themselves. Early the next year another Spartak fan, Alexei Ershov, was murdered in the city of Maloyaroslavets. Three thousand fans, drawn from all of the Moscow clubs, noisily demonstrated in the city, demanding and getting a long sentence for the accused. They were all back in 2013 for the Biryulovo riots, when reports of a murder in this southern immigrant district of Moscow ignited a massive anti-migrant riot. As one ultra leader, reflecting on the composition of the crowd, put it,

> Of course, most of the fans in the stands have nationalistic views. We all strongly dislike migrants and people from the Caucasus, but at the same time we are not members of any political movement. Five to six per cent are ideological nationalists, another 30 per cent are those who might throw a Nazi salute when they're drunk. The rest are those that do not accept any Nazi symbols . . . but when there is a murder in Biryulovo . . . we know which side we're on.[19]

These incidents were just the tip of a vast iceberg of racist acts and attitudes in Russian football, laid bare in a pair of minutely detailed reports compiled by the human rights organization SOVA, built on eyewitness accounts of games played at all levels of Russian football between 2013 and 2017.[20] At the most mundane level, stadiums and fans have been plastered, quite literally, with a huge array of neo-Nazi symbols, Nordic runes – which take on a distinctly Nazi or white supremacist hue in contemporary Russia – and esoteric numbers. This includes swastikas, Celtic crosses and the Odal rune (a favourite of the Nazis) emblazoned on club banners, the use of 88 (a reference to the eighth letter of the Roman alphabet, and thus HH, and thus *Heil Hitler!*), and slogans like 'White Power' and 'White Pride, World Wide'. These all come in the form of stickers, tattoos, badges and club/ultra-branded clothing. They are also used in graffiti, widely visible in Russian cities, and on flags and banners displayed at games. The chanting that accompanies these displays, especially when Russian teams are playing against Caucasian clubs, run to the general, like 'Fuck Caucus, Fuck!' and 'Kill the Hach' – one of many derogatory terms for Caucasian peoples – to the more specific: 'Dagestan is an animal capital', or 'FC Anzhi is an animal circus'. Just in case any of Russia's migrant Africans thought they were out of the picture, Spartak fans put them right in 2016, displaying a banner of Russian actor Bodorv and the opening words of a famous quote, 'You're not a brother to me, black bastard.' So too Russia's Jews. In 2017, when CSKA coach Leonid Slutsky featured in a club video celebrating Jewish New Year, the ultras replied with a banner saying, 'Listen to the Shofar in your free time, lousy coach.'

Not content with mere chanting, many groups have been active supporters of imprisoned neo-Nazi figures, many of them football ultras too, providing money for legal aid and medical care, while in 2012 Zenit's ultras published an open letter to the club in which they argued 'dark-skinned players are all but forced down Zenit's throat now, which only brings out a negative reaction' and said gay players were 'unworthy of our great city'. CSKA Moscow fan Olga Kuzkov won the 2015 Russian Premier League beauty pageant, and posted pictures of herself on social media giving a Nazi salute, against a backdrop of Nazi numerals and the nice tagline, 'Jews and gooks burn well in the oven.' The winner of Miss Spartak in 2017, Yana Bondarchuk, pulled the same trick, showing off her Odal rune tattoo. However, they have all been busiest when it comes to attacking antifascists and Caucasian fans inside the stadium and on the street. Antifa groups in Russian football are few and far between. In the more supportive environment of the big Caucasian clubs, Nalchik, Anzhi and Terek, they can show their face, and some survive at tiny clubs like Zvezda Irkuts and Okean Nakhodka, but they are a minuscule and usually invisible presence at the bigger clubs. No wonder: in 2011, anti-fascist campaigner Ilya Dzhaparidze was killed by a neo-Nazi group the night before leading an anti-racism rally at Dynamo.[21] Caucasians, be they Chechens, Dagastanis or Osettians, cannot be invisible. In 2013 alone travelling fans of Anzhi were violently assaulted in Krasnador, Mordovia, Moscow, St Petersburg and Ramenskoe: the fate of innumerable migrants to Russia's cities.

Despite such a broad agenda, Russia's football firms have still found time for the more traditional pleasures of a straight riot with the police in the stands. In 2013 Spartak were drawn away against second division club Shinnik Yaroslavl, where security was considerably laxer than at home and in the top league.[22] The Spartak fans spent the first half letting off enormous numbers of flares and smoke bombs, and then fought with the police who entered their stand early in the second half. The game was stopped in the fifty-third minute, the police deploying water cannons, and a restarted game finished with a 1–0 win to Spartak.

The Russian government had for some time become increasingly concerned about the impact of this kind of event on the World Cup they planned to host in 2018, and the potential political power of such people. Having toyed with surveillance, infiltration and co-option, the Kremlin opted for repression. Since 2014, at home at any rate, the Russian police and intelligence services steadily squeezed the ultra movement, bringing many of its key leaders in for questioning, arresting them when it suited. They also introduced stronger crowd control legislation and stiffer policing practice.

As such, *okolofutbola*, as the fighting subculture amongst football ultras is referred to, shifted out of the stadiums and the streets and into more discreet locations – urban peripheries, forests, etc. – where the police were less likely to intervene in prearranged fights between different clubs.[23] This pugilistic elite of the football scene, in contrast to the vodka-soaked revelries of the mainstream, opted for sobriety. In keeping with the teetotal, gimlet-eyed man-of-steel model beloved of Putin himself, these football ultras were not down the pub, but in the gym working out, and training in any number of martial arts. In effect, they became football-themed fight clubs with an ultra-nationalist flavour. But if the regime had steadily controlled them at home, they permitted, even applauded, a few outings overseas. In 2012, at the end of Russia's game against the Czech Republic in Wrocław at the European Championships, Russian fans attacked and hospitalized four security guards. Russians also got themselves into plenty of other fights in the Ukraine that summer, but they saved the best for the 2016 Euros in France.

Russia were drawn in the same group as England and, given the enduring if now absurdly anachronistic vision of English supporters still common amongst the devotees of *okolofutbola*, their match in Marseilles offered a perfect opportunity to go to work and test themselves again the old masters. Around 300 Russian ultras gathered in the city, where they were loosely organized by Alexander Shprygin, parliamentary assistant to Igor Lebedev, the ultra-nationalist parliamentarian, and chair of the All-Russia Football Supporters' Union, an organization notionally representing Russian fans at the national football federation, but designed as an instrument of top-down surveillance and control over troublesome ultras. The first encounter was in the Old Port, where thousands of beery England fans had gathered before the game. As one Russian recalled, 'We literally hadn't managed to get to the end of the first beer before a call rang out and our guys shouted, "So what: we are doing this?" We went into the square and started to just really work.'[24] Many were dressed in mixed martial arts gear, others wore masks and strapped go-pro cameras to their chests to capture the moment.[25] The English were sent flying. At the match itself, on the final whistle, the same crew charged the England crowd behind the goal, and cleared the stands. The French arrested and deported dozens of Russians, but things looked just fine from Moscow. Igor Lebedev was delighted: 'I don't see anything wrong with the fans fighting. Quite the opposite. Our guys are great. Keep it up!' President Putin condemned the violence, but made mockery nonetheless: 'I truly don't understand how 200 of our fans could beat up several thousand English?'[26] There was a great deal of online boasting, and ferocious promises from the overexcited ultras that England fans, indeed the world, could expect a rough ride, a 'festival of violence', at the 2018 World Cup. The Kremlin had decided otherwise. Ultra groups were more closely policed than ever. The Confederations Cup in 2017 was preceded by a widespread round-up of key figures in the movement. The All-Russia Football Supporters' Union was kicked out of the football federation and closed down. At the same time Alexander Shprygin had his car torched. The message from the Kremlin, that there would be no trouble at the World Cup, was loud and terrifyingly clear.[27]

IV

Since 1992, when the CIS team bowed out at the 1992 European Championships, all formal relationships between Russian football and that of the newly independent ex-Soviet states ceased. Despite a number of attempts to create new transnational footballing connections, like a super league in the post-Soviet space, all have been stillborn. Yet such is the historical weight and political interests of Russia, that it continues to cast a shadow of what is known in Moscow as the 'near abroad'. Football has its place beneath that penumbra.

Nowhere more so than in Transnistria, a narrow slice of land on the eastern flank of Moldova, abutting the Ukrainian border. While a new nationalism swept the western Romanian-speaking parts of Moldova in the final days of the Soviet Union, the majority Russian speakers of Transnistria declared their independence. A short border war was adjourned in 1992 and Transnistria, recognized by only the Russians, continues to exist in a strange limbo: it remains the case that there are no phone lines between Moldova's capital, Chişinău, and Transnistria's Tiraspol. However, in the realm of football Transnistria remained very much part of the Moldovan scene. Indeed, FC Sheriff Tiraspol has won almost every single Moldovan national championship since independence, and is thus an almost daily thorn in the side of Romanian Moldova, made tangible every other week when the club's small body of away fans persistently chant 'Russia, Russia' in their opponents' stadiums.[28] The club was owned and run by Sheriff, a holding company established by ex-KGB agents Viktor Gushan and Ilya Kazmaly, who also controlled much of the enclave's economy, its trucking firms and hotels and, according to the US State Department, the ruling political party. However they get their money, it has been enough to field a team of foreigners, a mix of Serbs and Brazilians especially, who outclass the meagre competition and in 2013 were good enough to make it to the group stage of the Europa Cup.

If football has served in Transnistria to establish a reputation, in Azerbaijan it is all about laundering one.[29] In 1993, Heydar Aliyev, previously a member of the Soviet Politburo and the head of the local KGB, took power in a coup that displaced elected President Abulfaz Elchibey. In 2003, he handed the post on to his son Ilham Aliyev, who has yet to relinquish it. Over two decades of unbroken rule stands, first and foremost, on total and virtually personal control of Azerbaijan's considerable oil revenues and the state oil company SOCAR. Secondly, the Aliyevs have proved effective, occasionally vicious authoritarians, rigging elections, harassing and imprisoning what little opposition emerges, and controlling and intimidating the press; they have justly acquired a reputation for the widespread abuse of human rights. In an effort to obscure that view the regime has turned to sport. Baku, the capital, has acquired a world-class multi-sport stadium, and in 2015 the government paid, almost in its entirety, for the European Games, an unloved multi-sport mini-Olympics, to be held there. They also paid up to be part of the Formula One circus and will stage four games at the multi-national 2020 European football championships. Atlético Madrid have played in a shirt bearing the words 'Azerbaijan: Land of Fire', while SOCAR have become a major sponsor of UEFA.[30] They were even prepared to go in, albeit as junior partners, with FIFA's extraordinary Hollywood vanity project, the movie *United Passions*.

On the pitch, the regime has directed its resources towards FK Qarabag,[31] a club founded in Ağdam, in the disputed territory of Nagorno-Karabakh, which sits inside Azerbaijan but is claimed by the Armenians. Its original stadium is now a ruin, sitting in a ruined city, thinly populated by Armenian security forces and snipers. From 1988 to 1994 Armenia and Azerbaijan waged a vicious war over Nagorno-Karabakh. For the duration of the war, the club was a practical symbol of Azeri resistance to the Armenian incursion, games increasingly played out to the sound of gunfire and air raids. It was not enough, and, with the war lost, the club, and what was left of the city's population, were evacuated to Baku, where it struggled on as a de facto representative of the many internally dispelled Azeris in the country. Rescued from bankruptcy in 2001 by the regime, through Aliyev's holding companies, the club was then turned into a national champion, whose name is a constant reminder to the Armenians of the government's enduring claim on Nagorno-Karabakh. When the team, miraculously, made the group stage of the Champions League in 2017 the President was unequivocal as to what it meant: 'Team Qarabag bears the name of Karabakh. Team Qarabag represents the city of Ağdam, which is under occupation. Therefore, your victory is not just a sporting victory, it is a victory of our state, and patriotic people.'[32]

In Belarus, the state most firmly and, for its leadership at any rate, most comfortably within the orbit of Russia, football is held in the same ambiguous esteem accorded it by the Kremlin. Like Putin, President Lukashenko, in power in Belarus since 1992, prefers ice hockey to football.[33] While the country's grassroots football pitches have rotted, there has been money for dozens of new 'ice palaces' in provincial towns. The domestic game is so poor that it gives its TV rights away for free. Average gates in the top division were no more than 2,000. The authorities were so cack-handed and greedy that, when presented with the prize of a home game against Spain in the qualifying rounds of the 2012 European Championships, they demanded so much from Spanish television that they got nothing, and set such high ticket prices (ten times the usual) that fans boycotted the game. Dinamo Minsk, the national champions, owned by the country's wealthiest man Yury Chyzh, also known as 'Lukashenko's Wallet', operated on a government-supported budget equal to that of the whole of football's top division. Their only competitors were FC BATE Borisov, the team of the giant Barysua automotive tractor plant, the country's largest single operation, who managed three trips to the group stages of the Champions League, even beating Bayern Munich 3–1 in 2013, but there has been precious little else to cheer since.

It was not the vagaries of football, or even Belarus's inevitably peripheral place in the European order, that bothered Lukashenko: it was the people who went to watch the game that troubled him. The first Belorussian football ultras appeared around Dinamo Minsk in the early 1980s, and grew in number under the more relaxed conditions of *perestroika* in the late 1980s. The turmoil of the 1990s saw Belorussian ultras, like their Russian counterparts, spread from the capital to every club, where they mixed and mutated with ultra-right-wing and white supremacist groups. In more recent years, this milieu took on a distinctly Belorussian ultra-nationalism, and has symbolically challenged the much more pro-Russian agenda of the government. In turn, the authorities have increasingly policed football fans, especially away fans, attempting to control what banners they display, and on occasion actually attacking them during games. Consequently, though they have had no official links with the country's small and fragmented opposition, they have become part of a wider culture of muted dissent and resistance.[34]

During the 'silent protests' of 2011 that followed another rigged presidential election and a sharp deterioration in the country's economy, the leader of Dinamo Minsk's ultras, also an activist in the protests, was arrested and detained, while FC BATE Borisov fans were heard chanting a coded call to the President, 'May he die.' The game played in 2014 in Minsk between Belarus and Ukraine saw the locals, emboldened, perhaps, by events in Kiev, singing the signature chant of the protests on the Ukrainian Maidan, where many citizens and Ukrainian football ultras were calling for the resignation of the pro-Russian President Victor Yanukovych. In addition to 'Slava Ukraine – glory to Ukraine', both Belorussian and Ukrainians enjoyed many rounds of the cult classic, *'Putin khuilo!'* – 'Putin is a dickhead!' Seven of them, as well as fans caught chanting the same at an FC BATE game, were arrested and sentenced.[35] This was all much less in evidence during the 2014 ice hockey World Championships held in Belarus later that year; but then the police had rounded up and detained most of the country's leading football ultras for the duration of the competition. However, in what was perhaps a sign of Lukashenko's weakness, the police held off arresting fans at recent national team games for flying the old white-red-white national flags and the *Pahonia*, the nation's historical coat of arms, that was abandoned in the 1990s.[36]

In time Ukrainian football would stir similar ultra-nationalist energies and, as the Belarus elite saw all too clearly, help staff the kind of social movements that could topple dictators; indeed, the game would wend its way through almost every key moment of the country's turbulent post-Communist history. In the first decade of Ukrainian independence, the team that had served as the nation's tribune in the Soviet League, Dynamo Kiev, ruled the roost. Acquired in 1993 by Grigori Surkis, till then an employee of Kiev City Council, and his younger brother Igor, Dynamo Kiev was a multifaceted prize: the leading force in the Ukrainian game, regular participants in European football, close to Ukraine's first two presidents, Leonid Kuchma and Leonid Kravchuk, and, through the Slavutych complex of companies attached to it, a very busy and profitable trading operation for the Surkis brothers. Both were known for their interest in referees, and in 1995 were behind the offer of $30,000 and two fur coats made to López Nieto, who would be in charge of Dynamo's Champions League game with Panathinaikos.[37] Once this was revealed, Dynamo and Igor Surkis, then acting president of the club, were banned from European football. President Kuchma, supported by his predecessor President Kravchuk, took personal charge of negotiations with UEFA, who would eventually rescind their bans on both

Dynamo and Surkis. It was these kind of connections that allowed the Surkises to add banking, energy, television and oil to their portfolio and acquire a record of corruption and electoral malpractice allegations against them that saw the US Department of Homeland Security refuse Grigori a visa in 2004. The older Surkis has not let the demise of his old political allies, or the irritant of the US immigration system, get in his way: rather, he left the club in his brother's hands, became an MP, ensuring his immunity from prosecution, ascended to the Presidency of the Ukrainian Football Federation, and secured himself a very comfortable perch as a vice-president on UEFA's executive committee where, no doubt, he has been paying special attention to the sartorial needs of officials.

By the beginning of the twenty-first century Dynamo Kiev and the old *nomenklatura*, like the Surkises, Kravchuk and Kuchma, were having to cede space to the enriched clubs of the new oligarchs and the new political forces emerging in the Ukraine. In the west of the country this included Igor Kolomoyskyi, one of the nation's richest bankers, who owned and backed Dnipro (FC Dnipropetrovsk), while in the east, Shakhtar Donetsk became the richest and most successful club in the country.[38] Once owned by Akhat Bragin, a proto-oligarch-cum-gang leader, Shakhtar was part of his fledgling business empire in coal and steel. In 1995, both passed to his deputy Rinat Akhmetov after Bragin was blown up during a Shakhtar match by a rival gang. Since then Akhmetov has built his business, SCM, into a multi-billion-dollar conglomerate with control of over 100 companies employing 300,000 people. In this context the near billion dollars he has spent on Shakhtar over the last twenty years, building them a five-star stadium and a team full of good Latin American imports, is small change. Moreover, the return on this investment has been considerable: domination of the Ukrainian league, victory in the UEFA Cup in 2009, and widespread goodwill amongst the public in the Donbass. However, Akhmetov's political investments have not always proved so bountiful.

In late 2004 the country's presidential elections pitted Viktor Yushchenko against Viktor Yanukovych, the titular heads of two political collations beginning to crystallize around long-established differences in the country; respectively, the West and the East, Ukrainian-speaking and Russian-speaking, pro-European and pro-Russian. All of Ukraine's oligarchs took sides, but Akhmetov's investment in Viktor Yanukovych and his Party of the Regions was perhaps the greatest. Initially it appeared a sound bet, as Yanukovych was declared the winner of the second round of voting, turning a huge deficit in the polls into a 3 per cent lead on the night. The urban publics of Ukraine, alert to reports of widespread electoral malpractice, had other ideas. In what became known as the Orange Revolution, mass occupations of public space broke out all over the country. In the east there were small demonstrations in support of Yanukovych, but the vast majority were against, and they called for the election result to be annulled. Kiev's Maidan, the great public square in front of parliament, saw up to a million people gathering in the fearsome cold of a Ukrainian winter. In a re-run of the vote, held in 2005, Yushchenko dispatched Yanukovych by a ten-point margin.

Thus, in 2007, it was to a European-oriented Ukraine that UEFA awarded, alongside Poland, the joint hosting of the 2012 European Championships. The president of the Ukrainian Football Federation made the link explicit: 'This is a decisive day for our country. It will provide new opportunities for our country as it strives to integrate with Europe.'[39] That, of course, would require European levels of infrastructure, and the government authorized the building of two new stadiums, four airports, the import of a fleet of South Korean high-speed trains, and the reconstruction of 1,000 miles of inter-city road, at an estimated cost of around $10 billion. Neither President Yushchenko or his Prime Minister Yulia Tymoshenko would get to enjoy the opening game in Kiev from the good seats. In the 2010 presidential election Viktor Yanukovych made a comeback to compare with Lazarus, beating Tymoshenko in a second ballot, 49 to 45. His four years in power were marked by the most sustained looting of public money yet conducted by the executive. Two footballing examples can stand proxy for a shameless and nationwide operation.

First, many of the major stadium and infrastructure projects for Euro 2012, until then open to competitive tender, were suddenly withdrawn from public competition and allocated to a small number of companies that were closely connected to a network of politicians and administrators around Yanukovych. The opposition's spokesperson on sport, Ostap Semerak, claimed that $4 billion of public money had been skimmed off the top of those contracts and passed into offshore, private hands. Altkom, one of the firms that got those Euro 2012 contracts, was traced back to a Ukrainian yoga teacher in

Cyprus who fronted dozens of other Russian and British firms too. Second, Oleksandr Yaroslavsky, a banking and property billionaire who had been a Green Party MP between 2002 and 2006 and a fervent opponent of Yanukovych, also owned Metalist Kharkiv and had invested heavily in the club. Suddenly, in 2012, he sold this prize to the unknown Sergey Kurchenko, and would later reveal that he had received an offer 'he couldn't refuse'. Sergey Kurchenko, it transpired, was a close friend of the older son of President Yanukovych and, in this and other business roles, was acting as a front for the family as they picked up a variety of assets.[40]

For good measure Yanukovych had Yulia Tymoshenko arrested, tried and imprisoned on the grounds that she did a bad gas deal with the Russians, but it was transparently an act of political spite and revenge. Just months before the tournament began she went on hunger strike, and was brutally treated during her transfer from prison to hospital. The German Chancellor Angela Merkel was just one of many European politicians who called for her release, and made it clear that they wouldn't be putting in an appearance at the tournament. Equally pointedly, the feminist activist group Femen disrupted a nationwide tour of the competition's trophy: Inna Shevchenko appeared by the Cup, bare-chested but for the words 'Fuck Euro 2012', highlighting the link between tourism, football and the country's large and often brutal sex industry. Such was the standing of the rule of law under Yanukovych that the Ukrainian TV channel 2+2, part of the Surkis brothers' empire, which had bought the domestic broadcast rights to the tournament from UEFA, refused to pay up and got away with it.[41] Ukraine, despite home advantage, managed just a single draw, and went home from their own party early.

In 2013, under considerable economic and diplomatic pressure from Russia, Yanukovych took the decision not to sign an Association Agreement with the European Union. This was met by a huge burst of spontaneous protest across the country, centring on the Maidan in Kiev where upwards of 400,000 people gathered. Met, in Kiev and elsewhere, with considerable police violence, the protests mutated into a wider challenge to the regime as a whole, but above all to Yanukovych and his corrupt networks. In their earliest days they were joined by tens of thousands of members of Ukraine's football ultra groups. Given the prevailing cultures of apolitical nihilism, fight club violence and overt racism prevalent amongst them over the previous decades, this might appear odd. However, their nationalism and loathing of the Yanukovych regime and its police force proved stronger than their divisions. In Kiev ultras had been explicitly politicized by the Pavlychenki case, in which a father and son, a Dynamo ultra, had been sentenced to life imprisonment for the murder of a judge on the very flimsiest of evidence. Ultras mobilized up to 5,000 protestors at a time against this, covered Kiev in Pavlychenki stickers and graffiti, and held up banners at their games demanding justice. All these tactics were deployed many times over in support for the Euromaidan protests as ultras helped occupy public squares, organize the collection and delivery of food and medicine and, where necessary, fight off the paid government thugs that came to disrupt protest camps. In Donetsk, Shakhtar ultras went as far as to call for a boycott of their own club given Akhmetov's past support for Yanukovych.[42]

By February Yanukovych had fled to Russia, his party dissolved. So too Ukraine, for while the Euromaidan protestors had a national reach, they were in a minority in the East and Crimea, where Yanukovych supporters and Russian speakers predominated. In February 2014 Russian military forces entered and annexed the Crimea, local supporters organized a swift referendum in which the fait accompli was garlanded with a majority. In the eastern regions of Ukraine, the Donbass in particular, armed separatists, with the tacit and active support of the Russian state, established a breakaway region, and ignited a civil war with the government in Kiev. Crimea's two leading teams, Sevastapol and Tavriya Smimferopol, both members of the Ukrainian top division, and both keen to stay there, were initially harassed and prevented from travelling, and were then forced to leave the Ukrainian premier league, before being dissolved. Sevastapol has been recreated in the lower Russian leagues, while Tavriya Smimferopol, like much of Crimea, is split. One version of the club has succumbed to reality and plays under the Russian football federation, the other has relocated itself to the city of Kherson in southern Ukraine, where the national government continues to house a putative Crimean administration.[43]

They are not the only clubs to have relocated. As the war in the east intensified through 2014, Shakhtar Donetsk moved its squad to Kiev, where they remain, and its home matches moved, first to Lviv and then to Kharkiv. Extraordinarily, the team managed to attract bigger crowds in Lviv than the local sides. Nonetheless, for a club of Shakhtar's size, once playing before 55,000 people, it has been a harsh landing. Shakhtar's owner was finding the new political geography equally difficult. As a long-term, if low-profile supporter of Yanukovych and his Party of the Regions, Akhmaetov has seen his political capital plummet. The war in the Donbass has robbed him of his local base and easy access to much of his business empire. Shakhtar survives, but many clubs have gone bankrupt, the league itself has been forced to shrink, foreign players have been departing at a canter, and Metalist Kharkiv, like its puppet masters, has disappeared altogether. In the wake of Yanukovych's departure the club president Sergey Kurchenko made himself scarce too. In his absence the club's debts accumulated, the squad was sold off and, given the absence of wages most of the time, it was hardly surprising when a huge match-fixing scandal was uncovered at the club in 2016. The entire first team was suspended and the club's licence to play has been revoked; like the rest of Ukrainian football its ruins remain in suspended animation.[44]

V

If President Putin had been, at best, lukewarm about football and, prior to its staging, reserved in his claims for the 2018 World Cup, there was no such reticence when it came to the Olympics. Anticipating the winter games of 2014, to be held in Sochi, he reminisced, 'We have strong memories of the emotional, uplifting enthusiasm we felt during the 1980 Moscow Olympics. The mighty, inspiring spirit of the Olympics is once again returning to our nation.'[45] Of course, such sentimentality required a good dose of cynicism and amnesia to make it plausible, but that was working for most popular reinterpretations of Russia's Soviet interregnum. In fact, preparations for the 1980 games were a case study in late Soviet self-loathing and paranoia, as organizers worried over the impression that Moscow, and its hapless phones and money-changing systems, would make on Western visitors. Subject to a boycott by the United States and many of its allies, in response to the 1979 Soviet invasion of Afghanistan, itself a precursor to the collapse of the Soviet Union, the games were politicized and lop-sided. Declared at the time to be the cleanest Olympics since drug testing had begun, they were later revealed to be the most chemically soaked of all. The Politburo and the party considered them a great patriotic success, much of the populace enjoying the relative freedoms of a long national holiday. For a few the enduring image of the Olympics was the release of a vast weeping Micah – the Games' ragged ursine mascot – into the Moscow night, carried away on bunches of helium balloons: a long goodbye to the Soviet Union, a state that had barely a decade to live.

In Putin's Russia, the ambiguities and uncertainties that accompanied the Moscow Games could be erased to produce a rose-tinted memory of a world in which Moscow really was the centre of attention, the Soviet Union really was an empire and a superpower at that, and, by whatever means, was the dominant Olympic sporting force. What better way, then, after over three decades of decline, break-up and humiliation, to announce a reassertion of Russian power in the new global order, than by staging the Games again. Moreover, in a situation where Russia remained in the most fundamental ways a weak global actor, it retained much of its Soviet-era strength in sporting diplomacy inside corrupt institutions, a strength that allowed it to win not only the 2014 Sochi Winter Olympics but the 2018 World Cup as well. The World Cup bid was so slick that, while the British Prime Minister, the heir to the throne and David Beckham humiliated themselves for England in front of the FIFA executive committee, Vladimir Putin did not even show up in Zurich until the victory had been announced. Later down the line, when investigators, both FIFA and the Swiss legal authorities, came looking for the bid committee's digital archive, they were informed that the entirety of its computers, leased for the occasion, had been incinerated.

Russia's initial forays into global football were notionally private matters for favoured oligarchs.[46] First off the mark, Roman Abramovich purchased Chelsea in 2003. In 2007, Alisher Usmanov bought 15 per cent of Arsenal and increased his stake to 29 per cent, but was thwarted in his ambitions by the implacability of American majority-owner Stan Kroenke. Even in exile, Boris Berezovsky sought to get into the game, backing the mysterious MSI fund that invested in clubs and third-party ownership of Latin American players. More recently Dmitry Rybolovlev, a billionaire who made his money by obtaining and selling the Russian state potash industry, purchased Monaco; Maxim Denim, a petro-chemical trader, bought Bournemouth; and in 2015 Portuguese police arrested a network of Russians who had bought into small clubs, like União de Leiria, as vehicles for money-laundering.[47] However, all of these projects have been dwarfed by those of Gazprom.

Gazprom, always an instrument of domestic economic policy, was increasingly used by Putin's governments as a tool of domestic and international politics.[48] The acquisition of a media empire, the creation of a new football channel with most of the country's sports rights, as well as its continuing support for Zenit St Petersburg, pointed to the former; the threat to raise gas prices to Moldova and Ukraine, on the eve of talks with the European Union, pointed to the latter. In addition to their huge investment in Zenit St Petersburg at home, they also signed leading sponsorship deals with Schalke 04 in Germany (the company's biggest foreign market), Red Star Belgrade in Serbia (where it owned a controlling stake in the national oil company and planned to build a new gas pipeline), and Chelsea (owned by the man who sold them his oil company Sibneft in 2005 in the country's biggest ever corporate deal). Extraordinarily, for a company that sells nothing direct to European consumers, Gazprom also became a major sponsor of the UEFA Champions League, and in 2015, when most other major corporations fought shy of the corruption-encrusted FIFA, a sponsor of the World Cup. Of these, Schalke, the great working-class miners' club of the Ruhr, was the jewel in the crown. Indeed, on the company's own website is the claim, 'Gazprom and Germany are linked together by football and FC Schalke 04.' Certainly relations were close and cordial. Schalke's President Clemens Tönnies established a personal friendship with President Putin, as his €5 billion meat processing company expanded into Russia. In 2011, when goalkeeper Manuel Neuer was poised to move to Bayern Munich, Putin called Tönnies, suggesting that more money be made available to prevent Neuer's departure. There was no holding Neuer, but Tönnies remained sufficiently thankful for Putin's input to suggest, in the midst of the Ukraine crisis, that the team visit him at the Kremlin.[49]

Sochi, marked by extravagant ceremonies, expensive stadiums and a lot of Russian gold medals, was deemed, the distractions of the Ukrainian situation aside, a great success. However, a grievous blow was dealt to the Games' legacy when Russian whistleblower Grigory Rodchenkov revealed widespread and organized doping practices in Russian elite sport. The chain of events and investigations that followed from the IOC, WADA, and a number of independent inquiries, most importantly the McClaren Commission, resulted in Russia being suspended from both the 2016 Rio and 2018 Pyeongchang Winter Olympics, as well as the retrospective loss of many of its medals. Amongst the throwaway lines of the McClaren report were the details of eleven footballers who tested positive at the London 2012 Olympics. This was picked up and investigated by FIFA's chief medical officer, the Czech Professor Jiri Dvorak, only for him to be abruptly sacked in late 2017.[50] As late as March 2018 FIFA had yet to complete investigations into thirty-four cases of possible doping by Russian players, including members of the 2014 World Cup squad. From hiding, and through his lawyer in the United States, whistleblower Grigory Rodchenkov was unambiguous: 'Mutko ordered protection for Russian footballers when he was the president of the Russian Football Union. He told me directly to "avoid any scandal by hiding positive results" and "doping would be handled internally," meaning that those doping irresponsibly or without protocols could be disciplined or reported.'[51]

Mutko is of course Vitaly Mutko, the golden thread that runs through all of these stories. He got his start in politics and sports administration in the 1990s as deputy mayor of St Petersburg, where amongst other things he worked with Vladimir Putin on international sporting events. His ascent has been steady ever since: President of Zenit St Petersburg, then President of the Russian Premier League, member of the Duma for Putin's United Russia, Minister of Sport from 2008 to 2016 and a key organizer of the Sochi games and the World Cup bid; and then Deputy Prime Minister of Russia and chair of the organizing committee of the 2018 World Cup. Along the way, he was also evidently central to the doping programme in Russia. He has since been banned from the Olympics by the IOC, and resigned his 2018 gig, but his domestic political position seems assured.

If they were doping they had better have been with good drugs, because, since the CIS team's dismal departure from the 1992 European Championships, Russia's national team had, with the glorious exception of 2008, been hopelessly mediocre, and on occasion embarrassingly anaemic, a shadow of the Soviet Union's once significant presence in global football. Thus, in headlines and chat rooms, both sports writers and the public quoted the sanguine fatalism of Viktor Chernomyrdin, the country's prime minister during the 1998 financial crisis, who looked back on the reforms of the Yeltsin era and thought, 'We hoped for the best, but, things turned out like they always do'; so too the Russian national team. It was not until 2002 that they would qualify for an international tournament again, and they would go on to miss out on the 2006 and 2010 World Cups. Even then, the team brought little joy. At the 2002 World Cup, after the team had lost their second game to their Japanese hosts 2–0, a riot broke out in central Moscow, where thousands had been watching on a big screen. Hundreds of windows were smashed, cars were set alight and visiting Japanese tourists were attacked. One man in the square was stabbed and killed, a police officer died later in hospital, dozens were injured and sixty people were arrested.[52]

It was a situation desperate enough for the Russian football authorities to hire, for the first time, a foreign coach – Guus Hiddink, who had steered South Korea to the semi-finals of the 2002 World Cup – and find the £6.25 million a year in hard currency to pay him. The press were contemptuous of 'the Dutch farmer', and his predecessor Valery Gazzaev wondered whether a foreigner could ever 'understand the complexities of the Russian soul'. Hiddink, unconventionally in the otherwise spartan and authoritarian training culture of Russian football, permitted joking, encouraged swearing, and at least got the team to the 2008 European Championships in Austria and Switzerland.[53] Hitherto almost entirely absent from international tournaments, significant numbers of Russians made the journey to watch them, testament to the booming oil economy of those years. Enthusiasm and optimism were nurtured on a strange concatenation of events as Russia, finally, regained the world ice hockey crown and won the Eurovision Song Contest.

Defeat in the opening game to Spain, the favourites, did not dampen spirits, and a victory in the next against Greece ignited a national wave of football fever. The Russian national team's games recorded unprecedented television audiences throughout the tournament, peaking at over 70 per cent of the nation. In their final group game Russia needed to beat Sweden to progress. The ultra-nationalist politician Vladimir Zhirinovsky offered to give the team a pep talk:

'The guys need a special psychological boost, a powerful emotional charge that will ensure their desire for victory.' The Russian media offered the same. Television stations, in their trailers for the match, rendered the game as a version of the Battle of Poltava. Columnists and commentators recalled the early eighteenth-century encounter at which the Russian forces defeated the Swedes, and established the core of modern imperial Russia.[54] Playing scintillating football, Russia won 2–0, the final whistle triggering a city-wide carnival in Moscow as hundreds of thousands of citizens, in face paint and bedecked in the national colours, flooded the streets; manufacturers reported a quintupling of flag sales. The quarter-final against the Dutch, which the Russians won 3–1 in extra time, saw a repeat, but with even bigger crowds, in a country where, for the first time, every news report, chat show, celebrity foghorn and politician was prefacing everything with a nod to football. The following day, even Patriarch Alexi II of the Orthodox Church, at a wreath-laying ceremony on the Day of Memory and Mourning for the dead of the Great Patriotic War, felt compelled to say that the nation's sorrow was 'mitigated by our joy over yesterday's victory.'[55] The semi-final was lost to Spain but, unlike 2002, the streets were peaceful, the mood deflated rather than angry. 'Our team has played so well,' argued *Izvestia*, 'that citizens can believe once again in their own country and its revival.'[56]

The boom, the euphoria, and the equanimity were short-lived. The same team, more or less, that won the Battle of Poltava lost a play-off to Slovenia and failed to even qualify for the 2010 World Cup. Under Italian Fabio Capello they did make it to the next one, and this time managed two dismal draws before departing. In France, at Euro 2016, while the *okolofutbola* crowd were winning in the street and the stands, the team itself was simply very poor, garnering a single point from a draw with England before going home. One viral video, made by fans, challenged the team to a game and offered to play for the nation for free: 'The whole country is tired of Russian football. Failure after failure, but the national team players only get richer!' Gennady Zyuganov, leader of the Communist Party, thought the team as soft as Putin's United Russia party, and that they needed 'a Stalinist mobilization' if things were to improve.[57] At the other end of the spectrum, Vladimir Zhirinovsky, leader of the LDPR, explained their defeat by Wales in terms of ultra-nationalist zeal, which the Welsh, oppressed by the English, had in spades. More nihilistically, perhaps realistically, 350,000 members of the public signed an online petition calling for the team to be simply dissolved.[58]

The team limped on, putting on a poor performance at the Confederations Cup in 2017. Attempts by Alexander Navalny, Boris Nemtsov's effective successor as the public face of political opposition in Russia, to stage protests around the tournament were crushed. The now ubiquitous hyper-security presence at mega-events ensured ultra-nationalist and hooligan firms were absent. The twelve stadiums, all effectively brand new, were completed, around one half of them doomed white elephants. Although all of these projects suffered from over-runs and backhanders, matters were at their worst in St Petersburg, where the Krestovsky Stadium cost 42 billion rubles, 580 per cent more than the original estimate, and was completed eight years late.[59] Thanks to a law passed in 2013 which exempted World Cup projects from Russia's already minimalist labour regulations, much of the construction workforce were North Koreans, most of whose pay went straight back to the government in Pyongyang, and whose living conditions were pitiful.[60] FIFA, although alerted to these facts, have glided over them.[61] For a riposte of any worth to this pharaonic project one must turn to Roman Ponomarev, a farmer from the village of Krasnoe south of the city, who built a replica of the Krestovsky from bales of straw: at its entrance hung the sign, 'Not a single ruble was stolen during the construction of this stadium.'[62] Neither the North Korean helots nor Ponomarev received tickets to the World Cup, but the government did issue an invitation to Sepp Blatter, the disgraced ex-president of FIFA and a man banned from football for life. President Putin had no expectations that Russia would win on the pitch, but as this, the clearest signal of all that Russia held the international rule of law in contempt, suggested, he was conducting the battle and making gains on other fronts.

CONCLUSION: THE GLOBAL POTEMKIN VILLAGE: WORLD CUP 2018

As of today, for one month, football will conquer Russia.
And from Russia, football will conquer the entire world.

Gianni Infantino

The new electronic interdependence re-creates the
world in the image of a global village.

Marshall McLuhan

I

Gianni Infantino's words, delivered as the punchline of his speech at the opening ceremony of the 2018 World Cup, managed to combine an extraordinary naivety with delusions of imperial grandeur. The latter, at least, had some basis in reality. Russia had certainly signed up to the usual onerous World Cup contract, with all the economic costs, temporary suspensions of sovereignty and tax exemptions for FIFA it entailed. Infantino was, no doubt, confident that the Russian public would warm to the spectacle, perhaps even be entranced by it. Yet that Infantino, with almost two decades of hands-on experience at UEFA and FIFA, should think that football would hold the whip hand in Russia defies belief. As the narrative of this book has made apparent, football has, more comprehensively than ever before, been colonized, shaped and used by the forces of economic and political power. Infantino's own role, when at UEFA, in aiding and abetting the royal houses of Abu Dhabi and Qatar, owners of Manchester City and PSG respectively, to 'cope' with the organization's Financial Fair Play strictures, alone suggests a remarkable familiarity with the current conjecture.[1] In fact, the real balance of power at the 2018 World Cup had been made clear a few days earlier at FIFA's annual congress, held in central Moscow. President Infantino, poised somewhere between items 7 and 8 on the agenda, suddenly informed the congress that they would not be moving on because, unannounced and unplanned, the president of the Russian Federation was popping in. Having stopped FIFA in its tracks, Putin's approach work was magnificent: shaking hands, working the room, charming the crowd, demonstrating exactly who was in charge. He delivered a speech of studied vacuity, claimed, with an entirely straight face, that 'sport and politics did not mix,' soaked up the applause, and departed, leaving the task of delivering the show to his factotums.[2]

In the lists of officials and organizers of the 2018 World Cup there is no mention of Grigory Potemkin, the eighteenth-century

Russian aristocrat, general and politician, but he was their spiritual forefather. In 1787, Potemkin took Catherine the Great on a tour of her empire's newly acquired southern lands. He was said to have ordered the construction of facades and fake houses to conceal the region's poverty. Quite how elaborate and how extensive his deceptions were is a matter of dispute, but the notion of a Potemkin village, coined by his twentieth-century German biographer, has acquired real currency, and was used to describe the showcase settlements of Stalin's Soviet Union and the sanitized Nazi concentration camps created for the benefit of the Red Cross. However, as Marshall McLuhan, the mercurial communications theorist of the 1960s, recognized, the modern global village is not made from plasterboard facades or even bricks and mortar, but is an electronic phenomenon: one that not only distracts and occludes, but also presents a convincing, alternative and deeply mendacious reality.

At one level, the World Cup could have been read as just a dazzling series of spectacles. The football itself was certainly compelling enough. The early rounds, unlike many recent tournaments, featured attacking rather than obsessively defensive teams, and a cascade of goals so great that there was just one goalless draw. The home team, against all expectations, went on a bravura run to the quarter-finals. Favourites, like the Germans, fell to exuberant giant-killers like Mexico and South Korea. The spectacle was captivating, and the world watched in even greater numbers than they had four years before in Brazil: over three billion people watched some of the tournament, and more than a billion tuned in for the final itself. In South America 97 per cent of the population engaged with the tournament. In Iceland 98 per cent of the TV audience watched their games. Powerful as these moments of the spectacle were, what turned the 2018 World Cup from sixty-four theatrically staged games of football into a five-week-long, twenty-four-hour-a-day global Potemkin village, was the unprecedented levels of reporting from journalists and the use of social media by fans, not just at the games, many of which were rather short on stadium atmosphere, but from Russia's public spaces.

For the duration of the tournament urban space, at least those zones in the World Cup cities where visitors congregated, were transformed. Normally these places would be strictly policed, with open drinking and carousing quickly snuffed out. Russia's police and security forces were, however, on their very best behaviour: with-drawing to the margins, permitting all manner of normally banned activities, and even summoning up a modicum of bonhomie. In these zones of permissible hedonism, a global digital village was temporar-ily erected. Americans and Europeans, normally the most visible of World Cup tourists, came in much smaller numbers than usual, deterred by the increasingly negative light in which Russia had been depicted in most of the Western press. Nonetheless, there were suffi-cient and colourful clusters of red-and-white checkerboard Croats, Swedes in yellow and Swiss with cow bells to ensure a European cameo. Much more prominent were Latin Americans: the usual pla-toons of wealthy and emigré Brazilians and Mexicans, indebted and indefatigable Argentinians, all reinforced by a huge contingent from Peru and its diaspora, who had qualified for the tournament for the first time in over thirty years. It was an event considered so unlikely during Peru's long, desperate years of economic crisis, civil war, and corrupt presidencies that one put off one's debts with the phrase, 'I'll pay you when Peru make it to the World Cup.' Now the country had qualified, and its citizens ran up more debt to get there. Some took redundancy money, others organized a whip round: 'There are people here who left their job because you get paid extra money when you leave somewhere you've been for a long time. A lot of others held a *pollada*, which involves cooking chicken and providing beer for money.'[3] Their overwhelming presence in Saransk, once a gulag city and almost entirely separated off from the rest of the world, brought a moment of warm, Latino carnival nationalism to the steppes.

China and India, although they failed to qualify, recorded unpre-cedented television audiences for the World Cup and, testament to the rising wealth of their new middle classes, sent their biggest con-tingent of fans to a World Cup ever.[4] Forty thousand Chinese bought tickets at home; 20,000 from the diaspora went too. As one AI engin-eer put it, 'Simply participating in this grand extravaganza makes us happy.' Three thousand more who bought 10,000 tickets from a mysterious Russian company, Anji MSK, were less happy. Scammed by these online hustlers, they were often seen standing disconso-lately outside World Cup stadiums they had been refused entry to.[5] Wealthy Indians spent their money on the expensive packages of premium tickets, five times as much money as they had spent on tickets for the Cricket World Cup in Australia just a few years before.

The availability of fan IDs for the duration of the tournament, as an alternative to expensive and cumbersome visas, saw hundreds of Nigerians make the journey. They had in fact been promised soccer try-outs and job opportunities by Lagos hucksters who, having taken their fee, abandoned them to their fate on the streets of Russia.[6] Invisible to visitors, and disdained by locals, all these spaces were cleaned and ordered by an army of migrant workers from the Caucuses and Central Asia.[7]

Russians were understandably confused by the change of regime, and even after their extraordinary opening 5–0 win over Saudi Arabia, they were cautious celebrants. A video that went viral on Twitter explained why. A Russian man, pointing to the cavorting visitors, asked a police officer whether he could join in. The policeman replies, sardonically, 'Are you a Russian guy? Then for you it won't be allowed.' The man pressed him: 'And if I'm not Russian?' The officer responded, 'For them everything is permitted.'[8] However, as Russia progressed into the knock-out stages, the public flooded into the main tourist zones, overwhelming their visitors at times, and by sheer weight of numbers forced the security apparatus to permit a bacchanalian public celebration.[9] The Russian press and government attempted to frame this as wholesome nationalism and patriotic joy, the Second World War, as ever, the touchstone for such moments. Russian fans displayed an officially approved banner for their team, 'You were born to make fairy tales a reality', paraphrasing a Soviet-era paean to the country's anti-aircraft batteries. After beating Spain in the round of sixteen, when the partying reached fever pitch, the official Kremlin spokesman thought, 'If we looked yesterday at the streets of many Russian cities, including Moscow, which I saw myself, it would be comparable to images of 9 May 1945.'[10] Others, including many of the revellers themselves, lived these moments not as a celebration of Russia as it was or had been, but as a tiny window on what it could be. Either way, the scenes of jubilation and hospitality were enough to temporarily banish, if not permanently erase, the dominant stereotypes of a dour, closed and xenophobic country. The imagery could not entirely dissolve the material realities of recent Russian foreign policy adventures, from the annexation of Crimea to interference in Western elections, and the poisoning of an ex-FSB agent, Sergei Skripal, in Britain, but it produced enough cognitive dissonance to blur, confuse and confound for a month; enough to

force every other global and national story, from Brexit to the rant-
ings of President Trump to global climate change, from the world's
media.[11]

Behind the great digital facade, and away from the zones of permitted hedonism, the Russian state had been busy. In the run-up to
the tournament the FSB conducted sweeps through the country's
football ultras and anti-fascist activists, forcibly reminding them to
keep a low profile, and where necessary arresting key figures in these
movements. More importantly, the Kremlin had been planning for
some time to announce a deeply controversial reform of the pension
system, and did so on the opening day of the World Cup.[12] Introduced by Prime Minister Medvedev, while Russia beat Saudi Arabia
5–0, the government proposed to raise the retirement age for women
from fifty-five to sixty-three, and for men from sixty to sixty-five.
Given the desperately short life expectancy of men in most of Russia,
this would see the average male citizen die before retirement. The
reforms were intended to save a trillion rubles year, but the population was well aware that just as much was lost to corruption. The
joke that circulated around the country, expressing the bitter anger
of the moment, ran, 'You say you'll never see your pension? Look,
we've held the Sochi Olympics, built a bridge to Crimea, and now
we're hosting the World Cup: there's your pension right there.'[13]

Alexei Navalny, the leading critic of the regime and only recently
released from prison, as well as other oppositional forces like liberal
party Yabloko, the leftist Sergei Udaltsov, and the Communists, called
for protests and attempted to gain official permission for demonstrations. Under laws passed before the tournament, they were all banned
from protesting in any World Cup city.[14] Through late June and early
July hundreds of demonstrations were held in non-World Cup cities,
in easily the biggest outbreak of public dissent since the huge protest
of 2011 against electoral manipulation, but they were rendered invisible by the news blackout from Russia's own media, and the absence
of the global media circus. While the regime continued to treat the
opposition, especially Navalny, with dismissive contempt, there was
also a hint of the paranoia and fear that afflicts regimes that know
their legitimacy is paper-thin. Indeed, the fear of Navalny was so
great that his name had been, in effect, banned from the airwaves.
Whilst commentating on Germany v Mexico, Leonid Slutsky, the griz-
zled Russian football coach, made a play on words – the Russian for

'high-pressure soccer' being almost identical to 'Navalny' – asking whether the opposition leader played football and, thinking aloud, remarked, 'That would be interesting to see.' The following day his commentary on the Tunisia v England game with Viktor Gusev produced a Twitter storm of political jokes: 'Gusev: I don't think there was a foul there. Slutsky: Of course – just like there are no Russian soldiers in Ukraine,' and, 'Gusev: The pass to Kane is very late. Slutsky: And now we'll be retiring much later too.' Slutsky managed one more game before his contract was suddenly and inexplicably terminated.[15]

In contrast to the brisk intervention that removed Slutsky, the Kremlin was happy to allow some its its favoured clients, like the President of Chechnya, Ramzan Kadyrov, rather more leeway. In a deal arranged between the Chechen government and the Egyptian Football Association (EFA) the national team based itself in the Chechen capital Grozny. Once there, Kadyrov paid them a visit in their hotel and had the team's star, Mo Salah, woken from his bed and required to join him for an impromptu trip to the city stadium where, miraculously, thousands had already gathered to greet them. Kadyrov filmed the whole thing on his phone and gleefully shared it on social media. The day after the team returned from the opening defeat by Uruguay, he had a 100-kilo cake, decorated in Chechen and Egyptian colours, delivered to the squad to celebrate Mo Salah's twenty-sixth birthday. The poor team then had to survive a visit from over a hundred Egyptian politicians, businessmen and celebrities orchestrated by the EFA, before losing their second game to Russia. Determined to extract every last mote of stardust, Kadyrov insisted that the squad attend a formal dinner the night before their last game, with Salah separated from his team mates, a trophy at the top table. Egypt promptly lost their third and last game and, after uproar in the Egyptian parliament, an official investigation into the EFA was launched.[16]

While the stadium crowds were often quiescent, lacking the great banks of organized, concentrated fans that have been the norm at recent World Cups, they could still deliver political messages that were, for the sorcerers of the spectacle, inconvenient.[17] FIFA fined the Russian football association because some fans displayed a neo-Nazi banner during their game with Uruguay. The Serbian FA was punished for a display of flags celebrating the Chetniks, the country's right-wing nationalist militia during the Second World War. So, too, the Swiss-Kosovans, Granit Xhaka and Xherdan Shaqiri, who both celebrated their goals against Serbia with hand gestures that evoked the Albanian double-headed eagle, and the politically explosive aspiration that Albanian-majority Kosovo should leave Serbia and become part of a Greater Albania. Sweden's Jimmy Durmaz was made the scapegoat for his side's defeat by Germany after giving away a last-minute free kick, converted by Toni Kroos. Born in Sweden to Assyrian migrant parents, he received a torrent of online racist abuse, was called a 'fucking immigrant' and a 'suicide bomber', and was, along with his family, subjected to death threats. The squad responded by posting their own online video in which, in unison, they backed Durmaz with the cheer, 'Fuck racism!'

World Cups had long featured the politics of ethnicity and race, and highlighted the complexity of contemporary citizenship and identity, but Russia 2018 was the first in which the politics of gender would be equally prominent. Women constituted, according to most estimates, 40 per cent of the global audience for the World Cup. The presence of women journalists, television presenters and commentators, though small, was more visible than at any previous tournament. Saudi women, in jeans and headscarves, made their first appearance in a World Cup crowd.[18] Supporters of women in Iran, still excluded from the football stadium at home, protested at all of their team's games, gaining substantial coverage for their cause.[19] Yet in other ways the depth of unreflective sexism in the football world seemed unchecked. For the first time, in a number of countries, women commentated on a men's World Cup match, like Vicki Sparks in Britain for the BBC, and Ally Wagner in the US on Fox Sports. Predictably, both were criticized and patronized, but Claudia Neumann, who commentated for German channel ZDF, received such a hail of online abuse that the company filed criminal charges against her trolls.[20] The Argentinian Football Association produced a manual for the tournament that included a section on 'How to stand a chance with a Russian girl', the main advice being, 'dress well, look clean and smell nice.' Even more crassly, Burger King were offering cash prizes and a lifetime's supply of Whopper burgers to Russian women who managed to get themselves impregnated by any visiting player, in the forlorn hope that it would improve the country's footballing gene pool. The venerable photo agency Getty put a 'Hottest Fans' gallery on its website; predictably enough, it contained just women as eye candy. Both initiatives came under fire and were withdrawn, though this did not deter the Russian broadcasters from tiresomely focusing on young, good-looking women whenever the opportunity arose.

Argentinian, Paraguayan and Brazilian men were all filmed teaching women who did not speak Spanish or Portuguese what they thought were football chants, but were in fact crude and sexually graphic doggerel. Other male fans were caught on camera harassing and assaulting women journalists as they tried to work. Amongst others, Malin Wahlberg, reporting for *Aftonbladet*, was ruffled and groped by three Swedes, while Julieth González Theran of *Deutsche Welle* was forcibly kissed by a man who had grabbed her breast mid interview. Social media and the growing confidence of women ensured this did not go unnoticed or challenged. Theran later posted on Instagram: 'I reject this type of Mysoginistic [*sic*] behavior in Soccer and other scenarios. I belong to the daily struggle of women who earn a space in a land full of male mistrust #metoo.' Brazilian Julia Guimarães dodged a man trying to kiss her as she was reporting, and then berated him for his insolence and disrespect: 'This is not polite. This is not right . . . never do this to a woman. Respect!'

If the Potemkin village did, in the end, reveal these scattered forms of resistance, the grand finale, France v Croatia, seemed much more sewn up. President Putin, an absent figure since Russia's opening game, and deeply reluctant to appear associated with any kind of national failure, must have felt on safe ground. In the VIP tribune he was flanked by friends and admirers – heads of state from Qatar, Gabon, Sudan, Belarus, Moldova, Armenia, Hungary and Kyrgyzstan – all of whom had been pursuing their own football and political projects. The only grit thrown into the spectacle was a four-person pitch invasion, early in the second half, by members of the Pussy Riot collective, calling for the release of political prisoners and decrying the impoverished and brutal state of Russia's politics. They were, of course, made invisible at the flick of a director's switch.

Simple as these technological solutions are, there remains a profound paradox in the attempts of the global political classes to try and control football. In this regard, the deep ludic basis of football's popularity is worth recalling. The game is simple and instantly comprehensible, with a tiny rule book and a mode of play so intuitive that every playground scuffle works out the necessity of offside for itself. It is cheap and flexible. It can be played with any number of players, requires just a ball, a sphere of almost any kind, and works on grass, sand, mud and concrete. It is accommodating of many body shapes and sizes, but privileges none. It provides space for individual brilliance and brio, but it is, above all, a collective effort that is only as good as its weakest links. It is a game of flow rather than sequence, truly three-dimensional in its movements, visually compelling and emotionally relentless, tumultuously punctuated by the orgasmic quality of its rare and precious goals. It remains the case that, by comparison with other sports, the odds on football's favourites are always longer, because the game is so much more unpredictable: most matches turn on a small number of chances, and an even smaller number of goals, football's entropy giving underdogs a better chance. It is a game that thrives upon chaos and uncertainty; that demands of individuals and collectives that they constantly adapt to an ever-changing milieu, yet retains the notion that anything is possible. Sudden changes of heart and fortune, last-minute reversals and rescues, are its true emotional and narrative currency. It is hard to imagine a game so unsuited to the inflexible sclerosis of authoritarian regimes. It is equally hard to imagine a form of play so well suited to serve as an avatar of our collective human dilemmas, and so suggestive of the virtues we might need to tackle them.[21]

World Cup 2018 was played in the midst of a long, northern hemisphere heatwave. It was just one of our era's mounting catalogue of extreme weather events, but in the global Potemkin village the long days and the warm nights were experienced as a blessing rather than as a harbinger of doom. Yet, despite every effort to seal this moment off from our material and meteorological reality, and to exclude all but the blandest interpretations of our world, the final delivered a tableau of devastating allegorical power. Late in the second half, the hot, humid weather of the Moscow night began to transform into a wild summer rainstorm. First there was mist, then drizzle, and by the time the final whistle blew and France had beaten Croatia 4–2 it had begun to rain and the sky was rent by thunder and lightning. There would be no repeat of the painful elongated ceremony that closed the 2014 Brazil World Cup. The organizers, seemingly eschewing grandeur for practicality, had settled for the creation of a small on-pitch stage where Infantino, Putin and

Presidents Macron and Grabar-Kitarovic lined up to hand out the medals to the participants. By the time the officials had been processed, the rain had gathered pace and began to soak the immaculate suits of the male presidents, and the Croatian top worn by Grabar-Kitarovic. A man with a single umbrella appeared and unfurled it above the head of President Putin alone. The others, now drenched, would have to wait until nearly all of the French team had passed them by before additional umbrellas could be mobilized. Even then there were not enough for most of the dignitaries, while the line of Qatar Airlines stewardesses behind them were left to maintain their excruciating rictus grins exposed to the elements. The French team, when they finally received their medals and the Cup itself, were exuberant and ecstatic, genuinely joyful, sliding and surfing on the soaking pitch, their blue shirts spotted by the golden confetti sticking to every rain-covered surface. Even in their most tightly controlled and televised forms these events exposed something of the uncertain and perilous world we share, but, viewed from the upper stands of the Luzhniki on the other side of the pitch, and filmed on a mobile phone, another truth was available.[22] At a distance, the participants appear like scurrying ants, the stage's dimensions are Lilliputian. The podium is awash in a landscape that is flooded. Facing the cameras, the players' backs are turned to most of the crowd in the arena: one can only connect with their euphoria by the medium of the big screens. At the same time, high above the stadium, the storm we have made is raging and indifferent to us all.

Acknowledgements

Over the last decade or so, I have had the immense privilege to travel widely in the world of football, and everywhere I have been fed, hosted, helped, steered and enlightened by a very generous crew of people. Thanks and blessings: in Argentina, to Paulo Alabarces, Carolina Duek, Ezequiel Fernandez-Moore, Martin Gottschalk, Marcela Mora y Arrujo, Ariel Scher, and Alejandro Wall; in Brazil, to Juliana Barbassa, Martin Curi, Christopher Gaffney and Tim Vickery; in Egypt to Shady Al-Mahmoudi; in England, to Ian Cusack, Dave Kelly and Mark Perryman; in Ghana, to Michael Oti Adjei; at the *Guardian* Long Read, to Jonathan Shanin and David Wolf; in Hungary to Dan Nolan and Andras Rakos; in Israel to Anna Raphael and Uri Sheradsky; in Italy to Paulo Maggioni; in Kenya to Bob Munroe and the MYSA crew; in Mexico to Tlatoani Carrera and Irex Irao; in Nigeria to Godwin Enakhena and Charity and Leonard Lawal; in Poland to Seweryn Dmowski; in Scotland, to Stewart Cosgrove, Daniel Grey, Gerry Hassan, Michael Roy, and Tom and Sophie Pilgrim Salter; in South Africa, to Judith Cherry, Gregory and Lindiwe Mthembu Salter, and Lungile Mdawaybe; in Uganda, to Opio Moses and everyone at Luzira prison; in Uruguay, to Carmen and Roberto Elissade, Bruno Mora and Luis Prats.

Thanks to those who have followed, watched or talked football with me, in one way and one mode or another – Johnny Acton, Peter Alegi, Perry Anderson, Lilli Barrett O'Keefe, Steve Bloomfield, Jules Boykoff, Mark Burman, Robert Colls, Simon Critchley, Claudine Domoney, Bob Edelman, David Edmonds, Mark Ellingham, Brenda Elsey, John Foot, Alix and Stanley Hughes, Alex Kee, Gabriel Kuhn, Hugh McKay, Martha Herrera Lasso, Werner Herzog, Daniel Howden, Alix Hughes, John Hughson, Sean Jacobs, Anthony Karon, Simon Kuper, Dan Levy, Tim Mansel, Steve Menary, James Montague, Paul Moss, Josh Nadel, Jefris Pakpahan, Lisa Parkinson, Martin Polley, George Quraishi, Tom Reed, Steve Roser, Tim Ruck, Tom Shakespeare,

Raja Shah, Derek Shearer, Alan Tomlinson, James Vernon, Manuel Veth, Jennie Walmsley, Kath and Steve Woodward and Robert Yates. Special shout out for Nigel Boyle, Andre Wakefield and my fabulous and generous Pitzer College, History of Football class (Spring 2019), who went through all this at its rawest. Publishing love and thanks to Matthew Cole, Graham Coster, Fraser Crichton, Andy Hawes, Kate Green, Robin Harvie, Sally Holloway, Chloe May, and Matt Weiland. As ever, bringing up the rear, but making it all possible, biggest love to Sarah, Molly and Luke.

Notes

Introduction

1. '2014 World Cup final attracted 1.01 billion viewers, FIFA says', http://www.espn.co.uk/football/world-cup-soccer/story/2759180/fifa-reports-101-billion-viewers-for-2014-world-cup-final. The fine-grain data can be examined in the official *TV Audience Report for the World Cup* at https://img.fifa.com/image/upload/n3z25ncdjj9qdwja1tet.pd

2. Transcript of Il Papa's blessing for the Cup at https://w2.vatican.va/content/francesco/en/messages/pont-messages/2014/documents/papa-francesco_20140612_videomessaggio-mondiale-calcio-2014-brasile.html. Castro cited in Watts, J., 'World Cup Diary', *Guardian*, 26 June 2014.

3. Rouhani can be seen in his sweats in Dehghan, S. K., 'Iranian president tweets World Cup chillout pic', *Guardian*, 17 June 2014.

4. Social media data at Woodford, D. and Prowd, K., 'Bigger than the Superbowl: the World Cup breaks viewing record': https://theconversation.com/bigger-than-the-superbowl-the-world-cup-breaks-viewing-records-27709. Gross, D., 'World Cup walloped social-media records': https://edition.cnn.com/2014/07/14/tech/social-media/world-cup-social-media/index.html.

5. https://colombiareports.com/10-dead-colombias-world-cup-celebration/; Markey, P., 'World Cup 2014: Wild celebrations in Algeria after they reach knock-out stage': *Independent*, 27 June 2014. Although released by the generally untrustworthy Russia Today, this film of French riot police at work in Paris amongst Algerian fans is very illuminating: https://www.youtube.com/watch?v=-JcgwDb7w8g. Serus, J., and Lopez, R., 'Mexico World Cup fans arrested; police horse struck in Huntington Park': *LA Times*, 24 June 2014. Boyd, S., 'There Were So Many World Cup Barbecues In Santiago When Australia Played Chile, It Triggered A Smog Emergency', https://www.businessinsider.com.au/there-were-so-many-world-cup-barbecues-in-santiago-when-australia-played-chile-it-triggered-a-smog-emergency-2014-6#iww3YAAO1MXkiQwQ.99".

6. Smith, D., 'Kenya attack: gunmen kill at least 48 people', *Guardian*, 16 June 2014.

7. 'Nigerian World Cup fans targeted by deadly bomb', *Guardian*, 18 June 2014.

8. Akram, F., 'In Rubble of Gaza Seaside Cafe, Hunt for Victims Who Had Come for Soccer', *New York Times*, 10 July 2014.

9. On the disaster that has befallen the Maracanã see: http://www.rioon watch.org/?p=15930; https://www.npr.org/sections/thetwo-way/2017/01/12/509465686/maracan-jewel-of-rios-olympics-now-languishes-in-disrepair.

10. Those in any doubt as to the tone of the FIFA anthem are encouraged to listen in here: https://www.youtube.com/watch?v=R9I7bn1b4oc.

11. The two most ethnically homogenous squads in the competition were Japan and South Korea, both of which have small immigrant populations.

12. Statistics on the player pyramid are taken from FIFPro (2016) *Global Employment Report 2016: Working Conditions in Professional Football* (Hoofddorp, FIFPro).

13. The actual list can be seen here: Gibson, O., 'World Cup final guest list has bizarre and random look', *Guardian*, 13 July 2014.

14. Details of who made it on onto the Nigerian World Cup gravy train are available at: http://www.theparadigmng.com/2014/06/14/national-waste-goodluck-jonathan-sends-massive-delegation-brazil-world-cup/. For choice details of the scams and overpayments that accompanied Ghana's official football ambassadors and their cooking staff and were investigated by a presidential commission of inquiry: https://www.todaygh.com/cooks-grabbed-67000-world-cup-campaign/.

15. Whelan was subsequently cleared: http://www.worldsoccer.com/features/two-years-on-and-world-cup-ticket-tout-ordeal-finally-over-392251. Match under investigation: https://www.theguardian.com/football/2016/feb/27/gianni-infantino-police-study-fifa-ticket-deals.

16. https://twitter.com/rihanna/status/488575114704076800?lang=en.

17. For the pitch invasion by said Russian, filmed from the stand: https://www.youtube.com/watch?v=XGBFRlA9TVQ.

18. Data drawn from Bershidsky, L., 'Why Adidas Beat Nike at the World Cup', https://www.bloomberg.com/view/articles/2014-07-11/why-adidas-beat-nike-at-the-world-cup. Parker, S., 'Nike vs Adidas: In a League of their Own', https://www.worldfinance.com/strategy/a-league-of-their-own-nike-vs-adidas.

19. Development NGOs, trade unions and other activists have been publishing reports about conditions in the sportswear industry alongside the Olympic Games, World Cups and European Championships since 2002. The most recent and comprehensive is Collectif Éthique Sur L'étiquette, *Foul Play* (BASIC, 2016). Older but insightful work includes Behind the Label, *Sweet FA? Football Associations, Workers' Rights and the World Cup* (TUC, London, 2006); *Clearing the Hurdles: Steps to*

improving wages and working conditions in the global sportswear industry
(Playfair, 2008); *Offside! Labour Rights and Sportswear Production in Asia*
(Oxfam International, 2006).

20. On hand stitching see International Labour Rights Forum, *Child Labour
in Football Stitching Activity in India* (2008). 'Eliminating Child Labour
from the Sialkot Soccer Ball Industry': http://www.fairplayforchildren.
org/pdf/1299571715.pdf; Kazim, H., 'The Football Stitchers of Sialkot'
(2010), http://www.spiegel.de/international/world/globalization-in-
pakistan-the-football-stitchers-of-sialkot-a-683873.html.

21. Parkin, S., '*FIFA* : the video game that changed football', *Guardian*, 21
December 2016.

22. Ibid.

23. Crisp, R., 'Argentine Football Fans, Rejoice! River Plate Now' (2015),
included in *FIFA 16* Demo, http://www.thebubble.com/fifa-16-demo-
includes-argentine-side/. Kariuki, N., 'How women finally made it into
the *FIFA* video game', https://www.pri.org/stories/2015-05-29/
how-women-finally-made-it-fifa-video-game.

24. Tweedle, A., 'Brexit is simulated in *Football Manager 2017*, and it's going
to make the game harder than ever', *Daily Telegraph*, 18 October 2016.

25. 'TC Freisenbruch are a German amateur team entirely run by 384 online
managers', *Four Four Two*, 31 March 2017, https://www.fourfourtwo.com/
news/tc-freisenbruch-are-a-german-amateur-team-entirely-run-384-online-
managers; Stuart, K., 'Why clubs are using *Football Manager* as a real-life
scouting tool', *Guardian*, 12 August 2017, https://www.theguardian.com/
technology/2014/aug/12/why-clubs-football-manager-scouting-tool.

26. McCarthy, J., 'Why top football teams are rushing to get *FIFA* eSports
players onside': http://www.thedrum.com/news/2016/11/02/why-top-
football-teams-are-rushing-get-fifa-esports-players-onside. Ramsey, G. and
Rideell, D., 'When football met eSports: PSG's tale of two sports at one
club', https://edition.cnn.com/2016/12/14/sport/esports-football-paris-
saint-germain-psg-bora-yellowstar-kim/index.html?no-st=1528475273.
Mclean, P., 'Premier League clubs kick off eSports participation', *Financial
Times*, 11 August 2016. PWC, *The burgeoning evolution of eSports: From
the fringes to Front and Centre* (PWC, 2016).

27. 'Football betting – the global gambling industry worth billions', *BBC
Sport*: https://www.bbc.co.uk/sport/football/24354124.

28. 'Illegal gambling networks across Asia targeted in INTERPOL-led
operation': https://www.interpol.int/en/News-and-media/News/2014/
N2014-133/.

29. Parkin, op. cit.

30. The Argentinian television coverage of the final can be seen at https://
www.youtube.com/watch?v=GDF3Yje35wQ and is infinitely superior to
the over-edited and manicured version available from FIFA.

Chapter 1

1. Alegi, P. and Bolsmann, C. (eds.), *Africa's World Cup: Critical Reflections on Play, Patriotism, Spectatorship and Space*, University of Michigan Press (2013); Bolsmann, C., 'Representation in the first African World Cup: "world-class", Pan-Africanism, and exclusion', *Soccer & Society* 13.2 (2012), pp. 156–72.

2. Essential background material for this chapter includes: Alegi, P., *African Soccerscapes: How a Continent Changed the World's Game*, Ohio University Press (2010); Darby, P., *Africa, Football and FIFA: Politics, Colonialism and Resistance*, Routledge (2013); Hawkey, I., *Feet of the Chameleon: The Story of African Football*, Anova Books (2009); Armstrong, G. and Giulianotti, R., *Football in Africa: Conflict, Conciliation and Community* (2004); Bloomfield, S., *Africa United: How Football Explains Africa*, Canongate (2011).

3. 'Shirt Sales 2014/15: Where Are Your Team's Supporters Really From?', http://blog.sportsdirect.com/post/shirt-sales-2014-15-where-are-your-team-s-supporters-really-from; Evans, N., 'The football stars of tomorrow: Meet the Ethiopian tribal people giving new life to old kits', https://www.mirror.co.uk/news/gallery/football-stars-tomorrow-meet-ethiopian-10955466

4. For useful background on Hayatou's football career see, Darby, P., 'Africa's place in FIFA's global order: A theoretical frame', *Soccer & Society* 1.2 (2000), pp. 36–61; Darby, P., 'Africa, the FIFA Presidency, and the Governance of World Football: 1974, 1998, and 2002', *Africa Today* (2003), pp. 3–24.

5. Okeleji, O., 'Nigeria's Super Falcons end protest', 19 December 2016, https://www.bbc.co.uk/sport/football/38345546; 'Ghana's Black Queens protest over unpaid bonuses in Accra', 22 December 2016, https://www.modernghana.com/news/744886/photos-ghanas-black-queens-protest-over-unpaid-bonuses-in.html

6. Smith, D., 'Eritrea's grand Italian cinemas shudder to the sound of English football', *Guardian*, 24 December 2015.

7. Wilson, J., 'The joys and surprises of watching Liverpool and Arsenal in Ethiopia (for 45p)', *Guardian*, 24 November 2015; Anderson, M., 'Cashing in on the beautiful game of Football', *Africa Report*, 17 May 2016, http://www.theafricareport.com/North-Africa/cashing-in-on-the-beautiful-game-of-football.html

8. Akindes, Gerard A., 'Transnational television and football in Francophone Africa: The path to electronic colonization?' Ohio University (2010); Akindes, Gerard A., 'Football bars: Urban sub-Saharan Africa's trans-local "stadiums"', *International Journal of the History of Sport* 28.15 (2011), pp. 2176–90.

9. Data quoted in Malik, S., 'English clubs battle for Africa fanbase', https://www.aljazeera.com/sport/football/2012/07/201271610434799895.html

10. Ross, E., 'Nigeria's Love Affair with Arsenal', *Guardian*, 5 September 2013, https://www.theguardian.com/world/2013/sep/05/nigeria-love-affair-arsenal-spurs

11. McLean, R., et al, 'Adama Barrow: from Argos Security Guard to President of the Gambia', *Guardian*, 2 December 2016.

12. Gondwe, S., 'President Mutharika emulates the Foxes' example not Arsenal dilly dally', 28 March 2017, https://www.nyasatimes.com/president-mutharika-emulate-foxes-example-not-arsenal-dilly-dally/

13. David, E., 'Hilarious! How Uhuru and Raila Behave Like English Premier League Teams', 27 September 2016, http://widenews.co.ke/uncategorized/hilarious-how-uhuru-and-raila-behave-like-english-premier-league-teams-3980/

14. Goldblatt, D., 'From London to Lagos, Exploring the Premier League's African Appeal', https://bleacherreport.com/articles/2711074-from-london-to-lagos-exploring-the-premier-leagues-african-appeal

15. BBC News, 'Nigeria United fan kills rivals', 28 May 2009, http://news.bbc.co.uk/1/hi/world/africa/8072356.stm

16. Malalo, H., 'Kenyan Arsenal fan hangs himself after Man Utd defeat', 6 May 2009, https://uk.reuters.com/article/soccer-champions-suicide-IDUKL62559420090506

17. On football, gender and domestic violence in Africa see: Daimon, A., 'The most beautiful game or the most gender violent sport? Exploring the interface between soccer, gender and violence in Zimbabwe', *Gender, sport and development in Africa: Cross-cultural perspectives on patterns of representations and marginalization* (2010), pp. 1–11; Tade, Oludayo, '"He is Father Christmas when Man-U wins": EUFA league and the dynamics of spousal relations in Nigeria', *Soccer & Society* 18.1 (2017), pp. 1–15.

18. Vokes, R., 'Arsenal in Bugamba: The Rise of English Premier League Football in Uganda', *Anthropology Today* 26.3 (2010), pp. 10–15.

19. BBC Sport, 'Man Utd 2–1 Portsmouth', 28 July 2008, http://news.bbc.co.uk/sport1/hi/football/africa/7527748.stm

20. On the 'Magic Cup affair', see: 'Scandal Exposed: Tourism CS Phyllis Kandie also named in Pewin Motors football tender', https://www.cnyakundi.com/scandal-exposed-tourism-cs-phyllis-kandie-also-named-in-pewin-motors-football-tender/; 'Everton break new ground in Africa with Tanzania trip as rewarding as it was brief', https://www.liverpoolecho.co.uk/sport/football/football-news/everton-break-new-ground-africa-13329298

21. 'The Dwindling Football Spectatorship In Our Local Football League', 7 January 2015, https://www.modernghana.com/news/590671/1/

the-dwindling-football-spectatorship.html; 'Low Stadium Attendance in Ghana because of European Leagues', 18 May 2010, https://www.ghanaweb.com/GhanaHomePage/SportsArchive/Low-Stadium-Attendance-in-Ghana-because-of-European-Leagues-182232

22. 'WE'RE LOSING THE FANS . . . record low crowd watch Battle of Zim showdown', https://www.herald.co.zw/were-losing-the-fans-record-low-crowd-watch-battle-of-zim-showdown/

23. Edwards, P., 'Is satellite TV killing African football?', BBC News, 29 January 2013, https://www.bbc.co.uk/news/world-africa-21206500

24. Walker, A., 'Is Premier League killing Nigerian football?', BBC News, 28 July 2008, http://news.bbc.co.uk/1/hi/world/africa/7526005.stm

25. Haxall, D., 'Pitch invasion: Football, contemporary art and the African diaspora', *Soccer & Society* 16.2–3 (2015), pp. 259–81.

26. On Drogba's cultural meanings see: Künzler, D., and Poli, R., 'The African footballer as visual object and figure of success: Didier Drogba and social meaning', *Global Perspectives on Football in Africa*, Routledge (2013), pp. 81–95.

27. Drogba is not alone in taking on such a role. Senegal's captain Mamadou Niang and Cameroon's Benoît Assou-Ekotto were champions of the UN's millennium development goals. Samuel Eto'o has been an ambassador for UNICEF.

28. On African footballer migration and the academy system see: Darby, P., 'The new scramble for Africa: the African football labour migration to Europe', *European Sports History Review* 3 (2001), p. 217; Darby, P., 'African football labour migration to Portugal: colonial and neo colonial resource', *Soccer & Society* 8.4 (2007), pp. 495–509; Darby, P., Akindes, G. and Kirwin, M., 'Football academies and the migration of African football labor to Europe', *Journal of Sport and Social Issues* 31.2 (2007), pp. 143–61; Darby, P., and Solberg, E., 'Differing trajectories: football development and patterns of player migration in South Africa and Ghana,' *Soccer & Society* 11.1–2 (2010), pp. 118–30; Poli, R., 'Migrations and trade of African football players: historic, geographical and cultural aspects', *Africa Spectrum* (2006), pp. 393–414; Poli, R., 'African migrants in Asian and European football: hopes and realities', *Sport in Society* 13.6 (2010), pp. 1001–11. On trafficking see Hawkins, E., *The Lost Boys: Inside Football's Slave Trade*, Bloomsbury (2015).

29. FIFPro (2016), *Working Conditions in Professional Football*, can be viewed at https://footballmap.fifpro.org/assets/2016_FIFPRO_GLOBAL_EMPLOYMENT_REPORT.pdf

30. 'Gunmen Wound Five Kano Pillars Players', http://www.bbc.co.uk/sport/football/31756677; 'Enyimba player feared death as team bus attacked in Nigeria', BBC Sport, 20 January 2016, https://www.bbc.co.uk/sport/football/35360068; 'Robbers attack Osun Utd players, machete officials',

June 7 2017, http://punchng.com/robbers-attack-osun-utd-players-machete-officials/

31. 'Katsina United fans attack Enyimba FC players, officials', http://dailypost.ng/2017/04/10/katsina-united-fans-attack-enyimba-fc-players-officials-video/

32. 'Gunshots fired in DOL game involving Tamale Utrecht and Berlin FC', 19 May 2016, https://www.myjoyonline.com/sports/2016/may-19th/gunshots-fired-in-dol-game-involving-tamale-utrecht-and-berlin-fc.php

33. The five most important exporters, all in the global top twenty, were West African (in descending order of players migrating – Nigeria, Ghana, Senegal, Cameroon and Côte d'Ivoire), but there are players abroad from almost everywhere. See Poli, R., Ravenel, L. and Besson, R., 'Exporting countries in world football', *CIES Football Observatory Monthly Report Issue* no. 8 (2015).

34. 'Playing Football on the Margins: West African Football Players in Poland', http://global-sport.eu/playing-football-on-the-margins-west-african-football-players-in-poland; Banas, P., 'For every Drogba there are hundreds of West African football hopefuls who struggle', 13 October 2016, https://theconversation.com/for-every-drogba-there-are-hundreds-of-west-african-football-hopefuls-who-struggle-66533

35. See Hawkins, 2016; Esson, J., 'Better off at home? Rethinking responses to trafficked West African footballers in Europe', *Journal of Ethnic and Migration Studies* 41.3 (2015), pp. 512–30; Esson, J., 'You have to try your luck: male Ghanaian youth and the uncertainty of football migration', *Environment and Planning A* 47.6 (2015), pp. 1383–97.

36. Poli, R., 'African migrants in Asian and European football: hopes and realities', *Sport & Society* 13.6 (2010), pp. 1001–11.

37. Alegi, P., '"Like cows driven to a dip": The 2001 Ellis Park stadium disaster in South Africa', *Soccer & Society* 5.2 (2004), pp. 233–47.

38. Sakyi-Addo, K., 'At least 126 die in Ghana football stadium stampede', *Guardian*, 11 May 2001.

39. Will, R., 'China's Stadium Diplomacy', *World Policy*, 6 June 2012, https://worldpolicy.org/2012/06/06/chinas-stadium-diplomacy/; Ross, E., 'China's Stadium Diplomacy in Africa', http://roadsandkingdoms.com/2014/chinas-stadium-diplomacy-in-africa/; Barrenguet, E., 'China: The Master Stadium Builder', *Africa Report*, 2 July 2010; Parmar, V., 'Stadium Diplomacy, White Elephants and Football's New Frontiers', *New African* 570.

40. For a useful overview of the Sino-African economic relationship see French, H., 'The next empire', *Atlantic* 305.4 (2010), pp. 59–69; French, H., *China's Second Continent: How a million migrants are building a new empire in Africa*, Vintage (2014).

41. Quoted in Shah, M., 'An Equal Playing Field?', *Yale Globalist*, 28 October 2009, http://tyglobalist.org/in-the-magazine/theme/an-equal-playing-field/

42. Op. cit. Ross (2014).

43. Chipande, H., 'China's Stadium Diplomacy: A Zambian Perspective', http://www.footballiscominghome.info/hosting/chinas-stadium-diplomacy-a-zambian-perspective/

44. 'Match crush kills Liberian fans', BBC Sport, 2 June 2008, http://news.bbc.co.uk/sport1/hi/football/africa/7429606.stm; Withnall, A., 'Deadly stampede at title-deciding football match in DR Congo sees at least 15 killed and dozens injured after police fire tear gas', *Independent*, 12 May 2014; Smith, D., 'Mali stadium stampede kills worshippers', *Guardian*, 22 February 2011; 'Seventeen killed in Angola stadium stampede', https://www.aljazeera.com/news/2017/02/seventeen-killed-angola-stadium-stampede-170211042836555.html; 'Stampede at Angolan stadium kills 17, injures scores', Reuters, 10 February 2017, https://www.reuters.com/article/us-soccer-angola-stampede-IDUSKBN15P2O0

45. Chadwick, S., 'How China is fuelling the African Cup of Nations through stadium diplomacy', http://www.scmp.com/sport/soccer/article/2061186/how-china-fuelling-african-cup-nations-through-stadium-diplomacy

46. Jackson, J., 'Angola's golden goals', *Observer*, 11 June 2006.

47. Redvers, L., 'Footballisation Pause', BBC Sport, http://news.bbc.co.uk/sport1/hi/football/africa/8713845.stm; Redvers, L., 'Nations Cup stadiums standing idle in Angola', http://news.bbc.co.uk/sport1/hi/football/africa/9416315.stm

48. Silva, C., 'The trouble with Angola', *Africa is a Country*, https://africasacountry.com/2013/01/the-trouble-with-angola; Silva, C., 'Afcon 2013 Preview: Angola's Palancas Negras and the Curse of the Quarter-finals', https://africasacountry.com/2013/01/afcon-2013-preview-angolas-palancas-negras-and-the-curse-of-the-quarterfinals

49. Sands, W., 'Equatorial Guinea: Empty Stadiums for Soccer Showcase', https://pulitzercenter.org/reporting/equatorial-guinea-empty-stadiums-soccer-showcase

50. Blas, J., 'All is forgotten: Equatorial Guinea rehabilitated to host of African Cup of Nations', *Financial Times*, 14 November 2014; O'Grady, S., 'Oh, You Thought FIFA Was Corrupt? Meet Equatorial Guinea', *Foreign Policy*, 14 November 2014; Wilson, J., 'Letter from Equatorial Guinea: Forget Human Rights – Here Comes the Football', *New Statesman*, 12 February 2015.

51. Onwumechilli, C., 'African Cup of Nations begins with an unlikely comeback from Equatorial Guinea', 16 January 2015, https://theconversation.com/african-cup-of-nations-begins-with-an-unlikely-comeback-from-equatorial-guinea-36373; Edwards, P., 'Equatorial

Guinea–Ghana riot: Joyous evening turns to night of shame', BBC News, 6 February 2015, https://www.bbc.co.uk/news/world-africa-31162971

52. Smith, D., 'Lionel Messi accused of undermining children's rights work with Gabon visit', *Guardian*, 4 August 2015; Wilson, J., 'Political unrest in Gabon casts shadow over 2017 Africa Cup of Nations draw', *Guardian*, 18 October 2016; Imray, G., 'African Cup returns to exotic Gabon, but with air of unease', AP, 11 January 2017, https://www.apnews.com/eb12c156cf854066b6bfb9936863e3a3

53. Quoted in Wilson, J., 'At the African Cup of Nations, football is overshadowed by political unrest', *New Statesman*, 5 February 2017.

54. AFP, 'Near Oyem, a white elephant in the Gabon rainforest?'; Lay, T., 'Africa Cup of Nations: Gabon's $75m stadium fails to impress in first match', *Africa Report*, 17 January 2017, http://www.theafricareport.com/Sports/africa-cup-of-nations-gabons-75m-stadium-fails-to-impress-in-first-match.html

55. Levy, U., 'African Cup of Nations' failures mirror Gabon's sorry state', https://africasacountry.com/2017/02/african-cup-of-nations-failures-mirror-gabons-sorry-state

56. Rookwood, J., 'Gabon 2017 – The Cup of African Nations', https://footballcollective.org.uk/2017/02/02/gabon-2017-the-cup-of-african-nations/

57. 'Violence mars World Cup games', BBC Sport, 28 March 2005, http://news.bbc.co.uk/sport1/hi/football/africa/4387389.stm

58. 'Guinea: Stadium Massacre, Rape Likely Crimes Against Humanity', Human Rights Watch, https://www.hrw.org/news/2009/12/17/guinea-stadium-massacre-rape-likely-crimes-against-humanity; Trenchard, T., 'Guineans remember rape and murder at stadium massacre', https://www.aljazeera.com/indepth/features/2016/09/massacre-stadium-guinea-confronts-160912114642137.html

59. Longman, J., 'Sierra Leone's Soccer team Struggles With Stigma Over Ebola Outbreak', *New York Times*, 13 October 2014; Solomon, B., 'Surviving and Soccer in Sierra Leone', *New York Times*, 23 July 2015; Barrie, M., 'Sierra Leone Fans and players turn to non-league football', BBC Sport, https://www.bbc.co.uk/sport/football/36833863; Oliver, B., 'Guinea's Africa Cup of Nations dream survives against all odds and Ebola taunts', *Guardian*, 31 January 2015; 'Ebola outbreak: Soccer stadium in Liberia to be converted to virus treatment centre, FIFA says', http://www.abc.net.au/news/2014-09-12/monrovia-soccer-stadium-to-house-ebola-centre-fifa/5738710

60. Doyle, P., 'Diouf and co miss the real party', *Guardian*, 1 February 2008, https://www.theguardian.com/football/2008/feb/01/africannationscup2008.africannationscup; Hann, M., 'Wrestling and

Football in Dakar, Senegal', http://global-sport.eu/wrestling-football-dakar-senegal

61. Smith, D., 'Nigerian president suspends team after poor showing', *Guardian*, 30 June 2010.

62. 'Detained Cameroon federation president wins election', BBC Sport, https://www.bbc.co.uk/sport/football/22983148

63. Ngouokou, E., *'Le football camerounais, corruption à tous les étages'*, https://mondafrique.com/le-football-camerounais-corruption-a-tous-les-etages/; Moore, G., 'World Cup 2014: Where did it all go wrong for shambolic Cameroon?' *Independent*, 22 June 2014.

64. Forum for African Investigative Reporters, *Killing Soccer in Africa*, https://fairreporters.files.wordpress.com/2011/11/fair_2010_soccer_proof7.pdf; p. 4.

65. Ibid.; 'Ghana to dissolve football association over bribery allegations', *Guardian*, 8 June 2018.

66. Lea, G., 'Didier Drogba: a man of peace', https://thesefootballtimes.co/2015/03/17/didier-drogba-a-man-of-peace/; Ritter Conn, J., 'The Legend of Les Elephants', http://grantland.com/features/world-cup-ivory-coast-dider-drogba-yaya-toure-civil-war-legend/; Nadarajah, S., 'Football as peacemaker? In Ivory Coast it might just work', http://www.worldsoccer.com/blogs/football-as-peacemaker-in-ivory-coast-it-might-just-work-339960#i8d1uDLL0acKlHBu.99

67. '"The curse is over!" declare Ivorians after African Cup win', https://www.vanguardngr.com/2015/02/curse-declare-ivorians-african-cup-win/

68. Quoted in Fumanti, M., 'Black chicken, white chicken: patriotism, morality and the aesthetics of fandom in the 2008 African Cup of Nations in Ghana', *Soccer & Society* 13.2 (2012), pp. 264–76.

69. Smith, D., 'World Cup 2010: Relaxed Ghana capture heart of a continent united', *Guardian*, 1 July 2010; 'Ghana sustains African pride at World Cup', BBC News, 27 June 2010, https://www.bbc.co.uk/news/10426866

70. Ferguson, E., 'World Cup 2010: Ghana weeps, but remains hopeful', *Guardian*, 4 July 2010.

71. 'Nigeria Olympic football team receive "$390,000 gift"', BBC Sport, https://www.bbc.co.uk/sport/football/37148817

72. 'Nigerian FA official banned for taking bribe', BBC Sport, https://www.bbc.co.uk/sport/football/25121568

73. Shaageee, O., 'Appeal Court clears Lulu of corruption charge', 7 February 2018, https://www.dailytrust.com.ng/appeal-court-clears-lulu-of-corruption-charge.html

74. Doyle, P., 'Why is Nigeria the world's toughest league in which to get an away win?', *Guardian*, 29 October 2013, https://www.theguardian.com/football/blog/2013/oct/29/nigeria-toughest-league-win-away

75. Oni, K., 'Fans attack referee Ozigbo in league game', http://www.goal.

com/en-ng/news/4111/npfl/2014/12/20/7248522/fans-attack-referee-ozigbo-in-league-game

76. Other rules included: no drinking, smoking, drug-taking, womanizing, foul language or cursing, no arguing with football officials, and to be MFM at all times.

77. Waliaula, S., 'Envisioning and visualizing English football in East Africa: the case of a Kenyan radio football commentator', *Soccer & Society* 13.2 (2012), pp. 239–49.

78. 'Somalia's Al-Shabab claims Baidoa attack killing 30', BBC News, 29 February 2016, https://www.bbc.co.uk/news/world-africa-35685648

79. Ngulu, D., 'Somali league structure gives prominence to world leagues', http://www.soka.co.ke/news/item/somali-league-structure-gives-prominence-to-world-leagues; Uurdoox, A. M. A., 'The unstoppable rise of Somalia Premier League', http://www.qaranimo.com/news/2016/07/29/the-unstoppable-rise-of-somalia-premier-league/; Edwards, P., 'Somalia moving towards brighter future', BBC Sport, 17 April 2015, https://www.bbc.co.uk/sport/football/32353183; Rogo, P., 'What's in a soccer game? For Somalia, a milestone goal', 17 December 2015, https://www.csmonitor.com/World/Africa/2015/1217/What-s-in-a-soccer-game-For-Somalia-a-milestone-goal; Mohamed, H., 'Somalia's football revival lures foreign players', 1 July 2015, https://www.aljazeera.com/indepth/features/2015/06/somalia-football-revival-lures-foreign-players-150630124818292.html

80. Teweldebirhan, S., 'Stop Mixing Politics with Sports', https://www.ezega.com/News/NewsDetails/3396/Stop-Mixing-Politics-with-Sports

81. Negussie, T., 'The Football-Politics Nexus in Ethiopia', 26 November 2013, http://addisstandard.com/the-football-politics-nexus-in-ethiopia/

82. Quote from Zere, A., 'The only safe thing to talk about in Eritrea is Football', *Africa is a Country*, https://africasacountry.com/2015/06/in-eritrea-the-only-safe-thing-to-talk-about-is-football

83. Rice, X., 'Eritrean footballers disappear after international match in Kenya', *Guardian*, 15 December 2009; Rice, X., 'Eritrean footballers go missing in Tanzania after tournament', *Guardian*, 12 July 2011; 'Eritrean players and coach missing in Kenya', BBC Sport, 17 December 2013, https://www.bbc.co.uk/sport/football/25415658; 'Ten players from Eritrean football team seek asylum after World Cup qualifier', *Guardian*, 15 October 2015; Okeowo, A., 'The Soccer-Star Refugees of Eritrea', *New Yorker*, 12 December 2016.

84. Howden, D., 'Football-mad president plays on while Burundi fears the return of civil war', *Guardian*, 6 April 2014; 'Burundi President Nkurunziza plays football amid protests', BBC News, 21 May 2015, https://www.bbc.co.uk/news/world-africa-32829176; Santora, M., 'In Burundi, President Pierre Nkurunziza's Push for Power Is Marked by

Bloodshed', *New York Times*, 20 July 2015; Vereni, J., 'On the Run in Burundi', *New Yorker*, 27 April 2016; 'President Pierre Nkurunziza: Officials in jail after Burundi leader is "roughed up" in game', BBC Sport, 2 March 2018, https://www.bbc.co.uk/sport/football/43265299

85. Ginnell, L., 'The rebirth of a footballing nation: how Congolese football is once again among Africa's best', https://thesefootballtimes. co/2017/01/12/the-rebirth-of-a-footballing-nation-how-congolese-football-is-once-again-among-africas-best/; Obayiuwana, O., 'TP Mazembe the Building of a Giant', *New African* 552, November 2012; Kazeem, Y., 'Kings of Africa: How Moise Katumbi redefined Congolese football club, TP Mazembe', http://venturesafrica.com/kings-of-africa-how-moise-katumbi-redefined-congolese-football-club-tp-mazembe/; Menary, S., 'For TP Mazembe, the richest club in Africa, the future looks bright', *World Soccer*, 3 September 2012, http://www.worldsoccer.com/columnists/steve-menary/339341-339341#WTha0cqIrYRi7EvF.99

86. 'Could football boss Moise Katumbi become DR Congo president?', BBC News, 7 March 2016, https://www.bbc.co.uk/news/world-africa-35726315; Gaffey, C., 'Who Is Moise Katumbi, Congo's Football Chief Challenging Joseph Kabila?', *Newsweek*, 5 May 2016, http://www. newsweek.com/who-moise-katumbi-congo-football-chief-455997

87. 'DR Congo halts football over fears of political violence', BBC Sport, 15 December 2016, https://www.bbc.co.uk/sport/football/38316676

88. 'Congolese football fans unite against President Kabila', https://www. ghanaweb.com/GhanaHomePage/NewsArchive/Congolese-football-fans-unite-against-President-Kabila-480821

89. Africa Centre for Open Governance, *Foul Play! The Crisis of Football Management in Kenya* (2010).

90. Doyle, P., 'Kenya leads way in ending blight of corruption in African football', *Observer*, 11 July 2010; Supporters Direct, First Africa Football Report attached: Club Structures and Licensing. https://supporters-direct. org/articles/club-structures-licensing-in-africa; Abshir, I., 'A League of their Own', http://roadsandkingdoms.com/2014/a-league-of-their-own/

91. Doyle, P., 'Zambia desperate to excel as they return to scene of their worst hour', *Guardian*, 19 January 2012, https://www.theguardian.com/football/blog/2012/jan/19/zambia-africa-cup-of-nations; Wilson, J., 'Victory Song: How Zambia's emotional triumph restored zest to the Cup of Nations', *Blizzard*, Issue 4.

92. This section draws on the wide body of scholarship on the topic: Ncube, L., 'The interface between football and ethnic identity discourses in Zimbabwe', *Critical African Studies* 6.2–3 (2014), pp. 192–210; Ncube, L., '"Bhora Mugedhi versus Bhora musango": The interface between football discourse and Zimbabwean politics', *International Review for the Sociology of Sport* 51.2 (2016), pp. 201–18; Ncube, L., and

Munoriyarwa, A., 'See no evil, hear no evil and speak no evil? The press, violence and hooliganism at the "Battle of Zimbabwe"', *Soccer & Society* (2017), pp. 1–16; Ncube, L., and Moyo, R., 'Can Highlanders FC break the jinx? Contesting press discourses on Highlanders FC's nine-year failure in the "Battle of Zimbabwe"', *African Identities* 15.4 (2017), pp. 387–97; Ncube, L., '"Highlander Ithimu yezwe lonke!": intersections of Highlanders FC fandom and Ndebele ethnic nationalism in Zimbabwe', *Sport in Society* (2017), pp. 1–18; Zenenga, P., 'Visualizing politics in African sport: political and cultural constructions in Zimbabwean soccer', *Soccer & Society* 13.2 (2012), pp. 250–63.; Chiweshe, M. K., 'Understanding the processes of becoming a football team fan in an African context: the case of Dynamos Football Club fans in Zimbabwe', *Soccer & Society* 12.2 (2011), pp. 174–83.

93. Smith, D., 'Robert Mugabe scores World Cup coup with Zimbabwe–Brazil football match', *Guardian*, 2 June 2010.

94. 'Zanu (PF) rigs peace-making soccer tourney', 9 May 2011, http://www.thezimbabwean.co/2011/05/zanu-pf-rigs-peace-making-soccer-tourney/.

95. Gleeson, M., 'Zimbabwe ban is new low for once-competitive team', 12 March 2015, https://www.reuters.com/article/us-soccer-africa-zimbabwe-analysis/zimbabwe-ban-is-new-low-for-once-competitive-team-IDUSKBN0M81QD20150312

96. David Goldblatt's picture can be seen here: http://www.tirochedeleon.com/item/304902

97. Dugger, C., 'South Africa Pushes to Make the Cup Its Own', *New York Times*, 23 May 2010.

98. Dubin, S. C., 'Imperfect pitch: pop culture, consensus, and resistance during the 2010 World Cup', *African Arts* 44.2 (2011), pp. 18–31.

99. Ibid.

100. Jethro, D., 'Vuvuzela Magic', *African Diaspora* 7.2 (2014), pp. 177–204; Kassing, J W., 'Noisemaker or cultural symbol: The vuvuzela controversy and expressions of football fandom', *African Football, Identity Politics and Global Media Narratives*, Palgrave Macmillan (2014), pp. 121–39; Hammond, N., 'The disharmonious honking of the vuvuzelas: homogenization and difference in the production and promotion of the 2010 Soccer World Cup in South Africa', *Soccer & Society* 12.1 (2011), pp. 46–55.

101. Quotation from Duane (2014).

102. Quoted in Smith, D., 'South Africans ponder life after the World Cup', *Guardian*, 11 July 2010.

103. Jacobs, S., 'Mr Big Bucks and the Mamelodi Sundowns', http://roadsandkingdoms.com/2014/mr-big-bucks-and-the-mamelodi-sundowns/

104. See also the English football photographer Stuart Roy Clarke, more at home in Burton Albion or Barnsley, who shot 'Bamako Twilight' in Mali's

capital on the eve of its civil war: a concise photo essay on the games'
place, from the matches played on rubbish-strewn wasteland with plastic
choked gutters for touchlines, to the eerie emptiness of the national
stadium. Clarke, S., 'Bamako Twilight', *Blizzard*, Issue 8.

105. O'Hagan, S., 'Omar Victor Diop: "I want to re-invent the heritage of
African studio photography"', *Observer*, 11 July 2015, https://www.
theguardian.com/artanddesign/2015/jul/11/mar-ictor-ioi-want-to-
reinvent-great-heritage-of-african-studio-photography; https://www.
theguardian.com/artanddesign/gallery/2015/jul/11/omar-victor-diops-
project-diaspora-in-pictures; Hilltout, J., 'Amen: Grassroots Football',
Cape Town: On the Dot (2010); http://www.andrewesiebo.com/
best-friends-1-2/

106. DeBarros, L., 'This is Phuti Lekoloane – South Africa's first openly gay
male footballer', http://www.mambaonline.com/2016/07/22/
phuti-lekoloane-south-africas-first-openly-gay-male-footballer/

107. Ahmadu, S., 'Lesbianism in women's football: Stakeholders take
Akinwunmi to task', http://www.goal.com/en-ng/news/12072/nigeria-
women/2016/06/23/24927142/lesbianism-in-womens-
football-stakeholders-take-akinwunmi-to; Walther-Ahrens, Tanja,
'Lesbianism as the Last Taboo in Women's Football',
https://www.idrottsforum.org/articles/walther-ahrens/walther-
ahrens101103.pdf

108. Mogorosi, R., 'Botswana's football has a new identity', *Mail and
Guardian*, 25 January 2017, https://mg.co.za/article/
2017-01-24-botswanas-football-has-a-new-identity

109. 'African amputees' cup kicks off', BBC News, 9 February 2007, http://
news.bbc.co.uk/1/hi/world/africa/6346363.stm; Bloomfield, S. 'Liberia's
amputee footballers: from civil war to African champions', *Observer*, 10
January 2010.

110. Egbejule, E., 'Nigerian football fans set up alternative Premier League –
on Twitter', *Guardian*, 1 October 2015, https://www.theguardian.com/
world/2015/oct/01/
nigerian-football-lovers-organise-their-own-premier-league-on-twitter

111. Goldblatt, D., 'Championing Kenya's hope after violence', http://news.
bbc.co.uk/1/hi/world/africa/7824135.stm

112. Kermeliotis, T., 'Alive & Kicking: Africa's football factory scoring big', 15
May 2013, https://edition.cnn.com/2013/05/15/business/alive-and-
kicking-football-africa/index.html

113. Goldblatt, D., 'The prison where murderers play for Manchester United',
Guardian, 28 May 2015.

Chapter 2

1. AFP, 'Ramadan-time Euro 2016 fever sweeps Arab world', 17 June 2016, https://www.dawn.com/news/1265465.
2. Hamsici, M., 'Barca or Real? Iraqi Kurdistan's big football faultline', BBC News, 1 March 2013, https://www.bbc.co.uk/news/magazine-21607705; see also https://www.youtube.com/watch?v=WILTUNmXehk
3. 'Why Spain's greatest football match, El Clasico, matters to Palestinians', BBC News, 7 October 2012, https://www.bbc.co.uk/news/world-middle-east-19861023
4. 'Morocco hit by Madrid fervour', 18 December 2014, https://www.fifa.com/clubworldcup/news/y=2014/m=12/news=morocco-hit-by-madrid-fervour-2494000.html
5. Cornwell, A., 'Real Madrid logo won't feature Christian cross in Middle East clothing deal', 24 January 2017, https://www.reuters.com/article/us-religion-soccer-realmadrid-IDUSKBN158235
6. Gamal, Muhammad Y., 'The final whistle: how football terminology took root in Arabic', na, 2008.
7. Awad's commentary can be heard here: https://www.youtube.com/watch?v=lnR__37JhQE
8. One translation, at https://www.reddit.com/r/Barca/duplicates/3551zg/my_translation_for_the_arabic_commentator_that/, goes:

> Messi's first goal: 'He gave it to him! Leo, Leo, Leo! Messi says goodnight! Grande Messi! Messi tastes Neuer's net. Messi shoots a magical ball! Messi! Messi! Messi! Messi! His ninth goal. Equals Cristiano! Goaaaaal! What a ball, what a ball! Messi controls, Messi goes backwards, Messi goes forwards, Messi puts the ball in. Bring on Kahn and bring on Neuer and even put Schmeichel at the corner of the goal! It's impossible to stop the Argentine when he decides to shoot and score.

> Messi's second goal: 'Messi goes in! Oh, daddy, oh, daddy, oh, daddy, oh, daddy, ohhhh, daddy! The Argentine is the daddy! Two nil! They murdered them in 120 seconds! Tiki taka del Argentino! Messi, Messi, Messi! Lionel has finished the game! Long live Argentina! because it brought us Maradona and Lionel. Crazy Messi, enthusiastic Messi. Messi, you made them nuts! Messi, you gave them headaches! Messi you have tortured them! Lewandowski, have a good trip! Messi has travelled deep into the earth and deep into Neuer's net. Ba, ba, Boateng, how is your back!!! How is your back doing,

Boateng? This is live! They have satisfied me, they have entertained me! Messi Golazo!! What a ball, what speed! What elegance, and what a foot! Messi, what a lad! Boateng had his sixth vertebra broken today! I'm sure of it!'

9. 'Politics takes back seat as Palestinians host soccer game', 27 October 2008, https://www.dawn.com/news/327291/politics-takes-back-seat-as-palestinians-host-soccer-game

10. Mahfouz, N., *Palace of Desire*, Random House (2016), p. 166.

11. Qandil, M., *Moon Over Samarqand*, American University in Cairo Press (2009).

12. Bisāṭī, M., *Drumbeat*, American University in Cairo Press (2010).

13. al-Berry, K., *Life is More Beautiful Than Paradise: A Jihadist's Own Story*, Oxford University Press (2009).

14. Writers in the diaspora, writing in English, have found their way back home through the game: see Awad, Y., 'Football in Arabic literature in diaspora: Global influences and local manifestations', *International Review for the Sociology of Sport* 51.8 (2016), pp. 1005–21; Alameddine, R., *I, the Divine: A Novel in First Chapters*, WW Norton & Company (2002); Aboulela, L., *Lyrics Alley*, Hachette UK (2010).

15. Al Salman/Sheikh Mohammed bin Ibrahim bin Abdul Latif Al Sheikh 3, 8. Mecca: Government Printing Press, 1399/1979, cited in Dorsey, J., 'Soccer v Jihad: A Draw', https://www.rsis.edu.sg/wp-content/uploads/2015/05/WP292.pdf.

16. Shaykh Mashoor Hasan Salmaan, *Football: Its Benefits and Ills According to the Divine Legislation*, Qurtuba (2016).

17. Ahmed, S., 'When women were forced to choose between faith and football', *Guardian*, 28 April 2018, https://www.theguardian.com/football/blog/2018/apr/28/women-faith-football-hijab-fifa-ban

18. The whole fatwa can be read at Morin, R., 'Fatwa Football', *Washington Post*, 18 December 2005, https://www.washingtonpost.com/archive/opinions/2005/12/18/fatwa-football/3b25cc48-82ae-4e54-86df-b9a68e2d9d08/?utm_term=.2341e4dff16f

19. Trabelsi, H., 'Islamists denounce "opium of football"', *Mail & Guardian*, 24 June 2006, http://mg.co.za/article/2006-06-24-islamists-denounce-opium-of-football

20. Terdman, M., 'Deliberations over Global Football among Radical Muslim "Fundamentalists"', in Mårtensson, U., Bailey, J., Ringrose, P., and Dyrendal, A., *Fundamentalism in the Modern World, Vol. 2: Fundamentalism and Communication: Culture, Media and the Public Sphere*, I.B. Taurus (2011), p. 314.

21. Ethnic minorities and stateless nations in the region are an occasional fourth side in these conflicts: JS Kabylie for Algeria's Berbers, Bnei

Sahknin for Israel's Arabs, Al-Wahad for Jordan's Palestinians, Erbil for Iraq's Kurds, Tractor Sazi for Iran's Azerbaijanis.

22. One for Max Weber here: in a splendid example of how the forces of rationalization can commandeer the avant-garde, see FIFA's version of the game, https://www.youtube.com/watch?v=EzbnKQKszm4

23. 'Transcript of Osama bin Laden videotape', 13 December 2001, http://edition.cnn.com/2001/US/12/13/tape.transcript/

24. http://www.independent.co.uk/news/half-an-hour-after-the-executions-kabul-stadium-opens-for-football-1171749.html

25. Court, L., 'Khalida Popal, Afghanistan football pioneer: "If the haters couldn't stop me, Trump can't"' Guardian, 15 March 2017.

26. Foster, R., 'Afghanistan's unlikely football league: eight teams, 18 matches and one city', Guardian, 20 July 2017, https://www.theguardian.com/sport/the-agony-and-the-ecstasy/2017/jul/20/football-afghanistan-premier-league-kabul; Qadiry, T., 'Roshan Afghan Premier League a hit with fans', 20 September 2012, https://www.bbc.co.uk/news/world-asia-19668215

27. 'Afghanistan suspends officials after women's soccer team abuse investigation', 9 December 2018, https://www.reuters.com/article/us-afghanistan-soccer-women/afghanistan-suspends-officials-after-womens-soccer-team-abuse-investigation-IDUSKBN1O807W

28. He also acquired Al Rasheed, a club team Uday set up using all of the best players in Iraq, and designed to play in Asian competition. They lost the final of what is now the Asian Champions League in 1986.

29. 'Iraqi footballers' fury at Bush', BBC News, 20 August 2004, http://news.bbc.co.uk/1/hi/world/middle_east/3584242.stm

30. Umm Haider, or 'Mother of Haider', whose twelve-year-old son was the boy killed, was subsequently awarded a trophy by the Prime Minister and gifted a house.

31. Quoted in 'Ten years on: How Iraq's soccer stars brought warring nation together', 28 July 2017, https://edition.cnn.com/2017/07/28/football/iraq-asia-cup-2007-anniversary/index.html. One member of the squad, Hawa Mulla Mohammed, saw his return rather more grimly: 'I had to pick up my two guns before going to practice because I'd been threatened. You can buy guns anywhere in Baghdad. You need them.'

32. Montague, J., 'Sectarianism threatens to blight Iraqi football's hopes', Guardian, 30 May 2008, https://www.theguardian.com/football/2008/may/30/iraq; Mubarak, H., 'Hussein Saeed: A True Machiavellian Prince', https://iraqsport.wordpress.com/2010/06/04/hussein-saeed-a-true-machiavellian-prince/; Cockburn, P., 'Fair play questioned in game of political football', https://www.independent.co.uk/news/world/middle-east/fair-play-questioned-in-game-of-political-football-2034066.html; Almasri, O., 'Iraqi Football: War, Corruption, Success and

Hope for the Future', https://www.goal.com/en-sg/news/3952/asia/2014/06/01/4826219/iraqi-football-war-corruption-success-and-hope-for-the

33. Losh, J., 'The rebel World Cup: on the road with Kurdistan's football team', *Guardian*, 14 October 2016, https://www.theguardian.com/global/2016/oct/14/football-alternative-world-cup-kurdistan-team-jack-losh-sebastien-rabas

34. Howard, M., 'Iraqis savour rare taste of unity as lions of Mesopotamia triumph', *Guardian*, 30 July 2007, https://www.theguardian.com/world/2007/jul/30/football.iraq; Walker, K., 'In Kurdistan, Tepid Support for Iraqi Football', 30 January 2014, http://www.rudaw.net/english/sports/30012014

35. Haddad, T., 'Kurdish football teams withdraw from Iraqi Premier League after Isis chants', 18 December 2016, https://www.ibtimes.co.uk/kurdish-football-teams-withdraw-iraqi-premier-league-after-isis-chants-1597079

36. 'Iraq's unlikely stadium boom', 13 October 2011, https://www.independent.co.uk/hei-fi/entertainment/iraqs-unlikely-stadium-boom-2369835.html; Almasri, O., 'Iraqi football: War, corruption, success and hope for the future', http://www.goal.com/en-sg/news/3952/asia/2014/06/01/4826219/iraqi-football-war-corruption-success-and-hope-for-the

37. Sherlock, R., 'How a talented footballer became world's most wanted man, Abu Bakr al-Baghdadi', *Daily Telegraph*, 11 November 2014, https://www.telegraph.co.uk/news/worldnews/middleeast/iraq/10948846/How-a-talented-footballer-became-worlds-most-wanted-man-Abu-Bakr-al-Baghdadi.html

38. Byrne, P., 'ISIS extremists behead four footballers after declaring the sport anti-Islamic', https://www.mirror.co.uk/news/world-news/isis-extremists-behead-four-footballers-8380263; Dearden, L., 'Isis kills at least 13 Real Madrid supporters in attack on cafe in Iraq', 13 May 2016, https://www.independent.co.uk/news/world/middle-east/iraq-balad-attacks-suicide-bomber-isis-daesh-islamic-state-a7027341.html

39. Miller, Q., 'How Football Survives on Islamic State's Turf', https://sports.vice.com/en_au/article/d7mp8x/how-football-survives-on-islamic-states-turf

40. Dorsey, J. M., 'The "Boytrap": When the Islamic State Goes to Play Soccer', 19 August 2016, https://www.theglobalist.com/islamic-state-is-boys-recruitment-soccer-football-terrorism-middle-east/

41. Dearden, L., 'Isis bans football referees in Syria because they enforce "laws of FIFA, not Sharia"', 31 August 2016, https://www.independent.co.uk/news/world/middle-east/isis-bans-football-referees-fifa-sharia-law-syria-commands-allah-a7218466.html

42. Janssen, B., 'Mosul: Liberated Iraqis free to play football without Isis's bizarre rules', 9 February 2017, https://www.independent.co.uk/news/world/middle-east/isis-mosul-football-iraq-battle-latest-rules-a7572046.html

43. Dartford, K., 'First football tournament played in Raqqa since ISIL insurgency', *Independent*, 4 April 2018, http://www.euronews.com/2018/04/04/first-football-tournament-played-in-raqqa-since-isil-insurgency

44. Tate, R., 'Iran football coach Ali Daei loses job following team's defeat', *Guardian*, 30 March 2009, https://www.theguardian.com/football/2009/mar/30/iran-football-ali-daei

45. 'Iranian football team shows support for Mousavi with green arm bands at Seoul World Cup qualifier', *Daily Telegraph*, 17 June 2009, https://www.telegraph.co.uk/news/worldnews/middleeast/iran/5559871/Iranian-football-team-shows-support-for-Mousavi-with-green-arm-bands-at-Seoul-World-Cup-qualifier.html

46. Hassett, S., 'Massive Iranian support has made Asian Cup "like playing in Tehran" says Ashkan Dejagah', 15 January 2016, https://www.smh.com.au/sport/soccer/massive-iranian-support-has-made-asian-cup-like-playing-in-tehran-says-ashkan-dejagah-20150115-12rbut.html

47. Gorman, J., 'Iranian women stand united in protest and hope at Asian Cup', *Guardian*, 23 January 2015, https://www.theguardian.com/football/blog/2015/jan/23/asian-cup-iran-fans-protest

48. 'How an Iranian woman snuck into a football stadium only open to men', 19 May 2016, http://observers.france24.com/en/20160519-iran-football-women-ban-stadium-woman

49. Dehghan, S. K., 'Iranian MPs speak out as women are barred from World Cup qualifier', *Guardian*, 6 September 2017, https://www.theguardian.com/world/2017/sep/06/iranian-mps-women-barred-world-cup-qualifier

50. Gumbel, A., 'Gaddafi's soccer foes pay deadly penalty', *Independent*, 15 July 1996, https://www.independent.co.uk/news/gadaffis-soccer-foes-pay-deadly-penalty-1328829.html

51. Quoted in Von Mittlestaedt, J., 'Libya's Soccer Rebellion: A Revolution Foreshadowed on the Pitch of Benghazi', http://www.spiegel.de/international/world/libya-s-soccer-rebellion-a-revolution-foreshadowed-on-the-pitch-of-benghazi-a-774594.html; Rice, X., 'Libya: a donkey taunt, the Gaddafis and a fatal footballing rivalry', *Guardian*, 25 May 2011.

52. 'Gaddafi's son suspended', BBC Sport, 6 November 2003, http://news.bbc.co.uk/sport1/hi/football/europe/3244269.stm. Check court case progress, 'Libyan court finds Gaddafi's son not guilty of murdering former football star Al-Riani', 5 April 2018, https://en.as.com/en/2018/04/05/football/1522950504_107459.html

53. Key research on the phenomenon includes: Amara, M., 'Football sub-culture and youth politics in Algeria', *Mediterranean Politics* 17.1 (2012), pp. 41–58; Amara, M., 'Football, the new battlefield of business in Algeria: Djezzy and Nedjma . . . RANA MĀK YA AL-KHDRA', *Journal of North African Studies* 16.3 (2011), pp. 343–60; Lyazghi, M., and Rharib, A.,

'Football and politics in Morocco,' *Sport in the African World* Routledge (2018), pp. 43–63; Rharib, A., and Amara, M., 'Ultras in Morocco', *Journal of International Centre of Sport Security*, July–August, vol. 2, 2014, pp. 40–5; Tuastad, D., 'From football riot to revolution. The political role of football in the Arab world', *Soccer & Society* 15.3 (2014), pp. 376–88.

54. Ayari, R., 'Tunisian Football Was Suffering Under Ben Ali – Tarak Dhiab', http://www.goal.com/en/news/89/africa/2011/01/19/2312586/tunisian-football-was-suffering-under-ben-ali-tarak-dhiab

55. 'Mounting Social Discontent Drives Late May Street Violence in Algiers and Oran', https://wikileaks.org/plusd/cables/08ALGIERS661_a.html

56. Rommel, C., 'A veritable game of the nation: on the changing status of football within the Egyptian national formation in the wake of the 2009 World Cup qualifiers against Algeria', *Critical African Studies* 6.2–3 (2014), pp. 157–75.

57. Elgohari, M., 'Egypt's Ultras: No More Politics', 30 June 2013, http://arabic.middleeastdigest.com/pages/index/12475/egypt's-ultras_no-more-politics

58. 'Malians cheer Gaddafi as they host Libya football team', BBC News, 29 March 2011, https://www.bbc.co.uk/news/world-africa-12891407

59. Shea, A., 'Tunisia: a team desperate for a nation's affection', https://thesefootballtimes.co/2018/06/11/tunisia-a-team-desperately-looking-for-a-nation/

60. Gritti, F., 'Ultras in Morocco: "They consider us animals"', 25 June 2014, https://cafebabel.com/en/article/ultras-in-morocco-they-consider-us-animals-5ae00945f723b35a145e4cc3/; Edwards, P., 'Morocco bans "ultra" fan groups following riot', 24 March 2016, https://www.bbc.co.uk/sport/football/35885404

61. 'Football v politics', *The Economist*, 26 May 2012, https://www.economist.com/middle-east-and-africa/2012/05/26/football-v-politics

62. AP, 'Soccer violence in Algeria reflects social unrest', 31 August 2014, https://www.cbc.ca/sports/soccer/soccer-violence-in-algeria-reflects-social-unrest-1.2751823

63. AP, 'Striker Albert Ebossé dies after being hit by object thrown from stands', *Guardian*, 24 August 2014, https://www.theguardian.com/football/2014/aug/24/striker-albert-ebosse-dies-hit-object-thrown-stands; Mezahi, M., 'JS Kabylie's return after Albert Ebossé's death shows lessons have not been learned', *Guardian*, 26 February 2015, https://www.theguardian.com/football/2015/feb/26/albert-ebosse-js-kabylie-alegria-nothing-changed; Okeleji, O., 'No answers a year after Ebossé's death', https://www.aljazeera.com/news/2015/09/answers-year-ebosse-death-150910103254836.html

64. These chants and the ones below all cited in Amara, M., 'Football sub-culture and youth politics in Algeria', *Mediterranean Politics* 17.1 (2012), pp. 41–58.

65. Boundaoui, A., 'Algerian football fans sing songs of freedom', 11 November 2014, https://www.middleeasteye.net/news/algerian-football-fans-sing-songs-freedom

66. Kingsley, P., 'Death of Zamalek fans in riot stirs political conspiracies in Egypt', *Guardian*, 13 February 2015, https://www.theguardian.com/football/2015/feb/13/death-of-zamalek-fans-in-riot-stirs-political-conspiracies-in-egypt

67. Accorsi, A., and Siegelbaum, M., 'Banning fandom: football and revolution in Egypt', 11 June 2015, http://www.middleeasteye.net/in-depth/features/banning-fandom-football-and-revolution-egypt-1885612941

68. '"Who isn't a migrant here?" says banner at Israeli soccer game', 13 September 2015, https://www.timesofisrael.com/who-isnt-a-migrant-here-says-banner-at-israeli-soccer-game/

69. Sorek, T., 'The Islamic Soccer League in Israel: setting moral boundaries by taming the wild', *Identities: Global Studies in Culture and Power* 9.4 (2002), pp. 445–70; Sorek, T., 'Arab football in Israel as an "integrative enclave"', *Ethnic and Racial Studies* 26.3 (2003), pp. 422–50; Sorek, T., 'Palestinian nationalism has left the field: a shortened history of Arab soccer in Israel', *International Journal of Middle East Studies* 35.3 (2003), pp. 417–37; Ben-Porat, A., 'Who are we? My club? My people? My state? The dilemma of the Arab soccer fan in Israel', *International Review for the Sociology of Sport* 49.2 (2014), pp. 175–89.

70. Watad, N., 'Ministers demand red card for Arab-Israeli football club', 19 October 2014, https://www.alaraby.co.uk/english/news/2014/10/22/ministers-demand-red-card-for-arab-israeli-football-club

71. Kaplan, A. S., 'Is Playing Soccer on Shabbat a Crime? Israel Redefines the Term "Political Football"', 10 September 2015, https://www.haaretz.com/.premium-israel-redefines-the-term-political-football-1.5397751

72. Ben-Porat, A., 'From community to commodity: the commodification of football in Israel', *Soccer & Society* 13.3 (2012), pp. 443–57; Ben-Porat, A., 'Six decades of sport, from a game to commodity: football as a parable', *Sport in Society* 12.8 (2009), pp. 999–1012.

73. Freedman, S., 'Israel's friendly football fans', *Guardian*, 21 December 2009, https://www.theguardian.com/commentisfree/2009/dec/21/israel-football-hapoel-ultras

74. On Hapoel Be'er Sheeva and the culture of small-town Israel see the delightful Adar, S., 'Light in the Darkness', *Blizzard*, Issue 22.

75. This account of Beitar draws upon: Goldblatt, D., 'Likud on the terraces', *Prospect*, September 2008; Ben-Porat, A., '"Biladi, Biladi": Ethnic and Nationalistic Conflict in the Soccer Stadium in Israel', *Soccer & Society*

2.1 (2001), pp. 19–38; Ben-Porat, A., 'Death to the Arabs: the right-wing fan's fear', *Soccer & Society* 9.1 (2008), pp. 1–13; Alfasi, Y., Levy, M., and Galily, Y., 'Israeli football as an arena for post-colonial struggle: the case of Beitar Jerusalem FC', *Journal of Comparative Research in Anthropology & Sociology* 6.1 (2015); Barshad, A., 'How Soccer Explains Israel', 19 March 2013, http://grantland.com/features/jerusalem-fc-beitar-signed-two-muslim-players-russia-february-stirred-national-controversy/

76. Tharoor, I., 'How Israeli soccer hooligans fanned flames of hate', *Washington Post*, 10 July 2014.

77. Beaumont, P., 'Beitar Jerusalem owner quits over fans' violence at European game', *Guardian*, 17 July 2015, https://www.theguardian.com/football/2015/jul/17/beitar-jerusalem-owner-quits-fans-violence-eli-tabib-israel-belgium-charleroi

78. Gellar, R., 'Israel may finally be doing something to stop its most racist soccer fans', *Washington Post*, 19 August 2019.

79. Masters, J., 'Hapoel Katamon: Football club brings Arabs and Israelis together', https://edition.cnn.com/2015/08/25/football/hapoel-katamon-israel-football/index.html; AFP, 'Fan-owned Hapoel Katamon look for tolerance in fractious Jerusalem', 9 April 2018, https://en.as.com/en/2018/04/09/football/1523277099_211113.html; Ha-Ilan, N., 'The (Re) Constitution of football fandom: Hapoel Katamon Jerusalem and its supporters', *Sport in Society* 21.6 (2018), pp. 902–18.

80. 'Fans of Beitar Jerusalem soccer team fed up with racism, form new club', 22 February 2018, https://www.jpost.com/Israel-News/Fans-of-Beitar-Jerusalem-soccer-team-fed-up-with-racism-form-new-club-543384; 'Maccabi Kabilio making waves', 10 May 2010, https://www.uefa.com/memberassociations/association=isr/news/newsid=1482733.html

81. Duerr, Glen M. E., 'Playing for identity and independence: the issue of Palestinian statehood and the role of FIFA', *Soccer & Society* 13.5–6 (2012), pp. 653–66.

82. 'Argentina scraps Israel World Cup friendly after campaign', BBC News, 6 June 2018, https://www.bbc.co.uk/news/world-middle-east-44378669

83. O'Hare, L., 'Celtic v Hapoel Be'er Sheva: Sport and politics collide', 16 August 2016, https://www.aljazeera.com/indepth/features/2016/08/celtic-hapoel-sheva-sport-politics-collide-160816055716847.html

84. 'FIFA will not take action on Israeli settlement teams', *Al Jazeera*, 27 October 2017, https://www.aljazeera.com/news/2017/10/fifa-delays-action-israeli-settlement-teams-171027124839956.html

85. Tuastad, D., 'The political role of football for Palestinians in Jordan', *The political role of football for Palestinians in Jordan* (1997), 105–21; Tuastad, D., '"A Threat to National Unity" – Football in Jordan: Ethnic Divisive or a Political Tool for the Regime?', *International Journal of the History of Sport* 31.14 (2014), pp. 1774–88; Mackenzie, J., '"Allah!

Wehdat! Al-Quds Arabiya!": Football, nationalism, and the chants of
Palestinian resistance in Jordan', diss., Arts & Social Sciences,
Department of History, Simon Fraser University (2015).

86. Reiche, D., 'War Minus the Shooting? The politics of sport in Lebanon as
a unique case in comparative politics', *Third World Quarterly* 32.2
(2011), pp. 261–77.

87. Antelava, N., 'Lebanon's political rivals meet in football "friendly"', 13
April 2010, http://news.bbc.co.uk/1/hi/8618829.stm; the last ten
minutes of the game, when the participants are at their most exhausted,
can be seen here: https://www.youtube.com/watch?v=fMa311oYcoE.

88. Habbab, B., 'World Cup raises foreign flags, Lebanese questions', 6 June
2014, https://english.al-akhbar.com/node/20072

89. Abdul Basit Saroot can be heard singing revolutionary songs here:
https://www.youtube.com/watch?v=U64qZPAGWWYAP, 'World Cup:
"This is not Assad's team, it's Syria's team"', 5 October 2017, https://
www.theguardian.com/football/2017/oct/05/football-this-is-not-assads-
team-its-syrias-team; 'Former captain of Syria's football team tortured to
death', 1 October 2016; https://www.alaraby.co.uk/english/society/
2016/10/1/former-captain-of-syrias-football-team-tortured-to-death

90. Almasri, O., 'Once full of promise, Syrian football has been destroyed by
civil war', *Guardian*, 7 September 2014, https://www.theguardian.com/
football/blog/2014/sep/07/syrian-football-civil-war; *Football: A Syrian
Elegy*, https://www.thealeppoproject.com/wp-content/uploads/2016/10/
Football-A-Syrian-Elegy-3.pdf

91. Fainaru, S., 'THE DICTATOR'S TEAM', http://www.espn.com/espn/
feature/story/_/id/19343630/how-syrian-government-brought-soccer-
campaign-oppression

92. 'Football in Saudi Arabia: Where the popular will matters', *The Economist*,
31 May 2014, https://www.economist.com/middle-east-and-africa/2014/
05/31/where-the-popular-will-matters

93. '#BBCtrending: The female football fan causing outrage in Saudi Arabia',
8 October 2014, https://www.bbc.co.uk/news/blogs-trending-29527556

94. AP, 'Only 14 Western Sydney Wanderers fans to travel to Riyadh for ACL
final', *Guardian*, 28 October 2014, https://www.theguardian.com/
football/2014/oct/28/only-14-western-sydney-wanderers-fans-to-travel-
to-riyadh-for-acl-final

95. Duerden, J., '"I can't describe my feelings" – Saudi women finally
allowed into games', *Guardian*, 11 January 2018.

96. Montague, J., 'From fairytale to tragedy: the betrayal of a Bahraini
dream', 24 February 2016, http://www.sportingintelligence.
com/2016/02/24/from-fairytale-to-tragedy-the-betrayal-of-a-bahraini-
dream-240201/

97. Cited in Corbett, J., 'Power Play', *Blizzard*, Issue 9.

98. Panja, T., 'Powerful Sheikh Linked to Sports Corruption Case Resurfaces in Prague', *New York Times*, 4 November 2017.

99. Rizvi, A., 'UAE team were lifted by a little magic from Metsu', https://www.thenational.ae/sport/uae-team-were-lifted-by-a-little-magic-from-metsu-1.396450

100. Abbot, S., *The Away Game: The Epic Search for Soccer's Next Superstars*, Norton (2018).

101. Booth, R., 'Qatar's migrant workers say they are paid to fill stadiums before World Cup', *Guardian*, 13 November 2015.

102. Duerden, J., 'Qatari Club Takes Curious Route to Asian Title', *New York Times*, 5 November 2011.

103. Brannagan, P. M., and Giulianotti, R., 'Soft power and soft disempowerment: Qatar, global sport and football's 2022 World Cup finals', *Leisure Studies* 34.6 (2015), pp. 703–19; Scharfenort, N., 'Urban development and social change in Qatar: the Qatar National Vision 2030 and the 2022 FIFA World Cup', *Journal of Arabian Studies* 2.2 (2012), pp. 209–30.

104. Pattisson, P., 'Revealed: Qatar's World Cup "slaves"', *Guardian*, 25 September 2013.

105. Gibson, O., 'French footballer trapped in Qatar asks Guardiola and Zidane for help', *Guardian*, 14 November 2013.

106. Quoted in Booth, R., and Pattisson, P., 'Trapped in Qatar: the migrants who helped build the "tower of football"', 28 July 2014, https://www.theguardian.com/global-development/2014/jul/28/-sp-qatar-migrants-tower-football-world-cup

107. On the post-boycott labour reforms see: AFP, 'Can Qatar deliver on its worker "revolution"?', 28 October 2017, http://www.france24.com/en/20171028-can-qatar-deliver-its-worker-revolution; Knecht, E., 'Its image at risk abroad, Qatar backs labor reforms at home', Reuters, 2 November 2017, https://uk.reuters.com/article/us-qatar-labour/its-image-at-risk-abroad-qatar-backs-labor-reforms-at-home-IDUKKBN1D21BU; Harwood, A., 'Qatar 2022 World Cup will honour workers' rights with the end of the kafala system, predicts ITUC head', *Independent*, 28 January 2018, https://www.independent.co.uk/sport/football/international/qatar-2022-world-cup-workers-rights-kafala-system-migraints-middle-east-a8182191.html; Keh, A., 'The 2022 World Cup Plants Some Trees and Prepares to Step Into the Spotlight', *New York Times*, 12 July 2018.

Chapter 3

1. Pink shirts include Palermo, Evian and Juventus away kits.

2. Note that in a world configured by cultural rather than FIFA geography, a proper survey of Latin America's rather than South America's Pink Tide

would acknowledge the advance of the Left in the Dominican Republic, Mexico, Nicaragua, Guatemala and Honduras.

3. Data on club turnovers broken down into these categories has been compiled in Soria, S., and Maldonado, A., 'The long and winding road of the football industry in Chile', *Sport in Latin America: Policy, Organization, Management* 5 (2016), p. 253; Kim, JH., 'Business development strategies among football clubs in Argentina', *Sport in Latin America: Policy, Organization, Management* 5 (2016), p. 270; Parrish, C., Lee, S. and Kim, JH., 'Innovative Business Development Strategies among Football Clubs in Argentina', *Sport in Latin America: Policy, Organization, Management* (2016), pp. 106–28; Ramallo, S., and Aguiar, F., 'Marketing in Argentine football: a snapshot', *Marketing and Football* (2007), p. 465.

4. Ferdman, R., and Yanovsky, D., 'Latin America earns more from exporting soccer players than live animals', 1 August 2013, https://qz.com/109317/latin-americas-soccer-player-exports-are-worth-more-than-its-animal-exports/; 'Uruguay exported 1,414 football players in the last decade', 6 January 2011, http://en.mercopress.com/2011/01/06/uruguay-exported-1.414-football-players-in-the-last-decade

5. Poli, R., Ravenel, L., and Besson, R., 'Exporting countries in world football', *CIES Football Observatory Monthly Report* issue no. 8 (2015); de Vasconcellos, R., Henrique, C., and Dimeo, P., 'The experience of migration for Brazilian football players', *Sport in Society* 12.6 (2009), pp. 725–36.

6. Mattos, C., 'Broadcasting football rights in Brazil: the case of Globo and "Club of 13" in the antitrust perspective', *Estudos Econômicos (São Paulo)* 42.2 (2012), pp. 337–62.

7. Richards, J., Double Trouble, *Blizzard* Issue 0.

8. Aranguren, L.P., and Podesta, R.G., 'Football in Peru', *Sport in Latin America: Policy, Organization, Management* 5 (2016), p. 244.

9. de Freitas Neto, R.M., et al., 'The Determinants of Brazilian Football Clubs' Debt Ratios', *Brazilian Business Review* 14, Special Ed. (2017), pp. 94–109.

10. Vickery, T., 'Club football in Uruguay struggling against global pressures', http://www.espn.co.uk/football/uruguayan-primera-division/0/blog/post/3371749/uruguay-club-football-struggling-against-global-pressures

11. 'Bolivian problems solved after strike threat', FIFPro, 1 March 2010, https://www.fifpro.org/news/bolivian-problems-solved-after-strike-threath/en/; 'Bolivian player strike threatens World Cup qualifiers', Reuters, 15 September 2015, https://uk.reuters.com/article/soccer-bolivia-strike/soccer-bolivian-player-strike-threatens-world-cup-qualifiers-IDUKL4N11L2YE20150915

12. 'Ecuador's players strike over $20 million salary backlog', Reuters, 27 November 2015, https://uk.reuters.com/article/soccer-ecuador-strike-IDUKL3N13M03I20151127

13. 'Colombian football can't be considered professional', FIFPro, 12 April 2011, https://www.fifpro.org/news/colombian-football-can-t-be-considered-professional/en/

14. Edwards, D., 'Strikes, Resignations, Molotov Cocktails: All Hell Breaks Loose At Colón', 20 November 2013, http://www.thebubble.com/strikes-resignations-molotov-cocktails-all-hell-breaks-loose-at-colon/

15. 'Alianza Lima fans beat own players after loss', *Sydney Morning Herald*, 6 February 2015, https://www.smh.com.au/sport/soccer/alianza-lima-fans-beat-own-players-after-loss-20150206-137wsi.html

16. Gowar, R., 'Peru takes steps to arrest decline', *World Soccer*, 21 August 2009; Dorrington, N., 'Striking Role,' *When Saturday Comes*, May 2012.

17. 'The magic word was democracy', FIFpro, 9 May 2016, https://fifpro.org/news/the-magic-word-was-democracy/en/

18. Bom Senso's manifesto: https://www.researchgate.net/profile/Fernando_Fleury/publication/267982438_Bom_Senso_FC_Proposal_Financial_Fair_Play_and_Brazilian_Soccer_Schedule/links/545ed7690cf2c1a63bfc2202.pdf

19. In English, at any rate, Casal and the Tenfield story is best covered at lacelesteblog.com, see 'No, Paco: The Mother Of All Crises, Part 2' and 'Adios, Eugenio! FIFA, Casal, and the Mother of All Crises: Part 3'.

20. https://www.elobservador.com.uy/mujica-cerro-expediente-la-dgi-casal-evitar-juicios-al-estado-n265786

21. 'Uruguayan stars force federation's financial hand over Tenfield's sponsor deal extension', 30 August 2016, http://keirradnedge.com/2016/08/30/celeste-stars-up-the-ante/; 'Player power pays off for Uruguay as Tenfield concedes contract defeat', 16 December 2016, http://keirradnedge.com/2016/12/16/tenfield-concedes/

22. Elsey, B., and Nadel, J., 'South American Soccer Is Ignoring Its Women', https://sports.vice.com/en_ca/article/pgnazz/south-american-soccer-is-ignoring-its-women

23. Mira, L., 'Santos close down futsal and female football teams to keep Neymar', http://www.goal.com/en/news/584/brazil/2012/01/03/2829228/santos-close-down-futsal-and-female-football-teams-to-keep

24. Rodriguez's goal can be seen at https://www.youtube.com/watch?v=hFHNnVFf9Iw

25. Elsey, B., 'From the ashes: South American women rise again for the Copa América Femenina', *Guardian*, 25 March 2018; Zirin, D., 'How a Feminist Uprising Is Saving South American Soccer', *Nation*, 20 April 2018, https://www.thenation.com/article/how-a-feminist-uprising-is-saving-south-american-soccer/; Elsey, B., 'Unbeaten Brazil claim women's

Copa América but everyone leaves happy', *Guardian*, 25 April 2018, https://www.theguardian.com/football/2018/apr/25/brazil-womens-copa-america-chile-everyone-happy

26. Elsey, B., 'Unbeaten Brazil claim Copa América but everyone leaves happy', *Guardian*, 25 April 2018.

27. AFP, 'Get in the kitchen!': life as a female football referee', http://sports.inquirer.net/212192/get-in-the-kitchen-life-as-a-female-football-referee#ixzz5MwSgfP8r

28. Watts, J., 'Outrage after Brazil football team signs goalkeeper convicted of killing girlfriend', *Guardian*, 13 March 2017.

29. 'Monkey chants aimed at Brazilian player in Peru', Reuters, 13 February 2014, https://uk.reuters.com/article/soccer-brazil-racism/soccer-monkey-chants-aimed-at-brazilian-player-in-peru-idUKL3N0LI56620140213

30. Reuters, 'Player walks off pitch in Peru over racist abuse from fans', *Guardian*, 2 March 2015, https://uk.reuters.com/article/uk-chile-soccer-racism/chile-football-match-suspended-after-racist-insults-idUKKCN0J700120141123

31. 'Chile football match suspended after racist insults', Reuters, 23 November 2014, https://uk.reuters.com/article/uk-chile-soccer-racism/chile-football-match-suspended-after-racist-insults-IDUKKCN0J700120141123

32. Valente, M., 'ARGENTINA: Bolivian Immigrants Complain of Racist Football Chants', 19 March 2003, http://www.ipsnews.net/2003/03/argentina-bolivian-immigrants-complain-of-racist-football-chants/

33. Candelaria, J., 'Journalist Condemned for Calling Afro-Ecuadorian Soccer Player a "Gorilla" Who Could Give Him Ebola', http://remezcla.com/sports/felipe-caicedo-condemns-racism; Montes, E., 'Racism Threatens to Overshadow the Copa America', 11 June 2015, https://sports.vice.com/en_uk/article/53vv75/racism-threatens-to-overshadow-the-copa-america

34. Mance, H., 'Local Speciality', *When Saturday Comes*, December 2009, http://www.wsc.co.uk/the-archive/922-South-America/5244-local-speciality; Wyss, J., 'In the cradle of Ecuadorean soccer, the beach is the fiercest field', *Miami Herald*, 5 June 2014, https://www.miamiherald.com/news/nation-world/world/americas/article1965552.html#storylink=cpy'; Thompson Hernandez, W., 'Afro-Ecuadorians and the Beating Heart of Soccer Culture in El Chota Valley', http://remezcla.com/features/sports/afro-ecuadorians-and-the-beating-heart-of-soccer-culture-in-el-chota-valley/; Jijon, I., 'The moral globalization of sport: Local meanings of football in Chota Valley, Ecuador', *International Review for the Sociology of Sport* 52.1 (2017), pp. 82–96.

35. Cited in Mora y Araujo, M., 'Ecuador's national team transforms through inclusion in face of racism', 11 June 2013, http://www.espn.com/soccer/blog/name/93/post/1840570/headline

36. Rahier, J., 'Race, Fútbol, and the Ecuadorian Nation: the Ideological

Biology of (Non-) Citizenship', e-misférica 5:2: Race and its Others (December 2008).

37. Pashley, A., 'Ecuador Going After "Ink Assassin" Over Controversial Political Cartoon', 17 February 2015, https://news.vice.com/article/ecuador-going-after-ink-assassin-over-controversial-political-cartoon

38. Vickery, T., 'The remarkable story of Independiente del Valle', *World Soccer*, 16 May 2016, https://www.worldsoccer.com/features/the-remarkable-story-of-independiente-del-valle-371075#WuD9YcujhS1HzLXf.99

39. Edwards, D., 'Peñarol clash postponed after man shot in Centenario toilets', 24 October 2016, http://www.goal.com/en/news/1662/uruguay/2016/10/24/28783812/Peñarol-clash-postponed-after-man-shot-in-centenario-toilets; 'Uruguayan football out of control: hooligans force the cancelling of the derby', 28 November 2016, http://en.mercopress.com/2016/11/28/uruguayan-football-out-of-control-hooligans-force-the-cancelling-of-the-derby

40. The full list of deaths in Argentinian football can be seen at http://salvemosalfutbol.org/lista-de-victimas-de-incidentes-de-violencia-en-el-futbol/; a good summary of the Brazilian situation is Murad, M., 'Práticas de violência e mortes de torcedores no futebol brasileiro', *Revista USP* 99 (2013), pp. 139–52.

41. A pretty comprehensive roster of Ecuadorian football violence can be read at 'Los actos de violencia en el fútbol ecuatoriano en una década', https://www.elcomercio.com/deportes/violencia-futbol-ecuador-barrasbravas-deportes.html; for Peru see de los Heros, M. A., 'Barras bravas y tiempos bravos: violencia en el fútbol peruano', *Avances en Psicología* 21.2 (2013), pp. 155–66.

42. 'Las sospechas tras el acribillamiento de tres barristas de U. de Chile', 19 March 2014, https://www.cooperativa.cl/noticias/pais/policial/las-sospechas-tras-el-acribillamiento-de-tres-barristas-de-u-de-chile/2014-08-19/132652.html

43. Watts, J., 'Latin America leads world on murder map, but key cities buck deadly trend', *Guardian*, 6 May 2015, https://www.theguardian.com/world/2015/may/06/murder-map-latin-america-leads-world-key-cities-buck-deadly-trend. For most recent homicide rates see Clavell, T., 'InSight Crime's 2017 Homicide Round-Up', 19 January 2018, https://www.insightcrime.org/news/analysis/2017-homicide-round-up/

44. Ramsey, G., '10 Ways Soccer and Organized Crime Mix in Latin America', 30 May 2014, https://www.insightcrime.org/news/analysis/10-ways-soccer-organized-crime-mix-latin-america/. On money-laundering specifically see Parkinson, C., 'Argentine Soccer at Center of Major Money-Laundering Network', 17 June 2013, https://www.insightcrime.org/news/brief/argentine-soccer-at-center-of-major-money-laundering-network/; De Michelle, R., 'Avocados, Soccer, Wire Transfers, and Money

Laundering', 10 January 2014, https://www.insightcrime.org/news/ analysis/avocados-soccer-wire-transfers-and-money-laundering/; La Susa, M., 'Argentina Soccer Crime Case Shows Evolution of Hooligan Groups', 1 December 2017, https://www.insightcrime.org/news/brief/ argentina-soccer-crime-case-shows-evolution-of-hooligan-groups/

45. *'Barra brava de Peñarol tiene a 400 "soldados"'*, 19 February 2017, https:// www.elpais.com.uy/informacion/barra-brava-Peñarol-soldados.html

46. Cited in Kelly, A., 'The barra bravas: the violent Argentinian gangs controlling football', *Observer*, 21 August 2011, https://www.theguardian. com/football/2011/aug/21/argentina-football-gangs-barra-bravas

47. On the situation in Rosario, at Newell's Old Boys, see 'Why Are The Soccer Hooligans Of Argentina Killing Each Other?', http://www. thefader.com/2016/06/01/argentina-soccer-hooligan-murders-old-boys- barra-brava

48. Cited in Schlotterbeck, I., 'Barras Bravas: The Dark Side of Soccer', http://www.coha.org/barras-bravas-the-dark-side-of-soccer/

49. For the whole sorry chronology of Cantero's presidency at Independiente, see https://www.lanacion.com.ar/1684473-gestion-cantero-barra-brava

50. Cited in Kelly (2011).

51. Longman, J., and Barnes, T., 'A Yellow Card, Then Unfathomable Violence, in Brazil', *New York Times*, 21 October 2013.

52. Worswick, C., 'Murders cast shadow over the game in Colombia', *World Soccer*, https://www.worldsoccer.com/blogs/murders-cast-shadow-over- the-game-in-colombia-343763#7uDiX42esuqZqGxs.99

53. 'Tougher sanctions against football hooligans in Chile', BBC News, 9 June 2015, https://www.bbc.co.uk/news/world-latin-america-33073170

54. Reuters, 'Violence mars Chilean title celebrations for Colo Colo', 7 December 2012, http://www.skysports.com/football/news/11095/ 10092097/violence-mars-chilean-title-celebrations-for-colo-colo

55. Gowar, R., 'Argentina takes aim at mafia-style gangs with new sports law', 19 April 2016, https://uk.reuters.com/article/uk-soccer-argentina- violence-IDUKKCN0XG218

56. On the Copa América 2007 see Kraul, C., 'Chavez's grand, risky dream', *LA Times*, 23 June 2007; NYT Blog, 'At the Stadium: A wave from Messi and a song for the fall of the government', *New York Times*, 10 July 2007; Richards, J., 'How the Vinotinto attempted to capture the mood of a nation', *Guardian*, 16 July 2007, https://www.theguardian.com/ football/2007/jul/16/sport.comment

57. Romero, S., 'World Cup 2014 . . . in Venezuela?', *New York Times*, 17 July 2007.

58. See https://carlesvinyas.wordpress.com/2013/05/11/hugo-chavez-el- legado-bolivariano-del-futbol-iii/; 'La cambiante historia de Zamora FC, el club del hermano de Hugo Chávez que será rival Boca', https://www.

lanacion.com.ar/1775207-la-cambiante-historia-de-zamora-fc-el-club-del-hermano-de-hugo-chavez-que-sera-rival-boca

59. For an overview of how football mourned Chavez, see https://carlesvinyas.wordpress.com/2013/06/19/hugo-chavez-el-legado-bolivariano-del-futbol-y-vi/

60. Rosati, A., 'World Cup in the middle: Venezuelans use soccer to push political agendas', 24 June 2014, https://www.csmonitor.com/World/Americas/Latin-America-Monitor/2014/0624/World-Cup-in-the-middle-Venezuelans-use-soccer-to-push-political-agendas

61. Protestors at the Copa América 2015 can be seen at 'IMPERDIBLES! Las pancartas en juego de la Copa América que Maduro no quiere que veas', https://maduradas.com/imperdibles-las-pancartas-en-juego-de-la-copa-america-que-maduro-no-quiere-que-veas-fotos/

62. 'Key Venezuela-Brazil football match interrupted by power cut', BBC News, 12 October 2016, https://www.bbc.co.uk/news/world-latin-america-37631085

63. Quoted in Jordan, D. C., 'Copa América Infrastructure Nowadays', 3 June 2016, https://www.caracaschronicles.com/2016/06/03/copa-america-infrastructure-nowadays/

64. 'Venezuela soccer players call on Maduro to halt repression', Reuters, 13 May 2017, https://uk.reuters.com/article/uk-venezuela-politics-soccer/venezuela-soccer-players-call-on-maduro-to-halt-repression-IDUKKBN188336

65. 'Venezuelan football teams hold minute's silence after kick-off to get around TV blackout', Daily Telegraph, 1 May 2017, https://www.telegraph.co.uk/football/2017/05/01/venezuelan-football-teams-hold-minutes-silence-kick-off-get/

66. Quoted in Goodhart, B., 'Evo Morales 2–1 Angela Merkel', Guardian, 7 July 2008, https://www.theguardian.com/football/2008/jul/07/bolivia.moralesfootball

67. The relationship between indigenous political movements in Bolivia and football is well explored in Villein Fiengo, S., 'DES-gol-ONIZACIÓN? Football and politics in indigenous movements in Bolivia', Critical Journal of Social Sciences 111 (2016). Profiles of Morales that give due weight to his sporting peccadilloes include: Walker, A., 'A Politician Who Plays Football, Or A Footballer Who Plays At Politics?', 25 June 2014, http://www.bolivianexpress.org/blog/posts/evo; Schiprani, A., 'Bolivia's Evo Morales: part-time pro footballer', Financial Times, 27 May 2014; Schiprani, A., 'Evo Morales: president, or President for life?', Financial Times, 26 October 2015.

68. 'Bolivian President Evo Morales signed by football club', BBC News, 19 May 2014, https://www.bbc.co.uk/news/world-latin-america-27463520

69. Caroll, R., 'Low blow Morales: Bolivian president knees football opponent in groin', *Guardian*, 5 October 2010.

70. The controversy is covered in Orihuela, R., 'Why FIFA's altitude ban is the height of stupidity', *Guardian*, 12 June 2007, https://www.theguardian.com/football/2007/jun/12/sport.comment; Reiche, D., 'Sport as a tool for deflecting political problems: Bolivia's President Morales' successful campaign against FIFA's ban on high-altitude football', *Sport in Society* 18.1 (2015), pp. 28–41.

71. Cited in Chakraboty, D., 'Bolivian Heights', http://www.goaldentimes.org/bolivian-heights/

72. Quoted in 'Maradona backs Morales on altitude', Al Jazeera, 18 May 2008, https://www.aljazeera.com/sport/2008/03/2008525185716688974.html

73. Quoted in Norman, G., 'No head for Heights', *When Saturday Comes*, June 2010.

74. 'Bolivia team given dose of military discipline before World Cup qualifier', *Guardian*, 3 October 2015, https://www.theguardian.com/football/2015/oct/03/bolivia-team-military-discipline-world-cup

75. El Tano Pasman, with English subtitles, can be seen here https://www.youtube.com/watch?v=XF30ZZ4Ahek. The World Cup couple, also with subtitles, can be seen here, https://www.youtube.com/watch?v=vUIGH-m8Lo8

76. Borges, J., and Bioy Casares, A., *Cronicas de Bustos Domecq*, Losada, Buenos Aires.

77. This body of work is well covered in Scher, A., *Contar el juego: literatura y deporte en la Argentina* (2014), and *Deportivo Saer: cuentos de deporte y literatura* (2016).

78. Bar-On, T., and De Gaetano, A.M., 'Fútbol para todos (soccer for all): democratization, populist legitimization or quasi-authoritarianism?' *International Journal of the History of Sport* 34.11 (2017), pp. 1061–87.

79. For the details of these transactions, including the account of Horacio Gennari's meeting with Grondona below, see Goldblatt, D., 'Could a row over football television rights bring down the Argentinian government?' *Prospect*, 19 July 2017.

80. Richards, J., 'Double Trouble', *Blizzard*, Issue 0.

81. Alabarces, P., *Football Fans and the Argentine Crisis of 2001–2002: The Crisis, the World Cup, and the Destiny of the Patria*, Greenwood (2011).

82. Franklin, J., 'He was sent from above,' *Guardian*, 12 November 2008, https://www.theguardian.com/football/2008/nov/12/diego-maradona-argentina; Selhi, M., 'Church of Maradona: Worshipping a (Former) Demi-God With Unusual Athletic Abilities', http://www.thebubble.com/

church-of-maradona-worshipping-a-former-demi-god-with-unusual-athletic-abilities/

83. Instead, Teixeira appointed himself as the chair, his daughter Joana Havelange to the number two spot, and added his lawyer, his press secretary, his personal secretary and factotum, and the man who had advised him during the 2001 Congressional investigation into football. He then garlanded the team with Carlos Langoni, a right-wing economist who had served as the president of the Bank of Brazil in the last days of the military dictatorship.

84. See inter alia, Manfred, T., 'Brazil's $3 Billion World Cup Stadiums Are Turning Into White Elephants 6 Months Later', https://www.businessinsider.com/brazil-world-cup-stadium-white-elephants-2015-1

85. 'Mineirão foi usado em esquema para repassar R$ 30 milhões a Pimentel, diz Joesley Batista em delação', Minas Gerais, 23 May 2017, https://g1.globo.com/minas-gerais/noticia/mineirao-foi-usado-em-esquema-para-repassar-r-30-milhoes-a-pimentel-diz-joesley-batista-em-delacao.ghtml

86. Readers can see the state of things for themselves at Dwyer, C., 'Maracanã, Jewel Of Rio's Olympics, Now Languishes In Disrepair', https://www.npr.org/sections/thetwo-way/2017/01/12/509465686/maracan-jewel-of-rios-olympics-now-languishes-in-disrepair

87. The poor state of Brazilian football attendance is explored in Moriera, B., 'The drama of Brazilian stadiums: a country without football fans', http://especiais.correiobraziliense.com.br/world-attendance-figures-football

88. The looks of disbelief amongst those present when the penny drops are worth viewing here: https://www.youtube.com/watch?time_continue=6&v=DtmBUv1lVls

89. The politics of this are covered at 'FIFA puts troubled Argentine FA under administration', Reuters, 24 June 2016, https://www.reuters.com/article/us-soccer-argentina-fifa/fifa-puts-troubled-argentine-fa-under-administration-IDUSKCN0ZA3NP

90. Macri's football and political careers are explored in Mattina, G., 'Popularity Leaders and the Changes in Political Representation: The Cases of Mauricio Macri and Luis Juez María Victoria López (UBA-Conicet)'; Kuper, S., 'The ultimate political goal', Financial Times, 20 November 2015.

91. 'AFA Boss "Chiqui" Tapia Consolidates Power with Conembol VP Seat', Perfil (Sabado), 12 May 2018, https://www.pressreader.com/argentina/perfil-sabado/20180512/284116386976300

92. For an overview in English of Futbol Para Todos see Duek, C., and Alabarces, P., 'Football for Everyone? Soccer, Television, and Politics in Argentina', Sport, Public Broadcasting, and Cultural Citizenship. Routledge (2013), pp. 112–25.

93. 'Macri's coffin and insulting songs MMSOB, the latest fad in Argentine football stadiums', 5 March 2018, http://en.mercopress.com/2018/03/05/macri-s-coffin-and-insulting-songs-mmsob-the-latest-fad-in-argentine-football-stadiums

94. Hughes, Rob, 'Soccer Capitulates to Terrorists as Copa America Is Put on Hold', *New York Times*, 4 July 2001; Lea, G., 'The Copa América of 2001 was an eventful tournament like few others in history', 11 October 2016, https://thesefootballtimes.co/2016/11/10/the-copa-america-of-2001-was-an-eventful-tournament-like-few-in-history/; 'Gold and Goals', *The Economist*, 25 July 2001.

95. Pachicho, E., 'Financial Head of Colombia "Soccer Cartel" Arrested', 28 April 2011, https://www.insightcrime.org/news/analysis/financial-head-of-colombia-soccer-cartel-arrested/

96. 'Colombia vows to eradicate drugs money from football', BBC News, 10 December 2010, https://www.bbc.co.uk/news/world-latin-america-11894601; 'Red card: A better country off the pitch is worse on it', *The Economist*, 19 May 2011.

97. Worswick, C., Lavigne, P., 'US Treasury clears America de Cali', 4 April 2013, http://www.espn.com/soccer/news/story/_/id/1397914/u.s.-clears-america-de-cali-from-%27clinton-list%27

98. 'Colombian Soccer Team Tries to Break from Narco Past', 26 September 2012, https://www.insightcrime.org/news/brief/millionarios-titles-colombia-soccer-crime/

99. Lohmuller, M., 'Eight Colombia Soccer Teams Suspected of Ties to Drug Traffickers', 8 June 2015, https://www.insightcrime.org/news/brief/eight-colombia-soccer-teams-suspected-ties-drug-traffickers/

100. 'Colombia Farc: The Norwegian who helped broker peace', BBC News, 26 August 2016, https://www.bbc.com/news/world-latin-america-37206714

101. 'Colombia Farc rebels to play Valderrama peace match', BBC News, 1 December 2013, https://www.bbc.co.uk/news/world-latin-america-25171390

102. AFP, 'Maradona juega "Partido por la Paz" de Colombia junto a Asprilla y Rincón', 10 April 2015, http://www.la-razon.com/marcas/Maradona-Partido-Colombia-Asprilla-Rincon_0_2250375091.html

103. Gendelman, D., 'The Rebirth of Colombia', *Paris Review*, 15 May 2014, https://www.theparisreview.org/blog/2014/05/15/the-rebirth-of-colombia/; Mackenna, E., 'Narco-Football Is Dead: Celebrating a Colombia Reborn', 2 June 2016, https://bleacherreport.com/articles/2642116-narco-football-is-dead-celebrating-a-colombia-reborn; Pizano, P., 'Colombia: Learning To Love Soccer Again', 24 June 2016, https://www.huffingtonpost.com/pedro-pizano/colombia-learning-to-love_b_10627114.html

104. Hunger, A., 'Colombia use fervent following to inflict comfortable defeat on Greece', *Guardian*, 14 June 2014, https://www.theguardian.com/football/2014/jun/14/world-cup-2014-colombia-greece-match-group-c-report

105. Alarcon, D., 'Colombia Forecast: A Day of World Cup Unity, Followed By an "Apocalyptic" Election', *New Republic*, 12 June 2014, https://newrepublic.com/article/118115/colombias-wild-weekend-world-cup-kickoff-and-presidential-election

106. 'World Cup: Euphoria grips soccer-mad Colombia ahead of Brazil clash', 4 July 2014, https://www.firstpost.com/sports/world-cup-euphoria-grips-soccer-mad-colombia-ahead-brazil-clash-1601243.html

107. 'Colombia coach Jose Pekerman gets over 400,000 votes in PRESIDENTIAL ELECTION after World Cup win', https://www.mirror.co.uk/sport/football/world-cup-2014/colombia-coach-jose-pekerman-gets-3710474

108. Alsema, A., 'Colombia gives soccer squad overwhelming welcome in Bogota', 6 July 2014, https://colombiareports.com/tens-thousand-welcome-colombias-soccer-team-home/

109. Torres, F., 'Football and war intertwine in Colombia', *Marca*, 18 February 2017, http://www.marca.com/en/football/international-football/2017/02/18/58a8a567e2704ea2488b4620.html; Iriarte, R., 'When Football Transcends Factions', https://worksthatwork.com/9/the-reconciliation-match

110. On Tabarez's work at home see Lee, S., 'Inside Tabarez's youth system that ensures tiny Uruguay will keep punching above their weight', https://www.goal.com/en-us/news/inside-tabarezs-youth-system-that-ensures-tiny-uruguay-will-keep-/10hrmw8fr3pow1p7gfsqu472s0

111. Some of them got to watch the football at the Estadio Nacional. In a grotesque tableau, Chile lined up for a World Cup qualifying match against the Soviet Union, except the Soviets had long refused to play such a game in such a place under such conditions. FIFA, it is worth recalling, had no problem at all with the game going ahead. While gaunt prisoners and gun-wielding guards watched blankly from the stands, the Chileans scored an open goal.

112. Worswick, C., 'The Caravan of Death', *Blizzard*, Issue 18; Waldenstein, D., 'In Chile's National Stadium, Dark Past Shadows Copa America Matches', *New York Times*, 17 June 2015.

113. Bielsa's time in Chile is well covered in Hunt, R., 'The Bespectacled Mutineer', *Blizzard*, Issue 25; Dorrington, N., 'Chile's transformation has had many authors over the years, but none as important as Marcelo Bielsa', *Independent*, 12 June 2017, https://www.independent.co.uk/sport/football/international/chile-marcelo-bielsa-manager-transformation-many-authors-important-as-a7786466.html

114. Franklin, J., 'World Cup 2010: Chile salutes its new kids on the block', *Guardian*, 30 June 2010, https://www.theguardian.com/football/blog/2010/jun/30/world-cup-2010-letter-from-chile

115. 'Chile: Bielsa and Piñera, When Football Meets Politics', 2 July 2010, https://globalvoices.org/2010/07/02/chile-bielsa-and-pinera-when-football-meets-politics/. The handshake in question can be seen here https://www.youtube.com/watch?v=AegtAdyoe6g

116. Colo Colo's role in Pinera's political career is covered in Cotterill, S., 'Electoral Role in Chile', *When Saturday Comes*, May 2010.

117. Cited in Dorrington (2017).

118. Kozak, P., 'Santiago prepares to come alive again as Jorge Sampaoli makes Chile believe', *Guardian*, 27 June 2014, https://www.theguardian.com/football/2014/jun/27/santiago-jorge-sampaoli-chile-world-cup; Elsey, B., 'A Team to Charm Even the Chilean Left', *New Republic*, 23 June 2014, https://newrepublic.com/article/118321/2014-world-cup-jorge-sampaoli-and-chile-change-minds-home; Thompson, W., 'Chile's new generation evident on pitch', 19 June 2014, http://www.espn.co.uk/football/blog/wright-thompson/94/post/1892634/wright-thompson-chiles-new-generation-carries-over-to-pitch

119. Young, J., 'The connection between Copa América and its hosts remains one of the tournament's unique charms', 2 July 2015, https://fusion.tv/story/160626/2015-copa-america-chile-atmosphere-protests-and-history/; Hawkins, M., 'Copa América 2015: A Final of Political Intrigue and Historical Merit', 4 July 2015, http://futebolcidade.com/copa-america-2015-a-final-of-political-intrigue-and-historical-merit/; Medina Uribe, P., 'Chile's Copa América – Can Football Still be Political?', 5 July 2015, https://africasacountry.com/2015/07/chiles-copa-america-can-football-still-be-political/; Wilson, J., 'The 99-year wait', *Blizzard*, Issue 18. Chile would retain the title the following year when a centennial version of the tournament was held in the United States.

120. Serrano, A., 'Student protests rock Chile ahead of soccer tournament', Al Jazeera, 10 June 2015, http://america.aljazeera.com/articles/2015/6/10/student-protests-rock-chile-ahead-of-continental-soccer-tournament.html; Staunton, P., and Alegria Torres, A., 'Teachers protest at Chile training ground ahead of Copa America opener', http://www.goal.com/en-gb/news/3710/copa-america/2015/06/09/12574292/teachers-protest-at-chile-training-ground-ahead-of-copa; Hodges-Ramon, L., 'Copa América – Students Protest Education Inequality', 13 June 2015, http://futebolcidade.com/copa-america-students-protest-education-inequality/

121. 'Arturo Vidal crash: Juventus and Chile midfielder "under the influence of alcohol" after crashing his Ferrari, say police', *Independent*, 17 June 2015, https://www.independent.co.uk/sport/football/international/arturo-

vidal-crash-arsenal-and-real-madrid-transfer-target-involved-in-ferrari-accident-while-under-10324979.html

122. http://www.coha.org/chile-an-adolescent-democracy-heads-to-the-polls/
123. Quoted in Edwards, D., 'Boca vs River is the Copa Libertadores final Argentina has craved – but will the country cope with the carnage?', *Independent*, 9 November 2018, https://www.independent.co.uk/sport/football/international/boca-vs-river-copa-libertadores-2018-final-juniors-plate-preview-prediction-watch-video-a8625831.html

Chapter 4

1. 'Theses on the Philosophy of History' in Benjamin, W., *Illuminations: Essays and Reflections*, Doubleday (2012).
2. AFP, 'German football team spends night at Stade de France after Paris attacks', *Guardian*, 14 November 2015.
3. Dearden, L., 'Belgian police arrest 12 terror suspects for "plotting imminent attacks during Euro 2016 match against Ireland"', *Independent*, 18 June 2016; 'Ukraine convicts Frenchman over Euro 2016 attack plot', http://www.france24.com/en/20180522-ukraine-terrorism-convicts-frenchman-over-euro-2016-football-france-attack-plot
4. Brown, G., 'Gordon Brown says "We need to lead Europe, not leave it – just ask Leicester City"', *Daily Mirror*, 10 May 2016, https://www.mirror.co.uk/news/uk-news/gordon-brown-says-we-need-7940337
5. Schuman, R., and Barnier, M., *Pour l'Europe*, Nagel (1963).
6. European Commission, *European Identity: Symbols to Sport* (1987), http://aei.pitt.edu/10610/1/10610.pdf
7. Szymanski, S., 'Fair Is Foul: A Critical Analysis of UEFA Financial Fair Play', *International Journal of Sport Finance* 9.3 (2014), pp. 218–229; Sass, M., 'Glory hunters, sugar daddies, and long-term competitive balance under UEFA Financial Fair Play', *Journal of Sports Economics* 17.2 (2016), pp. 148–58.
8. *The Book Sector in Europe: Facts and Figures*, Federation of European Publishers (2017), http://www.impalamusic.org/node/9; IFPI, *Global Music Industry Report 2017*, http://www.ifpi.org/downloads/GMR2017.pdf
9. Paramio, J.L., Buraimo, B., and Campos, C., 'From modern to postmodern: the development of football stadia in Europe', *Sport in Society* 11.5 (2008), pp. 517–34.
10. 'UEFA Elite Club Injury Study Report 2015/16', http://www.uefa.com/MultimediaFiles/Download/uefaorg/Medical/02/40/27/65/2402765_DOWNLOAD.pdf UEFA Elite Club Injury Study Report 2015/16
11. Maennig, W., *The feel-good effect at mega sport events: Recommendations*

for public and private administration informed by the experience of the FIFA World Cup 2006. No. 18, Hamburg contemporary economic discussions (2008); Schreiber, M., and Adang, O., 'Fiction, facts and a summer's fairy tale – mixed messages at the World Cup 2006', *Policing & Society* 20.2 (2010), pp. 237–55.

12. Lukaku, R., 'I've Got Some Things to Say', https://www.theplayerstribune. com/en-us/articles/romelu-lukaku-ive-got-some-things-to-say

13. See this extraordinary video of Bulgarian celebrations, and the homecoming parade for the team in Sofia: https://www.youtube.com/ watch?v=2omstWOly1I

14. Quoted in Alexandu, A., 'The Slow Death of Romanian Football', https://thesefootballtimes.co/2016/06/21/the-slow-death-of-romanian-football/

15. Gazdov, N., 'Bulgarian Footbolitics', *Vagabond*, 1 January 2009, https:// www.vagabond.bg/forum/politics/item/306-bulgarian-footbolitics.html; CSKA Sofia Live, 'The Long and Sad Demise of CSKA Sofia', futbolgrad. com, 1 April 2016, http://futbolgrad.com/long-sad-demise-cska-sofia/

16. The cable written by US diplomat Susan Sutton on Bulgarian football, 'Bulgarian football receives red card for corruption', makes for terrific reading on the question of ownership and match-fixing: see https:// wikileaks.org/plusd/cables/10SOFIA32_a.html

17. OCCRP, 'Dead Bulgarian Football Leaders', https://www.occrp.org/en/ 43-other/tracking/353-football-dead-bulgarian-football-leaders; Wilson, J., 'The Most Dangerous Job in Football', *Guardian*, 18 May 2007.

18. Alvad, S., 'Corruption and match-fixing in Bulgarian football', http:// www.playthegame.org/news/news-articles/2008/corruption-and-match-fixing-in-bulgarian-football/

19. Cotterill, S., 'Europe's Most Dysfunctional Club', *When Saturday Comes*, April 2010; Robinson, J., 'Would the real CSKA please stand up?' *Blizzard*, Issue 23, https://www.theblizzard.co.uk/article/would-real-cska-please-stand

20. The CSKA fans' assault on the BFF office can be seen here: https:// www.youtube.com/watch?v=OenmGtk9OGY

21. 'Bulgarian Soccer Tycoon charged over Tax Fraud', Reuters, 24 May 2012, https://in.reuters.com/article/bulgaria-crime-tycoon/prosecutors-charge-bulgarian-tycoon-with-tax-evasion-idINLI22544920090818

22. 'Former Prime Minister becomes Bulgaria's oldest player', Reuters, 26 August 2013, https://uk.reuters.com/article/uk-soccer-bulgaria-borisov/ former-prime-minister-becomes-bulgarias-oldest-player-IDUKBRE97P0AU20130826

23. Quoted in Gazdov (2009).

24. 'How To Get Into the Champions League With A Few Million Quid: The Story Of Unirea Urziceni', 8 December 2014, http://theraumdeuter.com/

european-football/get-champions-league-million-quid-story-unirea-urziceni/

25. https://www.tolo.ro/2017/02/23/stan-dan-adamescu-a-fost-un-agent-sie-exportat-de-regimul-comunist-in-germania-apoi-readus-in-romania-si-improprietarit-de-statul-roman-cu-unirea-shopping-center-si-cu-astra-asigurari/

26. 'Romania: Eight Top Football Officials Jailed for Corruption', OCCRP, 6 March 2014, https://www.occrp.org/en/daily/2359-romania-eight-top-football-officials-jailed-for-corruption

27. Gillet, K., 'Book 'em: the loophole undermining Romania's anti-corruption drive', *Guardian*, 3 January 2016.

28. 'Jail sentence for former head of the Romanian Professional Football League', https://www.romania-insider.com/jail-sentence-romanian-professional-football-league/; Romania Corruption Watch, 'White Collar Hooligans: Romanian Corruption and Football', https://medium.com/romania-corruption-watch/white-collar-hooligans-romanian-corruption-and-football-ab735c6bebb0; Ernst, I., 'Ex-head of Romanian Football League jailed for seven years for corruption', https://www.intellinews.com/ex-head-of-romanian-football-league-jailed-for-seven-years-for-corruption-100571/

29. https://www.prosport.ro/fotbal-intern/liga-1/breaking-news-mircea-sandu-dragomir-frf-lpf-achitati-dosarul-dezafilierii-universitatii-craiova-decizie-ne-lasa-cuvinte-mititelu-pierdut-despagubirile-240-milioane-euro-16394864

30. Taylor, I., 'Gigi Becali: combustible, proud, and rich . . . meet Steaua Bucharest's owner', *Guardian*, 7 March 2013; Konzett, E., 'Steaua Bucharest and Romanian Club Football's Perpetual Crisis', http://balkanist.net/steau-bucharest-and-the-perpetual-crisis-of-romanian-club-football/

31. Rosu, E., 'Where the team has no name: the fight over Steaua Bucharest's identity', *Guardian*, 27 December 2014, https://www.theguardian.com/football/blog/2014/dec/27/steaua-bucharest-romania-european-cup; Montague, J., 'Owner and Army Fight for a Soccer Club's Name', *New York Times*, 4 April 2017.

32. A detailed account of the game can be read here: https://romaniaballs.wordpress.com/2018/04/15/rapid-rising/

33. On the whole gamut of Tudjman's sporting politics see Brentin, Dario, '"A lofty battle for the nation": the social roles of sport in Tudjman's Croatia', *Sport in Society* 16.8 (2013), pp. 993–1008.

34. Brentin, D., 'The Nation's Most Holy Institution: football and the construction of Croatian national identity', *Open Democracy*, 1 July 2013, https://www.opendemocracy.net/dario-brentin/nations-most-holy-institution-football-and-construction-of-croatian-national-identity

35. Sindbæk, Tea, '"A Croatian champion with a Croatian name": national

identity and uses of history in Croatian football culture – the case of Dinamo Zagreb', *Sport in Society* 16.8 (2013), pp. 1009–24.

36. Wilson, J., 'Another rant in the life of Mamić', *Guardian*, 3 October 2007, https://www.theguardian.com/football/2007/oct/03/europeanfootball.sport

37. Holiga, A., 'How Hajduk Split Supporters Started an Uprising in Croatian Football', https://bleacherreport.com/articles/2280834-how-hajduk-split-supporters-started-an-uprising-in-croatian-football

38. Brentin, D., 'The Democratic "Hooligan"? Radical Democracy and Social Protest Amongst Football Fans in Croatia', *Balkanist*, 14 December 2014, http://balkanist.net/democratic-hooligan-radical-democracy-social-protest-amongst-football-fans-croatia/

39. Strickland, P., 'Croatia's anti-fascist football club battles far right', https://www.aljazeera.com/news/2018/03/croatia-anti-fascist-football-club-battles-180320183135441.html

40. Brentin, D., 'Ready for the homeland? Ritual, remembrance, and political extremism in Croatian football', *Nationalities Papers* 44.6 (2016), pp. 860–76.

41. Holiga, A., 'Croatia fans' act of terrorism in Italy was a planned cry for attention', *Guardian*, 17 November 2015, https://www.theguardian.com/football/blog/2014/nov/17/croatia-fans-terrorism-italy-planned-cry-attention

42. Holiga, A., 'Croatia's footballers may become biggest losers in swastika fallout', *Guardian*, 17 June 2015, https://www.theguardian.com/football/blog/2015/jun/17/modric-rakitic-mandzukic-swastika-croatian-football-federation

43. Holiga, A., 'Transfers, bungled testimony and old friendships – how Luka Modric became Croatia's public enemy number two', *Independent*, 14 June 2017, https://www.independent.co.uk/sport/football/european/luka-modric-real-madrid-zdravko-mamic-trial-court-case-a7790026.html; https://www.fourfourtwo.com/features/croatian-football-kingpin-zdravko-mamic-shot-assassination-attempt; 'Zdravko Mamic, Croatian football's Mr Big, given jail term', BBC News, 8 June 2018, https://www.bbc.co.uk/news/world-europe-44381167

44. Traynor, I., 'Serbian thugs are the toys of nationalist and neo-fascist leaders', *Guardian*, 13 October 2010, https://www.theguardian.com/football/blog/2010/oct/13/serbia-hooligans-italy-riot; Windelspecht, D., 'Serbia's Deadly Mix: Football, Politics and Crime', https://www.occrp.org/en/blog/6016-serbia-s-deadly-mix-football-politics-and-crime; Manalsev, A., 'Political Football: The Balkans' Belligerent Ultras Avoid Penalties', http://www.balkaninsight.com/en/article/political-football-the-balkans-belligerent-ultras-avoid-penalties; Gibson, O., 'Serbia deny racism in England U-21 game amid calls on UEFA to issue ban',

Guardian, 17 October 2012; Ames, N., 'Serbian football's eye-watering racism problem shows no sign of abating', *Observer*, 25 March 2017.

45. Montague, J., 'Ending an Albania-Serbia Game and Inciting a Riot, With a Joystick', *New York Times*, 6 October 2015. A video of the incident can be seen here: https://www.theguardian.com/football/video/2014/oct/15/serbia-albania-drone-brawl-video

46. Balkan Insight, 'Serbian Football Fans Show Support for Ratko Mladic', http://www.balkaninsight.com/en/article/soccer-clubs-line-up-to-show-mladic-support-11-27-2017

47. Ginnell, L., 'Bosnia Divided', http://roadsandkingdoms.com/2014/bosnia-divided/; Main, D., 'Bosnia's Ethnic Tensions Give Birth to New Rivalry', *World Soccer*, 21 September 2013.

48. Vulliamy, E., 'How Bosnia's pioneering footballers are succeeding where the politicians failed', *Guardian*, 5 November 2011; Dedovic, E., 'The Bosnian national football team: a case study in post-conflict institution building', https://www.opendemocracy.net/can-europe-make-it/edin-dedovic/bosnian-national-football-team-case-study-in-post-conflict-instituti; Kristjánsson, T., 'From rubble to Rio: the rise of Bosnian football', https://thesefootballtimes.co/2015/01/10/from-rubble-to-rio-the-rise-of-bosnian-football/

49. Vulliamy, E., 'How Edin Džeko United Bosnia', *Observer*, 8 June 2014.

50. Ibid.

51. In Poland's case, the depth of indifference is best gauged from the straight-faced denials issued by Wisla Krakow's management, despite obvious video evidence to the contrary, that Parma's Dino Baggio had been struck on the forehead by a knife during their UEFA Cup game in 1997. A more recent example of incompetence was Legia Warsaw fielding an ineligible player in their Champions League qualifying game against Celtic in 2014 – an error that saw UEFA turn their 6–1 two-leg victory into a defeat.

52. Wilson, J., 'Backhanders, bullets and bent refs as Polish football reaches a crisis', *Guardian*, 6 February 2007, https://www.theguardian.com/football/2007/feb/06/europeanfootball.sport1; 'Polish soccer plagued by cronyism and corruption', http://www.dw.com/en/polish-soccer-plagued-by-cronyism-and-corruption/a-15980132

53. 'A World of Ultras: Legia Warsaw', https://thesefootballtimes.co/2014/10/22/a-world-of-ultras-legia-warsaw/

54. FARE, *Never Again*, FARE (2011).

55. Belenkowski, S., 'Polish Football Fights Anti-Semitism', http://www.worldsoccer.com/blogs/polish-football-fights-anti-semitism-329946

56. 'Responding to racism during EURO 2012', http://theredcard.ie/2012/06/29/responding-to-racism-during-euro-2012/

57. See the photos of the 2015 gathering at https://followmyfreedom.

wordpress.com/2015/01/11/7th-patriotic-pilgrimage-for-polish-fans-10-01-15/; Davies, C., 'Faith, flag and football: how the Polish game developed a white supremacist fringe', *New Statesman*, 6 March 2017.

58. 'Poland Independence Day march turns violent', BBC News, https://www.bbc.co.uk/news/world-europe-20286409; Taylor, M., ' "White Europe": 60,000 nationalists march on Poland's independence day', *Guardian*, 12 November 2017.

59. Masters, J., 'Polish prosecutor: "Auschwitz" football chants are not anti-semitic', https://edition.cnn.com/2014/01/15/sport/football/poland-football-anti-semitism/index.html

60. Orynski, T., 'Fighting anti-semitism with surrealism', https://orynski.eu/fighting-antisemitsm-with-surrealism/

61. A video of the banner being unveiled can be seen here (best to mute the volume though): https://www.youtube.com/watch?v=dM-3GHN1HAs

62. A whole gallimaufry of racism and Islamophobia in Polish football grounds in the autumn of 2015 can be seen and heard here (with subtitles): https://www.youtube.com/watch?v=MCZWvxuqwG4

63. 'Czech football fans hang up Islamophobic banner during match, team later apologizes', http://www.romea.cz/en/news/czech/czech-football-fans-hang-up-islamophobic-banner-during-match-team-later-apologizes

64. 'Hungary: Football hooligans assault and injure refugees at Budapest train station', http://www.romea.cz/en/news/world/hungary-football-hooligans-assault-and-injure-refugees-at-budapest-train-station

65. 'Sparta Prague fans skip match to protest against migrant donations', https://www.eurosport.com/football/europa-league/2015-2016/sparta-prague-fans-skip-match-to-protest-against-migrant-donations_sto4933702/story.shtml

66. 'Robert Lewandowski w ogniu krytyki KRYSTYNY PAWŁOWICZ. "Czy da z siebie tyle, ile . . ." TA sugestia nas ROZWALIŁA', http://www.plotek.pl/plotek/1,153344,20231765,krystyna-pawlowicz-komentuje-gre-roberta-lewandowskiego.html

67. The photo accompanying the post can be seen here: 'A Hungarian mayor makes a show of "migrant-hunting" ', http://observers.france24.com/en/20160802-hungary-mayor-migrant-hunting-asotthalom

68. Orbán's early career in football is well covered in Nolan, D., 'Orbàn Planning', *Blizzard*, Issue 14, (2014).

69. This is all admirably covered in Ligeti, M., and Mucsi, G., 'Opening the door to corruption in Hungary's sport financing', in *Transparency International, Global Corruption Report: Sport*, 2017.

70. The Fidesz mayor of Újpest has made it clear that he would like to take the team from its current Belgian owners, which would put half of the first division in the party's hands.

71. Novak, B., 'Is Felcsut Mayor Lorinc Meszaros Viktor Orbán's straw man?', 17 November 2013, https://budapestbeacon.com/is-felcsut-mayor-lorinc-meszaros-viktor-orbans-straw-man/

72. Quoted in Goldblatt, D., and Nolan, D., 'Viktor Orbán's Reckless Football Obsession', *Guardian*, 11 January 2018, https://www.theguardian.com/news/2018/jan/11/viktor-orban-hungary-prime-minister-reckless-football-obsession

73. The Nordic sports model is dealt with in more detail in Andersson, T., and Carlsson, B., 'Football in Scandinavia: a fusion of welfare policy and the market', *Soccer & Society* 10.3–4 (2009). Its variations are covered on pp. 299–304 of Gammelsæter, H., Storm, R. and Söderman, S., 'Diverging Scandinavian approaches to professional football', *The Organization and Governance of Top Football Across Europe. An Institutional Perspective*, Routledge, NY (2011), p. 77; Gammelsæter, H., 'The organization of professional football in Scandinavia', *Soccer & Society* 10.3–4 (2009), pp. 305–23.

74. On the origins and legacy of the *rooligans* see Peitersen, B., 'Supporter culture in Denmark: the legacy of the 'World's Best Supporters''', *Soccer & Society* 10.3–4 (2009), pp. 374–85.

75. On Scandinavia's love-in with foreign football, especially English football, see: Hognestad, H., 'Long-distance football support and liminal identities among Norwegian fans', *Sport, dance and embodied identities* (2003), pp. 97–114; Hognestad, H. K., 'Transnational passions: a statistical study of Norwegian football supporters', *Soccer & Society* 7.4 (2006), pp. 439–62; Nash, R., 'Globalized football fandom: Scandinavian Liverpool FC supporters', *Football Studies* 3.2 (2000), pp. 5–23; Armstrong, G., and Hognestad, H., 'Hitting the bar: Alcohol, football identities and global flows in Norway', *European Studies* (2006), p. 85; Hognestad, H., 'Transglobal Scandinavian? Globalization and the contestation of identities in football', *Soccer & Society* 10.3–4 (2009), pp. 358–73.

76. Denmark's programme of commercialization is covered in: Storm, R. K., 'Winners and losers in Danish football: commercialization and developments in European and Danish first-tier clubs', *Soccer & Society* 12.6 (2011), pp. 737–53; Storm, R. K., 'The rational emotions of FC København: a lesson on generating profit in professional soccer', *Soccer & Society* 10.3–4 (2009), pp. 459–76.

77. Norway's pattern of commercialization is covered in Tuastad, S., 'The Scandinavian sport model: myths and realities. Norwegian football as a case study', *Soccer & Society* (2017), pp. 1–19.

78. 'Man handed suspended sentence in Danish match-fixing case', Reuters, 5 May 2015, https://uk.reuters.com/article/uk-soccer-denmark-matchfixing/man-handed-suspended-sentence-in-danish-match-

fixing-case-IDUKKBN0NQ1NS20150505; 'Three players jailed for match-fixing in Norway', Reuters, 29 April 2015, https://uk.reuters.com/article/uk-soccer-norway-matchfixing/three-players-jailed-for-match-fixing-in-norway-IDUKKBN0NK1PT20150429

79. On the recent growth of Finnish football, see Itkonen, H., and Arto, N., 'A popular game in Father Christmas Land? Football in Finland', *Soccer & Society* 13.4 (2012), pp. 570–83. On its vulnerability to scams, see Peurala, J., 'Match-manipulation in football – the challenges faced in Finland', *International Sports Law Journal* 13.3–4 (2013), pp. 268–86.

80. Associated Press, 'Trial of 10 men accused of rigging football matches begins in Finland', *Guardian*, 9 June 2011, https://www.theguardian.com/football/2011/jun/09/match-fixing-trial-finland-football

81. Andersson, T., and Carlsson, B., 'A diagnosis of the commercial immaturity of Swedish club football', *Soccer & Society* 12.6 (2011), pp. 754–73.

82. Andersson, T., 'Immigrant teams in Sweden and the case of Assyriska FF', *Soccer & Society* 10.3–4 (2009), pp. 398–417; Stokes, D., 'Dalkurd FF: The football club that's also a "country" for the Kurdish diaspora', 28 October 2017, https://edition.cnn.com/2017/10/24/football/dalkurd-kurdish-football-team-in-sweden/index.html

83. See Eivind, Å., 'Biggest but smallest: female football and the case of Norway', *Soccer & Society* 9.4 (2008), pp. 520–31.

84. Nelson, F., 'Turning rejects into champions – the miracle of Östersund FC, *Spectator*, 27 October 2017, https://blogs.spectator.co.uk/2017/10/the-miracle-of-ostersund/; Nelson, F., 'The secret of Östersund, the tiny Swedish team who beat Arsenal', *Spectator*, 23 February 2018, https://blogs.spectator.co.uk/2018/02/the-secret-of-ostersund-the-tiny-swedish-team-who-beat-arsenal/

85. See Clapham, A., 'A day inside Benfica's academy, the production line for European football', *Guardian*, 11 January 2018; Clapham, A., 'Inside the Sporting Lisbon academy, where Ballon d'Or winners are made', *Guardian*, 16 February 2018; Fieldsend, D., *The European Game: The Secrets of European Football Success* (2017); Panja, T., Lima, J., and Almeida, H., 'Soccer Factory That Made Ronaldo Tries to Find Another Ronaldo', Bloomberg, 30 June 2017, https://www.bloomberg.com/news/features/2017-06-30/soccer-factory-portugal-searches-for-another-cristiano-ronaldo

86. Darby, P., 'African football labour migration to Portugal: Colonial and neo-colonial resource', *Soccer & Society* 8.4 (2007). Club economics is surveyed in Barros, C. P., 'Portuguese football', *Journal of Sports Economics* 7.1 (2006), pp. 96–104.

87. These questions are well explored in Nuno Coelho, J., and Tiesler, N. C., 'The paradox of the Portuguese game: The omnipresence of football and

the absence of spectators at matches', *Soccer & Society* 8.4 (2007), pp. 578–600.

88. Khalip, A., 'Benfica club president named suspect in corruption probe', Reuters, 31 January 2018, https://uk.reuters.com/article/uk-portugal-benfica-corruption/benfica-club-president-named-suspect-in-corruption-probe-IDUKKBN1FK2B0; Wright, C., 'Porto Director Claims Benfica Executives Spent €150,000 On "Tribal Witchcraft" To Win Champions League Match', 28 June 2017, http://www.whoateallthepies.tv/international_football/258172/porto-director-claims-benfica-executives-spent-e150000-on-tribal-witchcraft-to-win-champions-league-match.html. In Portuguese see http://www.record.pt/futebol/futebol-nacional/liga-nos/fc-porto/detalhe/francisco-j-marques-benfica-monitoriza-as-sms-de-fernando-gomes

89. OCCRP, 'Portugal: Authorities Dismantle Russian Football Money Laundering Ring', 5 May 2016, https://www.occrp.org/en/daily/5198-portugal-authorities-dismantle-russian-football-money-laundering-ring

90. Quoted in Ames, P., 'Portuguese football's parable of populism', 22 June 2018, https://www.politico.eu/article/sporting-lisbon-bruno-de-carvalho-portugal-football-cautionary-populist-parable/; see also Aarons, E., 'Sporting meltdown casts shadow over Portugal's World Cup build-up', *Guardian*, 14 June 2018, https://www.theguardian.com/football/2018/jun/14/sporting-lisbon-meltdown-portugal-world-cup

91. Cruyff was speaking to the Spanish newspaper *El Periodico*, cited in BBC Sport, 'World Cup 2010: Dutch tactics upset Johan Cruyff', 12 July 2010, http://news.bbc.co.uk/sport1/hi/football/world_cup_2010/8812484.stm

92. The takeover at Ajax, and the debates around it, are well covered in Born, E., 'The Velvet Revolution', *Blizzard*, Issue 14.

93. Lechner, F. J., 'Imagined communities in the global game: Soccer and the development of Dutch national identity', *Global networks* 7.2 (2007), pp. 215–29; van Sterkenburg, J., 'National bonding and meanings given to race and ethnicity: watching the football World Cup on Dutch TV', *Soccer & Society* 14.3 (2013), pp. 386–403.

94. Kassimeris, Christos, 'Football and Prejudice in Belgium and the Netherlands, *Sport in Society* 12.10 (2009), pp. 1327–35.

95. 'The aftermath of a football tragedy', *The Economist*, 10 January 2013.

96. On the character and course of Dutch hooliganism see Spaaij, R., 'Football hooliganism in the Netherlands: Patterns of continuity and change', *Soccer & Society* 8.2–3 (2007), pp. 316–34; Spaaij, R., 'Men like us, boys like them: Violence, masculinity, and collective identity in football hooliganism', *Journal of Sport and Social Issues* 32.4 (2008), pp. 369–92.

97. McVitie, P., 'Death threats, racism and hangings – Dutch football has embarrassed itself enough already in 2016', 16 February 2016, http://

www.benefoot.net/dutch-football-has-embarrassed-itself-enough-already-in-2016/

98. FARE, 'Dutch team selfie sparks racism and new debate over "Black Pete"', 17 November 2014, http://farenet.org/news/dutch-team-selfie-speaks-racism-new-debate-black-pete/

99. As one ex-professional, coaching a predominantly black youth team in Belgium, put it, 'Everywhere they go they face racism, it's the black team playing against the white team.' Quoted in Kunti, S., 'Ex-player Paul Beloy says racism is still an issue in Belgium', BBC Sport, 26 December 2016, https://www.bbc.co.uk/sport/football/38365293

100. Amongst the best of the pieces on the rise of the Red Devils and their meanings are: Martiniello, M., and Boucher, G.W., 'The colours of Belgium: Red Devils and the representation of diversity', Visual Studies 32.3 (2017), pp. 224–35; Knight, S., 'The Rise of the Red Devils', Grantland; Mudde, C., 'Can soccer unite the Belgians?' Washington Post, 16 June 2014.

101. See AP, 'Marc Wilmots' Belgium uniting a nation under threat', Observer, 28 June 2014, https://www.theguardian.com/football/2014/jun/28/world-cup-2014-marc-wilmots-belgium-nation-threat-usa

102. Cendrowicz, L., 'Belgium's citizens put differences aside to cheer on World Cup team', Guardian, 5 July 2015, https://www.theguardian.com/world/2014/jul/05/belgium-world-cup-team-fans-unite

103. McCall, C., 'Poll: More than a third of Scots want England to lose every game', Scotsman, 14 June 2018.

104. 'Bertie's vision well and truly bowled out', Irish Times, 3 March 2010.

105. McDonald, H., 'Kevin McDaid's killing took us back to the dark ages, priest tells mourners', Guardian, 1 June 2009.

106. Conn, D., 'Memories of Belfast Celtic reawakened as IFA tries to soothe old wounds', Guardian, 23 February 2011.

107. Hassan, D., 'A people apart: Soccer, identity and Irish nationalists in Northern Ireland', Soccer & Society, 3(3), 65–83, p. 79.

108. Booth, D., 'The most supported football team in Wales has been revealed, and it's not Swansea City or Cardiff City', https://www.walesonline.co.uk/sport/football/football-news/most-supported-football-team-wales-12862174

109. O'Toole, F., https://www.irishtimes.com/news/the-croker-conversion-1.1194801

110. Ibid.

111. Bleakney, J., and Darby, P., 'The pride of east Belfast: Glentoran Football Club and the (re) production of Ulster unionist identities in Northern Ireland', International Review for the Sociology of Sport (2017), pp. 687–703; Hassan, D., and Murray, C., 'The Good Friday dis-agreement: Sport and contested identities in Northern Ireland since 1998', Sport and Contested Identities, Routledge (2017), pp. 30–48;

Hassan, D., 'An opportunity for a new beginning: soccer, Irish nationalists and the construction of a new multi-sports stadium for Northern Ireland', *Soccer & Society* 7.2–3 (2006), pp. 339–52.

112. See 'Northern Ireland Fans Singing "Will Grigg's On Fire" Against Germany in Parc des Princes! 21.06.2016', https://www.youtube.com/watch?v=dyzvwBR1FmM

113. Murray, C., and Hassan, D., '"They're just not my team": the issue of player allegiances within Irish football, 2007–2012', *Soccer & Society* 19. 5–6 (2018).

114. 'Celtic Northern Ireland player McGinn admits supporting Republic', *Belfast Telegraph*, 27 May 2011.

115. 'Why Northern Ireland are on the right path to attracting a Catholic fan base', *Irish Post*, 24 June 2016; Dreenan, J., 'How peace on the streets changed the spirit in the stands for Northern Ireland', *Guardian*, 11 June 2016; Brolly, J., 'Northern Ireland is a different world and my kids know nothing of the Troubles', *Independent*, 27 June 2016, https://www.independent.ie/sport/soccer/euro-2016/euro-2016-teams/northern-ireland/joe-brolly-northern-ireland-is-a-different-world-and-my-kids-know-nothing-of-the-troubles-34836702.html; Lowrty, M., '"I know of some people who won't go into the ground, who stay on the concourse until the anthem is played"', 11 June 2016, http://www.the42.ie/northern-ireland-euro-2016-republic-of-ireland-support-2787887-Jun2016/

116. For an overview of these issues, and the anti-English dimension of Welsh sports culture, see Johnes, M., 'Anglo-Welsh football relations', *Sport and English National Identity* in a 'Disunited Kingdom' 76 (2017); Johnes, M., '"We Hate England! We Hate England" National Identity and Anti-Englishness in Welsh Soccer Fan Culture', *Soccer Review* (2008); Johnes, M., ,"Every day when I wake up I thank the Lord I'm Welsh": Sport and national identity in post-war Wales', *Sport and National Identity in the Post-War World*, Routledge (2013), pp. 59–75.

117. This proposition is usefully and entertainingly explored in 'In Wales, the Ball is Round', https://www.bbc.co.uk/programmes/b07fm3ct

118. Quoted in Rogers, G., and Rookwood, J. 'Cardiff City Football Club as a vehicle to promote Welsh national identity', *Journal of Qualitative Research in Sports Studies*, 1(1), 57–68.

119. https://www.bbc.co.uk/sport/wales/36465608

120. Morris, S., '"Do it for Wales!": eager nation's hopes rise before Euro 2016 semi-final', *Guardian*, 6 July 2018.

121. Cross, T., 'The hope doesn't kill you. Wales and Euro 2016', 1 July 2017, https://medium.com/@tristandross/the-hope-doesnt-kill-you-fefb53183738

122. Giulanotti, R., 'Celtic, Cultural Identities and the Globalization of Football: Notes from the 2003 UEFA Cup Final in Seville', *Scottish Affairs* 48.1 (2004), pp. 1–23.

123. Millward, P., 'Glasgow Rangers supporters in the city of Manchester: The degeneration of a "fan party" into a "hooligan riot"', *International Review for the Sociology of Sport* 44.4 (2009), pp. 381–98.

124. Cosgrove, S., 'The Tartan Army just Scots version of Morris Dancers', *Daily Record*, 5 May 2005.

125. Quoted in Millan, D., 'Song Sung Blue', *When Saturday Comes* 232, June 2006.

126. Lennon speaks candidly for himself on these topics in McKenna, K., 'Football: Why do People Want to Kill Neil Lennon?', *Guardian*, 17 September 2011.

127. Drysdale, N., 'End of a romantic dream for the Roman Abramovich of Gretna', *Observer*, 23 March 2008.

128. On the Barcelona game see McCourt, I., 'Ex-Hearts manager claims he was sacked for not picking owner against Barcelona', *Guardian*, 28 July 2015.

129. '11 surprising facts that show how Scottish football has changed over the last 30 years', http://www.bbc.co.uk/programmes/articles/3lSm9mmbFJ WytR6gy6tSOQK/11-surprising-facts-that-show-how-scottish-football-has-changed-over-the-last-30-years

130. Knight, S., 'Terminal Blues', *Prospect*, 18 July 2012.

131. Much of the sorry tale of Rangers is covered in Spiers, G., 'How the mighty Glasgow Rangers have fallen', *Observer*, 18 January 2015, and McDermott, J., 'Glasgow Rangers: a club in danger of losing its identity', *Financial Times*, 16 January 2015.

132. Ruthven, G., 'Soccer Fans Supply Strong Voice in Scottish Independence Debate', *New York Times*, 12 September 2014.

133. The helicopter incident can be seen at https://www.youtube.com/watch?v=QHMXgLdPulw. For a masterly dissection of Berlusconi's political project see Ginsborg, P., *Silvio Berlusconi: Television, power and patrimony*, Verso (2005).

134. It is interesting that Paul Ginsborg, an English historian, albeit now an Italian citizen, has produced by some way the best histories of post-war Italy; so too in football. This account of Italian football draws heavily on two English-language overviews of the game: Foot, J., *Calcio: A history of Italian football*, Fourth Estate (2006) and Doidge, M., *Football Italia: Italian football in an age of globalization*, Bloomsbury (2015). See also, amongst English writers on Italian football, Jones, T., *The Dark Heart of Italy*, Faber (2008), which sets football alongside the country's other social and political pathologies. For a participatory view of the ultra movement see the fabulously well observed and funny Parks, T., *A Season With Verona*, Fourth Estate (2002).

135. Foot, J., 'How Italian Football Creates Italians: The 1982 World Cup, the "Pertini Myth" and Italian National Identity', *International Journal of the History of Sport* 33.3 (2016), pp. 341–58.

136. Doyle, M., 'Why Italy fans sing the pop anthem "Seven-Nation Army" by the White Stripes', http://www.goal.com/en-gb/news/6815/hyundai/2014/06/11/4873120/why-italy-fans-sing-the-pop-anthem-seven-nation-army-by-the

137. The scooter incident can be seen here: https://www.youtube.com/watch?v=L_Nu6HKVSmk

138. Guschwan, M. C., 'La Tessera della Rivolta: Italy's failed fan identification card', *Soccer & Society* 14.2 (2013), pp. 215–29; Testa, A., 'The All-Seeing Eye of State Surveillance in the Italian Football (Soccer) Terraces: The Case Study of the Football Fan Card', *Surveillance & Society* 16.1 (2018), pp. 69–83; Testa, A., 'Normalization of the exception: Issues and controversies of the Italian counter-hooliganism legislation', *Sport in Society* 16.2 (2013), pp. 151–66.

139. Bandini, P., 'Genoa Ultras get shirty as protest forces match suspension', *Guardian*, 23 April 2013, https://www.theguardian.com/football/blog/2012/apr/23/genoa-ultras-match-suspension-serie-a

140. Hooper, J., 'Coppa Italia officials and police accused of capitulating to football hooliganism', *Observer*, 4 May 2014.

141. Cited in Agnew, P., 'Is there something rotten in the state of Italian football?', *World Soccer*, 1 February 2017.

142. Jones, T., 'Inside Italy's ultras: the dangerous fans who control the game', *Guardian*, 1 December 2016.

143. Testa, A., and Armstrong, G., 'Purity and danger: policing the Italian neo-fascist football Ultras', *Criminal Justice Studies* 23.3 (2010), pp. 219–37; Testa, A., and Armstrong, G., 'Words and actions: Italian ultras and neo-fascism', *Social Identities* 14.4 (2008), pp. 473–90.

144. Doidge, M., '"The birthplace of Italian communism": political identity and action amongst Livorno fans', *Soccer & Society* 14.2 (2013), pp. 246–61.

145. de Menezes, J., 'Lazio "Ultras" tell women to stay away from their "sacred space" inside Stadio Olimpico stadium', *Independent*, 20 August 2018, https://www.independent.co.uk/sport/football/european/lazio-fans-ultras-women-stay-away-sacred-space-stadium-stadio-olimpico-flyers-a8499496.html

146. Mauro, M., *The Balotelli generation: Issues of inclusion and belonging in Italian Football and Society*, Peter Lang (2016); Doidge, Mark, '"If you jump up and down, Balotelli dies": Racism and player abuse in Italian football', *International Review for the Sociology of Sport* 50.3 (2015), pp. 249–64.

147. Bandini, P., 'The racism aimed at Mario Balotelli and Kevin-Prince Boateng shames Italy', *Guardian*, 13 May 2013, https://www.

theguardian.com/football/blog/2013/may/13/racism-mario-balotelli-kevin-prince-boateng-italy

148. Davies, L., 'Carlo Tavecchio still set for top job in Italian football despite racist comment', *Guardian*, 29 July 2014, https://www.theguardian.com/football/blog/2014/jul/29/carlo-tavecchio-italy-racism; Marinelli, M., 'The Ugly Side Of Italian Football: Blatant, Widespread Racism', 24 May 2015, https://www.ibtimes.com/ugly-side-italian-football-blatant-widespread-racism-1935667

149. Andreff, W., 'French football: A financial crisis rooted in weak governance', *Journal of Sports Economics* 8.6 (2007), pp. 652–61; Senaux, B., and Gammelsaeter, H., 'The regulated commercialization of French football', *The Organization and Governance of Top Football Across Europe* (2011), pp. 123–37; Hare, G., *Football in France: A Cultural History*, Berg Publishers (2003); Dauncey, H., and Hare, G., *France and the 1998 World Cup: The national impact of a world sporting event*, Routledge (2014).

150. Auclair, P., 'Only in Marseille: where ultras rule and temptation is never far away', *Guardian*, 6 January 2015, https://www.theguardian.com/football/blog/2015/jan/06/marseille-ultras-rule-temptation-never-far-away

151. Shea, A., 'The last of the ultras: Paris Saint-Germain and the repression of football fans in France', 28 February 2018, https://thesefootballtimes.co/2018/02/28/the-last-of-the-ultras-psg-and-the-repression-of-football-fans-in-france/

152. Dauncey, H., and Hare, G., 'World Cup France 98: metaphors, meanings and values', *International Review for the Sociology of Sport* 35.3 (2000), pp. 331–47.

153. Gordon, D., and Parreno, P., *Zidane: a 21st-century portrait*, Artificial Eye (2006); Dauncey, H., and Morrey, D., 'Quiet contradictions of celebrity: Zinedine Zidane, image, sound, silence and fury', *International Journal of Cultural Studies* 11.3 (2008), pp. 301–20; Rowe, D., 'Stages of the global: Media, sport, racialization and the last temptation of Zinedine Zidane', *International Review for the Sociology of Sport* 45.3 (2010), pp. 355–71; Haxall, D., 'From Galáctico to Head Butt: Globalization, Immigration and the Politics of Identity in Artistic Reproductions of Zidane', *Football and the Boundaries of History*, Palgrave Macmillan (2017), pp. 31–53.

154. Dubois, L., *Soccer Empire: The World Cup and the future of France*, University of California Press (2011); Dubois, L., 'Racism and the specter of "dual nationality" in French football', *Contemporary French Civilization* 39.1 (2014), pp. 111–32; Thompson, C. S., 'From Black-Blanc-Beur to Black-Black-Black?: "L'Affaire des Quotas" and the Shattered "Image of

1998" in Twenty-First-Century France', *French Politics, Culture & Society* 33.1 (2015), pp. 101–21.

155. 'French football mired in fresh racism row', *World Soccer*, 7 November 2014, https://www.worldsoccer.com/news/french-football-mired-in-fresh-racism-row357554-357554#y3jmzeE3VhYQXOQY.99

156. Auclair, P. 'The Face of a Nation', 10 June 2016, *Eight By Eight*.

157. Llopis-Goig, R., 'The predominance of soccer in the sport and leisure habits of Spanish society', *Sport in Society* 17.6 (2014), pp. 824–41; Llopis-Goig, R., 'From "socios" to "hyper-consumers": an empirical examination of the impact of commodification on Spanish football fans', *Soccer & Society* 13.3 (2012), pp. 392–408.

158. Hamilos, P., 'Spanish wealth gap biggest in Europe, says charity', *Guardian*, 10 October 2013.

159. This is admirably covered in Lowe, S., *Fear and Loathing in La Liga: Barcelona, Real Madrid, and the World's Greatest Sports Rivalry*, Nation Books (2014).

160. 'Twenty-Two Spanish Soccer Clubs Have Entered Bankruptcy Protection', 11 June 2011, https://www.businessinsider.com/twenty-two-spanish-soccer-clubs-have-entered-bankruptcy-protection-2011-7?IR=T; Jenson, P., 'Pain in Spain: La Liga in financial turmoil', *Independent*, 20 July 2013.

161. Tremlett, G., 'EU prepares to blow final whistle on Spain's debt-ridden football clubs', *Guardian*, 21 March 2013.

162. Storere, A., 'How Málaga went from rags to riches to relegation', 18 May 2018, https://thesefootballtimes.co/2018/05/18/how-malaga-went-from-rags-to-riches-to-relegation/

163. https://www.20minutos.es/deportes/noticia/espana-bandera-polemica-243094/0/

164. Keely, G., 'Spain revels in new spirit of unity as football team heals divisions', *Observer*, 29 June 2008; De La Serna, V., 'Political fútbol', *Guardian*, 1 July 2008, https://www.theguardian.com/commentisfree/2008/jul/01/spain.euro2008; Lowe, S., 'Proud Spain almost lost for words as old jinx finally ends', *Guardian*, 30 June 2008.

165. Tremlett, G., 'World Cup 2010: Spain's success puts nationalists in the shade', *Guardian*, 11 July 2010; 'Viewpoint: Does football unite Spain?', BBC News, 13 July 2010, https://www.bbc.com/news/10610414

166. West, A., 'Spain's year: Football glory, economic gloom', BBC News, 29 December 2012, https://www.bbc.co.uk/news/world-europe-20769031

167. De La Serna, V., 'Political fútbol', *Guardian*, 1 July 2008, https://www.theguardian.com/commentisfree/2008/jul/01/spain.euro2008

168. https://www.youtube.com/watch?v=BXSz76uRAfE

169. https://www.youtube.com/watch?v=FsmvJbD30cg

170. Cited in Vaczi, M., 'Football, the Beast, and the Sovereign: The Politics of Joking Relationships in Spain', *Ethnos* (2017), pp. 1–17.

171. Honigstein, R., *Das Reboot: How German Football Reinvented Itself and Conquered the World*, Random House (2015).

172. Merkel, U., 'German football culture in the new millennium: ethnic diversity, flair and youth on and off the pitch', *Soccer & Society* 15.2 (2014), pp. 241–55.

173. Merkel, U., 'Football fans and clubs in Germany: conflicts, crises and compromises', *Soccer & Society* 13.3 (2012), pp. 359–76.

174. Daniel, P., and Kassimeris, C., 'The Politics and Culture of FC St. Pauli: from leftism, through anti-establishment, to commercialization', *Soccer & Society* 14.2 (2013), pp. 167–82; Totten, M., 'Sport activism and political praxis within the FC Sankt Pauli fan subculture', *Soccer & Society* 16.4 (2015), pp. 453–68.

175. Knight, B., 'Cult club 1. FC Union Berlin sells stadium to fans', 11 November 2011, https://www.dw.com/en/cult-club-1-fc-union-berlin-sells-stadium-to-fans/a-15524651

176. Honigstein, R., 'Are German fans really turning against the beautiful game?', *Guardian*, 7 April 2008, https://www.theguardian.com/football/2008/apr/07/europeanfootball.sport2

177. Honigstein, R., 'Ultras play with fire as Bundesliga engulfed by flares and violence', *Guardian*, 26 November 2012, https://www.theguardian.com/football/blog/2012/nov/26/bundesliga-flares-violence-safety-measures

178. Knight, B., 'Silent protests support Bundesliga fan culture', *Deutsch Welle*, 2 December 2012, https://www.dw.com/en/silent-protests-support-bundesliga-fan-culture/a-16423746

179. Hardin, J., 'Bundesliga clubs step up in refugee crisis', 3 September 2015, https://www.dw.com/en/bundesliga-clubs-step-up-in-refugee-crisis/a-18691678; Uersfeld, S., 'German clubs to wear "refugees welcome" logo, St Pauli raise questions', 16 September 2015, http://www.espn.co.uk/football/german-bundesliga/story/2615258/german-clubs-to-wear-refugees-welcome-logo; Montague, J., 'Refugees welcome . . . in Germany at least', *World Soccer*, 24 October 2015, https://www.worldsoccer.com/features/refugees-welcome-in-germany-at-least-365379; Aarons, E., 'Welcome to Football: How Borussia Dortmund help give refugees hope', *Guardian*, 5 December 2017, https://www.theguardian.com/football/2017/dec/05/borussia-dortmund-refugees-bundesliga-german-football-league; Edwards, T., 'Bayern Munich donate €1m and set up training camps for refugees in Germany', *Daily Telegraph*, 3 September 2015.

180. Oltermann, P., 'How RB Leipzig became the most hated club in German football', *Guardian*, 8 September 2016, https://www.theguardian.com/football/2016/sep/08/why-rb-leipzig-has-become-the-most-hated-club-in-german-football; Honigstein, R., 'RB Leipzig's genuine glee gives haters

something different to consider', *Guardian*, 12 September 2016, https://www.theguardian.com/football/blog/2016/sep/12/rb-leipzig-fans-borussia-dortmund-bundesliga

181. 'Modern football is rubbish – German fans make silent protest', *World Soccer*, 26 August 2015, https://www.worldsoccer.com/news/modern-football-is-rubbish-german-fans-make-silent-protest-364076#kQmye6DfsDl8mDG8.99'; Ford, M., 'Borussia Dortmund fans plan RB Leipzig protest amid increased police presence', 12 October 2017, https://www.dw.com/en/borussia-dortmund-fans-plan-rb-leipzig-protest-amid-increased-police-presence/a-40920587

182. Dynamo Dresden-Fans: Randale in Karlsruhe auf dem Weg zum Stadion, https://www.youtube.com/watch?v=gΛT5xghVo9Q

183. '"No to Monday night football": Frankfurt fans protest against Bundesliga plans', *Guardian*, 20 February 2018.

184. 'Eastern German soccer clubs struggle to stay in the game', 5 September 2010, https://www.dw.com/en/eastern-german-soccer-clubs-struggle-to-stay-in-the-game/a-5967469; Fildew, J., 'The East German curse: how footballing reunification failed', 30 March 2018, https://thesefootballtimes.co/2018/03/30/the-east-german-curse-how-footballing-reunification-failed/

185. Kern, S., 'Germany: Hooligans Declare War on Islamic Radicals', 10 November 2014, https://www.gatestoneinstitute.org/4859/germany-hooligans-salafists; 'Germany's New Right: The Unholy Alliance of Neo-Nazis and Football Hooligans', 4 November 2015, http://www.spiegel.de/international/germany/new-right-wing-alliance-of-neo-nazis-and-hooligans-appears-in-germany-a-1000953.html

186. 'Leipzig police arrest hundreds after far-right hooligans' violent rampage', 12 January 2016, https://www.dw.com/en/leipzig-police-arrest-hundreds-after-far-right-hooligans-violent-rampage/a-18974153

187. Knight, B., 'Anti-Semitic Anne Frank football stickers appear in Germany,' 31 October 2017, https://www.dw.com/en/anti-semitic-anne-frank-football-stickers-appear-in-germany/a-41188645

188. Ford, M., '"Not a neo-Nazi club": Energie Cottbus supporters battling right-wing image', 29 May 2018, https://www.dw.com/en/not-a-neo-nazi-club-energie-cottbus-supporters-battling-right-wing-image/a-43979910

189. Ford, M., 'From the stands to the streets: What does Chemnitz violence have to do with football?', 28 August 2018, https://www.dw.com/en/from-the-stands-to-the-streets-what-does-chemnitz-violence-have-to-do-with-football/a-45258812

190. Martin, M., 'Ozil quits German national side citing racism over Turkish heritage', *Reuters*, 22 July 2018, https://www.reuters.com/article/

us-soccer-germany-turkey/soccer-ozil-quits-german-national-side-citing-racism-over-turkish-heritage-IDUSKBN1KC0UQ

191. Cleland, J., and Cashmore, E., 'Football fans' views of racism in British football', *International Review for the Sociology of Sport* 51.1 (2016), pp. 27–43.

192. Buxton, R., 'Malky Mackay: The "sexist, racist, homophobic" texts which cost him the Crystal Palace job', https://metro.co.uk/2014/08/21/malky-mackay-the-sexist-racist-homophobic-texts-which-cost-him-the-crystal-palace-job-4841142/?ito=cbshare

193. Taylor, D., 'Eni Aluko accuses England manager Mark Sampson of "racist" Ebola remark', *Guardian*, 21 August 2018; Steinberg, J., 'Eni Aluko accuses FA of actions "bordering on blackmail" as Glenn and co. grilled – as it happened', *Guardian*, 18 October 2017.

194. Kelner, M., 'How a day of drama unfolded for the FA at Westminster', *Guardian*, 19 October 2017.

195. https://www.instagram.com/sterling7/p/BrKYvF3gH9e/

196. Gayle, D., 'Anti-fascists block route of Democratic Football Lads Alliance London march', *Guardian*, 13 October 2018.

197. Hills, D., 'Neil Warnock on Brexit: "I can't wait to leave. To hell with the rest of the world"', *Observer*, 13 January 2019; Nakrani, S., '"Do your duty": Boreham Wood FC demand MPs sort out Brexit', *Guardian*, 15 January 2019.

198. https://www.bbc.com/sport/football/47041871, transcript https://www.indy100.com/article/brexit-jurgen-klopp-liverpool-bbc-news-interview-watch-video-8754651

199. Aarons, E., 'Richard Scudamore will accept £5m departure bonus from Premier League', Guardian, 15 November 2018, https://www.theguardian.com/football/2018/nov/15/premier-league-5m-richard-scudamore-gift

200. Pomonis, P., 'Unmasking tape', When Saturday Comes, 185, July 2002, https://www.wsc.co.uk/the-archive/923-Europe/2846-unmasking-tape

201. Both Karamanlis quotes in 'Greece welcomes back squad', BBC Sport, 5 July 2004, http://news.bbc.co.uk/sport1/hi/front_page/3866949.stm

202. Pomonis, P., 'Remembering Greece's abysmal Euro 2008', http://www.wsc.co.uk/wsc-daily/1036-Euro-2012/8703-remembering-greece-s-abysmal-euro-2008

203. Zaimakis, Y., 'Football fan culture and politics in modern Greece: the process of fandom radicalization during the austerity era', *Soccer & Society* 19.2 (2018), pp. 252–70.

204. Makris, A., http://greece.greekreporter.com/2011/02/01/greek-football-affected-by-economic-crisis/; Dabilis, A., http://greece.greekreporter.com/2012/09/09/in-crisis-greek-football-teams-prefer-greek-players/

205. Slater, M., 'Greek football crisis adds to national blues', BBC Sport, http://www.bbc.co.uk/blogs/mattslater/2011/06/an_economy_in_

pieces_a.html; Manoli, A. E., and Antonopoulos, G. A., '"The only game in town?": football match-fixing in Greece', *Trends in Organized Crime* 18.3 (2015), pp. 196–211; Manoli, A. E., Antonopoulos, G. A., and Bairner, A., 'The inevitability of corruption in Greek football', *Soccer & Society* (2017), pp. 1–17.

206. http://www.open.ac.uk/arts/research/finance-crisis-protest/comment-and-debate/football-politics-and-crisis-greece-1; http://www.open.ac.uk/arts/research/finance-crisis-protest/comment-and-debate/football-politics-and-crisis-greece-2

207. Barrett, M., 'Plagued by problems in football and society, is Euro 2012 Greece's beacon of hope?', http://www.sportingintelligence.com/2012/06/07/plagued-by-problems-in-football-and-society-does-euro-2012-offer-greece-a-beacon-on-hope-070602/

208. Anthony, S., 'Olympiakos' political party gaining support in Greece', http://www.wsc.co.uk/wsc-daily/1177-may-2014/11551-olympiakos-political-party-gaining-support-in-greece

209. Spyros T., and Balabanidis, Y., 'Football, Politics and Crisis in Greece 1', http://www.open.ac.uk/arts/research/finance-crisis-protest/comment-and-debate/football-politics-and-crisis-greece-1; Spyros, T., and Balabanidis, Y., 'Football, Politics and Crisis in Greece 2', http://www.open.ac.uk/arts/research/finance-crisis-protest/comment-and-debate/football-politics-and-crisis-greece-2

210. Wood, G., 'Owner of Greek champions banned over corruption probe', https://uk.reuters.com/article/uk-soccer-greece-olympiakos/owner-of-greek-champions-banned-over-corruption-probe-IDUKKBN0OY1L320150618

211. 'Evangelos Marinakis: Nottingham Forest owner cleared of forming Greek match-fixing ring', BBC Sport, 26 March 2018, https://www.bbc.co.uk/sport/football/43546409; 'Greek club owners and players prosecuted for match-fixing', Andy Brown, The Sports Integrity Initiative, 1 March 2018, https://www.sportsintegrityinitiative.com/greek-club-owners-players-prosecuted-match-fixing/

212. 'Law amendments save Greek football from international ban', http://www.playthegame.org/news/news-articles/2015/0035_greek-football-row/

213. 'Crowd violence delays the start of the Greek Cup final', BBC Sport, 10 May 2017, https://www.bbc.co.uk/sport/football/39833037. See also, 'Greece: Over 40 injured as violent clashes mar Greek Cup final', https://www.youtube.com/watch?v=ZZcJkcPHCiw

214. Veth, M., 'Ivan Savvidis and the power struggle over Greek football', 15 March 2018, http://futbolgrad.com/ivan-savvidis-paok-gun/; Smith, H., 'Greek Superleague suspended after team owner invades pitch with a gun', *Guardian*, 12 March 2018; 'Gun-toting PAOK owner "deeply sorry"

for his role in chaotic scenes', *Guardian*, 13 March 2018; Keddie, P., 'The New Greek Oligarchs' Path to Power: Soccer', https://www.ozy.com/fast-forward/the-new-greek-oligarchs-path-to-power-soccer/85458

215. Svetkovska, S., 'Russian Businessman Behind Unrest in Macedonia', 16 July 2018, https://www.occrp.org/en/investigations/8329-russian-businessman-behind-unrest-in-macedonia; Montague, J., 'Macedonia's ultra-important referendum', https://www.politico.eu/article/macedonias-ultra-important-referendum-greece-footbal-thessaloniki-ivan-savvidis/

216. Kozanoglu, C., 'Beyond Edirne: Football and the national identity crisis in Turkey', *Football Cultures and Identities*, Palgrave Macmillan (1999), pp. 117–25.

217. Korkmaz, A., 'New stadiums testify to the death of Turkish football', *Hurryiet Daily News*, 24 December 2015, http://www.hurriyetdailynews.com/opinion/ozgur-korkmaz/new-stadiums-testify-to-the-death-of-turkish-football—92935

218. Erdoğan's hat trick can be seen here: https://www.youtube.com/watch?v=EWFK-IAP3DU; on the more recent history of Başakşehir, Murray, T., 'Başakşehir: the controversial state-backed club threatening Turkey's established order', 1 March 2018, see, https://thesefootballtimes.co/2018/03/01/basaksehir-the-controversial-state-backed-club-threatening-turkeys-established-order/

219. For the basics, see Demircan, M., 'Background to the match-rigging scandal that has rocked Turkey', *World Soccer*, August 2011, https://www.worldsoccer.com/blogs/turkey-match-fixing-scandal-revealed-330963#5OAXe1mdk6RsViBw.99; and for a detailed legal overview of the case, Yilmaz, S., Manoli, A. E., and Antonopoulos, G. A., 'An anatomy of Turkish football match-fixing', *Trends in Organized Crime* (2018), pp. 1–19.

220. For those with a taste for conspiracy theory in Turkish football, the pitch invasion at the 2013 Turkish Cup, see here: https://www.youtube.com/watch?v=38hjr9J0dSU, is a rich field of study, with no agreement on who or what ignited the event, but with candidates including Besiktas ultras, Çarşı, a new ultra group of AKP loyal fans *Eagles 1453*, and the security services.

221. https://www.youtube.com/watch?v=JM4r-PRiDpg

222. Gezi; https://www.youtube.com/watch?v=70WjAoKWqbw; https://www.youtube.com/watch?v=Ck0AP6xO08I

223. Kytö, M., '"We are the rebellious voice of the terraces, we are Çarşı": constructing a football supporter group through sound', *Soccer & Society* 12.1 (2011), pp. 77–93; Coskun, G. B., and Coskun, B. B., 'From Stadia to the Gezi Park: On ÇARŞI, Public Sphere and Political Agency of a

Football Fan Group' (2014). Turan, Ö., and Özçetin, B., 'Football fans and contentious politics: The role of Çarşı in the Gezi Park protests', *International Review for the Sociology of Sport* (2017); Battini, A., and Koşulu, D., 'When ultras defend trees: framing politics through subcultural fandom-comparing UltrAslan and Çarşı before and during Occupy Gezi', *Soccer & Society* 19.3 (2018), pp. 418–39. Topless protest here: https://www.youtube.com/watch?v=ji7yQp_IjPk

224. Irak, D., '"Shoot some pepper gas at me!" Football fans vs. Erdoğan: organized politicization or reactive politics?', *Soccer & Society* 19.3 (2018), pp. 400–17.

225. 'Fenerbahçe team bus attacked on journey home from Rizespor match', *Observer*, 4 April, 2015, https://www.theguardian.com/football/2015/apr/04/fenerbahce-team-bus-attacked

226. Sweeney, S., 'Amedspor: resistance is everywhere', *Region*, 6 February 2018, https://theregion.org/article/12748-amedspor-resistance-is-everywhere

227. Ibid.

228. Lewis, B., 'Hakan Sukur – Turkey's fallen hero who can never return home', *Observer*, 18 February 2018, https://www.theguardian.com/football/2018/feb/18/hakan-sukur-turkey-fallen-hero-exile

229. Atherton, M., and Macbeth, J., 'Disability and football', *Routledge Handbook of Football Studies* (2016). García, B., et al, 'Facilitating inclusivity and broadening understandings of access at football clubs: the role of disabled supporter associations', *European Sport Management Quarterly* 17.2 (2017), pp. 226–43.

230. Magrath, R., and Anderson, E., 'Football, homosexuality and the English Premier League', *The English Premier League: A socio-cultural analysis*, Routledge (2017), pp. 150–64. Schallhorn, C., and Hempel, A., 'Media Coverage of Thomas Hitzlsperger's Coming-out in German Newspapers', *Journalism Studies* 18.9 (2017), pp. 1187–205.

231. The scale of the effort can be gleaned from FARE's database of projects, https://farenet.org/campaigns/refugees-football-database/

232. For an overview of these developments see Williams, J., *Women's Football, Europe and Professionalization 1971–2011* (2011); Williams, J., *Globalizing Women's Football: Europe, Migration and Professionalization*, Peter Lang (2013).

233. McRae, D., 'Cork City's Lisa Fallon: "The lads don't make exceptions. I'm just a coach"', *Guardian*, 4 February 2019; Wilsher, K., 'Helena Costa: I walked from Clermont Foot 63 after being sidelined by men', *Guardian*, 25 June 2014; Doyle, P., 'Corinne Diacre's drive and spirit of adventure wins over fans and critics', *Guardian*, 29 November 2016; '"I pick my team based on penis size" – German coach's withering response to

journalist', *BBC Sport*, 17 January 2019, https://www.bbc.com/sport/
football/46903807

234. Friend, N., 'Bilbao set European women's soccer attendance record,' 1
February 2019, http://www.sportspromedia.com/news/athletic-bilbao-
women-attendance-record

235. Grez, M., 'Women's team fed sandwiches at gala while men enjoy
three-course meal', 13 November 2018, https://www.cnn.
com/2018/11/22/football/fc-basel-anniversary-gala-womens-team-
tombola-tickets-spt-intl/index.html

236. For an overview see Pope, S., 'Female fans of men's football', Hughson,
J., Maguire, J., Moore, K., and Spaaij, R. (eds.), *Routledge Handbook of
Football Studies*, Routledge (2016); Pope, S., and Pfister, G. (eds.),
Female Football Players and Fans: Intruding into a Man's World, Palgrave
Macmillan (2018).

237. http://www.girlfans.co.uk, https://www.season-zine.com/home

238. Taylor, L., 'Women and children first, with the men nowhere, works at
Fenerbahçe', *Guardian*, 21 September 2011, https://www.theguardian.
com/football/blog/2011/sep/21/women-children-men-fenerbahce-ban.
See the real thing here: https://www.youtube.com/watch?v=H6VXdH_
Tat4. Erhart, I., 'Ladies of Besiktas: A dismantling of male hegemony at
Inönü Stadium', *International Review for the Sociology of Sport* 48.1
(2013), pp. 83–98. https://edition.cnn.com/2011/09/21/sport/football/
fenerbahce-all-female-crowd/index.html; 'More Turkish women flock to
stadiums, Beşiktaş boasts most female supporters', https://www.
dailysabah.com/life/2018/02/07/more-turkish-women-flock-to-
stadiums-besiktas-boasts-most-female-supporters

239. Key surveys of these developments include: Kennedy, P., '"Left-wing"
supporter movements and the political economy of football', *Soccer &
Society* 14.2 (2013), pp. 277–90; Kennedy, P., and Kennedy, D. (eds.),
Fan Culture in European Football and the Influence of Left-Wing Ideology,
Taylor & Francis (2017); García, B., and Zheng, J. (eds.), *Football and
Supporter Activism in Europe: Whose game is it?*, Springer (2017).
Cleland, J., et al, *Collective Action and Football Fandom: A Relational
Sociological Approach*, Springer (2018).

240. https://www.huckmag.com/outdoor/sport-outdoor/italian-football-
club-fighting-racism-pitch/

241. Kossakowski, R., 'From the Bottom to the Premiership: The Significance
of the Supporters' Movement in the Governance of Football Clubs in
Poland', *Football and Supporter Activism in Europe*, Palgrave Macmillan
(2017), pp. 233–55.

242. Turner, M., '"Football without fans is nothing": contemporary fan
protests and resistance communities in the English Premier League era',

The English Premier League, Routledge (2017), pp. 126–46; Cleland, J., and Dixon, K., '"Black and whiters": the relative powerlessness of "active" supporter organization mobility at English Premier League football clubs', *Soccer & Society* 16.4 (2015), pp. 540–54.

243. Hill, T., Canniford, R. and Millward, P., 'Against modern football: Mobilising protest movements in social media', *Sociology* (2016).

244. Football leaks at footballleaks2015.wordpress.com. All of *Der Spiegel*'s work: http://www.spiegel.de/international/topic/football_leaks/

245. Ronay, B., 'Football, fire and ice: the inside story of Iceland's remarkable rise', *Guardian*, 8 June 2016; Harper, D., 'Volcano! The incredible rise of Iceland's national football team', *Guardian*, 30 Jan 2016.

Chapter 5

1. Gluttons for punishment might enjoy the entirety of the AFC's vision document, http://www.the-afc.com/about-afc_1/visionmission/

2. Mabley, B., 'Big in Japan: how Chelsea are winning the hearts of fans in a football-mad country', *Guardian*, 12 May 2015, https://www.theguardian.com/football/blog/2015/may/12/chelsea-japan-yokohama-rubber-yoshinori-muto

3. Bland, B., 'European football clubs see a chance to score in China', *Financial Times*, 22 April 2017.

4. Duerden, J., 'Is a new colonialism taking place as football's big fish look east?', *Guardian*, 8 July 2008, https://www.theguardian.com/football/2008/jul/07/premierleague.europeanfootball

5. 'Ultras Malaya calls for boycott of Spurs, Liverpool "circus" matches', 29 April 2015, https://www.thestar.com.my/news/nation/2015/04/29/ultras-want-boycott-epl-circus/; Johnston, P., 'Malaysian fans call for boycott of Premier League "circus"', 29 April 2015, https://uk.reuters.com/article/uk-soccer-malaysia-england/malaysian-fans-call-for-boycott-of-premier-league-circus-IDUKKBN0NK0BX20150429

6. 'Thai company completes £30m takeover of Sheffield Wednesday', *Guardian*, 29 January 2015; Montague, J., *The Billionaires Club: The Unstoppable Rise of Football's Super-rich owners*, Bloomsbury (2017).

7. Lowe, S., 'From "Ali the Saviour" to "Ali Baba"? A cautionary tale from Santander', *Guardian*, 27 April 2017, https://www.theguardian.com/football/blog/2011/apr/27/racing-santander-la-liga; Alhamado, B., 'Fraud-friendly Bahrain: Is the Gulf kingdom's royal family hiding a wanted fraudster?', https://correctiv.org/en/investigations/stories/2016/09/29/fraud-friendly-bahrain/

8. 'The Italian job: Erick Thohir, Inter Milan', *Financial Times*, 5 October 2014, https://www.ft.com/content/6e2769c0-4970-11e4-9d7e-00144feab7de

9. 'Singapore businessman Lim buys Valencia', 17 May 2014, https://uk.reuters.com/article/uk-soccer-spain-valencia-IDUKKBN0DX0AJ20140517

10. 'FIFA bans Myanmar from 2018 World Cup after crowd', Reuters, 30 September 2011, https://uk.reuters.com/article/uk-soccer-fifa-myanmar/fifa-bans-myanmar-from-2018-world-cup-after-crowd-IDUKTRE78T1X120110930

11. AFP, 'Riots follow Myanmar football exit from Southeast Asian Games', 17 December 2013, https://www.thenational.ae/sport/riots-follow-myanmar-football-exit-from-southeast-asian-games-1.601758

12. https://www.youtube.com/watch?v=XZngYo387y4; 'Thai Football Fans Run Amok In Laos During AFF U-19 Final', 5 September 2015, https://aecnewstoday.com/2015/thai-football-fans-run-amok-in-laos-during-aff-u-19-final/#axzz5JFdI8zZU

13. CNN, 'Chinese riot after Japan win final', 8 August 2004, http://edition.cnn.com/2004/SPORT/football/08/07/china.japan/; AP, 'Unrest after China loses Asian Cup Final to Japan', https://www.youtube.com/watch?v=CzKE0DhaYzY; 'In Soccer Loss, a Glimpse of China's Rising Ire at Japan', *New York Times*, 9 August 2004.

14. Lu, Z., and Hong, F., *Sport and Nationalism in China*, Routledge (2013).

15. Yeon SY., 'Flags and banners mar East Asian Cup', *When Saturday Comes*, http://www.wsc.co.uk/wsc-daily/1165-august-2013/10110-korea-friday

16. 'Football officials urge corruption action at Malaysia meeting', BBC News, 20 February 2013, https://www.bbc.co.uk/news/world-asia-21515491

17. LERPONG AMSA-NGIAM, 'Thai football rocked as 12 arrested for match-fixing', 22 November 2017, http://www.nationmultimedia.com/detail/national/30332202

18. 'AFC bans 22 individuals from Laos, Cambodia for match-fixing', 15 February 2017, https://www.reuters.com/article/uk-soccer-asia-laos-matchfixing-IDUKKBN15U1LA

19. AFP, 'Hun Sen Warns Against Football Betting', 10 June 2010, http://www.malaysia-today.net/2010/06/10/hun-sen-warns-against-football-betting/

20. Eimer, D., 'Cambodia's football betting Mecca fuels rise in match-fixing scandals', *Daily Telegraph*, 7 April 2013.

21. Vickers, S., 'Zimbabwe FA bans 15 players and officials for life', 19 October 2012, https://www.bbc.co.uk/sport/football/19962706; PA, 'Fake Togo team played friendly against Bahrain, claim reports', 15 September 2010, https://www.theguardian.com/football/2010/sep/15/fake-togo-friendly-bahrain; Phillips, B., 'Africa's Soccer Impostors: The

bizarre, sad tale of Togo's fake national team', *Slate*, http://www.slate.com/articles/sports/sports_nut/2010/10/africas_soccer_impostors.html

22. Hill, D., and Longman, J., 'Fixed Soccer Matches Cast Shadow Over World Cup', *New York Times*, 31 May 2014; Hill, D., 'Inside the Fixing: How a Gang Battered Soccer's Frail Integrity', *New York Times*, 1 June 2014.

23. Borden, S., 'Police Call Match-Fixing Widespread in Soccer', *New York Times*, 4 February 2013.

24. Cotterill, S., 'The unique experience of watching football in Japan', *When Saturday Comes*, http://www.wsc.co.uk/wsc-daily/1001-November-2010/5915-the-unique-experience-of-watching-football-in-japan

25. Mabley, B., 'The Gaijin of Gamba', *Blizzard*, Issue 5.

26. Longman, J., and Suzuki, K., 'Japanese Team Comes of Age, and Lifts a Country', *New York Times*, 14 July 2011; Gottleib, B., 'Women's soccer a "beautiful flower" for post-disaster Japan', CNN, 17 July 2011, http://edition.cnn.com/2011/SPORT/football/07/15/japan.world.cup.final/index.htm; McCurry, J., 'Women's World Cup victory brings joy to Japan', *Guardian*, 18 July 2011, https://www.theguardian.com/world/2011/jul/18/japan-womens-world-cup-reaction-jo

27. Mandujano, Y., 'Japanese Media Ideologies Behind The National Football Teams Representing Japan and Portraying Archetypes of Men and Women?', *EJCJS*, vol. 14, issue 1, http://www.japanesestudies.org.uk/ejcjs/vol14/iss1/mandujano1.html

28. 'Tears in Tokyo as Japan thumped in World Cup final', Reuters, 6 July 2015, https://www.reuters.com/article/us-soccer-women-final-japan-reaction/tears-in-tokyo-as-japan-thumped-in-world-cup-final-IDUSKCN0PG0B720150706; 'Women's World Cup: Japan reacts with sadness and pride', BBC News, 6 July 2015, https://www.bbc.co.uk/news/world-asia-33405105

29. Duerden, J., 'K League struggles to attract fans', 4 May 2015, https://asia.nikkei.com/Business/K-League-struggles-to-attract-fans; Duerden, J., 'Interest in K-League on the wane as South Korea hope for World Cup success', http://www.espn.com/soccer/blog/football-asia/153/post/3459660/interest-in-k-league-on-the-wane-as-south-korea-hope-for-world-cup-success; Williams, P., 'Struggling K-League turning to Southeast Asia for assistance', *FourFourTwo*, 10 May 2016, https://www.fourfourtwo.com/sg/features/struggling-k-league-turning-southeast-asia-assistance#7veoLQaATsO5UspT.99

30. 'South Korea pelted with toffees on return home', *Guardian*, 30 June 2014, https://www.theguardian.com/football/2014/jun/30/world-cup-2014-south-korea-toffee

31. 'Rotten Shot: A Football Scandal fouls South Korea's Modernizing Image', *The Economist*, 21 July 2011; Sung-Hun, C., 'In South Korea Sport, a

Culture of Corruption', *New York Times*, 13 July 2011; Duerden, J., 'South Korea's ongoing battle against match-fixing', https://thesetpieces.com/world-football/south-koreas-ongoing-battle-match-fixing/

32. See, for example, 'PAUL POGBA DANCING "GANGNAM STYLE" – 2017', https://www.youtube.com/watch?v=R_9kLlMjDCI

33. Montague, J., 'Inside the Secret World of Football in North Korea', 12 December 2017, https://bleacherreport.com/articles/2746418-inside-the-secret-world-of-football-in-north-korea; 'North Koreans get "Soccer Fierce Battle" computer game', BBC News, 4 August 2017, https://www.bbc.com/news/blogs-news-from-elsewhere-40824431; 'A joint North-South Korean football World Cup – a diplomatic fantasy?', *Deutsche Welle*, https://www.dw.com/en/a-joint-north-south-korean-football-world-cup-a-diplomatic-fantasy/a-39305923

34. Georgakis, S., and M., Simone, 'From old soccer to new football? Expert accounts of transformations on the world game in Australia post-Crawford Report', *Soccer & Society* 17.1 (2016), pp. 72–89.

35. Pajic, Z., '"A" is for Australia: New Football's billionaires, consumers and the "Asian Century". How the A-League defines the new Australia', *Soccer & Society* 14.5 (2013), pp. 734–50.

36. Ticher, M., 'Respect the A-League boycott. The fans make the games worth watching', 4 December 2015, https://www.theguardian.com/football/2015/dec/04/respect-the-aleague-boycott-the-fans-make-the-games-worth-watching

37. Hallinan, C., and Hughson, J., 'The beautiful game in Howard's "Brutopia": football, ethnicity and citizenship in Australia', *Soccer & Society* 10.1 (2009), pp. 1–8.

38. Hallinan, C. J., and Hughson, J. E. (eds.), *The Containment of Soccer in Australia: Fencing Off the World Game*, Routledge (2013), p. 6.

39. Hallinan, C., and Heenan, T., 'Australia, Asia and the new football opportunity', *Soccer & Society* 14.5 (2013), pp. 751–67.

40. 'FFA falls short on indigenous talent', 31 March 2017, https://www.sbs.com.au/news/ffa-falls-short-on-indigenous-talentony

41. McCafferty, G., 'Australian women's soccer team boycott sell-out U.S. tour over pay', 11 September 2015, https://edition.cnn.com/2015/09/11/football/australia-matildas-women-soccer-pay/index.html; Connoly, P., '"They ARE feminine": the Matildas' long road from sexism in '79 to sellouts in '17', *Guardian*, 15 September 2017, https://www.theguardian.com/football/2017/sep/16/they-are-feminine-the-matildas-long-road-from-sexism-in-79-to-sellouts-in-17

42. Ticher, M., 'Australia's Asian Cup an example for World Cups', *When Saturday Comes*, http://www.wsc.co.uk/wsc-daily/1190-january-2015/12123-australia-s-asian-cup-an-example-for-world-cups

43. 'Australian Prime Minister, Tony Abbott, booed at Asian Cup 2015', https://www.youtube.com/watch?v=LjZr4xRz78k

44. 'Malaysia celebrates, declares holiday', Reuters, 30 December 2010, https://www.eurosport.com/football/international-football/2010/malaysia-declares-holiday_sto2600207/story.shtml

45. 'Step on it, people', 6 September 2015, https://www.thestar.com.my/opinion/columnists/on-the-beat/2015/09/06/step-on-it-people/

46. Jegathesan, M., 'Malaysia flares as Asian football's problem child', AFP, 10 September 2015, http://www.businessinsider.com/afp-malaysia-flares-as-asian-footballs-problem-child-2015-9?IR=T

47. 'Football Hooliganism a Growing Threat in Malaysia', 18 February 2014, http://www.malaysiandigest.com/opinion/488446-football-hooliganism-a-growing-threat-in-malaysia.html

48. 'FA Cup quarter-final wrap: Ugly scenes mar Perak win while JDT record goal fest back home', *FourFourTwo*, https://www.fourfourtwo.com/my/features/fa-cup-quarter-final-wrap-ugly-scenes-mar-perak-win-while-jdt-record-goal-fest-back-home#W6p1iIf9kG0JABjC.99

49. Yusoff, N. H., 'Football disorder among football fans in Malaysia: a study of Kelantan, Johor, Perak and Selangor football fans', http://www.iarjournal.com/wp-content/uploads/05-P26-31.pdf

50. Booth, R., 'WikiLeaks cables: Burma general considered Manchester United buyout', *Guardian*, 6 December 2010, and for the cable itself, 'US embassy cables: Burma general urged to bid $1bn for Manchester United', https://www.theguardian.com/world/us-embassy-cables-documents/211733

51. https://www.treasury.gov/press-center/press-releases/Pages/hp837.aspx

52. 'Amid Myanmar's Gloom, Pro Soccer Gives Locals a Chance to Cheer', *WSJ*, 23 June 2009, https://www.wsj.com/articles/SB124570662948438629; Pye, D., 'Football and pagodas galore, but no bread at Burma's circus', *New Internationalist*, 10 December 2010, https://newint.org/blog/2010/12/10/football-and-pagodas

53. Khaing, H., 'Politics fouls football as MNL teams mull future', 14 October 2016, https://frontiermyanmar.net/en/politics-fouls-football-as-mnl-teams-mull-future

54. Sipilan, J., 'Malaysia debates pulling out of soccer cup over Myanmar's Rohingya crackdown', https://www.reuters.com/article/us-myanmar-rohingya-malaysia-soccer-IDUSKBN13I0XG; AFP, 'Kyrgyzstan scraps Myanmar football match over concerns', http://www.mizzima.com/news-international/kyrgyzstan-scraps-myanmar-football-match-over-concerns; 'Iranian head coach of Myanmar *futsal* team resigns over Rohingya mass killing', https://www.dhakatribune.com/sport/other-sports/2017/09/11/iranian-head-coach-myanmar-futsal-team-resigns-rohingya-mass-killings/

55. 'Muangthong United and Buriram United – A History of Hatred', http://

backpagefootball.com/muangthong-united-buriram-united-history-hatred/115111/

56. Duerden, J., 'When Football Meets Politics', *Diplomat*, 26 December 2011, https://thediplomat.com/2011/12/when-football-meets-politics/; '"Kingmaker" of Thai politics transforms rural hometown into sporting boomtown', 8 June 2017, https://www.straitstimes.com/asia/se-asia/kingmaker-of-thai-politics-transform-rural-homtown-into-sporting-boomtown; Murphy, P., 'The unrelenting rise of Buriram United', 30 October 2015, https://thesefootballtimes.co/2015/10/30/unrelenting-rise-of-buriram-united/

57. Duerden, J., 'FAT Shaming', *Blizzard*, Issue 23.

58. 'Vietnam officials jailed on graft', BBC News, 7 August 2007, http://news.bbc.co.uk/1/hi/world/asia-pacific/6935264.stm

59. Barrett, T., 'Football in Hanoi, where Premier League clubs trump the Vietnamese champions', *Guardian*, 17 October 2016, https://www.theguardian.com/football/in-bed-with-maradona/2016/oct/17/football-vietnam-hanoi-manchester-united

60. 'Club chair criticizes VFF, wants to set up new league', 13 September 2011, http://english.vietnamnet.vn/fms/sports/12660/club-chair-criticizes-vff—wants-to-set-up-new-league.html

61. 'Vietnam banking tycoon given 30-year jail term', *Tuổi Trẻ*, 9 June 2014, https://tuoitrenews.vn/society/20198/vietnam-banking-tycoon-given-30year-jail-term

62. These events can be seen here, 'Vietnam football team stage bizarre "mannequin" protest', https://www.youtube.com/watch?v=1uWc4Ke62VM&feature=player_embedded

63. Denyer, S., 'Vietnamese soccer team's goal isn't on the field; it's in politics', *Washington Post*, 20 December 2015, https://www.washingtonpost.com/world/asia_pacific/a-soccer-team-in-vietnam-doubles-as-a-club-for-dissidents/2015/12/19/4bed4fef-4eab-4940-841d-fcecec107440_story.html?utm_term=.2e427cd0b6e7; AFP, 'Vietnam's dissident footballers take aim at politics', http://www.nationmultimedia.com/detail/breakingnews/30321837

64. Szep, J., 'In Vietnam, anti-Chinese protesters find a new outlet: soccer', 23 December 2012, https://www.reuters.com/article/us-vietnam-china-dissidents/in-vietnam-anti-chinese-protesters-find-a-new-outlet-soccer-IDUSBRE8BM0BB20121223

65. Ibid.

66. Fuller, A., 'Ultras In Indonesia', 29 February 2016, http://readingsideways.net/ultras-in-Indonesia/

67. On Joseph Revo, 'World Cup Bid Executive Found Guilty of Murder' https://worldfootballinsider.com/world-cup-bid-executive-found-guilty-of-murder/?mode=list; On Halid and his jail cell, Duerden,J., 'Protest

Vote', *When Saturday Comes*, 291, 2011, https://www.wsc.co.uk/
the-archive/917-International-football/8792-protest-vote, and Belford,
A., 'In Indonesia, A Scandal Over Soccer' *New York Times*, 3 March 2011,
https://www.nytimes.com/2011/03/04/world/asia/04iht-indonesia04.
html; On Halid's brother see, 'More Woes for Disgraced Indonesia
Football Chief Nurdin Halid', World Football Insider, 14 April 2011,
https://worldfootballinsider.com/
more-woes-for-disgraced-indonesia-football-chief-nurdin-halid/

68. Kane, R., 'Protests, Politics, and Corruption: The Fight to Control
Indonesian Soccer', 30 April 2015, https://sports.vice.com/en_au/
article/ez3ea7/protests-politics-and-corruption-the-fight-to-control-
indonesian-soccer

69. 'Edy Rahmayadi: We are starting from a position of less than zero', 29
November 2016, https://en.tempo.co/read/news/2016/11/29/
241823966/Edy-Rahmayadi-We-are-starting-from-a-position-of-less-
than-zero

70. Huda, L., 'Jakarta's hooligan problem: violence and deaths surround
"Jakmania" football fans', *Guardian*, 21 November 2016, https://www.
theguardian.com/cities/2016/nov/21/jakarta-hooligan-violence-
jakmania-persija-football-fans; Renaldi, A., 'Fans Keep Dying At
Indonesian Football Matches', 5 September 2017, https://
www.vice.com/en_id/article/vbbk93/fans-keep-dying-at-indonesian-
football-matches

71. Fuller, A., 'Ultras in Indonesia', http://readingsideways.net/ultras-in-
indonesia/; Fuller, A., 'BONEK 1927 AS ULTRAS', 27 August 2015,
http://readingsideways.net/bonek-1927-as-ultras/; Fuller, A., and
Junaedi, F., 'Ultras in Indonesia: conflict, diversification, activism', *Sport
in Society* 21.6 (2018), pp. 919–31.

72. Fuller, A., 'Warkop Pitulikur and Football Activism', 24 June 2015,
http://readingsideways.net/warkop-pitulikur-and-football-activism/

73. 'Nepal: land of the puppet president', *World Soccer*, April 2016, http://
www.worldsoccer.com/features/nepal-land-of-the-puppet-president-
369644

74. Cowan, S., 'Corruption in world football and the fall of Ganesh Thapa',
http://www.recordnepal.com/wire/corruption-in-world-football-and-the-
fall-of-ganesh-thapa/

75. '"BFF rotten, football dead"', 11 October 2016, http://www.newagebd.
net/article/669/bff-rotten-football-dead

76. Ahsan, A., 'Faisal Saleh Hayat: The feudal lord of Pakistani football',
Nation, 8 September 2016, https://nation.com.pk/08-Sep-2016/
faisal-saleh-hayat-the-feudal-lord-of-pakistani-football

77. Adkin, R., and Hassan, S., 'Blatter's corroded legacy on South Asian

soccer fields', 7 September 2015, https://www.reuters.com/article/us-fifa-southasia-insight-IDUSKCN0R72AP20150907

78. Ray, S., 'How India's ISL became world football's fourth biggest league', *Guardian*, 23 December 2014, https://www.theguardian.com/football/blog/2014/dec/23/india-super-league-fourth-biggest-league

79. Caless, K., 'In Search of India's Football Culture with Mumbai FC's Yellow Brigade', 6 February 2017, https://sports.vice.com/en_uk/article/bmq75a/in-search-of-indias-football-culture-with-mumbai-fcs-yellow-brigade

80. Ullal, N., 'How Bengaluru FC's "West Block Blues" fan group are making noise for right reasons', 28 June 2017, http://www.marca.com/en/football/international-football/2017/06/28/5953a978e2704ed8688b4644.html

81. Narayan, M., 'India's champions Bengaluru spark revolution with uncertain future', *Observer*, 15 January 2017, https://www.theguardian.com/football/2017/jan/15/india-champions-bengaluru-football-revolution-fans

82. Lawrence, J., 'The world's worst football team', *Esquire*, 19 January 2016, https://www.esquireme.com/sports/meet-worlds-worst-football-team

83. The impact of television in Bhutan and the many social problems that emerged after its introduction are explored in Scott-Clark, C. and Levy, A., 'Fast forward into trouble', *Guardian*, 14 June 2003.

84. Burt, J., 'Kazakhs' oil-powered pipe dream is a mission impossible', *Independent*, 10 October 2008.

85. 'Kazakh leader's ex-son-in-law Rakhat Aliyev found dead in Austrian jail', Reuters, 24 February 2015.

86. Baumgartner, P., 'FC Astana – the little club with deep pockets', *Guardian*, 11 September 2015, https://www.theguardian.com/world/2015/sep/11/astana-benfica-champions-league-kazakhstan; Veth, M., 'FC Astana – Reaching for the Stars In Kazakhstan', 27 July 2015, http://futbolgrad.com/fc-astana-reaching-for-the-stars-in-kazakhstan/

87. Rickleton, C., 'Football in Kazakhstan: A Tale of Two Cities', https://eurasianet.org/s/football-in-kazakhstan-a-tale-of-two-cities, 27 July 2015, http://futbolgrad.com/fc-astana-reaching-for-the-stars-in-kazakhstan/

88. 'Tajik President's Son Named Head Of Football Federation', *RFERL*, 5 January 2012, https://www.rferl.org/a/tajikistan_rustam_emomali_football_federation/24443401.html; Rickleton, C., 'Tajik Football Match Erupts into Violence', 20 November 2012, http://futbolgrad.com/tajik-football-violence/

89. 'Tajik Soccer Fans Riot After "Favoritism" For President's Son's Team', *RFERL*, 14 June 2011, https://www.rferl.org/a/tajik_soccer_fans_riot_after_game_presidential_son_team/24235176.html

90. Sherkhanov, A., 'Tajik Football Club Sanctioned After Beating Team

Founded By President's Son', 26 April 2012, https://www.rferl.org/a/ tajik_football_club_fined_rustam_emamoli/24561390.html

91. Putz, C., 'Thanks, Dad! Tajik President's Son Gets A New Job', 12 January 2017, https://thediplomat.com/2017/01/thanks-dad-tajik-presidents-son-gets-a-new-job/

92. O'Flynn, K., 'Death and glory', *Observer*, 15 March 2009.

93. Bennets, M., 'Rivaldo Revolution', *When Saturday Comes* 261, November 2008.

94. 'Uzbekistan: Brazilian Football Star Rivaldo Seeks Unpaid Wages From Tashkent Club', https://eurasianet.org/s/uzbekistan-brazilian-football-star-rivaldo-seeks-unpaid-wages-from-tashkent-club; Duerden, J., 'The bursting of the Bunyodkor bubble', http://www.espn.com/soccer/columns/story/_/id/1418061/the-bursting-of-the-bunyodkor-bubble

95. 'Former Chinese football chiefs jailed over bribes', Reuters, 13 June 2017, https://uk.reuters.com/article/uk-soccer-china-corruption/former-chinese-football-chiefs-jailed-over-bribes-IDUKBRE85C03D20 120613

96. 'Ex-World Cup ref known as "golden whistle" jailed for match-fixing', CNN, 17 February 2012, https://edition.cnn.com/2012/02/16/sport/football/football-china-referee-fixing/index.html

97. AP, 'Shanghai Shenhua stripped of 2003 title in China match-fixing inquiry', *Guardian*, 19 February 2013, https://www.theguardian.com/football/2013/feb/19/shanghai-shenhau-stripped-match-fixing

98. Miner, A., 'China shows how to crack down on soccer', https://www.japantimes.co.jp/opinion/2015/06/02/commentary/world-commentary/china-shows-how-to-crack-down-on-soccer/#.Wy_CLS2ZPuQ

99. Van de Ven, J., 'Death of an institution: The Dalian Shide Story', 25 April 2013, https://wildeastfootball.net/2013/04/death-of-an-institution-the-dalian-shide-story; Herman, R., 'Murder, Corruption, and the Demise of a Chinese Football Giant', https://sports.vice.com/en_uk/article/qkyp7v/murder-corruption-and-the-demise-of-a-chinese-football-giant

100. The whole document can be seen here: Wilson, C., 'Read Chinese Football's 50-point reform plan in full – exclusive translation', https://wildeastfootball.net/2016/02/read-chinese-footballs-50-point-reform-plan-in-full-exclusive-translation/

101. Clover, C., 'TV rights deal confirms China football's rise', *Financial Times*, 23 February 2016, https://www.ft.com/content/7e00e7aa-da14-11e5-98fd-06d75973fe09

102. Jaffe, G., 'Beijing's Green Army', 15 April 2014, http://roadsandkingdoms.com/2014/beijings-green-army/

103. Wilson, C., 'Shanghai Shenhua fans' Xi Jinping protest banner confiscated amid ruckus', 18 March 2014, https://wildeastfootball.

net/2014/03/shanghai-shenhua-fans-xi-jinping-protest-banner-confiscated-amid-ruckus/

104. Wilson, C., 'The radical, contrary Chinese football fans who support Japanese opponents', *Guardian*, 15 Match 2017, https://www.theguardian.com/football/2017/mar/15/chinese-fans-support-japanese-club-football-shanghai-urawa-asian-champions-league

Chapter 6

1. 'Exclusive video of Jack Warner apparently offering "gifts" of £25,000 to Caribbean delegates – full transcript': the transcript and video of this amazing speech can be accessed at *Daily Telegraph*, 12 October 2011, https://www.telegraph.co.uk/sport/football/international/8821695/Exclusive-video-of-Jack-Warner-apparently-offering-gifts-of-25000-to-Caribbean-delegates-full-transcript.html

2. McTear, E., 'Cuban revolution: Cuba embraces pro soccer after years out in the cold', CNN, 1 March 2016, https://www.cnn.com/2016/03/01/football/cuban-professional-football-players-mexico/index.html

3. 'World Cup 2018: Panama declares public holiday after qualifying', BBC News, 11 October 2017, https://www.bbc.co.uk/news/world-latin-america-41579670; Davison, D., 'Ecstasy in the Caribbean: how Panama reached their first ever World Cup', https://thesefootballtimes.co/2017/12/07/ecstasy-in-the-caribbean-how-panama-reached-their-first-ever-world-cup/

4. Longman, J., 'For 90 Minutes, a Political Crisis Will Take a Back Seat in Honduras', *New York Times*, 4 October 2009.

5. Rosenberg, M., 'Honduras coup rivals use soccer triumph in crisis', 24 October 2009, https://www.reuters.com/article/us-honduras-soccer/honduras-coup-rivals-use-soccer-triumph-in-crisis-IDUSTRE59N1GH20091024; Fletcher, P., 'How football helped to heal Honduras', BBC Sport, 25 May 2010, http://www.bbc.co.uk/blogs/paulfletcher/2010/05/how_football_helped_to_heal_ho.html; Plenderleith, I., 'Fantasy Football,', http://www.wsc.co.uk/the-archive/1013-World-Cup-2010/5236-fantasy-football; Rogers, T., 'Can the World Cup Save Honduras?', *Time*, 3 June 2010, http://content.time.com/time/specials/packages/article/0,28804,1991933_1991952_1993681,00.html

6. Soca Warriors can be seen here: https://www.youtube.com/watch?v=BC1mSOY1hmI

7. Bunton, S., 'World Cup stunning moments: Haiti shock Dino Zoffs Italy', *Guardian*, 24 April 2018.

8. Montague, J., 'Qualifying after the quake: Haiti soccer's World Cup dream', http://edition.cnn.com/2011/SPORT/football/09/06/football.

haiti.world.cup/index.html; Olukotun, D., 'Soccer in Haiti: 2 Years After the Quake', https://www.huffingtonpost.com/deji-olukotun/haiti-soccer_b_1201999.html

9. Davis, D. H., *The industrialization of football: a cultural analysis of Jamaica's Reggae Boyz 1998 road to France World Cup campaign*. Diss., 2013 (University of the West Indies).

10. Branford, A., 'PURELY POLITICAL: Political football', 25 September 2011, http://www.nationnews.com/nationnews/news/2024/purely-political-political-football; 'The House of David', *Barbados Underground*, 10 April 2011, https://barbadosunderground.net/2011/10/04/the-house-of-david/; 'Opposition MP does more for Barbados Football than ruling party minister who has FIFA ties: Sept 2011 is first "LIME Pelican Football Challenge Barbados"', 7 August 2011, https://www.bajanreporter.com/2011/08/opposition-mp-does-more-for-barbados-football-than-ruling-party-minister-who-has-fifa-ties-sept-2011-is-first-lime-pelican-football-challenge-barbados/

11. 'Patrick John's football woes', *Dominica News Online*, 25 June 2012, http://dominicanewsonline.com/news/homepage/news/sports/patrick-johns-football-woes/

12. The full roll-call of dishonour included five resignations (including the presidents of the federations of the Cayman Islands, St Lucia and the Bahamas) and thirteen bans from football dispensed by FIFA's ethics committee.

13. Kapuściński, R., *The Soccer War*, Vintage (2013).

14. Reuters, 'Ex-head of Salvadoran soccer federation given eight years in prison', Reuters, https://www.reuters.com/article/us-el-salvador-soccer-IDUSKBN16E05F

15. Jackson, E., 'Corruption wins a round: judge throws out bribery charges against former soccer boss', http://www.thepanamanews.com/2017/11/corruption-in-panamanian-soccer-wins-a-round/

16. Kaplan, S., 'What Guatemala can teach fragile states about cleaning up the justice system', *Guardian*, 20 October 2015; Guy, J., 'Can Anyone Save Guatemala's Soccer Federation Before It's Kicked Out of FIFA?', http://remezcla.com/features/sports/guatemala-fifa-corruption/; Witz, B., 'Guatemala's Soccer Scandal drains Fans' Interest in the Game', *New York Times*, 25 March 2016; Gagne, D., 'Brother of "Narco Leader" Becomes Top Guatemala Soccer Official', https://www.insightcrime.org/news/brief/brother-of-narco-leader-becomes-top-guatemala-soccer-official/

17. Yagoub, M., 'Why Are So Many Honduras Soccer Bosses Involved in Crime?', https://www.insightcrime.org/news/analysis/why-are-so-many-honduras-soccer-bosses-involved-in-crime/

18. Perason, B., 'Ex-Honduran minister gets nearly two-and-a-half years

prison in U.S. drug case', Reuters, 19 January 2018, https://www.
reuters.com/article/us-usa-honduras-moneylaundering/ex-honduran-
minister-gets-nearly-two-and-a-half-years-prison-in-u-s-drug-case-
idUSKBN1F82C1

19. Yagoub, op. cit.

20. Tuckman, J., 'World Cup 2014: "'We showed them who we are." Costa
Rica is proud of its team', *Observer*, 27 June 2014.

21. Simpson, J., 'Netherlands vs Costa Rica: Best World Cup performance
marred as three Costa Rican fans stabbed at match screening in
country's capital', *Independent*, 6 July 2014.

22. Lopez, J., 'Football Hooliganism on the Rise in Costa Rica', *Costa Rica
Star*, 23 October 2014, https://news.co.cr/football-hooliganism-on-the-
rise-in-costa-rica/33314/; Dyer, Z., '53 arrested in soccer hooligan brawl
at Costa Rica's National Stadium', *Tico Times*, 17 February 2014, http://
www.ticotimes.net/2014/02/17/53-arrested-in-soccer-hooligan-brawl-at-
costa-ricas-national-stadium; '"The Classic" turns violent: A
horse-punching teenager and 69 others arrested at Sunday match
between rivals La Liga and Saprissa', *Tico Times*, 21 July 2014, http://
www.ticotimes.net/2014/07/21/the-classic-turns-violent-a-horse-
punching-teenager-and-69-others-arrested-at-sunday-match-between-
rivals-la-liga-and-saprissa

23. AP, 'Two killed and 16 injured as football fans clash', *Guardian*, 27 July
2009; '*Suspendido el partido Real Espana-Marathon for relay de la barras*',
https://www.laprensa.hn/deportes/1134694-410/en-vivo-transmision-
real-espa%C3%B1a-marathon-semifinales-torneo-apertura-2017-2018-
honduras

24. Valencia, R., 'How Gangs Have Disturbed the Math of Soccer in El
Salvador', https://www.insightcrime.org/news/analysis/
how-gangs-have-disturbed-the-math-of-football-in-el-salvador/

25. 'Alfredo Pacheco, El Salvador ex-footballer, murdered', BBC News, 27
December 2015, https://www.bbc.co.uk/news/world-latin-america-
35187900; Murillo, A., 'In one of the world's most violent areas, soccer
can be a deadly game', *El Pais*, 23 December 2015; 'Violencia en el fútbol',
https://impresa.prensa.com/deportes/Violencia-futbol_0_4735776430.
html; Lakhani, N., 'Arnold Peralta shooting: autopsy results show Rangers
footballer shot 18 times', *Guardian*, 11 December 2015.

26. Quoted in Archibold, R., 'Mexican Writer Mines the Soccer Field for
Metaphors', *New York Times*, 25 October 2013. See also Bar, T., on 'El
Tri: A pagan religion for all', 4 June 2014, https://www.washingtonpost.
com/news/monkey-cage/wp/2014/06/04/el-tri-a-pagan-religion-for-
all/?noredirect=on&utm_term=.b97237bb7266

27. Subcomandante Marcos's letter to Galeano can be read here: https://

javiersoriaj.wordpress.com/2011/05/23/textos-fundamentales-del-zapatismo-3-carta-del-sup-marcos-a-eduardo-galeano-2-de-mayo-de-1995/

28. 'Damos, pero recibimos de los zapatistas mucho más: Moratti', La Journada, 13 May 2005, http://www.jornada.unam.mx/2005/05/13/index.php?section=deportes&article=a25n1dep

29. Simpson, W., 'Easton Cowboys and Cowgirls: anatomy of an alternative sports club', Soccer & Society 17.5 (2016), pp. 721–31; Simpson, Will, Freedom Through Football: The story of the Easton cowboys and cowgirls, Tangent Books (2017).

30. Arie, S., and Tuckman, S., 'Soccer stars support guerrillas', Guardian, 19 October 2004; Magee, W., 'Javier Zanetti, Inter Milan and the Rebel Football Match That Never Took Place', 30 January 2017, https://sports.vice.com/en_us/article/wnmgdw/javier-zanetti-inter-milan-and-the-rebel-football-match-that-never-took-place

31. The full details of the epistolary exchange between Subcomandante Marcos and Massimo Moratti can be read here: http://www.schoolsforchiapas.org/wp-content/uploads/2014/07/Zapatista-FC-Football-in-Rebel-Territory.pdf

32. https://www.poblanerias.com/2012/12/epn-premia-a-seleccion-olimpica-de-futbol-por-medalla-de-oro/

33. Chicago Tribune, 11 August 2012.

34. Quoted in Archibold (2013).

35. Grillo, I., 'Mexico's billionaire brawl', PRI, 18 August 2011, https://www.pri.org/stories/2011-08-18/mexicos-billionaire-brawl; Nicholson, P., 'Carlos Slim exits Mexican club ownership but holds on to broadcast rights', 11 September 2017, http://www.insideworldfootball.com/2017/09/11/carlos-slim-exits-mexican-club-ownership-holds-broadcast-rights/; Turner, E., 'Know your oligarch, Club América: The family behind Mexico's most successful club', 8 January 2015, https://fusion.tv/story/88822/club-america-azcarraga-family-televisa/

36. Nicholson, op. cit.

37. Elder, A., 'Tijuana Rising', New York Times Soccer Blog, 18 April 2012; 'Polemic PRI politician pins hopes on Tijuana soccer team', 28 November 2012, https://thetequilafiles.com/2012/11/28/polemic-pri-politician-pins-hopes-on-tijuana-soccer-team/; Abnos, A., 'In new documentary, the astounding rise of Club Tijuana explored in full', Sports Illustrated, 19 September 2016, https://www.si.com/planet-futbol/2016/09/19/club-tijuana-xolos-club-frontera-documentary; said documentary can be seen here: http://www.clubfrontera.com

38. Homewood, B., 'Identity Crisis: Unpicking the convoluted threads of Mexico's franchise system', Blizzard, 1 March 2014, https://www.

theblizzard.co.uk/article/identity-crisis; Turner, E., 'Decades of suffering plagues the soccer team, or teams, of Irapuato, Mexico', 4 February 2015, https://fusion.tv/story/93266/irapuato-mexico-history-soccer/

39. https://mlmcompanies.org/omnilife/

40. Munoz, D., *'El origen de las "barras bravas" que manchan al futbol mexicano'*, 28 September 2018, https://lasillarota.com/especialeslsr/el-origen-de-las-barras-bravas-que-manchan-al-futbol-mexicano-barras-tito-tepito-origen-aldo-fascci/249484

41. Menedez, J. F. *'Futbol, corrupción y narcotráfico'*, http://www.excelsior.com.mx/opinion/jorge-fernandez-menendez/2014/03/04/946753; Aceves, J., 'The Wiseguy's Guide to Liga MX: How Mexican Futbol is used to Launder Money', http://futmexnation.com/2017/08/10/the-wiseguys-guide-to-liga-mx-how-mexican-futbol-is-used-to-launder-money/; 'Mexican soccer remains tainted by links to drug trafficking', 6 June 2014, https://thetequilafiles.com/2014/06/06/mexican-soccer-remains-tainted-by-links-to-drug-trafficking/

42. Heydari, K. A., 'In Mexico, Violence scars the Game', *New York Times Soccer Blog*, 11 January 2012. Watch at https://www.youtube.com/watch?v=qf7C3VYPe3s

43. Lists *'La violencia no ha perdonado a los estadios de fútbol'*, http://www.marca.com/claro-mx/futbol/liga-mx/2017/02/20/58ab0ab846163f1e508b4575.html

44. Gault, M., 'Football in Juarez, Mexico, the murder capital of the world', https://thesefootballtimes.co/2014/06/28/football-in-the-murder-capital-of-the-world/; Powell, R., 'Life After Death in Juarez: Football Returns to a City Damaged by Narco Violence', https://sports.vice.com/en_uk/article/gvage4/life-after-death-in-juarez-football-returns-to-a-city-damaged-by-narco-violence

45. See Corcoran, P., 'Mexico Soccer Shoot-out Reflects Nation's Struggle', 26 August 2011, https://www.insightcrime.org/news/analysis/mexico-soccer-shootout-reflects-nations-struggle/

46. Lopez, G., 'Mexico goalkeeper arrested for helping kidnap gang', Reuters, 8 January 2012, https://www.reuters.com/article/us-crime-mexico-goalkeeper/mexico-goalkeeper-arrested-for-helping-kidnap-gang-IDUSTRE8060N020120108

47. Aceves, J., 'The Wiseguys Guide to Liga MX: How Mexican Futbol is Used to Launder Money', 10 August 2017, http://futmexnation.com/2017/08/10/the-wiseguys-guide-to-liga-mx-how-mexican-futbol-is-used-to-launder-money/; On Alvarez, and Tirso Martinez see 'Mexican soccer remains tainted by links to drug trafficking', 6 June 2014, https://thetequilafiles.com/2014/06/06/mexican-soccer-remains-tainted-by-links-to-drug-trafficking/; On Rios and much more, see ,

Mendez, J. F., 'Futbol, corrupción y narcotráfico', Excelsior, 3 March 2014, https://www.excelsior.com.mx/opinion/jorge-fernandez-menendez/2014/03/04/946753

48. Stewaret, J., 'Xolos reserve soccer player charged with smuggling meth from Mexico', *San Diego Tribune*, 12 April 2017, https://www.sandiegouniontribune.com/news/courts/sd-me-soccer-arrest-20170412-story.html

49. Hoenig, C., 'The Measure of Diversity That Only One U.S. Pro Sport Meets', https://www.diversityinc.com/news/measure-diversity-one-u-s-pro-sport-meets; Kehow III, R., 'Why Are There No Black Coaches in MLS?', 5 May 2015, https://sports.vice.com/en_us/article/yp79yx/why-are-there-no-black-coaches-in-mls

50. King, J. C., 'The Dark Side of American Soccer Culture', 12 July 2016, *New York Times Magazine*; Nachman, G., 'Beers, bandanas and boos: the "American Outlaws" grapple with frat-boy soccer', *Guardian*, 6 July 2016, https://www.theguardian.com/football/blog/2016/jun/06/american-outlaws-us-soccer-team-supporters-group; Clare, S., 'The Rise and Rise of the American Outlaws', *Huffington Post*, 6 December 2017, https://www.huffingtonpost.com/steve-clare/the-rise-and-rise-of-the-_1_b_3844519.html

51. Dundas, Z., 'Are Portland Thorns the first "real club" in women's football?' *Guardian*, 10 April 2015, https://www.theguardian.com/football/blog/2015/apr/10/are-portland-thorns-the-first-real-club-in-womens-football

52. Baxter, K., 'Women's World Cup: Success measured by competition and ticket sales', *LA Times*, 7 July 2015; Murray, C., 'Women"s World Cup: bigger, better – but still treated as the poor relation', *Guardian*, 4 July 2015; Ahmed, S., 'Women's World Cup May Seem Like a Feminist Fairy Tale, But the Fight's Not Over', 10 July 2015, https://rewire.news/article/2015/07/10/womens-world-cup-may-seem-like-feminist-fairy-tale-fights/

53. Bonestell, M., and Bieler, D., 'USWNT set to be first women's team to get ticker-tape parade in New York', *Washington Post*, 7 July 2015.

54. Conn, D., 'Hope Solo accuses Sepp Blatter of sexual assault at awards ceremony', *Guardian*, 10 November 2017; Pentz, M., 'Megan Rapinoe: "God forbid you be a gay woman and a person of color in the US"', *Guardian*, 25 March 2017, https://www.theguardian.com/football/2017/mar/25/megan-rapinoe-gay-woman-person-color-us

55. Coulter, A., 'Any growing interest in soccer a sign of nation's moral decay', 2 July 2014, https://eu.clarionledger.com/story/opinion/columnists/2014/06/25/coulter-growing-interest-soccer-sign-nations-moral-decay/11372137/

56. Gendelman, D., 'Why Mexico, Not USA, will enjoy home advantage at

Copa América', *Guardian*, 5 June 2016, https://www.theguardian.com/football/2016/jun/05/mexico-fans-usa-home-advantage-copa-america; Evans, S., 'Mexico is winning Copa America on U.S. turf – and also at the gate and on TV', *Washington Post*, 17 June 2016, https://www.washingtonpost.com/news/soccer-insider/wp/2016/06/17/mexico-is-winning-copa-america-on-u-s-turf-and-also-at-the-gate-and-on-tv/?utm_term=.fbd9cb6c7cb3

57. Quoted in Yoestig, T., 'What It's Like Living In The U.S. As A Mexico Soccer Fan', https://the18.com/soccer-news/mexico-soccer-fans-in-usa

58. Quoted in Tucker, D., 'Mexico's complex rivalry with USA divides Mexican American soccer fans', *Guardian*, 8 October 2015.

59. Rodriguez, E., 'Choosing Sides When the U.S. Plays Mexico', *New Yorker*, 20 October 2015; Echegaray, L. M., 'America's new soccer fans: why the children of immigrants are cheering USA', *Guardian*, 12 July 2015, https://www.theguardian.com/football/2015/jul/12/americas-new-soccer-fans-immigrants-usa

60. French, S., 'Liga MX sees United States as land of opportunity', *Four Four Two*, 14 July 2016, https://www.fourfourtwo.com/us/features/liga-mx-united-states-land-opportunity-mls-competition-tv-ratings#rWweuRUk20qvA606.99'

61. Fujita, A., 'To get on the US national men's soccer team, you may need to cross the border into Mexico', https://www.pri.org/stories/2014-07-08/get-us-national-mens-soccer-team-you-may-need-cross-border-mexico

62. Turner, E., 'Know your oligarch: Jorge Vergara's Omnilife money has Chivas on track for the second division', https://fusion.tv/story/90199/jorge-vergara-chivas-omnilife/

63. Keyes, D., *Making the Mainstream: The Domestication of American Soccer*. Unpublished research paper supported by the CIES Joao Havelange Scholarship (2014).

64. Quoted in Bandini, P., 'Roosevelt lookalike goes viral in show of rising US soccer power', *Guardian*, 30 June 2014, https://www.theguardian.com/football/blog/2014/jun/30/usa-fan-teddy-goalsevelt-world-cup-2014

65. Chen, A., 'Reborn in the USA: Why the World Cup makes it OK to love America', https://medium.com/matter/reborn-in-the-usa-2567f4b81b9b

Chapter 7

1. This chapter is based primarily on a reading of the key investigative texts into FIFA and world football over the last thirty years. Pride of place goes to Andrew Jennings, without which none of this would be

possible: see Jennings, A., *Foul!: The Secret World of FIFA: Bribes, Vote-Rigging and Ticket Scandals*, HarperSport (2006); Jennings, A., *The Dirty Game: Uncovering the Scandal at FIFA*, Random House (2016). On the academic side the pioneers have been John Sugden and Alan Tomlinson: see Sugden, J., and Tomlinson, A., *FIFA and the Contest for World Football: Who Rules the People's Game?*, Polity Press (1998); Sugden, J., and Tomlinson, A., *Badfellas: FIFA Family at War*, Mainstream (2003); Tomlinson, A., and Sugden, J., *Football, Corruption and Lies: Revisiting 'Badfellas', the Book FIFA Tried to Ban*, Routledge (2017); Tomlinson, A., *FIFA (Fédération internationale de Football Association): The Men, the Myths and the Money*, Routledge (2014). Honourable mentions also to David Yallop for his early biography of Havelange; Yallop, D., *How They Stole the Game*, Hachette UK (2011), and to Barbara Smit, whose work on the Adidas/FIFA/ISL nexus is brilliant: Smit, B., *Sneaker Wars: The Enemy Brothers Who Founded Adidas and Puma and the Family Feud that Forever Changed the Business of Sports*, Harper Perennial (2008). On the Qatari bid for the World Cup, the *Sunday Times* Insight team came up trumps: see Blake, H., and Calvert, J., *The Ugly Game: The Qatari Plot to Buy the World Cup*, Simon and Schuster (2015). Bringing it all together over many years of coverage is the excellent, Conn, D., *The Fall of the House of FIFA*, Random House (2017). See also Papenfuss, M., and Thompson, T., *American Huckster: How Chuck Blazer Got Rich From – and Sold Out – the Most Powerful Cabal in World Sports*, Harper Paperbacks (2017), for more eye-watering detail on CONCACAF.

2. Cited in Barry, D., 'FIFA Film: An Epic Fantasy', *New York Times*, 1 June 2015.
3. Cited in Riach, J., 'FIFA film *United Passions* is PR exercise that rankles even with its stars', *Observer*, 25 October 2014.
4. Roxborough, S., and Richford, R., 'FIFA Movie Director Breaks Silence on Bomb: "It's a Disaster; My Name Is All Over [This Mess]"', *Hollywood Reporter*, 17 June 2015.
5. Hoffman, J., '*United Passions* review – FIFA propaganda is pure cinematic excrement', *Guardian*, 4 June 2015.
6. Op. cit. Barry (2015).
7. Cited in Tomlinson (2014), p. 133.
8. 'Quotes from British Parliament Meeting with Sebastian Coe', 2 December 2015, https://www.flotrack.org/articles/5047713-quotes-from-british-parliament-meeting-with-sebastian-coe
9. See Ziegler, M., 'FIFA sack four over lies to sponsors', *Independent*, 13 December 2006; 'Jerome Valcke: He's scored the worst ever own goal. Now he's running football', *Independent*, 28 October 2007, https://www.

independent.co.uk/news/people/profiles/j-r244me-valcke-he-scored-the-worst-ever-own-goal-now-hes-running-football-398086.html

10. Cited in Marek, M., and Beckmann, S., 'Underground skyscraper serves as FIFA's unique headquarters', DW.Com, 18 May 2010, http://www.dw.com/en/underground-skyscraper-serves-as-fifas-unique-headquarters/a-5565834

11. Valcke's comment here quoted in Collett, M., 'Valcke comments on 2022 World Cup timing stir controversy', 8 January 2014, https://uk.reuters.com/article/uk-soccer-world-qatar/valcke-comments-on-2022-world-cup-timing-stir-controversy-IDUKBREA070IF20140108

12. Cited in Conn (2017), p. 69.

13. Check in at about 15.49 on this: https://www.youtube.com/watch?v=YfyPi5MnPSY

14. Triesman's performance at the select committee for Culture, Media and Sport can be enjoyed here: https://www.telegraph.co.uk/sport/football/international/8504841/Lord-Triesman-alleges-Fifa-corruption-in-World-Cup-bidding-process-at-Commons-committee-hearing.html

15. 'Exclusive video of Jack Warner apparently offering "gifts" of £25,000 to Caribbean delegates – full transcript', *Daily Telegraph*, 12 October 2011.

16. He also let it be known, via the German press, that 'with the English bid I said: "Let us be brief. If you give back the Falkland Islands, which belong to us, you will get my vote." They then became sad and left.' 'FIFA's Julio Grondona apologises for "unacceptable" attack on England', *Guardian*, 5 October 2011.

17. Gibson, O., 'Sepp Blatter wants singer Plácido Domingo to join FIFA's wise men', *Guardian*, 7 June 2013.

18. The whole sorry performance can be seen here: https://www.youtube.com/watch?v=YxFn61pOMgI

19. Panja, T., 'FIFA Anti-Corruption Adviser Quits "Least Productive Project"', Bloomberg, 22 April 2013.

20. See the excellent overview of both the process of production and the contents of these various reports: Pielke, R., 'An Evaluation of the FIFA Governance Reform Process of 2011–2013', *Managing the Football World Cup*, Palgrave Macmillan (2014), pp. 197–221; Pielke, R., 'How can FIFA be held accountable?', *Sport Management Review* 16.3 (2013), pp. 255–67.

21. The booing at the London 2012 Olympics can be heard here: https://www.youtube.com/watch?v=ysjZYIeeMP8, and that at the opening of the Confederations Cup in 2013 here: https://www.youtube.com/watch?v=c7Qq_XeQY2A. 'FIFA chief Blatter booed at Asian Cup final', Reuters, 31 January 2015, https://in.reuters.com/article/soccer-asia-blatter-IDINKBN0L40KG20150131

22. The spat between FIFA and the Nobel Foundation that ensued after the latter withdrew from the partnership is nicely covered here (FIFA's sense

of hurt and surprise is simply beyond all belief): Gibson, O., 'FIFA says Nobel board's termination of relationship against "spirit of fair play"', *Guardian*, 16 June 2015, https://www.theguardian.com/football/2015/jun/16/fifa-nobel-handshake-for-peace-termination-fair-play

23. The museum was launched planning to attract 250,000 visitors annually but, given that it is in Zurich, it has actually done very well to attract 132,000. Now headed by actual archivists and scholars, it may yet prove to be a valuable cultural resource for global football.

24. But for D'Hooghe, the 'straights' (Geoff Thompson, Junji Ogura, Senes Erzik) have all left the FIFA executive committee if not football altogether. The Cypriot Marios Lefkaritis has left the committee to spend more time, no doubt, with the Qatari Investment Authority.

25. Cited in the *Guardian*'s live coverage of the event, stored as 'Sepp Blatter re-elected as FIFA president after Prince Ali Bin al-Hussein concedes defeat', https://www.theguardian.com/football/live/2015/may/29/fifa-to-vote-on-sepp-blatter-presidential-bid-amid-corruption-scandal-live

26. Rice, S., '"I am the president of everybody": What Sepp Blatter said after winning re-election as FIFA president', *Independent*, 29 May 2015.

27. Cited in Borden, S., 'Gianni Infantino to Lead FIFA Into New Era', *New York Times,* 26 February 2016.

Chapter 8

1. Nemtsov cited in Osbourne, A., 'World Cup 2018: Troubled times at Russia's other great international sporting venue', *Daily Telegraph*, 5 December 2010. Putin is quoted in the Russian government's own transcript of the press conference in Zurich that followed the award of the 2018 World Cup, http://archive.premier.gov.ru/eng/events/pressconferences/13186/

2. Nemtsov, B., and Martynyuk, L., *Winter Olympics in the Sub Tropics: Corruption and Abuse in Sochi* (2013), available at https://www.putin-itogi.ru/cp/wp-content/uploads/2013/05/ReporT_ENG_SOCHI-2014_preview.pdf

3. Brown, O., 'Spurs striker Roman Pavlyuchenko delves into Russian politics with Vladimir Putin', *Daily Telegraph*, 14 October 2008.

4. 'Russian footballer Dmitri Tarasov reveals Putin shirt in Turkey match', BBC News, 17 February 2016, https://www.bbc.co.uk/news/world-europe-35593324

5. For this and almost everything else in this chapter the essential source is Manuel Veth's superb but sadly unpublished Ph.D. thesis: Veth, K. M., 'Selling the "people's game": football's transition from Communism to

capitalism in the Soviet Union and its successor state', Diss., King's College, London (2016). The other key academic texts are Edelman, R., *Serious Fun: A History of Spectator Sport in the USSR*, Oxford University Press (1993); Edelman, R., 'The Professionalization of Soviet Sport: The Case of the Soccer Union', *Journal of Sport History* 17.1 (1990), pp. 44–55; Edelman, R., *Spartak Moscow: A History of the People's Team in the Workers' State,* Cornell University Press (2009).

6. Russian government's own transcript of the press conference in Zurich that followed the award of the 2018 World Cup: http://archive.premier. gov.ru/eng/events/pressconferences/13186/

7. See Edelman (2009); Rabiner, I., Fallen Idol (2011), *Blizzard*, https:// www.theblizzard.co.uk/article/fallen-idol; Veth, M., 'A New House is Not a Home: The Continued Demise of Spartak Moscow', futbolgrad.com, 16 December 2014, http://futbolgrad.com/new-house-not-home-continued-demise-spartak-moscow/

8. Spartak's fags-and-booze sideline brought the club into direct contact and conflict with local organized crime, which provides one of the theories to explain why, in 1997, Spartak's chief executive Larisa Nechayeva was shot on the way home from the club's training ground.

9. Nickels, J., 'Leonid Fedun – From Apparatchik to Affluence', *Russian Football News*, 18 January 2018, http://russianfootballnews.com/leonid-fedun-from-apparatchik-to-affluence/; Theilade, T. M., 'Russian Club Owners: Leonid Fedun (Spartak Moscow) – A Dinamo Fan in Charge of Spartak Moscow', http://russianfootballnews.com/russian-club-owners-leonid-fedun-spartak-moscow-a-dinamo-fan-in-charge-of-spartak-moscow/

10. Williams, S., 'The Downfall of a Russian Soccer Team', *New Yorker*, 11 February 2016; Leonov, V., 'Dinamo Moscow: A monument of corruption and incompetence?', 5 September 2018, http://russianfootballnews.com/dinamo-moscow-a-monument-of-corruption-and-incompetence/

11. The scale of artificial sponsorship deals in Russian football, and UEFA's collusion with them, is laid out in Shaw, C., 'UEFA hid financial doping at Russian state football clubs', https://theblacksea.eu/stories/football-leaks-2018/uefa-hid-financial-doping-russian-state-football-clubs/

12. Torpedo's sorry tale can be followed in detail in Veth, M., 'Torpedo Moscow – Between Extinction and Hope', futbolgrad.com, 4 December 2015.

13. McArdle, D., 'Alania Vladikavkaz – Russian Football's Endangered Snow Leopards', http://futbolgrad.com/alania-vladikavkaz-russian-footballs-endangered-snow-leopards/

14. Veth, M., 'Anzhi Makhachkala – Russia's weirdest club is out of money', 30 July 2018, http://futbolgrad.com/anzhi-makhachkala-money/

15. Appell, J., 'Eastern Promise', *When Saturday Comes*, January 2009; Law,

M., 'Russian football faces fresh controversy as Rubin Kazan fail to pay players for past four months', *Daily Telegraph*, 6 December 2017; Martynov, A., 'Revolution in Kazan – A New Direction for Rubin', *Russian Football News*, 4 June 2017, http://russianfootballnews.com/author/andreymartynov/

16. Walter, K., 'FC Akhmat Grozny: The Establishment of a Kadyrov Dynasty', http://jerichoonline.com/2017/08/24/fc-akhmat-grozny-the-establishment-of-a-kadyrov-dynasty/; 'Football in the shadows of Islam and politics', http://sportexecutive.dk/football-shadows-islam-politics/; Theilade, T. M., 'Terek Grozny's Name Change – A Political Tool', *Russian Football News*, 8 June 2017, http://russianfootballnews.com/terek-groznys-name-change-kadyrovs-political-tool/

17. http://old.themoscowtimes.com/sitemap/free/1999/6/article/spartak-fans-clash-with-riot-police/275850.html

18. Clover, C., *Black Wind, White Snow: The Rise of Russia's New Nationalism*, Yale University Press (2016), pp. 279–82.

19. Quoted in Matusevich, Y., 'Russian Football Hooliganism – the Caucasian Divide', 2 December 2013, http://futbolgrad.com/russian-football-hooliganism-caucasian-divide/

20. SOVA/FARE (2015), 'Time For Action: Incidents of discrimination in Russian football', May 2012–May 2014; SOVA/FARE (2018), 'Incidents of discrimination in Russian football', 2017–May 2018.

21. See 'Interview with Antifa Ultra Petr From Ekaterinburg', http://russianfootballnews.com/interview-with-antifa-ultra-petr-from-ekaterinburg/; 'Russian neo-Nazi Ilya Goryachev was jailed for life for a string of hate killings in Russia", https://www.news.com.au/world/europe/russian-neonazi-ilya-goryachev-was-jailed-for-life-for-a-string-of-hate-killings-in-russia/news-story/b12ac7c043dc2a741a4d96030257e400

22. Key elements of the evening's proceedings can be seen here: https://www.youtube.com/watch?v=brBDSzM_VW0; https://www.youtube.com/watch?v=0C0RN-8IbwY

23. Reevell, P., 'Russian Hooligans' Toughest Opponents? Russia's Police', *New York Times*, 28 April 2017; Parkin, S., 'The Rise of Russia's Neo-Nazi Football Hooligans', *Guardian*, 24 April 2018.

24. Quoted in Reevell, 2017; other coverage, Boffery, D., 'Russian Hooligans Were Savage and Organized, Say England Fans', *Guardian*, 12 June 2016.

25. One of many examples of this can be seen at https://youtu.be/izrEi293-Xw

26. Lebedev quoted in https://www.independent.co.uk/sport/football/international/russia-fan-violence-russian-official-tells-hooligans-well-done-lads-keep-it-up-after-condoning-euro-a7079861.html; Putin is cited

in https://sports.vice.com/en_uk/article/78nqja/vladimir-putin-asks-how-can-200-russian-fans-beat-up-several-thousand-english

27. RFE, 'From Hero To Hounded: Russian Soccer-Fans Head Under Fire', https://www.rferl.org/a/russia-soccer-shprygin-excluded-head-fans-association-/28014729.html; Reevell, P., 'Russian Hooligans: "In 2018, God willing, I will beat someone"', *Irish Times*, https://www.irishtimes.com/sport/soccer/russian-hooligans-in-2018-god-willing-i-will-beat-someone-1.3067068

28. Montague, J., 'In a Sliver of the Old USSR, Hot Soccer Team is a Virtual State Secret', *New York Times*, 19 August 2012; Walk, I., 'Across the Dniester: How Football Is Bridging Moldova's Cultural Divide', https://thesefootballtimes.co/2016/11/22/across-the-dniester-how-football-is-bridging-moldovas-cultural-divide/

29. Amnesty International UK, 'Azerbaijan, "the Russian linesman" and other dodgy sporting decisions', https://www.amnesty.org.uk/blogs/global-voices/azerbaijan-russian-linesman-european-games-baku-sports-human-rights; Gibson, O., 'Turning black gold into sporting glitter: what Azerbaijan tells us about modern sport', *Guardian*, 19 December 2014; Abbasov, I., 'Baku 2015's gleaming stadiums a facade covering corrupt Azerbaijan regime', *Guardian*, 11 June 2015, https://www.theguardian.com/sport/blog/2015/jun/11/baku-2015-european-games-azebaijan-corrupt-regime-free-speech

30. Gibson, O., 'Azerbaijan's sponsorship of Atlético Madrid proves spectacular success', *Guardian*, 1 May 2014, https://www.theguardian.com/football/2014/may/01/azerbaijan-sponsorship-atletico-madrid-spectacular-suc

31. O'Connor, R., 'Flying the flag for Azerbaijan: the story of FK Qarabag', https://thesetpieces.com/features/flying-flag-azerbaijan-story-fk-qarabag/; O'Connor, R., 'The story of FK Qarabag: how a team born from war now prepares to host Chelsea in the Champions League', *Independent*, 22 November 2017, https://www.independent.co.uk/sport/football/european/fk-qarabag-champions-league-chelsea-preview-how-born-from-war-to-champions-league-debut-a8069506.html

32. He continued: 'We achieve victories both on the battlefield and on sports grounds. Similarly, in April of last year, the heroic Azerbaijani soldiers showed great courage and freed some of our lands from occupiers. Life now boils on these lands. Our people have returned to the lands liberated from occupation. Now they live and create there. The flag of Azerbaijan now flies over these lands. You also raised the flag of Azerbaijan in football yesterday.'

33. On Belarus see Rainbow, J., 'Football in Belarus and Tale of False Promise', *World Soccer*, 7 December 2013.

34. On all of this see Bylina, V., 'Football in Belarus – Ultras Versus the Authoritarian Regime', futbolgrad.com, 19 December 2016.

35. Bylina, V., 'Belarusian Authorities Crack Down on Football Fans', *Belarus Digest*, 23 February 2015, https://belarusdigest.com/story/belarusian-authorities-crack-down-on-football-fans/; BBC News, 'Belarus: Football fans jailed for anti-Putin chant', 10 October 2014, https://www.bbc.co.uk/news/blogs-news-from-elsewhere-29567246

36. On the Pahonia and football see: 'Protest against police brutality: Football fans boycott matches', https://charter97.org/en/news/2015/7/24/161232/

37. On the reign of the Surkis brothers see: Misura, V., 'Ukrainian Football: the Case of the Surkis', http://www.brusselstimes.com/opinion/9141/ukrainian-football-the-case-of-surkis

38. Veth, M., 'The empire that is Shakhtar Donetsk FC', *Open Democracy*, 11 March 2015, https://www.opendemocracy.net/od-russia/manuel-veth/empire-that-is-shakhtar-donetsk-fc

39. Quoted in 'Poland and Ukraine host Euro 2012', BBC Sport, 18 April 2007, http://news.bbc.co.uk/sport1/hi/football/europe/6562527.stm

40. Harding, L., and Leigh, D., 'Euro 2012: UEFA urged to investigate $4bn corruption allegations in Ukraine', *Guardian*, 20 June 2012.

41. Harding, L., 'Euro 2012 turning into a PR disaster for Ukraine as racism fears scare off fans', *Guardian*, 28 May 2012; Lasocki, J., and Jasoina, L., 'Football and Politics: The Legacy of Euro 2012 in Ukraine', *Open Democracy*, https://www.opendemocracy.net/od-russia/janek-lasocki-łukasz-jasina/football-politics-legacy-of-euro-2012-in-ukraine

42. On Ukraine's Ultras and politics before the 2014 uprising, and the left–right division see Veth, M., 'Ukranian Ultras – Where Two Worlds Collide', fubtolgrad.com, 20 July 2013, http://futbolgrad.com/ukrainian-ultras-where-two-wings-collide/; after 2014 see Volkvava, E., and Bartkowski, M., 'The Ukrainian soccer ultras: allies of the resistance', *Open Democracy*, https://www.opendemocracy.net/civilresistance/elena-volkava-maciej-bartkowski/ukrainian-soccer-ultras-allies-of-resistance; Lukov, Y., 'Ultras United: Football Fans Rally for Ukraine's Sake', https://www.bbc.co.uk/news/world-europe-27540360; Zafesova, A., 'The ultras' role in the war', https://eastwest.eu/en/east-58/the-ultras-role-in-the-war; Fresko, A., 'From hooligans to warriors: the metamorphosis of Ukrainian ultras', https://journey2016.atavist.com/from-hooligans-to-warriors-the-metamorphosis-of-ukrainian-ultras

43. 'Premier League's Crimea Crisis', *World Soccer*, 18 April 2014; Rothwell,

E., 'A Soccer Secession', http://roadsandkingdoms.com/2014/a-soccer-secession/

44. Veth, M., 'The End of Metalist Kharkiv', futbolgrad.com, 6 June 2016, http://futbolgrad.com/end-metalist-kharkiv/; 'Kharkiv Metalist Stadium Returns to State Ownership', *Kharkiv Observer*, 13 April 2018, http://kharkivobserver.com/kharkiv-metalist-stadium-returns-to-state-ownership/

45. 'Olympics – At Sochi Games, Putin evokes spirit of 1980', https://www.reuters.com/article/olympics-1980/olympics-at-sochi-games-putin-evokes-spirit-of-1980-IDUSL5N0L90SG20140206

46. Parfitt, T., 'Vladimir Putin tells Roman Abramovich to pay for World Cup 2018', *Guardian*, 5 December 2010.

47. http://russianfootballnews.com/the-russian-mafia-in-world-football/

48. Theilade, T. M., 'Gazprom, Zenit and European Football', https://thesefootballtimes.co/2016/06/22/gazprom-zenit-european-football/; 'Gazprom's Colossal Football Empire', https://thesefootballtimes.co/2015/01/15/the-gazprom-empire/; Veth, M., 'Gazprom Football Empire – the creation of a global image campaign', http://futbolgrad.com/gazprom-football-empire-creation-global-image-campaign/; Veth, M., 'Gazprom, Schalke, and Putin: How Schalke is a Metonym for Germany's Dependence on Russia's Resources', http://bundesligafanatic.com/20140312/gazprom-schalke-metonym-for-german-dependence-russian-resouces/

49. At the time, Russian Prime Minister Vladimir Putin wanted Schalke to keep Manuel Neuer instead of selling him to Bayern Munich, http://www.goal.com/en/news/15/german-football/2011/10/26/2729254/russian-prime-minister-vladimir-putin-wanted-schalke-to-keep

50. Warshaw, A., 'Dvorak's FIFA exit reveals open wounds of Infantino's hiring and firing policy', *Inside World Football*, 14 November 2016, http://www.insideworldfootball.com/2016/11/14/dvoraks-fifa-exit-reveals-open-wounds-infantinos-hiring-firing-policy/

51. Quoted in 'Rodchenkov insists Mutko ordered him to hide any positive drug tests of Russian players', *Inside World Football*, 20 February 2018, http://www.insideworldfootball.com/2018/02/20/rodchenkov-insists-mutko-ordered-hide-positive-drug-tests-russian-players/

52. 'Moscow riot prompts World Cup rethink', BBC News, http://news.bbc.co.uk/1/hi/world/europe/2034878.stm; 'Two die in Moscow World Cup rioting', *Guardian*, 10 June 2002.

53. Wilson, J., 'Guus Hiddink's spell in Russian football took them into the fast lane', *Guardian*, 16 February 2010.

54. Wier, F., 'Euro 2008: Russian soccer team revives nationalism', *Christian Science Monitor*, 27 June 2008.

55. Cited in Borusyak, L., 'Football as a catalyst for Patriotism', https://www.opendemocracy.net/article/russia-theme/football-as-a-catalyst-for-patriotism

56. Cited in Wier (2008).

57. Magee, W., 'Communist Party of Russia Claims National Team Need "Stalinist Mobilisation" After Wales Defeat', *Vice Sports*, 21 June 2016, https://sports.vice.com/en_ca/article/3dgezb/communist-party-of-russia-claims-national-team-need-stalinist-mobilisation-after-wales-defeat

58. '"We can play for free": Russian football fans challenge national team after Euro 2016 failure', https://www.rt.com/sport/349045-football-fans-team-russia/; Sharkov, D., 'Euro 2016: More Than 350,000 Call for Russia's Football Team to be Dissolved', http://www.newsweek.com/euro-2016-over-350000-call-russias-team-be-dissolved-478763

59. Seddon, M., 'St Petersburg's World Cup stadium project tainted by corruption', *Financial Times*, 18 November 2016.

60. Luhn, A., '"Like prisoners of war": North Korean labour behind Russia 2018 World Cup', *Observer*, 4 June 2017; Melnæs, H., 'The Salves of St Petersburg', http://www.josimar.no/artikler/the-slaves-of-st-petersburg/3851/

61. Conn, D., 'World Cup 2018: FIFA admits workers have suffered human rights abuses', *Guardian*, 25 May 2017.

62. 'Russian farmer builds straw stadium to mock World Cup cost and corruption', *Global Construction Review*, 24 July 2017.

Conclusion

1. 'How Oil Money Distorts Global Football', 2 November 2018, http://www.spiegel.de/international/world/financial-fair-play-manchester-city-and-psg-pact-with-the-sheikhs-a-1236414.html

2. Those with the stomach for the football world's most grating and disingenuous clichés can read the whole of Putins's speech here: http://en.kremlin.ru/events/president/news/57738

3. Panja, T., 'Peru Invades Russia. Well, At Least Many of its Fans Have', *New York Times*, 16 June 2018; James, S., 'Heard the one about the Peru fan who put on 24kg to get a World Cup ticket?', *Guardian*, 15 June 2018; Savarese, M., 'Passionate Peruvian fans flood World Cup's smallest city', 15 June 2018, https://www.apnews.com/450d0f8b56f242d1ba11cb12705c8c04

4. Bhushan, R., 'India stars in football world cup – with off-the-field presence', 23 June 2018, //economictimes.indiatimes.com/

articleshow/64703835.cms?utm_source=contentofinterest&utm_
medium=text&utm_campaign=cppst"

5. Yu, K., 'China and its influence at the World Cup in Russia', 2 July 2018, https://www.aljazeera.com/indepth/features/china-influence-world-cup-russia-180701095302734.html

6. Soric, M., 'Football brought Nigerians to Moscow; now they're stranded', 8 July 2018, https://www.dw.com/en/football-brought-nigerians-to-moscow-now-theyre-stranded/a-44578779

7. Charlton, A., and Ellingworth, J., 'Migrant workers the key to Russia's smooth-running World Cup', 5 July 2018, https://www.apnews.com/ca3c6f1119d64666ac7d0310eba324c8

8. Rothwell, E., 'Amazing night of partying is a cherished memory for Russia – but World Cup provoking questions too', 2 July 2018, https://www.eurosport.com/football/world-cup/2018/amazing-night-of-partying-is-a-cherished-memory-for-russia-but-world-cup-provoking-questions-too_sto6828805/story.shtml

9. Smith, R., 'Finally, a loss for Russia. But only on the field', *New York Times*, 25 June 2018.

10. Roth, A., 'A wild night: Russia win and Moscow parties as never before', *Guardian*, 2 July 2018; Tetrault-Farber, G., 'After shock Russia win, Moscow cleans up huge party mess', 2 July 2018, https://www.reuters.com/article/us-soccer-worldcup-rus-garbage/after-shock-russia-win-moscow-cleans-up-huge-party-mess-IDUSKBN1JS16B

11. 'Which news stories captured the public's attention in June?', https://www.populus.co.uk/insights/2018/07/which-news-stories-captured-the-publics-attention-in-june/

12. Dobtokhotov, R., 'What the Kremlin did while Russians were watching the World Cup', 24 June 2018, https://www.aljazeera.com/indepth/opinion/kremlin-russians-watching-world-cup-180624101121762.html

13. Gutterman, S., 'The Week In Russia: World Cup Hosts Advance, Retirement Recedes', 22 June 2018, https://www.rferl.org/a/the-week-in-russia-world-cup-hosts-advance-retirement-recedes/29313888.html

14. 'Russian opposition leader Navalny freed ahead of World Cup', 14 June 2018, https://www.france24.com/en/20180614-russian-opposition-leader-navalny-freed-ahead-world-cup

15. 'Russian soccer commentator who mentioned Putin critic goes off air', 20 June 2018, https://www.reuters.com/article/us-soccer-worldcup-russia-commentator/russian-soccer-commentator-who-mentioned-putin-critic-goes-off-air-IDUSKBN1JG2BL

16. Smith, R., 'In Cairo, All Roads Lead to Image of Salah', *New York Times*, 18 June 2018; Islam, S., 'How Mohamed Salah managed the impossible: to unite Egypt', *Guardian*, 14 June 2018, https://www.theguardian.com/football/2018/jun/14/

mohamed-salah-brought-happiness-and-pride-to-egypt-world-cup-liverpool; Zidan, K., 'The Egyptian Football Association Turned Mo Salah's World Cup Into An Embarrassing Disaster', 27 June 2018, https://deadspin.com/the-egyptian-football-association-turned-mo-salahs-worl-1827167435; Mo getting his Chechen citizenship: https://www.youtube.com/watch?time_continue=10&v=B_AjTidjWMk

17. One report from the Belgium–France semi-final depicted a kind of cosmopolitan lassitude: 'The man who'd chanted "Brazil" to my immediate right was from Israel. To the left, a France-supporting Russian banged two inflatable air sticks. To the left of him, a South African drinking Budweiser from a plastic glass with red flashing lights. On the row in front, five excitable young men from Libya who spent longer facetiming their friends to show them where they were than watching the game': Mitten, A., 'The World Cup in Russia has been a big success, but it's been a tournament for the rich', https://www.unibet.co.uk/blog/football/world-cup/the-world-cup-in-russia-has-been-a-big-success-but-it%27s-been-a-tournament-for-the-rich-1.1050717

18. Hendaway, H., 'Saudi women in Russia to support team, reinforce new image', 14 June 2018. https://www.apnews.com/d0db935be5d148f5b43c6148375627de

19. Ferris-Rotman, A., '"Let us be free": Iranian women mount protest over stadium ban at World Cup match', 15 June 2018, https://www.washingtonpost.com/world/europe/let-us-be-free-iranian-women-mount-protest-over-stadium-ban-at-world-cup-match/2018/06/15/9755dd1e-6fdb-11e8-b4d8-eaf78d4c544c_story.html?utm_term=.8628e0778778

20. All of these incidents were well covered in more detail in 'Fare blog: We need to talk about sexism at the World Cup', 26 June 2018, https://farenet.org/news/women-in-football-term-slug/fare-blog-we-need-to-talk-about-sexism-at-the-world-cup-2018/; Morin, S., 'Female Sports Reporters Are Blowing the Whistle on Sexist Behavior at the World Cup', *Time*, 3 July 2018; Aziz, S., 'Man's World Cup? Sexism and harassment at Russia 2018', 9 July 2018, https://www.aljazeera.com/indepth/features/man-world-cup-sexism-harassment-russia-2018-1807040 85133765.html

21. I have explored these arguments at greater length in the conclusion of Goldblatt, D., *The Ball is Round: A Global History of Football*, Penguin (2006).

22. See this video for example: https://www.youtube.com/watch?v=LK5qaabE-yg

Index

Picture Credits

1. (Erdoğan) Kayhan Ozer / Anadolu Agency / Getty Images
   (Morales) AIZAR RALDES / AFP / Getty Images
2. Jean Catuffe / Getty Images
3. Andrew Esiebo
4. Li Jing / Xinhua / Alamy Live News
5. Jon Hrusa / EPA / Shutterstock
6. Claudia Wiens / Alamy Stock Photo
7. Saeid Zareian / dpa / Alamy Live News
8. LOUAI BESHARA / AFP/Getty Images
9. jbdodane / Alamy Stock Photo
10. Felipe Dana / AP / Shutterstock
11. Geraldo Bubniak / Fotoarena
12. Photo by Mario Tama / Getty Images
13. Realy Easy Star / Alamy Live News
14. http://josper.com/en/portfolio/puskas-akademia-felcsut-stadium-2/
15. East News sp. z o.o. / Alamy Stock Photo
16. Peppe Iovino / Alamy Stock Photo
17. Anonymous / AP / Shutterstock
18. Allstar Picture Library / Alamy Stock Photo
19. Jan Huebner / Imago / PA Images
20. Brazil Government / Alamy Stock Photo
21. SIPA Asia / ZUMA Wire / Alamy Live News
22. SIRIOH Co., LTD / Alamy Stock Photo
23. Jonathan Larsen / Diadem Images / Alamy Stock Photo
24. Marmaduke St. John / Alamy Stock Photo
25. Christian Palma / AP / Shutterstock
26. FABRICE COFFRINI / AFP / Getty Images
27. Christian Charisius / dpa / Alamy Live News